Microeconomics:
Theory and Applications

MICROECONOMICS:
THEORY AND APPLICATIONS

Dominick Salvatore

Chairman and
Professor,
Department of
Economics,
Fordham University

MACMILLAN PUBLISHING COMPANY

New York

COLLIER MACMILLAN PUBLISHERS

London

To My Parents

Macmillan Publishing Company
866 Third Avenue, New York, New York 10022

Collier Macmillan Canada, Inc.

Library of Congress Cataloging in Publication Data

Salvatore, Dominick.
   Microeconomics: Theory and Applications

   Includes bibliographical references and indexes.
   1. Microeconomics.   I. Title.
HB172.S14   1986   338.5   85-7175
ISBN 0-02-405320-1

Printing: 1 2 3 4 5 6 7 8   Year: 6 7 8 9 0 1 2 3 4 5

ISBN   0-02-405320-1

Preface

Microeconomic theory studies the economic behavior of individual consumers, resource owners, and business firms, and the operation of markets in a free-enterprise economy. While macroeconomic issues, such as the rate of national unemployment and inflation, usually receive more attention in the media, it is the sum total of all the individual decisions by consumers, resource owners, and firms that actually determines the overall performance of the economy. Because it presents many of the basic tools of economic analysis, microeconomic theory is one of the most important courses in all economics and business programs.

This is a text for the standard undergraduate course in intermediate microeconomics in economics and business programs. Only a prior course in principles of economics is required and only simple geometry is used. The presentation is clear and concise, and it is reinforced throughout with numerous pertinent real-world *examples* and extensive *applications* from economics and business. There are no mathematical footnotes, but there is an optional mathematical appendix at the end of the text for students who have had calculus.

Useful and Unique Features of the Text

Although the structure of this text is traditional, there are a number of very useful features which, together, makes it unique.

Each chapter includes several extensive and current *real-world applications*. These applications serve to highlight the relevance of microtheory in analyzing (and offering possible solutions to) important present-day economic problems. The recurrent theme throughout the text is that only by "putting theory to work" does theory truly come alive. Applications deepen understanding of the theory and motivate the student by demonstrating the great usefulness of the theory.

Each chapter progresses smoothly *from theory to applications*. Many texts present applications in separate chapters, with the result that applications seem to be mere appendages and are seldom covered. Other texts present applications throughout the chapter, interrupting the continuity in the presentation of the theory.

This text also introduces *greater realism* than most others by presenting numerous real-world examples of the theories examined. The oligopoly chapter (Chapter 13) includes an extensive discussion of *managerial theories of the firm* and *game theory*. These important topics are often omitted from other texts.

A very important feature of the text is the presentation of *important recent developments in consumer demand theory* (Chapter 6) and important *extensions of production theory* (Chapter 9). These examine revealed preference, index numbers, choices subject to risk, the demand for characteristics, and empirical demand curves (in Chapter 6); and the Cobb-Douglas production function, empirical production and cost curves, technological progress, and linear programming (in Chapter 9). While these chapters are optional, many professors may want to expose their students to at least some of these current developments and extensions in demand and production theory. In other texts, either these important topics are not covered at all (a serious omission) or they are presented at too high a level to be accessible to most undergraduates.

There is also a chapter (16) on interest and capital theory and one (Chapter 19) on public goods, externalities, and the role of the government.

Graphs are drawn on a light background grid with real numbers to add realism to the analysis and to facilitate reading off answers. For example, instead of saying that a reduction in the price of X from P_1 to P_2 results in an increase in the quantity demanded from Q_1 to Q_2 per unit of time, we examine how a reduction from \$2 to \$1 in the price of hamburgers leads an individual to increase the quantity demanded from 2 to 6 per week. This also allows us to separate numerically the substitution from the income effect of the price reduction, thus making the analysis more realistic and much more easily and thoroughly comprehensible to students.

Organization of the Book

The text is organized into six parts. Part I (Chapters 1–2) presents an introduction to microeconomic theory and a review of some principles of economics. Chapter 1 deals with scarcity as the fundamental economic fact facing every society, examines the function or purpose of microeconomic theory and its methodology, and discusses the overall organization of the text and of each of its chapters. Chapter 2 is a brief review of the concepts of demand, supply, equilibrium, and elasticity.

Part II (Chapters 3–6) presents the theory of consumer behavior and demand. Chapter 3 examines the tastes of the consumer and how the consumer maximizes utility or satisfaction in spending his or her income. These concepts are then utilized and extended in Chapter 4 to derive the consumer's demand curve for a commodity. Chapter 5 shows how, by aggregating or summing up individual consumer's demand curves, we get the market demand curve for the commodity. Chapter 5 also examines in detail the usefulness and measurement of the various demand elasticities. Finally, Chapter 6 presents more advanced topics and more recent important developments in consumer demand theory. The presentation of the theory is reinforced throughout with many real-world examples and important applications.

Part III (Chapters 7–9) presents the theory of production and cost. Chapter 7 examines production theory or how firms combine resources or inputs to produce final commodities. These concepts are then utilized and extended in Chapter 8 to examine costs of production and to derive the short-run and the long-run cost curves of the firm. Finally, Chapter 9 presents more advanced topics in the theory of production and costs. As in the previous parts, the presentation of the theory is reinforced throughout with many real-world examples and important applications.

Part IV (Chapters 10–13) presents the theory of the firm and market structure. It brings together the theory of consumer behavior and demand (from Part II) and the theory of production and costs (from Part III) to analyze how price and output are determined under various types of market organization. Chapter 10 shows how price and output are determined under perfect competition. Chapter 11 shows price and output determination under pure monopoly. Chapter 12 does the same for monopolistic competition, and Chapter 13 does so for oligopoly.

Part V (Chapters 14–16) presents the theory of input pricing and employment. Until this point, input prices were assumed to be given. In this part we examine how input prices and the level of their employment are determined in the market. Chapter 14 examines input pricing and employment under perfect competition in the output and input markets. Chapter 15 deals with input pricing and employment under imperfect competition in the output and/or input markets. Chapter 16 presents interest and capital theory; that is, it deals with choices in the allocation of inputs over time. Many real-world examples and applications add an important dose of realism to the theoretical analysis.

Part VI (Chapters 17–19) presents the theory of general equilibrium and welfare economics, and examines the role of government. Chapter 17 presents general equilibrium theory. This examines the interdependence or relationship among all products and input markets, and shows how the various individual markets (studied in Parts II–V) fit together to form an integrated economic system. Chapter 18 studies welfare economics within a general equilibrium framework. It examines questions of economic efficiency in the production of output and equity in the distribution of income. Finally, Chapter 19 examines externalities, public goods, and the role of government. It studies why externalities (such as pollution) and the existence of public goods (such as national defense) lead to economic inefficiencies. It also presents policies that can be used to overcome these inefficiencies.

The eight core chapters are: 3–5, 7–8, 10–11, 14.

Audience and Level

There are several choices in the use of the text.

(1) For a solid, popular, "no-frills" undergraduate course in microeconomics, I would include Chapters 1 and 2 and the eight core chapters (3–5, 7–8, 10–11, 14) with their applications.

(2) With a stronger background (such as a two-semester course in principles of economics), I would skip Chapter 2 and cover parts of one or two other chapters, as follows:

(2a) If the aim is to give a stronger theoretical background, I would choose topics from Chapter 6 (Extensions of Consumer Demand Analysis) and Chapter 9 (Extensions of Production Theory), or Chapters 17 (General Equilibrium Analysis) and 18 (Welfare Economics).

(2b) For a more "applied" course, I would choose topics from Chapter 15 (Input Price and Employment under Imperfect Competition) and Chapter 19 dealing with public goods, externalities, and the role of government.

(2c) For business majors, I would cover the following topics (time permitting) in addition to the eight core chapters: choices subject to risk, index numbers, and empirical demand curves (from Chapter 6); empirical production and cost curves, and linear programming (from Chapter 9); managerial theories of the firm and game theory (from Chapter 13); and Chapter 16 on interest rates and capital theory.

Thus, the book is designed for flexibility, depending on the background of the student and the aims of the course—keeping in mind that in most cases no more than 11 or 12 chapters can be covered in one semester.

Teaching Aids

Each chapter contains a number of teaching aids to make the text easier to use in the classroom. The sections of each chapter are numbered for easy reference. Longer sections are broken into two or more subsections. All of the graphs and diagrams are carefully explained in the text and then summarized briefly in the captions. Most diagrams are drawn on a light background grid to facilitate reading off answers.

Each chapter ends with the following teaching aids:

Summary—Reviews the main points covered in the text.
Chapter Glossary—Gives the definition of important terms introduced in bold-face in the chapter. A separate index of glossary terms in alphabetical order is provided at the end of the book for easy cross-reference.

Questions for Review—At least one question for each section in the chapter.

Problems—These ask the student to calculate a specific measure or explain a particular theory or issue. Brief answers to selected problems are provided at the end of the book for feedback. These problems are indicated by a star (★).

Supplementary Readings—The most important references are included along with specific notes indicating the topic they cover. A separate author index is included at the end of the book.

For those interested, a short *mathematical appendix* is available at the end of the text.

A substantial *Instructor's Manual* prepared *by the author* is available which includes chapter objectives, lecture suggestions, detailed answers to the end-of-chapter problems, a set of 25 multiple-choice questions with answers for each chapter, and additional problems with answers for each chapter for examinations and/or class discussions. The *Manual* was prepared with as much care as the text itself.

A *Study Guide*, prepared by Dr. Mary Acker of Iona College, is available which includes chapter summaries, an annotated bibliography for each chapter, multiple choice questions, review questions, and problems.

Acknowledgments

This text grew out of the undergraduate and graduate courses in microeconomics that I have been teaching at Fordham University during the past 15 years. I was very fortunate to have had many excellent students who with their questions and comments have contributed much to the clarity of exposition of this text.

I owe a great intellectual debt to my brilliant former teachers of economics: William Baumol, Arthur Bloomfield, Victor Fuchs, Jack Johnston, Lawrence Klein, W. A. Lewis, Michael Michaely, Bernard Okun, Hans Singer, and Peter Wiles. It is incredible how many of the insights that one gains as a student of a superb economist and teacher live on for the rest of one's life.

My colleague in the Economic Department, Professor Joseph Cammarosano, read through the entire manuscript and made numerous suggestions that significantly improved the final product. I have received also much useful advice from my other colleagues, Clive Daniels, James Heilbrun, John Piderit, Edward Sheehey, Siamack Shojai, and Timothy Weithers, and much support from Richard E. Doyle, Academic Vice-President, Gerald M. Quinn, Associate Academic Vice-President; Mary G. Powers, Dean of the

Graduate School, and Edward Dowling, Dean of Fordham College. Anita Longobardi assisted me throughout this project. No professor could ask for a better assistant. I also received much help from my other assistants, Bernard Appia, Cristina Cadac, Joan Combs, John Connelly, Cristina Gaspar, John Gilleaudeau, and Luis Mejia-Maya.

The following Professors reviewed the manuscript and made many valuable suggestions: Taeho Bark, Georgetown University; Gordon Bennett, University of Southern Florida; Charles Berry, University of Cincinnati; Josef Brada, Arizona State University; Charles Breeden, Marquette University; Joseph Cammarosano, Fordham University; Jacques Cremer, Virginia Tech; Clive Daniel, Fordham University at Lincoln Center; David Gay, University of Arkansas; Roy Hensley, University of Miami; Joseph Jadlow, Oklahoma State University; W. E. Kuhn, The University of Nebraska–Lincoln; Mike Magura, University of Toledo; Stephen Miller, University of Connecticut; Peter Murrell, University of Maryland; Patricia Nichol and Donald Owen, Texas Tech University; David Salant, Virginia Tech; Charles Stuart, University of California, Santa Barbara; Allen Wilkins, University of Wisconsin at Madison.

The following professors have also offered much useful advice: Mary Acker and John Spagnolo of Iona College; Francis Colella of Simpson College, Iowa; Reza Ghorashi of Stockton State College, New Jersey; Stanley Lawson of St. John's University; Louis Lopilato and Gregory Clare of Marcy College; Joseph Kiernan and Richard Kjetsaa of the College of Business Administration at Fairleigh Dickinson University; George Mungia of the University of Santo Domingo; Patrick O'Sullivan and Cecilia Winters of the State University of New York. Other useful comments were made by Dr. John McAuley, Vice-President, Economic Research Department, Chemical Bank; Dr. Vincent Malanga, Vice-President of Shilling & Company; and Dr. Glenn DeSouza, Senior Economist at Arthur D. Little. To all of them, I am deeply grateful.

Finally, I would like to express my gratitude to the entire staff at Macmillan, especially Chip Price, Jack Repcheck, John Travis, Jackie Kennen, David Cloughen, Harold Stancil, Victoria Sandvik, and Nick Sklitsis for their kind and skillful assistance, and to Angela Bates, Cathryn McCarthy, Eileen McCauley, Aida Napolitano, Adelaide Mottola, and Marie Sundberg, the department secretaries, for their efficiency and cheerful disposition.

D.S.

Brief Contents

ONE INTRODUCTION   1

Chapter 1 Introduction   2

Chapter 2 Demand and Supply: A Review   25

TWO THEORY OF CONSUMER BEHAVIOR AND
DEMAND   57

★Chapter 3 Consumer Preferences and Choice   58

★Chapter 4 Consumer Behavior and Individual Demand   94

★Chapter 5 Market Demand and Elasticities   127

Chapter 6 Extensions of Consumer Demand Theory   159

THREE THEORY OF PRODUCTION AND COST   193

★Chapter 7 Production Theory   194

★Chapter 8 Costs of Production   228

Chapter 9 Extensions of Production and Cost Theory   262

FOUR THEORY OF THE FIRM AND MARKET
STRUCTURE   297

★Chapter 10 Price and Output Under Perfect Competition   298

★Chapter 11 Price and Output Under Pure Monopoly   334

Chapter 12 Price and Output Under Monopolistic Competition   374

Chapter 13 Price and Output Under Oligopoly   401

FIVE PRICING AND EMPLOYMENT OF INPUTS   445

★Chapter 14 Input Price and Employment Under Perfect Competition   446

★ Core Chapter.

xi

Chapter 15 Input Price and Employment Under Imperfect
Competition   483

Chapter 16 Intertemporal Choice: Interest and Capital   512

SIX GENERAL EQUILIBRIUM, WELFARE ECONOMICS, AND THE ROLE OF GOVERNMENT   551

Chapter 17 General Equilibrium Analysis   552

Chapter 18 Welfare Economics   581

Chapter 19 Externalities, Public Goods, and the Role of
Government   611

APPENDICES   634

A Mathematical Appendix   A1

B Answers to Selected Problems   B1

Glossary Index   I1

Name Index   I5

Subject Index   I7

Detailed Contents

ONE INTRODUCTION   1

Chapter 1   Introduction   2

1.1   The Fundamental Economic Fact   4
   1.1a   Human Wants and Resources   4
   1.1b   Scarcity   5
1.2   The Functions of an Economic System   7
1.3   Microeconomic Theory and the Price System   10
   1.3a   The Circular Flow of Economic Activity   10
   1.3b   Determination and Function of Prices   12
   1.3c   Effect of Government   13
1.4   Models and Methodology   15
1.5   Positive and Normative Economics   16
1.6   Organization of the Book   19
   1.6a   Organization of the Text   19
   1.6b   Chapter Organization   20
Summary   21
Glossary   21
Questions for Review   22
Problems   23
Supplementary Readings   24

Chapter 2   Demand and Supply: A Review   25

2.1   Market Analysis   26
2.2   Market Demand   27
   2.2a   Demand Schedule and Demand Curve   27
   2.2b   Changes in Demand   29
   2.2c   Price Elasticity of Demand   31
2.3   Market Supply   34
   2.3a   Supply Schedule and Supply Curve   34
   2.3b   Changes in Supply   36
   2.3c   Price Elasticity of Supply   37
2.4   Equilibrium   39
2.5   Adjustment to Changes in Demand and Supply   41
   2.5a   Adjustment to Changes in Demand   41
   2.5b   Adjustment to Changes in Supply   43
2.6   Applications   44
Summary   51
Glossary   52
Questions for Review   53

Problems   54
Supplementary Readings   55

TWO THEORY OF CONSUMER BEHAVIOR AND DEMAND   57

Chapter 3 Consumer Preferences and Choice   58

3.1 Utility Analysis   60
   3.1a Total and Marginal Utility   60
   3.1b Cardinal and Ordinal Utility   63
3.2 Indifference Curves   64
   3.2a Definition of Indifference Curves   64
   3.2b Characteristics of Indifference Curves   66
   3.2c The Marginal Rate of Substitution   68
   3.2d Some Special Types of Indifference Curves   69
3.3 Budget Line   72
   3.3a Definition of the Budget Line   72
   3.3b Changes in the Budget Line   74
3.4 Consumer's Choice   76
   3.4a Utility Maximization   76
   3.4b Corner Solutions   78
   3.4c Marginal Utility Approach to Utility Maximization   80
3.5 Applications   83
Summary   89
Glossary   89
Questions for Review   90
Problems   91
Supplementary Readings   93

Chapter 4 Consumer Behavior and Individual Demand   94

4.1 Changes in Income   96
   4.1a Income-Consumption Curve and Engel Curve   96
   4.1b Normal and Inferior Goods   99
4.2 Changes in Price   101
   4.2a Price-Consumption Curve and Individual Demand Curve   102
   4.2b Price-Consumption Curve and Price Elasticity of Demand   105
4.3 Substitution and Income Effects   108
   4.3a Separation of the Substitution and Income Effects   108

4.3b   Substitution and Income Effects for Inferior
Goods   111
4.4   Applications   114
Summary   123
Glossary   123
Questions for Review   124
Problems   125
Supplementary Readings   126

Chapter 5   Market Demand and Elasticities   127

5.1   The Market Demand for a Commodity   129
5.2   Price Elasticity of Market Demand   132
5.2a   Price Elasticity Graphically   132
5.2b   Price Elasticity and Total Expenditures   134
5.2c   Factors Affecting Price Elasticity   135
5.3   Income Elasticity of Demand   138
5.4   Cross Elasticity of Demand   141
5.5   Marginal Revenue and Elasticity   144
5.5a   Demand, Total Revenue, and Marginal
Revenue   144
5.5b   The Geometry of Marginal Revenue
Determination   145
5.5c   Marginal Revenue, Price, and Elasticity   148
5.6   Applications   150
Summary   154
Glossary   155
Questions for Review   156
Problems   157
Supplementary Readings   158

Chapter 6   Extensions of Consumer Demand Theory   159

6.1   The Substitution Effect According to Slutsky   161
6.2   The Theory of Revealed Preference   163
6.3   Index Numbers   165
6.3a   Expenditure, Laspeyres, and Paasche
Indices   166
6.3b   Measures of Changes in Consumer
Welfare   167
6.4   Utility Theory Under Uncertainty   170
6.5   The Characteristics Approach to Consumer
Theory   174
6.6   Empirical Demand Curves   176
6.7   Applications   180
Summary   187
Glossary   188

Questions for Review   189
Problems   190
Supplementary Readings   191

THREE THEORY OF PRODUCTION AND COST   193

Chapter 7 Production Theory   194

7.1 Organization of Production and Classification of
Inputs   196
    7.1a   The Organization of Production   196
    7.1b   Classification of Inputs   197
7.2 Production with One Variable Input   198
    7.2a   Total, Average, and Marginal Product   199
    7.2b   The Geometry of Average and Marginal Product
Curves   200
    7.2c   The Law of Diminishing Returns and Stages of
Production   202
7.3 Production with Two Variable Inputs   205
    7.3a   Definition of Isoquants   206
    7.3b   Derivation of Total Product Curves from the
Isoquant Map   207
7.4 The Shape of Isoquants   209
    7.4a   Characteristics of Isoquants   209
    7.4b   Economic Region of Production   212
    7.4c   Fixed-Proportions Production Functions   214
7.5 Constant, Increasing, and Decreasing Returns to
Scale   216
7.6 Applications   219
Summary   223
Glossary   224
Questions for Review   225
Problems   226
Supplementary Readings   227

Chapter 8 Costs of Production   225

8.1 The Nature of Production Costs   229
8.2 Optimal Combination of Inputs   232
    8.2a   Isocost Lines   232
    8.2b   Least-Cost Input Combination   234
    8.2c   Cost Minimization in the Long and Short
Runs   235
8.3 Theory of Cost in the Short Run   236
    8.3a   Total Costs   236

8.3b   Per-Unit Costs   238

8.3c   The Geometry of Per-Unit Cost Curves   241

8.4   Long-Run Theory of Costs   244

8.4a   Expansion Path and the Long-Run Total Cost Curve   244

8.4b   Derivation of the Long-Run Average Cost Curve   246

8.4c   Relationship Between Short- and Long-Run Cost Curves   247

8.5   The Shape of the Long-Run Average Cost Curve   250

8.6   Applications   251

Summary   257

Glossary   258

Questions for Review   258

Problems   259

Supplementary Readings   261

Chapter 9   Extensions of Production and Cost Theory   262

9.1   The Cobb-Douglas Production Function   263

9.1a   The Formula   264

9.1b   Illustration   264

9.1c   Empirical Estimation   268

9.2   The Elasticity of Substitution   270

9.3   Technological Progress   272

9.4   Linear Programming: The Basic Concepts   274

9.4a   Introduction to Linear Programming   274

9.4b   Some Basic Linear Programming Concepts   275

9.5   Linear Programming: a More Complete Picture   278

9.5a   Solution of Linear Programming Problems   279

9.5b   Illustration of Profit Maximization   279

9.5c   Illustration of Cost Minimization   282

9.6   Applications   286

Summary   292

Glossary   293

Questions for Review   293

Problems   294

Supplementary Readings   295

FOUR   THEORY OF THE FIRM AND MARKET STRUCTURE   297

Chapter 10   Price and Output Under Perfect Competition   298

10.1   Market Structure: Perfect Competition   300

10.2   Price Determination in the Market Period   302

10.3 Short-Run Equilibrium of the Firm   304
    10.3a Total Approach   304
    10.3b Marginal Approach   306
    10.3c Profit Maximization or Loss
        Minimization   308
10.4 Short-Run Supply Curve and Equilibrium   310
    10.4a Short-Run Supply Curve of the Firm and
        Industry   310
    10.4b Short-Run Equilibrium of the Industry and
        Firm   313
10.5 Long-Run Equilibrium of the Firm and Industry   315
    10.5a Long-Run Equilibrium of the Firm   315
    10.5b Long-Run Equilibrium of the Industry and
        Firm   315
10.6 Constant, Increasing, and Decreasing Cost
Industries   319
    10.6a Constant Cost Industries   319
    10.6b Increasing Cost Industries   320
    10.6c Decreasing Cost Industries   321
10.7 Applications   323
    Summary   329
    Glossary   330
    Questions for Review   331
    Problems   332
    Supplementary Readings   333

Chapter 11 Price and Output Under Pure Monopoly   334

11.1 Pure Monopoly   336
    11.1a Definition and Sources of Monopoly   336
    11.1b The Monopolist's Demand Curve   339
11.2 Short-Run Equilibrium Price and Output   341
    11.2a Total Approach   341
    11.2b Marginal Approach   342
    11.2c Profit Maximization or Loss
        Minimization   345
    11.2d Short-Run Marginal Cost and Supply   348
11.3 Long-Run Equilibrium Price and Output   349
    11.3a Profit Maximization in the Long Run   349
    11.3b Comparison with Perfect Competition: The
        Social Cost of Monopoly   351
11.4 Multiplant Monopolist   354
    11.4a Short-Run Equilibrium   354
    11.4b Long-Run Equilibrium   356
11.5 Price Discrimination   356
    11.5a Charging Different Prices for Different
        Quantities   356

        11.5b   Charging Different Prices in Different
               Markets   358
  11.6 Applications   362
       Summary   369
       Glossary   370
       Questions for Review   370
       Problems   371
       Supplementary Readings   373

Chapter 12 Price and Output Under Monopolistic Competition   374

  12.1 Monopolistic Competition   376
        12.1a   The Nature of Monopolistic Competition   376
        12.1b   Demand Curves Under Monopolistic
                Competition   378
  12.2 Short-Run Equilibrium Price and Output   379
  12.3 Long-Run Equilibrium Price and Output   382
  12.4 Product Variation and Selling Expenses   385
        12.4a   Product Variation   385
        12.4b   Selling Expenses   386
  12.5 Evaluation of Monopolistic Competition   389
        12.5a   Comparison with Perfect Competition   389
        12.5b   Evaluation of the Theory of Monopolistic
                Competition   392
  12.6 Applications   393
       Summary   397
       Glossary   398
       Questions for Review   398
       Problems   399
       Supplementary Readings   400

Chapter 13 Price and Output Under Oligopoly   401

  13.1 Oligopoly: Definition and Sources   403
  13.2 No Rivalry Recognized: The Cournot and the Edgeworth
      Models   405
        13.2a   The Cournot Model   405
        13.2b   The Edgeworth Model   407
  13.3 Rivalry Recognized: The Chamberlin and the Kinked-
      Demand Curve Models   409
        13.3a   The Chamberlin Model   409
        13.3b   The Kinked-Demand Curve Model   411
  13.4 Theory of Games and Oligopolistic Behavior   413
        13.4a   Zero-Sum Games   413
        13.4b   Mixed Strategies   415

13.4c   Non-Zero Sum Games   416
13.4d   The Prisoners' Dilemma   417
13.5   Collusion: Cartels, Price Leadership Models, and Antitrust Laws   419
13.5a   The Centralized Cartel   419
13.5b   Market-Sharing Cartel   422
13.5c   Price Leadership   424
13.5d   Oligopoly and Antitrust Laws   427
13.6   Long-Run Adjustments and Efficiency Implications   428
13.6a   Long-Run Adjustments   428
13.6b   Nonprice Competition   429
13.6c   Welfare Effects   430
13.7   Applications   431
Summary   439
Glossary   441
Questions for Review   442
Problems   443
Supplementary Readings   444

FIVE   PRICING AND EMPLOYMENT OF INPUTS   445

Chapter 14   Input Price and Employment Under Perfect Competition   446

14.1   Profit Maximization and Optimal Input Employment   448
14.2   The Demand Curve of a Firm for an Input   450
14.2a   The Demand Curve of a Firm for One Variable Input   450
14.2b   The Demand Curve of a Firm for One of Several Variable Inputs   452
14.3   The Market Demand Curve for an Input and Its Elasticity   454
14.3a   The Market Demand Curve for an Input   455
14.3b   Determinants of the Price Elasticity of Demand for an Input   456
14.4   The Supply Curve of an Input   458
14.4a   The Supply of Labor by an Individual   459
14.4b   The Substitution and the Income Effects of a Wage Increase   461
14.4c   The Market Supply Curve for an Input   462
14.5   Pricing and Employment of an Input   464
14.6   Economic Rent   466

14.7 Applications   470
Summary   478
Glossary   479
Questions for Review   480
Problems   481
Supplementary Readings   482

Chapter 15 Input Price and Employment Under Imperfect Competition   483

15.1 Profit Maximization and Optimal Input Employment   485
15.2 The Demand Curve of a Firm for an Input   486
15.2a The Demand Curve of a Firm for One Variable Input   486
15.2b The Demand Curve of a Firm for One of Several Variable Inputs   488
15.3 The Market Demand Curve, and Input Price and Employment   489
15.4 Monopsony   491
15.5 Monopsony Pricing and Employment of One Variable Input   494
15.6 Monopsony Pricing and Employment of Several Variable Inputs   497
15.7 Applications   500
Summary   507
Glossary   508
Questions for Review   509
Problems   510
Supplementary Readings   511

Chapter 16 Intertemporal Choice: Interest and Capital   512

16.1 Lending–Borrowing Equilibrium   514
16.1a Lending   514
16.1b Borrowing   517
16.1c The Market Rate of Interest with Borrowing and Lending   519
16.2 Saving–Investment Equilibrium   522
16.2a Saving-Investment Equilibrium without Borrowing and Lending   522
16.2b Saving-Investment Equilibrium with Borrowing and Lending   524
16.2c The Market Rate of Interest with Saving and Investment, Borrowing and Lending   526

16.3 Investment Decisions   528

    16.3a   Present-Value Rule for Investment Decisions: The Two-Period Case   528

    16.3b   Present-Value Rule for Investment Decisions: The Multiperiod Case   530

16.4 Determinants of the Market Rates of Interest   535

16.5 Applications   537

Summary   546

Glossary   546

Questions for Review   547

Problems   548

Supplementary Readings   549

SIX GENERAL EQUILIBRIUM, WELFARE ECONOMICS, AND THE ROLE OF GOVERNMENT 551

Chapter 17 General Equilibrium Analysis 552

17.1 Partial vs. General Equilibrium Analysis   554

17.2 General Equilibrium of Exchange   557

17.3 General Equilibrium of Production   561

17.4 Derivation of the Production Possibilities Frontier   563

17.5 General Equilibrium of Production and Exchange   565

17.6 Applications   569

Summary   576

Glossary   577

Questions for Review   577

Problems   578

Supplementary Readings   580

Chapter 18 Welfare Economics 581

18.1 Welfare Economics—The General Concept   583

    18.1a   The Meaning of Welfare Economics and Pareto Optimality   583

    18.1b   Marginal Conditions for Economic Efficiency and Pareto Optimum   585

18.2 Utility-Possibilities Frontiers   586

    18.2a   The Utility-Possibilities Frontier   586

    18.2b   The Grand Utility-Possibilities Frontier   588

18.3 The Social Welfare Function and the Point of Maximum Social Welfare   590

    18.3a   The Social Welfare Function   590

    18.3b   The Point of Maximum Social Welfare   591

18.4 Perfect Competition and Economic Efficiency   593
18.5 Social Policy Criteria   595
    18.5a Measuring Changes in Social Welfare   596
    18.5b Arrow's Impossibility Theorem   598
    18.5c The Theory of the Second Best   599
18.6 Applications   600
    Summary   606
    Glossary   607
    Questions for Review   608
    Problems   609
    Supplementary Readings   611

Chapter 19 Externalities, Public Goods, and the Role of Government   611

19.1 Externalities   612
    19.1a Externalities Defined   613
    19.1b Externalities and Market Failure   613
19.2 Externalities and Property Rights   616
19.3 Public Goods   618
    19.3a The Nature of Public Goods   618
    19.3b The Provision of Public Goods   621
19.4 Benefit–Cost Analysis   622
19.5 Applications   624
    Summary   629
    Glossary   630
    Questions for Review   631
    Problems   631
    Supplementary Readings   633

APPENDICES   634

A Mathematical Appendix   A1

B Answers to Selected Problems   B1

Glossary Index   I1

Name Index   I5

Subject Index   I7

Microeconomics:
Theory and Applications

Introduction

ONE

Part One (Chapters 1–2) presents an introduction to microeconomic theory and a review of some principles of economics. Chapter 1 deals with scarcity as the fundamental economic fact facing every society, examines the function or purpose of microeconomic theory and its methodology, and discusses the overall organization of the text and of each of its chapters. Chapter 2 is a brief review of the concepts of demand, supply, equilibrium, and elasticities. As such, Chapter 2 can be skipped by those who remember well these concepts from principles of economics.

Introduction

Chapter 1

1-1　The Fundamental Economic Fact

1-2　The Functions of an Economic System

1-3　Microeconomic Theory and the Price System

1-4　Models and Methodology

1-5　Positive and Normative Economics

1-6　Organization of the Book

Examples

1-1　Why Do Economists Earn More Than Sociologists?

1-2　The 1981 Florida Freeze and the Price of Orange Juice

1-3　Agreement and Disagreement Among Economists

> **Preview Questions**
>
> Why can human wants never be fully satisfied?
>
> Who decides how many color TV's are produced in the U.S. each year?
>
> Why are textiles produced with much machinery and few workers in the U.S.?
>
> Why are there few automakers but many wheat farmers?
>
> Why do economists earn more than sociologists?
>
> Should the minimum wage be raised?
>
> Should government initiate a guaranteed job program?
>
> How can we distinguish between a good economic theory and bad one?

Microeconomic theory is perhaps the most important course in all economics and business programs. It provides the tools for understanding how the U.S. economy and most other economies operate. That is, microeconomic theory can help us answer such questions as why if society spends more on defense it may have to accept less public housing; why the price of housing has risen sharply in recent years; why the price of beef is higher than the price of chicken; why the price of gasoline rose sharply during the 1970s and is declining in the 1980s; why textiles are produced with much machinery and few workers in the U.S. but with many workers and a small amount of machinery in India; why there are only a handful of automakers but many wheat farmers in the U.S.; why the courts ordered the breakup of AT&T in 1982; why physicians earn more than cab drivers and college professors; why raising the minimum wage leads to increased youth unemployment; why environmental pollution arises and how it can be regulated; why some goods and services (such as national defense) are provided by the government. These are only a few of the important questions that microeconomic theory helps us answer.

More generally, microeconomic theory examines how a consumer spends his or her income to maximize satisfaction, how a firm combines resources to minimize production costs and maximize profits, how a particular form of market structure (perfect competition, monopoly, monopolistic competition, and oligopoly) arises and how each affects the well-being of society, how the pricing and employment of resources or inputs are determined, and how government can increase the well-being of society by taxes and subsidies. Surely these are important questions. Microeconomic theory provides the tools that enable us to answer these questions.

Microeconomic theory is also the basis for most "applied" fields of economics such as industrial economics, labor economics, natural resources and environmental economics, agricultural economics, regional economics, public finance, development economics, and international economics. One cannot understand well these other fields without a thorough understanding of microeconomic theory. This is why students are usually required to take microeconomic theory before taking courses in these other fields.

In this introductory chapter, we define the subject matter and the methodology of microeconomics. We begin by examining the meaning of scarcity as the fundamental economic fact facing every society. We then go on to discuss the basic economic functions that all economic systems must somehow perform and the way they are performed in a free-enterprise economic system such as our own. Subsequently, we go on to examine the role of theory or models in microeconomics, discuss the basic methodology of economics, and distinguish between positive and normative economics. Finally, we examine briefly the organization of the book and of each of its chapters.

1-1

The Fundamental Economic Fact

According to the usual definition, **economics** deals with the allocation of scarce resources among alternative uses to satisfy human wants. The essence of this definition rests on the meaning of human wants and resources and on the scarcity of economic resources in relation to insatiable human wants. These concepts are now examined in turn.

1-1a Human Wants and Resources

Human wants refer to all the goods, services, and the conditions of life that individuals desire. That is, human wants refer to the quality, variety, and quantity of foods we want; to the quality, location, and size of housing we wish; to the clothes we want to wear, the car we want to drive, the appliances we desire, the education, the entertainment, the vacations we wish, and so on. Human wants vary, of course, among different people, over different periods of time, and in different locations. However, human wants always seem to be greater than the goods and services available to satisfy those wants. While we may be able to get all we desire of hamburgers, beer, pencils, and magazines, there are always more and better things that we are unable to obtain. No matter how good our clothes, house, car, education, or vacation, we always seem to wish for more and better ones. In short, the sum total of all human wants are insatiable or can never be fully satisfied.

Resources are the inputs, the factors or the means of producing the goods and services we want. **Economic resources** or inputs can be classified broadly into land or natural resources, labor or human resources, and capital. These are the resources that firms must pay to hire. Land or natural resources refer to the fertility of the soil, the climate, the forests, and the mineral deposits present in the soil. Labor refers to all human effort, both physical and mental, that can be directed toward producing desired goods and services. It includes entrepreneurial talent to combine other labor, capital, and natural resources to produce new, better, or cheaper products. Finally, capital is all the "produced" means of production such as the machinery, factories, equipment, tools, inventories, drainage and irrigation on agricultural land, and the transportation and communication networks. All of these greatly facilitate the production of other goods and services. Note that the economist's definition of capital differs from that of the "man in the street," who instead uses the word "capital" to mean "money." In the economist's sense, money is not capital because money, as such, produces nothing but simply facilitates the exchange of goods and services. Note also that this broad threefold classification of resources into land, labor, and capital is only a convenient way to organize the discussion and does not convey the enormous variety of specific resources that each category encompasses.

1-1b Scarcity

It is important to note that the same resource could be used either to produce some specific goods and services or others. That is, resources have alternative uses. For example, a particular piece of land could be used to build a factory, for housing, for roads, or for a park. A laborer could provide cleaning services, be a porter, construct bridges, or provide other manual services. A student could be trained to become an accountant, a lawyer, or an economist. A tractor could be used to construct a road or a dam. Steel could be used to build a car or a bridge. An even more crucial aspect of all **economic resources** is that they are scarce or limited in supply rather than unlimited. Thus, economic resources command a price; they are not free. While air may be unlimited and free for the purpose of operating an internal-combustion engine, *clean* air to breathe is not free if it requires the installation and operation of antipollution equipment. In economics, we are interested in economic resources and **economic goods** rather than in free ones. **Free resources** and **free goods** are those of which the quantity supplied exceeds the quantity demanded at zero price.

Since resources are generally limited in supply, the amount of goods and services that any society can produce is also limited. That is, society cannot produce all of the comfortable housing, nutritious food, and elegant clothing that all members of society want. It also cannot provide all the education nor satisfy all the vacation desires of the population. Society simply cannot have all the goods and services that it wants, but must choose which commodities to produce and which to sacrifice. In short, society can only satisfy some wants rather than all wants. Thus, every society faces

5

scarcity. If human wants were limited or resources unlimited, there would be no scarcity and there would be no need to study economics.

The pervasiveness of scarcity facing all societies is clearly shown by the **production possibilities frontier** or **transformation curve** of Figure 1-1. In the figure, *ABDE* is a hypothetical production possibilities frontier of a nation producing two commodities, food and clothing. It shows the alternative combinations of food and clothing that the economy can produce by fully utilizing all of its resources with the best technology available to it. For example, point *B* indicates that the nation can produce 6 units of food (6F) and 8 units of clothing (8C) by fully employing all labor, capital, and natural resources with the best technology available to the nation. The nation does not presently have the resources to reach a point such as *G* (9F, 8C) outside the production frontier. On the other hand, point *H* (6F, 4C) inside the frontier indicates that the nation is not fully utilizing all of its resources with the best technology available.

Starting at any point on production frontier *ABDE*, the nation can produce more food only by producing less clothing. A reduction in the output of clothing is necessary in order to release resources for the production of additional food. This makes the transformation curve negatively sloped. Thus, if starting at point *B* (6F, 8C), the nation wants to produce an additional 3 units of food, it must give up 4 units of clothing (the movement from point *B* to point *D* along the frontier). The economy simply does not

FIGURE 1-1.
Production
Possibilities
Frontier

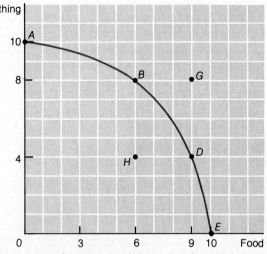

ABDE is a production possibilities frontier. It shows the alternative combinations of food and clothing that the economy can produce by fully utilizing all the resources at its disposal with the best technology available to it. A point such as G above the frontier can be reached only with growth. A point such as H inside the frontier is inefficient. Starting at a point such as B on the frontier, the nation can produce an additional 3 units of food only by giving up 4 units of clothing (the movement from point B to point D) because resources are scarce.

have enough resources to produce 9 units of food without reducing the quantity of clothing produced to 4 units (point *D*). No society can produce all the goods and services it wants. That is, every society faces scarcity.

Over time, resources may increase as the size and skills of the labor force rise, as new mineral resources are discovered and new uses are found for available land and natural resources, as the nation's stock of capital is increased, and as **technology** improves (i.e., as more productive ways are found to organize production). With growth, the nation's production possibilities frontier shifts outward and the nation can produce more of both food and clothing than before growth. However, while society's ability to produce goods and services generally rises over time, human wants always seem to move well ahead of society's ability to satiate or fully satisfy them. Thus, scarcity remains. Perhaps the first economic lesson that a toddler learns is that he or she must choose between this toy and that toy and cannot have both. Thus, scarcity is all-pervasive. One must choose between going to college or going to work, watching TV or studying during the same period of time, going to the movies or going to a game on a limited budget. In a nutshell, scarcity is the **fundamental economic fact** of every society. As such, scarcity is an important unifying theme found throughout the text and economics.

1-2

The Functions of an Economic System

Faced with the pervasiveness of scarcity, all societies, from the most primitive to the most advanced, must somehow determine (1) what to produce, (2) how to produce, (3) for whom to produce, (4) how to provide for the growth of the system, and (5) how to ration a given quantity of a commodity over time. Let us look at each of these five basic functions to see exactly what they mean and examine how the **price system** performs each of these functions under a **free-enterprise system** (i.e., in a system where the government allows private property and private economic decisions by individuals and firms).

What to produce refers to which goods and services to produce and in which quantities to produce them. Since no society can produce all the goods and services it wants, it must choose which to produce and which to forego. In a free-enterprise system, the function of what to produce is accomplished by the price system. That is, only those goods and services for which consumers are willing and able to pay a price sufficiently high to cover at least all costs of production will generally be produced over time. Automobile manufacturers will simply not produce cars costing $1 million if no one is there to purchase them. Consumers can generally induce firms to produce more of a commodity by paying a higher price for it. On the other hand, a reduction in the price that consumers are willing to pay for a commodity will usually result in a decline in the output of the commodity. For example, an increase in the price of milk and a reduction in the price of eggs are signals to farmers to raise more cows and fewer chickens.

How to produce refers to the way in which resources or inputs are organized to produce the goods and services that consumers want. Should textiles be produced with a great deal of labor and little capital or, alternatively, with little labor and a great deal of capital? Since resources are scarce, it is important for society to use the available resources as efficiently as possible. In a free-enterprise system, the way in which resources are oganized in production is also determined by the price system. That is, since the price of resources reflects their relative scarcity, firms will combine them in such a way as to minimize costs of production. By doing so, they will use resources in the most efficient and productive way to produce those commodities that society wants and values the most. When the price of a resource rises, firms will attempt to economize on the use of that resource and substitute cheaper resources so as to minimize their production costs. For example, a rise in the minimum wage leads firms to substitute machinery for some unskilled labor.

For whom to produce deals with the way that the output is distributed among the members of society. This function is also performed by the price system. Those individuals who possess the most valued skills (i.e., those skills that are used to produce the most valued commodities) or own a greater amount of other resources will receive higher incomes and will be able to pay and coax firms to produce more of the commodities they want. Their greater monetary "votes" enable them to satisfy more of their wants. For example, society produces more goods and services for the average physician than for the average clerk because the former has a much greater income than the latter.

Example 1-1 Why Do Economists Earn More Than Sociologists?

The Facts: Table 1-1 gives salaries for college professors in various fields in 1981.

Comment: Economics professors earn more than professors of other social sciences because of the more valuable opportunities for rewarding occupations in business, government, and consulting that are available to economists. It may also take longer and cost more to train economists than other social scientists. Therefore, in order to keep economists teaching, colleges and universities must pay higher salaries than those required to keep other social scientists teaching. This also means that, on the average, more of society's resources are directed at producing the goods and services wanted by the former than by the latter.

In all but the most primitive societies there is still another function that the economic system must perform. That is, it must provide for the growth

8

TABLE 1-1   Salaries of University or College Professors with Ph.D.'s in 1981

Field	Median Salary
Engineers	$34,600
Medical Scientists	33,900
Physicists	31,500
*Economists	31,100
Computer Specialists	30,300
Chemists	29,700
Mathematicians	29,700
Statisticians	29,500
Biological Scientists	28,800
Psychologists	28,600
Political Scientists	28,200
*Sociologists/Anthropologists	27,400

Source: National Science Foundation, *Characteristics of Doctoral Scientists and Engineers in the United States: 1981* (Washington, D.C.: 1982), p. 59.

of the nation over time. While governments can crucially affect the rate of **economic growth** by tax incentives, and by incentives for research, education, and training, the price system is also important. For example, interest payments provide the incentive to savers to postpone present consumption, thereby releasing resources to increase society's stock of capital goods. Capital accumulation and technological improvements are stimulated by the expectations of profits. Similarly, the incentive of higher wages (the price of labor services) induces people to acquire more training and education which increases their productivity. It is through capital accumulation, technological improvements, and increases in the quantity and quality (productivity) of labor that a nation grows over time. These are all affected by the operation of the price system.

Finally, an economic system must allocate a given quantity of a commodity over time. **Rationing over time** is also accomplished by the price system. For example, the price of wheat is not so low immediately after harvest that some wheat does not last until the next harvest. This results because some people (speculators) will buy some wheat soon after harvest (when the price is low) and sell it later (before the next harvest) when the price is higher. By doing so, the price of wheat is not so low after harvest that all of the harvested wheat is exhausted (consumed) before the next harvest.

Thus, we see that under a free-enterprise economic system, the price system organizes and coordinates economic activity and determines which commodities are produced and in what quantities, how production is organized, and how the output is distributed. The price system is also important for the growth of the nation and in the rationing of a given quantity of a commodity over time.

1-3

Microeconomic Theory and the Price System

In this section, we define the subject matter of microeconomic theory, briefly examine the determination and function of prices in a system of free enterprise, and show how governments affect the operation of the economic system. We will see that prices play such an important role that microeconomic theory is often referred to as "price theory."

1-3a The Circular Flow of Economic Activity

Microeconomic theory studies the economic behavior of *individual* decision-making units such as individual consumers, resource owners, and business firms, and the operation of individual markets in a free-enterprise economy. This is to be contrasted with **macroeconomic theory** which studies the total or *aggregate* level of output and national income, and the level of national employment, consumption, investment, and prices for the economy *viewed as a whole.* Both microeconomics and macroeconomics provide very useful tools of analysis and both are important. While macroeconomics often makes the headlines, microeconomics attempts to explain some of the most important economic and social problems of the day. These range from the high cost of energy, to welfare programs, environmental pollution, rent control, minimum wages, safety regulations, rising medical costs, monopoly, discrimination, labor unions, wages and leisure, crime and punishment, taxation and subsidies, and so on.

Microeconomics focuses attention on two broad categories of economic units: households and business firms, and it examines the operation of two types of markets: the market for goods and services, and the market for economic resources. The interaction of households and business firms in the markets for goods and services and in the markets for economic resources represents the core of the free-enterprise economic system. Specifically, households own the labor, the capital, the land, and the natural resources that business firms require to produce the goods and services households want. Business firms pay to households wages, salaries, interest, rents, and so on, for the services and resources that households provide. Households then use the income that they receive from business firms to purchase the goods and services produced by business firms. The income of households are the production costs of business firms. The expenditures of households are the receipts of business firms. The so-called **circular flow of economic activity** is complete.

The circular flow of economic activity can be visualized in Figure 1-2. The inner loop shows the flow of economic resources from households to business firms and the flow of goods and services from business firms to households. The outer loop shows the flow of money incomes from busi-

FIGURE 1-2.
*The Circular Flow
of Economic
Activity*

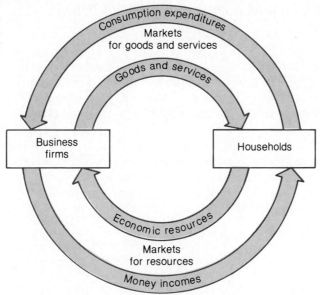

The inner loop shows the flow of resources from households to business firms and the flow of goods and services from business firms to households. The outer loop shows the flow of money incomes from business firms to households and the flow of consumption expenditures from households to business firms. The prices of goods and services are determined in the top half of the figure and the prices of resources in the bottom half of the figure.

ness firms to households and the flow of consumption expenditures from households to business firms. Thus, the inner loop represents production flows while the outer loop represents financial flows.

Looking at it from a different perspective, we see that the top part of Figure 1-2 shows the flow of goods and services from business firms to households and the opposite flow of consumption expenditures from households to business firms. Here are the markets where goods and services are bought and sold. The bottom part of Figure 1-2 shows the flow of resources from households to business firms and the opposite flow of money incomes to households. Here are the markets where resources or their services are bought and sold.

Specifically, the top loop shows consumers' purchases of foods, clothing, housing, health care, education, transportation, recreation, vacations, and so on, and the expenditures that consumers incur to pay for them. The bottom loop shows the labor time, the capital, the land, and the entrepreneurship that individuals provide to firms in return for wages, interest, rent, and profits, which represent the incomes with which consumers purchase the goods and services they want.

1-3b Determination and Function of Prices

The prices of goods and services are determined in the markets for goods and services (the top half of Figure 1-2), while the prices of resources and their services are determined in the markets for resources (the bottom half of Figure 1-2). If households want to purchase more of a commodity than is placed on the market by business firms, the price of the commodity will be bid up until the *shortage* of the commodity is eliminated. This occurs because at a higher price households will want to *purchase less* of the commodity while business firms will want to *produce more* of the commodity. For example, if automobile prices rise, consumers will want to purchase fewer automobiles while automakers will want to produce more automobiles. Automakers can produce more automobiles at higher prices because they are able to bid resources (labor, capital, and land) away from other uses.

On the other hand, if households want to purchase less of a commodity than business firms place on the market, the price of the commodity will fall until the *surplus* of the commodity disappears. This occurs because at a lower price households will want to *purchase more* of the commodity while business firms will want to *produce less* of the commodity. For example, if consumers want to purchase less beef than farmers send to market, the price of beef falls until the quantity demanded of beef matches the quantity supplied. In the process, farmers will hire fewer resources so that some resources will be freed to produce more of other commodities that consumers value more highly. Thus, it is the system of commodity prices that determines which commodities are produced and in what quantities (the "what to produce" question of the previous section) and how resources are utilized.

Example 1-2 The 1981 Florida Freeze and the Price of Orange Juice

The Facts: On Tuesday, January 13, 1981, Florida registered the coldest temperature since 1977. The freeze dehydrated oranges and reduced juice yields by about 28 percent, thus raising the price of orange juice by over 40 percent. The increase in the price of orange juice was expected to keep orange juice consumption in the U.S. below the 230 million gallons reached in 1980 and to increase imports from Brazil from less than 20 million gallons in 1980 to over 50 million gallons in 1981.

Comment: This example vividly portrays the workings of the price system. The freeze reduced the domestic supply of orange juice. As consumers wanted to purchase more orange juice than was available at existing prices, they bid prices up. This discouraged consumption and encouraged imports (which made up for part of the reduction in domestic production) until the reduced quantity of orange juice that consumers wanted to purchase at the higher price matched the reduced supply. Thus, we see how a shortage of orange juice was automatically eliminated by the workings of the price system.

Source: Commodities, April 1981, pp. 62–63.

Turning to factor markets, if households provide less of a resource or service than business firms want to hire at a given price, the price of the resource will be bid up until the shortage of the resource is eliminated. This occurs because at higher resource prices, households will usually provide more of the resource or service while business firms will economize on the use of the resource (so as to minimize production costs). For example, if hospitals want to hire more nurses than are available, nurses' salaries rise. This results in more people entering nursing schools and in hospitals economizing on the use of nurses (for example, by employing more orderlies at lower salaries to perform some of the tasks previously performed by nurses). The process continues until the adjustment (i.e., the shortage of nurses) is eliminated.[1]

On the other hand, if too much of a resource is made available at a given price, the price falls until the surplus is eliminated. This occurs because at lower resource prices, households will usually provide less of the resource or service while business firms will substitute in production the cheaper resource for the more expensive one (so as to minimize production costs). Thus, in a free-enterprise economy it is the system of resource prices that determines how production is organized and how the income of resource owners is established (the "how to produce" and the "for whom to produce" questions of the previous section).

It is because of the crucial function of prices in determining what goods are produced and in what quantities, how production is organized, and how output or income is distributed that microeconomic theory is often referred to as **price theory.**[2]

1-3c Effect of Government

So far our discussion has deliberately excluded government. Bringing government into the picture will modify somewhat the operation of the system but will not, in a free-enterprise system such as our own, replace the operation of markets. Governments affect the circular flow of economic activity

---

[1] The shortage of nurses may last many years if the demand for hospital care and for nurses outstrips the increasing number of nurses being trained or if market imperfections and government involvement prevents wages from rising to the equilibrium level. This is what seems to have happened in fact in many areas of the U.S.

[2] In imperfectly competitive markets (monopoly, monopolistic competition, and oligopoly) the price system does not function as smoothly as indicated above and the determination of commodity and resource prices and quantities is more complex.

by purchasing goods and services for public consumption (education, defense, police, and so on) that compete with privately consumed goods and services. Governments may themselves produce some goods and services, thus leaving fewer resources for business firms to use. Most importantly, governments, through taxes and subsidies, usually redistribute income from the rich to the poor. By doing so, they can greatly affect the circular flow of economic activity. Governments also use taxes to discourage the consumption of certain commodities such as alcohol and tobacco and provide incentives for the consumption of others such as housing and education. Thus, ours is a **mixed economy** comprising private enterprise and government actions and policies.

While government policies certainly affect the circular flow of economic activity in a free-enterprise system, they do not replace the price system.[3] This is to be contrasted with a centrally planned economy such as the U.S.S.R. or China, where most economic decisions are made by government officials or planning committees. There, it is the government rather than the markets that sets prices. This represents an alternative to the free-enterprise system as to how the basic economic questions are answered. More often than not, when government sets prices, persistent shortages of certain commodities result (as evidenced by the long lines in front of some stores) while some other commodities are unwanted and go to waste. This results because it is very difficult for the government to determine the correct (i.e., the market-clearing) prices of goods and services. Thus, long lines can often be seen in front of many Moscow restaurants and a car can only be purchased in the Soviet Union after waiting periods ranging from months to years.

In contrast, in the U.S. and other free-enterprise or mixed economies, the price system operates so smoothly that people are not even aware of it. Only on rare occasions (usually as a result of government interference), do we become aware that something is wrong. The long lines to get gasoline at most gas stations in 1979 resulted because of the attempt on the part of the U.S. government to keep gasoline prices below the market level. When price controls were eliminated and the price of gasoline was allowed to rise to the market level, gasoline lines disappeared. When bad weather sharply reduced the output of Florida oranges in 1977 and 1981, and that of fresh fruits and vegetables in 1984, no waiting lines were seen outside food stores in the U.S. The price of oranges and vegetables simply rose, and this rationed available supplies to match the amounts that consumers wanted to purchase at the higher prices.

---

[3] Government sometimes does replace the price system in some markets by imposing price controls, such as rent ceilings and minimum wages. In general, however, in a free-enterprise economy such as our own, government works through the market (with taxes and subsidies) rather than supplanting it.

1-4

Models and Methodology

In microeconomic theory we seek to predict and explain the economic behavior of individual consumers, resource owners and business firms, and the operation of individual markets. For this purpose we use models. A **model** abstracts from the many details surrounding an event and identifies a few of the most important determinants of the event. For example, the amount of a commodity that an individual demands over a given period of time depends on the price of the commodity, the individual's income, and the price of related commodities (i.e., substitute and complementary commodities). It also depends on the individual's age, sex, education, background, whether the individual is single or married, whether he or she owns a house or rents, the amount of money he or she has in the bank, the stocks the individual owns, the individual's expectations of future income and prices, geographic location, climate, and many other considerations.

However, given the consumer's tastes and preferences, demand theory identifies the price of the commodity, the individual's income, and the price of related commodities as the most important determinants of the amount of a commodity demanded by an individual. While it may be *unrealistic* to focus only on these three considerations, demand theory postulates that these are generally capable of predicting accurately and explaining consumer behavior and demand. One could, of course, include additional considerations or variables to gain a fuller or more complete explanation of consumer demand, but that would defeat the main purpose of the theory or model, which is to simplify and generalize.

A theory or model usually results from casual observation of the real world. For example, we may observe that consumers, in general, purchase less of a commodity when its price rises. However, before such a theory of demand can be accepted, we must go back to the real world to test it. We must make sure that individuals in different places, and over different periods of time do indeed, as a group, purchase less of a commodity when its price rises. Only after many such successful tests and the absence of contradictory results, can we accept the theory and make use of it in subsequent analysis to predict and explain consumer behavior. If, on the other hand, test results contradict the model, then the model must be discarded and a new one formulated.

To summarize, a theory or model is usually developed by casual observation of the real world, but we must then go back to the real world to determine whether or not the implications or predictions of the theory are indeed correct. Only then can we accept the theory or model. We should emphasize that a model is not tested by the realism or lack of realism of its assumptions but rather by its ability to predict accurately and explain. The assumptions of the model are usually unrealistic in that they must necessarily represent a simplification and generalization of reality. However, if the model predicts accurately and explains the event, it is tentatively accepted. In a nutshell, the accepted **methodology of economics** (and science in general) is that a model is tested not by the realism or lack of realism of its assumptions but only by its predictive ability.

For example, demand theory, as originally developed, was based on the assumption that utility (i.e., the satisfaction that a consumer receives from the consumption of a commodity) is cardinally measurable (i.e., we can attach specific numerical values to it). This assumption is clearly unrealistic. Nevertheless, we accept the theory of demand because it leads to the correct prediction that a consumer will purchase less of a commodity when its price rises (other things, such as the consumer's income and the price of related commodities, remaining equal).

In microeconomic theory, we will be presenting and applying many economic theories or models that seek to predict and explain the economic behavior of consumers, resource owners, and business firms as they interact in the markets for goods, services, and resources. The models presented are generally those that have already been successfully tested. In a microeconomic theory course, we are not concerned with the actual testing of these theories or models, but rather with their presentation, usefulness, and applications.

1-5

Positive and Normative Economics

An important distinction made in economics is that between positive economics (or analysis) and normative economics.

Positive economics or analysis studies what *is*. It is concerned with how the economic system performs the basic economic functions of what to produce, how to produce, for whom to produce, how it provides for growth, and how it rations the available supply of a good over time. That is, how is the price of a commodity, service, or resource actually determined in the market? How do producers combine resources to minimize costs of production? How does the number of firms in a market and the type of product they produce affect the determination of the price and quantity sold of the commodity? How does the number and type of owners and users of a resource affect the price and quantity of the resource placed on the market? How do specific taxes and subsidies affect the production and consumption of various commodities and the use of various resources? What effect do minimum wages have on employment and incomes? The level of real wages on work and leisure? Rent control on the availability of housing? Deregulation of gas on gas prices and consumption? How does the economic system provide for the growth of the nation? How does it ration the available supply of a commodity over time? All of these and many more topics fall within the realm of positive economics. Positive economics is entirely statistical in nature and is devoid of ethical or value judgements.

Normative economics, on the other hand, studies what *ought* to be. It is concerned with how the basic economic functions *should* be performed. Normative economics is thus based on value judgments and, as such, is subjective and controversial. While positive economics is independent of normative economics, the latter is based both on the former and the value judgments of society. Controversies in positive economics can be (and are) usually resolved by the collection of more or better market data. On the other hand, controversies in normative economics usually are not and cannot be resolved. Take, for example, the case of national defense expenditures. Many people believe that national defense expenditures should be reduced. Others are against reductions, and no amount of economic analysis is going to resolve the controversy. Economists can provide an analysis of the *economic* costs and benefits of national defense expenditures. This can be very useful in clarifying the economic issues involved, but it is not likely to lead to general agreement on the proposition that national defense expenditures should or should not be reduced. The reason is that value judgements are involved. This is to be contrasted to the statement that rent ceilings result in a housing shortage, which economic analysis and real-world observation demonstrate to be generally true (and with which all but a tiny minority of people agree).

Example 1-3   Agreement and Disagreement Among Economists

The Facts: Table 1-2 shows the responses to various propositions of the more than 200 economists who responded to a questionnaire sent to a random sample of 600 economists. These responses can help us determine which of the propositions belong to positive economics and which to normative economics.

Comment: The first two propositions in Table 1-1 can be taken to be propositions of positive economics because they elicit general agreement. That is, the vast majority of economists agree that a ceiling on rents reduces the quality and quantity of housing and that a minimum wage increases unemployment among young and unskilled workers. The last four propositions are normative and give rise to wide disagreement, as indicated by the substantial minority of economists who disagree. To be noted is that economic analysis and the collection of more and better data (facts) can resolve many controversies among people in society as a whole. Only those disagreements that remain and which are based on ethical or value judgements belong to normative economics.

Except for the last two chapters and some of the applications at the end of each chapter, this book is primarily concerned with positive economics. Statements such as national defense expenditures should be reduced and

TABLE 1-2   **Responses of Economists to Various Propositions**

Proposition	Percentage of Respondents Who Agreed	Disagreed
1. A ceiling on rents reduces the quality and quantity of housing	98	2
2. A minimum wage increases unemployment among young and unskilled workers	90	10
3. The distribution of income in the U.S. should be more equal	71	29
4. National defense expenditures should be reduced from the present level	66	34
5. The level of government spending should be reduced (disregarding expenditures for stabilization)	57	43
6. The government should be the employer of last resort and initiate a guaranteed job program	53	47

Source: J. Kearl, et al., "A Confusion of Economists?" *American Economic Review,* Vol. 69, No. 2 (May 1979), p. 30. See also B. S. Frey, et al., "Consensus and Dissension Among Economists: An Empirical Inquiry," *American Economic Review,* Vol. 74, No. 5 (December 1984), p. 991.

government should initiate guaranteed job programs are propositions of normative economics, because they are based on value judgements. The economists' tools of analysis and logic can be applied to determine the economic benefits and costs of normative questions, leaving for society as a whole (through elected representatives) the task of making normative decisions. It is extremely important in economics to specify exactly when we are leaving the realm of positive economics and entering that of normative economics. That is, when disagreements can be resolved by the collection of more or better data (facts) and when ethical or value judgements are involved.

The unifying theme throughout positive and normative economics is **economic efficiency.** This refers to the situation in which consumers cannot reorganize their consumption expenditures so as to increase their satisfaction and producers cannot reorganize production to increase output. That is, consumption and production are efficient when, respectively, consumers maximize satisfaction in spending their income and producers combine scarce resources to produce as many as possible of the goods and services that consumers want the most. Economic efficiency is closely related to scarcity. Because resources are scarce, it is essential to utilize them most efficiently. In striving for economic efficiency, government policies may sometimes be required.

Most people in the free world believe (normative statement follows) that a free-enterprise system is more efficient than a system in which the government itself owns the means of production and directly allocates resources and incomes. Recently, even the Soviet Union and communist

China have implicitly acknowledged the importance of the price system by allowing some private and more decentralized decision-making. For example, starting in fall 1984, state-owned enterprises in China were given greater independence and they were made to compete to survive. Many purely economic functions were left to plant managers operating within guidelines, and the prices of many products were left to be determined by the market forces of demand and supply.[4]

1-6

Organization of the Book

In this section we briefly describe the organization of the book and of each of its chapters. We briefly outline the content of each of the six parts of the text and examine how each of the 19 chapters is organized. This is like the examination of a road map before a trip.

1-6a Organization of the Text

The text is organized into six parts. Part I provides an introduction to microeconomic theory (this chapter) and a review of demand and supply (Chapter 2).

Part II (Chapters 3–6) deals with the theory of consumer behavior and demand. It examines consumer preference and choice (Chapter 3), it derives the consumer's demand for a commodity (Chapter 4), and then it shows how to obtain the market demand curve for the commodity and how to measure its responsiveness to price and income changes (Chapter 5). Chapter 6 extends traditional consumer demand theory in some important directions (such as choice in the face of risk).

Part III (Chapters 7–9) deals with the theory of production and costs. Chapter 7 examines how firms combine resources to produce goods and services and Chapter 8 shows the costs of production incurred by firms when hiring resources. Chapter 9 extends traditional production theory in several important ways (such as linear programming).

Part IV (Chapters 10–13) covers the theory of the firm and markets. It shows how the price and output of a final commodity are determined under perfect competition (Chapter 10), pure monopoly (Chapter 11), monopolistic competition (Chapter 12), and oligopoly (Chapter 13).

Part V (Chapters 14–16) presents the theory of input pricing and employment. Chapter 14 examines input pricing and employment under perfect competition, and Chapter 15, under imperfectly competitive markets.

---

[4] See, "Chinese Announce Sweeping Changes in Their Economy," *The New York Times*, October 21, 1984, p. 1. The subtitles of the above article read: "Competition Is Stressed" and "Government Control Is to Be Eased and Many Prices Set by Supply and Demand."

Chapter 16 presents interest and capital theory. That is, it deals with choices in the allocation of inputs over time.

The last part of the text (Part VI) deals with general equilibrium analysis (Chapter 17), welfare economics (Chapter 18), and externalities, public goods, and the role of government (Chapter 19).

1-6b Chapter Organization

Each chapter is organized as follows. The chapter opens with a series of thought-provoking questions. They serve to motivate the student as he reads the chapter. The student should attempt to answer these questions before reading the chapter. After reading the chapter, the student should go back to these questions and possibly revise his or her answers or thoughts on the subject.

The presentation in each chapter is clear and concise, and is reinforced throughout with numerous pertinent real-world examples. The sections of the chapter are numbered for easy reference. Longer sections are broken into two or more numbered subsections. All graphs and diagrams are carefully explained in the text and then summarized briefly in the captions.

Each chapter progresses smoothly *from theory to applications*. Several extensive and current *real-world applications* are included after the presentation of the theory. These carefully chosen applications serve to highlight the relevance of microtheory in analyzing (and offering possible solutions) to important present-day economic problems. The recurrent theme throughout the text is that only by "putting theory to work" does theory "truly" come alive. Applications thus serve to deepen one's understanding of the theory and to demonstrate its usefulness.

Each chapter ends with a number of teaching aids. Each section of the chapter is summarized in one paragraph in the **summary.** Important terms are printed in boldface type when they are first introduced and explained (as in this chapter), and are then collected with their definitions in the **glossary** at the end of the chapter. There are then 12 **questions for review,** which deal with the most important concepts or theories presented in each chapter. This is followed by 12 **problems** (10 in this chapter). Problems differ from the questions for review in that the problems usually ask the student to draw a graph illustrating a particular theory or to calculate a specific measure. These problems are challenging but not tricky or time consuming. They are intended to show whether or not the student understands the material in the chapter and can use it to analyze similar problems. The answers to problems marked by an asterisk are provided at the end of the book for feedback. Finally, there is a short list of **supplementary readings** with an indication of their relevance. For the interested student, a **mathematical appendix** is available at the end of the book.

In short, this text is student oriented. Its aim is to facilitate and enhance student understanding and participation in learning and applying microeconomic analysis.

Summary

1. Economics deals with the allocation of scarce resources among alternative uses to satisfy human wants. Scarcity of resources and commodities is the fundamental economic fact of every society.
2. Faced with the pervasive problem of scarcity, all societies, from the most primitive to the most advanced, must somehow decide what to produce, how to produce, for whom to produce, how to provide for the growth of the system, and how to ration a given amount of a commodity over time. Under a free-enterprise or mixed economic system, such as our own, it is the price system that performs these functions, for the most part.
3. Microeconomic theory studies the economic behavior of individual decision-making units such as individual consumers, resource owners, and business firms, and the operation of individual markets, in a free-enterprise economy. This is contrasted with macroeconomic theory, which studies the economy viewed as a whole. Microeconomic theory focuses attention on households and business firms as they interact in the markets for goods and services and resources. This can be represented by the circular flow of economic activity.
4. Theories make use of models. A model abstracts from the very large number of details surrounding an event and seeks to identify a few of the most important determinants of the event. A theory or model is usually developed by casual observation of the real world. We then must go back to the real world to test that the implications or predictions of the theory or model are indeed correct. Only then can we accept the theory or model. The accepted methodology of eco-

nomics (and science in general) is that a model is tested not by the realism or lack of realism of its assumptions but only by its predictive ability.
5. Positive economics or analysis refers to what is, or how the economic system performs the basic economic functions of what to produce, how to produce, for whom to produce, how to provide for growth, and how to ration the available supply of a commodity over time. Positive economics is entirely statistical in nature and is devoid of ethical or value judgements. Normative economics, on the other hand, studies what ought to be or how the basic economic functions should be performed. Normative economics is based both on positive economics and on value judgements.
6. The book is organized into six parts. Part I (Chapters 1–2) provides an introduction to microeconomic theory and a review of demand and supply. Part II (Chapters 3–6) deals with the theory of consumer behavior and demand, Part III (Chapters 7–9) with the theory of production and cost, Part IV (Chapters 10–13) with the theory of firms and markets, Part V (Chapters 14–16) with the theory of input pricing and employment, and Part VI (Chapters 17–19) with general equilibrium analysis, welfare economics, and externalities, public goods, and the role of government. Each chapter opens with a series of incisive questions and includes numerous examples and applications. All graphs come with captions. End-of-chapter materials include a summary, glossary, questions for review, problems, and supplementary readings. A mathematical appendix is at the end of the book.

Glossary

Economics A field of study that deals with the allocation of scarce resources among alternative uses to satisfy human wants.

Human wants All the goods, services, and the conditions of life that individuals desire, and which provide the driving force for economic activity.

Resources The inputs, the factors, or the means of producing the goods and services that consumers want.

Economic resources Resources that are limited in supply or scarce and thus command a price.

Economic goods Goods that are limited in supply or scarce and can be obtained only at a price.

Free resources Resources of which the quantity supplied exceeds the quantity demanded at zero price.

Free goods Goods of which the quantity supplied exceeds the quantity demanded at zero price.

Technology The state of the arts or techniques available to combine resources or inputs to produce goods and services.

Production possibilities frontier or **transformation curve** It shows the alternative combinations of commodities that a nation can produce by fully utilizing all of its resources with the best technology available to it.

Fundamental economic fact The scarcity of resources and, therefore, of goods and services.

Price system The system whereby the organization and coordination of economic activity is determined by commodity and resource prices.

Free-enterprise system The form of market organization where economic decisions are made by individuals and firms.

What to produce Which goods and services to produce and in what quantities.

How to produce The way resources or inputs are combined to produce the goods and services that consumers want.

For whom to produce The way that output is distributed among the members of society.

Economic growth The increase in resources, commodities, and incomes and the improvements in technology over time.

Rationing over time The allocation of a given amount of a commodity over time.

Microeconomic theory The study of the economic behavior of *individual* decision-making units such as individual consumers, resource owners, and business firms, and the operation of individual markets, in a free-enterprise economy.

Macroeconomic theory The study of the total or *aggregate* level of output, national income, national employment, consumption, investment, and prices for the economy *viewed as a whole*.

Circular flow of economic activity The flow of resources from households to business firms and the opposite flow of money incomes from business firms to households. Also, the flow of goods and services from business firms to households and the opposite flow of consumption expenditures from households to business firms.

Price theory Another name for microeconomic theory that stresses the importance of prices in the determination of what goods are produced and in what quantities, the organization of production, and the distribution of output or income.

Mixed economy An economy, such as our own, characterized by private enterprise and government actions and regulations.

Model Another name for theory or the set of assumptions from which the result of an event is deduced or predicted.

Methodology of economics The proposition that a model is tested not by the realism or lack of realism of its assumptions but by its predictive ability.

Positive economics The study of what *is* or how the economic system performs the basic economic functions. It is entirely statistical in nature and devoid of ethical or value judgements.

Normative economics The study of what *ought* to be or how the basic economic functions *should* be performed. It is based both on positive economics and value judgements.

Economic efficiency The situation in which consumers maximize their satisfaction in spending their income and producers combine resources most productively.

Questions for Review

1. **(a)** What is meant by human wants? Why are they insatiable?
   (b) What is meant by resources? How are they broadly classified? What is the distinction between capital and money in economics?
   (c) What is the distinction between economic resources and noneconomic resources? Between economic goods and noneconomic goods?
   (d) What is meant by technology? Is technology the same in different nations? How can technology be improved over time?

2. **(a)** What is the fundamental fact of every society? Why does it arise?

(b) Will this fundamental fact disappear over time as standards of living rise? Why?

3. (a) What is meant by an economic system? A free-enterprise system? By the price system?

(b) What are the basic functions of any economic system?

(c) How does the price system answer the questions of what, how, and for whom to produce in a free-enterprise system?

4. (a) What is meant by economic growth? Why do modern societies seek economic growth? How do they achieve it?

(b) How does the price system provide for economic growth?

(c) How does the price system ration the given supply of a commodity over time?

5. (a) What is meant by microeconomic theory? How does this differ from macroeconomic theory?

(b) On what broad economic units and markets does microeconomic theory focus attention?

(c) What is meant by the circular flow of economic activity? What is its purpose?

(d) Which are the "real" and which are the "financial" flows in the circular flow of economic activity?

6. (a) What is the relationship between the circular flow of economic activity, and commodity and factor prices?

(b) Why is microeconomic theory often called price theory?

(c) What is meant by a mixed economic system? How are basic economic functions performed in a centrally planned economy?

7. (a) What is the meaning of a theory or model?

(b) What is the purpose of a model?

(c) How are models constructed?

8. (a) How do we distinguish between a good model and a bad model?

(b) Can you give an example of a good economic model?

(c) Can you give an example of a bad economic model?

9. (a) What is meant by positive economics? By normative economics?

(b) What is the relationship between positive economics and normative economics?

10. (a) What is the contribution that economists can make in normative economics?

(b) Can you give an example of positive economics?

(c) Can you give an example of normative economics?

Problems

1. Indicate which characteristic of the production possibilities frontier reflects scarcity.

★2. Show on Figure 1-1 the effect of
(a) an increase in the resources of the nation.
(b) an improvement in technology.
(c) Can the increase in resources and technology eliminate the problem of scarcity? Why?

3. Briefly explain how the sharp increase in petroleum prices since the fall of 1973 affected driving habits and the production of cars in the U.S.

4. Explain why India produces textiles with much more labor relative to capital than the U.S.

5. Explain how the introduction of government affects the circular flow of economic activity.

★6. Explain the effect of government setting the price of a commodity
(a) below that which would prevail without the price ceiling.
(b) above that which would prevail without the price floor.

7. (a) If two models predict equally well but one is more complicated than the other, indicate which model you would use and why.

(b) Indicate how you would determine which of the two models is more complex.

8. (a) Explain how you would go about con-

★ = answer provided at the end of book.

23

structing a model to predict total sales of American-made cars in the U.S. next year.
(b) Indicate how you would test your model.

9. Since economists often disagree on economic matters, economics is not a science. True or false? Explain.

★10. Briefly indicate which aspects of the redistribution of income from higher to lower income people involve
(a) positive economics
(b) normative economics.

Supplementary Readings

A paperback in the Schaum's Outline Series in Economics that gives a problem-solving approach to microeconomic theory and that can be used with this and other texts is

Dominick Salvatore, *Microeconomic Theory,* 2nd ed. (New York: McGraw-Hill, 1983), Chapter 1.

For a classic discussion of the operation of the price system, see

George J. Stigler, *The Theory of Price,* 3rd ed. (New York: Macmillan, 1966), Chapter 2.

The methodology of economics is discussed in detail in

Milton Friedman, "The Methodology of Positive Economics," in *Essays in Positive Economics* (Chicago: University of Chicago Press, 1953), pp. 1–43.

Lionel Robbins, *The Nature and Significance of Economic Science,* 2nd ed. (London: Macmillan, 1935).

Chapter 2

Demand and Supply: A Review

2-1 Market Analysis

2-2 Market Demand

2-3 Market Supply

2-4 Equilibrium

2-5 Adjustment to Changes in Demand and Supply

2-6 Applications

Examples

2-1 Price Elasticity of Demand for Selected Commodities

2-2 Price Elasticity of Supply for Selected Commodities

2-3 The Pope and the Price of Fish

2-4 Heavy Rains, Higher Vegetable Prices

Applications

Application 1: Rent Control

Application 2: Agricultural Price Support Programs

Application 3: The Effect of an Excise Tax

Application 4: The Cobweb Model

This chapter provides an overview of the functioning of markets. It shows how the forces of demand and supply determine the market price of a commodity and how price is affected by changes in demand and supply. So widespread is the applicability of the market model that one could safely start answering any question of economics by saying that it depends on demand and supply.

We begin the chapter by defining the concept of a market. Next we review the meaning of demand, changes in demand, and price elasticity of demand. After reviewing supply, we examine how the interaction of the forces of market demand and supply determine the equilibrium price and quantity of a commodity. Finally, we examine how the equilibrium price and quantity of a commodity are affected by changes in demand and supply.

This chapter is, for the most part, a review of material covered in principles of economics. However, this basic material is supplemented by several real-world examples and important applications that demonstrate the great relevance of the market model. The chapter also provides a brief overview of the topics to be examined in detail in subsequent chapters.[1]

2-1

Market Analysis

Most of microeconomic analysis is devoted to the study of how individual markets operate. A **market** is the network of communications between

---

[1] The student who is familiar with and remembers well the concepts presented in this chapter can go on to Chapter 3 without loss of continuity.

individuals and firms for the purpose of buying and selling goods and services. Markets provide the framework for the analysis of the forces of demand and supply that, together, determine commodity and resource prices. As explained in Chapter 1, prices play the central role in microeconomic analysis.

A market can, but need not, be a specific place or location where buyers and sellers actually come face to face for the purpose of transacting their business. Some markets are indeed specific places or locations. For example, the New York Stock Exchange is located in a building at 11 Wall Street in New York City. On the other hand, the market for college professors has no specific location but refers to all the formal and informal information network on teaching opportunities throughout the nation. There is a market for each good, service, or resource bought and sold in the economy. Some of these markets are local, some are regional, while others are national or international in character.

Throughout this chapter, we assume that markets are perfectly competitive. A **perfectly competitive market** is one where no buyer or seller can affect the price of the product, all units of the product are homogeneous or identical, resources are mobile, and knowledge of the market is perfect. For the purpose of our present chapter, this definition of a perfectly competitive market suffices. A more detailed definition and analysis of this and other types of markets is given in Part IV of the text.

2-2
Market Demand

In this section we review the concepts of the market demand schedule and the market demand curve, examine the meaning of changes in demand, and review the measure of price elasticity of demand. These concepts will be used extensively in this chapter and in the rest of the text. Indeed, the concept of demand is one of the most crucial in microeconomic theory and in all of economics.

2-2a Demand Schedule and Demand Curve

A **market demand schedule** is a table showing the quantity of a commodity that consumers are willing and able to purchase over a given period of time at each price of the commodity, while holding constant all other relevant economic variables on which demand depends. The other economic variables held constant for the purpose of defining a demand schedule are consumers' incomes, their tastes, the price of related commodities (substitutes and complements), and the number of consumers in the market.

For example, Table 2-1 provides a hypothetical daily demand schedule for hamburgers in a large market (say New York City, Chicago, or Los

27

TABLE 2-1 Market Demand Schedule for Hamburgers

Price per Hamburger	Quantity Demanded per Day (Million Hamburgers)
$2.00	2
1.50	4
1.00	6
0.75	7
0.50	8

Angeles). Table 2-1 shows that at the price of $2.00 per hamburger, the quantity demanded is 2 million hamburgers per day. At the lower price of $1.50, the quantity demanded is 4 million hamburgers per day. At the price of $1.00, the quantity demanded is 6 million hamburgers, while at the price of $0.75 and $0.50, the quantity demanded is 7 and 8 million hamburgers, respectively.

Note that at lower prices, greater quantities of hamburgers are demanded. This is true for most commodities. Lower commodity prices will induce consumers to buy more of the commodity and will also bring more consumers into the market. The inverse price-quantity relationship (indicating that a greater quantity of the commodity is demanded at lower prices, and a smaller quantity at higher prices) is called the **law of demand.**

By plotting on a graph the various price-quantity combinations given by the market demand schedule, we obtain the **market demand curve** for the commodity. The price per unit of the commodity is usually measured along the vertical axis while the quantity demanded of the commodity per unit of time is measured along the horizontal axis. For example, Figure 2-1 shows the market demand curve for hamburgers corresponding to the market demand schedule of Table 2-1. The *negative slope* of the demand curve (i.e., its downward-to-the-right inclination) is a reflection of the law of demand or inverse price-quantity relationship. That is, the negative slope of the demand curve shows that a reduction in the price of the commodity leads to an increase in the quantity demanded while a rise in price results in a reduction in the quantity demanded.

The various points on the demand curve represent *alternative* price-quantity combinations. For example, at the price of $2.00 per hamburger, the quantity demanded is 2 million hamburgers (point *B* in Figure 2-1). If instead the price is $1.50, the quantity demanded is 4 million hamburgers (point *C*), and so on. A demand curve also shows the maximum price consumers are willing to pay to purchase each quantity of a commodity per unit of time. For example, the demand curve of Figure 2-1 shows that for 2 million hamburgers, consumers are willing to pay the maximum price of $2.00 per hamburger (point *B*); for 4 million hamburgers, consumers are willing to pay the maximum price of $1.50 (point *C*), and so on. Finally, a

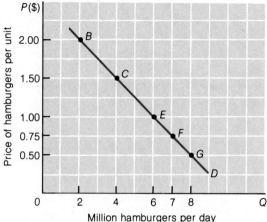

FIGURE 2-1.
The Market
Demand Curve for
Hamburgers

Market demand curve D shows the quantity of hamburgers purchased per day at each price, while holding constant consumers' incomes, tastes, the price of substitute and complementary commodities, and the number of consumers in the market. D shows that at lower hamburger prices, greater quantities are demanded. This is reflected in the negative slope of the demand curve and is referred to as the law of demand.

particular demand curve refers to a specific period of time. Thus, the demand curve of Figure 2-1 is for one day. The demand curve for hamburgers for a month is correspondingly larger.[2]

2-2b Changes in Demand

A change in (1) consumers' incomes, (2) their tastes, (3) the price of related commodities, and (4) the number of consumers in the market (the variables held constant in drawing a market demand curve) causes the entire demand curve to shift. For example, with a rise in consumers' incomes the demand curve for most commodities (normal goods) shifts to the right since consumers can then afford to purchase more of each commodity at each price. The same is true if consumers' tastes change so that they demand more of the commodity at each price, or if the number of consumers in the market increases.

    A demand curve also shifts to the right if the price of a substitute commodity rises or if the price of a complementary commodity falls. For example, if the price of hot dogs (a substitute of hamburgers) rises, people will

---

  [2] Note that the demand curve in Figure 2-1 is drawn on a light background grid to facilitate the reading of the various price-quantity alternatives on the demand curve. The grid is used as a visual aid in most figures in the text. A demand curve could be drawn and the analysis could be conducted more generally without numerical values and without the grid. However, most students seem to find the grid useful.

switch some of their purchases away from hot dogs and demand more hamburgers at each and every price of hamburgers (a rightward shift in the demand for hamburgers). Similarly, if the price of the bun (a complement of hamburgers) *falls*, the demand for hamburgers also shifts to the right (since the price of a hamburger *with the bun* is then lower).

On the other hand, the demand curve for a commodity usually shifts to the left (so that less of it is demanded at each price) if consumers' incomes, the price of substitute commodities, and the number of consumers in the market decline, if the prices of complements rise, or if consumers' tastes change so that they demand less of the commodity at each price.

In Figure 2-2, D is the original demand curve for hamburgers (from Figure 2-1) and D' is a higher demand curve for hamburgers. With D', consumers demand more hamburgers at each price. For example, at the price of $1.00, consumers demand 12 million hamburgers per day (point E') as compared with the original 6 million demanded (point E) with D. Indeed, the shift from D to D' leads consumers to demand 6 million *additional* hamburgers per day at each price.

A shift in demand is referred to as a *change in demand* and must be clearly distinguished from a *change in quantity demanded* (which refers instead to a movement along a given demand curve as a result of a change in the commodity price). Thus, the shift in demand from D to D' is an

FIGURE 2-2.
Change in Demand
for Hamburgers

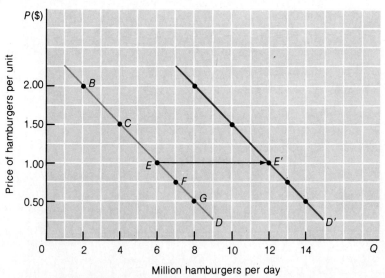

The rightward shift from D to D' in the demand curve for hamburgers results from an increase in consumers' incomes or taste for hamburgers, from an increase in the price of substitutes (such as hot dogs), from a decline in the price of complements (such as buns), or from an increase in the number of consumers in the market. At each price, consumers demand more hamburgers with D'. Thus, at P= $1.00, consumers purchase 12 million hamburgers with D' instead of 6 million hamburgers with D.

increase in demand, while the movement along D, say, from point E to point F is a change in the quantity demanded. The change in demand is caused by the change in the economic variables that are held constant in drawing a given demand curve, while a change in the quantity demanded is a movement along a given demand curve as a result of a change in the price of the commodity (with all the other economic variables on which demand depends remaining constant).

2-2c Price Elasticity of Demand

The responsiveness in the quantity demanded of a commodity to a change in its price is very important to consumers and producers alike. For example, when the price of gasoline rose sharply in the fall of 1973, consumers reduced their purchases of gasoline somewhat, but they ended up spending much more on gasoline because they could not quickly and easily replace their gas guzzlers with more fuel-efficient compact cars, and because they could not easily find alternative means of transportation quickly enough. Similarly, a producer may consider lowering the price of a commodity if the increase in the quantity demanded increases his or her total revenue (price times quantity), but not if he or she expects the total revenue from the sale of the commodity to decline.

The responsiveness in the quantity demanded of a commodity to a change in its price could be measured by the inverse of the slope of the demand curve (i.e., by $\Delta Q/\Delta P$).[3] The disadvantage is that the inverse of the slope is expressed in terms of the units of measurement. Thus, a change of 100,000 units in the quantity demanded of a commodity is very large if the commodity is new housing units, but it is not very large if the commodity is hamburgers. Similarly, a price change of $1.00 is insignificant for houses but very large for hamburgers. Thus, measuring the responsiveness in the quantity demanded of a commodity to a change in price by the inverse of the slope of the demand curve is not very useful. Furthermore, comparison of changes in quantity to changes in price across commodities is meaningless.

In order to have a measure of the responsiveness in the quantity demanded of a commodity to a change in its price that is independent of the units of measurement, Alfred Marshall, the great English economist of the turn of the century, refined and popularized the concept of the price elasticity of demand. This is defined in terms of *relative* or *percentage* changes in quantity demanded and price. As such, price elasticity of demand is a pure number (i.e., it has no units attached to it), and its value is not affected by changes in the units of measurement. As shown in Exam-

---

[3] Since the turn of the century, the convention in economics (started by Alfred Marshall) is to plot price on the vertical axis and quantity on the horizontal axis. Therefore, the quantity response to a change in price could be measured by $\Delta Q/\Delta P$, which is the inverse of the slope of the demand curve.

31

ple 2-1 which follows, this also allows meaningful comparisons in the price elasticity of demand of different commodities.

The **price elasticity of demand** is given by the percentage change in the quantity demanded of a commodity divided by the percentage change in its price. Letting η (the Greek letter eta) stand for the coefficient of price elasticity of demand, ΔQ for the change in quantity, and ΔP for the change in price, we have the formula for the price elasticity of demand:

$$\eta = -\frac{\Delta Q/Q}{\Delta P/P} = -\frac{\Delta Q}{\Delta P} \cdot \frac{P}{Q} \tag{2-1}$$

Since quantity and price move in opposite directions, we use (as a convention) the negative sign in the formula (i.e., we multiply by -1) in order to make the value of η positive. Note that the inverse of the slope of the demand curve (i.e., $\Delta Q/\Delta P$) is a component, but only a component, of the elasticity formula.

Formula (2-1) measures **point elasticity of demand** or the elasticity at a particular point on the demand curve. More frequently, we measure **arc elasticity of demand** between two points on the demand curve. If we used Formula (2-1) to measure arc elasticity, we would get different results depending on whether the price rises or falls.[4] To avoid this, we use the *average* of the two prices and the *average* of the two quantities in the calculations. Letting P_1 refer to the higher of the two prices (with Q_1 the quantity at P_1) and P_2 refer to the lower of the two prices (with Q_2 the corresponding quantity), we have the formula for arc elasticity of demand[5]:

$$\eta = -\frac{\Delta Q}{\Delta P} \cdot \frac{(P_1 + P_2)/2}{(Q_1 + Q_2)/2} = -\frac{\Delta Q}{\Delta P} \cdot \frac{(P_1 + P_2)}{(Q_1 + Q_2)} \tag{2-2}$$

For example, using Formula (2-1) to measure elasticity for a *price decline* from point C to point E on the demand curve of Figure 2-1, we get

$$\eta = \left(-\frac{2}{-0.50}\right)\left(\frac{1.50}{4}\right) = \frac{3}{2} = 1.5$$

On the other hand, measuring elasticity for a *price increase* from point E to point C on the same demand curve, we get

$$\eta = \left(-\frac{-2}{0.50}\right)\left(\frac{1}{6}\right) = \frac{2}{3} = 0.67$$

---

[4] As we will see below, this results because a different base is used in calculating percentage changes for a price increase than for a price decrease.

[5] For the second ratio in the formula, we could use $\overline{P}/\overline{Q}$, where the bar on P and Q refers to their average value.

Using instead Formula (2-2) for arc elasticity, we get

$$\eta = -\left(-\frac{2}{0.50}\right)\frac{(1.50 + 1.00)/2}{(4 + 6)/2} = \frac{2.5}{2.5} = 1$$

Price elasticity of demand is usually different at and between different points on the demand curve, and it can range anywhere from zero to very large or infinite. Demand is said to be elastic if $\eta > 1$; unitary elastic if $\eta = 1$; and inelastic if $\eta < 1$. In general, the greater and the closer are the number of substitutes available for a commodity, the larger is the price elasticity of demand. The reason for this is that an increase in the price of a commodity, such as hamburgers, that has very close substitutes (hot dogs, for example) results in a very large *relative* decline in the number of hamburgers purchased (as consumers readily switch to hot dogs), and so the price elasticity of demand for hamburgers is very large.[6]

Example 2-1   **Price Elasticity of Demand for Selected Commodities**

The Facts: Table 2-2 presents estimates of the price elasticity of demand for selected commodities in the United States when sufficient time is allowed for consumers to adjust fully to the price change.

Comment: The price elasticity of demand for radio and TV repairs of 3.84 means that a 1% reduction in the price of radio and TV repairs increases the quantity demanded by 3.84%, so that total expenditures (price times quantity) on radio and TV repairs increase. Whenever, as in this case, η exceeds 1, demand is said to be elastic. If $\eta = 1$, a 1% reduction in price increases quantity by 1%, leaving total expenditures unchanged. Demand is then said to be unitary elastic. Finally, if η is smaller than 1, a 1% reduc-

TABLE 2-2   **Estimates of Price Elasticity of Demand (η) for Selected Commodities, United States**

Commodity	Elasticity	Commodity	Elasticity
Radio and TV repair	3.84	Bus transportation (local)	1.20
Motion pictures	3.67	Medical insurance	0.92
China and glassware	2.55	Jewelry and watches	0.67
Tobacco products	1.89	Stationery	0.56
Electricity (household)	1.89	Potatoes	0.31
Foreign travel	1.77	Sugar	0.31

Sources: H. Houthakker and L. D. Taylor, *Consumer Demand in the United States: Analyses and Projections* (Cambridge, Mass.: Harvard University Press, 1970) and H. Schultz, *The Theory and Measurement of Demand* (Chicago: University of Chicago Press, 1951).

---

[6] A more extensive discussion of the factors affecting price elasticity of demand is given in Section 5.2c.

tion in price increases quantity by less than 1% so that total expenditures on the commodity decline. For example, a 1% reduction in the price of sugar increases the quantity of sugar demanded by only 0.31% so that total expenditures on sugar decline. Demand is then said to be inelastic.[7]

A natural question at this point might be "Why is the price elasticity of demand for radio and TV repair and for motion pictures so large while that for sugar so low?" The answer is that very good substitutes are available for radio and TV repair (such as the purchase of a new, higher quality radio and TV) and for motion pictures (such watching cable TV at home) but not for sugar (saccharin and honey being poor substitutes).

2-3

Market Supply

In this section we review the concepts of the market supply schedule and the market supply curve, examine the meaning of changes in supply, and review the measure of price elasticity of supply. The concept of supply is very important because together with demand it determines the equilibrium price and quantity of a commodity, and to show how equilibrium is determined is one of the most important aims of microeconomic theory.

2-3a Supply Schedule and Supply Curve

A **market supply schedule** is a table showing the quantity supplied of a commodity over a given period of time at each price of the commodity, while holding constant technology, resource prices and, for agricultural commodities, weather conditions. For example, Table 2-3 gives a hypothetical daily supply schedule for hamburgers. Starting at the bottom, the table shows that at the price of $0.50 per hamburger, the quantity supplied is 2 million hamburgers per day. At the higher price of $0.75 per hamburger, the quantity supplied is 4 million hamburgers per day. At the price of $1.00, the quantity supplied is 6 million hamburgers per day, and so on. Higher hamburger prices allow producers to bid resources away from other uses and supply greater quantities of hamburgers.

By plotting on a graph the various price-quantity combinations given by the market supply schedule, we obtain the **market supply curve** for the commodity. For example, Figure 2-3 shows the market supply curve for hamburgers corresponding to the market supply schedule of Table 2-3. It is called a supply curve even though it is a straight line in this case. The

---

[7] It should be noted that the elasticity estimates in Table 2-2 refer to the period when they were calculated (i.e., 1951 and 1970). Over time, these coefficients can change because of changes in incomes, tastes, availability of substitutes and complements, and in the number of consumers in the market.

TABLE 2-3 Market Supply Schedule for Hamburgers

Price per Hamburger	Quantity Supplied per Day (Million Hamburgers)
$2.00	14
1.50	10
1.00	6
0.75	4
0.50	2

positive slope of the supply curve (i.e., its upward-to-the-right inclination) is a reflection of the fact that higher prices must be paid to induce producers to supply greater quantities of the commodity.

As with the demand curve, the various points on the supply curve represent *alternative* price-quantity combinations. For example, at the price of $0.50 per hamburger, the quantity supplied is 2 million hamburgers per day (point *R* in Figure 2-3). If instead the price is $0.75, the quantity supplied is 4 million hamburgers (point *N*), and so on. A supply curve also shows the *minimum* price that producers must receive to supply each quantity of the commodity. For example, the supply curve of Figure 2-3 shows that suppliers must receive the minimum price of $0.50 per hamburger in order to supply 2 million hamburgers per day (point *R*); producers must receive the minimum price of $0.75 per hamburger to supply 4 mil-

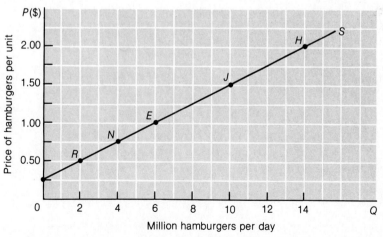

FIGURE 2-3. The Market Supply Curve for Hamburgers

Market supply curve S shows the quantity of hamburgers supplied per day at each price, while holding constant technology and resource prices. S shows that higher hamburger prices must be offered to induce producers to supply greater quantities. This is reflected in the positive slope of the supply curve.

lion hamburgers (point N), and so on. A particular supply curve also refers to a specific period of time. Thus, the supply curve of Figure 2-3 is for one day. The supply curve of hamburgers for a month is correspondingly larger.

2-3b Changes in Supply

An improvement in technology, a reduction in the price of the resources used in the production of the commodity and, for agricultural commodities, more favorable weather conditions cause the entire supply curve of the commodity to shift to the right. Producers would then supply more of the commodity at each price. For example, at the price of $1.00, producers supply 12 million hamburgers per day (point E') with S' as opposed to only 6 million hamburgers per day with S (see Figure 2-4).

The shift to the right from S to S' in Figure 2-4 is referred to as *an increase in supply*. This must be clearly distinguished from *an increase in the quantity supplied*, which is instead a movement along a given supply curve in the upward direction (as, for example, from point E to point J, in Figure 2-4) resulting from an increase in the commodity price (from $1.00 to $1.50). On the other hand, a decrease in supply refers to a leftward shift in the supply curve and must be clearly distinguished from a decrease in the quantity supplied of the commodity (which is a movement along a given supply curve and results from a decline in the commodity price).

FIGURE 2-4.
Change in the
Supply of
Hamburgers

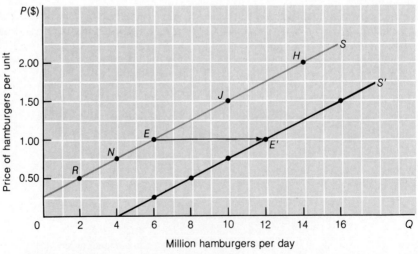

The rightward shift from S to S' in the supply curve of hamburgers results from an improvement in technology or from a reduction in resource prices. With S', producers supply more hamburgers at each price than with S. Thus, at P = $1.00, producers supply 12 million hamburgers with S' instead of only 6 million with S.

36

2-3c Price Elasticity of Supply

The **price elasticity of supply** measures the responsiveness or sensitivity in the quantity supplied of a commodity as a result of a change in its price. It is given by the percentage change in the quantity supplied of a commodity divided by the percentage change in its price. Being expressed in terms of relative or percentage changes, the price elasticity of supply is a pure number (i.e., it has no units attached to it), and its value does not change when the units of measurement are changed. As we will see in Example 2-2 which follows, this allows meaningful comparisons in the price elasticity of supply of different commodities.[8]

Letting ϵ (the Greek letter epsilon) stand for the coefficient of price elasticity of supply, ΔQ for the change in the quantity *supplied*, and ΔP for the change in price, we can measure **point elasticity of supply** by the following formula:

$$\epsilon = \frac{\Delta Q/Q}{\Delta P/P} = \frac{\Delta Q}{\Delta P} \cdot \frac{P}{Q} \qquad (2\text{-}3)$$

Note that the inverse of the slope of the supply curve is a component, but only a component, of the formula for the price elasticity of supply. Since quantity and price move in the same direction (i.e., since the supply curve is usually positively sloped), ϵ is positive.

Formula (2-3) measures **point elasticity of supply** or the elasticity at a particular point on the supply curve. More frequently, we measure **arc elasticity of supply** between two points on the supply curve. If we used Formula (2-3) to measure arc elasticity, we would get different results depending on whether the price rises or falls. To avoid this, we use the average of the two prices and the average of the two quantities (as was done in measuring arc elasticity of demand). Letting P_1 now refer to the lower of the two prices (with Q_1 the quantity at P_1) and P_2 to the higher of the two prices (with Q_2 the corresponding quantity), we can measure arc elasticity of supply by

$$\epsilon = \frac{\Delta Q}{\Delta P} \cdot \frac{(P_1 + P_2)/2}{(Q_1 + Q_2)/2} = \frac{\Delta Q}{\Delta P} \cdot \frac{(P_1 + P_2)}{(Q_1 + Q_2)} \qquad (2\text{-}4)$$

For example, using Formula (2-4) to measure arc elasticity between points E and J on the supply curve of Figure 2-4, we get

$$\epsilon = \frac{4}{0.50} \cdot \frac{(1.00 + 1.50)/2}{(6 + 10)/2} = \frac{5}{4} = 1.25$$

[8] The discussion in Section 2-2c on the advantages of using the price elasticity of demand rather than the inverse of the slope of the demand curve as a measure of the responsiveness in the quantity demanded of a commodity to a change in its price also applies here.

The longer the time period involved, the larger usually is the price elasticity of supply (i.e., the greater usually is the percentage change in quantity supplied as a result of a given percentage change in price). The reason for this is that it takes time for producers to bid resources away from other uses and expand production (when the price of the commodity rises) or to release resources (at the expiration of contracts) when the price of the commodity falls. Thus, the longer the period of time involved, the more producers are able to adjust their output to sales, and the greater usually is the price elasticity of supply.

The supply curve is said to be *elastic* if ε is larger than 1, *unitary elastic* if ε = 1, and *inelastic* if ε is smaller than 1. A straight-line supply curve is elastic throughout if (as S in Figure 2-4) it crosses the price axis; it is unitary elastic if it crosses the origin (as S in Problem 3a), and inelastic if (as S′ in Figure 2-4) it crosses the quantity axis. The reason is that the relative change in the quantity supplied is greater than, equal to, or smaller than the relative change in price depending upon whether the straight line supply curve crosses the price axis, the origin, or the quantity axis, respectively.[9]

Example 2-2 Price Elasticity of Supply for Selected Commodities

The Facts: Table 2-4 presents estimates of the price elasticity of supply for selected commodities in the United States.

Comment: The price elasticities of supply given in the table are long-run elasticities. That is, they refer to periods of time long enough for producers to be able to change all resources required in the production of the various products. For shorter periods of time, price elasticities of supply would be smaller, and in some cases, much smaller. Note the great difference in the

TABLE 2-4   Estimates of Price Elasticity of Supply (ε) for Selected Commodities, United States

Commodity	Elasticity	Commodity	Elasticity
Green peppers	0.26	Onions	1.00
Watermelons	0.48	Cabbage	1.20
Tomatoes	0.90	Cucumbers	2.20
Celery	0.95	Green peas	4.40
Carrots	1.00	Spinach	4.70

Source: M. Nerlove and W. Addison, "Statistical Estimation of Long-run Elasticities of Supply and Demand," *Journal of Farm Economics* (now *Journal of Agricultural Economics*), Vol. 40, November 1958, pp. 861–880.

[9] The student can convince himself or herself of this by drawing on graph paper three straight-line supply curves, one crossing the price axis, one going through the origin, and the other crossing the quantity axis, and then calculating arc elasticity between any two points on each supply curve.

price elasticity of supply between, say, green peppers and green peas. This means that the type of land and other resources used in the production of green peas is much less specialized and can be transferred much more easily to and from other uses than the resources used in the production of green peppers. Thus, a given change in the price of green peas leads to proportionately much greater production response than for green peppers (i.e., the price elasticity of supply is much greater for the former than for the latter).[10]

2-4

Equilibrium

We now examine how the interaction of the forces of demand and supply determines the equilibrium price and quantity of a commodity in a perfectly competitive market. The **equilibrium price** of a commodity is the price at which the quantity demanded of the commodity equals the quantity supplied and the market clears. The process by which equilibrium is reached in the market place can be shown with a table and illustrated graphically.

Table 2-5 brings together the market demand and supply schedules for hamburgers from Tables 2-1 and 2-3. From Table 2-5, we see that only at $P = \$1.00$ is the quantity supplied of hamburgers equal to the quantity demanded and the market clears (the third line in Table 2-5). Thus, $P = \$1.00$ is the equilibrium price and $Q = 6$ million hamburgers per day is the equilibrium quantity.

At prices above the equilibrium price, the quantity supplied exceeds the quantity demanded and there is a **surplus** of the commodity, which drives the price down. For example, at $P = \$2.00$, the quantity supplied (QS) is 14 million hamburgers, the quantity demanded (QD) is 2 million hamburgers, so that there is a surplus of 12 million hamburgers per day (see the first

TABLE 2-5   Market Supply Schedule, Market Demand Schedule, and Equilibrium

Price per Hamburger	Quantity Supplied per Day (Million Hamburgers)	Quantity Demanded per Day (Million Hamburgers)	Surplus (+) or Shortage (−)	Pressure on Price
$2.00	14	2	12	Downward
1.50	10	4	6	↓ Downward
★1.00	6	6	0	Equilibrium
0.75	4	7	−3	↑ Upward
0.50	2	8	−6	Upward

[10] More will be said on the price elasticity of supply in Section 10-6.

line of Table 2-5). Sellers must reduce price to get rid of their unwanted inventory accumulations of hamburgers. At lower prices, producers supply smaller quantities and consumers demand larger quantities until the equilibrium price of $1.00 is reached, at which the quantity supplied of 6 million hamburgers per day equals the quantity demanded and the market clears.

On the other hand, at prices below the equilibrium price, the quantity supplied falls short of the quantity demanded and there is a **shortage** of the commodity which drives the price up. For example, at $P = \$0.50$, $QS = 2$ million hamburgers while $QD = 8$ million hamburgers, so that there is a shortage of 6 million hamburgers per day (see the last line of Table 2-5). The price of hamburgers is then bid up by consumers who want more hamburgers than are available at the low price of $0.50. As the price of hamburgers is bid up, producers supply greater quantities while consumers demand smaller quantities until the equilibrium price of $P = \$1.00$ is reached, at which $QS = QD = 6$ million hamburgers per day and the market clears. Thus, bidding drives price and quantity to their equilibrium level.

The determination of the equilibrium price can also be shown graphically by bringing together on the same graph the market demand curve of Figure 2-1 and the market supply curve of Figure 2-3. In Figure 2-5, the intersection of the market demand curve and the market supply curve of hamburgers at point E defines the equilibrium price of $1.00 per hamburger and the equilibrium quantity of 6 million hamburgers per day.

FIGURE 2-5.
Demand, Supply,
and Equilibrium

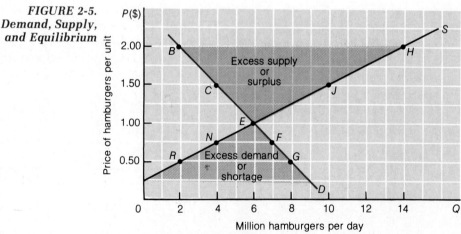

The intersection of D and S at point E defines the equilibrium price of $1.00 per hamburger and the equilibrium quantity of 6 million hamburgers per day. At P larger than $1.00, the resulting surplus will drive P down toward equilibrium. At P smaller than $1.00, the resulting shortage will drive P up toward equilibrium. The price of $1.00 tends to persist because at P = $1.00, QS = QD.

At higher prices, there is an excess supply or surplus of the commodity (the top shaded area in the figure). Suppliers then lower price in order to sell their excess supplies. The surplus is eliminated only when suppliers have lowered their price to the equilibrium level. On the other hand, at below equilibrium prices, the excess demand or shortage (the bottom shaded area in the figure) drives the price up to the equilibrium level. This results because consumers are unable to purchase all of the commodity they want at below-equilibrium prices and bid up the price. The shortage is eliminated only when consumers have bid up the price to the equilibrium level. That is, only at $P = \$1.00$, $QS = QD = 6$ million hamburgers per day and the market is in equilibrium (clears). So to the question "Does demand or supply determine price?," the answer is "both."[11]

Equilibrium is the condition which, once achieved, tends to persist in time. That is, as long as D and S do not change, the equilibrium point remains the same. It should be noted that, at a particular point in time, the observed market price may or may not be the equilibrium price. All we know is that market forces always push the market price toward the equilibrium price when they are not equal. This may occur very rapidly or not. Yet, before the market price reaches a particular equilibrium price, demand and supply may change (shift) defining a new equilibrium price. Thus, only when the market price does not change can we be sure that the two are identical. In what follows, we assume that, in the absence of price controls, the market price *is* the equilibrium price.

2-5

Adjustment to Changes in Demand and Supply

We now analyze the effect of a change in the demand and supply of a commodity on the equilibrium price and quantity of the commodity. Since the demand and supply curves of a commodity often shift over time, it is very important to analyze how these shifts affect equilibrium.

2-5a Adjustment to Changes in Demand

In Section 2-2, we have seen that the market demand curve for a commodity shifts as a result of a change in consumers' incomes, their tastes, the price of related commodities (i.e., substitutes and complements), and as a result of a change in the number of consumers in the market. Given the market supply curve of a commodity, an increase in its demand (i.e., a rightward shift of the entire demand curve) results both in a higher equi-

---

[11] For a mathematical presentation of how equilibrium is determined using rudimentary calculus, see Section A10 of the Mathematical Appendix.

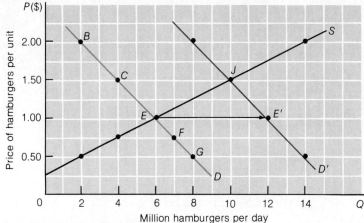

FIGURE 2-6.
Adjustment to an
Increase in Demand

In the figure, D and S are the original demand and supply curves (as in Figure 2-5) and D′ is a higher demand curve. The shift from D to D′ results in a temporary short-age of hamburgers, which drives the price up to P = $1.50 at which QS = QD = 10 million hamburgers. Note that as price rises, the quantity demanded declines while the quantity supplied increases until the new equilibrium point J is reached at which both P and Q are higher than at the old equilibrium point E.

librium price and a higher equilibrium quantity. A reduction in demand has the opposite effect.

In Figure 2-6, *D* and *S* are the original demand and supply curves (as in Figure 2-5) and *D′* is a higher demand curve (as in Figure 2-2) resulting, for example, from an increase in consumers' incomes. Figure 2-6 shows that the shift from *D* to *D′* results in a temporary shortage of 6 million ham-burgers (*EE′* in the figure) at the original equilibrium price of *P* = $1.00 (point *E*). As a result, the price of hamburgers is bid up to *P* = $1.50 at which *QS* = *QD* = 10 million hamburgers. Note that as the price of ham-burgers rises to *P* = $1.50, the quantity demanded declines (from point *E′* to point *J* along *D′*) while the quantity supplied increases (from point *E* to point *J* along *S*) until the new equilibrium point *J* is reached. At the new equilibrium point *J*, both *P* and *Q* are higher than at the old equilibrium point *E* and the market, once again, clears.

Example 2-3   The Pope and the Price of Fish

The Facts: In 1966, the Roman Catholic Church abolished the over-one-thousand-year-old requirement that Catholics not consume meat on Fri-days. The result was that the demand for fish declined (i.e., the demand curve for fish shifted to the left). Given the supply curve of fish, the fall in demand resulted in a price decline ranging from 2% for scrod to 21% for large haddock, for a weighted average decline in the price of fish equal to 12.5% in New England, where about 45% of the population is Catholic.

Comment: Abolishment of the meatless Friday requirement for Catholics affected (reduced) the demand for fish but did not affect the supply of fish. That is, the demand curve for fish shifted to the left but the supply curve of fish remained unchanged (did not shift). Given the supply curve of fish, the decline in demand resulted in a reduction in the price of fish and a decline *in quantity supplied of fish* (a movement down along the given supply curve) until a new and lower equilibrium price and quantity of fish was established in New England.

Source: F. W. Bell, "The Pope and the Price of Fish," *American Economic Review*, December 1968, pp. 1346–1350.

2-5b Adjustment to Changes in Supply

In Section 2-3, we have seen that the market supply curve for a commodity shifts as a result of a change in technology, resource prices, and weather conditions (for agricultural commodities). Given the market demand curve for the commodity, an increase in supply (i.e., a rightward shift of the entire supply curve) results in a lower equilibrium price but a larger equilibrium quantity. On the other hand, a reduction in supply has the opposite effect.

In Figure 2-7, *D* and *S* are the original demand and supply curves (as in Figure 2-5) and *S'* is a higher supply curve (as in Figure 2-4) resulting, for example, from a reduction in the price of beef. Figure 2-7 shows that the shift from *S* to *S'* results in a temporary surplus of 6 million hamburgers

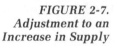
FIGURE 2-7.
Adjustment to an
Increase in Supply

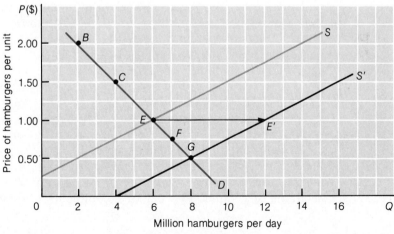

In the figure, D and S are the original demand and supply curves (as in Figure 2-5) and S' is a larger supply curve. The shift of S to S' results in a temporary surplus of hamburgers, which drives the price down to P = $0.50 at which QS = QD = 8 million hamburgers. Note that as price falls, the quantity demanded increases while the quantity supplied decreases until new equilibrium point G is reached, at which P is lower and Q is higher than at equilibrium point E.

43

(*EE'* in the figure) at the original equilibrium price of $P = \$1.00$ (point *E*). In order to get rid of their surplus, sellers reduce price to $P = \$0.50$, at which $QS = QD = 8$ million hamburgers. Note that as the price of hamburgers falls to $P = \$0.50$, the quantity demanded increases (from point *E* to point *G* along *D*) while the quantity supplied decreases (from point *E'* to point *G* along *S'*) until the new equilibrium point *G* is reached. At new equilibrium point *G*, *P* is lower and *Q* is higher than at old equilibrium point *E* and the market, once again, clears.

Example 2-4 **Heavy Rains, Higher Vegetable Prices**

The Facts: Torrential rains in early 1983 turned many of California's vegetable and fruit fields into swamp holes. The result was sparser crops and higher prices for the consumer. For example, the cost of a case of broccoli rose from about $10 to $20. The price of asparagus also doubled from $1.50 to $3 per bunch. Most supermarket executives expected higher prices and supply problems for the subsequent six months.

Comment: Torrential rains in California affected (reduced) the supply of fresh vegetables but did not affect demand. Given the demand for fresh vegetables, a leftward shift in the supply curve resulted in an increase in the price of vegetables and a reduction *in the quantity demanded* until a new higher equilibrium price and lower equilibrium quantity was established.

Source: Newsweek, April 11, 1983, p. 55.

Using Figure 2-5, the student should be able to show what happens to the equilibrium price and quantity if both the demand and supply of hamburgers increase, if both decrease, or if one increases and the other decreases (see Problems 7 and 8). It should be noted that in the above analysis, we have implicitly assumed that there are no price controls and that price and quantity adjust instantaneously or immediately to changes in demand or supply. With effective price controls, the market is not allowed to operate and a shortage or surplus persists. This is examined in Applications 1 and 2 that follow. Sometimes, as in the case of agricultural commodities, quantity adjusts with a lag or delay to changes in price. To examine this, we use the cobweb model (see Application 4). In Application 3, the market model is used to measure the relative burden of a tax imposed on each unit of a commodity that falls on buyers and sellers of the commodity.

2-6

Applications

We now apply the tools of demand and supply to examine several important issues. These range from an analysis of rent control, agricultural price support programs, the effect of an excise tax, and the cobweb model. These applications clearly show the great importance and relevance of the tools of demand and supply that we have reviewed in this chapter.

Application 1: Rent Control

Since 1940, New York City (and since the late 1970s many other cities including Boston, Washington, D.C., and Los Angeles) have imposed rent controls on apartments to help tenants. Rent controls are **price ceilings** or maximum rents below equilibrium rents. These result in a shortage of apartments.

For example, Figure 2-8 might refer to the market for apartment rentals in New York City. Without rent control, the equilibrium rent is $500 and the equilibrium number of apartments rented is 2.4 million. At the controlled rent of $300 per month, 3 million apartments could be rented. Since only 1.8 million apartments are available at that rent, there is a shortage of 1.2 million apartments. Indeed, apartment seekers would be willing to pay a rent of $700 per month rather than go without an apartment when only 1.8 million apartments are available (see the figure).[12]

FIGURE 2-8.
Rent Control

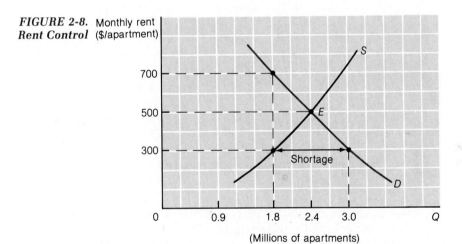

Without rent control, the equilibrium rent is $500 and the equilibrium number of apartments rented is 2.4 million. At the controlled rent of $300 per month, 3 million apartments could be rented. Since only 1.8 million apartments are available at that rent, there is a shortage of 1.2 million apartments. Apartment seekers would be willing to pay a rent of $700 per month rather than go without an apartment when only 1.8 million apartments are available.

[12] A price ceiling at or above the equilibrium price has no effect. For example, rent is $500 and the number of apartments rented is equal to 2.4 million in Figure 2-8, regardless of whether a rent ceiling of $500 or higher is imposed or not. Only if rent control or the maximum rent allowed by law is below the equilibrium rent of $500 does a shortage of apartments for rent result.

Rent control introduces many predictable distortions into the housing market. First, as we have seen above, rent control results in a shortage of apartments for rent. This is evidenced by the great difficulty and time required to find a vacant rent-controlled apartment to rent. Second, owners of rent-controlled apartments usually cut maintenance and repairs to reduce costs, and so the quality of housing deteriorates. The reason is that if some tenants vacated their rent-controlled apartments because of inadequate maintenance, landlords could fill vacant apartments very easily and quickly. Third, rent control reduces the return on investment in rental housing and so fewer rental apartments will be constructed. That is, resources do not flow into the rental housing market in sufficient amounts.[13] Fourth, conversion into cooperatives and condominiums is encouraged, which further reduces the supply of rent-controlled apartments.[14] Fifth, with rent control, there must be a substitute for market price allocation. That is, nonprice rationing is likely to take place as landlords favor families with few or no children or pets and families with higher incomes.

In summary, we can predict that rent control leads to a (1) a shortage of rental housing; (2) lower maintenance; (3) inadequate allocation of resources to the construction of new rental housing; (4) reduction in the stock of rental housing through conversion into cooperatives and condominiums; and (5) nonprice rationing of apartments for rent. For example, one study revealed that the vacancy rate of rent-controlled apartments in New York City was less than 1%, expenditures on repairs was only about half as much as on noncontrolled apartments, and the shortage of new rental housing construction amounted to over $3 billion.[15]

Similar distortions result from the imposition of price ceilings on other commodities. For example, it was estimated that the price ceiling on gasoline in the U.S. in the summer of 1979 resulted in $200 million in lost time and 100 million gallons of gas wasted per month from waiting on long lines to obtain gasoline. Black markets also sprung up as some consumers were willing to pay a higher price for gasoline rather than stand on lines, and some suppliers were willing to accommodate them at higher prices. When price control was abolished, gasoline prices rose to the equilibrium level and long lines at the pumps and other market distortions soon disappeared.

Application 2: Agricultural Price Support Programs

From the 1930s until 1973, the federal government operated a price support program (i.e., it established a **price floor** or a minimum price above the equilibrium price) for several agricultural commodities in order to increase farm incomes. This resulted in a surplus of agricultural commodities,

---

[13] To overcome this, rent control laws usually exempt new apartments.

[14] Many localities have passed laws restricting this practice.

[15] G. Sternlieb, *The Urban Housing Dilemma* (New York: New York Housing and Development Administration, 1972).

46

which was purchased by the government. The government then used part of the surplus to assist low-income people, to subsidize school lunch programs, and for foreign aid, but a great deal of the surplus had to be stored and some spoiled. From the early 1960s, the government also provided incentives for farmers to keep part of their land idle to avoid ever-increasing surpluses. Starting in 1973, the government gave farmers a direct subsidy if the market price of certain commodities fell below a target price.

We can analyze the effect of these various farm support programs with the aid of Figure 2-9, which refers to the wheat market. In the absence of any support program, wheat farmers produce the equilibrium quantity of 2 billion bushels per year, sell it at the equilibrium price of $3 per bushel, and realize a total income of $6 billion. If the government established a price floor of $4 per bushel for wheat, farmers supply 2.2 billion bushels per year, consumers purchase only 1.8 billion bushels, and the government must purchase the surplus of 0.4 billion bushels at the support price of $4 per bushel, for a total cost of $1.6 billion. This does not include the cost of storing the surplus. The price floor has no effect if the market price rises above it.

If through acreage restriction, output falls from 2.2 to 2.1 billion bushels at the supported price of $4 per bushel, the surplus declines to 0.3 billion bushels, and the cost of the price support program falls to $1.2 billion. With direct subsidies, farmers sell the equilibrium quantity of 2 billion bushels

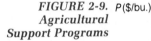

FIGURE 2-9.
Agricultural
Support Programs

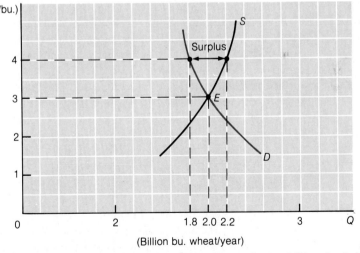

(Billion bu. wheat/year)

At the price floor of $4 per bushel, farmers supply 2.2 billion bushels, consumers purchase 1.8 billion bushels, and the government purchases the surplus of 0.4 billion bushels at a total cost of $1.6 billion. If through acreage restriction, output falls to 2.1 billion bushels, the surplus is 0.3 billion bushels and the cost of the price support program falls to $1.2 billion. With direct subsidies, farmers sell 2 billion bushels at $3 per bushel and the government provides a direct subsidy of $1 per bushel at a total cost of $2 billion.

47

at the equilibrium price of $3 per bushel, and the government then provides farmers a direct subsidy of $1 per bushel at a total cost of $2 billion (if the government sets the target price for wheat at $4 per bushel). With a direct subsidy, however, there is no storage problem and consumers obtain wheat at the lower market price of $3 per bushel.

During the 1960s and early 1970s the stored surplus of wheat resulting from the price support program was sometimes over 1 billion bushels and the total cost of the entire farm support program was more than $5 billion dollars, which represented more than 35% of farm income in the early 1970s. In fiscal year 1983, the total cost of the program had skyrocketted to $28 billion. This was $3 billion more than all farm income in 1983. Most of the benefit also seemed to have gone to owners of large farms rather than to small poor farmers. Under the acreage limitation program, about 20% of agricultural land was kept idle (in so-called "soil banks"). Since the least fertile land was kept idle and farmers cultivated the remaining land more intensively, output declined by less than 5%. Today, the government uses price floors, incentives to keep land idle, and gives direct subsidies to sustain agricultural incomes. Despite these programs, farm incomes are still depressed.

Application 3: The Effect of an Excise Tax

An **excise tax** is a tax on each unit of a commodity.[16] If collected from sellers, the tax causes the supply curve to shift up by the amount of the tax, since sellers require that much more per unit to supply each amount of the commodity. The result is that consumers purchase a smaller quantity at a higher price, while sellers receive a smaller *net* price after payment of the tax. Thus consumers and producers share the burden or **incidence of the tax.**

We can analyze the effect of an excise tax collected from sellers through the use of Figure 2-10. In the figure, D and S are the demand and supply curves of hamburgers with the equilibrium defined at point E (at which P = $1.00 and Q = 6 million hamburgers, as in Figure 2-5). If a tax of 75¢ per hamburger is collected from sellers, S shifts up by the amount of the tax to S″ since sellers now require a price 75¢ higher than before to realize the same net after-tax price. Now D and S″ define equilibrium point C with Q = 4 million hamburgers and P = $1.50, or 50¢ higher than before the imposition of the tax. Thus, at the new equilibrium point consumers purchase a smaller quantity and pay a higher price. Sellers also receive the smaller *net* price of 75¢ (the price of $1.50 paid by consumers minus the 75¢ collected by the government on each hamburger sold).

In the case shown in Figure 2-10, two thirds of the burden of the tax falls

---

[16] An excise tax can be of a given dollar amount *per unit* of the commodity or of a given percentage of the price of the commodity (*ad valorem*). If all units of the commodity are of equal quality and price (as we assume here), the per-unit and the *ad valorem* excise tax are equal and the distinction is unnecessary.

FIGURE 2-10.
The Effect of an
Excise Tax

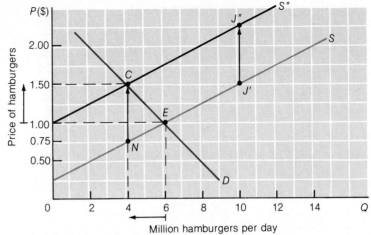

With D and S, P = $1.00 and Q = 6 million hamburgers (point E), as in Figure 2-5. If the tax of 75¢ per hamburger is collected from sellers, S shifts up by 75¢ to S". With D and S", Q = 4 million hamburgers and P = $1.50 for consumers (point C), but sellers receive a net price of only 75¢ after paying the 75¢ tax per unit. Thus, in this case, ⅔ of the burden or incidence of the tax falls on buyers and ⅓ falls on sellers.

on consumers and one third on sellers. That is, consumers pay 50¢ more and sellers receive a net price that is 25¢ less than before the imposition of the excise tax. Thus, even though the tax is collected from sellers, the forces of demand and supply are such that sellers are able to pass on or shift part of the burden of the tax to consumers in the form of a higher price for hamburgers. Given the supply of a commodity, the less sensitive the quantity demanded is to price (i.e., the steeper and less elastic is the demand curve), the greater is the share of the tax paid by consumers in the form of higher prices. On the other hand, given the demand for a commodity, the less sensitive the quantity supplied is to price (i.e., the steeper and less elastic is the supply curve), the smaller is the share of the tax paid by consumers and the larger is the share left to be paid by sellers (see Problem 11).

If the government collected the tax of 75¢ per hamburger from buyers or consumers rather than from sellers, D would shift down by 75¢ to D" (pencil D" in Figure 2-10). With D" and S, Q = 4 million hamburgers, P = $0.75 (that buyers pay to sellers) and then buyers have to pay the tax of 75¢ per hamburger to the government. Again, consumers pay $1.50, which is 50¢ more than the previous equilibrium price, and sellers receive 25¢ less. Therefore, the net result is the same whether the tax is collected from sellers or from buyers.

Application 4: The Cobweb Model
The **cobweb model** explains what happens when the quantity supplied of a commodity in a given time period depends on the price in the *previous*

FIGURE 2-11.
The Cobweb Model

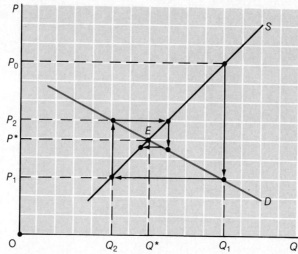

Q_1 is the quantity supplied in period one in response to the disequilibrium price of P_0 in the previous time period. However, Q_1 can only be sold in period one at P_1 (the demand price for Q_1). Then, given P_1 in period one, producers supply only Q_2 in period two. However, in the second time period, the unit price for Q_2 is bid up to P_2. The process continues until the equilibrium price and quantity of P^* and Q^* are reached.

period. The cobweb model can be used to explain the fluctuation in the price and quantity of some agricultural commodities, where this year's output was determined (planted) last year, based on last year's prices.

The cobweb model is illustrated by Figure 2-11.[17] Higher subscripts for the P's and the Q's in the figure refer to successive time periods. In Figure 2-11, Q_1 is the quantity supplied in period one in response to the disequilibrium price of P_0 in the previous time period. However, Q_1 can only be sold in period one at P_1 (the demand price for Q_1). Then, given P_1 in period one, producers supply only Q_2 in period two. However, in period two, the unit price for Q_2 is bid up to P_2. The process continues until the equilibrium price and quantity of P^* and Q^* are reached.

Equilibrium is reached in Figure 2-11 because the supply curve is drawn steeper or less elastic than the demand curve. Had the supply curve been drawn flatter or more elastic than the demand curve, price and quantity would have moved further and further away from equilibrium in ever widening cycles (see Problem 12a). With a demand and a supply curve of equal steepness or elasticity, price and quantity oscillate above and below equilibrium indefinitely without converging or diverging. That is, periods with small quantities and high prices alternate indefinitely with periods with large quantities and low prices (see Problem 12b).

---

[17] It is from the appearance of this figure that the model takes its name.

While this model has some validity and can explain some price fluctuation for agricultural commodities, the model is simplistic since it assumes no production adjustment to expectations of future prices. That is, cobwebs disappear if producers correctly predict future prices of the commodity and use these predicted prices, rather than current prices, to plan or determine next year's output. Since it is very difficult to predict future prices accurately, cobweb cycles remain.

We have one year cycles for wheat, corn, hog, and other products where the basic production period is one year. For some commodities or products, the cycle is longer than one year. For example, it takes about three years to raise a steer. Cobweb cycles also occur in labor markets. For example, when wages of engineers are high, more students enter engineering schools. However, the greater number of engineers graduating five years later drives their wages down. As a result, fewer students opt for engineering five years later, and this drives their wages up in ten years when fewer of them graduate.[18]

Summary

1. Most of microeconomic analysis is devoted to the study of how individual markets operate. A market is the network of communication between individuals and firms for the purpose of buying and selling goods, services, and resources. Markets provide the framework for the analysis of the forces of demand and supply that determines commodity and resource prices. A market can, but need not, be a specific place or location. We assume a perfectly competitive market. This is a market where no buyer or seller can affect the price of the product, all units of the product are homogeneous, resources are mobile, and knowledge is perfect.

2. A market demand schedule is a table showing the quantity demanded of a commodity at each price over a given time period while holding constant all other relevant economic variables on which demand depends. The market demand curve is the graphic representation of the demand schedule. It is negatively sloped and this reflects the inverse price-quantity relationship or the law of demand. A change in consumers' incomes, tastes for the commodity, the number of consumers in the market, and the price of substitutes or complements shifts the demand curve. The price elasticity of demand is measured by the percentage change in quantity demanded divided by the percentage change in price. To measure arc elasticity of demand, the average prices and quantities are used in the calculations.

3. A market supply schedule is a table showing the quantity supplied of a commodity at each price over a given time period. The market supply curve is the graphic representation of the supply schedule. It is usually positively sloped, indicating that producers supply more of the commodity at higher prices. A change in technology, resource prices and, for agricultural commodities, weather conditions shifts the supply curve. The price elasticity of supply is measured by the percentage change in the quantity supplied divided by the percentage change in price.

4. The equilibrium price and quantity of a commodity is defined at the intersection of the market demand and supply curves of the commodity. At higher than equilibrium prices, there is a surplus of the commodity, which leads sellers to lower price to the equilibrium level. At lower

---

[18] For a mathematical presentation of the cobweb model using rudimentary calculus, see Section A11 of the Mathematical Appendix.

than equilibrium prices, there is a shortage of the commodity, which leads consumers to bid prices up to the equilibrium level. Equilibrium is the condition that, once achieved, tends to persist.

5. An increase in demand (i.e., a rightward shift in the demand curve) results in an increase in both the equilibrium price and quantity of the commodity. A decrease in demand has the opposite effect. On the other hand, an increase in supply (i.e., a rightward shift in the supply curve) results in a lower equilibrium price but a higher equilibrium quantity. A decrease in supply has the opposite effect.

6. A price ceiling below the equilibrium price (such as rent control) leads to a shortage of the commodity and possibly black markets. A price floor above the equilibrium price (as for some agricultural commodities) leads to a surplus of the commodity. Given the supply of a commodity, the steeper or the less elastic is the demand for the commodity, the greater is the burden or incidence of a per-unit tax on consumers. In a cobweb model, the quantity supplied of a commodity in a given time period depends on the price in the previous period. It can be used to explain fluctuations in the price of agricultural products and of some resources.

Glossary

Market The network of communication between individuals and firms for the purpose of buying and selling goods, services, and resources.

Perfectly competitive market A market where no buyer or seller can affect the price of the product, all units of the product are homogeneous, resources are mobile, and knowledge is perfect.

Market demand schedule A table showing the quantity of a commodity that consumers are willing and able to purchase during a given period of time at each price of the commodity, while holding constant all other relevant economic variables on which demand depends.

Law of demand The inverse price-quantity relationship illustrated by the negative slope of the demand curve.

Market demand curve The graphic representation of the market demand schedule showing the quantity demanded of a commodity per time period at each commodity price, while holding constant all other relevant economic variables on which demand depends.

Price elasticity of demand (η) The percentage change in the quantity demanded of a commodity during a specific period of time divided by the percentage change in its price.

Point elasticity of demand The price elasticity of demand at a specific point on the demand curve.

Arc elasticity of demand The price elasticity of demand between two points on the demand curve; it uses the average price and the average quantity in calculating the percentage change in price and quantity.

Market supply schedule A table showing the quantity supplied of a commodity during a given period of time at each price of the commodity, while holding constant all other relevant economic variables on which supply depends.

Market supply curve The graphic representation of the market supply schedule showing the quantity supplied of a commodity per time period at each commodity price, while holding constant all other relevant economic variables on which supply depends.

Price elasticity of supply (ϵ) The percentage change in the quantity supplied of a commodity during a specific period of time divided by the percentage change in its price.

Point elasticity of supply The price elasticity of supply at a specific point on the supply curve.

Arc elasticity of supply The price elasticity of supply between two points on the supply curve; it uses the average price and the average quantity in calculating the percentage change in price and quantity.

Equilibrium price The price at which the quantity demanded of a commodity equals the quantity supplied and the market clears.

Surplus The excess quantity supplied of a commodity at higher than equilibrium prices.

Shortage The excess quantity demanded of a commodity at lower than equilibrium prices.

Equilibrium The condition that, once achieved, tends to persist. It occurs when the quantity demanded of a commodity equals the quantity supplied and the market clears.

Price ceiling The maximum price allowed for a commodity. If it is below the equilibrium price, it leads to a shortage of the commodity.

Price floor A minimum price for a commodity. If it is above the equilibrium price, it leads to a surplus of the commodity.

Excise tax A tax on each unit of the commodity.

Incidence of the tax The relative burden of the tax on buyers and sellers.

Cobweb model It explains price fluctuations for agricultural products when the quantity supplied of the product in a given time period depends on the price in the previous period.

Questions for Review

1. (a) What is a market?
   (b) Must a market be a specific place or location?
   (c) What is the primary function of markets?
   (d) How many markets are there in the U.S. economy?
   (e) What is a perfectly competitive market?

2. (a) What is meant by market demand schedule? By market demand curve?
   (b) What economic variables are held constant in defining a demand schedule and demand curve?
   (c) What is meant by the law of demand? What characteristic of the demand curve reflects the law of demand?
   (d) What is the difference between "a change in the quantity demanded" and "a change in demand"?

3. Will the demand curve shift to the right or to the left if
   (a) consumers' incomes increase?
   (b) the price of substitutes decrease?
   (c) the price of complements increase?
   (d) the number of consumers in the market decreases?

4. (a) What is the formula for point elasticity of demand?
   (b) What is the formula for the arc elasticity of demand?
   (c) Why do we use the average price and the average quantity to calculate arc elasticity?
   (d) What is the difference between slope and price elasticity of demand?
   (e) What is the advantage of using the price

elasticity of demand instead of the slope of the demand curve?

5. (a) What is meant by a market supply schedule? By market supply curve?
   (b) What economic variables are held constant in defining a supply schedule and supply curve?
   (c) What is the usual shape of the supply curve?
   (d) What is the difference between "a change in the quantity supplied" and "a change in supply"?
   (e) What are the formulas for point and arc elasticity of supply?

6. Will the supply curve shift to the right or to the left if
   (a) technology improves?
   (b) the price of resources increases?
   (c) the weather is less favorable (for agricultural products)?

7. (a) What is meant by equilibrium? Equilibrium price? Equilibrium quantity?
   (b) How is the equilibrium price and quantity of a commodity defined graphically?
   (c) What is meant by a surplus? A shortage?
   (d) How does a surplus drive the price down? A shortage drive the price up?

8. (a) What is meant by an increase in demand? A decrease in demand?
   (b) Given the supply curve of a commodity, will an increase in demand lead to a temporary surplus or shortage of the commodity at the original equilibrum price?
   (c) Will an increase in demand lead to an

increase or decrease in the equilibrium price?

(d) Will a decrease in demand lead to an increase or decrease in the equilibrium quantity?

9. (a) What is meant by an increase in supply? A decrease in supply?

(b) Given the demand curve for a commodity, will an increase in supply lead to a temporary surplus or shortage of the commodity at the original equilibrium price?

(c) Will an increase in supply lead to an increase or decrease in the equilibrium price?

(d) Will a decrease in supply lead to an increase or decrease in the equilibrium quantity?

10. (a) What is meant by a price ceiling? When is a price ceiling ineffective?

(b) What is the result of an effective price ceiling? Was this the effect of rent control laws?

(c) What is meant by a price floor? When is a price floor ineffective?

(d) What is the result of an effective price floor? What was the result of the price support program in U.S. agriculture?

11. (a) What is an excise tax? What is meant by the "incidence of the tax"?

(b) Does it make any difference whether the excise tax is collected from sellers or from buyers? Why?

(c) Under what condition is the burden of the tax greater on buyers than on sellers?

(d) When is the relative burden of the tax greater on sellers?

12. (a) What is meant by the cobweb model?

(b) How does the cobweb model explain price fluctuations for some agricultural commodities?

(c) Why is the cobweb model simplistic?

Problems

1. Given the following demand schedule of a commodity

P($)	6	5	4	3	2	1	0
QD	0	10	20	30	40	50	60

show that by substituting the prices given in the above table into the following demand equation or function, you obtain the corresponding quantities demanded given in the above table:

$$QD = 60 - 10P$$

★2. (a) Derive the demand schedule from the following demand function:

$$QD' = 80 - 10P$$

(b) On the same graph, plot the demand schedule of Problem 1 and label it D and the demand curve of part (a) of this problem and label it D'.

(c) Does D' represent an increase in demand or an increase in the quantity demanded? Why?

3. (a) Derive the supply schedule from the following supply function:

$$QS = 10P$$

(b) Derive the supply schedule from the following supply function:

$$QS' = 20 + 10P$$

(c) On the same graph, plot the supply schedule of part (a) and label it S and the supply curve of part (b) and label it S'.

(d) What may have caused S to shift to S'?

4. (a) Find the price elasticity of demand curve D of Problem 1 for a price decline from $P = \$5$ to $P = \$4$, for a price increase from $P = \$4$ to $P = \$5$, and then find the arc elasticity between the two points.

(b) Find the price elasticity of supply curve S of Problem 3a for a price increase from

★ = answer provided at the end of book.

$P = \$4$ to $P = \$5$, for a price decrease from $P = \$5$ to $P = \$4$, and then find the arc elasticity between the two points.

★5. (a) Construct a table similar to Table 2-5 giving the supply schedule of Problem 3a and the demand schedule of Problem 1. In the same table identify the equilibrium price and quantity of the commodity, the surplus or shortage at prices other than the equilibrium price, and the pressure on price with a surplus or a shortage.

   (b) Show your results of part (a) graphically.

6. (a) Repeat the procedure in Problem 5a for the supply schedule of Problem 3b and the demand schedule of Problem 2a.

   (b) Show your results of part (a) graphically.

   (c) On the same graph, draw D and S from Problem 5b and D' and S' from Problem 6b. What general conclusion can you reach as to the effect of an increase in the demand and supply of a commodity on the equilibrium price and quantity of the commodity?

7. On separate sets of axes, show that

   (a) a decrease in demand reduces the equilibrium price and quantity of the commodity.

   (b) a decrease in supply increases price but reduces quantity.

   (c) a decrease in both demand and supply will reduce quantity but may increase, reduce, or leave price unchanged.

8. On separate sets of axes, show that

   (a) an increase in both demand and supply will increase quantity and may increase, reduce, or leave price unchanged.

   (b) a decrease in demand and an increase in supply will reduce price but may increase, decrease, or leave quantity unchanged.

   (c) an increase in demand and a decrease in supply will increase price but may increase, decrease, or leave quantity unchanged.

★9. Indicate what happens in the market for hamburgers if

   (a) the price of hot dogs increases.

   (b) a disease develops that kills a large proportion of cattle.

   (c) a new breed of cattle is developed with much faster growth.

   (d) a medical research proves that this new breed results in hamburgers with less cholesterol.

   (e) a direct subsidy on each head of cattle is given to farmers raising cattle.

10. With reference to your answer to Problem 5a, indicate the effect of the government imposing on the commodity a

   (a) price ceiling of $P = \$2$.

   (b) price ceiling of $P = \$3$.

   (c) price ceiling higher than $P = \$3$.

   (d) price floor of $P = \$5$.

   (e) price floor of $P = \$4$.

   (f) price floor equal or smaller than $P = \$3$.

★11. Draw a figure showing that

   (a) given the supply of a commodity, the less sensitive the quantity demanded is to price (i.e., the steeper is the demand curve), the greater is the share of the tax paid by consumers in the form of higher prices.

   (b) given the demand for a commodity, the less sensitive the quantity supplied is to price (i.e., the steeper is the supply curve) the smaller is the share of the tax paid by consumers and the larger is the share paid by sellers.

12. Draw a figure illustrating the cobweb model for the case where the price and quantity oscillate by

   (a) increasing amounts in ever widening cycles.

   (b) constant amounts without either converging or diverging.

Supplementary Readings

A paperback in the Schaum's Outline Series in Economics that gives a problem-solving approach to the topics discussed in this chapter is

Dominick Salvatore, *Microeconomic Theory* (New York: McGraw-Hill, 1983), Chapters 2 and 3.

For the earliest clear exposition of the concept and measurement of price elasticity of demand, see

Alfred Marshall, *Principles of Economics,* 9th ed. (London: Macmillan, 1920), Book III, Chapter IV.

An early clear exposition of the concepts of demand, supply, and equilibrium is found in

Alfred Marshall, *Principles of Economics,* 9th ed. (London: Macmillan, 1920), Book V, Chapter I–III.

Theory of Consumer Behavior and Demand

TWO

Part Two (Chapters 3–6) presents the theory of consumer behavior and demand. Chapter 3 examines the tastes of the consumer and how the consumer maximizes utility or satisfaction in spending his or her income. These concepts are then utilized and extended in Chapter 4 to derive the consumer's demand curve for a commodity. Chapter 5 shows how, by aggregating or summing up individual consumer's demand curves, we get the market demand curve for the commodity. Chapter 5 also examines in detail the usefulness and measurement of various demand elasticities. Finally, Chapter 6 presents more advanced topics and more recent important developments in consumer demand theory. The presentation of the theory is reinforced throughout with many real-world examples and important applications.

Chapter 3

Consumer Preferences and Choice

3-1   Utility Analysis

3-2   Indifference Curves

3-3   Budget Line

3-4   Consumer's Choice

3-5   Applications

Examples

3-1   Experimental Determination of Indifference Curves

3-2   Utility Maximization by Criminals and Psychiatric Patients

3-3   Noneconomic Optimization in Consumer Product Safety Regulation

Applications

Application 1:   The Effect of Government Warnings

Application 2:   Rationing

Application 3:   Charitable Behavior

Application 4:   The Economics of Fringe Benefits

Preview Questions

Why does a consumer purchase some commodities and not others?

What constrains or limits consumer purchases?

What is the aim of a rational consumer in spending income?

Why do most consumers purchase many commodities rather than only one or a few?

What is the effect of government warnings on the use of some products?

What is the effect of government rationing of a product?

Why do some people give to charity?

Why do firms give some fringe benefits rather than higher wages?

In this chapter, we begin the formal study of microeconomics by studying the economic behavior of the consumer. A consumer is an individual or a household composed of one or more individuals. The consumer is the basic economic unit determining which commodities are purchased and in what quantities. Millions of such decisions are made each day on the more than $2 trillion worth of goods and services produced by the American economy each year.

In this chapter we inquire into what guides these individual consumer decisions. Why do consumers purchase some commodities and not others? How do they decide how much to purchase of each commodity? What is the aim of a rational consumer in spending income? These are but a few of the important questions to which we seek answers in this chapter. The theory of consumer behavior and choice is the first step in the derivation of the market demand curve, the importance of which was clearly demonstrated in Chapter 2.

We begin the study of the economic behavior of the consumer by examining tastes. The consumer's tastes can be related to utility concepts or indifferences curves. These are discussed in the first two sections of the chapter. We then introduce the budget line. This gives the constraint or limitations faced by the consumer in purchasing goods and services. This constraint arises because the commodities that the consumer wants command a price in the market place (i.e., they are not free) and the consumer has limited income. Thus, the budget line reflects the familiar and pervasive economic fact of scarcity as it pertains to the individual consumer.

Since the consumer's wants are unlimited or, in any event, exceed his or her ability to satisfy them all, it is important that he or she spend income so as to maximize satisfaction. Thus, we provide a model to illustrate and predict how a rational consumer maximizes satisfaction, given his or her tastes (indifference curves) and the constraints he or she faces (the budget line). The several real-world examples and important applications presented in the chapter demonstrate the relevance and usefulness of the theory of consumer behavior and choice.

3-1

Utility Analysis

In this section we discuss the meaning of utility, distinguish between total utility and marginal utility, and examine the important difference between cardinal and ordinal utility. The concept of utility is used here to introduce the consumer's tastes. The analysis of consumer tastes is a crucial step in determining how a consumer maximizes satisfaction in spending income.

3-1a Total and Marginal Utility

Goods are desired because of their ability to satisfy human wants. For example, the individual of Chapter 2 desired hamburgers because they satisfied his or her appetite. Similarly, the individual desired soft drinks because they satisfied his or her thirst. The property of a good that enables it to satisfy a want is called **utility.**

As an individual consumes more of a good per time period, his **total utility** (TU) or satisfaction increases. For example, the total utility of the individual increases when he consumes more hamburgers because this enables him to satisfy more of his appetite. While total utility generally increases as the individual consumes more of a commodity, his extra or marginal utility diminishes. **Marginal utility** (MU) is the extra utility received from consuming one additional unit of the good. Marginal utility declines as the individual consumes more units of the commodity per time period (while holding constant the quantity consumed of all other commodities).

For example, Table 3-1 indicates that one hamburger per day (or more generally, one unit of good X per period of time) gives the consumer a total utility of $TU = 10$ utils, where a **util** is an arbitrary unit of utility. For two hamburgers, $TU = 16$ utils, $TU = 20$ utils for three hamburgers, and $TU = 22$ utils for four hamburgers. Total utility remains unchanged at $TU = 22$ for five hamburgers and actually declines to $TU = 20$ for six hamburgers.

The highest utility that an individual can get from consuming a particular commodity is called the saturation point. Consuming more units of the commodity past the saturation point leads to a *decline* in total utility. For example, in Table 3-1, the saturation point is reached after the individual consumes the fourth hamburger. The increase in consumption from five to

TABLE 3-1   Total and Marginal Utility

Q_x	TU_x	MU_x
0	0	. . .
1	10	10
2	16	6
3	20	4
4	22	2
5	22	0
6	20	−2

six hamburgers per day then reduces the individual's total utility from TU = 22 utils to TU = 20 utils. This decline in total utility arises because of storage or disposal problems.[1]

The third column of Table 3-1 gives the extra or marginal utility result-ing from the consumption of each *additional* hamburger. Since total utility increases from TU = 0 when the individual does not consume any ham-burgers to TU = 10 when he or she consumes one hamburger, MU = 10 utils for the first hamburger. The second hamburger increases total utility from TU = 10 to TU = 16 utils, and so MU = 6 utils. For the third ham-burger MU = 4 utils and MU = 2 utils for the fourth hamburger. Since consumption of the fifth hamburger leaves total utility unchanged at TU = 22 utils; MU = 0 utils for the fifth hamburger. Consumption of the sixth hamburger actually reduces TU by 2 utils, and so MU = −2 utils.

Plotting the values given in Table 3-1, we obtain Figure 3-1, with the top panel showing total utility and the bottom panel showing marginal utility. The total and marginal utility curves are obtained by joining the midpoints of the bars measuring TU and MU at each level of consumption. Note that the TU rises by smaller and smaller amounts (the shaded areas) and so the MU declines. The consumer reaches saturation after consuming the fourth hamburger. Thus, TU remains unchanged with the consumption of the fifth hamburger and MU is zero. After the fifth hamburger, TU declines and so MU is negative. The negative slope or downward-to-the-right inclination of the MU curve reflects the **law of diminishing marginal utility.**

There is a possibility that **MU** might first rise for a while before it begins to fall. For example, having only one television set in the house might not result in much satisfaction because of strong disagreements as to which program to view. The marginal utility of the second television set might then be more than for the first set by allowing more choice of programs by the various family members (for example, the parents may watch one TV set and the children watch the other set). This might be shown by the dashed-line portion of the TU and MU curves in Figure 3-1. More than two TV sets might still increase TU but MU will eventually decline. We will

---

[1] That is, some effort (disutility), no matter how small, is required to get rid of the sixth hamburger. Assuming that the individual cannot sell the sixth hamburger, he or she would not want it even for free.

FIGURE 3-1.
Total and Marginal
Utility

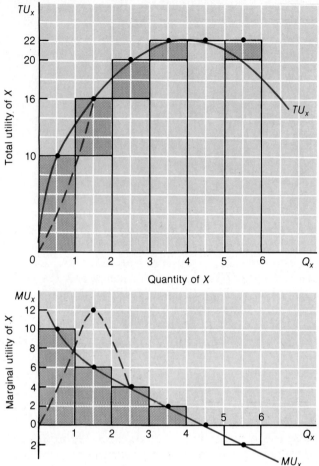

In the top panel, total utility (TU) increases by smaller and smaller amounts (the shaded areas) and so the marginal utility (MU) in the bottom panel declines. The consumer reaches saturation after he or she consumes the fourth hamburger (good X). Thus, TU remains unchanged with the consumption of the fifth hamburger, and MU is zero. After the fifth hamburger per day, TU declines and MU is negative. The negative slope or the downward-to-the-right inclination of the MU curve reflects the law of diminishing marginal utility.

see later that, for our purposes, the economically relevant portion of the MU curve is the range over which marginal utility is positive and declining.

It should be noted that utility schedules refer to the tastes of a particular individual. That is, they are unique to the individual and reflect his or her own particular subjective preferences and perceptions. Different individuals may have different tastes and different utility schedules. Utility schedules remain unchanged so long as the individual's tastes remain the same.

Utility schedules also refer to a specific period of time. Thus, the *TU* and *MU* schedules given in Table 3-1 might refer to one day. For a different period of time, the utility schedules of the individual will be different. For example, the sixth hamburger results in a decline in the total utility of the individual if he or she must consume all six hamburgers (and a given amount of other foods) during one day, but may not if he or she consumes the six hamburgers over a week's time. The utility schedules for a particular good are also based on the assumption that the individual does not change the quantity consumed of other goods. For example, if an individual eats nothing but hamburgers during a day, then the sixth hamburger may not yield negative marginal utility.

3-1b. Cardinal and Ordinal Utility

The concept of utility discussed in the previous section was introduced at about the same time, in the early 1870s, by William Stanley Jevons of Great Britain, Karl Menger of Austria, and Léon Walras of France. They believed that the utility that an individual receives from consuming each quantity of a good or basket of goods could be measured cardinally just like weight, height, or temperature.[2]

Cardinal utility means that an individual can attach specific values or number of utils from consuming each quantity of a good or basket of goods. Thus, in Table 3-1 we saw that the individual received 10 utils from consuming one hamburger. He received 16 utils or six additional utils from consuming two hamburgers. The consumption of the third hamburger gave this individual four extra utils, or two-thirds as many extra utils as the second hamburger. Thus, Table 3-1 and Figure 3-1 reflect cardinal utility. They actually provide an index of satisfaction for the individual.

This is to be contrasted to **ordinal utility,** which only *ranks* the utility received from consuming various amounts of a good or baskets of goods. Thus, ordinal utility only specifies that consuming two hamburgers gives the individual more utility than he receives from consuming one hamburger, without specifying exactly how much additional utility the second hamburger provides. Similarly, ordinal utility would only say that three hamburgers give this individual more utility than two hamburgers, but *not* how many more utils.[3]

---

[2] A market basket of goods can be defined as containing specific quantities of various goods and services. For example, one basket may contain one hamburger, one soft drink, and a ticket to a ball game, while another basket may contain two soft drinks and two movie tickets.

[3] To be sure, numerical values could be attached to the utility received by the individual from consuming various hamburgers, even with ordinal utility. However, with ordinal utility, higher utility values only indicate higher rankings of utility and no importance can be attached to actual numerical differences in utility. That is, with ordinal utility, 20 utils can only be interpreted as being more utility than 10 utils, but not twice as much. Thus, to indicate rising utility rankings, numbers such as 5, 10, 20; 8, 15, 17; or I (lowest), II, and III are equivalent.

Ordinal utility is a much weaker notion than cardinal utility since it only requires that the consumer be able to rank baskets of goods in order of his or her preference. That is, when presented with a choice between any two baskets of goods, ordinal utility only requires that the individual be able to indicate if he or she prefers the first basket, the second basket, or is indifferent between the two. It does not require that the individual be able to specify how many more utils he or she receives from the preferred basket. *In short, ordinal utility only ranks various consumption bundles whereas cardinal utility provides an actual index or measure of satisfaction.*

The distinction between cardinal and ordinal utility is important because a theory of consumer behavior can be developed on the weaker assumption of ordinal utility, without the need for a cardinal measure. And a theory that reaches the same conclusion as another on weaker assumptions is a superior theory.[4] Nevertheless, cardinal utility does add an important dimension to the analysis of consumer choice and is important for the analysis of consumer choices in the face of risk (presented in Chapter 6). Utility analysis is also a convenient way to introduce the concept of consumer tastes and to highlight the crucial difference between cardinal and ordinal utility. Furthermore, some attempts are still being made to measure utility cardinally.

3-2

Indifference Curves

In this section we define indifference curves and examine their characteristics. Indifference curves were first introduced by the English economist F. Y. Edgeworth in the 1880s. The concept was refined and extensively used by the Italian economist V. Pareto in the early 1900s. They were popularized and greatly extended in application in the 1930s by two other English economists: R. D. G. Allen and J. R. Hicks. Indifference curves are a crucial tool of analysis. They are used to represent an ordinal measure of the tastes and preferences of the consumer and to show how he or she maximizes utility in spending income.

3-2a Definition of Indifference Curves

Consumers' tastes can be examined with ordinal utility. An ordinal measure of utility is based on three assumptions. First, we assume that when faced with any two baskets of goods, the consumer can determine whether he or she prefers basket A to basket B, B to A, or whether he or she is indifferent between the two. Second, we assume that the tastes of the con-

---

[4] This is like producing a given output with fewer or cheaper inputs, or achieving the same medical result (such as control of high blood pressure) with less or weaker medication.

TABLE 3-2   Indifference Schedule

Hamburgers (X)	Soft Drinks (Y)	Combination
1	10	A
2	6	B
4	3	C
7	1	F

sumer are *consistent* or *transitive*. That is, if the consumer states that he prefers basket A to basket B and also that he prefers basket B to basket C, then he will prefer A to C. Third, we assume that more of a commodity is preferred to less. That is, we assume that the commodity is a **good** rather than a **bad,** and the consumer is never satiated with the commodity.[5] The above three assumptions can be used to represent an individual's tastes with indifference curves. In order to conduct the analysis by plane geometry, we will assume throughout that there are only two goods, X and Y.

An **indifference curve** shows the various combinations of two goods that give the consumer equal utility or satisfaction. A higher indifference curve refers to a higher level of satisfaction and a lower indifference curve refers to less satisfaction. However, we have no indication as to how much additional satisfaction or utility a higher indifference curve refers. That is, different indifference curves simply provide an ordering or ranking of the individual's preferences.

For example, Table 3-2 gives an indifference schedule showing the various combinations of hamburgers (good X) and soft drinks (good Y) that give the consumer equal satisfaction. This information is plotted as indifference curve U_1 in the left panel of Figure 3-2. The right panel repeats indifference curve U_1 along with a higher indifference curve (U_2) and a lower one (U_0).

Indifference curve U_1 shows that one hamburger and ten soft drinks per unit of time (combination A) give the consumer the same level of satisfaction as two hamburgers and six soft drinks (combination B), four hamburgers and three soft drinks (combination C), or seven hamburgers and one soft drink (combination F). On the other hand, combination R (4 hamburgers and 7 soft drinks) has both more hamburgers and more soft drinks than combination B (see the right panel of Figure 3-2) and so it refers to a higher level of satisfaction. Thus, combination R and all the other combinations that give the same level of satisfaction as combination R define higher indifference curve U_2. Finally, all combinations on U_0 give the same satisfaction as combination T, and combination T refers to both fewer hamburgers and fewer soft drinks than (and therefore is inferior to) combination B on U_1.

Although in Figure 3-2 we have drawn only three indifference curves, there is an indifference curve going through each point in the XY plane (i.e., referring to each possible combination of good X and good Y). Another

---

[5] Examples of bads are pollution, garbage, and disease, of which less is preferred to more.

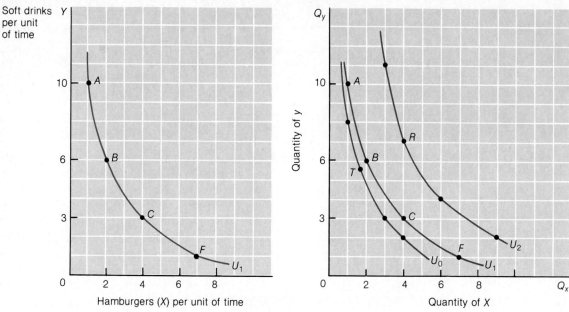

FIGURE 3-2.   Indifference Curves

An indifference curve shows the various combinations of two goods that give the con-sumer equal satisfaction or utility. Thus, the individual is indifferent between com-binations A (1X and 10Y), B (2X and 6Y), C (4X and 3Y), and F (7X and 1Y) since they all lie on indifference curve U_1. Combination R (4X and 7Y) gives more satisfac-tion than combination B and lies on higher indifference curve U_2 in the right panel. Indifference curve U_0 refers to a lower level of satisfaction than U_1 and U_2.

way of saying this is that between any two indifference curves, an addi-tional one can always be drawn. The entire set of indifference curves is called an **indifference map** and reflects the entire set of tastes and prefer-ences of the consumer.

3-2b Characteristics of Indifference Curves

Indifference curves are usually negatively sloped, cannot intersect, and are convex to the origin (see Figure 3-2). Indifference curves are negatively sloped because if one basket of X and Y goods contains more of X, it will have to contain less of Y than another basket for the two baskets to give the same level of satisfaction and be on the same indifference curve. For example, since basket B on indifference curve U_1 in Figure 3-2 contains more hamburgers (good X) than basket A, basket B must contain fewer soft drinks (good Y) for the consumer to be on indifference curve U_1.

A positively sloped curve would indicate that one basket containing more of both commodities gives the same utility or satisfaction to the consumer as another basket containing less of both commodities (and no other commodity). Since we are dealing with goods rather than bads, such a curve could not possibly be an indifference curve. For example, in the left panel of Figure 3-3, combination B' contains more of X and more of Y than combination A', and so the positively sloped curve on which B' and A' lie cannot be an indifference curve. That is, B' must be on a higher indifference curve than A' if X and Y are both goods.

Indifference curves also cannot intersect. Intersecting curves are inconsistent with the definition of indifference curves. For example, if curve 1 and curve 2 in the right panel of Figure 3-3 were indifference curves they would indicate that basket A* is equivalent to basket C* since both A* and C* are on curve 1, and also that basket B* is equivalent to basket C* since both B* and C* are on curve 2. By transitivity, B* should then be equivalent to A*. However, this is impossible since basket B* contains more of both good X and good Y than basket A*. Thus, indifference curves cannot intersect.

Indifference curves are usually convex to the origin. That is, they lie above any tangent to the curve. Convexity results from or is a reflection of decreasing marginal rate of substitution, which is discussed next.

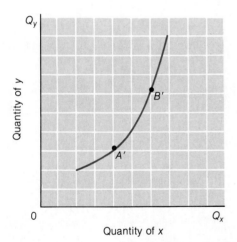
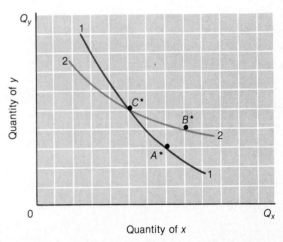

FIGURE 3-3. Indifference Curves Cannot Be Positively Sloped or Intersect

In the left panel, the positively sloped curve cannot be an indifference curve because it shows that combination B', which contains more of X and more of Y than combination A', gives equal satisfaction to the consumer as A'. This is impossible if X and Y are both goods. In the right panel, if curves 1 and 2 were indifference curves they would indicate that A* is equivalent to C* since both A* and C* are on curve 1, and also that B* is equivalent to C* since both B* and C* are on curve 2. Thus, B* should be equal to A*. However, this is impossible since B* contains more of both good X and good Y than A*. Thus, indifference curves cannot intersect.

3-2c The Marginal Rate of Substitution

The marginal rate of substitution (*MRS*) refers to the amount of one good that an individual is willing to give up for an additional unit of another good while maintaining the same level of satisfaction or remaining on the same indifference curve. For example, the marginal rate of substitution of good X for good Y (MRS_{xy}) refers to the amount of Y that the individual is willing to exchange per unit of X and maintain the same level of satisfaction. Note that MRS_{xy} measures the downward vertical distance (the amount of Y that the individual is willing to give up) per unit of horizontal distance (i.e., per additional unit of X required) to remain on the same indifference curve. That is, $MRS_{xy} = -\Delta Y/\Delta X$. Because of the reduction in Y, MRS_{xy} is negative. However, we multiply by -1 and express MRS_{xy} as a positive value.

For example, starting at point A on U_1 in Figure 3-4, the individual is willing to give up four units of Y for one additional unit of X and reach point B on U_1. Thus, $MRS_{xy} = -(-4/1) = 4$. This is the absolute (or positive value of the) slope of the chord from point A to point B on U_1. Between point B and point C on U_1, $MRS_{xy} = 3/2 = 1.5$ (the absolute slope of chord BC). Between points C and F, $MRS_{xy} = 2/3 = 0.67$. At a particular point on the indifference curve, MRS_{xy} is given by the absolute slope of the tangent

FIGURE 3-4.
The Marginal Rate
of Substitution
(MRS)

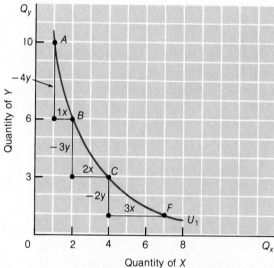

Starting at point A, the individual is willing to give up 4 units of Y for one additional unit of X and reach point B on U₁. Thus, MRS_{xy} = 4 (the absolute slope of chord AB). Between points B and C, MRS_{xy} = 3/2. Between C and F, MRS_{xy} = 2/3. MRS_{xy} declines because as an individual is left with fewer and fewer units of Y, each remaining unit of Y becomes very valuable to him or her, and so he or she is willing to give up less and less of Y to obtain each additional unit of X. Diminishing MRS_{xy} is a reflection of the convexity of the indifference curve.

to the indifference curve at that point. Different individuals usually have different indifference curves and different MRS_{xy} (at points where their indifference curves have different slopes).

We can relate indifference curves to the preceding utility analysis by pointing out that all combinations of goods X and Y on a given indifference curve refer to the same level of total utility for the individual. Thus, for a movement down a given indifference curve, the gain in utility in consuming more of good X must be equal to the loss in utility in consuming less of good Y. Specifically, the increase in consumption of good X (ΔX) times the marginal utility that the individual receives from consuming each additional unit of X (MU_x) must be equal to the reduction in Y ($-\Delta Y$) times the marginal utility of Y (MU_y). That is,

$$(\Delta X)\,(MU_x) = -(\Delta Y)\,(MU_y) \qquad\qquad (3\text{-}1)$$

so that

$$MU_x/MU_y = -\Delta Y/\Delta X = MRS_{xy} \qquad\qquad (3\text{-}2)$$

Thus, MRS_{xy} is equal to the absolute slope of the indifference curve and to the ratio of the marginal utilities.[6]

Note that MRS_{xy} (i.e., the absolute slope of the indifference curve) declines as we move down the indifference curve. This follows from, or is a reflection of, the convexity of the indifference curve. That is, as the individual moves down an indifference curve and is left with less and less Y (say, soft drinks) and more and more X (say, hamburgers), each remaining unit of Y becomes more valuable to him and each additional unit of X becomes less valuable. Thus, he is willing to give up less and less of Y to obtain each additional unit of X. It is this property that makes MRS_{xy} diminish and indifference curves convex to the origin. We will see in Section 3-4 the crucial role that convexity plays in consumer utility maximization.[7]

3-2d Some Special Types of Indifference Curves

While indifference curves are usually negatively sloped and convex to the origin, they may sometimes assume other shapes, as shown in Figure 3-5. Horizontal indifference curves, as in the top left panel of Figure 3-5, would indicate that commodity X is a **neuter;** that is, the consumer is indifferent between having more or less of the commodity. On the other hand, vertical indifference curves, as in the top right panel, would indicate that commodity Y is a neuter.

---

[6] For a mathematical presentation of indifference curves and their characteristics using rudimentary calculus, see Section A1 of the Mathematical Appendix.

[7] It should be noted that a movement along an indifference curve in the *upward* direction measures MRS_{yx}, which also diminishes.

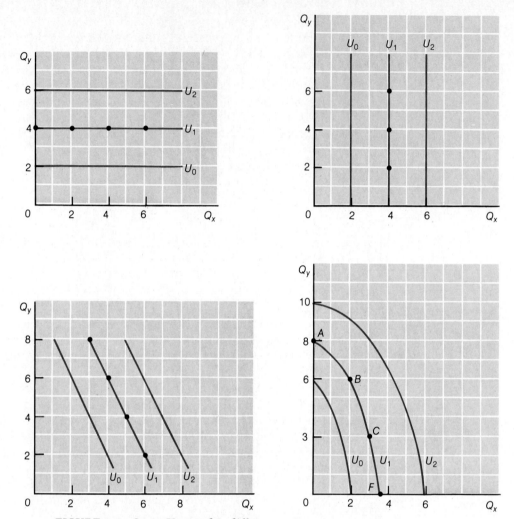

FIGURE 3-5. *Some Unusual Indifference Curves*

Horizontal indifference curves, as in the top left panel, indicate that X is a neuter; that is, the consumer is indifferent between having more or less of it. Vertical indifference curves, as in the top right panel, indicate that Y is a neuter. The bottom left panel shows indifference curves that are negatively sloped straight lines. Then MRS_{xy} is constant, and X and Y are perfect substitutes for the individual. The bottom right panel shows indifference curves that are concave to the origin (i.e., MRS_{xy} increases).

The bottom left panel shows indifference curves that are negatively sloped straight lines. Here, MRS_{xy} or the absolute slope of the indifference curves is constant. This means that an individual is always willing to give up the same amount of good Y (say, two cups of tea) for each additional unit of good X (one cup of coffee). Therefore, good X and two units of good Y are *perfect substitutes* for this individual.

70

Finally, the bottom right panel shows indifference curves that are concave rather than convex to the origin. This means that the individual is willing to give up more and more units of good Y for each additional unit of X (i.e., MRS_{xy} increases). For example, between points A and B on U_1, $MRS_{xy} = 2/2 = 1$; between B and C, $MRS_{xy} = 3/1 = 3$; and between C and F, $MRS_{xy} = 3/0.5 = 6$. In Section 3-4, we will see that in this unusual case, the individual will end up consuming only good X or only good Y.

While indifference curves can assume any of the shapes shown in Figure 3-5, they are usually negatively sloped, nonintersecting, and convex to the origin. As the following example indicates, these characteristics of indifference curves have been confirmed experimentally when neither commodity is a bad.

Example 3-1   Experimental Determination of Indifference Curves

The Facts: In May 1967, an experiment was conducted at the University of California at Los Angeles to derive indifference curves between money and ball-point pens for each of seven college students (five males and two females). First, each student was given $20 and no pens, and then less and less money and more and more pens so as to leave him or her at the same level of satisfaction. Lower indifference curves were then obtained by starting with smaller amounts of money and no pens. The indifference curves so derived did not intersect, were negatively sloped and, with the exception of only one indifference curve for one of the subjects, were convex to the origin. The experiment was then repeated to derive indifference curves between money and French pastries (to be eaten on the spot) for each of the same seven college students. For the two female students in the group, indifference curves were positively sloped throughout (as in the left panel of Figure 3-3), indicating that for them French pastries were a bad rather than a good, and that they had to be paid to eat any pastry. For the five male subjects, indifference curves became positively sloped after about three pastries (their saturation point), after which pastries became a bad.

Comment: Weight consciousness was probably responsible for the two female subjects regarding French pastries always as bads. This was less true for the male subjects (for whom pastries became a bad only after they ate three of them). In the experiment, money served as a generalized consumption good. Since we are ultimately interested in market behavior, the sample should be broadened to include also noncollege students and other commodities. However, a careful reading of the full description of the above experiment makes it clear that it is very difficult to determine indifference curves experimentally. Yet, the above experiment does show that when the commodity was a good rather than a bad the indifference curves between money and the good were negatively sloped, nonintersecting, and convex to the origin (i.e., they exhibited all of the characteristics deemed

71

essential for indifference curves to accurately portray an individual's tastes and preferences).

Source: K. R. MacCrimmon and M. Toda, "The Experimental Determination of Indifference Curves," *Review of Economic Studies,* October 1969, pp. 433–451.

3-3

Budget Line

In this section we introduce the constraints or limitations faced by a consumer in satisfying his or her wants. In order to conduct the analysis by plane geometry, we assume that the consumer spends all income on only two goods, *X* and *Y*. We will see that the constraints of the consumer can then be represented by a line called the budget line. The position of the budget line and changes in it can best be understood by looking at its endpoints.

3-3a Definition of the Budget Line

In Section 3-2a, we have seen that we can represent a consumer's tastes by an indifference map. We now introduce the constraints or limitations that a consumer faces in attempting to satisfy his or her wants. The amount of goods that a consumer can purchase over a given period of time is limited by the consumer's income and by the prices of the goods that he or she must pay. In what follows we assume (realistically) that the consumer cannot affect the price of the goods he or she purchases. In economics jargon, we then say that the consumer faces a **budget constraint** due to his or her limited income and the given prices of goods.

By assuming that a consumer spends all of his or her income on good *X* (hamburgers) and on good *Y* (soft drinks), we can express the budget constraint as

$$P_xQ_x + P_yQ_y = I \tag{3-3}$$

where P_x is the price of good *X*, Q_x is the quantity of good *X*, P_y is the price of good *Y*, Q_y is the quantity of good *Y*, and *I* is the consumer's money income. Equation (3-3) postulates that the price of *X* times the quantity of *X* plus the price of *Y* times the quantity of *Y* equals the consumer's money income. That is, the amount of money spent on *X* plus the amount spent on *Y* equals the consumer's income.[8]

---

[8] Equation (3-3) could be generalized to deal with any number of goods. However, as pointed out above, we deal with only two goods for purposes of diagrammatic analysis.

Suppose that $P_x = \$2$, $P_y = \$1$, and $I = \$10$ per unit of time. This could, for example, be the situation of a student who has $10 per day to spend on snacks of hamburgers (good X) priced at $2 each, and on soft drinks (good Y) priced at $1 each. By spending all income on Y the consumer could purchase 10Y and 0X. This defines endpoint J on the vertical axis of Figure 3-6. Alternatively, by spending all income on X, the consumer could purchase 5X and 0Y. This defines endpoint K on the horizontal axis. By joining endpoints J and K with a straight line we get the consumer's **budget line.** This shows the various combinations of X and Y that the consumer can purchase by spending all income at the given price of the two goods. For example, starting at endpoint J, the consumer could give up two units of Y and use the $2 not spent on Y to purchase the first unit of X and reach point L. By giving up another 2Y, he or she could purchase the second unit of X. The slope of -2 of budget line JK shows that for each 2Y the consumer gives up, he or she can purchase 1X more.

By rearranging Equation (3-3), we can express the consumer's budget constraint in a different and more useful form. By subtracting the term P_xQ_x from both sides of Equation (3-3) we get

$$P_yQ_y = I - P_xQ_x \tag{3-3A}$$

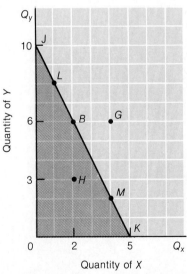

FIGURE 3-6.
The Budget Line

With an income of $I = \$10$, and $P_y = \$1$ and $P_x = \$2$, we get budget line JK. This shows that by spending all income on X and Y, the consumer can purchase 10Y and 0X (endpoint J), 8Y and 1X (point L), 6Y and 2X (point B), . . . , or 0Y and 5X (endpoint K). $I/P_y = \$10/\$1 = 10 = Q_y$ is the vertical or Y-intercept of the budget line. $-P_x/P_y = -\$2/\$1 = -2$ is the slope. If the consumer does not spend all income, he or she will be at a point such as H in the shaded area below the budget line (budget space). The consumer cannot reach a point such as G above the budget line.

By then dividing both sides of Equation (3-3A) by P_y, we isolate Q_y on the left-hand side and define Equation (3-4):

$$Q_y = I/P_y - (P_x/P_y)Q_x \qquad (3-4)$$

The first term on the right-hand side of Equation (3-4) is the vertical or Y-intercept of the budget line and $-P_x/P_y$ is the slope of the budget line. For example, continuing to use $P_x = \$2$, $P_y = \$1$, and $I = \$10$, we get $I/P_y = Q_y = 10$ for the Y-intercept (endpoint J in Figure 3-6) and $-P_x/P_y = -2$ for the slope of the budget line. The slope of the budget line refers to the rate at which the two goods can be exchanged for one another in the market (i.e., $2Y$ for $1X$).

The consumer can purchase any combination of X and Y on the budget line or in the shaded area below the budget line (called *budget space*). For example, at point B the individual would spend \$4 to purchase $2X$ and the remaining \$6 to purchase $6Y$. At point M, he or she would spend \$8 to purchase $4X$ and the remaining \$2 to purchase $2Y$. On the other hand, at a point such as H in the shaded area below the budget line (i.e., in the budget space), the individual would spend \$4 to purchase $2X$ and \$3 to purchase $3Y$ and be left with \$3 of unspent income. In what follows, we assume that the consumer does spend all of his or her income and is on the budget line. Because of the income and price constraints, the consumer cannot reach combinations of X and Y above the budget line. For example, the individual cannot purchase combination G ($4X$, $6Y$) because it requires an expenditure of \$14 (\$8 to purchase $4X$ plus \$6 to purchase $6Y$).

Savings could be introduced into the model by treating it as a good. Savings allows the consumer to purchase goods in the future. For example, if good Y were savings, the budget line would show the various combinations of savings and good X (hamburgers) that the consumer could achieve with his or her income and the price of X that he or she faces. A point such as B would then refer to the consumer spending \$4 to purchase $2X$ and saving \$6.

3-3b Changes in the Budget Line

A particular budget line refers to a specific level of the consumer's income and prices of the two goods. If the consumer's income and/or the price of good X or good Y change, the budget line will also change. When only the consumer's income changes, the budget line will shift up if income (I) rises and down if I falls, but the slope of the budget line remains unchanged. For example, the left panel of Figure 3-7 shows budget line JK (the same as in Figure 3-6 with $I = \$10$), higher budget line $J'K'$ with $I = \$15$, and still higher budget line $J''K''$ with $I = \$20$ per day. Since P_x and P_y do not change, the three budget lines are parallel and their slopes are equal. (With an income of only \$5, we would have the dashed budget line in the left panel.)

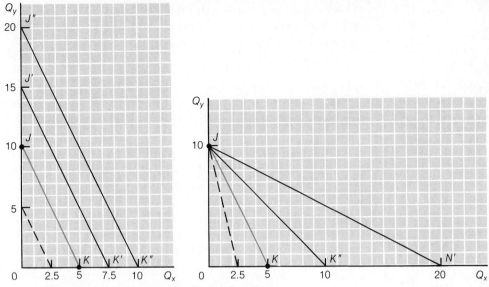

FIGURE 3-7.   Changes in the Budget Line

The left panel shows budget line JK (the same as in Figure 3-6 with I = $10), higher budget line J'K' with I = $15, and still higher budget line J"K" with I = $20 per day. It also shows the lower dashed budget line with I = $5. Since P_x and P_y do not change, the four budget lines are parallel and their slopes are equal. The right panel shows budget line JK with P_x = $2, budget line JK" with P_x = $1, and budget line JN' with P_x = $0.50. It also shows the dashed budget line with P_x = $4. The vertical or Y-intercept (endpoint J) remains the same because income and P_y do not change. The slope of budget line JK" is $-P_x/P_y$ = $-$1/$1 = -1$, for budget line JN', it is $-\frac{1}{2}$, and for the dashed budget line, it is -4.

If only the price of good X changes, the vertical or Y-intercept remains unchanged and the budget line rotates upward or counterclockwise if P_x falls and downward or clockwise if P_x rises. For example, the right panel of Figure 3-7 shows budget line JK (the same as in Figure 3-6 at P_x = $2), budget line JK'' with P_x = $1, and budget line JN' with P_x = $0.50. The vertical intercept (endpoint J) remains the same because I and P_y do not change. The slope of budget line JK'' is $-P_x/P_y = $1/$1 = -1$. The slope of budget line JN' is $-\frac{1}{2}$. (With P_x = $4, we would have the dashed budget line with $-P_x/P_y = -4/1 = -4$).

On the other hand, if only the price of Y changes, the horizontal or X-intercept will be the same but the budget line will rotate upward if P_y falls and downward if P_y rises. For example, with I = $10, P_x = $2, and P_y = $0.50 (rather than P_y = $1), the new vertical or Y-intercept is Q_y = 20 and the slope of the new budget line is $-P_x/P_y = -4$. With P_y = $2, the new Y-intercept is Q_y = 5 and $-P_x/P_y = -1$ (the student should be able to sketch these lines). Finally, with a proportionate reduction in P_x and

P_y and constant I there will be a parallel upward shift in the budget line, and with a proportionate increase in P_x and P_y and constant I there will be a parallel downward shift in the budget line.

3-4

Consumer's Choice

We will now bring together the tastes and preferences of the consumer (given by his or her indifference map) and the income and price constraints faced by the consumer (given by his or her budget line) to examine how the consumer determines which goods to purchase and in what quantities in order to maximize utility or satisfaction. As we will see in the next chapter, utility maximization is essential for the derivation of the consumer's demand curve for a commodity (which is a major objective of this part of the text).

3-4a Utility Maximization

Given the tastes of the consumer (reflected in his or her indifference map), the **rational consumer** seeks to maximize the utility or satisfaction received in spending his or her income. A rational consumer maximizes utility by trying to attain the highest indifference curve possible, given his or her budget line. This occurs where an indifference curve is tangent to the budget line so that the slope of the indifference curve (the MRS_{xy}) is equal to the slope of the budget line (P_x/P_y). Thus, the condition for **constrained utility maximization, consumer optimization,** or **consumer equilibrium** occurs where the consumer spends all income (i.e., he or she is on the budget line) and

$$MRS_{xy} = P_x/P_y \tag{3-5}$$

Figure 3-8 brings together on the same set of axes the consumer indifference curves of Figure 3-2 and the budget line of Figure 3-6 to determine the point of utility maximization. Figure 3-8 shows that the consumer maximizes utility at point B where indifference curve U_1 is tangent to budget line JK. At point B, the consumer is on the budget line and $MRS_{xy} = P_x/P_y = 2$. Indifference curve U_1 is the highest that the consumer can reach with his or her budget line. Thus, to maximize utility the consumer should spend \$4 to purchase $2X$ and the remaining \$6 to purchase $6Y$. Any other combination of goods X and Y that the consumer could purchase (those on or below the budget line) provides less utility. For example, the consumer could spend all income to purchase combination L, but this would be on lower indifference curve U_0.

FIGURE 3-8.
Constrained Utility
Maximization

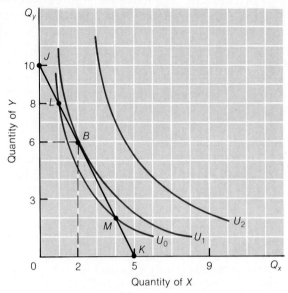

The consumer maximizes utility at point B, where indifference curve U_1 is tangent to budget line JK. At point B, $MRS_{xy} = P_x/P_y = 2$. Indifference curve U_1 is the highest that the consumer can reach with his or her budget line. Thus, the consumer should spend \$4 to purchase 2X and the remaining \$6 to purchase 6Y. Any other combination of X and Y that the consumer can purchase (those on or below the budget line) provides less utility.

Note that at point L, the consumer is willing to give up more of Y than he has to in the market to obtain one additional unit of X. That is, MRS_{xy} (the absolute slope of indifference curve U_0 at point L) exceeds the value of P_x/P_y (the absolute slope of budget line JK). Thus, starting from point L, the consumer can increase his or her satisfaction by purchasing less of Y and more of X until he or she reaches point B or U_1, where the slopes of U_1 and the budget line are equal (i.e., $MRS_{xy} = P_x/P_y = 2$). On the other hand, starting from point M, where $MRS_{xy} < P_x/P_y$, the consumer can increase his or her satisfaction by purchasing less of X and more of Y until he or she reaches point B on U_1, where $MRS_{xy} = P_x/P_y$. One tangency point such as B is assured by the fact that there is an indifference curve going through each point in the XY commodity space. The consumer cannot reach indifference curve U_2 with the present income and the given prices of goods X and Y.[9]

Utility maximization is more prevalent (as a general aim of individuals) than it may seem at first. It is observed not only in consumers as they attempt to maximize utility in spending income but also in many other

[9] For a mathematical presentation of utility maximization using rudimentary calculus, see Section A2 of the Mathematical Appendix.

individuals, including criminals and psychiatric patients. That is, at least some of the behavior of criminal and psychiatric patients is consistent with utility maximization. As the following example shows, even these individuals often respond rationally to economic incentives!

Example 3-2 Utility Maximization by Criminals and Psychiatric Patients

The Facts: A 1973 study reported that criminals often respond to incentives in much the same way as people engaged in legitimate economic activities. The rate of robberies and burglaries was found to be positively related to the gains and inversely related to the costs of (i.e., punishment for) criminal activity. For example, it was found that for each 1 per cent increase in the probability of being caught and sent to jail, the rate of robberies declined by 0.85 per cent. For each 1 per cent increase in the duration of imprisonment, the rate of burglaries declined by 0.90 per cent. Another study published in 1972 found that even institutionalized psychiatric patients often were willing to perform simple tasks such as bedmaking in exchange for tokens that could be used to obtain goods such as coffee, cigarettes, movies, and clothing. They also responded to changes in the token compensation rate for specific tasks in a way remarkably similar to the way that workers in the economy at large respond to changes in wage rates.

Comment: The assumption that individuals seek to maximize utility is basically an assumption that they behave rationally. While criminals exhibit a great deal of "deviant" and antisocial behavior, and psychiatric patients often behave abnormally and irrationally, both seem to respond rationally to some economic incentives. Thus, utility maximization is more prevalent than it might seem, and economics has something to contribute (together with sociology, psychology, and medicine) to the analysis of illegal activity and psychiatric behavior. One conclusion that follows from economic analysis, at least as far as criminal activity is concerned, is that increasing the efficiency of police in apprehending criminals and the imposition of stiffer sentences (i.e., increasing the cost of engaging in criminal activity) discourage crime.

Source: I. Ehrlich, "Participation in Illegitimate Activities: A Theoretical and Empirical Investigation," *Journal of Political Economy,* May/June 1973, pp. 521–561, J. H. Kagel, "Token Economies and Experimental Economics," *Journal of Political Economy,* July/August 1972, pp. 779–785.

3-4b Corner Solutions

If indifference curves are everywhere either flatter or steeper than the budget line, or if they are concave rather than convex to the origin, then the consumer maximizes utility by spending all income on either good Y or good X. These are called **corner solutions.**

In the left panel of Figure 3-9, indifference curves U_0, U_1, and U_2 are everywhere flatter than budget line JK, and U_1 is the highest indifference curve that the consumer can reach by purchasing $10Y$ and $0X$ (endpoint J). Point J is closest to the tangency point, which cannot be achieved. The individual could purchase $2X$ and $6Y$ and reach point B, but point B is on lower indifference curve U_0. Since point J is on the Y-axis (and involves the consumer spending all his or her income on good Y) it is called a corner solution.

The middle panel shows indifference curves that are everywhere steeper than the budget line, and U_1 is the highest indifference curve that the consumer can reach by spending all income to purchase $5X$ and $0Y$ (endpoint K). The individual could purchase $1X$ and $8Y$ at point L, but this is on lower indifference curve U_0. Since point K is on the horizontal axis and involves the consumer spending all his or her income on good X, point K is also a corner solution.

In the right panel, *concave* indifference curve U_1 is tangent to the budget line at point B but this is not optimum because the consumer can reach higher indifference curve U_2 by spending all income to purchase $10Y$ and

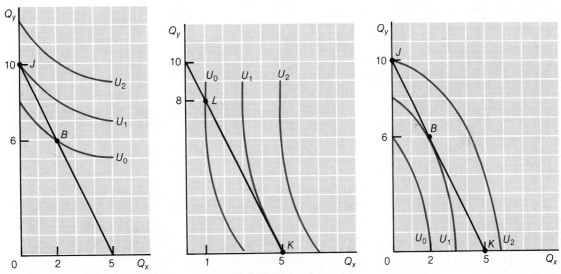

FIGURE 3-9. *Corner Solutions*

In the left panel, indifference curves are everywhere flatter than the budget line and U₁ is the highest indifference curve that the consumer can reach by purchasing 10Y only (point J). The middle panel shows indifference curves everywhere steeper than the budget line, and U₁ is the highest indifference curve that the consumer can reach by spending all income to purchase 5X (point K). In the right panel, concave indifference curve U₁ is tangent to the budget line at point B but this is not the optimum point because the consumer can reach higher indifference curve U₂ by consuming only good Y (point J).

79

0X (endpoint J). This is also a corner solution. Thus, the condition that an indifference curve must be tangent to the budget line for optimization is true only when indifference curves assume their usual convex shape and are neither everywhere flatter nor steeper than the budget line.

Finally, it must be pointed out that while a consumer in the real world does not spend all of his or her income on one or a few goods, there are many more goods that he or she does not purchase because they are too expensive for the utility they provide. For example, few people purchase a $2,000 watch because the utility that most people get from the watch does not justify its $2,000 price. The nonconsumption of many goods in the real world can be explained by indifference curves which, though convex to the origin, are everywhere either flatter or steeper than the budget line, yielding corner rather than interior solutions.

3-4c Marginal Utility Approach to Utility Maximization

If utility were cardinally measurable, then the condition for constrained utility maximization would be for the consumer to spend all income on X and Y in such a way that

$$\frac{MU_x}{P_x} = \frac{MU_y}{P_y} \tag{3-6}$$

Expression (3-6) reads, the marginal utility of good X divided by the price of good X equals the marginal utility of good Y divided by the price of good Y. MU_x/P_x is the extra or marginal utility per dollar spent on X. Likewise MU_y/P_y is the marginal utility per dollar spent on Y. Thus, for constrained utility maximization or optimization, the marginal utility of the last dollar spent on X and Y should be the same.[10]

For example, Table 3-3 shows a portion of the declining marginal utility schedule for good X (from Table 3-1) and good Y, on the assumption that MU_x is independent of MU_y (i.e., that MU_x is not affected by how much Y the individual consumes, and MU_y is not affected by Q_x consumed). If the

TABLE 3-3   Marginal Utility of X and Y

Q_x	MU_x	Q_y	MU_y
1	10	4	5
2	6	5	4
3	4	6	3
4	2	7	2
5	0	8	1

[10] We will see later that Condition (3-6) holds also for the indifference curve approach.

80

consumer's income is I = \$10, and P_x = \$2 and P_y = \$1, the consumer should spend \$4 to purchase $2X$ and the remaining \$6 to purchase $6Y$ so that Condition (3-6) is satisfied. That is,

$$\frac{6 \text{ utils}}{\$2} = \frac{3 \text{ utils}}{\$1} \qquad (3\text{-}6A)$$

If the consumer spent only \$2 to purchase $1X$ and the remaining \$8 to purchase $8Y$, $MU_x/P_x = 10/2 = 5$ and $MU_y/P_y = 1/1 = 1$. The last (second) dollar spent on X thus gives the consumer 5 times as much utility as the last (eighth) dollar spent on Y and the consumer would not be maximizing utility. To be at optimum, the consumer should purchase more of X (MU_x falls) and less of Y (MU_y rises) until he or she purchases $2X$ and $6Y$, where Condition (3-6) is satisfied.[11] This is the same result obtained with the indifference curve approach in Section 3-4a. Note that even when the consumer purchases $1X$ and $4Y$ Condition (3-6) is satisfied ($MU_x/P_x = 10/2 = MU_y/P_y = 5/1$), but the consumer would not be at optimum because he or she would be spending only \$7 of the \$10 income.

The fact that the marginal utility approach gives the same result as the indifference curve approach (i.e., $2X$ and $6Y$) should not be surprising. In fact, we can easily show why this is so. By cross multiplication in Equation (3-6), we get

$$\frac{MU_x}{MU_y} = \frac{P_x}{P_y} \qquad (3\text{-}7)$$

But we have shown in Section 3-2c that $MRS_{xy} = MU_x/MU_y$ [see Equation (3-2)] and in Section 3-4a that $MRS_{xy} = P_x/P_y$ when the consumer maximizes utility [see Equation (3-5)]. Therefore, bringing together Equations (3-2), (3-5), and (3-7), we can express the condition for consumer utility maximization as

$$MRS_{xy} = \frac{MU_x}{MU_y} = \frac{P_x}{P_y} \qquad (3\text{-}8)$$

Thus, the condition for consumer utility maximization with the marginal utility approach [i.e., Equation (3-6)] is equivalent to that with the indifference curve approach [Equation (3-5)], except for corner solutions. With both approaches, the value of Equation (3-8) is 2.

From the above discussion of utility maximization, it must not be inferred that all individuals and institutions do or should engage in *eco-*

---

[11] By giving up the eighth and the seventh unit of X, the individual loses 3 utils. By using the \$2 not spent on X to purchase the second unit of Y, the individual receives 6 utils, for a net gain of 3 utils. Once the individual consumes $6X$ and $2Y$, Equation (3-6) holds and he or she maximizes utility.

nomic optimization. Some individuals and institutions optimize other objectives. As the following example shows, noneconomic institutions operate under different constraints and optimize *noneconomic* objectives. For example, political institutions maximize political objectives and this is likely to result in an economic misallocation of resources.

Example 3-3   Noneconomic Optimization in Consumer Product Safety Regulation

The Facts: Table 3-4 gives the benefit-cost ratio of safety-regulation projects for ten products implemented by the Consumer Product Safety Commission (CPSC) in 1977. Both benefits and costs were estimated in dollars. For example, a benefit-cost ratio of 2 means that the total benefit of regulation is twice the total cost of implementation.

Comment: Since the benefit-cost ratio differed widely for the ten products tested, and since for all but the first three products tested the benefit-cost ratio was smaller than one, CPSC did not optimize the *economic* use of resources. However, as a political rather than as an economic institution, this was to be expected. That is, as a political institution, the CPSC had different constraints (i.e., political pressures) and, if anything, was expected to optimize political rather than economic objectives. The CPSC may also have used different values than the ones given in the above table. Furthermore, government costs may not have been the only ones entering into the calculations of the benefit-cost ratios. Thus, in discussing utility maximization, we must be careful not to infer that all individuals and institutions seek or should seek economic optimization. Since some individuals and institutions have noneconomic objectives, it is only natural that they attempt to optimize those objectives rather than economic ones.

Source: H. G. Grabowski and J. M. Vernon, "Consumer Product Regulation," *American Economic Review,* May 1978, pp. 284–289.

TABLE 3-4   Benefit-Cost Ratios of CPSC Projects

Project	Benefit-Cost Ratio
Bathtubs and showers	2.70
Public playground equipment	2.02
Drain cleaners	1.08
Ladders	0.94
Ranges and ovens	0.87
Power mowers	0.40
Matches	0.37
Ammonia	0.11
Extension cords	0.10
Television	0.09

3-5

Applications

In this section we apply the tools developed in the chapter to analyze several important issues. These applications clearly show the great importance and relevance of the tools of analysis introduced. We examine the effect of government warnings on consumption, government rationing of a good (such as gasoline during wartime), charitable behavior, and the economics of fringe benefits. In all of these applications the crucial importance and analytical usefulness of indifference curve analysis is clearly brought out.

Application 1: The Effect of Government Warnings

Suppose that in Figure 3-10, good X refers to regular soda and good Y to diet soda, $P_x = \$1$, $P_y = \$1$, and the consumer spends his entire weekly allowance of $10 on sodas. Suppose also that the consumer maximizes utility by spending $3 to purchase three regular sodas and $7 to purchase seven diet sodas (point B on indifference curve U_1) before any government warning on the possible danger of cancer from diet sodas. After the warn-

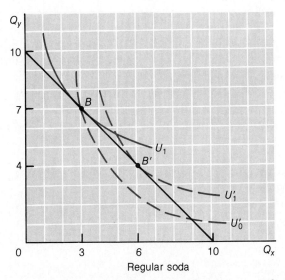

FIGURE 3-10.
Effect of
Government
Warnings

The consumer maximizes utility by spending $3 to purchase three regular sodas and $7 to purchase seven diet sodas (point B on indifference curve U_1) before any government warning on the possible danger of cancer from diet sodas. After the warning, the consumer's tastes change and are given by dashed indifference curves U_0' and U_1'. Now U_0' can intersect U_1 because of the change in tastes. After the warning, the consumer maximizes utility by purchasing six regular sodas and only four diet sodas (point B', where U_1' is tangent to the budget line).

ing, the consumer's tastes may change away from diet and toward regular sodas.[12] This can be shown by dashed indifference curves U'_0 and U'_1. Note that U'_0 is steeper than U_1 at the original optimization point B, indicating that after the warning the individual is willing to give up more diet sodas for an additional regular soda (i.e., MRS_{xy} is higher for U'_0 than for U_1 at point B). Now U'_0 can intersect U_1 because of the change in tastes. Note also that U'_0 involves less utility than U_1 at point B because the seven diet sodas (and the three regular sodas) provide less utility after the warning. After the warning, the consumer maximizes utility by consuming six regular sodas and only four diet sodas (point B', where U'_1 is tangent to the budget line).

The above analysis clearly shows how indifference curve analysis can be used to examine the effect of any government warning on consumption patterns.[13] Indeed, we can analyze the effect on consumption of any new information by examining the effect it has on the consumer's indifference map. Similarly, indifference curve analysis can be used to analyze the effect on consumer purchases of any regulation such as the one requiring drivers in many states to wear seat belts.

Application 2: Rationing
Because goods are scarce, some method of allocating them among individuals is required. In a free-enterprise economy such as our own, the price system accomplishes this for the most part. Sometimes, however, the government rations goods, such as gasoline during World War II. If the maximum amount of a good that the government allows is less than the individual would have purchased, the **rationing** will reduce the individual's level of satisfaction.

The effect of rationing on utility maximization and consumption can be examined with Figure 3-11. In the absence of rationing, the individual maximizes satisfaction at point B, where indifference curve U_1 is tangent to budget line JK and consumes 2X and 6Y (as in Figure 3-8). If the government did not allow the individual to purchase more than 1X per day, the budget line becomes JLK', with a kink at point L. Thus, rationing changes the constraints under which utility maximization occurs. The highest indifference curve that the individual can reach with budget line JLK' is now U_0 at point L by consuming 1X and 8Y. The incentive would then arise for the consumer to purchase more of X on the black market at a higher price.[14]

---

[12] It may be argued that government warnings change the information available to consumers rather than tastes. That is, the warning affects consumers' perception as to the ability of various goods to satisfy their wants.

[13] Another example of a government warning is provided by the 1965 law requiring manufacturers to print on each pack of cigarettes the warning that cigarette smoking is dangerous to health.

[14] Since the price of good X in the black market is higher, the individual would still be unable to reach point B that he or she can reach without rationing. Thus, rationing leads to price distortions and inefficiencies.

FIGURE 3-11.
Rationing

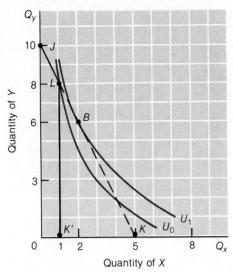

In the absence of rationing, the individual maximizes satisfaction at point B, where indifference curve U_1 is tangent to budget line JK and consumes 2X and 6Y (as in Figure 3-8). If the government did not allow the individual to purchase more than 1X per day, the budget line becomes JLK', with a kink at point L. The highest indifference that the individual can reach with budget line JLK' is now U_0 at point L by consuming 1X and 8Y.

If rations were 2X or more per day, the rationing system would not affect this consumer since he or she maximizes utility by purchasing 2X and 6Y (point B in the figure). Rationing is more likely to be binding or restrictive on high-income people than on low-income people (who may not have sufficient income to purchase even the allowed quantity of the rationed commodity). Thus, our model predicts that high-income people are more likely to make black market purchases than low-income people. Effective rationing leads not only to black markets but also to a "spill over" of consumer purchases on other goods not subject to rationing (or into savings). Both occurred in the U.S. during World War II.

Application 3: Charitable Behavior

The assumption that consumers seek to maximize utility may leave the impression that there is no room in our analysis for concern on the part of some individuals for the well-being of others. This is not the case. For example, indifference curve analysis can be used to analyze charitable behavior.

We can do this by plotting the donor's income along the vertical axis and the recipient's income along the horizontal axis, as in Figure 3-12. The well-being of the recipient is an economic good for the donor, and so the donor's indifference curves assume the usual negative shape. That is, moving down along a donor's indifference curve in either panel of Figure 3-12

85

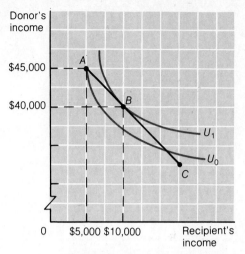
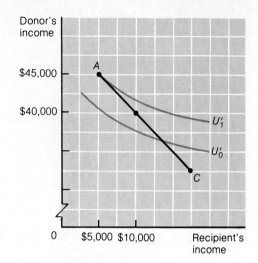

FIGURE 3-12.   Charitable Behavior

Point A *shows the initial income of $45,000 per year for the donor and $5,000 for the recipient. Moving down along a donor's indifference curve indicates how much charity the donor is willing to give while remaining at the same level of utility. Budget line AC shows that each dollar transferred from the donor increases the recipient's income by one dollar. If the donor's indifference curves are as in the left panel, the donor maximizes utility by giving $5,000 in charity (point B, where the donor reaches* U_1*). In the right panel, the donor reaches* U_1' *at point A by giving no charity.*

indicates how much charity the unselfish donor is willing to give to the poor recipient and remain at the same level of utility.

Suppose that the initial income of the donor is $45,000 per year and the income of the potential recipient is only $5,000 per year (point *A*). If the donor's indifference curves were as in the left panel, the donor would maximize utility by giving $5,000 in charity to the poor recipient (point *B*, where the donor reaches indifference curve U_1). If, on the other hand, the donor's indifference curves were as in the right panel, the donor would reach U_1' (the highest indifference curve possible) at point *A* by giving no charity (a corner solution). Note that budget line *AC* has a slope of -1, indicating that for each dollar of income transferred by the donor, the recipient's income rises by one dollar.[15]

The difference in outcome in the two panels is due to the difference in the intensity of the preferences of the donor. In the left panel, the donor is willing to transfer more than $1 of his or her income to increase the recipient's income by $1 (i.e., indifference curve U_1 is steeper than budget line *AC* at point *A*). Thus, the donor maximizes utility by transferring income

---

[15] The budget line does not extend above point *A* (the initial distribution of income) because the donor cannot take income away from the recipient. On the other hand, below point *C* the budget line is irrelevant because it would imply that the recipient ends up with a larger income than the donor.

to the recipient until he or she reaches point B, at which U_1 is tangent to AC. On the other hand, in the right panel, the donor is willing to transfer less than $1 of his or her income to increase the recipient income by $1 at point A, and so the donor maximizes utility by giving no charity (i.e., by remaining at point A).

Application 4: The Economics of Fringe Benefits

Indifference curve analysis can also be used to examine the economics of fringe benefits. **Fringe benefits** are goods and services provided to employees and paid for by employers. These include medical and dental services, life insurance, contributions to pension funds, and so on. Many employees prefer some fringe benefits to higher cash compensation because fringe benefits are not subject to income taxes. In fact, fringe benefits have been growing faster than cash compensation in recent decades and, in some cases, account for as much as 25 per cent of total labor compensation in the U.S. and even more in many European nations.[16]

The economics of fringe benefits can be examined with the aid of Figure 3-13. Suppose that initially the employee's income is $200 per week (point A on the vertical axis). If the employee spent all income on medical services with a unit price of $10, he or she could purchase 20 units of medical services per week (point C on the horizontal axis). The initial budget line is then AC. If the employer subsequently offered fringe benefits to the employee in the form of free medical services worth $100 per week, the budget line of the employee becomes $AB'C'$, where $AB' = CC' = 10$. Dashed segment $A'B'$ is irrelevant because the employee does not receive the additional compensation in cash. Were the employer to increase cash compensation by $100 (instead of providing $100 dollars worth of free medical services), the employee's budget line would then be $A'C'$.

Thus, we have three alternative budget lines for the employee. Budget line AC without either fringe benefits or increased cash compensation, budget line $AB'C'$ with $100 in fringe benefits, and budget line $A'C'$ with $100 in increased cash compensation. The important question now is whether the employee would be better off with $100 in fringe benefits or with $100 in cash. For simplicity, we assume for now that there are no tax benefits to employees from receiving fringe benefits rather than higher money incomes.

Figure 3-13 shows that if the employee's indifference curves are U_0, U_1, and U_2, the employee maximizes utility at point B, where U_0 is tangent to AC before any increase in compensation, at point B' on U_1 with free medical services, and at point B'' ($> B'$) on U_2 with increased cash compensation. In this case, increased cash compensation allows the employee to reach a higher indifference curve than with free medical services.[17] How-

---

[16] Recent proposals in the United States would tax some fringe benefits.
[17] Both cost the employer $100.

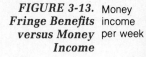

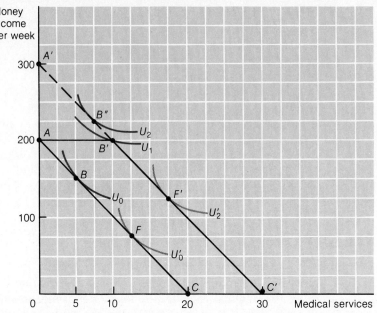

FIGURE 3-13.
Fringe Benefits
versus Money
Income

The employee's budget line before any increase in compensation is AC. It is AB'C' with $100 worth of free medical services, and A'C' with $100 increased cash compensation. With U_0, U_1, and U_2 the employee maximizes utility at point B on U_0 before the increase in compensation, at B' on U_1 with free medical services, and at B'' on U_2 with increased cash compensation. On the other hand, another employee with a stronger preference for medical services may go from point F on U_0' to point F' on U_2' either with increased cash compensation or with free medical services.

ever, another employee with a strong preference for medical services and facing indifference curves U_0' and U_2' will move instead from point F on U_0' to point F' on U_2', either with increased cash compensation or with free medical services. Thus, depending on the tastes of the employee, *an increase in cash compensation will not be worse than receiving fringe benefits and may be better.*

This conclusion can change if we consider that cash income is taxable while fringe benefits are not. For example, $100 worth of free and nontaxable medical services may be worth more than $100 in cash subject to a 30% tax rate. This may be the reason for the great increase in fringe benefits in recent decades. However, increasing compensation by providing tax-deductible fringe benefits may lead to the consumption of a socially wasteful bundle of goods. For example, the employee in Figure 3-13 can reach indifference curve U_1 by consuming less medical services and more of other goods than at point B' with less than a $100 increase in untaxed cash compensation (see Figure 3-13).

Summary

1. The want-satisfying quality of a good is called utility. More units of a good increases total utility (TU) but the extra or marginal utility (MU) declines. The saturation point is reached when TU is maximum and MU is zero. Afterwards, TU declines and MU is negative. MU may at first rise, but eventually it will decline. This is known as the law of diminishing marginal utility. Cardinal utility actually provides an index of satisfaction for a consumer whereas ordinal utility only ranks various consumption bundles.

2. The tastes of a consumer can be represented by indifference curves. These are based on the assumptions that the consumer can rank baskets of goods according to his or her preferences, tastes are consistent and transitive, and he or she prefers more of a good to less. An indifference curve shows the various combinations of two goods that give the consumer equal satisfaction. Higher indifference curves refer to more satisfaction and lower indifference curves to less. Indifference curves are negatively sloped, cannot intersect, and are convex to the origin. The marginal rate of substitution (MRS) measures how much of a good the consumer is willing to give up for one additional unit of the other good and remain on the same indifference curve. Indifference curves are generally convex to the origin and exhibit diminishing MRS.

3. The budget line shows the various combinations of two goods (say X and Y) that a consumer can purchase by spending all income (I) on the two goods at the given prices (P_x and P_y). The vertical or Y-intercept of the budget line is given by I and $-P_x/P_y$ is the slope. The budget line shifts up if I increases and down if I decreases, but the slope remains unchanged. The budget line rotates upward if P_x falls and downward if P_x rises.

4. A rational consumer maximizes utility when reaching the highest indifference curve possible with the budget line. This occurs where an indifference curve is tangent to the budget line so that their slopes are equal (i.e., $MRS_{xy} = P_x/P_y$). If indifference curves are everywhere either flatter or steeper than the budget line or if they are concave, utility maximization requires the consumer to spend all income on either good Y or good X only. These are called corner solutions. The marginal utility approach postulates that the consumer maximizes utility when he or she spends all income and the marginal utility of the last dollar spent on X and Y are the same. Since $MRS_{xy} = MU_x/MU_y = P_x/P_y$, the marginal utility and the indifference curve approaches are equivalent.

5. Government warnings or new information may change the shape and location of a consumer's indifference curves and the consumption pattern. Rationing reduces utility if it restricts the individual to purchase less of a good than he or she wants. Indifference curve analysis can also be used to analyze charitable behavior. Fringe benefits are goods and services provided to employees and paid for by employers. An equivalent increase in money income can provide the employee with equal or greater utility, except that money income is taxable and fringe benefits are not.

Glossary

Utility   The ability of a good to satisfy a want.

Total utility (*TU*)   The aggregate amount of satisfaction received from consuming various amounts of a good or baskets of goods.

Marginal utility (*MU*)   The extra utility received from consuming one additional unit of the good.

Util   The arbitrary unit of measure of utility.

Law of diminishing marginal utility   Each additional unit of a good eventually gives less and less extra utility.

Cardinal utility   The ability to actually provide an index of utility from consuming various amounts of a good or baskets of goods.

Ordinal utility   The rankings of the utility received by an individual from consuming various amounts of a good or various baskets of goods.

Good   A commodity of which more is preferred to less.

Bad   An item of which less is preferred to more.

Indifference curve   The curve showing the various combinations of two commodities that give the consumer equal satisfaction and among which the consumer is indifferent.

Indifference map   The entire set of indifference curves reflecting the consumer's tastes and preferences.

Marginal rate of substitution (MRS)   The amount of a good that a consumer is willing to give up for an additional unit of the other good while remaining on the same indifference curve.

Neuter   A commodity of which an individual is indifferent between having more or less.

Budget constraint   The limitation on the amount of goods that a consumer can purchase imposed by his or her limited income and the prices of the goods.

Budget line   A line showing the various combinations of two goods that a consumer can purchase

by spending all income at the given prices of the two goods.

Rational consumer   An individual who seeks to maximize utility or satisfaction in spending his or her income.

Constrained utility maximization   The process by which the consumer reaches the highest level of satisfaction given his or her income and the prices of goods. This occurs at the tangency of an indifference curve with the budget line.

Consumer optimization   Constrained utility maximization.

Consumer equilibrium   Constrained utility maximization.

Corner solution   Constrained utility maximization with the consumer spending all of his or her income on only one or some goods.

Rationing   Quantitative restrictions imposed by the government on the amount of a good that an individual can purchase per unit of time.

Fringe benefits   Goods and services provided to employees and paid for by employers.

Questions for Review

1. What is meant by
   (a) total utility? marginal utility? saturation point?
   (b) the law of diminishing marginal utility?
   (c) cardinal utility? ordinal utility?
2. (a) Do utility schedules refer to the tastes of a consumer or to the constraints faced by a consumer?
   (b) Do different consumers have the same utility schedules?
   (c) Do utility schedules refer to a specific period of time or to different periods of time?
   (d) What assumption is made in specifying a particular set of utility schedules with regard to the amount of other goods consumed?
3. (a) On what assumptions do indifference curves rest? In what way are these assumptions weaker than cardinal utility?
   (b) What does an indifference curve show? A higher indifference curve? A lower indifference curve?
   (c) What are the characteristics of indifference curves?

4. Why are indifference curves
   (a) negatively sloped?
   (b) nonintersecting?
   (c) convex to the origin?
5. (a) What is meant by the marginal rate of substitution?
   (b) Why does the marginal rate of substitution diminish along an indifference curve?
   (c) What characteristic of indifference curves is a reflection of diminishing marginal rate of substitution?
6. What would be the shape of indifference curves if the marginal rate of substitution were
   (a) constant? What kind of goods would these be?
   (b) zero? What would then be the relationship between the two goods?
   (c) increasing?
7. (a) What is meant by a budget constraint? By a budget line?
   (b) What is the vertical intercept of the budget line?
   (c) What is the slope of the budget line?
8. (a) What happens to the budget line if the con-

sumer's income rises? If the consumer's income falls?

(b) How is the budget line affected by a decline in the price of good X? By an increase in the price of X?

(c) How is the budget line affected by a decline in the price of good Y? By an increase in the price of Y?

(d) How is the budget line affected by the same relative change in the price of good X and good Y?

9. (a) What is meant by constrained utility maximization? How is it achieved?

(b) What is meant by corner solutions? When do they occur?

(c) What are the conditions for constrained utility maximization with the marginal utility approach?

(d) Are the marginal utility and the indiffer-

ence curve approaches for constrained maximization equivalent? Why?

10. (a) What is the effect of government warnings?

(b) What is meant by rationing?

(c) What is the effect of rationing?

11. (a) What does the indifference curve of a potential donor to charity show?

(b) How can the giving of charity be explained by the slope of the donor's indifference curve and budget line?

(c) How can indifference curve analysis be used to explain why some high-income people do *not* give to charity?

12. (a) What are fringe benefits?

(b) Do fringe benefits provide more utility than an equivalent amount of money income?

(c) Why have fringe benefits been rising faster than cash compensation?

Problems

1. From the following total utility schedule

Q_x	0	1	2	3	4	5	6	7
TU_x	0	4	14	20	24	26	26	24

(a) derive the marginal utility schedule.

(b) plot the total and the marginal utility schedules.

(c) Where does the law of diminishing marginal utility begin to operate?

(d) Where is the saturation point?

2. The following table gives four indifference schedules of an individual.

(a) Using graph paper, plot the four indifference curves on the same set of axes.

(b) Calculate the marginal rate of substitution of X for Y between the various points on U_1.

(c) What is MRS_{xy} at point C on U_1?

(d) Can we tell how much better off is the individual on U_2 than on U_1?

★3. (a) Starting with a given *equal* endowment of good X and good Y by individual A and individual B, draw A's and B's indifference curves on the same set of axes showing that individual A has a preference for good X over good Y with respect to individual B.

Combination	U_1		U_2		U_3		U_4	
	Q_x	Q_y	Q_x	Q_y	Q_x	Q_y	Q_x	Q_y
A	3	12	6	12	8	15	10	13
B	4	7	7	9	9	12	12	10
C	6	4	9	6	11	9	14	8
F	9	2	12	4	15	6	18	6.4
G	14	1	15	3	19	5	20	6

★ = answer provided at the end of the book.

(b) Explain the reason for drawing as you did individual A's and individual B's indifference curves in part (a).

4. Draw an indifference curve for an individual showing that
   (a) good X and good Y are perfect complements.
   (b) item X becomes a bad after 4 units.
   (c) item Y becomes a bad after 3 units.
   (d) MRS is increasing for both X and Y.

5. Suppose an individual has an income of $15 per time period, the price of good X is $1 and the price of good Y is also $1. That is, $I = \$15$, $P_x = \$1$, and $P_y = \$1$.
   (a) Write the equation of the budget line of this individual in the form that indicates that the amount spent on good X plus the amount spent on good Y equals the individual's income.
   (b) Write the equation of the budget line in the form that you can read off directly the vertical intercept and the slope of the line.
   (c) Plot the budget line.

6. This problem involves drawing three graphs, one for each part of the problem. On the same set of axes, draw the budget line of Problem 5 (label it 2) and two other budget lines:
   (a) One with $I = \$10$ (call it 1), and another with $I = \$20$ (label it 3), and with prices unchanged at $P_x = P_y = \$1$.
   (b) One with $P_x = \$0.50$, $P_y = \$1$, and $I = \$15$ (label it 2A), and another with $P_x = \$2$ and the same P_y and I (label it 2B).
   (c) One with $P_y = \$2$, $P_x = \$1$, and $I = \$15$ (label it 2C), and another with $P_x = P_y = \$2$ and $I = \$15$ (label it 2F).

★7. (a) On the same set of axes, draw the indifference curves of Problem 2 and the budget line of Problem of 5c.
   (b) Where is the individual maximizing utility? How much of X and Y should he or she purchase to be at optimum? What is the general condition for constrained utility maximization?
   (c) Why is the individual not maximizing utility at point A? At point G?
   (d) Why can't the individual reach U_3 or U_4?

8. On the same set of axes (on graph paper), draw the indifference curves of Problem 2 and budget lines

(a) 1, 2, and 3 from Problem 6a; label the points at which the individual maximizes utility with the various alternative budget lines.
(b) 2 and 2A from Problem 6b; label the points at which the individual maximizes utility the various alternative budget lines.

★9. Given the following marginal utility schedule for good X and good Y for the individual, and given that the price of X and the price of Y are both $1, and that the individual spends all income of $7 on X and Y,

Q	1	2	3	4	5	6	7
MU_x	15	11	9	6	4	3	1
MU_y	12	9	6	5	3	2	1

(a) indicate how much of X and Y the individual should purchase to maximize utility.
(b) show that the condition for constrained utility maximization is satisfied when the individual is at his or her optimum.
(c) How much total utility does the individual receive when he or she maximizes utility? How much utility would the individual get if he or she spent all income on X or Y?

10. Show on the same figure the effect of (1) an increase in cigarette prices, (2) an increase in consumers' incomes, and (3) a government warning that cigarette smoking is dangerous to health, all in such a way that the net effect of all three forces together leads to a net decline in cigarette smoking.

11. (a) Draw a figure showing indifference curve U_2 tangent to the budget line at point B ($8X$), and a lower indifference curve (U_1) intersecting the budget line at point A ($4X$) and at point G ($12X$).
   (b) What happens if the government rations good X and allows the individual to purchase no more than $4X$? No more than $8X$? No more than $12X$?
   (c) What would happen if the government instead mandated (as in the case of requiring auto insurance, seat belts, and so on) that the individual purchase at least $4X$? $8X$? $12X$?

⋆**12.** Do you expect the growth of fringe benefits in relation to cash compensation to grow faster in periods of low or rapid inflation? Why? What effect can you predict from the federal government indexing of taxes for inflation that started in 1985?

Supplementary Readings

A paperback in the Schaum's Outline Series in Economics that gives a problem-solving approach to the topics discussed in this chapter is

Dominick Salvatore, *Microeconomic Theory*, 2nd ed. (New York: McGraw-Hill, 1983), Chapters 4 and 5.

For a discussion of the development of the utility approach to consumer demand theory see

George J. Stigler, "The Development of Utility Theory," *Journal of Political Economy*, August 1950.

The complete utility approach to consumer demand theory is found in

Alfred Marshall, *Principles of Economics*, 9th ed. (London: Macmillan, 1920), Book III.

The indifference curve approach to consumer demand theory is presented in

John R. Hicks, *Value and Capital*, 2nd ed. (Oxford: Oxford University Press, 1946), pp. 1–25.

Consumer Behavior and Individual Demand

4-1 Changes in Income

4-2 Changes in Price

4-3 Substitution and Income Effects

4-4 Applications

Examples

4-1 Consumption Expenditures by Income Class

4-2 Negatively Sloped Demand Curves

4-3 Gasoline Tax and Rebate Proposal

Applications

Application 1: The Food Stamp Program

Application 2: Consumer Surplus

Application 3: Exchange

Application 4: Time as an Economic Good

Chapter 4

Preview Questions

How much more of a good does a consumer purchase when his or her income rises?

Does a consumer purchase more of every good when his or her income rises?

How much more of a good does a consumer purchase when the price of the good falls?

Why does a consumer purchase more of a good when its price falls?

Which is better: a subsidy in cash or in kind?

Is a consumer willing to pay more for the first unit of a good than for subsequent units?

Does voluntary exchange between two individuals benefit both?

How can time be incorporated as an additional constraint on consumption?

In Chapter 3, we have seen that a consumer maximizes utility by reaching the highest possible indifference curve with the given budget line. This fact is now utilized to examine how the consumer responds to changes in income and prices, while holding tastes constant. Since income and prices change frequently in the real world, it is important to examine their individual effect on consumer behavior.

We begin by examining how the consumer responds to changes in his or her income, while holding prices and tastes constant. This will allow us to derive a so-called Engel curve and to distinguish between normal and inferior goods. Then, we examine the consumer's response to a change in the price of the good and derive the individual's demand curve for the good. This is the basic building block for the market demand curve of the good (to be derived in Chapter 5), the importance of which was clearly outlined in Chapter 2.

After deriving an individual's demand curve, we show how to separate the substitution from the income effect of a price change for normal and inferior goods. The ability to separate graphically the income from the substitution effect of a price change is one of the most powerful tools of analysis of microeconomic theory, with wide applicability to evaluate many important issues. It is also used to examine the possible, but rare, exception to the law of negatively sloped demand. Finally, we examine some important applications of the theory presented in the chapter. These applications, together with the real-world examples included in the theory sections, highlight the importance of the theory of consumer behavior and demand.

95

4-1

Changes in Income

A change in the consumer's income shifts his or her budget line and this affects consumer purchases. In this section we examine how a consumer reaches a new optimum position when his or her income changes but with prices and tastes unchanged. We will first show this for normal goods and then for inferior goods.

4-1a Income-Consumption Curve and Engel Curve

By changing the consumer's money income while holding constant prices and tastes, we can derive the consumer's income-consumption curve. The **income-consumption curve** is the locus of or joins consumer optimum points resulting when only the consumer's income varies. From the income-consumption curve we can then derive the consumer's Engel curve.

For example, the top panel of Figure 4-1 shows that with budget line JK the consumer maximizes utility or is at optimum at point B, where indifference curve U_1 is tangent to budget line JK and the consumer purchases $2X$ and $6Y$ (the same as in Figure 3-8). That is (continuing with the example of Chapter 3), the best way for the student to spend his or her daily income allowance of $10 on snacks of hamburgers (good X) and soft drinks (good Y) is to purchase 2 hamburgers and 6 soft drinks per day. If the prices of hamburgers and soft drinks remain unchanged at $P_x = \$2$ and $P_y = \$1$ but the daily income allowance rises from $10 to $15 and then to $20, budget line JK shifts up to $J'K'$ and then to $J''K''$ (the same as in the left panel of Figure 3-7). The three budget lines are parallel because the prices of X and Y do not change.

With an income of $15 and budget line $J'K'$, the consumer maximizes utility at point R, where indifference curve U_2 is tangent to budget line $J'K'$ and the consumer purchases $4X$ and $7Y$ (see the top panel of Figure 4-1). Indifference curve U_2 is the same as in the right panel of Figure 3-2 because tastes have not changed. Finally, with an income of $20 and budget line $J''K''$, the consumer maximizes utility or is at optimum at point S on U_3 by purchasing $5X$ and $10Y$ per unit of time (per day). By joining optimum points B, R, and S we get (a portion of) the income-consumption curve for this consumer (student). Thus, the income-consumption curve is the locus of consumer optimum points resulting when only the consumer's income varies.[1]

---

[1] Note that at each point along the income-consumption curve the value of the MRS_{xy} is the same. This is so because $-P_x/P_y$ is the same for each of the budget lines (i.e., parallel lines have identical slopes).

FIGURE 4-1.
Income-
Consumption Curve
and Engel Curve

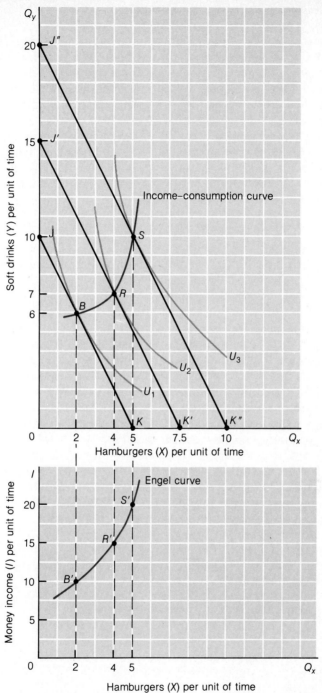

In the top panel and with $P_x = \$2$ and $P_y = \$1$, the individual budget line is JK with income I of $10, J'K' with I = $15, and J"K" with I = $20. Given indifference curves U_1, U_2, and U_3, the individual maximizes utility at points B, R, and S, respectively. By joining optimum points B, R, and S we get the income-consumption curve (top panel). By then plotting income on the vertical axis and the various optimum quantities purchased of good X along the horizontal axis, we can derive corresponding Engel curve B'R'S' in the bottom panel.

From the income-consumption curve in the top panel of Figure 4-1 we can derive the Engel curve in the bottom panel. The **Engel curve** shows the amount of a good that the consumer would purchase per unit of time at various income levels. To derive the Engel curve we keep the same horizontal scale as in the top panel but measure money income on the vertical axis.

The derivation of the Engel curve proceeds as follows. With a daily income allowance of $10, the student maximizes utility by purchasing two hamburgers per day (point B) in the top panel. This gives point B′ (directly below point B) in the bottom panel. With an income allowance of $15, the student is at optimum by purchasing four hamburgers (point R) in the top panel. This gives point R′ in the bottom panel. Finally, with a daily income allowance of $20 the student maximizes utility by purchasing five hamburgers (point S in the top panel and S′ in the bottom panel). By joining points B′, R′, and S′ we get (a portion of) the Engel curve in the bottom panel. Thus, the Engel curve is derived from the income-consumption curve and shows the quantity of hamburgers per day (Q_X) that the student would purchase at various income levels (i.e., with various income allowances).

Engel curves are named after Ernst Engel, the German statistician of the second half of the 19th century who pioneered studies of family budgets and expenditure patterns. Sometimes Engel curves show the relationship between income and *expenditures* on various goods rather than the *quantity* purchased of various goods. However, since prices are held constant, we get the same result (i.e., the same Engel curve).

For some goods, the Engel curve may rise only gently. This indicates that a given increase in income leads to a proportionately larger increase in the quantity purchased of the good. These goods are sometimes referred to as "luxuries." Examples of these may be education, recreation, and steaks and lobsters (for some people). On the other hand, the Engel curve for other goods rises rather rapidly, indicating that a given increase in income leads to a proportionately smaller increase in the quantity purchased of these goods. These are called "necessities." Basic foodstuffs are usually regarded as necessities. A more precise definition of luxuries and necessities is given in Chapter 5.

Example 4-1 Consumption Expenditures by Income Class

The Facts: Table 4-1 gives the percentage of total consumption expenditures by selected income classes for U.S. families in 1980–1981. The table shows that higher income families spend a smaller percentage of their income than lower income families on food, housing, and medical and educational services, but proportionately more on clothing, personal care, and transportation.

Comment: That the proportion of total expenditures on food declines as family income rises has been found to be true not only for the U.S. in the

TABLE 4-1   Percentage of Total Consumption by Income Class for All U.S. Families, 1980–1981

Consumption Item	Annual Income		
	$5,000–$9,999	$10,000–$14,999	$15,000–$19,999
Food	23.9%	22.1%	20.8%
Clothing	4.6	5.0	5.2
Housing (incl. Furniture, Light, and Fuel)	33.1	29.6	28.0
Medical and Educational Services	7.4	6.1	5.8
Personal Care, Comfort, and Recreation	9.3	10.0	10.9
Transportation and Other	21.7	27.2	29.3
Total	100.0	100.0	100.0

Source: U.S. Dept. of Labor, Bureau of Labor Statistics, *Consumer Expenditure Survey: Results from the 1980–81 Interview*, USDL: 84-514 (Washington, D.C., December 19, 1984), Table 2.

period of the survey but also at other times and in other nations. Thus, food in general is a necessity rather than a luxury. This regularity is sometimes referred to as "Engel's law." Indeed, the higher the proportion of income spent on food in a nation, the poorer the nation is usually taken to be. For example, in India more than 50% of income is spent on food on the average. Less regularity has been found in the proportion of expenditures on other goods.

4-1b Normal and Inferior Goods

A **normal good** is one of which the consumer purchases more with an increase in income. An **inferior good** is one of which the consumer purchases less with an increase in income. Good X in Figure 4-1 is a normal good because the consumer purchases more of it with an increase in income. For example, an increase in the student income allowance from $10 to $15 leads to an increase in his or her purchase of hamburgers from two to four per day. Thus, for a normal good, the income-consumption curve and the Engel curve are both positively sloped, as in Figure 4-1.

Figure 4-2 shows the income-consumption curve and the Engel curve for an inferior good. This results from supposing that the student, instead of spending his daily income allowance on soft drinks (good Y) and hamburgers (good X), spends it on soft drinks and candy bars (good Z), and he or she views candy bars as an inferior good.[2] With the price of soft drinks at $1 and the price of candy bars also at $1, the budget line of the student is JK'

[2] Other commodities which are, perhaps, even more readily recognized as inferior goods in the U.S. today than candy bars are potatoes, rice, bologna, and cheaper cuts of meats.

FIGURE 4-2.
Income-
consumption curve
and Engel Curve for
an Inferior Good

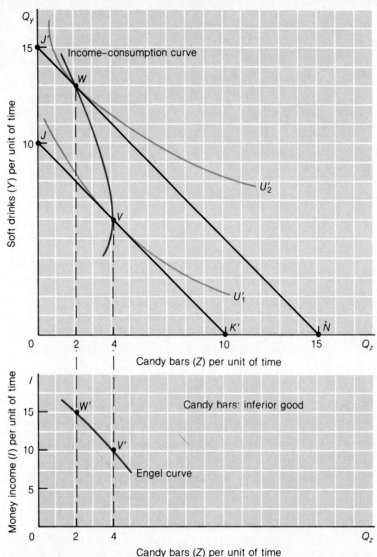

In the top panel and with $P_z = \$1$ and $P_y = \$1$, the individual budget line is JK' with income I of \$10 and J'N with I = \$15. Given indifference curves U'_1 and U'_2, the individual maximizes utility at points V and W, respectively. By joining points V and W we get the income-consumption curve (top panel). By then plotting income on the vertical axis and the optimum quantities purchased of good Z along the horizontal axis, we derive corresponding Engel curve V'W' in the bottom panel. Since the income-consumption curve and Engel curve are negatively sloped, good Z is an inferior good.

with a daily income allowance of $10 and $J'N$ with an income of $15 (see the top panel of Figure 4-2).

If indifference curves between soft drinks and candy bars are U'_1 and U'_2, the student maximizes satisfaction at point V, where indifference curve U'_1 is tangent to budget line JK' with a daily income allowance of $10, and he or she maximizes utility at point W, where indifference curve U'_2 is tangent to budget line $J'N$ with an income of $15 (see the top panel of Figure 4-2). Thus, the consumer purchases four candy bars with an income of $10 and only two candy bars with an income of $15. Candy bars are, therefore, inferior goods for this student. The income-consumption curve for candy bars (VW in the top panel of Figure 4-2) and the corresponding Engel curve ($V'W'$ in the bottom panel) are both negatively sloped, indicating that the student purchases fewer candy bars as his or her income allowance increases.

Note that the classification of a good into normal or inferior depends only on how a specific consumer views the particular good. Thus, the same candy bar can be regarded as a normal good by another student. Furthermore, a good can be regarded as a normal good by a consumer at a particular level of income and as an inferior good by the same consumer at a higher level of income. For example, with an allowance of $40 dollars per day, the student of the previous section may begin to regard hamburgers as an inferior good since he or she now can afford steaks and lobsters. Also note that an inferior good is not "bad" because more is preferred to less and indifference curves remain negatively sloped (refer back to Section 3-2).

In the real world, most broadly defined goods such as food, clothing, housing, health care, and education and recreation are normal goods. Inferior goods are usually narrowly defined cheap goods, such as bologna, for which good substitutes are available. As pointed out earlier, a normal good can be further classified as a luxury or a necessity, depending on whether the quantity purchased increases proportionately more or less than the increase in income.

4-2

Changes in Price

Commodity prices frequently change in the real world and it is important to examine their effect on consumer behavior. A change in commodity prices changes the consumer budget line and this affects his or her purchases. In this section we examine how the consumer reaches a new optimum poisiton when the price of a good changes but the price of the other good, income, and tastes remain unchanged.

4-2a Price-Consumption Curve and Individual Demand Curve

By changing the price of good X while holding constant the price of good Y, income, and tastes, we can derive the consumer's price-consumption curve for good X. The **price-consumption curve** for good X is the locus of or joins consumer optimum points resulting when only the price of good X varies. From the price-consumption curve we can then derive the consumer's demand curve for good X.

For example, the top panel of Figure 4-3 shows once again that with budget line JK, the consumer maximizes utility or is at optimum at point B, where indifference curve U_1 is tangent to budget line JK and the consumer purchases $2X$ and $6Y$ (the same as in Figure 3-8). Suppose that the consumer's income (i.e., the student allowance) remains unchanged at $I = \$10$ per day and the price of good Y (soft drinks) also remains constant at $P_y = \$1$. A reduction in the price of good X (hamburgers) from $P_x = \$2$ to $P_x = \$1$ and then to $P_x = \$0.50$ would cause the consumer's budget line to become flatter or to rotate counterclockwise from JK to JK'' and then to JN' (the same as in the right panel of Figure 3-7).[3]

With $P_x = \$1$ and budget line JK'', the consumer maximizes utility at point E, where indifference curve U_2 is tangent to budget line JK'' and the consumer purchases $6X$ and $4Y$ (see the top panel of Figure 4-3). Indifference curve U_2 is the same as in the right panel of Figure 3-2 because tastes have not changed. Finally, with $P_x = \$0.50$ and budget line JN', the consumer maximizes utility or is at optimum at point G on U_4 by purchasing $10X$ and $5Y$ per unit of time (per day). By joining optimum points B, E, and G we get (a portion of) the price-consumption curve for this consumer (student). Thus, the price-consumption curve for good X is the locus of consumer optimum points resulting when only the price of X changes.[4]

From the price-consumption curve in the top panel of Figure 4-3 we can derive the individual consumer's (student's) demand curve for good X in the bottom panel. The **individual's demand curve** for good X shows the amount of good X that the consumer would purchase per unit of time at various alternative prices of good X while holding everything else constant. It is derived by keeping the same horizontal scale as in the top panel but measuring the price of good X on the vertical axis.

The derivation of the individual's demand curve proceeds as follows. With $I = \$10$, $P_y = \$1$, $P_x = \$2$, the student maximizes utility by purchasing $2X$ (two hamburgers) per day (point B) in the top panel. This gives point B' (directly below point B) in the bottom panel. With $P_x = \$1$, the consumer

---

[3] Remember that the X-intercept of the budget lines are obtained by I/P_x. Thus, with $I = \$10$ and $P_x = \$2$, we get endpoint K and budget line JK. With $P_x = \$1$, we get endpoint K'' and budget line JK'', and with $P_x = \$0.50$, we get end point N' and budget line JN'.

[4] At each point along the price-consumption curve, $MRS_{xy} = P_x/P_y$. However, unlike the case of the income-consumption curve, these ratios will vary because the budget lines are no longer parallel.

102

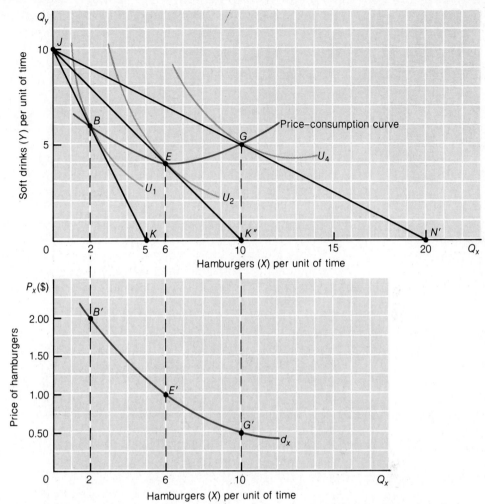

FIGURE 4-3. The Price-Consumption Curve and the Individual's Demand Curve

The top panel shows that with I = $10 and P_y = $1, the consumer is at optimum at point B by purchasing 2X with P_x = $2, at point E by purchasing 6X with P_x = $1, and at point G by purchasing 10X with P_x = $0.50. By joining points BEG, we get the price-consumption curve for good X. In the bottom panel, by plotting the optimum quantities of good X on the horizontal axis and the corresponding prices of good X on the vertical axis, we derive the individual's negatively sloped demand curve for good X, d_x.

is at optimum by purchasing 6X (point E) in the top panel. This gives point E' in the bottom panel. Finally, with P_x = $0.50, the consumer maximizes utility by purchasing 10X (point G in the top panel and G' in the bottom panel). Other points could be similarly obtained. By joining points B', E', and G' we get the individual consumer's demand curve for good X, d_x, in the bottom panel. Thus, the demand curve is derived from the price-consumption curve and shows the quantity of the good that the consumer would purchase per unit of time at various alternative prices of the good while holding everything else constant.

We will see in Chapter 5 that the market demand curve for a good (our ultimate aim in Part II of the text) is obtained from the addition or the horizontal summation of all individual consumer's demand curves for the good. Note that the individual consumer's demand curve for a good (d_x in the bottom panel of Figure 4-3) is negatively sloped. This reflects the *law of demand*, which postulates that the quantity purchased of a good per unit of time is inversely related to its price. Thus, the individual purchases more hamburgers per unit of time when its price falls and less of it when the price rises. Also note that an individual consumer's demand curve for a good is derived by holding constant the individual's tastes, his or her income, and the price of other goods. If any of these change, the entire demand curve will shift. This is referred to as a change in demand as opposed to a change in the quantity demanded, which refers instead to a movement along a given demand curve as a result of a change in the price of the good while holding everything else constant (refer back to Section 2-5).

Example 4-2 Negatively Sloped Demand Curves

The Facts: Since the Arab oil embargo in the fall of 1973, proposals have been advanced for increasing the gasoline tax. This would raise the price of gasoline and lead to a reduction in the quantity of gasoline demanded per year by motorists, and reduce American dependence on foreign oil. These recommendations were all based on the knowledge that the demand curve of gasoline (as the demand curve for practically all goods) is negatively sloped. Even the demand curve for alcohol by alcoholics seems to be negatively sloped. For example, an experiment showed that the greater is the number of pulls of a one-pound lever to get a drink (i.e., the greater the effort or price to get a drink), the smaller is the number of drinks demanded by alcoholics. Laboratory rats also "demanded" fewer "drinks" when the price of a drink was increased (by requiring a greater number of presses of a lever). Even the "demand" for airline hijackings seems to be negatively sloped. This can be inferred from the fact that with the increased probability of apprehension and severity of punishment (the price) for hijacking an airline rising sharply since 1973, the number of hijackings per year dwindled.

Comment: While our concern here is only that the demand curve of the "typical" consumer be negatively sloped, it is interesting that the law of negatively sloped demand seems to have wider applicability. As we have seen, even the demand curve for alcohol of alcoholics and rats seems to be negatively sloped, and so is the "demand" curve for crime (hijacks). Thus, as the effort or price to get a drink increases, alcoholics and rats demand

104

fewer drinks. Similarly, as the probability of apprehension and punishment for (i.e., as the price of) crime increases, the number of crimes committed decreases (see also Example 3-2).

Sources: "The Energy Disaster," *The New York Times*, November 1, 1979, p. 23. "Deterrence," *The Public Interest*, Summer 1973, pp. 119–120 (on alcohol). J. Kagel *et al.*, "Experimental Studies of Consumer Demand Behavior Using Laboratory Animals," *Economic Inquiry*, March 1975, pp. 22–38. W. Landes, "An Economic Study of U.S. Aircraft Hijacking, 1961–1976," *The Journal of Law and Economics*, April 1978, pp. 1–31.

4-2b Price-Consumption Curve and Price Elasticity of Demand

We can determine whether an individual's demand curve for a commodity is elastic, unitary elastic, or inelastic directly from the slope of the price-consumption curve. From Section 2-2 we know that the price elasticity of demand (η) is given by the percentage change in the quantity demanded of a good divided by the percentage change in its price. Demand is said to be elastic, unitary elastic, or inelastic depending on whether η exceeds 1, is equal to 1, or is smaller than 1, respectively. This can be determined directly from the shape of the price-consumption curve. That is, the demand curve is elastic, unitary elastic, or inelastic depending on whether the price-consumption curve falls, is horizontal, or rises.

We can show this with Figure 4-4. The horizontal axis in each of the three panels measures the quantity of good X purchased per unit of time (as before). Instead of measuring the quantity of good Y along the vertical axes, we now measure *money spent on all goods other than X*. With money income of $I = \$10$ and $P_x = \$2$, we get budget line JK in each panel. That is, if the consumer spent all money for other goods and purchased no X, he or she would be at vertical intercept or endpoint J of budget line JK. However, by spending all income on good X, the individual can purchase $5X$ (endpoint K in each panel). Joining endpoints J and K we get budget line JK in each panel. On the other hand, with $P_x = \$1$, we would get budget line JK'' in each panel.

Each indifference curve in the three panels would then show the various combinations of money for all other goods and the quantity of X purchased that give the individual the same level of utility. As a starting point, each panel shows that with budget line JK, the individual maximizes utility at point B by purchasing $2X$ and spending \$6 ($0R$) on all other goods. Thus, $JR = \$4$ is the amount spent on X. That is, with $I = \$10$ ($0J$) and \$6 ($0R$) spent on all other goods, \$4 (JR) is the remaining amount spent on X. The distance from the vertical intercept of the budget line down to the point directly across from the point of consumer utility maximization always measures the amount of money spent on good X in this type of figure.

105

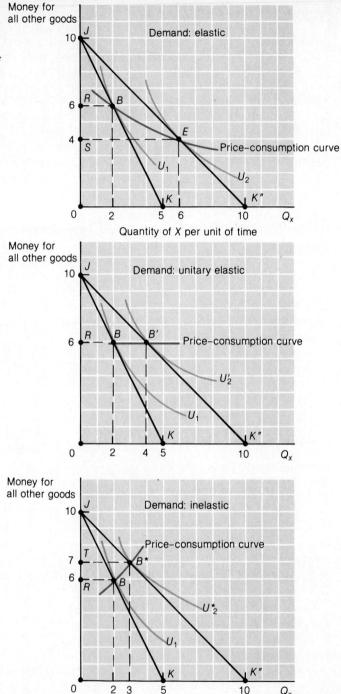

FIGURE 4-4. *The Price-Consumption Curve and the Price Elasticity of Demand*

In each panel, the vertical axis measures money spent on all goods other than good X (rather than Q_y). Then the vertical distance from the point where the budget line crosses the vertical axis to the point directly across from where the consumer is at optimum gives the amount of money spent on X. The top panel shows that as P_x falls, money spent on X increases. This gives a price-consumption curve (PCC) that slopes downward, and the demand for X is price elastic. In the middle panel, a reduction in P_x leaves expenditures on X constant. Thus, the PCC is horizontal and demand is unitary elastic. In the bottom panel, the PCC slopes upward and demand is inelastic.

With $P_x = \$1$ and budget line JK'' in each panel, we now have three alternative situations. With indifference curve U_2 in the top panel, the individual is at optimum at point E by purchasing $6X$ and spending $\$6$ (JS) on X. Since the amount of money income spent on X increases (from $JR = \$4$ to $JS = \$6$) when P_x falls, the percentage increase in the quantity purchased of X (the numerator of the elasticity formula) must be greater than the percentage decline in the price of X (the denominator of the elasticity formula), and so the demand curve is price elastic over this range. This is reflected in the negatively sloped price-consumption curve in the top panel. Thus, whenever total expenditures on a good increase when its price falls, the price-consumption curve is negatively sloped and the demand for the good is price elastic.

The middle and the bottom panels show that with *alternative* indifference curves U'_2 and U^*_2, we get a different situation. With budget line JK'' and indifference curve U'_2 in the middle panel, the consumer maximizes utility at point B' by purchasing $4X$ and spending $JR = \$4$ on X. Since the amount of money income spent on X is the same ($JR = \$4$) when $P_x = \$1$ as when $P_x = \$2$, the increase in Q_x must be proportionately equal to the decline in P_x, and so d_x is unitary elastic over this range. This is reflected in the horizontal (zero sloped) price-consumption curve in the middle panel. Thus, whenever the price-consumption curve is horizontal, a change in the price of the good will leave total expenditures on the good unchanged, and the demand curve has a price elasticity of 1.

Finally, with budget line JK'' and indifference curve U^*_2 in the bottom panel, the consumer is at optimum at point B^* by purchasing $3X$ and spending only $JT = \$3$ on X (down from $JR = \$4$). This means that the percentage increase in Q_x must be smaller than the percentage decline in P_x, so that d_x is inelastic over this range. This is reflected in a postively sloped price-consumption curve in the bottom panel of Figure 4-4. Thus, whenever total expenditures on a good decreases when its price falls, the price-consumption curve is positively sloped, and the demand for the good is price inelastic.

Summarizing, we can say that the demand curve for a commodity is price elastic, unitary elastic, or inelastic if the price-consumption curve is negatively, zero, or positively sloped, respectively. This can be confirmed by using Formula (2-2) for measuring arc elasticity (see Section 2-2). By doing so, the student would find that $\eta = 6/4 = 1.5$ over the range of the demand curve that could be derived from the top panel of Figure 4-4, $\eta = 1$ for the middle panel, and $\eta = 0.6$ for the bottom panel.

As pointed out in Chapter 2, the price elasticity of demand usually changes at different points on the demand curve. Thus, d_x in the bottom panel of Figure 4-3 is price elastic over range $B'E'$ (because the price-consumption curve falls over range BE) and is inelastic over the $E'G'$ range (because the price-consumption curve rises over the EG range). At point E the slope of the price-consumption curve is zero and so d_x has unitary price elasticity at point E'. More will be said on this in Chapter 5, where we return to the topic of elasticities in greater detail.

4-3

Substitution and Income Effects

In this section we separate the substitution from the income effect of a price change for both normal and inferior goods. This will give us an important analytical tool with wide applicability and will also allow us to examine the exception to the law of downward sloping demand.

4-3a Separation of the Substitution and Income Effects

We have seen in the previous section that when the price of a good falls the consumer buys more of it. This is the combined result of two separate forces at work called the substitution effect and the income effect. We now want to separate the total effect of a price change into these two components. We begin by first reviewing how the total effect of a price change (discussed in Section 4-2a) operates.

In Figure 4-5, $I = \$10$ and $P_y = \$1$ and these remain constant. With $P_x = \$2$, we have budget line JK and the consumer maximizes utility at point B on indifference curve U_1 by purchasing $2X$. When the price of good X falls to $P_x = \$1$, the budget line becomes JK'' and the consumer maximizes utility at point E on indifference curve U_2 by purchasing $6X$ (so far this is the same as in Figure 4-3). The increase in the quantity purchased from $2X$ to $6X$ is the total effect or the sum of the substitution and income effects. We are now ready to separate this total effect into these two components.

First, consider the **substitution effect.** In Figure 4-5, we see that when the price of X falls from $P_x = \$2$ to $P_x = \$1$, the individual moves from point B on U_1 to point E on U_2 so that his or her level of satisfaction increases. Suppose that as P_x falls we could reduce the individual's money income sufficiently to keep him or her on original indifference curve U_1. We can show this by drawing hypothetical or imaginary budget line J^*K^* in Figure 4-5. Imaginary budget line J^*K^* is parallel to budget line JK'' so as to reflect the *new* set of relative prices (i.e., $P_x/P_y = \$1/\$1 = 1$) and is below budget line JK'' in order to keep the individual at the original level of satisfaction (i.e., on indifference curve U_1).[5] The individual would then maximize satisfaction at point T, where indifference curve U_1 is tangent to imaginary budget line J^*K^*.

[5] Budget line J^*K^* is imaginary in the sense that we do not actually observe it, unless the reduction in P_x is in fact accompanied, for example, by a lump-sum tax that in fact removes $\$3$ ($JJ^* = K''K^*$) from the money income of the individual.

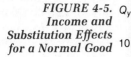

FIGURE 4-5.
Income and
Substitution Effects
for a Normal Good

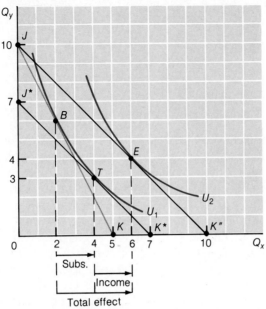

The optimum point is B with P_x = $2 and E with P_x = $1 (as in the top panel of
Figure 4-3). To isolate the substitution effect, we draw imaginary budget line J*K*,
which is parallel to JK'' and tangent to U_1 at T. The movement along U_1 from point
B to point T is the substitution effect and results from the relative reduction in P_x only
(with real income constant). The shift from point T on U_1 to point E on U_2 is then the
income effect. The total effect (BE = 4X) equals the substitution effect (BT = 2X) plus
the income effect (TE = 2X).

The movement along indifference curve U_1 from original point B to imaginary point T measures the substitution effect only (since the individual
remains on the same indifference curve or level of satisfaction). From Figure 4-5, we see that the substitution effect, by itself, leads the individual
to increase the quantity purchased of good X from 2 to 4 units when P_x falls
from $2 to $1. That is, the individual substitutes hamburgers for, say, hot
dogs and purchases two additional hamburgers and fewer hot dogs per unit
of time. The substitution effect results exclusively from the reduction in
the **relative price** of X (from P_x/P_y = $2/$1 = 2 to P_x/P_y = $1/$1 = 1)
with the level of satisfaction held constant. Note that because indifference
curves are negatively sloped, the substitution effect always involves an
increase in the quantity demanded of a good when its price falls.

Next, consider the **income effect.** The shift from the imaginary point T
on U_1 to the actual new point E on U_2 can be taken as a measure of the
income effect. The shift from point T to point E does not involve any price
change. That is, since the imaginary budget line J*K* and the actual new
budget line JK'' are parallel, relative prices are the same (i.e., P_x/P_y = 1 in
both). The shift from indifference curve U_1 to U_2 can thus be taken as a
measure of the increase in the individual's real income or purchasing

109

power.[6] Since good X is a normal good, an increase in the consumer's purchasing power or real income leads him or her to purchase more of X (and other normal goods). In Figure 4-5, the income effect, by itself, leads the consumer to purchase two additional hamburgers (i.e., to go from $4X$ to $6X$).[7]

Thus, the total effect of the reduction in P_x ($BE = 4X$) equals the substitution effect ($BT = 2X$) plus the income effect ($TE = 2X$). The substitution effect reflects the increase in Q_x resulting only from the reduction in P_x and is independent of any change in the consumer's level of satisfaction or real income. On the other hand, the income effect reflects the increase in Q_x resulting only from the increase in satisfaction or real income. Only the total effect of the price change is actually observable in the real world, but we have been able, at least conceptually or experimentally, to separate this total effect into a substitution effect and an income effect.

Note that in Figure 4-5, the substitution and the income effect are of equal size. In the real world, the substitution effect is likely to be much larger than the income effect. The reason is that most goods have suitable substitutes and when the price of a good falls, the quantity of the good purchased is likely to increase very much as consumers substitute the now-cheaper good for others. On the other hand, with the consumer purchasing many goods and spending only a small fraction of his or her income on any one good, the income effect of a price decline of any one good is likely to be small. There are, however, exceptional cases where the income effect exceeds the substitution effect.

Finally, it should be noted that while the substitution effect of a price reduction is always positive (i.e., it always leads to an increase in the quantity demanded of a good), the income effect can be positive if the good is normal or negative if the good is inferior.

Example 4-3 Gasoline Tax and Rebate Proposal

The Facts: Since the Arab oil embargo in the fall of 1973, various proposals have been advanced to impose a gasoline excise tax ranging from 25¢ to 50¢ per gallon. This would increase gasoline prices to motorists, and lead to a reduction in gasoline consumption and American dependence on foreign oil. In order to avoid the deflationary effect of the tax on the economy (i.e., to avoid the reduction in purchasing power in an already recessionary economy), it was proposed either to return to consumers the amount of the tax collected on gasoline in the form of a *general* tax rebate unrelated to gasoline consumption or to reduce other taxes.

---

[6] The shift from point T to point E could be observed by giving back to the consumer the hypothetical lump-sum tax of $3 collected earlier. Only with such an increase in real income or purchasing power can the consumer move from point T on U_1 to point E on U_2.

[7] It also leads the individual to purchase one additional soft drink (i.e., to go from $3Y$ to $4Y$). See the figure.

110

Comment: All of these proposals relied on the distinction between the substitution and the income effect of an increase in gasoline prices. The substitution effect would result as people switched to cheaper means of transportation (trains, buses, subways), to car pools, and to more fuel efficient cars. The general income subsidy would then neutralize the reduction in real income associated with the increase in the price of gasoline. It should be noted parenthetically, however, that one could not arrange such a subsidy so that *everybody individually* could be exactly compensated for his or her fall in real income. While never adopted, this policy proposal highlights the usefulness of the distinction between the substitution and the income effects of a price change.

Source: "The Energy Disaster," *The New York Times,* Nov. 1, 1979, p. 23, and "On the Issues: John B. Anderson," *The New York Times,* March 29, 1980, p. 9.

4-3b Substitution and Income Effects for Inferior Goods

For a normal good, the substitution and the income effects of a price decline are both positive and reinforce each other in leading to a greater quantity purchased of the good. On the other hand, when the good is inferior, the income effect moves in the opposite direction from the substitution effect. That is, when the price of an inferior good falls, the substitution effect continues to operate as before to *increase* the quantity purchased of the good. This results from the convex shape of indifference curves. However, the increase in purchasing power or real income resulting from the price decline leads the consumer to purchase *less* of an inferior good. Thus, for an inferior good, the substitution effect of a price decline leads the consumer to purchase more of the good while the income effect leads the consumer to purchase less of it. However, since the substitution effect is usually larger than the income effect, the quantity demanded of the inferior good increases when its price falls and the demand curve is still negatively sloped.

We can separate the substitution from the income effect of a price decline for an inferior good by returning to the candy bar (inferior good Z) example of the previous section. In the top panel of Figure 4-6, the consumer is originally at optimum at point V, where indifference curve U'_1 is tangent to budget line JK' and the consumer purchases four candy bars (as in the top panel of Figure 4-2). If now the price of candy bars declines from $P_z = \$1$ to $P_z = \$0.50$, the consumer moves to optimum point S, where indifference curve U'_2 is tangent to budget line JN' and the consumer purchases 6Z. The movement from point V to point S (+2Z) is the sum or net effect of the substitution and income effects.

To separate the substitution effect from the income effect, we now draw the imaginary budget line J*N*, which is lower than, but parallel to, budget

111

FIGURE 4-6.
Income and
Substitution Effects
for Inferior Goods

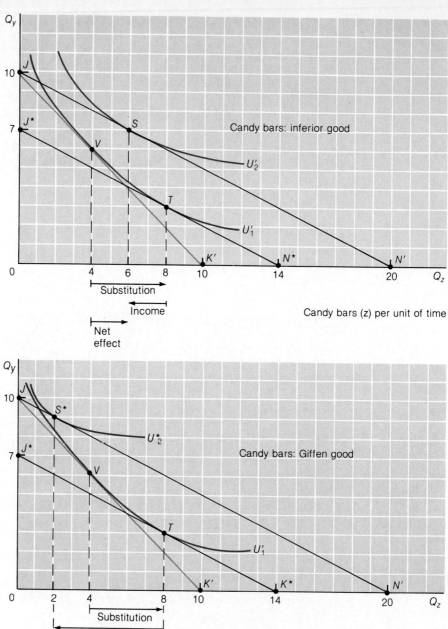

In the top panel the optimum point is V with P_z = $1 and S with P_z = $0.50. To isolate the substitution effect, we draw J^*N^* parallel to JN' and tangent to U_1' at point T. The movement along U_1' from point V to point T is the substitution effect. The movement from point T on U_1' to points S on U_2' is the income effect. Since the income effect is negative, good Z is inferior. However, since the positive substitution effect exceeds the negative income effect, Q_z increases when P_z falls. In the bottom panel, the positive substitution effect (VT = 4Z) is smaller than the negative income effect (TS^* = −6Z), so that Q_z declines by 2Z when P_z falls. Good Z is then a Giffen good.

line JN' and tangent to U_1' at point T. The movement along U_1' from the original point V to imaginary point T is the *substitution effect*. It results exclusively from the reduction in P_z relative to P_y and is independent of any increase in real income. Thus, the substitution effect, by itself, leads the individual to purchase four additional units of good Z per unit of time (from $4Z$ to $8Z$).

On the other hand, the movement from imaginary point T on U_1' to the new point S on U_2' can be taken as a measure of the *income effect*. It results exclusively from the increase in the level of satisfaction of the consumer with relative prices constant ($P_z/P_y = \$0.50/\$1 = \frac{1}{2}$ for imaginary budget line J^*N^* and for new budget line JN'). The income effect, by itself, leads the consumer to purchase two *fewer* units of good Z per unit of time (from $8Z$ to $6Z$) because good Z is an inferior good. That is, the decline in P_z causes the consumer's real income to rise, but since good Z is an inferior good, the consumer purchase two *fewer* units of good Z.

Thus, the total effect ($VS = 2Z$ given by the movement from point V on U_1' to point S on U_2') equals the positive substitution effect ($VT = 4Z$ given by the movement from point V to T on U_1') plus the negative income effect ($TS = -2Z$ given by the movement from point T on U_1' to point S on U_2'). However, since the positive substitution effect exceeds the negative income effect, the consumer purchases two additional units of good Z when its price declines. Thus, the demand curve for good Z is negatively sloped, even though good Z is an inferior good. That is, the consumer purchases $4Z$ at $P_x = \$1$ and $6Z$ at $P_z = \$0.50$.

On the other hand, if the positive substitution effect is smaller than the negative income effect when the price of an inferior good falls, then the demand curve for the inferior good is positively sloped. This very rarely, if ever, occurs in the real world, and is referred to as the **Giffen paradox,** after the 19th century English economist, Robert Giffen, who first discussed it. Note that a Giffen good is an inferior good but not all inferior goods are Giffen goods. If it exists, a Giffen good would lead to a positively sloped demand curve for the individual and would represent an exception to the law of negatively sloped demand.

The bottom panel of Figure 4-6 is drawn on the assumption that good Z is now a Giffen good. That is, good Z is assumed to be an inferior good for which the positive substitution effect is *smaller* than the negative income effect when the price of the good falls. In the bottom panel, the consumer is originally at optimum point V and hypothetically moves to point T because of the substitution effect (as in the top panel). However, with *alternative* indifference curve U_2^* in the bottom panel (as opposed to U_2' in the top panel), the income effect is given by the movement from point T to point S^*. Point S^* is to the left of point T because good Z is an inferior good, so that an increase in real income leads to less of it being purchased. The total effect is now VS^* ($-2Z$) and is equal to substitution effect VT ($4Z$) plus income effect TS^* ($-6Z$). Since the positive substitution effect is smaller than the negative income effect, the quantity demanded of good Z *declines*

113

when its price falls, and d_z would be positively sloped over this range. That is, the individual would purchase $4Z$ at $P_z = \$1$ but only $2Z$ at $P_z = \$0.50$.

While theoretically interesting, the Giffen paradox rarely, if ever, occurs in the real world. The reason is that inferior goods are usually narrowly defined goods for which suitable substitutes are available (so that the substitution effect usually exceeds the opposite income effect). Giffen thought that potatoes in 19th century Ireland provided an example of the paradox, but subsequent research did not lend credence to his belief. Note that the separation of the substitution from the income effect (and all of the analysis in this chapter) could easily be shown for a price increase rather than for a price decline. These alternatives are assigned as end-of-chapter problems.

4-4

Applications

In this section we apply the tools developed in this chapter to analyze the economics of the food stamp program, consumer surplus, exchange, and time as an economic good. While these applications deal only with the demand for goods (including services), the tools developed in this chapter have many other applications (as we will see in other parts of the text). For example, the distinction between the substitution and the income effects is very useful to analyze the effect of overtime pay on the number of hours worked and on leisure time. However, as this topic deals with the supply of labor, it is appropriately postponed until Chapter 14, which deals with input price and employment.

Application 1: The Food Stamp Program
Under the federal food stamp program, low-income families receive free food stamps, which they can use only to purchase food. In 1980, over 4.4 million eligible low-income families received free food stamps at a cost of over $9.6 billion to the federal government. The important question is whether it would have been better (i.e., provided more satisfaction) to give an equal amount of subsidy in cash to poor families.

We can examine this question with Figure 4-7. Suppose that, initially, a typical poor family has a weekly income of $100. If the poor family spent its entire weekly income on nonfood items, it could purchase $100 worth of nonfood items per week (point A on the vertical axis). On the other hand, if the poor family spent the entire $100 on food, it could purchase 100 units of food per week if the unit price of food is $1 (point C on the horizontal axis). The initial budget line of the family is then AC.

With free food stamps that allow the family to purchase $50 worth of food per week, the budget line of the family becomes $AB'C'$, where $AB' = CC' = 50$. Combinations on dashed segment $A'B'$ are not available with the

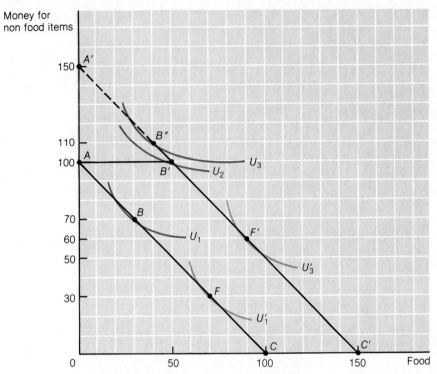

FIGURE 4-7.
Food Stamps versus Cash Aid

A poor family spending its weekly income of $100 (and no food stamps) either entirely on nonfood items or entirely on food (with a unit price of $1) faces budget line AC. The family's budget line becomes AB'C' with $50 worth of free food stamps per week, and A'C' with a $50 cash subsidy instead. The family maximizes utility at point B on U_1 without any aid, at point B' on U_2 with food stamps, and at point B" on U_3 with the cash subsidy. However, another family with the same original income and budget line AC but with stronger preference for food may go instead from point F on U_1' to point F' on U_3' either with the cash subsidy or with food stamps.

food stamp program because the family would have to spend more than its $100 money income on nonfood items and less than the $50 of food stamps on food (and this is not possible). Were the government to provide $50 in cash rather than in food stamps, the budget line would then be A'C'. Thus, we have three alternative budget lines for the family: budget line AC without any aid, budget line AB'C' with $50 in food stamps, and budget line A'C' with $50 cash aid instead.

If the family's indifference curves are U_1, U_2, and U_3, the family maximizes utility at point B where U_1 is tangent to AC before receiving any aid, at point B' on U_2 with food stamps, and at point B" (> B') on U_3 with the cash subsidy. In this case, the cash subsidy allows the family to reach a higher indifference curve than food stamps.[8] However, *another family with*

[8] Both cost the government $50.

the same initial income of $100 (and budget line *AC*) but stronger prefer-
ence for food and facing indifference curves U_1' and U_3' will move instead
from point *F* on U_1' to point *F'* on U_3, either with the cash subsidy or with
food stamps. Thus, depending on the family's tastes, *a cash subsidy will not
be worse than food stamps and may be better* (i.e., provide more
satisfaction).

Application 2: Consumer Surplus

Consumer surplus is the difference between what a consumer is willing to
pay for a good and what he actually pays. It results because the consumer
pays for *all* units of the good only as much as he or she is willing to pay for
the *last* unit of the good (which gives less utility than earlier units). We can
see how consumer surplus arises and how it can be measured with the aid
of Figure 4-8.

The figure shows that $5 is the maximum amount that the consumer is
willing to pay for the first unit of good *X* (say, hamburgers) rather than go
without it. Thus, the area of the first rectangle (with height of $5 and width
of 1) measures the marginal value or benefit that the consumer gets from

FIGURE 4-8.
Consumer Surplus

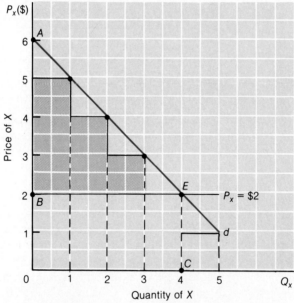

The maximum amount that the consumer is willing to pay for good X rather than go
without it is $5 for the first unit (the area of the first rectangle), $4 for the second unit
(the area of the second rectangle), $3 for the third unit, and $2 for the fourth. If
$P_x = \$2$, all 4X can be purchased for $8. The difference between what the consumer
is willing to pay for 4X ($5 + $4 + $3 + $2 = $14) and what he or she actually pays
($8) is the consumer surplus (the shaded area that equals $6). If good X could be
purchased in infinitesimally small units, the consumer surplus would equal the area
under d_x and above $P_x = \$2$ (area AEB = $8).

116

the first hamburger. After all, by being willing to purchase the first hamburger for $5, the consumer indicates that he or she prefers paying $5 for the first hamburger rather than keeping the $5 in cash or spending the $5 on other goods. The second unit of good X (hamburger) gives the consumer less utility than the first, and the consumer would be willing to pay $4 for it rather than go without it. Thus, $4 (the area of the second rectangle) can be taken as a measure of the marginal value or benefit of the second hamburger to the consumer. The third hamburger gives the consumer less utility than either the first or the second and so the consumer is willing to pay only $3 for it. Thus, the marginal value or benefit of the third hamburger is $3 and is given by the area of the third rectangle. For the fourth hamburger, the consumer would be willing to pay $2 (the area of the fourth rectangle) and this is a measure of the marginal value or benefit of the fourth hamburger, and so on.

To summarize, the consumer would be willing to pay $5 for the first hamburger, $4 for the second, $3 for the third, and $2 for the fourth, for a total of $14 for all four hamburgers. Thus, $14 is the total benefit that the consumer receives from purchasing 4 hamburgers. However, if the market price is $2 per hamburger, the consumer can purchase all four hamburgers at a total cost of (i.e., by actually spending) only $8. Since the consumer would be willing to pay $14 for the first four hamburgers rather than go entirely without them, but actually pays only $8, he or she enjoys a net benefit or *consumer surplus* equal to the difference ($6).

To put it another way, the consumer is willing to pay $5 for the first hamburger, but since he or she can purchase it for only $2, he or she receives a surplus of $3 for the first hamburger. Since he or she is willing to pay $4 for the second hamburger but pays only $2, there is a surplus of $2 on the second hamburger. For the third hamburger, the consumer is willing to pay $3 but since he or she pays only $2, the surplus is $1. For the fourth hamburger, the consumer is willing to pay $2 and since he or she has to pay $2 for it, there is no surplus on the fourth hamburger. The consumer would not purchase the fifth hamburger because he or she is not willing to pay the $2 market price for it.

By adding the consumer surplus of $3 on the first hamburger, $2 on the second, $1 on the third, and $0 on the fourth, we get the consumer surplus of $6 obtained earlier. This is given by the sum of the shaded areas in the figure. The same result would have been obtained if the consumer had been asked for the maximum amount of money that he or she would have been willing to pay for four hamburgers rather than do entirely without them—*all or nothing*.

If hamburgers could have been purchased in smaller and smaller fractions of a whole hamburger, then the consumer surplus would have been given by the entire area under demand curve d_x above the market price of $2. That is, the consumer surplus would have been the area of triangle AEB, which is $\frac{1}{2}(4)(4) = \$8$. This exceeds the consumer surplus of $6 that we have found by adding only the shaded areas in the figure. Specifically, the consumer would have been willing to pay \$16 (the area of *OAEC*) for four hamburgers. Note that *OAEC* is composed of triangle *AEB* plus rectangle *OBEC*. Since he or she only pays \$8 (*OBEC*), the consumer surplus is \$8 (*AEB*). If P_x fell to \$1, the consumer would purchase five hamburgers and the consumer's surplus would be \$12.50 (the area under d_x and above $P_x = \$1$ in the figure) if hamburgers could be purchased by infinitely small fractions of a whole hamburger.[9]

The concept of the consumer surplus was first used by Dupuit in 1844 and was subsequently refined and popularized by Alfred Marshall. The concept helped resolve the so-called **water-diamond paradox,** which plagued classical economists until 1870. That is, why is water, which is essential for life, so cheap while diamonds, which are not essential, so expensive? The explanation is that because water is so plentiful (relatively cheap) and we use so much of it, the utility of the last unit is very little (washing the car) and we pay for all units of water as little as we are willing to pay for the last *nonessential* unit of it. On the other hand, diamonds are scarce in relation to demand and since we use very little of them, the utility and price of the *last unit* are very great. The *total* utility and the consumer surplus from all the water used are far greater than the total utility and the consumer surplus from all the diamonds purchased. However, demand depends on marginal utility, not on total utility. In a desert, the first glass of water would be worth much more than any glassful of diamonds.

Application 3: Exchange

Suppose that two individuals, A and B, have a given amount of good *X* and good *Y* and decide to trade some of these goods with each other. If the exchange is voluntary, the strong presumption is that both individuals gain from the exchange (otherwise, the individual who loses would simply refuse to trade). We can examine the process of voluntary exchange by indifference curve analysis.

Suppose that individual A's tastes and preferences for good *X* and good *Y* are shown by indifference curves U_1, U_2, and U_3 in the top left panel of Figure 4-9. On the other hand, individual B's tastes and preferences are given by indifference curves U_1', U_2', and U_3' (with origin *O'*) in the top right panel. Initially, individual A has an allocation of 3*X* and 6*Y* (point *C* in the top left panel) and individual B has 7*X* and 2*Y* (point *C* in the top right panel).

We now rotate individual B's indifference diagram by 180 degrees (so that origin *O'* appears in the top right corner) and superimpose it on individual A's indifference diagram in such a way that the axes of the two dia-

---

[9] Measuring consumer surplus by the area under the demand curve and above the prevailing market price is only an approximation, but for most purposes it is sufficiently accurate to be a useful tool of analysis. For a mathematical measure of consumer surplus using rudimentary calculus, see Section A5 of the Mathematical Appendix.

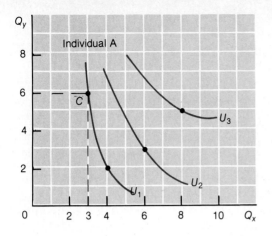

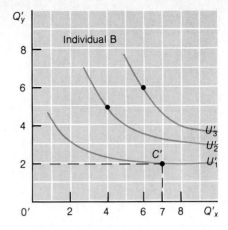

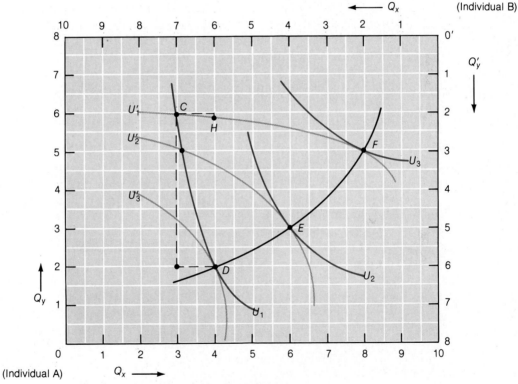

FIGURE 4-9. Edgeworth Box Diagram

The top left panel shows individual A's indifference curves and the top right panel shows B's indifference curves. The box in the bottom panel is obtained by rotating by 180 degrees B's indifference map diagram and superimposing it on A's diagram in such a way that the dimension of the box equals the initial combined amount of goods X and Y owned by A and B. Any point in the box refers to a particular distribution of X and Y between A and B. At point C, MRS_{xy} for the two individuals differs (U_1 and U_1' cross) and there is a basis for mutually beneficial exchange until a point between D and F on curve DEF is reached (where MRS_{xy} for A and B are equal).

119

grams form the so-called **Edgeworth box diagram,** shown in the bottom panel of Figure 4-9. The length of the box (10X) measures the combined amount of X initially owned by individual A (3X) and individual B (7X). The height of the box (8Y) measures the amount of Y initially owned by individual A (6Y) and individual B (2Y). A's indifference curves are convex to origin O (as usual), while B's indifference curves are convex to origin O'.

Any point inside the box indicates how the total amount of X and Y may be distributed between the two individuals. For example, the initial distribution of X and Y given by point C indicates that individual A has 3X and 6Y (viewed from origin O) and individual B has the remainder of 7X and 2Y (when viewed from origin O') for a total of 10X and 8Y (the dimension of the box). Individual A is on indifference curve U_1 and individual B is on indifference curve U_1'.

Since at point C (where U_1 and U_1' intersect), the marginal rate of substitution of good X for good Y (MRS_{xy}) for individual A exceeds MRS_{xy} for individual B, there is a basis for mutually beneficial exchange between the two individuals. Starting at point C, individual A would be willing to give up 4Y to get one additional unit of X (and move to point D on U_1). On the other hand, individual B would be willing to give up about 0.2Y for one additional unit of X (and move to point H on U_1'). Since A is willing to give up more of Y than necessary to induce B to give up 1X, there is a basis for trade in which individual A gives up some of Y in exchange for some of X from individual B.

Whenever the MRS_{xy} for the two individuals differ at the initial distribution of X and Y, either or both may gain from exchange. For example, starting from point C, if individual A exchanges 4Y for 1X with individual B, A would move from point C to point D along indifference curve on U_1, while B would move from point C on U_1' to point D on U_3'. By moving from indifference curve U_1' to indifference curve U_3', individual B receives all of the gains from the exchange while individual A gains or loses nothing (since A remains on U_1). At point D, U_1 and U_3' are tangent and so their slopes (MRS_{xy}) are equal. Thus, there is no basis for further exchange (at point D, the amount of Y that A is willing to give up for 1X is exactly equal to what B requires to give up 1X). Any further exchange would make either one or both individuals worse off than they are at point D.

Alternatively, if individual A exchanged 1Y for 5X with individual B, individual A would move from point C on U_1 to point F on U_3, while individual B would move from point C to point F along U_1'. Then, A would reap all the benefits from exchange while B would neither gain nor lose. At point F, MRS_{xy} for A equals MRS_{xy} for B and there is no further basis for exchange. Finally, starting again from point C on U_1 and U_1', if A exchanges 3Y for 3X with B and gets to point E, both individuals gain from the exchange since point E is on U_2 and U_2'.

Starting from any point not on curve DEF, both individuals can gain from

120

exchange by moving to a point on curve *DEF* between points *D* and *F*. The closer individual A gets to point *F* (i.e., the more shrewd A is as a bargainer), the greater is the proportion of the total gain from the exchange accruing to A and the less is left for B. The Edgeworth box is named after the English economist F. Y. Edgeworth, who in 1881 first outlined its construction. (We will return to exchange in greater detail in Chapter 17.)

Application 4: Time as an Economic Good

So far we have considered income as the only constraint on consumption. However, the consumption of most goods and services (such as eating a meal in a restaurant or going to a baseball game) involves spending time as well as money. Therefore, it is only appropriate to consider time as an additional constraint on consumption.

Suppose an individual has a maximum income $100 and 24 hours *per month* available to attend baseball games (good *Y*) or to consume restaurant meals (good *X*). Suppose that the admission price for a baseball game and the price of a restaurant meal are each $10. Suppose also that it takes 3 hours to watch a game and 2 hours to consume a restaurant meal. The usual income constraint is given by budget line *CF* in the left panel of Figure 4-10. That is, if the individual spent the entire income to attend baseball games, he or she could attend 10 games per month (point F, given by $100/$10). On the other hand, if the individual spent the entire income on meals, he or she could purchase 10 meals per month (point C, given by $100/$10). By joining points *C* and *F*, we obtain the usual income budget line. The individual can purchase any combination of *X* and *Y* on or below *income* budget line *CF*. Budget line *CF* reflects only the individual's income constraint.

We can similarly derive the individual's **time budget line.** That is, if the individual spent the entire 24 hours per month for baseball games, he or she could attend 8 games per month (point G, given by 24 hours/3 hours). On the other hand, if the individual spent the entire 24 hours on restaurant meals, he or she could consume 12 meals per month (point H, given by 24 hours/2 hours). By joining points *G* and *H*, we get the individual's time budget constraint. The individual can achieve any combination of *X* and *Y* on or below time budget line *GH* in the left panel (ignoring the income constraint). That is, budget line *GH* reflects only the individual's time constraint.

Let us now look at both budget lines together. The combination of *X* and *Y* given by point *L* in the left panel is above and can be achieved neither with income budget line *CF* nor with time budget line *GH*. Point *N* is on *CF* but above *GH*. Thus, the individual would have the income to purchase combination *N* but does not have sufficient time per month to enjoy *N*. The individual can achieve combination *R* because *R* is on *GH* and below *CF*. The individual can also achieve combination *S* since *S* is below both *CF* and *GH*. Thus, only combinations on or below *GEF* satisfy both the income

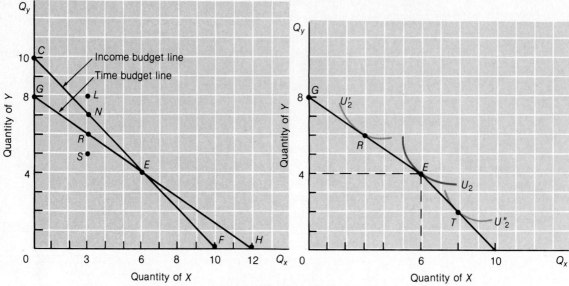

FIGURE 4-10. *Time as a Constraint*

In the left panel, CF is a usual income budget line and GH is a time budget line. The binding constraint is time over segment GE and income over EF. GEF is the boundary of the region showing all combinations of X and Y that satisfy both constraints simultaneously. With indifference curve U_2 in the right panel, the individual maximizes utility at point E by purchasing 6X and 4Y. At point E both income and time are binding constraints. If the individual's indifference curve is instead U_2', only the time constraint is binding and he or she can reach a higher indifference curve by working less. If the individual's indifference curve is U_2'' instead, only income is the binding constraint and he or she can reach a higher indifference curve by working more.

and the time constraint simultaneously.[10] Over the range GE, time is the binding constraint, while over segment EF, income is the binding constraint. The area bounded by the axes and GEF is the feasible region (what the individual can achieve with both his or her income and time constraints). The feasible region is repeated in the right panel.

In the right panel, if the individual's indifference curve is U_2, he or she would maximize satisfaction at point E (where both constraints are binding) by purchasing 6X (meals) and 4Y (games). If the individual's indifference curve were instead U_2', only the time constraint would be binding at tangency point R. It would then pay for the individual to work less (and have less money to spend) in order to have more time for meals and games. This would shift down the income budget line and shift up the time budget line. The individual would then be able to reach an indifference curve higher than U_2' at the point where both budget lines cross so that both constaints would just be binding (not shown in the figure).

[10] Note that GEF is not a straight line but bends at point E.

The opposite is true if the individual's indifference curve is U_2''. That is, with U_2'', income is the only binding constraint at tangency point T. The individual, therefore, should work more (so as to have more money to spend). As he or she does, the income budget line shifts up and the time budget line shifts down. This individual should continue to substitute work for free time until both constraints become binding. The individual would then reach the highest indifference curve of type U_2'' (higher than U_2'') possible (not shown in the figure).

Summary

1. The income-consumption curve joins consumer optimum points resulting when only the consumer's income is varied. The Engel curve is derived from the income-consumption curve and shows the amount of a good that the consumer would purchase per unit of time at various income levels. A normal good is one of which the consumer purchases more with an increase in income. An inferior good is one of which the consumer purchases less with an increase in income. The income-consumption curve and the Engel curve are positively sloped for normal goods and negatively sloped for inferior goods.

2. The price-consumption curve for a good joins consumer optimum points resulting when only the price of the good varies. This shows the amount of the good that the consumer would purchase per unit of time at various prices of the good, while holding everything else constant. The individual consumer's demand curve for a good is negatively sloped, reflecting the law of demand. Demand is elastic, unitary elastic, or inelastic depending on whether the price-consumption curve is negatively sloped, horizontal, or positively sloped.

3. When the price of a good falls, consumers substitute this for other goods and their real income rises. If the good is normal, the income effect reinforces the substitution effect in increasing the quantity purchased of the good. If the good is inferior, the substitution effect tends to increase while the income effect tends to reduce the quantity demanded of the good. Since the former usually exceeds the latter, the quantity demanded of the good increases and the demand curve is negatively sloped. Only in the rare case where the income effect overwhelms the opposite substitution effect for an inferior good will the quantity demanded of the good decrease when its price falls, and the demand curve slopes upward. This is very rare and is known as the Giffen paradox.

4. A cash subsidy leads to an equal or greater increase in utility than a subsidy in kind (such as the food stamp program) that costs the same. The consumer surplus is given by the difference between what the consumer is willing to pay for a good and what he actually pays for it. Its value can be approximated by the area under the demand curve and above the market price of the good. An Edgeworth box diagram is constructed by rotating by 180 degrees an individual's indifference map diagram and superimposing it on another's, so that the dimensions of the box equal the combined initial distribution of the two goods between the two individuals. It can be used to analyze voluntary exchange. Since the consumption of most goods involves the expenditure of both time and money, time should be included as an additional constraint.

Glossary

Income-consumption curve   The locus of consumer optimum points resulting when only the consumer's income varies.

Engel curve   It shows the amount of a good that a consumer would purchase at various income levels.

Normal good   A good of which the consumer purchases more with an increase in income.

Inferior good   A good of which a consumer purchases less with an increase in income.

Price-consumption curve   The locus of consumer
optimum points resulting when only the price of
a good varies.

Individual's demand curve   It shows the quantity
that the individual would purchase of the good
per unit of time at various alternative prices of
the good, while keeping everything else constant.

Substitution effect   The increase in the quantity
demanded of a good when its price falls resulting
only from the relative price decline and independent of the change in real income.

Relative price   The ratio of the price of a good to
the price of another.

Income effect   The increase in the quantity purchased of a good resulting only from the increase
in real income that accompanies a price decline.

Giffen paradox   An inferior good for which the

positive substitution effect is smaller than the
negative income effect so that less of the good is
purchased when its price falls.

Food stamp program   A federal program under
which eligible poor families receive free food
stamps to purchase food.

Consumer surplus   The difference between what
the consumer is willing to pay for a given quantity of a good and what he actually pays for it.

Water-diamond paradox   The question of why is
water, which is essential to life, so cheap while
diamonds, which are not essential, are so
expensive.

Edgeworth box diagram   A diagram constructed
from the indifference map diagrams of two individuals that can be used to analyze voluntary
exchange.

Time budget line   A line showing the various combinations of two goods that an individual can
obtain with his or her time available.

Questions for Review

1. (a) What does an income-consumption curve
   show?
   (b) How is an income-consumption curve
   derived?
   (c) What is the slope of indifference curves
   along the income-consumption curve?
   Why?

2. (a) What is an Engel Curve?
   (b) How is an Engel curve derived?
   (c) What are Engel curves used for?

3. (a) What is a normal good? An inferior good?
   (b) What is the shape of the income-consumption curve and Engel curve for a normal
   good?
   (c) What is the shape of the income-consumption curve and Engel curve for an inferior
   good?
   (d) Can a good be normal for one individual
   and at one income level and inferior for
   another individual and at another income
   level?

4. (a) What does the price-consumption curve
   show?
   (b) How is a price-consumption curve derived?

   (c) What does an individual's demand curve
   for a good show?
   (d) How is an individual's demand curve for a
   good derived?

5. Why is the demand curve for a good
   (a) elastic when the price-consumption curve
   is negatively sloped?
   (b) unitary elastic when the price-consumption
   curve is horizontal?
   (c) inelastic when the price-consumption
   curve is positively sloped?

6. (a) What is meant by the substitution effect? By
   the income effect?
   (b) How can the substitution effect of a price
   decline be conceptually separated from the
   income effect?
   (c) When the price of a normal good declines,
   does the substitution effect tend to increase
   or decrease the quantity purchased of the
   good per unit of time? What about the
   income effect?

7. (a) When the price of an inferior good declines,
   does the substitution effect tend to increase
   or decrease the quantity purchased of the

good per unit of time? What about the income effect?

(b) When the price of an inferior good declines, will more of it or less of it be purchased per unit of time? Why?

(c) Is the demand for an inferior good negatively or positively sloped?

8. (a) What is meant by the Giffen paradox?

(b) Must a Giffen good be an inferior good?

(c) Must an inferior good be a Giffen good?

9. (a) What is meant by the food stamp program? How does it operate?

(b) Does an equal amount of cash aid increase utility more than the food stamp program?

(c) To what other application in Chapter 3 is the figure for examining the food stamp program similar?

10. (a) What is meant by the consumer surplus?

(b) How can the consumer surplus be measured with a demand diagram?

(c) How did the concept of the consumer surplus help resolve the water-diamond paradox?

11. (a) What is an Edgeworth box diagram? How is it constructed? What is its use?

(b) What does any point inside the box indicate?

(c) What condition is required for voluntary exchange to take place?

(d) When will voluntary exchange come to an end?

12. (a) What is meant by a time budget line? How is it constructed?

(b) What is the relationship between the income and the time budget lines?

(c) How is utility maximization affected by consideration of both the income and the time constraints?

Problems

1. (a) Derive the income-consumption curve and Engel curve from the indifference curves of Problem 2 in Chapter 3 and the budget lines from Problem 6a in Chapter 3. Is good X a normal or an inferior good? Why?

(b) Derive the Engel curve for good Y. Is good Y a normal or an inferior good? Why?

2. (a) For the budget lines of Problem 6a in Chapter 3, draw indifference curves that show that good X is inferior; derive the income-consumption curve and the Engel curve for good X.

(b) Draw the Engel curve for good Y. Must good Y be normal?

★3. (a) Derive the price-consumption curve and demand curve for good X from the indifference curves of Problem 2 in Chapter 3 and the budget lines from Problem 6b in Chapter 3 when the price of X falls from $P_x = \$2$ to $P_x = \$1$ and then to $P_x = \$0.50$.

(b) Use the figure for your answer to part (a) to explain how you would derive the

price-consumption curve and demand curve for good X when the price of X rises from $P_x = \$0.50$ to $P_x = \$1$ and then to $P_x = \$2$.

4. (a) Is the demand curve for good X (d_x) that you derived in Problem 3 elastic, unitary elastic, or inelastic? Why?

(b) Use the formula for arc elasticity to measure the price elasticity of d_x between points B' and E' and between points E' and G'.

5. Using the indifference curves of Problem 2 in Chapter 3 and the budget lines of Problem 6b in Chapter 3, separate the substitution from the income effect when the price of X falls from $P_x = \$2$ to $P_x = \$1$ and then from $P_x = \$1$ to $P_x = \$0.50$.

★6. Separate the substitution effect from the income effect for an *increase* in the price of an inferior good.

7. Separate the substitution effect from the income effect for an increase in price of a Giffen good.

★ = answer provided at the end of the book.

★8. It is sometimes asserted that rice in very poor Asian countries might be an inferior good. While there is no evidence that this is indeed the case, explain the reasoning behind the assertion.

9. Since the average number of children per family has declined in the face of rapidly rising family incomes, children must be an inferior good. True or false? Explain.

★10. Show with indifference curve analysis that a poor family can be made to reach a given higher indifference curve with a smaller cash subsidy than with a subsidy in kind (such as, for example, by the government paying half of the market price of food for the family). Why might the government still prefer a subsidy in kind?

11. With reference to Figure 4-8 in the text, indicate the size of the consumer surplus when $P_x = \$3$ if
   (a) good X can only be purchased in whole units.
   (b) good X can be purchased in infinitesimally small fractional units.

12. With reference to Figure 4-9 in the text, indicate how exchange could take place starting from the initial distribution of good X and good Y between individual A and individual B given by the intersection of U_1 and U_2'.

Supplementary Readings

For a problem-solving approach to the topics discussed in this chapter see

Dominick Salvatore, *Microeconomic Theory,* 2nd ed. (New York: McGraw-Hill, 1983), Chapter 5, Sections 5.6–5.9.

The ground-breaking work for the topics discussed in this chapter is found in

John R. Hicks, *Value and Capital,* 2nd ed. (Oxford: Oxford University Press, 1946), pp. 26–38.

For a discussion of the Giffen paradox, see

George J. Stigler, "Notes on the History of the Giffen Paradox," *Journal of Political Economy,* 1947, pp. 152–156.

The analysis of time as an economic good is found in

Gary S. Becker, "A Theory of the Allocation of Time," *Economic Journal,* 1965, pp. 493–517.

Market Demand and Elasticities

5-1 The Market Demand for a Commodity

5-2 Price Elasticity of Market Demand

5-3 Income Elasticity of Demand

5-4 Cross Elasticity of Demand

5-5 Marginal Revenue and Elasticity

5-6 Applications

Examples

5-1 The Market Demand for Potatoes

5-2 Estimated Short-Run and Long-Run Price Elasticities of Demand

5-3 Estimated Income Elasticities of Demand

5-4 Estimated Cross Elasticities of Demand

Applications

Application 1: Price Elasticity of Demand in Agriculture

Application 2: The Short-Run and Long-Run Demand for Gasoline

Application 3: Other Price Elasticities and Their Usefulness

Application 4: The Income Elasticity of Demand and the Negative Income Tax Proposal

Application 5: Cross Elasticities in the Courtroom

Chapter 5

Preview Questions

How is the market demand curve for a commodity obtained? What is its use?

How can the price elasticity at a point on the demand curve be measured?

What does the income elasticity of demand measure? What is its usefulness?

What does the cross elasticity of demand measure? What is its usefulness?

What is meant by marginal revenue?

What is the relationship between marginal revenue, price, and elasticity?

What are some important real-world applications of elasticities?

In Chapter 3, we have seen how the consumer maximizes the utility or satisfaction in spending his or her income. In Chapter 4, we have examined how the concept of utility maximization is used to derive an individual's demand curve for a commodity or good. We now want to see how the *market* demand curve for a commodity is obtained by summing up the individuals' demand curves for the commodity. As seen in Chapter 2, our interest in the market demand curve for a commodity arises from the fact that (together with the market supply curve) it determines the equilibrium price of the commodity.

After we have derived the market demand curve for a commodity, we will discuss the various elasticities of demand and their usefulness. It is often crucial in the analysis of many economic issues to have a measure of the responsiveness or sensitivity in the quantity demanded of a particular commodity to a change in its own price, in consumers' incomes, and in the price of other commodities. These define respectively, the price elasticity of demand (first examined in Section 2-2), the income elasticity of demand, and the cross elasticity of demand. We will see that whether the quantity demanded of a commodity changes very much or very little as a result of changes in prices and incomes makes a great deal of difference to the outcome of the analysis. An important dose of realism is introduced into the discussion by several examples that present real-world estimates of the various elasticities for many commodities.

Finally, since consumers' expenditures on a commodity represent the revenues of the producers or sellers of the commodity, the discussion is extended to the producers' side of the market. This is done by examining total and marginal revenues from the sale of the commodity and their relationship to the price elasticity of demand. The chapter concludes with several important applications of the various elasticity measures to highlight their usefulness and importance in the analysis of current economic issues.

5-1

The Market Demand for a Commodity

In this section we examine how the market demand curve for a commodity is derived from the individuals' demand curves. The **market demand curve** for a commodity is simply the *horizontal summation* of the demand curves of all the consumers in the market. Thus, the market quantity demanded at each price is the sum of the individual quantities demanded at that price. For example, in the top of Figure 5-1, the market demand curve for hamburgers (commodity X) is obtained by the horizontal summation of the demand curve of individual 1 (d_1) and individual 2 (d_2), on the assumption that they are the only two consumers in the market. Thus, at the price of $1, the market quantity demanded of 10 hamburgers is the sum of the 6 hamburgers demanded by individual 1 and the 4 hamburgers demanded by individual 2.

If instead there were one million individuals in the market, each with demand curve d_x, the market demand curve for hamburgers would be D_x (see the bottom part of Figure 5-1). Both D_x and d_x have the same shape, but the horizontal scale refers to millions of hamburgers. Note that d_x is the individual's demand curve for hamburgers derived in Chapter 4 (see Figure 4-3).

The market demand curve for a commodity shows the various quantities of the commodity demanded in the market per unit of time at various alternative prices of the commodity, while holding everything else constant. The market demand curve for a commodity (just as an individual's demand curve) is negatively sloped, indicating that price and quantity are inversely related. That is, the quantity demanded of the commodity increases when its price falls and decreases when price rises. The things held constant in drawing the market demand curve for a commodity are incomes, the prices of substitute and complementary commodities, tastes, and the number of consumers in the market. A change in any of these will cause the market demand curve for the commodity to shift (see Section 2-2b).[1]

Finally, it must be pointed out that a market demand curve is simply the horizontal summation of the individual demand curves *only if* the con-

---

[1] A change in expectations about the future price of the commodity will also affect its demand curve. For example, the expectation that the price of the commodity will be lower in the future will shift the market demand curve to the left (so that less is demanded at each price in the current period) as consumers postpone some of their purchases of the commodity in anticipation of a lower price in the future.

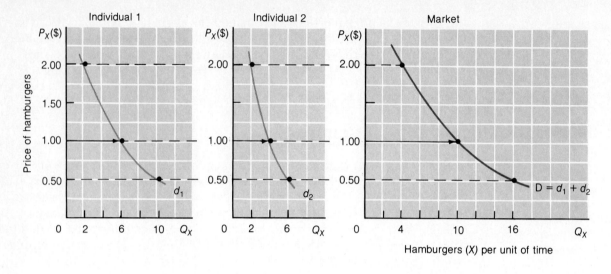

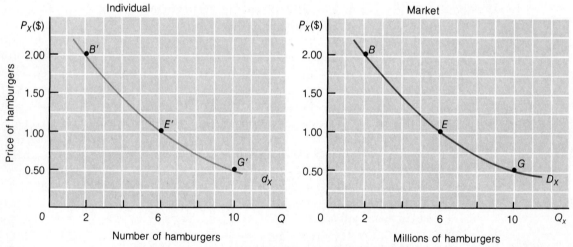

FIGURE 5-1.   From Individual to Market Demand

The top part of the figure shows that the market demand curve for hamburgers, D, is obtained from the horizontal summation of the demand curve for hamburgers of individual 1 (d₁) and individual 2 (d₂). The bottom part of the figure shows an individual's demand curve, dₓ, and the market demand curve, Dₓ, on the assumption that there are one million individuals in the market with demand curves for hamburgers identical to dₓ.

sumption decisions of individual consumers are independent. This is not always the case. For example, people sometimes demand a commodity because others are purchasing it and in order to be "fashionable." The result is a **bandwagon effect** to "keep up with the Joneses." That is, sometimes, the greater is the number of people purchasing a commodity as its price falls, the more people join in purchasing it in order to be fashionable and not feel left out. This results in the market demand curve for the commodity being flatter or more elastic than otherwise.

At other times, the opposite or **snob effect** occurs as many consumers seek to be different and exclusive by demanding less of a commodity as more people consume it. That is, as the price of a commodity falls and more people purchase the commodity, some people will stop buying it in order to stand out and be different. This tends to make the market demand curve steeper or less elastic than otherwise. There are then some individuals who, in order to impress people, demand more of certain commodities (such as diamonds, mink coats, Rolls Royces, etc.) the more expensive these goods are. This form of "conspicuous consumption" is called the **Veblen effect** (after Thorstein Veblen, who introduced it). For example, some high-income people may be less willing to purchase a $4,000 mink coat than a $10,000 one when the latter clearly looks much more expensive. This also results in a steeper or less elastic market demand curve for the commodity than otherwise.[2]

In what follows, we assume that the bandwagon, snob, and Veblen effects are not significant so that the market demand curve for the commodity can be obtained simply by the horizontal summation of the individual demand curves. An example of an actual demand function for a commodity estimated for the "average" consumer and the aggregation over all the consumers in the market is provided by the following example.

Example 5-1 The Market Demand for Potatoes

The Facts: The following demand function for potatoes was estimated for the U.S. over 1959–1973 period:

$$Q = 163.6 - 17.7P + 9.3I$$

where Q is the annual consumption of potatoes in pounds per capita or per person, P is the average price in dollars per one hundred pounds of potatoes, I is the average per capita income in thousands of 1958 dollars. Substituting the average income per capita of $2.344 (in thousands of dollars at 1958 prices) into the demand function, we get

$$Q = 163.6 - 17.7P + 9.3(2.344)$$
$$Q = 185.4 - 17.7P$$

---

[2] Conceivably, in some cases, the snob and Veblen effects could even make the market demand curve of the commodity positively sloped.

By then substituting various prices per one hundred pounds of potatoes into the above demand function, we get

P	$4.00	3.50	3.00	2.50	2.00	1.50
Q	115	123	132	141	150	159

Thus, at the price of $4 the average person demanded 115 pounds of potatoes per year in the U.S. over the period of the study. At $P = \$3.50$, he or she demanded 123 pounds, and so on.

Comment: When plotted, the above price-quantity data give a straight-line demand curve. This is the estimated per capita demand curve. It shows how many pounds of potatoes the average person demands per year at various prices. With one million persons in the market, only the horizontal scale need be changed to refer to millions of pounds to get the aggregate or market demand curve. (The student should sketch these demand curves, as in the bottom part of Figure 5-1.) Note that income is *explicitly* held constant in drawing such demand curves. On the other hand, by not including the prices of related commodities (substitutes and complements of potatoes) in the estimation of the above demand function we implicitly assumed that they did not affect the demand for potatoes. A detailed discussion of how empirical demand functions and demand curves are estimated in the real world is given in Chapter 6.

Source: Adapted from D. Suits, "Agriculture," in W. Adams, *The Structure of the American Economy,* 5th ed. (New York: Macmillan, 1977), pp. 1–39.

5-2

Price Elasticity of Market Demand

In this section, we show how we can measure graphically the price elasticity at any point on a demand curve. We also examine the important relationship between the price elasticity of demand and the total expenditures of consumers on the commodity. That is, when the price of a commodity changes, will consumers' expenditures on the commodity increase, decrease, or remain unchanged? Finally, we examine the determinants or the factors that affect the size of the price elasticity of demand. This section is an extension of the discussion of the price elasticity of demand presented in Section 2-2c, and so it may be useful for the student to go back to review that material.

5-2a Price Elasticity Graphically

In Section 2-2c, we defined the price elasticity of demand as -1 times the percentage change in the quantity demanded of a commodity divided by

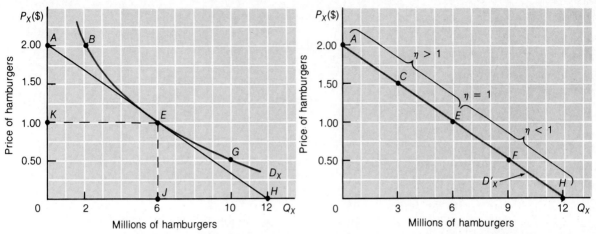

FIGURE 5-2. Measurement of Price Elasticity of Demand Graphically

In the left panel, the price elasticity at point E on D_x is measured by drawing tangent AEH to point E on D_x and dropping perpendicular EJ to the horizontal axis. At point E, η = JH/OJ = 6/6 = 1. In the right panel, η = 1 at point E (the midpoint of D'_x), η > 1 above the midpoint, and η < 1 below the midpoint.

the percentage change in its price. We now show how to measure graphically price elasticity at any point on a linear or nonlinear demand curve.

To measure the price elasticity at point E on D_x in the left panel of Figure 5-2, we proceed as follows. We draw tangent AEH to point E on D_x, and drop perpendicular EJ to the quantity axis. Minus 1 times the slope of tangent line AEH is constant throughout and can be measured by

$$-\frac{\Delta P}{\Delta Q} = \frac{JE}{JH}$$

The first component of the price elasticity formula is given by -1 times the inverse of the slope of the demand curve or

$$-\frac{\Delta Q}{\Delta P} = \frac{JH}{JE}$$

The second component of the price elasticity formula is

$$\frac{P}{Q} = \frac{JE}{OJ}$$

Reassembling the two components of the elasticity formula, we have

$$\eta = -\frac{\Delta Q}{\Delta P} \cdot \frac{P}{Q} = \frac{JH}{JE} \cdot \frac{JE}{OJ} = \frac{JH}{OJ} = \frac{6}{6} = 1$$

That is, the price elasticity of D_x at point E in the left panel of Figure 5-2 is equal to 1. Since EJH, AKE, and AOH are similar triangles (see the left panel of Figure 5-2), the price elasticity of D_x at point E can be measured by any of the following ratios of distances:

$$\eta = \frac{JH}{OJ} = \frac{OK}{KA} = \frac{EH}{AE} \qquad (5\text{-}1)$$

The price elasticity of demand at any other point on D_x can be found in a similar way by drawing a tangent to D_x at that point and then proceeding as indicated above (see Problem 1). This provides a very convenient and easy way to measure the price elasticity of demand at any point on a non-linear demand curve.

The same procedure can also be used to measure the price elasticity at any point on a straight-line demand curve. For example, by inspecting the right panel of Figure 5-2, we can find that $\eta = 9/3 = 3$ at point C on D'_x, $\eta = 3/9 = 1/3$ at point F, and $\eta = 6/6 = 1$ at point E (the midpoint of D'_x). Furthermore, $\eta \rightarrow \infty$ (infinity) at point A and $\eta = 0$ at point H (see Problem 2). Thus, while the slope of a straight-line demand curve is constant throughout, its price elasticity varies between each point on (and declines as we move down) the demand curve. As a general rule, a straight-line demand curve is unitary elastic at its geometric midpoint, price elastic above its midpoint, and inelastic below the midpoint (see the right panel of Figure 5-2).[3]

Two other simple rules are useful in considering the price elasticity of demand. The first is that, of two parallel demand curves (linear or nonlinear), the one further to the right has a smaller price elasticity at each price (see Problem 3a, with answer at the end of the text). Also, when two demand curves intersect, the flatter of the two is more price elastic at the point of intersection (see Problem 3b, with the answer also provided at the end of the text).

5-2b Price Elasticity and Total Expenditures

There is an important relationship between the price elasticity of demand and the total expenditures of consumers on the commodity. This relationship is often used in economics. It postulates that a decline in the commodity price results in an increase in total expenditures if demand is elastic, leaves total expenditures unchanged if demand is unitary elastic, and results in a decline in total expenditures if demand is inelastic.

Specifically, when the price of a commodity falls, total expenditures (price times quantity) increase if demand is elastic because the percentage

[3] For a mathematical derivation of the formula for point (price) elasticity of demand (as well as other elasticities) using rudimentary calculus, see Section A3 of the Mathematical Appendix.

TABLE 5-1   Total Expenditures and Price Elasticity of Demand

Point	P_x ($)	Q_x (Million Units)	Total Expenditures (Million $)	n
A	2.00	0	0	∞
C	1.50	3	4.5	3
E	1.00	6	6.0	1
F	0.50	9	4.5	⅓
H	0	12	0	0

increase in quantity (which by itself tends to increase total expenditures) exceeds the percentage decline in price (which by itself tends to reduce total expenditures). Total expenditures are maximum when $\eta = 1$ and decline thereafter. That is, when $\eta < 1$, a reduction in the commodity price leads to a percentage increase in the quantity demanded of the commodity that is smaller than the percentage reduction in price, and so total expenditures on the commodity declines. This is shown in Table 5-1, which refers to D'_x in Figure 5-2.

From Table 5-1, we see that between points A and E, $\eta > 1$ and total expenditures on the commodity increase as the commodity price declines. The opposite is true between points E and F over which $\eta < 1$. Total expenditures are maximum at point E (the geometric midpoint of D'_x in Figure 5-2). The general rule summarizing the relationship among total expenditures, price, and the price elasticity of demand is that *total expenditures and price move in opposite directions if demand is elastic and in the same direction if demand is inelastic* (see Table 5-1).

Figure 5-3 shows a demand curve that is unitary elastic throughout. Thus, $\eta = JH/JO = 6/6 = 1$ at point E on D^*, $\eta = LJ/OL = 3/3 = 1$ at point B', and $\eta = HN/OH = 12/12 = 1$ at point G'. Note that total expenditures (price times quantity) are constant ($6 million) at every point on D^*. This type of demand curve is a *rectangular hyperbola*. Its general equation is

$$Q = \frac{C}{P} \tag{5-2}$$

where Q is the quantity demanded, P is its price, and C is a constant (total expenditures). Thus, $P \cdot Q = C$. For example, at point B', $(P)(Q) = (\$2)(3) = \$6$. At point E, $(\$1)(6) = \$6$, and at point G', $(\$0.50)(12) = \$6$ also.

5-2c Factors Affecting Price Elasticity

Since the price elasticity of demand is so useful (i.e., it tells us, among other things, what happens to the level of total expenditures on the commodity when its price changes), it is very important to identify the forces that

135

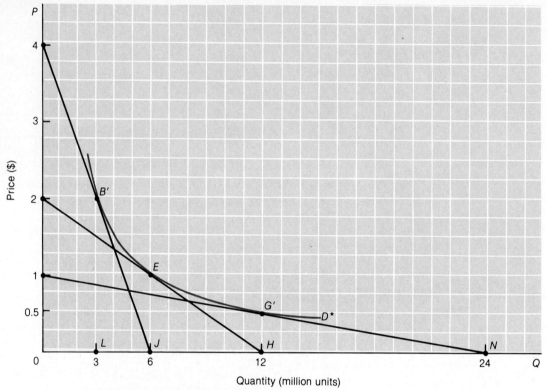

FIGURE 5-3. Unitary Elastic Demand Curve

Demand curve D* has unitary elasticity throughout. Thus, η = JH/OJ = 6/6 = 1 at point E, η = LJ/OL = 3/3 = 1 at point B', and η = HN/OH = 12/12 = 1 at point G'. Total expenditures (P Q) are the same ($6 million) at every point on D*. This demand curve is a rectangular hyperbola.

determine its value. The size of the price elasticity of demand depends primarily on two factors. *First* and foremost, *the price elasticity of demand for a commodity is larger the closer and the greater is the number of available substitutes.* For example, the demand for coffee is more elastic than the demand for salt because coffee has better and more substitutes (tea and cocoa) than salt. Thus, the same percentage increase in the price of coffee and salt elicits a larger percentage reduction in the quantity demanded of coffee than of salt.

In general, a commodity has closer substitutes and thus a higher price elasticity of demand the more narrowly the commodity is defined. For example, the price elasticity for Marlboro cigarettes is much larger than for cigarettes in general, and still larger than for all tobacco products. If a commodity is defined so that it has perfect substitutes, its price elasticity of demand is infinite. For example, if a wheat farmer attempted to increase his or her price above the market price, he or she would lose all sales as buyers switch all their wheat purchases to other farmers (who produce identical wheat).

Second, *price elasticity is larger, the longer is the period of time allowed for consumers to adjust to a change in the commodity price.* The reason for this is that it usually takes time for consumers to learn of a price change and to fully respond or adjust their purchases to it. For example, consumers may not be able to reduce the quantity demanded of electricity very much, soon after they learn of an increase in the price of electricity. However, over a period of several years, households can replace electric with gas heaters, purchase electrical appliances that consume less electricity, and so on. Thus, for a given price change, the quantity response *per unit of time* is usually much greater in the long run than in the short run, and so η is larger in the former than in the latter time period. This is clearly shown in the following example.[4]

Example 5-2 **Estimated Short-Run and Long-Run Price Elasticities of Demand**

The Facts: Table 5-2 gives estimated price elasticities of demand (η) for selected commodities in the United States right after the price change (i.e., in the short run) and after sufficient time is allowed for consumers to fully adjust to the price change (i.e., in the long run).

TABLE 5-2 Estimated Short-Run and Long-Run Price Elasticity of Demand (η) for Selected Commodities, United States

Commodity	Elasticity	
	Short Run	Long Run
Radio and TV repairs	0.47	3.84
Motion pictures	0.87	3.67
China and glassware	1.54	2.55
Tobacco products	0.46	1.89
Electricity (household)	0.13	1.89
Foreign travel	0.14	1.77
Bus transportation (local)	0.20	1.20
Medical insurance	0.31	0.92
Jewelry and watches	0.41	0.67
Stationery	0.47	0.56

Source: H. S. Houthakker and L. D. Taylor, *Consumer Demand in the United States: Analyses and Projections* (Cambridge, Mass.: Harvard University Press, 1970).

[4] Sometimes it is stated that the price elasticity of demand is larger the greater is the number of uses of the commodity. However, no satisfactory reason has been advanced as to why this should be so. It is also sometimes said that price elasticity is lower the smaller is the importance of the commodity in consumers' budgets (i.e., the smaller is the proportion of the consumers' incomes spent on the commodity). However, empirical estimates often contradict this.

137

Comment: Table 5-2 shows that long-run price elasticities for most commodities are much larger than corresponding short-run price elasticities. (It was these long-run elasticities that were presented in Table 2-2). For example, the price elasticity of demand for radio and TV repairs (the first row in the table) is only 0.47 in the short run but becomes 3.84 in the long run. This means, for example, that a 1 per cent increase in price leads to a reduction in the quantity demanded of radio and TV repairs of only 0.47 per cent in the short run but of 3.84 per cent in the long run. Evidently, people get frustrated by rising radio and TV repair prices and purchase new radios and TV sets in the long run rather than have their old sets repaired. On the other hand, η rises only from 0.47 in the short run to 0.56 in the long run for stationery (the last row of Table 5-2). Evidently, people cannot find suitable substitutes for stationery even in the long run, and so the long run price elasticity remains very low. It should be noted that estimated price elasticity of demand for any commodity is likely to vary (sometimes widely) depending on the nation under consideration, the time period examined, and the estimation technique used. Thus, estimated price elasticity values should be used cautiously.

5-3

Income Elasticity of Demand

In Section 4-1 we defined an **Engel curve** as showing the amount of a commodity that a consumer would purchase per unit of time at various income levels, while holding prices and tastes constant. We can measure the responsiveness or sensitivity in the quantity demanded of a commodity at any point on the Engel curve by the **income elasticity of demand.** This is defined as

$$\eta_I = \frac{\Delta Q/Q}{\Delta I/I} = \frac{\Delta Q}{\Delta I} \cdot \frac{I}{Q} \tag{5-3}$$

where ΔQ is the change in the quantity purchased, ΔI is the change in income, Q is the original quantity, and I is the original money income of the consumer.

A commodity is normal if η_I is positive and inferior if η_I is negative. A normal good can be further classified as a **necessity** if η_I is less than 1 and as a **luxury** if η_I is greater than 1. In the real world, most broadly defined commodities such as food, clothing, housing, health care, education, and recreation are normal goods. Inferior goods are usually narrowly defined inexpensive goods, such as bologna, for which good substitutes are available. Among normal goods, food and clothing are necessities while education and recreation are luxuries.

TABLE 5-3 Income Elasticity and Classification of Hamburgers (*X*) at Various Daily Income Allowances

I	Q_x	$\%\Delta Q_x$	$\%\Delta I$	η_I	Classification
10	2	. . .	. . .	. . .	. . .
15	4	100	50	2.00	Luxury
20	5	25	33	0.76	Necessity
30	6	20	50	0.40	Necessity
40	4	−33	33	−1.00	Inferior

The above classification of goods into inferior and normal, and necessity and luxury cannot be taken too seriously, however, since the same commodity can be regarded as a luxury by some individuals or at some income level, and as a necessity or even as an inferior good by other individuals or at other income levels.[5] There is a very simple geometric method to determine if a commodity is a luxury, a necessity, or an inferior good at each income level. If the tangent to the Engel curve is positively sloped and crosses the income axis, η_I exceeds 1 and the good is a luxury at that income level. If the tangent crosses the origin, $\eta_I = 1$. If the tangent crosses the horizontal axis, η_I is less than 1 and the commodity is a necessity at that income level. Finally, if the tangent to the Engel curve is negatively sloped, the commodity is an inferior good.

For example, Figure 5-4 and Table 5-3 show that the student of Chapters 3 and 4 would regard hamburgers as a luxury at income levels (allowances) of up to $15 per day. Hamburgers would become a necessity for daily allowances of between $15 and $30 and would be regarded as an inferior good at higher incomes (where the student can afford steaks and lobsters).

The concept and measurement of the income elasticity of demand and Engel curve can refer to a single consumer or to the entire market. When referring to the entire market, Q and ΔQ are the total or the market quantity purchased and its change, while I and ΔI are the total or aggregate money income of all consumers in the market and its change.[6]

As pointed out in Section 4-1, the proportion of total expenditures on food declines as family incomes rise. This is referred to as **Engel's law.** Indeed, the higher the proportion of income spent on food, the poorer a family or nation is taken to be. For example, in the U.S. less than 20 per cent of total family incomes is spent on food as compared with over 50 per cent for India (a much poorer nation).

[5] Indeed, some economists feel that the necessity/luxury classification of goods is entirely spurious and meaningless.

[6] However, it should be remembered that the income elasticity of market demand is not well defined unless it is also specified on which commodities income increments are spent.

FIGURE 5-4.
Engel Curve and
Income Elasticity

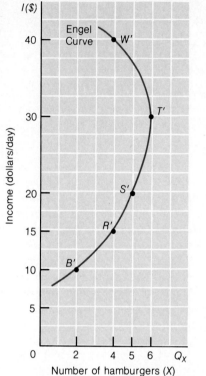

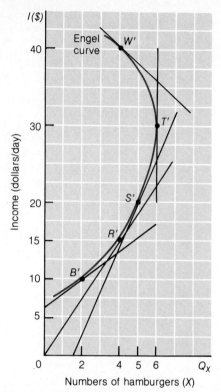

Since the tangent to the Engel curve is positively sloped and crosses the income axis up to the daily income allowance of $15, hamburgers are a luxury for this individual (student). Since the tangent goes through the origin at I = $15, $\eta_I = 1$ at that income level. Since the tangent is positively sloped and crosses the quantity axis at I from $15 to $30, hamburgers are a necessity between these income levels. For I higher than $30, the Engel curve is negatively sloped and hamburgers become an inferior good for this individual.

Example 5-3   Estimated Income Elasticities of Demand

The Facts: Table 5-4 gives estimated income elasticities of demand (η_I) for selected commodities in the United States.

Comment: All commodities listed in Table 5-4 can be taken to be luxuries except for tobacco products and china and glassware (which are necessities) and margarine and flour (which are inferior goods). More recent studies on margarine, however, seem to indicate that it is no longer an inferior good. The income elasticities given in Table 5-4 are measured as the percentage change in expenditures on the various commodities (rather than the percentage change in the *quantity* purchased of the various goods) resulting from a given percentage change in income. To the extent that prices are held constant, however, we get the same results as if the per-

140

TABLE 5-4   Estimated Income Elasticity of Demand (η_I) for Selected Commodities, United States

Commodity	Income Elasticity	Commodity	Income Elasticity
Radio and TV repairs	5.20	Stationery	1.83
Motion pictures	3.41	Jewelry and watches	1.64
Foreign travel	3.09	Tobacco products	0.86
Medical insurance	2.02	China and glassware	0.77
Electricity (household)	1.94	Margarine	−0.20
Bus transportation (local)	1.89	Flour	−0.36

Source: H. S. Houthakker and L. D. Taylor, *Consumer Demand in the United States: Analyses and Projections* (Cambridge, Mass.: Harvard University Press, 1970), and H. Wold and L. Jureen, *Demand Analysis* (New York: Wiley, 1953).

centage change in quantity were used. Table 5-4 shows that a 1 per cent increase in income leads to a 5.2 per cent increase in consumers' expenditures on radio and TV repairs but to a 0.36 per cent *decline* in expenditures on flour. However, as pointed out earlier, the interpretation of these income elasticity values is not as clear-cut and precise as the price elasticity of demand discusssed earlier.

5-4

Cross Elasticity of Demand

We have seen in Section 2-2a that one of the things held constant in drawing the market demand curve for a commodity is the price of substitute and complementary commodities. Commodities X and Y are **substitutes** if more of X is purchased when the price of Y goes up. For example, consumers usually purchase more coffee when the price of tea rises. Thus, coffee and tea are substitutes. Other examples of substitutes are butter and margarine, hamburgers and hot dogs, Coca Cola and Seven Up, electricity and gas, and so on.

On the other hand, commodities X and Y are **complements** if less of X is purchased when the price of Y goes up. For example, consumers usually purchase fewer lemons when the price of tea goes up. Thus, lemons and tea are complements. Other examples of commodities that are complements are coffee and cream, hamburgers and buns, hot dogs and mustard, cars and gasoline, and so on.

An increase in the price of a commodity leads to a reduction in the quantity demanded of the commodity (a movement along the demand curve for the commodity) but causes the demand curve for a substitute to shift to the right and the demand curve for a complement to shift to the left. For example, an increase in the price of tea will cause the demand for coffee (a substitute of tea) to shift to the right (so that more coffee is demanded at each

141

coffee price) and the demand for lemons (a complement of tea) to shift to the left (so that fewer lemons are demanded at each lemons price).

We can measure the responsiveness or sensitivity in the quantity purchased of commodity X as a result of a change in the price of commodity Y by the **cross elasticity of demand** (η_{xy}). This is given by:

$$\eta_{xy} = \frac{\Delta Q_x / Q_x}{\Delta P_y / P_y} = \frac{\Delta Q_x}{\Delta P_y} \cdot \frac{P_y}{Q_x} \tag{5-4}$$

where ΔQ_x is the change in the quantity purchased of X, ΔP_y is the change in the price of Y, P_y is the original price of Y, and Q_x is the original quantity of X. Note that in measuring η_{xy}, we hold constant P_x, consumers' incomes, their tastes, and the number of consumers in the market.

If η_{xy} is greater than zero, X and Y are substitutes because an increase in P_y leads to an increase in Q_x, as X is substituted for Y in consumption. On the other hand, if η_{xy} is less than zero, X and Y are complements because an increase in P_y leads to a reduction in (Q_y and) Q_x. The absolute value (i.e., the value without the sign) of the cross elasticity of demand measures the degree of substitution or complementarity. For example, if η_{xy} between coffee and tea is found to be larger than that between coffee and hot chocolate, this means that coffee and tea are better substitutes than coffee and hot chocolate. If η_{xy} is close to zero, X and Y are independent commodities. This may be the case with cars and pencils, telephones and chewing gum, pocket calculators and beer, and so on.

Several additional things must be kept in mind with respect to the cross elasticity of demand. *First*, the value of η_{yx} need not equal the value of η_{xy} since the responsiveness of Q_x to a change in P_y need not equal the responsiveness of Q_y to a change in P_x. For example, a change in the price of coffee is likely to have a greater effect on the quantity of sugar (a complement of coffee) demanded than the other way around, since coffee is the more important of the two in terms of total expenditures.

Second, a high positive cross elasticity of demand is often used to define an industry since it indicates that the various commodities are very similar. For example, the cross elasticity of demand between Chevrolets and Oldsmobiles is very high and so they belong to the same (auto) industry. This can lead to some difficulty, however. For example, how high must the positive cross elasticity between two commodities be for them to be in the same industry? Also, if the cross elasticity between cars and station wagons and between station wagons and trucks is "high" but the cross elasticity of demand between cars and trucks is "low," are cars and trucks in the same industry? In these cases the definition of the industry usually depends on the problem to be studied.

Third, the above definition of substitutes and complements is sometimes referred to as a "gross" definition; as such, it refers to the entire market response and reflects both the income and the substitution effects. For an individual consumer, there is a more rigorous definition (in terms of the substitution effect only) discussed in more advanced texts (the interested reader is referred to the work of Hicks in the Supplementary Readings).

Example 5-4 Estimated Cross Elasticities of Demand

The Facts: Table 5-5 gives estimated cross elasticity of demand (η_{xy}) for selected commodities in the United States (except for sugar and fruits, and cheese and butter, which refer to the United Kingdom).

Comment: The cross elasticity of demand for the first six sets of commodities (referring to the U.S.) are all positive, indicating that these commodities are substitutes. Note that the values of η_{xy} differ from the values of η_{yx}. Only sugar and fruits, and cheese and butter have negative cross elasticities of demand (for the U.K.), indicating that they are complements. From the table, we can see that a 1 per cent increase in the price of butter (Y) results in an increase in the quantity purchased of margarine (X) of 0.81 per cent. However, a 1 per cent increase in the price of margarine results in an increase in the quantity purchased of butter of 0.67 per cent. On the other hand, a 1 per cent increase in the price of butter leads to a *reduction* in the quantity purchased of cheese of 0.61 per cent in the U.K. It should also be noted that it is possible that in some situations a particular pair of commodities will be substitutes while in other situations the same pair of goods will be complements.

TABLE 5-5   Estimated Cross Elasticity of Demand (η_{xy}) between Selected Commodities, United States

Commodity	Cross Elasticity with Respect to Price of Following Commodity	Cross Elasticity
Margarine	Butter	+0.81
Butter	Margarine	+0.67
Natural gas	Fuel oil	+0.44
Electricity (household)	Natural gas	+0.20
Beef	Pork	+0.28
Pork	Beef	+0.14
Sugar	Fruits	−0.28*
Cheese	Butter	−0.61*

*United Kingdom
Source: H. Wold and L. Jureen, *Demand Analysis* (New York: Wiley, 1953); R. Halvorsen, "Energy Substitution in U.S. Manufacturing," *The Review of Economics and Statistics*, Nov. 1977; R. Stone, *The Measurement of Consumer's Expenditures and Behavior in the U.K., 1920–1938*, Vol. 1 (Cambridge University Press, 1954).

Marginal Revenue and Elasticity

Up to this point, we have examined demand from the consumers' side only. However, consumers' expenditures on a commodity are the receipts or the total revenues of the sellers of the commodity. In this section, we look at the sellers' side of the market. We begin by defining marginal revenue and showing how the marginal revenue curve can be derived geometrically from the demand curve. Then we examine the relationship between marginal revenue, price, and the price elasticity of demand. Thus, the material of this section represents the link or bridge between the theory of demand (Part II of the text) and the theory of the firm (Part IV: Chapters 10–13).

5-5a Demand, Total Revenue, and Marginal Revenue

The total amount of money earned by sellers of a commodity is called **total revenue (TR)**; it is equal to the price per unit of the commodity times the quantity of the commodity sold. **Marginal revenue (MR)** is then the change in total revenue per unit change in the quantity sold; MR is calculated by dividing the change in total revenue (ΔTR) by the change in the quantity sold (ΔQ):

$$MR = \frac{\Delta TR}{\Delta Q} \tag{5-5}$$

We can also show that the sum of the marginal revenues on all units of the commodity sold equals total revenue.

In Table 5-6, price (column 1) and quantity (column 2) give the demand schedule of the commodity. Price times quantity gives total revenue (column 3). The change in total revenue resulting from each additional unit of

TABLE 5-6 Demand, Total Revenue, and Marginal Revenue

P (1)	Q (2)	TR (3)	MR (4)	Sum of MR's (5)
$11	0	$ 0	. . .	. . .
10	1	10	$10	$10
9	2	18	8	18
8	3	24	6	24
7	4	28	4	28
6	5	30	2	30
5	6	30	0	30
4	7	28	−2	28
3	8	24	−4	24

the commodity sold gives the marginal revenue (column 4). As a check on the calculations, we see that the sum of the marginal revenues equals total revenues (column 5). Note that TR/Q equals **average revenue (AR),** and $AR = P$ (the height of the demand curve).

The information given in Table 5-6 is plotted in Figure 5-5. The top panel gives the total revenue curve. The bottom panel gives the corresponding demand (D) and marginal revenue curves. Since MR is defined as the change in TR per unit change in Q, the MR values are plotted at the mid-point of each quantity interval in the bottom panel of Figure 5-5. On the other hand, points on the TR and D curves are plotted at each level of output. For example, at $P = \$11$, $Q = 0$ and so TR (which equals P times Q) is zero and is plotted at the origin in the top panel of Figure 5-5. At $P = \$10$, $Q = 1$ and so $TR = \$10$ and MR ($\Delta TR/\Delta Q$) is also $\$10$. This TR value is plotted at $Q = 1$ in the top panel, while the corresponding MR is plotted between $Q = 0$ and $Q = 1$ (i.e., at $Q = 0.5$) in the bottom panel.

The MR curve starts at the same point on the vertical axis as the D curve and is everywhere else below the D curve. The reason is that to sell one more unit of the commodity, price must be lowered not only for the additional unit sold but also on all previous units. For example, we see in Table 5-6 that to sell the second unit of the commodity, price must be lowered from $\$10$ to $\$9$ on both units. Therefore, the MR on the second unit is given by $P = \$9$ (a point on D) minus the $\$1$ reduction on the price of the first unit. That is, $MR = \$8$, which is lower than P, so the MR curve is below the D curve (see the bottom panel of Figure 5-5). When D is elastic, MR is positive because an increase in Q increases TR. When D is unitary elastic, $MR = 0$ because an increase in Q leaves TR unchanged (at its maximum level). When D is inelastic, MR is negative because an increase in Q reduces TR (see the bottom panel of Figure 5-5). We will make a great deal of use of the relationship between the demand curve and the marginal revenue curve in Part IV of the text, where we deal with the theory of the firm and market structure.

5-5b The Geometry of Marginal Revenue Determination

The marginal revenue curve for a straight-line and for a nonlinear demand curve can easily be found geometrically. This is shown in Figure 5-6. In the left panel, we can find the marginal revenue corresponding to point C on D_x' by dropping perpendicular CJ to the vertical axis and CW to the horizontal axis, and then subtracting distance AJ from CW. This identifies point C'. Thus, at $Q = 3$, $P = WC = \$1.50$ and $MR = WC' = \$1.00$. Similarly, by dropping perpendiculars EK and EE' from point E on D_x' and subtracting distance AK from EE', we get point E'. Thus, at $Q = 6$, $P = E'E = \$1$ and $MR = 0$. By joining points C' and E' we derive the MR_x' curve shown in the left panel of Figure 5-6. Note that the MR_x' curve starts at point A (as the D_x' curve) and every point bisects (i.e., cuts in half) the distance from the D_x' curve to the vertical or price axis. (Indeed, this provides an alter-

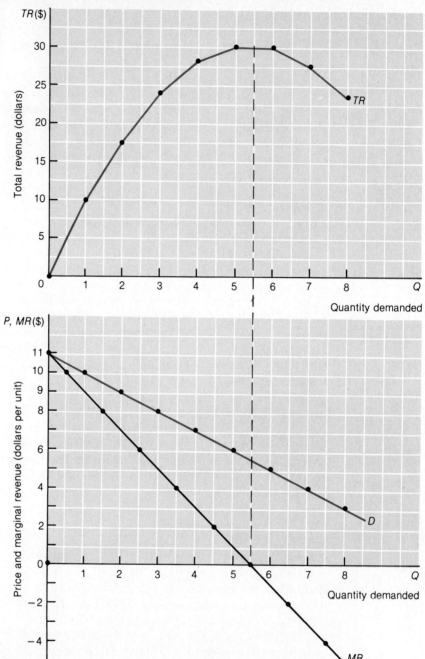

FIGURE 5-5.
*Total Revenue,
Demand, and
Marginal Revenue*

Total revenue rises up to 5 units of the commodity sold, remains constant between 5
and 6 units, and declines thereafter. When D is elastic, MR is positive because TR
increases. When D is unitary elastic, MR = O because TR is constant (at its maximum), and when D is inelastic, MR is negative because TR declines.

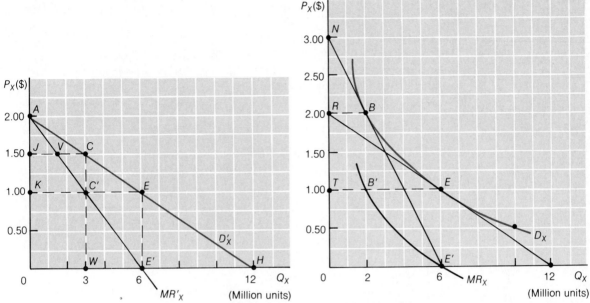

FIGURE 5-6. Marginal Revenue Determination

In the left panel, for point C on the D'x curve, MR = C'W and is obtained by sub-tracting distance AJ from price CW. For point E, MR = O and was obtained by sub-tracting distance AK = EE' from Px. In the right panel, to find the MR at point B we draw a tangent to the Dx curve at point B and then we move down distance NR from point B. This identifies point B' on the MRx curve. By moving down distance RT from point E on the Dx curve, we define point E' (MR = O) on the MRx curve.

native but equivalent method of deriving the MR curve geometrically for a straight-line demand curve.) Thus, JV = ½JC, KC' = ½KE, and OE' = ½OH (see the figure).

To find the marginal revenue curve corresponding to any point on a non-linear demand curve, we draw a tangent to the demand curve at that point and then proceed as above. Thus, to find the marginal revenue correspond-ing to point B on D_x in the right panel of Figure 5-6, we draw the tangent to demand curve D_x at point B and move distance NR downward from point B. This identifies point B' on the MR_x curve. Another point on the MR_x curve is obtained by moving distance RT down from point E. This identifies point E'. Other points on the MR_x curve can similarly be obtained. By join-ing these points we get the MR_x curve for the D_x curve (see the right panel of Figure 5-6). Note that when the demand curve is nonlinear, the marginal revenue curve is also nonlinear.

We can prove that this method gives the value of the marginal revenue corresponding to any point on a demand curve by returning to the left panel of Figure 5-6. At point C on the D'_x curve, TR = OJCW. However, TR is also equal to the sum of the *MR*'s. Thus, we must identify point C' such that $OAC'W = OJCW$. These two areas would have $OJVC'W$ in common. Now, only if $CC' = AJ$ will triangle AJV and VCC' be congruent and equal in area, so that $OAC'W = OJCW$. Thus, to find point C' we must move distance AJ downward from point C (as, indeed, we have done earlier in deriving the value of MR_x' corresponding to D_x' at $Q = 3$).

5-5c Marginal Revenue, Price, and Elasticity

There is an important and often-used relationship among marginal revenue, price, and the price elasticity of demand given by

$$MR = P(1 - 1/\eta) \tag{5-6}$$

For example, at point C on D_x' in the left panel of Figure 5-6, $\eta = WH/OW = 9/3 = 3$, and

$$MR = \$1.50(1 - 1/3) = \$1.00$$

(the same as WC' found earlier geometrically). At point E, $\eta = E'H/OE' = 6/6 = 1$, and $MR = \$1.00(1 - 1/1) = \$1.00(0) = 0$. At point A, $\eta = OH/O = 12/0 = \infty$ (infinity), and $MR = \$2.00(1 - 1/\infty) = \$2.00(1 - 0) = \$2.00$.

Formula (5-6) also applies to nonlinear demand curves. For example, at point B on D_x in the right panel of Figure 5-6, $\eta = 4/2 = 2$ and

$$MR = \$2.00(1 - 1/2) = \$1.00$$

FIGURE 5-7.
Demand Curve for
the Output of a
Perfectly
Competitive Firm

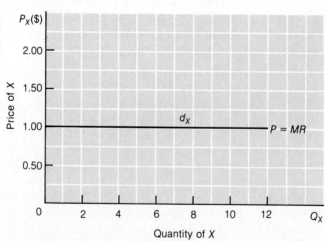

The demand curve for the output of a perfectly competitive firm is horizontal or infinitely elastic. Thus, MR = P and the demand curve and the marginal revenue curve coincide.

(the same as found earlier geometrically). Similarly, at point E,
$\eta = 6/6 = 1$ and $MR = \$1.00(1 - 1/1) = 0$.

Formula (5-6) can be derived with reference to the straight-line demand curve in the left panel of Figure 5-6. Take, for example, point C on D'_x. At point C,

$$\eta = WH/OW = CH/AC = JO/AJ$$

But $JO = CW$ and, by congruent triangles, $AJ = CC'$. Hence,

$$\eta = JO/AJ = CW/CC' = CW/(CW - WC')$$
$$= P/(P - WC') = P/(P - MR)$$

With this result, we manipulate the equation algebraically, to isolate MR on the left-hand side:

$$\eta(P - MR) = P$$
$$P - MR = P/\eta$$
$$-MR = P/\eta - P$$
$$MR = P - P/\eta$$
$$MR = P(1 - 1/\eta) \text{ [Expression (5-6)}^7\text{]}$$

So far, we have discussed the market demand curve for a commodity (D'_x or D_x in Figure 5-6). If there is only one producer or seller in the market (a monopolist), the firm faces the market demand curve for the commodity. When there is more than one producer or seller of the commodity, each firm will face a demand curve that is more elastic than the market demand curve because of the possible substitution among the products of the different firms. With a very large number of sellers of a homogeneous or identical product, the demand curve for the output of each firm might be horizontal or infinitely elastic (perfect competition). Then the change in total revenue in selling one additional unit of the commodity (i.e., the marginal revenue) equals price. This is confirmed by using Formula (5-6). That is,

$$MR = P(1 - 1/\infty) = P$$

For example, in Figure 5-7, if the firm sells $5X$, its $TR = \$5$. If it sells $6X$, $TR = \$6$. Thus, $MR = P = \$1$, and the demand curve and the marginal revenue curves coincide. (The perfectly competitive model will be examined in Chapter 10.)

---

[7] For a more straightforward derivation of Expression (5-6) using simple calculus, see Section A6 of the Mathematical Appendix.

5-6

Applications

In this section, we apply the various elasticities of demand examined in this chapter to analyze a number of important economic problems and uses. These amply demonstrate the importance of elasticities in (1) understanding the economic problems faced by American farmers, (2) evaluating the response of motorists to the sharp increase in petroleum prices during the 1970s, and (3) reaching correct decisions in business and government. We will see that the actual value of the elasticity coefficients often makes a crucial difference to the outcome of the analysis.

Application 1: Price Elasticity of Demand in Agriculture

The price elasticity of demand for agricultural commodities is central to understanding the economic problems faced by American farmers and the economics of farm aid programs. Only by making use of the price elasticity of demand in agriculture can we provide correct answers to such crucial questions as the following: Why are farmers often better off with bad than with good harvests? Why do individual farmers then strive to produce as much as possible each year? By how much should the government raise or lower the price of agricultural commodities in order to raise farmers' income to a specific target level?

Many empirical studies have found that the market demand curve for most agricultural commodities is price inelastic. As a result, a bad harvest and a smaller quantity brought to market will lead to higher prices and larger total revenues (incomes) of farmers than a good harvest. For example, suppose that D_w in Figure 5-8 is the market demand curve for wheat. With 6 billion bushels of wheat brought to market under normal weather conditions, the price of wheat would be $1 per bushel (point E) and the total revenue of wheat farmers would be $6 billion. With a bad harvest of $Q_w = 4$ billion bushels, $P_w = \$2$ (point E') and $TR = \$8$ billion. On the other hand, with a good harvest of $Q_w = 8$ billion bushels, $P_w = \$0.50$ (point E'') and $TR = \$4$ billion. However, given that the wheat production of each individual farmer is too small to affect wheat prices, each farmer must produce as much wheat as possible in times of good or bad harvests to maximize his or her income.

The fact that the market demand curve for agricultural commodities is inelastic also explains why government farm aid programs seek to increase farm prices in order to raise farmers' incomes. How high farm prices must be raised in order to increase farmers' incomes by a given amount depends on how inelastic the market demand curve is.

Application 2: The Short-Run and Long-Run Demand for Gasoline

It was estimated that a 50% increase in the price of gasoline (about the size of the increase in 1973–1974 and 1979–1980 in the U.S.) would reduce gas-

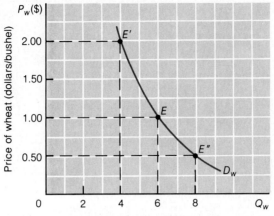

FIGURE 5-8.
Market Demand for
Wheat and Total
Revenue of Wheat
Farmers

D_w is the market demand curve for wheat. With 6 billion bushels of wheat brought to market under normal weather conditions, the price of wheat would be $1 per bushel (point E) and the total revenue (income) of wheat farmers would be $6 billion. With a bad harvest of Q_w = 4 billion bushels, P_w = $2 (point E'), and TR = $8 billion. With a good harvest of Q_w = 8 billion bushels, P_w = $0.50 (point E") and TR = $4 billion.

oline consumption in the U.S. by about 15% in the year immediately following the price increase.[8] This implies a short-run price elasticity of demand of about 0.3 (i.e., η = %ΔQ/%ΔP = 15%/50% = 0.3). The reduction in gasoline consumption would be achieved in the short run mostly through a reduction in the number of miles driven and through an increase in the miles per gallon (resulting from better tuned cars and lower highway speeds).

In the long run (i.e., over a period of 5 years or more following the price increase), it was estimated that yearly gasoline consumption in the U.S. would decrease by about 28% primarily as a result of shifting from gas guzzlers to more fuel-efficient cars. This implies a long-run price elasticity of demand for gasoline of about 0.56 (i.e., η = 28%/50% = 0.56). If correct, this long-run price elasticity would be much higher than originally anticipated for a product such as gasoline for which few if any good substitutes are available. However, it would take several years for consumers to adjust fully to a sharp price increase.

Figure 5-9 gives a hypothetical short-run and long-run demand curve of gasoline for automobiles in the United States. The figure shows gasoline consumption of 80 billion gallons at the price of $1 per gallon (point E) before the price increase. Gasoline consumption would fall to 70 billion gallons the year after the price rose to $1.50 per gallon (point A on short-run demand curve D_G) and to 60 billion gallons several years later (point B

[8] See, C. A. Dahl, "Consumer Adjustment to a Gasoline Tax," *The Review of Economics and Statistics*, August 1979, pp. 427–431.

FIGURE 5-9.
Short-Run and Long-
Run Demand for
Gasoline

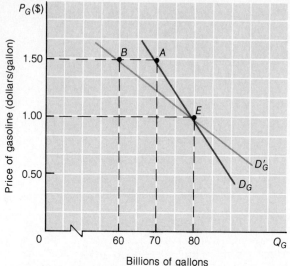

The figure shows that at the gasoline price of $1 per gallon, 80 billion gallons per year are demanded. At the price of $1.50, 70 billion gallons per year are demanded the year after the price increase (point A on short-run demand curve D_G) and 60 billion gallons several years later (point B on long-run demand curve D'_G).

on long-run demand curve D'_G). In reality, most of the reduction in gasoline consumption resulting from price increases was neutralized in the U.S. by the long-run growth of the economy. However, without the price increases, gasoline consumption would have been that much higher.

Application 3: Other Price Elasticities and Their Usefulness

Knowledge of price elasticities of demand is very useful and often necessary in reaching correct decisions in business and government. For example, following deregulation in 1978, airlines lowered air fares in order to increase their total revenues because each faced an elastic demand. On the other hand, the increase in fares by railroads in the 1930s in the face of an elastic demand sharply reduced their revenues. Railroads should have reduced, not increased, fares in order to increase their total revenues.

A tax imposed on the consumption of a commodity with a price-inelastic demand such as gasoline, cigarettes, or coffee will raise a great deal of revenues without substantially cutting consumption. If a large cut in consumption is in fact desired (for example, for gasoline and cigarettes), a very large tax is required (the precise size of the tax can be calculated by using the estimated value of the price elasticity of demand). On the other hand, an increase in the tax *rate* on legal gambling, which has a price-elastic demand, will lead to a more than proportionate decline in quantity (as many people turn to illegal gambling) and will reduce government revenues.

152

It was estimated that tax laws in the U.S. reduce the effective cost (price) of owner-occupied housing by about 28% for a home owner in the 40% tax bracket (due to deduction of mortgage interest and real property taxes in determining taxable income). With a price elasticity of demand for owner-occupied housing estimated at 1.22, the federal personal income tax benefit increases the quantity demanded of owner-occupied housing by about 34% (1.22 times 28%) for potential home owners in the 40% tax bracket. In order to estimate the cost of a national health insurance plan that reduces the cost (price) of medical care, we must have knowledge of the price elasticity of demand for the various medical services included in the plan. Knowledge of the value of the price elasticity of demand is important even in combatting crime. For example, it was seen in Example 3-2 that a rise in expenditures for law enforcement devoted to apprehend and prosecute criminals (i.e., increasing the probability of catching and sending criminals to jail) reduces the rate of robberies by about 0.85% and the rate of burglaries by about 0.90%. These are but a few crucial applications of price elasticity of demand in the real world.

Application 4: The Income Elasticity of Demand and the Negative Income Tax Proposal

An important criterion for evaluating the so-called **negative income tax** proposal was the income elasticity of demand of low-income families for various commodities. A negative income tax involves using cash subsidies to raise poor families' income to a guaranteed minimum level. Public support for this program would certainly be greater if it could be shown that recipient families would spend the increased income on such commodities as housing, food, and education rather than on alcohol, gambling, and drugs. This involves estimating the income elasticity of demand of recipient families for various commodities. The first experiment that attempted to do that involved twelve hundred families receiving cash grants over a three year period from 1969 to 1972 in the state of New Jersey.[9] The result demonstrated that recipient families used most of their increased income to move from public housing into better living quarters and to purchase refrigerators, washing machines, and other durable commodities. Such behavior by recipient families provided support for the program. (An evaluation of the effect of a negative income tax on incentives to work is examined in Applicaiton 5 in Chapter 14.)

Application 5: Cross Elasticities in the Courtroom

The well-known *cellophane* case was decided in the courts primarily on the basis of high cross elasticities of demand estimates between cellophane and other "flexible packaging materials." Briefly, the background of the

---

[9] See, H. W. Watts and A. Rees, eds., *Final Report of the New Jersey Graduated Work Incentive Experiment* (Madison, Wisconsin: Institute for Research on Poverty and Mathematics, 1974).

153

case is as follows. In 1947, the U.S. Justice Department brought suit against the duPont Company (which then sold 75 per cent of all the cellophane used in the United States) for illegally monopolizing the production and sale of cellophane. DuPont argued in court that cellophane was just one of many flexible packaging materials. These included cellophane, waxed paper, aluminum foil, and many others. Based on the high cross elasticity of demand between cellophane and these other products, duPont argued that the relevant market was not cellophane but flexible packaging materials, and duPont had less than 20% of this market. Therefore, according to duPont, it had not monopolized the market. The prosecution, on the other hand, argued that cellophane was sufficiently distinct as a product and that no good substitutes were available for some of its uses. After years of litigation, the courts finally ruled that the government could not prove its charges and dismissed the case in 1953.[10]

Summary

1. The market demand curve for a commodity is obtained from the horizontal summation of the demand curves of all the individual consumers in the market and shows the total quantity demanded at various prices. It is negatively sloped and, in drawing it, we must hold constant the consumers' incomes, the price of substitutes and complementary commodities, tastes, and the number of consumers in the market. The market demand curve will be flatter or more elastic than otherwise with a bandwagon effect, and steeper and less elastic when a snob effect is present, or with conspicuous expenditures or the Veblen effect.

2. By drawing a tangent to a point on a nonlinear demand curve and dropping a perpendicular to either axis we can measure price elasticity at that point by the ratio of two distances. A straight-line demand curve is unitary elastic at its midpoint, elastic above the midpoint, and inelastic below the midpoint. Total expenditures and price move in opposite directions if demand is elastic and in the same direction if demand is inelastic. A rectangular hyperbola demand curve has unitary elasticity and constant total expen-

ditures throughout. A demand curve is more elastic (a) the closer and the better are the available substitutes and (b) the longer the adjustment period to the price change.

3. The income elasticity of demand (η_I) measures the percentage change in the quantity purchased of a commodity divided by the percentage change in consumers' incomes. A commodity is usually taken to be a necessity if η_I is between 0 and 1 and a luxury if η_I exceeds 1. η_I exceeds 1 if the tangent to the Engel curve is positively sloped and crosses the income axis. η_I is between 0 and 1 if the tangent to the Engel curve is positively sloped and crosses the quantity axis. If η_I is negative, the commodity is an inferior good and the Engel curve is negatively sloped. According to Engel's law, the proportion of total expenditures on food declines as family incomes rise.

4. Commodities X and Y are substitutes if more of X is purchased when the price of Y goes up, and complements if less of X is purchased when the price of Y goes up. The cross elasticity of demand between commodities X and Y (η_{xy}) measures the percentage change in the quantity purchased of

---

[10] See *U.S. Reports*, Vol. 351 (Washington, D.C.: U.S. Government Printing Office, 1956), p. 400.

X divided by the percentage change in the price of Y. If η_{xy} is positive, X and Y are substitutes. If η_{xy} is negative, X and Y are complements, and if $\eta_{xy} = 0$, X and Y are independent commodities.

5. The total revenue (TR) of sellers equals price times quantity. Marginal revenue (MR) is the change in TR per unit change in the quantity of the commodity sold. MR is positive when demand (D) is elastic because a reduction in price increases TR. When D is unitary elastic, MR = 0 because TR is constant (at its maximum). When D is inelastic, MR is negative because a reduction in price reduces TR. The MR curve for a straight-line D curve bisects the quantity axis. The MR at a point on a nonlinear D curve is found geometrically by drawing a tangent to the demand curve at that point. Marginal revenue, price, and price elasticity of demand

are related by $MR = P(1 - 1/\eta)$. The demand curve facing a perfectly competitive firm is horizontal and $P = MR$ because η is infinite.

6. Because the demand for most agricultural commodities is price inelastic, farmers' incomes tend to be higher with bad harvests than with good ones. It was estimated that the long-run price elasticity of demand for gasoline in the U.S. is well below 1, but it is about twice as large as the short-run price elasticity. Knowledge of price elasticities of demand are often essential in reaching correct decisions in business and government. One of the many real-world uses of income elasticities of demand was to evaluate the negative income tax proposal. The cross elasticity of demand found its way into the courts in defining a market or industry in the cellophane antitrust case.

Glossary

Market demand curve It shows the quantity demanded of a commodity in the market per time period at various alternative prices of the commodity, while holding everything else constant. It is obtained from the horizontal summation of the demand curve of all the consumers in the market, and it is negatively sloped.

Bandwagon effect The situation where some people demand a commodity because other people purchase it (i.e., in order to "keep up with the Joneses").

Snob effect The situation where some people demand a smaller quantity of a commodity as more people consume it, in order to be different and exclusive.

Veblen effect The situation where some people purchase more of certain commodities the more expensive they are; also called conspicuous consumption.

Income elasticity of demand (η_I) The percentage change in the quantity purchased of a commodity over a specific period of time divided by the percentage change in consumers' income.

Necessity A commodity with income elasticity of demand between 0 and 1.

Luxury A commodity with income elasticity of demand greater than 1.

Engel's law The proportion of total expenditures on food declines as family incomes rise.

Substitutes Two commodities are substitutes if an increase in the price of one of them leads to more of the other being purchased.

Complements Two commodities are complements if an increase in the price of one of them leads to less of the other being purchased.

Cross elasticity of demand (η_{xy}) The percentage change in the quantity purchased of a commodity divided by the percentage change in the price of another commodity.

Total revenue (TR) The price of the commodity times the quantity sold of the commodity.

Average revenue (AR) Total revenue divided by the quantity sold.

Marginal revenue (MR) The change in total revenue per unit change in the quantity sold.

Negative income tax The proposal to use cash subsidies to raise poor families' incomes in the U.S. to a guaranteed minimum level.

Questions for Review

1. (a) What is meant by the market demand curve? How is it obtained?
   (b) What is the shape of the market demand curve? Why?
   (c) What are the things that are held constant in drawing a market demand curve?
   (d) What is meant by the bandwagon, snob, and Veblen effects? How do they alter the shape of the market demand curve?

2. (a) How can the price elasticity at a point on a demand curve be measured geometrically?
   (b) What is the price elasticity of a straight-line demand curve at its midpoint, above its midpoint, and below its midpoint?
   (c) What is the relationship between the slope and the price elasticity of a demand curve?

3. Do total expenditures increase, decrease, or remain unchanged if
   (a) price rises and demand is elastic?
   (b) price rises and demand is inelastic?
   (c) price rises and demand is unitary elastic?
   (d) What is the relationship between total expenditures and price elasticity for a price decline?

4. (a) What is the shape of a demand curve that is unit elastic throughout?
   (b) How can you tell if a demand curve is unit elastic throughout by simply looking at total expenditure?
   (c) What is the general equation of a unit-elastic demand curve?

5. (a) Under what condition are there closer substitutes for a commodity, when the commodity is defined narrowly or broadly?
   (b) What is the most important factor determining the price elasticity of demand for a commodity?
   (c) Is the price elasticity of demand greater in the short or in the long run? Why?

6. (a) What does the income elasticity of demand measure?
   (b) What are the things held constant in measuring the income elasticity of demand?
   (c) Does the income elasticity of demand measure a movement along a given demand curve or a shift in demand?

7. (a) What is meant by a necessity? A luxury? Are these concepts very precise?
   (b) How can we determine graphically if a particular commodity is a necessity or a luxury? Normal or inferior?
   (c) What is meant by Engel's law? How can it be used as a rough measure of the standard of living of a family or nation?

8. (a) What is meant by substitutes? Complements?
   (b) What does the cross elasticity of demand measure?
   (c) How can the cross elasticity of demand be used to define substitutes and complements?
   (d) How can the cross elasticity of demand be used to define an industry?

9. (a) What is meant by total revenue? By marginal revenue? By average revenue?
   (b) What is the relationship between demand, total revenue, and marginal revenue?
   (c) How can the marginal revenue curve be derived geometrically for a straight-line demand curve? For a curvilinear demand curve?

10. (a) What is the general relationship among (i.e., the formula relating) marginal revenue, price, and the price elasticity of demand?
    (b) If price is $3 and the price elasticity of demand is 2, what is the marginal revenue?
    (c) What is the relationship among marginal revenue, price, and the price elasticity of demand when the demand curve for the output of a firm is horizontal?

11. (a) Why are farmers' incomes usually higher with bad than with good harvests?
    (b) Why then do farmers strive to produce as much as they can in each year?
    (c) Is the short-run price elasticity of demand for gasoline in the U.S. zero? Is the long-run price elasticity of demand larger than 1?

12. (a) Can you give some examples of applications of price elasticity of demand in the real world?
    (b) How was the income elasticity of demand of poor families for various commodities used

to evaluate the negative income tax proposal?

Problems

1. Measure graphically the price elasticity of demand curve D_x in the left panel of Figure 5-2
   (a) at point B.
   (b) at point G.
2. Using the general formula for the price elasticity of demand (i.e., equation 2-1), prove that
   (a) $\eta = \infty$ at point A on D'_x in the right panel of Figure 5-2.
   (b) $\eta = 0$ at point H in the same diagram.
★3. Explain the following.
   (a) Of two parallel demand curves, the one further to the right has a smaller price elasticity at each price.
   (b) When two demand curves intersect, the flatter of the two is more elastic at the point of intersection.
4. Using only the total expenditures criterion, determine if the demand schedules given in the following table are elastic, inelastic, or unitary elastic.

$P(\$)$	5	4	3	2	1
Q_x	100	130	180	275	560
Q_y	100	120	150	220	430
Q_z	100	125	167	250	500

5. If the price elasticity of demand for Marlboro cigarettes is 6 and its price rose by 10%
   (a) by how much would the quantity demanded decrease?
   (b) would the consumers' total expenditures on Marlboro cigarettes increase, decrease, or remain unchanged?
   (c) If the price of all other brands of cigarettes also increased by 10% what would happen to the quantity demanded of Marlboro? To consumers' expenditures on Marlboro?

★ = answer found at the end of the book.

(c) How were cross elasticities of demand used in the courts to decide the cellophane case?

6. From the following table

Q_x	100	250	350	400	300
I	\$10,000	15,000	20,000	25,000	30,000

   (a) calculate the income elasticity of demand for commodity X between various income levels and determine what type of good is commodity X;
   (b) plot the Engel curve; how can you tell from the shape of the Engel curve what type of good is commodity X?
★7. (a) Explain why in a two-commodity world both commodities cannot be luxuries.
   (b) What would be the effect on the quantity of cars purchased if consumers' incomes rose by 10% and the income elasticity of demand is 2.5?
8. Which of the following sets of commodities are likely to have positive cross elasticity of demand?
   (a) aluminum and plastics.
   (b) wheat and corn.
   (c) pencils and paper.
   (d) private and public education.
   (e) gin and tonic.
   (f) ham and cheese.
   (g) men's and women's shoes.
★9. Using the values for the price and income elasticity of demand for electricity and for the cross elasticity of demand between electricity and natural gas given in Tables 5-2, 5-4, and 5-5, answer the following questions.
   (a) Is the demand for electricity elastic or inelastic in the short run? In the long run? How much would the quantity demanded of electricity change as a result of a 10% increase in its price in the short run? In the long run?

(b) Is electricity a necessity or a luxury? How much would electricity consumption change with a 10% increase in consumers' incomes?

(c) Is natural gas a substitute or complement of electricity? By how much would electricity consumption change with a 10% increase in the price of natural gas?

10. Given the following demand schedule

P	$8	7	6	5	4	3	2	1	0
Q	0	1	2	3	4	5	6	7	8

(a) find the total revenue and the marginal revenue.

(b) plot the total revenue curve, the demand curve, and the marginal revenue curve.

(c) Using the formula relating marginal revenue, price and elasticity, confirm the values of the marginal revenue found geometrically for $P = \$8$, for $P = \$4$, and for $P = \$2$.

11. Explain why a firm should never operate in the inelastic range of its demand curve.

12. The following proposition (proved in Section A4 of the Mathematical Appendix at the end of the text) is given:

$$K_x \eta_{Ix} + K_y \eta_{Iy} = 1$$

where K_x is the proportion of the consumer's income I spent on commodity X (i.e., $K_x = P_x Q_x / I$), η_{Ix} is the income elasticity of demand for commodity X, K_y is the proportion of income spent on Y (i.e., $K_y = P_y Q_y / I$), and η_{Iy} is the income elasticity of demand for Y. Aslo, suppose that a consumer spends 75% of his or her income on commodity X and the income elasticity of demand for commodity X is 0.9. Assume also that the individual consumes only commodities X and Y.

(a) Find the income elasticity of demand for commodity Y.

(b) What kind of commodity is Y? X? How high would the income elasticity of demand for X have to be before commodity Y becomes inferior?

Supplementary Readings

For a problem-solving approach to the topics discussed in this chapter, see

Dominick Salvatore, *Microeconomic Theory,* 2nd ed. (New York: McGraw-Hill, 1983), Section 2-4 and Chapter 3.

For a more extensive discussion of the bandwagon, snob, and Veblen effects, see

Harvey Leibenstein, *Beyond the Economic Man: A New Foundation for Microeconomics* (Cambridge, Mass.: Harvard University Press, 1976), Chapter 4.

For a more extensive and advanced discussion of price and income elasticities of demand, together wtih estimates for many more commodities, see

Hendrik S. Houthakker and **Lester D. Taylor,** *Consumer Demand in the United States: Analyses and Projections* (Cambridge, Mass.: Harvard University Press, 1970).

The definition of substitutes in terms of the substitution effect only is found in

John R. Hicks, *Value and Capital* (New York: Oxford University Press, 1946), p. 44.

Extensions of Consumer Demand Theory

Chapter 6

6-   The Substitution Effect According to Slutsky

6-2   The Theory of Revealed Preference

6-3   Index Numbers

6-4   Utility Theory Under Uncertainty

6-5   The Characteristics Approach to Consumer Theory

6-6   Empirical Demand Curves

6-7   Applications

Examples

6-1   Gasoline Tax and Rebate Proposal Revisited

6-2   Changes in Average Real Weekly Earnings

6-3   Estimation of Implicit or Hedonic Prices

6-4   The Demand for Electricity in the United States

Applications

Application 1:   Compensated Demand Curve

Application 2:   Usual and Compensated Demand Curve by Revealed Preference

Application 3:   Choosing a Portfolio

Application 4:   Forecasting Residential Demand for Electricity

Preview Questions

How can the substitution effect be measured in the real world?

How can an indifference curve be derived from observed market behavior?

What is meant by index numbers? What is their usefulness?

How can traditional economic theory be extended to deal with choices involving risk?

How can the introduction of a new product and quality changes be analyzed?

How are market demand curves actually estimated in the real world?

This chapter extends traditional demand theory in some important directions. While some of these extensions are theoretical in nature (such as the theory of revealed preference), most seek to bridge the gap between theory and the real world. That is, they deal with ways to make the theory of demand more operational and more readily applicable to the analysis of real-world problems. Thus, we examine a more practical and very useful method of measuring the substitution effect from actual market data that does not require knowledge of the individual's indifference curves (which, as we have seen in Example 3-1, are not easy to obtain). We will see how index numbers can help us determine how the standard of living has changed over time.

We also examine a method for dealing with choices involving risk and with the introduction of new commodities and quality changes. These are not dealt by the traditional theory of demand presented in Chapters 3–5. Since most economic choices that individuals make in the real world do involve risk or uncertainty (for example, if an automobile will turn out to be a good one or an occupation as rewarding as anticipated), the extension of demand theory to deal with choices subject to risk is very important indeed. Similarly, quality changes and new goods are constantly being introduced in the economy and to the extent that theory can be extended to deal with them its usefulness will be greatly enhanced. Finally, we will examine how demand curves are actually estimated from quantity-price data.

We postponed dealing with these important topics until this chapter because either they are not yet universally accepted or fully developed, or because they are somewhat more difficult and advanced. The average undergraduate should, however, with a little more effort, be able to go through them. He or she will find that the extra effort will be fully justified by the extra insights obtained. The numerous examples and useful applications presented in this chapter attest to the great importance of these extensions of traditional demand theory.

6-1

The Substitution Effect According to Slutsky

We have seen in Chapter 4 that it is very useful to separate the substitution from the income effect of a price change. In Section 4.3 and Figure 4-5 we measured the substitution effect by a movement along an individual's indifference curve. This required knowledge of the exact shape of the individual's indifference curve, which, as we have seen in Example 3-1, is difficult to obtain. Fortunately, there is another more practical method of measuring the substitution effect of a price change that does not involve knowledge of the exact shape of the individual's indifference curve but which relies entirely on readily available quantity-price observations in the market. This is shown in Figure 6-1.

FIGURE 6-1.
The Slutsky
Substitution Effect

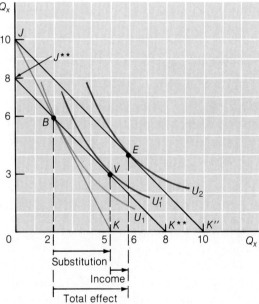

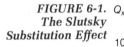

With I = \$10 and P_y = \$1, the consumer is at optimum at point B on U_1 with P_x = \$2 and at point E on U_2 with P_x = \$1. The increase in the quantity purchased from 2X to 6X is the total effect. We can isolate the Slutsky substitution effect by rotating original budget line JK through original optimum point B until it is parallel to budget line JK″. This gives budget line J**K**, which is tangent to U_1' at point V. The movement from point B to point V (3X) is the Slutsky substitution effect, while the movement from point V to point E (1X) is the income effect.

161

Figure 6-1 is drawn on the assumptions that the consumer's money income (I) is \$10, the price of commodity Y (P_y) is \$1, and the price of commodity X (P_x) is originally \$2 and subsequently falls to \$1. This gives budget line JK and JK'', respectively. With I = \$10 and P_y = \$1, the consumer is at optimum at point B on U_1 by purchasing $2X$ with P_x = \$2, and at point E on U_2 by purchasing $6X$ with P_x = \$1 (so far, this is the same as in the top panel of Figure 4-3 and in Figure 4-5). The increase in the quantity purchased from $2X$ to $6X$ is the total effect or the sum of the substitution and income effects.

The new method of measuring the substitution effect involves rotating original budget line JK through original optimum point B, until it is parallel to budget line JK''. This gives budget line $J^{**}K^{**}$ (see Figure 6-1). Budget line $J^{**}K^{**}$ is parallel to budget line JK'' so as to reflect the new lower price of P_x = \$1. By going through point B, budget line $J^{**}K^{**}$ keeps real income constant as at point B but with the new ratio of prices. Real income is here kept constant in the sense that the consumer could purchase, if he or she wanted, the same bundle of commodities ($2X$ and $6Y$) as at point B. In fact, the consumer purchases more of X and less of Y with budget line $J^{**}K^{**}$ (because of the fall in P_x relative to P_y) and moves to point V ($5X$ and $3Y$) because by doing so he or she reaches higher indifference curve U_1'.

The movement from point B to point V ($3X$) is the **Slutsky substitution effect** (after the Russian-born economist Eugene Slutsky, who introduced it), while the movement from point V to point E ($1X$) is the income effect. We eliminated the income effect (so as to identify the Slutsky substitution effect) by imposing an imaginary tax that allows the consumer to purchase, if he or she wants, the same bundle of goods (i.e., $2X$ and $6Y$) that he or she purchased before the price change. This measure of the income effect can easily be estimated from price-quantity observations in the market and does not require knowledge of the exact shape of either indifference curve U_1 or U_1' (see Figure 6-1).

This is to be contrasted with the **Hicksian substitution effect** (shown in Figure 4-5), which was reflected by a movement down along original indifference curve U_1. With the Hicksian substitution effect, real income is held constant by keeping the consumer on original indifference curve U_1. Elimination of the income effect was reflected by the movement from a higher to a lower (the original) indifference curve—a quantity that is not directly or cardinally measurable. Another way of saying this is that in order to separate the substitution from the income effect as we have done in Section 4-3 and Figure 4-5, we need to know the exact shape of the individual's indifference curve, which is very difficult to obtain.

To summarize, the Slutsky method of measuring the substitution effect is more useful in empirical work than the Hicksian method because it can be obtained from actual quantity-price observations and does not require (as the Hicksian method) knowledge of the exact shape of the indifference curve. This is clearly demonstrated by the gasoline tax and rebate proposal revisited in Example 6-1. However, it should be noted that for small price changes, the difference between the Slutsky and the Hicksian substitution effect is very small.

Example 6-1　Gasoline Tax and Rebate Proposal Revisited

The Facts: Using 1980 data, it can be estimated that a tax which increases the price of gasoline by 50% would reduce gasoline consumption by about 260 gallons per family per year in the long run and result in the collection of about $558 in excise tax per family. The 260 gallons reduction in family gasoline-consumption per year is the total effect or the sum of the substitution and income effects of the tax. If, subsequently, to avoid the deflationary effect of the tax, the amount collected was returned to consumers in the form of a *general* tax rebate of $558 per family, gasoline consumption would increase by about 34 gallons per family per year. This is the income effect of the tax. It would leave a substitution effect of about 226 (260 − 34) gallons reduction in family gasoline consumption per year. Note that, as usual, the substitution effect is much larger than the income effect.

Comment: The above calculations are based on the following U.S. data for 1980: median family income of $21,000; gasoline price of $1.20 per gallon; average family gasoline consumption of 930 gallons per year; long-run price elasticity of demand for gasoline of 0.56, and long-run income elasticity of demand for gasoline of 1.36. (Problem 3 asks you to show how these data were used to obtain the above results; the answer to the problem is then provided in the back of the book.) Note that the above results are estimates and do not involve knowledge of the shape of the indifference curves to calculate the substitution effect. Measuring the substitution effect of a price change this way (i.e., as proposed by Slutsky) is thus more practical and empirically useful than measuring it as a movement along an individual's indifference curve as proposed by Hicks. We will see that whenever we need to keep real income constant in what follows, we will use the Slutsky method.

Sources: Example 4-3; Application 2 in Chapter 5; *U.S. Statistical Abstract* (Washington, D.C.: U.S. Government Printing Office, 1983), and H. S. Houthakker and L. D. Taylor, *Consumer Demand in the United States: Analyses and Projections* (Cambridge, Mass.: Harvard University Press, 1970).

6-2

The Theory of Revealed Preference

Until now we have assumed that indifference curves are derived by asking the consumer to choose between various market baskets of commodities, as described in Example 3-1. Not only is this difficult and time consuming to do but we also cannot be sure that the consumer can or will provide trustworthy answers to direct questions as to their preferences. According to the **theory of revealed preference** (developed by Paul Samuelson and John Hicks), a consumer's indifference curves can be derived from observing the actual market behavior of the consumer and without any need to inquire directly about his or her preferences. For example, if the consumer purchases basket A rather than basket B, even though A is not cheaper than B, we can infer that he or she prefers A to B.

The theory of revealed preference rests on the following assumptions:

1. The tastes of the consumer do not change over the period of the analysis.
2. The consumer's tastes are **consistent,** so that if the consumer purchases basket A rather than basket B, he or she will never prefer B to A.
3. The consumer's tastes are **transitive,** so that if the consumer prefers A to B and B to C, he or she will prefer A to C.
4. The consumer can be induced to purchase any basket of commodities if its price is lowered sufficiently.

Figure 6-2 shows how a consumer's indifference curve can be derived by revealed preference. Suppose that the consumer is observed to be at point A on budget line NN in the left panel. Then, he or she prefers A to any point on or below NN. On the other hand, points above and to the right of A are superior to A since they involve more of commodity X and commodity Y. Thus the consumer's indifference curve must be tangent to budget line NN at point A and be above NN everywhere else. It must also be to the left and below shaded area LAM. Such an indifference curve would be of the usual shape (i.e., negatively sloped and convex to the origin).

To locate more precisely the indifference curve in the **zone of ignorance** (i.e., in the area between LAM and NN), consider point B on NN. Point B is inferior to A since the consumer preferred A to B. However, the consumer could be induced to purchase B with budget line PP (i.e., with P_x/P_y sufficiently lower than with NN). Since A is preferred to B and B is preferred to any point on BP, the indifference curve must be above BP. We have thus eliminated shaded area BPN from the zone of ignorance. Similarly, by choosing another point, such as D, we can, by following the same reasoning as for B, eliminate shaded area DSN. Thus, the indifference curve must lie *above SDBP* and be tangent to NN at point A.

The right panel of Figure 6-2 shows how we can chip away from the zone of ignorance immediately to the left of LA and below AM. Suppose that with budget line P'P' (which goes through point A and thus refers to the same real income as at A), the consumer chooses combination G (with more of X and less of Y than at A) because P_x/P_y is lower than on NN.[1] Then points in the shaded area above and to the right of G are preferred to G, which is preferred to A. Thus, we have eliminated some of the upper zone

---

[1] Note that this is the Slutsky definition of constant real income.

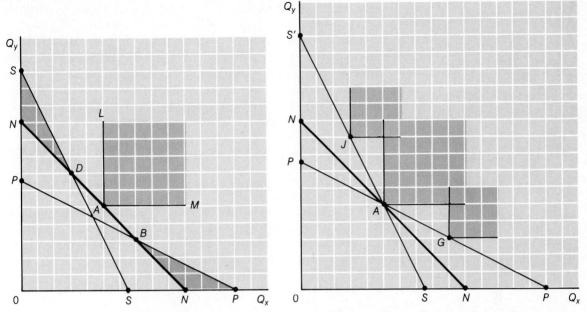

FIGURE 6-2. *Derivation of an Indifference Curve by Revealed Preference*

In the left panel, the consumer is originally at optimum at point A on NN. Thus, the indifference curve must be tangent to NN at point A and above NN everywhere else. It must also be to the left and below shaded area LAM. If the consumer is induced to purchase combination B (which is inferior to A) with budget line PP, we can eliminate shaded area BPN. Similarly, with combination D on budget line SS, shaded area DSN can be eliminated. Thus, the indifference curve must be above SDBP. In the right panel, the consumer prefers G to A with budget line P′P′ and prefers J to A with Budget line S′S′. Thus, the indifference curve must be below points G and J.

of ignorance. Similarly, choosing another budget line, such as S′S′, we can eliminate the area above and to the right of a point such as J, which the consumer prefers to A at the higher P_x/P_y given by S′S′. Thus, the indifference curve on which A falls must lie *below* points G and J. The process can be repeated any number of times to further reduce the upper and lower zones of ignorance, thereby locating the indifference curve more precisely.

While not very practical as a method for actually deriving an indifference curve, the theory of revealed preference can be used to identify the Slutsky substitution effect and derive a consumer's demand curve without using indifference curves (see Application 2).

6-3

Index Numbers

In this section, we discuss index numbers and their use in measuring changes in standards of living or welfare, especially during inflationary periods. For example, workers and their unions are very keen to know if money wages are keeping up with rising prices. Cost-of-living indices are often used for inflation adjustment in wage contracts, for pensions and welfare payments and, since 1984, even for tax payments. In this section, we will define three indices and, by comparing the values of these indices in two different time periods, determine if the standard of living has increased, decreased, or remained unchanged. For simplicity, we will assume that the consumer spends all income on only two commodities, X and Y.

6-3a Expenditure, Laspeyres, and Paasche Indices

In order to measure changes in the standard of living or welfare from one time period to another, we begin by defining three indices: the income or expenditure index, the Laspeyres price index, and the Paasche price index.

The **income** or **expenditure index** *(E)* is the ratio of period 1 to base period money income or expenditures. That is,

$$E = \frac{x_1 P_{x1} + y_1 P_{y1}}{x_0 P_{x0} + y_0 P_{y0}} \tag{6-1}$$

where x and y refer to the quantities of commodities X and Y purchased, respectively; P refers to price, and the subscripts "1" and "0" refer to period 1 and the base period, respectively.

Thus, the income or expenditure index is the sum of the product of period 1 quantities and their respective period 1 prices divided by the sum of the product of base period quantities and their respective base period prices. In short, E measures the ratio of the consumer's period one expenditures or income to the base period expenditures or income. If $E > 1$, the individual's *money* income or expenditures has increased from the base period to period 1. However, since prices usually also rise we cannot determine simply from the value of E whether the individual's *real* income or standard of living has also increased. To do that, we need to define the Laspeyres and the Paasche price indices and compare their value to that of the income or expenditure index.

The **Laspeyres price index** *(L)* is the ratio of the cost of *base period quantities* at period 1 prices relative to base period prices. That is,

$$L = \frac{x_0 P_{x1} + y_0 P_{y1}}{x_0 P_{x0} + y_0 P_{y0}} \tag{6-2}$$

In the Laspeyres price index, we use the base period quantities as the weights and measure the cost of purchasing these base period quantities at period 1 prices relative to base period prices.

TABLE 6-1 Hypothetical Quantity-Price Data in a Base Period and in Period 1

Period	x	P_x	y	P_y
0 (base)	4	$1	3	$2
1	3	2	6	1

The **Paasche price index** *(P)* is the ratio of the cost of *period 1 quantities* at period 1 prices relative to base period prices. That is,

$$P = \frac{x_1 P_{x1} + y_1 P_{y1}}{x_1 P_{x0} + y_1 P_{y0}} \qquad (6\text{-}3)$$

In the Paasche price index, we use period 1 quantities as the weights and measure the cost of purchasing period 1 quantities at period 1 prices relative to base period prices. Thus, the difference between the Laspeyres and the Paasche price indices is that the former uses the base period quantities as the weights while the latter uses the period 1 quantities.

For example, using the hypothetical data in Table 6-1, we can calculate

$$E = \frac{x_1 P_{x1} + y_1 P_{y1}}{x_0 P_{x0} + y_0 P_{y0}} = \frac{(3)(\$2) + (6)(\$1)}{(4)(\$1) + (3)(\$2)} = \frac{\$12}{\$10} = 1.2 \text{ or } 120\%$$

$$L = \frac{x_0 P_{x1} + y_0 P_{y1}}{x_0 P_{x0} + y_0 P_{y0}} = \frac{(4)(\$2) + (3)(\$1)}{\$10} = \frac{\$11}{\$10} = 1.1 \text{ or } 110\%$$

$$P = \frac{x_1 P_{x1} + y_1 P_{y1}}{x_1 P_{x0} + y_1 P_{y0}} = \frac{\$12}{(3)(\$1) + (6)(\$2)} = \frac{\$12}{\$15} = 0.8 \text{ or } 80\%$$

6-3b Measures of Changes in Consumer Welfare

Since some quantities and prices rise over time while others fall, it is often impossible to determine by simple inspection of the quantity-price data whether an individual's standard of living or welfare has increased, decreased, or remained unchanged from one time period to the next. To measure changes in the standard of living we compare the value of the income or expenditure index to the value of the Laspeyres and the Paasche price indices.

An individual's standard of living is higher in period 1 than in the base period if E > L. That is, the individual is better off in period 1 than in the base period if the increase in his or her money income (E) exceeds the increase in the cost of living using base-period quantities as weights (L). For example, since we calculated from Table 6-1 that E = 1.2 or 120% while L = 1.1 or 110%, the individual's standard of living increased from the base period to period 1 because his or her income has risen more than his or her costs or prices.

On the other hand, *the individual's standard of living is higher in the base period than in period 1 if E < P.* That is, the individual is better off in the base period than in period 1 if the increase in his or her money income (E) is smaller than the increase in the cost of living using period 1 quantities as the weights (P). If E is not smaller than P, the individual's standard of living is not higher in the base period. For example, since $E = 120\%$ and $P = 80\%$ from Table 6-1, the individual is not better off in the base period than in period 1. Thus, with $E > L$ and E not smaller than P, the individual of the above numerical example is definitely better off in period 1 than in the base period.

Figure 6-3 presents a graphical interpretation of the numerical example of Table 6-1. In the figure, I_0I_0 is the individual's budget line in the base period. That is, with $x = 4$, $P_x = \$1$, $y = 3$, and $P_y = \$2$, the individual's total income (I) and expenditure in the base period is $10 (obtained from 4X times $1 plus 3Y times $2). If the individual had spent the entire base-period income of $10 on commodity X he or she could have purchased 10X. If instead the individual had spent his or her entire base period income of

<table>
<tr><td>

FIGURE 6-3.
Changes in
Consumer Welfare

</td><td>

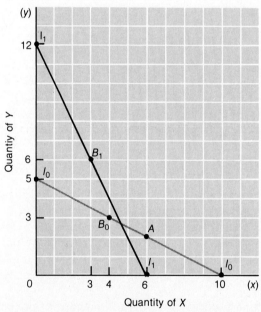

Quantity of X

</td></tr>
</table>

The individual purchases 4X and 3Y (B_0) on budget line I_0I_0 in the base period and 3X and 6Y (B_1) on budget line I_1I_1 in period 1. Since point B_0 is below budget line I_1I_1, the individual must be better off in period 1 than in the base period. That is, since B_0 was available to the individual in period 1 but was not chosen, the individual must be better off with B_1 in period 1 than with B_0 in the base period. Had the individual been at point A in the base period, we would need the individual's indifference curves to determine if B_1 is superior, inferior, or equal to A.

168

$10 on commodity Y he or she could have purchased $5Y$. This defines I_0I_0 as the individual's budget line in the base period. The individual's purchase of $4X$ and $3Y$ in the base period (see the first row of Table 6-1) is indicated by point B_0 on budget line I_0I_0. We can similarly determine from the second row of Table 6-1 that in period 1 the individual's income is $12 (obtained from $3X$ times $2 plus $6Y$ times $1) so that his or her budget line is I_1I_1. The individual's purchase of $3X$ and $6Y$ in period 1 is indicated by point B_1 on budget line I_1I_1.

From Figure 6-3 we can conclude that since point B_0 is below budget line I_1I_1, the individual must be better off in period 1 than in the base period. That is, since B_0 was available to the individual in period 1 but was not chosen, the individual must be better off in period 1. Specifically, in period 1 the individual could have purchased the base period bundle (B_0) at period 1 prices by spending only $11 ($4X$ times $2 plus $3Y$ times $1) of his or her period 1 income of $12. On the other hand, in the base period the individual could not have purchased period 1 quantities at base period prices since that would require an expenditure of $15 ($3X$ times $1 plus $6Y$ times $2), which exceeded his or her base period income of $10. Thus, the individual must be better off with B_1 in period 1 than with B_0 in the base period.

Had the individual been at a point such as A rather than at point B_0 on budget line I_0I_0 in the base period (see Figure 6-3), we could no longer determine without the individual's indifference curves whether the individual was better off in period 1, in the base period, or was equally well off in period 1 as in the base period. This would depend on whether point B_1 was on a higher, lower, or on the same indifference curve as point A, respectively. The student should be able to calculate from comparing point A on I_0I_0 in the base period to point B_1 on I_1I_1 in period 1 that $E = 120\%$, $L = 140\%$, and $P = 80\%$. Since E is not larger than L (so that the individual is not better off in period 1) but E is not smaller than P (so that the individual is not better off in the base period), we have conflicting results and we cannot tell whether the standard of living is higher, lower, or equal in period 1 as compared with the base period. This confirms the inconclusive results of the graphical analysis (in the absence of the individual's indifference curves) in Figure 6-3.

Because the Laspeyres price index (L) uses base period quantities as the weights, L becomes available sooner than the Paasche price index (P).[2] The most common of the price indices is the consumer price index (CPI), which has been published monthly by the Bureau of Labor Statistics for over sixty years. This is a Laspeyres index for a "typical" urban family of four. It is the weighted average of the price of 400 goods and services purchased by consumers in the United States. The weights of the various commodities in the basket are periodically changed to reflect variations in consumption patterns. Other important (Laspeyres) price indices are the wholesale price

---

[2] The Laspeyres price index also uses period 1 prices. However, period 1 prices become available much sooner than period 1 quantities.

TABLE 6-2   Weekly Money and Real Earnings in the United States, 1977–1982

Year	Total Private Nonagricultural Weekly Money Earnings	CPI (1977 = 100)	Total Private Nonagricultural Weekly Real Earnings
1977	$189.00	100.0	$189.00
1978	203.70	107.6	189.31
1979	219.91	119.9	183.41
1980	235.10	136.1	172.74
1981	255.20	150.0	170.13
1982	267.26	159.0	168.09
1983	280.70	163.9	171.26

Source: U.S. Department of Labor, Bureau of Labor Statistics, *Employment and Earnings* (Washington, D.C.: U.S. Government Printing Office, Monthly).

index *(WPI)* and the *GNP* deflator. The latter is used to calculate *GNP* in real terms.

Example 6-2 Changes in Average Real Weekly Earnings

The Facts: Table 6-2 gives average weekly earnings in private nonagricultural occupations in the United States from 1977 to 1982 and the consumer price index *(CPI)*. By dividing weekly *money* earnings by the *CPI* (with base 1977 = 100), we get weekly *real* earnings in 1977 prices (shown in the last column of the table).

Comment: While weekly money earnings increased from $189.00 in 1977 to $280.70 in 1983, real earnings declined from $189.00 to $171.26. Thus, the standard of living of nonagricultural workers in the U.S. declined by about 10 per cent from 1977 to 1983. Since it is known that the *CPI* imparts an upward bias to the increase in the cost of living (see the book by Allen in the Supplementary Bibliography), the true decline in real earnings is somewhat smaller than the above figures indicate. It should be pointed out, however, that using the change in real income or earnings as a measure of the change in the standard of living is appropriate only if tastes have not changed over the period of the analysis. If tastes did change, we could not reach any conclusion as to how welfare was affected by changes in real income or earnings.

6-4

Utility Theory under Uncertainty

Traditional demand theory implicitly assumes a riskless world. It assumes that consumers face complete certainty as to the results of the choices they make. Clearly, this is not the case in most instances. For example, when

170

we purchase an automobile we cannot be certain as to how good it will turn out and how long it will last. Similarly, when we choose an occupation, we cannot be exactly certain as to how rewarding it will be in relation to alternative occupations. Thus, the applicability of traditional economic theory is limited by the fact that it is based on the assumption of riskless world while most economic decisions are made in the face of risk.

Traditional economic theory could not deal with choices subject to risk or uncertainty because of its strict adherence to the principle of diminishing marginal utility of money (MU). This explains why an individual would not accept a fair (i.e., a 50–50) bet of winning or losing a given sum of money, say, $1,000. That is, because of diminishing MU, the individual's loss of utility in losing $1,000 exceeds his or her gain in utility in winning $1,000. Thus, an individual would not accept a fair bet and certainly would not accept an unfair one (i.e., one where the odds of winning are less than 50%).

By postulating a total utility of money function (as in Figure 6-4) which first increases at a decreasing rate (MU declines) and then increases at an increasing rate (MU increases), Milton Friedman and L. J. Savage could explain or at least rationalize why a family would purchase insurance against the small chance of a large loss (say, through a fire), and also purchase a lottery ticket offering a small chance of a large win (i.e., gamble). Such seemingly contradictory behavior was left entirely unexplained by traditional economic theory.

Figure 6-4 gives a total utility curve which first faces down and then faces up when plotted against income. Suppose that the family's income is OA with utility AA' without a fire, and OB with utility BB' with a fire. If the probability of no fire is p (so that the probability of a fire is $1 - p$), the **expected income** of the family is

$$\bar{I} = (p)(OA) + (1 - p)(OB) \tag{6-4}$$

For example, suppose a family owns a small business that generates a daily income of $OA = \$200$ without a fire and $OB = \$20$ after a fire, and the probability of no fire is $p = 0.9$, so that $1 - p = 0.1$. Then $\bar{I} = (0.9)(\$200) + (0.1)(\$20) = \$182$. The income of $182 is not actually available to the family. That is, the family faces only two alternatives: (1) an income of $200 with probability of 90 per cent and (2) an income of $20 with probability of 10 per cent. The expected income of $182 is a weighted average of these two alternatives using the probabilities as weights. However, the family would never actually have the income of $182. Different probabilities of occurrence attached to incomes $OA = \$200$ and $OB = \$20$ result in a different expected income. For example, if $p = 0.8$, $\bar{I} = (0.8)(\$200) + (0.2)(\$20) = \$164$.

The utility of the expected income is given by the height of dashed line $B'A'$ at the point directly above the level of the expected income. For example, the utility of expected income $OC = \$182$ is CC', with endpoint C' on

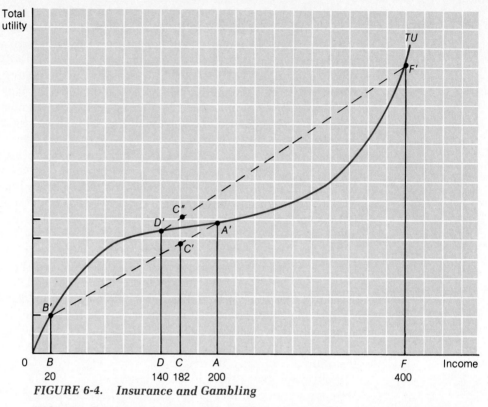

FIGURE 6-4.   Insurance and Gambling

With a family's income of OA with probability p of no fire, and OB with probability 1 − p of a fire, the family's expected income Ī = (p)(OA) + (1 − p)(OB). If Ī = OC, the family should purchase insurance at cost AD because DD' (the utility of insured income OD) exceeds CC' (the utility of expected income OC without insurance). Furthermore, if a lottery ticket costs AD with probability 1 − p' of winning and thereby raise the family's income to OF, the expected income would be Ī' = (p')(OD) + (1 − p')(OF). If Ī' = OC, the family would also purchase the ticket because CC" exceeds AA'.

straight dashed line B'A' (see the figure). This convenient geometric property results directly from the definition of the expected income (i.e., as the weighted average of the two alternative incomes using objective probabilities as the weights). The utility of the expected income does not fall on the total utility curve because the expected income is not an income that the family can actually achieve (such as OA or OB).

Now suppose that in fact Ī = OC = \$182 with utility CC'. If the cost of insurance is AD = \$60 (see the figure), the family's actual daily income after the purchase of the insurance is OD = \$140 (given by OA − AD). The utility of assured income OD = \$140 is DD' on the total utility curve (because income *OD* is actually achieved by the family with the purchase of the insurance). Since the utility associated with income *OD* with insurance (i.e., *DD'*) exceeds the utility of the expected income of *OC* without insurance (i.e., *CC'*) the family would purchase the insurance. That is, since the family receives the utility of *DD'* with the secure (insured) income of *OD* as compared with the lower utility of *CC'* with the uninsured expected income of *OC* (made up of income *OA* with probability *p* or income *OB* with probability 1 − *p*), the family would be better off by purchasing the insurance.

Next we turn to the analysis of gambling. Starting again with income *OA*, the family will also contemplate purchasing a lottery ticket costing *AD* = \$60.[3] With the lottery ticket, the family's income will be *OD* = \$140 (from *OA* − *AD*) with utility *DD'* without winning, and *OF* = \$400 with utility *FF'* by winning (see the figure). If the probability of *not* winning is *p'*, the expected income ($\bar{I}'$) is

$$\bar{I}' = (p')(OD) + (1 - p')(OF) \tag{6-4A}$$

If $\bar{I}' = OC$ with utility *CC''*, with endpoint *C''* on dashed line *D'F'*, the family would purchase the lottery ticket because *CC''* exceeds *AA'* (the utility of income *OA* without purchasing the ticket).[4]

Thus, the family buys insurance and also gambles—a seemingly contradictory behavior that traditional theory could not explain. By postulating a total utility function that first rises at a decreasing rate (so that the marginal utility declines) and then increases at an increasing rate (so that marginal utility rises) as shown in Figure 6-4, Friedman and Savage were able to rationalize a great deal of market behavior involving risk that traditional economic theory could not deal with. Note that in choices subject to risk, the consumer maximizes *expected* utility rather than utility (see Problem 8 with answer at the end of the text). While the above theory faces many shortcomings,[5] it does provide at least an indication of the factors to consider in the analysis of decisions involving risk. This is clearly shown in Application 3 dealing with the choice of a portfolio of stocks and bonds.

[3] In order to keep Figure 6-4 simple, we assume that the cost of the lottery ticket is the same as the cost of the previous insurance premium for the family, but the two analyses are independent.

[4] Point *CC''* is on straight dashed line *D'F'* and gives the utility of the family's expected income with the purchase of the lottery ticket. Since *CC''* exceeds *AA'* (the utility of income *OA* without the purchase of the ticket), it pays for the family to purchase the lottery ticket. Note that point *C* on the horizontal axis is much closer to point *D* than to point *F* because the probability of winning is very small.

[5] One of the shortcomings is that the theory *rationalizes* more than *explains* economic behavior in the face of risk.

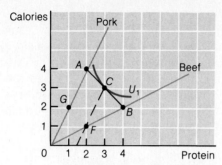 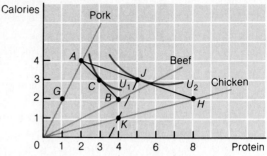

FIGURE 6-5.   The Characteristics Approach to Consumer Theory

In the left panel, $10 worth of pork gives the combination of protein and calories indicated by point A and $10 worth of beef gives point B. Thus, AB is the budget line. The consumer maximizes utility at point C where U_1 is tangent to AB, by spending $5 on pork and $5 on beef, and receiving OF characteristics from beef and FC (equals OG) from pork. In the right panel, $10 worth of chicken gives point H, so that the budget line is AH. The consumer maximizes utility at point J on U_2 by spending $5 on pork and $5 on chicken, and obtaining OK characteristics from chicken and KJ (equals OG) characteristics from pork, with no beef purchased.

6-5

The Characteristics Approach to Consumer Theory

The **characteristics approach to consumer theory,** pioneered by Kelvin Lancaster, postulates that a consumer demands a good because of the characteristics, properties, or attributes of the good, and it is these characteristics that give rise to utility. For example, a consumer does not demand beef, as such, but rather the characteristic of protein, which is the direct source of utility. Beef also provides calories, and protein and calories are also provided (though in different proportions) by pork and chicken. Thus, a good usually possesses more than one characteristic, and any given characteristic is present in more than one good.

The new characteristics approach to consumer theory can be shown graphically. In the left panel of Figure 6-5, the horizontal axis measures the characteristic of protein and the vertical axis measures calories. Suppose that the consumer's income is $10 and that $10 worth of pork provides the combination of protein and calories given by point *A*, while $10 worth of beef gives *B*.[6] The budget line is then *AB*. Area *OAB* is called the **feasible region** and budget line *AB* is the **efficiency frontier.** That is, the consumer can purchase any combination of protein and calories in area *OAB*, but he

---

[6] Note that the characteristics ray for pork has a slope four times larger than the characteristics ray for beef. Thus, pork provides four times as many calories per unit of protein as beef.

or she will maximize utility or satisfaction by choosing combinations on budget line *AB*.

If U_1 is a consumer's indifference curve in characteristics space (i.e., with characteristics protein and calories measured along the axes), the consumer maximizes utility at point *C*, where indifference curve U_1 is tangent to budget line *AB*. The consumer reaches point *C* by obtaining *OF* characteristics from spending $5 on beef and *FC* characteristics from spending the remaining $5 on pork. *OF* = ½*OB* and *OG* = ½*OA*. Note that *FC* equals *OG*, both in length and direction.[7]

In the right panel, a new good is introduced, chicken, which has half as many calories per unit of protein as beef. If $10 worth of chicken provides the combination of protein and calories given by point *H*, the new budget line or efficiency frontier becomes *AH*. The consumer now maximizes utility at point *J*, where indifference curve U_2 is tangent to budget line *AH*. He or she reaches point *J* by obtaining *OK* characteristics from spending $5 on chicken and *KJ* (equals *OG*) characteristics from spending the remaining $5 on pork. No beef is now purchased.

The reduction in the price of a good can be shown by a proportionate outward movement along the characteristics ray of the good, while an increase in income can be shown by a proportionate outward shift of the entire budget line. These will permit the consumer to reach a higher indifference curve as in traditional consumer theory (see Problem 9, with answer at the end of the text).

The new characteristics approach to consumer theory has several important advantages over traditional demand theory. First, substitution among goods can easily be explained in terms of some common characteristics of the goods. For example, according to this theory coffee and tea are substitutes because they both have the characteristic of being stimulants.

Second, the introduction of a new good can easily be taken care of by drawing a new ray from the origin reflecting the combination of the two characteristics of the new good. This was shown by the introduction of chicken in the right panel of Figure 6-5. However, the new good will only be purchased if its price is sufficiently low (e.g., chicken in the right panel of Figure 6-5). Had $10 worth of chicken provided only the combination of protein and calories given by point *K* on the characteristics ray for chicken, the budget line would become *ABK* and the consumer would maximize utility by remaining at point *C* and purchasing no chicken.

Third, a quality change can be shown by rotating the characteristics ray for the good. For example, the introduction of a new breed of leaner hogs resulting in pork with less calories per unit of protein can be shown by a clockwise rotation of the characteristics ray for pork. Finally, by comparing the price of two goods that are identical except for a particular character-

---

[7] *FC* and *OG* are called vectors. Thus, the above is an example of vector analysis, whereby vector *OC* (not shown in the left panel of Figure 6-5) is equal to the sum of vectors *OF* and *OG*.

istic, this approach permits the estimation of the implicit or **hedonic price** of the characteristic. This is shown in Example 6-3.

One disadvantage of the new theory is that some characteristics, such as taste and style, are subjective and cannot be measured explicitly. The problem is even more serious in dealing with the characteristics of services. Nevertheless, the hedonic approach is very useful because it allows at least an *implicit* measure of the various characteristics of each good (as the following example clearly demonstrates).

Example 6-3 Estimation of Implicit or Hedonic Prices

The Facts: Two researchers compared the price of houses that were identical except for being exposed to different levels of the pollutant nitrogen oxide in the Boston metropolitan area in 1970. They found that buyers of residential properties seemed willing to pay more for houses that were exposed to less atmospheric pollution. Specifically, for each one-part-per-hundred-million lower level of nitrogen oxide in the air, buyers were disposed to pay $1,600 for the same house in the less polluted area.

Comment: By comparing prices of houses that are otherwise identical except for some other characteristic, such as lower noise pollution, proximity to good schools, parks, and a good transportation network, we can estimate the implicit or hedonic price of each of these other characteristics. Similarly, we can estimate the hedonic price for each characteristic of an automobile by comparing the price of two automobiles that are identical except for the characteristic under consideration. Thus, the characteristics approach to consumer demand theory has the very useful property of allowing us to implicitly measure the various characteristics of each good.

Source: D. Harrison and D. Rubinfeld, "Hedonic Prices and the Demand for Clean Air," *Journal of Environmental Economics and Management,* March 1978, pp. 81–102.

6-6

Empirical Demand Curves

So far, we have discussed the theory of demand and theoretical demand curves. However, to analyze a real-world situation, we need the actual or empirical market demand curve. There are several different approaches to estimate market demand curves. One involves *interviews or questionnaires.* These ask consumers how much of a commodity they would purchase at various prices. However, it is generally agreed today that this procedure yields very biased results since consumers either cannot or will not give trustworthy answers.

Another approach is *consumer clinics*, where consumers are given a sum of money and asked to spend it in a simulated store to see how they react to price changes. However, the sample of consumers must necessarily be small because this procedure is expensive. Also, the results are questionable because consumers are aware that they are in an artificial situation. Still another approach is a *market experiment*, whereby the seller increases the price of the commodity in one market or store and lowers it in another, and then records the different quantities purchased in the two markets or stores. This procedure is questionable because (1) a small sample is involved, (2) the seller can permanently lose customers in the high-priced market or store, and (3) only the immediate or short-run response to the price change is obtained.

Today, market demand curves are generally estimated from actual market data of the quantities purchased of the commodity at various prices over time (i.e., using time series data) or for various consuming units or areas at one point in time (i.e., using cross-section data). However, only when the scatter of quantity-price observations (points) fall as in the left panel of Figure 6-6 can we estimate a demand curve from the data. When the points fall as in the right panel, we face an **identification problem** and may be able to estimate neither a reliable demand curve nor a supply curve for the commodity from the data.[8]

When quantity-price observations (points) fall as in the left panel of Figure 6-6, we can estimate the average demand curve for the good by correcting for the forces that cause the demand curve to shift (i.e., by correcting for the changes or differences in incomes and in the prices of related commodities). This is accomplished by the **multiple regression** statistical technique.[9] Regression analysis allows the economist to disentangle the independent effect of the various determinants of demand, so as to identify from the data the average market demand curve for the commodity (such as dashed line *D* in the left panel).

To conduct the regression analysis, the researcher collects data on the quantity purchased of the good in question, its price, the income of consumers, and the price of one or more related commodities (substitutes and complements). Regression analysis allows the researcher to correct for the effect of changes or differences in consumers' incomes and in the price of

---

[8] Each quantity-price observation (point) is usually given by the intersection of a different (and unknown) demand and supply curve for the commodity. The reason for this is that demand and supply curves usually shift over time and are usually different for different consumers and in different places. When the points fall as in the left panel, we can correct for the forces that cause the demand curve to shift and derive an average demand curve from the data. When the points fall as in the right panel and the shifts in demand and supply are not independent, we are unable to do so.

[9] Regression analysis is explained in a course in statistics. For an introduction to regression analysis, see D. Salvatore, *Statistics and Econometrics* (New York: McGraw-Hill, 1982), Chapters 6 and 7.

177

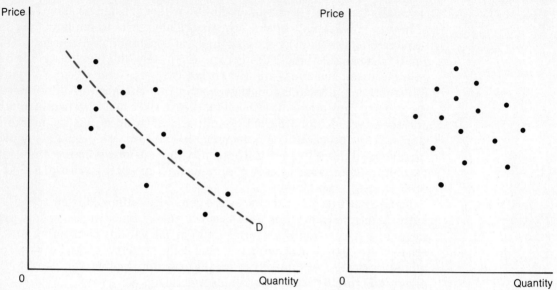

FIGURE 6-6.   *Empirical Estimation of Demand Curves*

When the scatter of quantity-price observations (points) fall as in the left panel we can estimate by regression analysis an average demand curve from the data, such as dashed line D. However, when the points fall as in the right panel, we may be unable to estimate or identify either a reliable demand or supply curve for the commodity from the data.

related commodities and permits the estimation of the average demand function that best fits the data (as, for example, D in the left panel of Figure 6-6). The values of all the collected variables are usually first transformed into logarithms because by doing so the estimated coefficients of the demand function are the various elasticities of demand.[10]

By regression analysis we estimate a demand function of the following form:

$$Q_x = a + bP_x + cI + eP_y \tag{6-6}$$

[10] In order for the estimated coefficients to be elasticities, the value of each variable collected must first be transformed into the natural logarithm. Natural logs are those to the base 2.718 (as opposed to common logs, which are to the base 10). For example, the natural log of 100, written ln100, is 4.61 (i.e., ln100 = 4.61). This is obtained by looking up the number 100 in a table of natural logs or more simply using a pocket calculator. The time series or the cross section data of each variable transformed into natural logs are then used to run the regression and obtain the various coefficients of the demand function. These estimated coefficients are themselves the elasticities. Why this is so is explained in a course of mathematics for economists. For an example of a demand curve estimated for data not transformed into natural logs, see Problem 12 (with answer at the end of the text).

where Q_x, P_x, I, and P_y usually refer to the logarithm of the quantity purchased of commodity X per unit of time, its price, the consumers' income, and the price of related commodity Y, respectively. $Q_x = a$ (the constant) when P_x, I, and P_y are all zero. The estimated coefficient of P_x, b, is the price elasticity of demand (when the regression is performed on the data transformed into logarithms). On the other hand, "c" is the estimated income elasticity of demand, while "e" is the estimated cross elasticity of demand of good X for good Y.

For the demand curve of good X to obey the law of demand, the estimated b coefficient (η_x) must be negative (so that quantity demanded and price are inversely related). Good X is a necessity if the estimated c coefficient (η_I) is positive but smaller than 1. On the other hand, good X is a luxury if $c > 1$ and an inferior good if $c < 0$. If the estimated e coefficient (η_{xy}) is positive, good Y is a substitute for good X. If $e < 0$, good Y is a complement of good X.

While regression analysis is not devoid of problems, it is the most extensively used technique today for the estimation of market demand curves and the one utilized in measuring all elasticities presented in Chapter 5. As the following example shows, the results of empirical demand studies are usually reported in the form of estimated elasticity coefficients.

Example 6-4   The Demand for Electricity in the United States

The Facts: Table 6-3 reports the actual or estimated elasticity of demand for electricity for residential use in the United States, with respect to the price of electricity, per capita income, the price of gas, and the number of customers in the market. These elasticities were obtained from the market demand function estimated by multiple regression analysis. The data used were cross-sectional data transformed into natural logarithms for the 48 contiguous states in the United States for the year 1969.

Comment: The above results indicate that the amount of electricity for residential use consumed in the United States would fall by 9.74 per cent as a result of a 10 per cent increase in the price of electricity, would increase by 7.14 per cent with a 10 per cent increase in per capita income, would increase by 1.59 per cent with a 10 per cent increase in the price of gas,

TABLE 6-3   Elasticities of Demand for Electricity for Residential Use in the United States

Variable	Value
Price	(−)0.974
Per capita income	0.714
Price of gas	0.159
Number of customers	1.000

and is proportional to the number of customers in the market. Thus, the market demand curve for electricity is negatively sloped, electricity is a normal good and a necessity, and gas is a substitute for electricity. Using the above estimated demand elasticities and projecting the growth in per capita income, in the price of gas, in the number of customers in the market, and in the price of electricity, public utilities could forecast the growth in the demand for electricity in the United States in subsequent years (see Application 4). This is extremely important to meet future electricity needs since it takes many years to plan and build for higher capacity.

Source: R. Halvorson, "Demand for Electric Energy in the United States," *Southern Economic Journal,* April 1976, pp. 610–625.

6-7

Applications

In this section, we apply the tools developed in the chapter to analyze a number of important economic problems and uses of the new tools. These range from deriving a compensated demand curve that keeps real (rather than money) income constant, deriving the usual and the compensated demand curve by revealed preference, choosing a portfolio of stocks and bonds, and forecasting residential demand for electricity in the United States. These applications show the great importance and relevance of the extensions of demand theory presented in this chapter.

Application 1: Compensated Demand Curve

From Figure 6-1, we can derive the usual demand curve (which shows both the substitution and the income effects) and the **compensated demand curve** (which shows only the Slutsky substitution effect). This is shown in Figure 6-7.

The top panel of Figure 6-7 repeats Figure 6-1 for ease of reference. Individual demand curves d_x and d_x^* in the bottom panel are derived from the top panel. Demand curve d_x is the usual demand curve as derived in Figure 4-3 and shows both the substitution and income effects. Demand curve d_x^* is the income-compensated demand curve. It shows only the Slutsky substitution effect.

Specifically, with $I = \$10$ and $P_y = \$1$, the individual maximizes utility at point B, where indifference curve U_1 is tangent to budget line JK when $P_x = \$2$, and he or she maximizes utility at point E, where indifference curve U_2 is tangent to budget line JK'' with $P_x = \$1$ (see the top panel of Figure 6-7). The movement from point B to point E (i.e., from $2X$ to $6X$) reflects the sum of the substitution and the income effects of the reduction in P_x from \$2 to \$1. This is shown by the movement from point B' to point E' along the usual demand curve d_x in the bottom panel. The Slutsky sub-

FIGURE 6-7.
Usual and
Compensated
Demand Curve

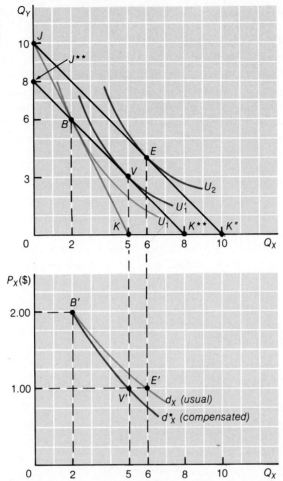

The top panel repeats Figure 6–1. The bottom panel is derived from the top panel
and shows the usual demand curve d_x as derived in Figure 4–3. d_x shows both the
substitution and income effects. d_x^* is the compensated demand curve. It shows the
Slutsky substitution effect only.

stitution effect is shown in the top panel of Figure 6-7 by the movement
from point B on indifference curve U_1 to point V on indifference curve U_1'.
This involves the increase from 2 to 5 units in the quantity demanded of
commodity X by the individual and is reflected by the movement from
point B' to point V' along the (Slutsky) compensated demand curve d_x^* in
the bottom panel.

Note that d_x^* is less elastic than d_x because d_x^* excludes the positive
income effect on normal commodity X. Specifically, since X is a normal
good, the substitution and the income effects reinforce each other in leading to a greater quantity demanded of X when P_x falls. Since d_x^* shows only

the substitution effect while d_x shows both the substitution and the income effects, d_x^* is steeper and less elastic than d_x. Furthermore, since d_x^* shows only the substitution effect, the Giffen case is ruled out. That is, while d_x could, in rare instances, slope upward for some inferior (Giffen) goods (thereby representing the exception to the law of downward-sloping demand), d_x^* is always negatively sloped because it only shows the substitution effect and this always leads to a greater quantity of the commodity being purchased when its price falls.[11] Finally, note that we can also derive a compensated demand curve showing only the Hicksian substitution effect (see Problem 1, with answer at the end of the text).

The great importance of the income-compensated demand curve stems from the fact that this is the general nature of statistical demand curves estimated from quantity-price observations. That is, as discussed in Section 6-6 and Example 5-1, a statistical demand function, by disentangling the independent effect of the change in the price of the commodity from that brought about by changes in *real* income and in the prices of related commodities, gives essentially an income-compensated demand curve. However, this does not mean that the usual demand curve (showing both the substitution and income effects) is not important also. Indeed, it is the usual demand curve that is relevant to businessmen when they decide what prices to charge. Thus, both the usual and the compensated demand curves are useful for some purposes.

Application 2: Usual and Compensated Demand Curve by Revealed Preference

The theory of revealed preference can be used to derive the usual and the compensated demand curve without using indifference curves. This is shown in Figure 6-8. The top panel of Figure 6-8 is identical to both Figure 6-1 and the top panel of Figure 6-7 except for the omission of all indifference curves. The consumer is originally *observed* to be at point B with budget line JK. When the price of X falls from $P_x = \$2$ to $P_x = \$1$, the budget line becomes JK″ and the consumer's real income rises. To keep real income constant as at point B, JK is rotated counterclockwise through point B until it is parallel to JK″. This can be accomplished with a lump-sum tax that allows the consumer to purchase combination B at the lower price of X. The result is budget line J**K**.

With budget line J**K**, the individual will not consume along J**B because it is below JB, and JB is inferior to B. Instead, the individual consumes along BK**, say, at point V. Point V involves more of X and less of Y than at point B because P_x/P_y has fallen. The movement from B to V (3X) is the substitution effect shown by compensated demand curve d_x^* in the

---

[11] For an inferior good that is not a Giffen good, the usual demand curve is steeper or less elastic than the compensated demand curve for a price reduction.

FIGURE 6-8.
Usual and
Compensated
Demand Curve by
Revealed
Preference

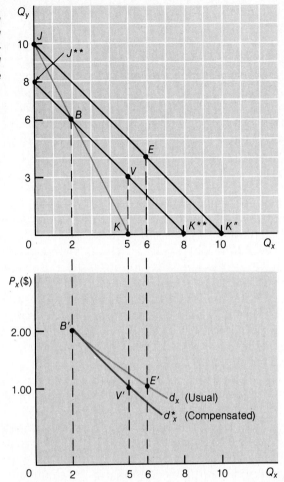

This figure is identical to Figure 6–7, except for the omission of indifference curves from the top panel. The consumer is observed to be at point B on JK with P_x = $2, and at point E on JK″ with P_x = $1. This is the total effect shown on the usual d_x in the bottom panel. With budget line J**K** (which keeps real income constant as at point B), the consumer is observed to purchase combination V. The movement from B to V is the Slutsky substitution effect (3X) shown by compensated demand curve d_x^* in the bottom panel.

bottom panel.[12] If the consumer's real income is then allowed to rise to the level indicated by budget line JK″ (by rebating the lump-sum tax), the consumer will purchase still more of commodity X, if X is a normal good. If the consumer is observed to be at point E with budget line JK″, the move-

---

[12] It is this positive substitution effect when the price of good X falls that makes compensated demand curve d_x^* in the bottom panel negatively sloped.

ment from point V to point E $(1X)$ is the income effect associated with the reduction in P_x (see the top panel of Figure 6-8).

Thus, we see that of the total increase of 4 units (from 2 to 6) in the quantity purchased of good X when its price falls from $P_x = \$2$ to $P_x = \$1$, three of the units are accounted for by the substitution effect and one by the income effect. Usual demand curve d_x shown in the bottom panel of Figure 6-8 reflects both the substitution and the income effects while compensated demand curve d_x^* shows only the (Slutsky) substitution effect. Note that d_x and d_x^* in the bottom panel of Figure 6-7 and in Figure 6-8 are identical, but in Figure 6-8 they were derived without using indifference curves.

Application 3: Choosing a Portfolio

An important application of the economic theory of choices involving risk is in the selection of a portfolio (stocks and bonds) in which to invest part of one's wealth. Each portfolio has an expected rate of return and an expected rate of risk (usually measured by the variability of the return). These are measured on the vertical and horizontal axes, respectively, of Figure 6-9. Since investors on the average, are risk averse, they will hold a more risky portfolio only if it provides a higher return. For example, the additional risk (a bad) that the individual faces at point E than at point C on indifference curve U_1 is just balanced by the higher return that he or she receives at point E. Thus, indifference curves are here positively sloped as indicated in the figure. Indifference curve U_1 represents more utility than U_0 because it involves either a higher return for a given risk or a smaller risk for a given return.

Suppose that for simplicity there exist only two assets, with return and risk given by points A and B, respectively. If the risk of assets A and B are independent, the investor can choose any mixed portfolio of assets A and B shown on curve AEB. To understand the shape of curve AEB, note that the investor has available mixed portfolios with a return anywhere between that of asset A and asset B alone, depending on the particular combination of assets A and B in the portfolio. As far as risk is concerned, there are portfolios on frontier AEB that have lower risks than those which are comprised exclusively of either asset A or asset B.[13] That is, by diversifying his or her investment, the investor can reduce overall risks. This accords with the old saying "don't put all your eggs in one basket."[14]

The optimum portfolio for the investor in Figure 6-9 is the mixed portfolio indicated by point E, where indifference curve U_1 is tangent to fron-

[13] For example, suppose that the probability of a low return is ¼ on asset A and ½ on asset B and that we now take the probability of a low return as the measure of risk. If these probabilities are independent, the probability of a low return on both A and B at the same time is $(½)(¼) = ⅛$ or smaller than for either A or B separately.

[14] If the return of asset A were inversely correlated with that of asset B, so that when the return of one asset is high, the return of the other asset is low, curve AEB would be even more bowed out than AEB.

FIGURE 6-9.
Choosing a Portfolio

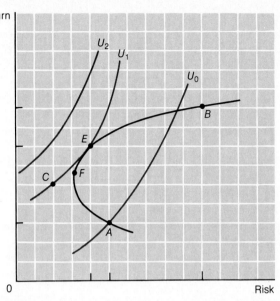

Indifference curves U_0, U_1, and U_2 show various levels of satisfaction, with $U_2 > U_1$ $> U_0$. Points on a given indifference curve (such as C and E on U_1) show the various combinations of return and risk that assure the investor equal satisfaction. On the other hand, frontier AEB represents those combinations of return and risk that are obtainable with a mixed portfolio of asset A and asset B with independent risk. The optimum portfolio for the investor is represented by point E, where U_1 is tangent to the frontier AEB. A more risk-averse investor would have steeper indifference curves and choose a mixed portfolio such as F with a lower risk and return than E.

tier *AEB*. A more risk-averse investor would have steeper indifference curves and would choose a less risky (but a lower-return) portfolio on *AEB* (as indicated, for example, by point *F*).

When faced with uncertainty in the market place, consumers often attempt to reduce it by searching for more information. They may do so by purchasing published information, by visiting more stores or dealers to get a better deal (for example, in purchasing a new car), or by hiring consultants. Such a search would end when the marginal return from the search has fallen to the level of the marginal or extra cost of additional search.

Application 4: Forecasting Residential Demand for Electricity

Using the elasticities presented in Table 6-3 and projecting the growth in per capita income, in the price of gas, in the number of customers in the market, and in the price of electricity, we can forecast the growth in the demand for electricity in the United States.

For example, if we assume that per capita incomes will grow at a rate of 3 percent per year, the price of gas at 20 percent per year, the number of customers by 1 percent per year, and the price of electricity at 4 percent per year, we can forecast that the demand for electricity for residential use in the United States will expand at a rate of 2.43 percent per year. This is obtained by adding the product of the value of each elasticity by the projected growth of the corresponding variable, as indicated in the following equation:

$$Q = (0.714)(3\%) + (0.159)(20\%) + (1.000)(1\%) - (0.974)(4\%)$$
$$= 2.142 + 3.180 + 1.000 - 3.896$$
$$= 6.322 - 3.896 = 2.426$$

With different projections as to the yearly growth in per capita income, the price of gas, the number of customers in the market, and the price of electricity, we will get correspondingly different results.

The above results are shown in Figure 6-10, where P_0 and Q_0 are the original price and quantity of electricity demanded in the United States on hypothetical demand curve D_0 in the base period (say, the current year). Demand curve D' results from the projected increase in per capita income, D'' from the increase in the price of gas also, and D_1 from the increase in

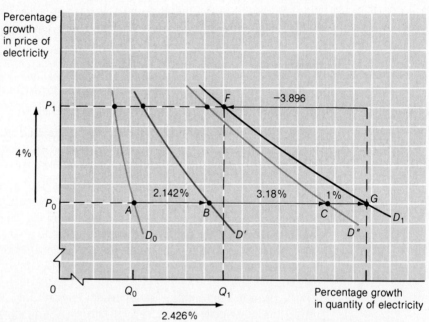

FIGURE 6-10.
Forecast of
Electricity in the
United States

P_0 and Q_0 are the original price and quantity of electricity demanded in the U.S. on hypothetical demand curve D_0 · Demand Curve D' results from projecting a 3 per cent increase in per capita incomes, D'' by also projecting a 20 per cent increase in the price of gas, and D_1 from a 1 percent increase in the number of customers in the market as well. If the price of electricity is also assumed to increase by 4 per cent (from P_0 to P_1), the demand for electricity increases by 2.426 per cent per year (the movement from point A on D_0 to point F on D_1).

the number of customers in the market as well. Thus, D_1 takes into account or reflects the cumulative effect of all the growth factors considered.

Were the price of electricity to remain constant, the demand for electricity would rise by 6.322 per cent per year (given by the movement from point A on D_0 to point G on D_1 in the figure). The projected increase in the price of electricity by 4 per cent per year (from P_0 to P_1), by itself, will result in a decline in the quantity demanded of electricity by 3.896 per cent (the movement from point G to point F on D_1). The net result of all forces at work gives rise to a net increase in Q of 2.426 per cent per year (the movement from point A on D_0 to point F on D_1).

The results of empirical studies on the demand for electricity in the United States and in other countries are very useful to evaluate changes in electricity use and to forecast future use. For example, studies of this nature led to forecasts that the growth of demand for electricity during the 1970s and 1980s was going to be much smaller than originally anticipated because of the increase in electricity rates (as a result of the sharp increase in petroleum prices and sluggish growth of the nation as a whole). This led to the cancellation of many major power plants projects. Demand studies have been conducted for practically every major commodity in the United States and are widely used by businessmen and managers to forecast future demand. This, in turn, greatly affects investments in new plants and equipment and the general level of economic activity.

Summary

1. The Slutsky substitution effect is obtained by rotating the original budget line through the original optimum point (before the price change) until it is parallel to the budget line after the price change. The movement from the original equilibrium point to the point where the rotated budget line is tangent to a higher (than the original) indifference curve is the Slutsky substitution effect. This is more practical and empirically useful than the Hicksian substitution effect.

2. According to the theory of revealed preference, a consumer's indifference curve can be derived from observing the actual market behavior of the consumer and without any need to inquire directly into his or her preferences. The theory is based on the assumption that tastes are constant, consistent, transitive, and such that the consumer can be induced to purchase any basket of commodities if its price is lowered sufficiently. According to this theory, the indifference curve is tangent to the original budget line at the original optimum point and everywhere else above the original budget line. By using additional observed market choices of the consumer at different money incomes and commodity prices, we can eliminate more and more of the zone of ignorance so as to pinpoint more and more precisely the location of the indifference curve.

3. Index numbers are used to measure changes in standards of living or welfare, especially during inflationary periods. The expenditure index (E) is the ratio of money income or expenditures in period 1 relative to the base period. The Laspeyres price index (L) is the ratio of the cost of purchasing base period quantities at period 1 prices relative to base period prices. The Paasche price index (P) is the ratio of the cost of purchasing period 1 quantities at period 1 prices relative to base period prices. The consumer is better off in period 1 if E exceeds L. He or she is better off

in the base period if $E < P$. The most important price index is the consumer price index (CPI). This is a Laspeyres price index.

4. Traditional demand theory is of limited applicability because it assumes a riskless world, while most economic decisions are made in the face of risk or uncertainty. Traditional economic theory could not deal with choices subject to risk because of its strict adherence to the principle of diminishing marginal utility of money. By postulating a total utility of money function that first increases at a decreasing rate (MU declines) and then increases at an increasing rate (MU increases), Friedman and Savage could rationalize why a family would purchase insurance and also buy a lottery ticket (i.e., choices involving risk).

5. The characteristics approach to consumer theory postulates that a consumer demands a good because of its characteristics or attributes. A good usually possesses more than one characteristic and any one characteristic is present in more than one good. With indifference curves drawn in characteristics space, we can show utility maximization and the effect of price and income changes (just as with the traditional approach). As opposed to traditional demand

theory, the characteristics approach can also deal with the introduction of new goods and quality changes.

6. To analyze a real world situation, an actual or empirical market demand curve is required. This is usually obtained by regression analysis using actual market data. Sometimes, however, it is very difficult or impossible to identify either the demand curve or the supply curve of a commodity from the data. When the regression analysis is conducted on data transformed into natural logarithms, the coefficients of the estimated demand function are the various elasticities of demand. These are very useful in forecasting.

7. A compensated demand curve keeps real income constant (i.e., reflects only the substitution effect). The theory of revealed preference can be used to derive the usual and the Slutsky income-compensated demand curves without using indifference curves. Utility theory under uncertainty is useful in choosing a portfolio of assets. From the actual estimated elasticities of demand and from the anticipated change in the various independent variables in the demand function we can forecast the change in the demand for the commodity.

Glossary

Slutsky substitution effect The change in the quantity purchased of a commodity from the original optimum point to the point where a new budget line (going through the original point and parallel to the budget line after the price change) is tangent to a higher (than the original) indifference curve.

Hicksian substitution effect The change in the quantity purchased of a commodity from the original optimum point to the point where a new budget line parallel to the budget line after the price change is tangent to the original indifference curve.

Theory of revealed preference The theory that postulates that a consumer's indifference curve can be derived from the consumer's market behavior and without any need to inquire directly into his or her preferences.

Consistent The property of consumers' tastes whereby if a consumer purchases basket A rather than basket B, he or she will never prefer B to A.

Transitive The property of consumers' tastes whereby if a consumer prefers A to B and B to C, he or she will prefer A to C.

Zone of ignorance The area above the original budget line and to the left and below perpendiculars to the axes from the original optimum point, in which the consumer's indifference curve is located.

Income or **expenditure index (E)** The ratio of period 1 to base period money income or expenditures.

Laspeyres price index (L) The ratio of the cost of purchasing base period quantities at period 1 prices relative to base period prices.

Paasche price index (P) The ratio of the cost of

purchasing period 1 quantities at period 1 prices relative to base period prices.

Expected income ($\bar{I}$)   The probability of one level of income (p) times that income level plus the probability of an alternative income ($1 - p$) times that alternative income level.

Characteristics approach to consumer theory   It postulates that a consumer demands a good because of its characteristics or attributes and it is these characteristics that give rise to utility.

Feasible region   The area in characteristics space showing all the combinations of characteristics that the consumer can purchase with his or her income and commodity prices.

Efficiency frontier   The budget line in characteristics space.

Hedonic price   The implicit price of a characteristic of a good.

Identification problem   The difficulty sometimes encountered in estimating the market demand or supply curve of a commodity from quantity-price observations.

Multiple regression   A statistical technique that allows the economist to disentangle the independent effect of the various determinants of demand, so as to identify from the data the average market demand curve for the commodity.

Compensated demand curve   A demand curve showing only the substitution effect.

Questions for Review

1. (a) Why is the budget line that is used to measure the Slutsky substitution effect parallel to the budget line after the price change?
   (b) Why does the budget line that is used to measure the Slutsky substitution effect pass through the original optimum point?
   (c) How is the size of the Slutsky substitution effect measured?

2. (a) How is the Hicksian substitution effect measured?
   (b) How do the Hicksian and the Slutsky substitution effects differ?
   (c) Which is larger: the Hicksian or the Slutsky substitution effect for a reduction in the commodity price? Why?

3. (a) What is meant by the theory of revealed preference?
   (b) In what way does the theory of revealed preference extend traditional demand theory?
   (c) What is the most important use of the theory of revealed preference?

4. (a) How is the point of tangency of the indifference curve to the original budget line determined by the theory of revealed preference?
   (b) What is meant by the zone of ignorance?
   (c) How can the size of the zone of ignorance be reduced?

5. Define the following in words and symbols:
   (a) the income or expenditure index.
   (b) the Laspeyres price index.
   (c) the Paasche price index.

6. Define an increase and a decrease in the standard of living
   (a) in words.
   (b) using the expenditure, the Laspeyres, and the Paasche price indices.
   (c) graphically.

7. (a) Why is traditional demand theory unable to explain or deal with choices involving risk?
   (b) What is meant by expected income?
   (c) Is an individual who refuses a 50–50 bet to win or lose a given amount of money an insurer or a gambler?

8. (a) Does the marginal utility of money increase or decrease for an insurer?
   (b) Does the marginal utility of money increase or decrease for a gambler?
   (c) How can we explain an individual being an insurer and a gambler at the same time?
   (d) Would an individual with constant MU of money accept a 50–50 bet?

9. What is meant by
   (a) the characteristics approach to consumer theory?
   (b) characteristics space?
   (c) feasible region? efficiency frontier?

10. (a) How can the characteristics approach to consumer theory deal with the effect of price and income changes?
    (b) Which are the most important advantages of the characteristics approach over traditional consumer theory?
    (c) What is a disadvantage of the characteristics approach to consumer theory?
11. What are the disadvantages of using each of the following procedures to obtain a market demand curve empirically?

(a) Interviews and questionnaires.
(b) Consumer clinics.
(c) Market experiments.

12. (a) How are most demand curves estimated today?
    (b) What is meant by the identification problem?
    (c) When are the coefficients of the estimated market demand function themselves the various elasticities of demand?

Problems

★1. (a) Draw a graph that in its top panel shows both the Hicksian and the Slutsky substitution effects for a decrease in commodity prices, and in its bottom panel shows the derivation of the usual demand curve, and the Hicksian and the Slutsky compensated demand curves.
   (b) Which is better, the Hicksian or the Slutsky substitution effect, for empirical work? Why?

 2. Repeat the procedure in Problem 1a for an increase in the commodity price.

★3. (a) Show how the total effect of a 260 gallon reduction per year in family gasoline consumption was obtained in Example 6-1 from the data given in the example.
   (b) Show how the income effect of about 34 gallons in Example 6-1 was obtained.

 4. (a) Redraw the left panel of Figure 6-2 and show on it how the zone of ignorance above budget line NN can be further reduced.
   (b) Redraw the right panel of Figure 6-2 and show on it how the zone of ignorance to the left of LA and below AM can be further reduced.
   (c) Draw a figure showing (on the same graph) the lower and the upper boundaries of the indifference curve found in parts (a) and (b).

 5. Given the following data, calculate the expenditure index, the Laspeyres price index, and

the Paasche price index, and determine if the standard of living of the consumer increased or decreased from the base period to period 1.

Year	x	P_x	y	P_y
1980 (base)	2	$2	3	$1
1985	3	3	2	2

6. Given the following hypothetical data, determine what happened to the consumer's standard of living in 1983, 1984, and 1985 in relation to 1977.

Year	x	P_x	y	P_y
1977 (base)	4	$2	3	$3
1983	4	4	4	4
1984	2	6	2	5
1985	3	6	4	7

7. With reference to Figure 6-4, if $OA = \$50,000$, $OB = \$10,000$ and the probability of income OB, $p = 95$ per cent,
   (a) find $\bar{I}$.
   (b) what is the maximum amount that this family would pay for the insurance?

★8. Suppose that an individual is just willing to accept a bet to win or lose $1,000 if the odds of winning are 60 percent. Suppose also that if the individual loses, he or she loses 150 utils.
   (a) Is the individual a gambler or an insurer?

★ = answer found at the end of the book.

190

(b) How much utility does the individual gain if he or she wins the bet?

(c) Is this a cardinal measure of utility?

★9. Starting with the left panel of Figure 6-5, show

(a) a 50 percent reduction in the price of pork and its effect on consumer utility maximization.

(b) a 50 per cent increase in the consumer's income and its effect on consumer utility maximization.

10. Starting with the right panel of Figure 6-5, indicate

(a) what producers of beef can do to regain their lost market.

(b) the general condition for a new good being purchased.

(c) the general relationship between the number of characteristics and the number of goods purchased.

(d) when a consumer will purchase only one good.

11. Given the following estimated elasticities of the demand for commodity X, $\eta_x = (-1)1.5$, $\eta_I = 3$, and $\eta_{xy} = -0.5$, answer the following questions.

(a) Does the demand for commodity X obey the law of demand? Is commodity X a necessity, a luxury, or an inferior good? Is good Y a substitute or a complement of X?

(b) By how much does the quantity purchased of X change if P_x falls by 5 per cent? If I rises by 5 per cent? If P_y rises by 1 percent? If all of the above occur?

12. Given the following estimated market demand function,

$$Q_x = 100 - 1.5P_x + 3.0I - 0.5P_y$$

where, Q_x is the quantity demanded of commodity X in million pounds per year, P_x is the price of X in dollars per pound, I is the income in thousands of dollars, and P_y is the price of commodity Y in dollars per pound. (Note that the above variables are not expressed in terms of natural logarithms.)

(a) indicate by how much Q_x changes as a result of a \$1 increase in P_x, a \$2,000 increase in income, a \$2 increase in P_y.

(b) if the average values (indicated by a bar on the variable) are $\overline{Q}_x = 20$, $\overline{P}_x = \$15$, $\overline{I} = \$10$, and $\overline{P}_y = \$8$, find the value of η_x, η_I, and η_{xy}.

Supplementary Readings

For a problem-solving approach to the topics discussed in this chapter, see

Dominick Salvatore, *Microeconomic Theory,* 2nd ed. (New York: McGraw-Hill, 1983), Chapter 6.

A more detailed and advanced presentation and comparison of the Slutsky and Hicksian substitution effects is found in

Milton Friedman, *Price Theory,* 2nd ed. (Chicago: Aldine, 1976), pp. 47–54.

An alternative presentation of the theory of revealed preference is found in

William J. Baumol, *Economic Theory and Operations Research* (Englewood Cliffs, N.J.: Prentice-Hall, 1977), pp. 343–353.

A more extensive discussion of index numbers is found in

R. D. G. Allen, *Index Numbers in Theory and Practice* (London: Macmillan, 1975).

The original (and difficult) paper on utility theory involving risk is

Milton Friedman and **L. J. Savage,** "The Utility Analysis of Choices Involving Risk," *Journal of Political Economy,* August 1948, pp. 279–304.

The original (and difficult) paper that introduced the characteristics approach to consumer demand theory is

Kelvin Lancaster, "A New Approach to Consumer Demand Theory," *Journal of Political Economy,* January–February 1966, pp. 132–157.

On the estimation of empirical demand curves, see

William J. Baumol, *op. cit.,* pp. 227–247.

THREE

Theory of Production and Cost

Part Three (Chapters 7–9) presents the theory of production and cost. Chapter 7 examines production theory or how firms combine resources or inputs to produce final commodities. These concepts are then utilized and extended in Chapter 8 to examine costs of production and to derive the short-run and the long-run cost curves of the firm. Finally, Chapter 9 presents more advanced topics in the theory of production and costs. The presentation of the theory is reinforced throughout with many real-world examples and important applications.

Production Theory

7-1 Organization of Production and Classification of Inputs

7-2 Production With One Variable Input

7-3 Production With Two Variable Inputs

7-4 The Shape of Isoquants

7-5 Constant, Increasing, and Decreasing Returns to Scale

7-6 Applications

Examples

7-1 Diminishing Returns in Potato Production

7-2 Isoquants in Corn Production

7-3 Returns to Scale in U.S. Manufacturing Industries

Applications

Application 1: Population, Technology, and Diminishing Returns

Application 2: Speed Limit and Gasoline Consumption

Application 3: Energy and Capital Substitution in Production

Application 4: Economies and Diseconomies of Scale and the Optimal Size of Tankers

Chapter 7

Preview Questions

How is production organized in the U.S. economy?

Why is it important for resources to be used efficiently in production?

How can production take place when only some resources can be varied?

Can the availability of resources be increased over time?

Why is production more efficient when all resources can be varied?

Are most commodities produced with fixed or variable input combinations?

If all inputs are doubled, will output double?

Has the size of most firms increased over time?

In Part II, we examined the theory of consumer behavior and demand. Our focus of attention was the consumer. In Part III, we examine the theory of production and cost. Here the focus of attention is the firm. This chapter examines the theory of production or how firms organize production. That is, we examine how firms combine resources or inputs to produce final commodities. The next chapter then builds on the discussion in this chapter and analyzes the costs of production of the firm.

This chapter begins with a discussion of the organization of production. Here we define the meaning of production, examine the reason for the existence of firms and their aim, classify resources or inputs into various categories, and define the meaning of the short run and the long run in production. From this, we go on to present the theory of production when only one input is variable. This is accomplished by defining the total, the average, and the marginal product curve of the variable input. Production theory will subsequently be extended to deal with two variable inputs by the introduction of isoquants.

From the theory of production where only one or two inputs are variable, we proceed to examine cases in which all inputs are variable. Here, we define the meaning of constant, increasing, and decreasing returns to scale, the conditions under which they arise, and their importance. Finally, we present some important applications of production theory. These, together with the real-world examples included in the theory sections, highlight the importance and relevance of the theory of production presented in the chapter.

195

Organization of Production and Classification of Inputs

In this section we examine the organization of production and classify inputs into various categories. We begin by focusing on the meaning and organization of production and the reason for the existence of firms and their aim. Then, we go on to classify inputs into various broad categories. This will serve as a general background for the theory of production presented in subsequent sections.

7-1a The Organization of Production

Production refers to the transformation of resources into outputs of goods and services. For example, General Motors hires workers who use machinery in factories to transform steel, plastic, glass, rubber, and so on, into automobiles. The output of a firm can either be a final commodity such as automobiles or an intermediate product such as steel (which is used in the production of automobiles and other goods). The output can also be a service rather than a good. Examples of services are education, medicine, banking, legal counsel, accounting work, communication, transportation, storage, wholesaling, retailing, and many others. Finally, production is a flow concept or has a time dimension. It refers to the rate of output over a given period of time. This is to be distinguished from the stock of a commodity or input that refers to the quantity of the commodity (such as the number of automobiles) or input (such as the tons of steel) at hand or available at a particular point in time.

More than 80 per cent of all goods and services consumed in the United States is produced by firms. The remainder is produced by the government and nonprofit organizations such as the Red Cross, private colleges, foundations, and so on. A **firm** is an organization that combines and organizes resources for the purpose of producing goods and services for sale at a profit. There are millions of firms in the United States. These include proprietorships (firms owned by one individual), partnerships (owned by two or more individuals), and corporations (owned by stockholders). The way the firm is organized is not of primary concern in the study of microeconomic theory; only what they *do* is. Firms arise because it would be very inefficient and costly for workers and for the owners of capital and land to enter into and enforce contracts with one another to pool their resources for the purpose of producing goods and services.

Just as consumers seek to maximize utility or satisfaction, firms generally seek to maximize profits. Both consumers and firms can be regarded as maximizing entities. Profits refer to the revenue of the firm from the sale of the output after all costs have been deducted. Included in costs are not only the actual wages paid to hired workers and payments for purchasing other inputs but also the income that the owner of the firm would earn by working for someone else and the return that he or she would receive from investing his or her capital in the best *alternative* use. For example, the owner of a delicatessen must include in his or her costs not only payments for the rental of the store, hired help, and for the purchase of the hams, cheeses, beers, milk, crackers, and so on in the store. He or she must also include as part of costs the foregone earnings of the money invested in the store as well as the earnings that he or she would receive by working for someone else in a similar capacity (e.g., as the manager of another delicatessen). The owner earns (economic) profits only if total revenue exceeds total costs (which includes actual expenses and the alternatives foregone).

The profit-maximizing assumption provides the framework for analyzing the behavior of the firm in microeconomic theory. It is from this assumption that the behavior of the firm can be studied most fruitfully. This assumption has recently been challenged by the so-called "managerial theories of the firm" (discussed in greater detail in Chapter 13), which postulate multiple goals for the firm. That is, after attaining "satisfactory" rather than maximum profits, the large modern corporation is said to seek to maintain or increase its market share, maximize sales or growth, maintain a large staff of executives and lavish offices, minimize uncertainty, create and maintain a good public image as a desirable member of the community and good employer, and so on. However, because many of these goals can be regarded as indirect ways to earn and increase profits in the long run, we will retain the profit-maximizing assumption.

7-1b Classification of Inputs

As stated above, firms tranform inputs into outputs. **Inputs,** resources, or factors of production are the means of producing the goods and services demanded by society. Inputs can be classified broadly into labor or human resources (including entrepreneurial talent), capital, and land or natural resources. However, this threefold classification of inputs is only a convenient way to organize the discussion and does not convey the enormous variety of specific resources in each category. For example, labor includes simple clerks and assembly-line workers as well as accountants, teachers, engineers, doctors, and scientists, and we must consider the specific types of labor and other inputs required for the analysis of production of a particular firm or industry.[1]

Particularly important among inputs is **entrepreneurship.** This refers to the ability on the part of some individuals to see opportunities to combine

---

[1] The reason is that different skills require varying training costs and wages to be supplied. Thus, to analyze the production process of a particular firm or industry, we must consider the *specific* types of labor and other inputs that are required. Yet, for general theoretical work, it is often convenient to deal with the broad input categories of labor, capital, and land.

resources in new and more efficient ways to produce a particular commodity or to produce entirely new commodities. The motivation is the great profit possibilities that an entrepreneur may believe to exist. The entrepreneur either uses his or her resources to exploit these profit opportunities or, more likely, attempts to convince other people with large sums of money to put some of that money at his or her disposal to introduce new production techniques or new products and share in the potential profits. We have many examples of this during the late 1970s and early 1980s in the field of microcomputers. This was a time when some young engineers and computer experts sought to combine new and more powerful chips (the basic memory component of computers) to produce cheaper or better microcomputers. Some of these entrepreneurs were successful and became rich overnight (e.g., the developers of the Apple Computers). Most had to abandon their dream after huge losses. In any event, entrepreneurs play a very crucial role in modern economies. They are responsible for the introduction of new technology and new products, and for most of the growth of the economy as a whole.

Inputs can be further classified into fixed and variable. **Fixed inputs** are those that cannot be varied or can be varied only with excessive cost during the time period under consideration. Examples of fixed inputs are the firm's plant and specialized equipment. For example, it takes many years for GM to build a new automobile plant and introduce robots to perform many repetitive assembly-line tasks. **Variable inputs,** on the other hand, are those that can be varied easily and on a short notice during the time period under consideration. Examples of these are raw materials and many types of workers, particularly those with low levels of skills. Thus, whether an input is fixed or variable depends on the time horizon being considered. The time period during which at least one input is fixed is called the **short run,** while the time period during which all inputs are variable is called the **long run.** Obviously, the length of time it takes to vary all inputs (i.e. to be in the long run), varies for firms in different industries. For a street vendor of apples, the long run may be a day. For an apple farmer, it is at least five years (this is how long it takes for newly planted trees to begin bearing fruit).

7-2

Production With One Variable Input

In this section, we present the theory of production when only one input is variable. Thus, we are dealing with the short run. We begin by defining the total, the average, and the marginal product of the variable input and examining their relationship graphically. We will then discuss the important law of diminishing returns and the meaning and importance of the stages of production. Production theory with more than one variable input is taken up in subsequent sections.

7-2a Total, Average, and Marginal Product

A **production function** is a unique relationship between inputs and outputs. It can be represented by a table, a graph, or an equation showing the maximum output of a commodity that can be produced per period of time with each set of inputs. Both output and inputs are measured in physical rather than monetary units. Technology is assumed to remain constant. A simple short-run production function is obtained by applying various amounts of labor to farm one acre of land and recording the resulting output or **total product (TP)** per period of time. This is illustrated by the first two columns of Table 7-1.

The first two columns of Table 7-1 provide a hypothetical production function for a farm using various quantities of labor (i.e., number of workers per year) to cultivate wheat on one acre of land (and using no other input). Note that when no labor is used, total output or product is zero. With one unit of labor (1L), total product (TP) is 3 bushels of wheat per year. With 2L, TP = 8 bushels. With 3L, TP = 12 bushels, and so on.[2]

From the total output or product schedule we can derive the (per-unit) average and marginal products schedules for the input. Specifically, the total (physical) output or total product (TP) divided by the quantity of labor employed (L) equals the **average product** of labor (AP_L). On the other hand, the change in output or total product per-unit change in the quantity of labor employed is equal to the **marginal product** of labor (MP_L).[3] That is,

$$AP_L = \frac{TP}{L} \tag{7-1}$$

$$MP_L = \frac{\Delta TP}{\Delta L} \tag{7-2}$$

Column 3 in Table 7-1 gives the average product of labor (AP_L). This equals TP (column 2) divided by the quantity of labor used (column 1). Thus, with one unit of labor (1L), the AP_L equals ¾ or 3 bushels. With 2L, AP_L is ⅘ or 4 bushels, and so on. Finally, column 4 reports the marginal product of labor (MP_L). This measures the change in total product per-unit change in labor. Since labor increases by one unit at a time in column 1, the MP_L in column 4 is obtained by subtracting successive quantities of the TP in column 2. For example, TP increases from 0 to 3 bushels when we add the first unit of labor. Thus, the MP_L is 3 bushels. For an increase in labor from 1L to 2L, TP increases from 3 to 8 bushels. Thus, the MP_L is 5 bushels. For an increase in labor from 2L to 3L, the MP_L is 4 bushels (12 − 8), and so on.

---

[2] The reason for the decline in TP when 6L are used will be discussed shortly.

[3] In subsequent chapters, when the possibility arises of confusing the AP and the MP with their monetary values, they will be referred to as the average *physical* product and the marginal *physical* product.

199

TABLE 7-1   Total, Average, and Marginal Product of Labor in the Cultivation of Wheat on One Acre of Land (Bushels per Year)

Labor (Workers per Year) (1)	Output or Total Product (2)	Average Product of Labor (3)	Marginal Product of Labor (4)
0	0	. . .	. . .
1	3	3	3
2	8	4	5
3	12	4	4
4	14	3.5	2
5	14	2.8	0
6	12	2	−2

Plotting the total, averge, and marginal product quantities of Table 7-1 gives the corresponding product curves shown in Figure 7-1. Note that TP grows to 14 bushels with $4L$. It stays at 14 bushels with $5L$ and then declines to 12 bushels with $6L$ (see the top panel of Figure 7-1). The reason for this is that laborers get into each other's way and actually trample the wheat when the sixth worker is employed. In the bottom panel, we see that the AP_L curve rises to 4 bushels and then declines. Since the marginal product of labor refers to the change in total product per-unit change in labor used, each value of the MP_L is plotted halfway between the quantities of labor used. Thus, the MP_L of 3 bushels, which results from increasing labor from $0L$ to $1L$, is plotted at $0.5L$; the MP_L of 5 bushels, which results from increasing labor from $1L$ to $2L$, is plotted at $1.5L$, and so on. The MP_L curve rises to 5 bushels at $1.5L$ and then declines. Past $4.5L$, the MP_L becomes negative.

7-2b The Geometry of Average and Marginal Product Curves

The shape of the average and marginal product of labor curves is determined by the shape of the corresponding total product curve. The AP_L at any point on the TP curve is equal to the slope of the straight line drawn from the origin to that point on the TP curve. Thus, the AP_L at point A on the TP curve in the top panel of Figure 7-1 is equal to the slope of OA. This equals ¾ or 3 bushels and is plotted directly below point A, as point A', in the bottom panel of Figure 7-1. Similarly, the AP_L at point B on the TP curve is equal to the slope of dashed line OB. This equals ⁸⁄₂ or 4 bushels and is plotted as point B' in the bottom panel. At point C, the AP_L is again equal to 4. This is the highest AP_L. Past point C, the AP_L declines but remains positive as long as the TP is positive.

The MP_L between any two points on the TP curve is equal to the slope of the TP between the two points. Thus, the MP_L between the origin and point A on the TP curve in the top panel of Figure 7-1 is equal to the slope of OA. This is equal to 3 bushels and is plotted halfway between $0L$ and $1L$

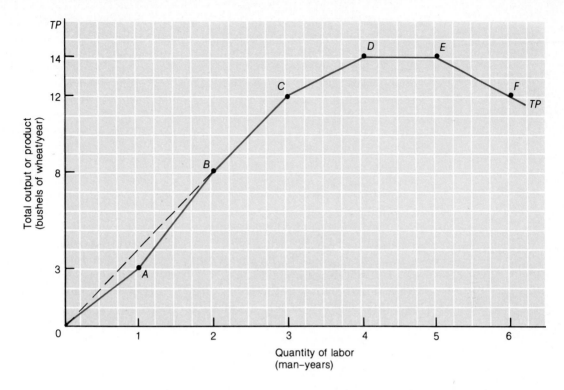

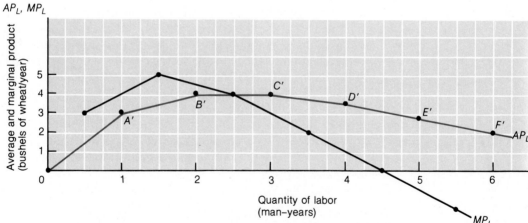

FIGURE 7-1.   The Total, Average, and Marginal Product Curves

The top panel shows the total output or total product (TP) curve. The AP_L at any point on the TP curve is given by the slope of a line from the origin to the point on the TP curve. Thus, the AP_L at point A is 3 bushels (the slope of OA) and is plotted as A′ in the bottom panel. The AP_L curve is highest between 2L and 3L. The MP_L between two points on the TP curve is given by the slope of the TP between the two points. Thus, the MP_L between A and B is 5 bushels (the slope of AB) and is plotted between A and B in the bottom panel. The MP_L is highest at 1.5L, $MP_L = AP_L$ at 2.5L, $MP_L = O$ at 4.5L, and it is negative thereafter.

(i.e., at 0.5L) in the bottom panel of Figure 7-1. Similarly, the MP_L between points A and B on the TP curve is equal to the slope of AB. This is equal to 5 (the highest MP_L) and is plotted as point G' at 1.5L in the bottom panel. The MP_L between B and C on the TP curve is equal to the slope of BC. This equals 4 and is the same as the highest AP_L (the slope of OB and OC). Between points D and E, TP remains unchanged and the $MP_L = 0$. Past point E, TP falls and MP_L becomes negative.

We have drawn the curves in Figure 7-1 under the assumption that labor is used in whole units. If this were not the case and labor time were infinitesimally divisible, we would have the smooth TP, AP_L, and MP_L curves shown in Figure 7-2. In this figure, the AP_L (given, as before, by the slope of a ray from the origin to the TP curve) rises up to point H on the TP curve in the top panel and then declines. Thus, the AP_L curve in the bottom panel rises up to point H' and declines thereafter (but remains positive as long as TP is positive). On the other hand, the MP_L at any point on the TP curve is equal to the slope of the tangent to the TP curve at that point. The slope of the TP curve rises up to point G (the point of inflection) and then declines. Thus, the MP_L curve in the bottom panel rises up to point G' and declines thereafter. The MP_L is zero at point I' directly below point I, where the TP is highest or has zero slope, and it becomes negative when TP begins to decline.[4]

Note that the MP_L curve reaches its maximum point before the AP_L curve. Furthermore, as long as the AP_L curve is rising, the MP_L curve is above it. When the AP_L curve is falling, the MP_L curve is below it, and when the AP_L curve is highest, the MP_L curve intersects the AP_L curve. The reason for this is that for the AP_L to rise, the MP_L must be greater than the average to pull the average up. For the AP_L to fall, the MP_L must be lower than the average to pull the average down. For the average to be maximum (i.e., neither rising nor falling) the marginal must be equal to the average (the slope of line OH). For example, for a student to increase his or her cumulative average test score, he or she must receive a grade on the next (marginal) test that exceeds his or her average. With a lower grade on the next test, the student's cumulative average will fall. If the grade on the next test equals the previous average, the cumulative average will remain unchanged.

7-2c The Law of Diminishing Returns and Stages of Production

The decline in the MP_L curve in Figures 7-1 and 7-2 is a reflection of the **law of diminishing returns**. This is an empirical generalization or a phys-

---

[4] Note that the TP curve in Figure 7-2 has an initial portion over which it faces up (so that the MP_L increases). That is, up to point G, labor is used so sparsely on one acre of land that the MP_L increases as more labor is employed. This is usual but not always true. That is, in some cases, the TP curve faces down from the origin (so that MP_L falls from the very start). An example of this is discussed in Chapter 9.

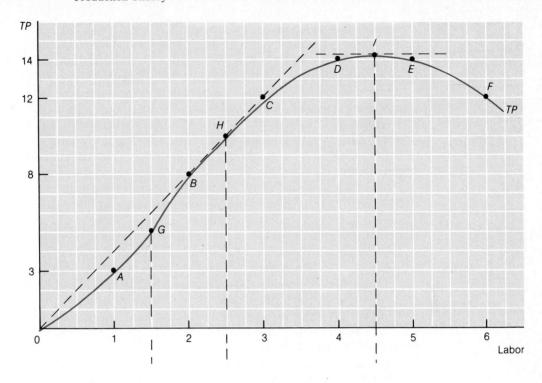

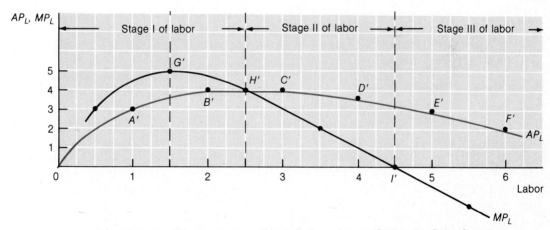

FIGURE 7-2. The Geometry of Total, Average, and Marginal Product Curves

With labor time infinitesimally divisible, we have smooth TP, AP, and MP curves. The AP_L (given by the slope of the line from the origin to a point on the TP curve) rises up to point H′ and declines thereafter (but remains positive as long as TP is positive). The MP_L (given by the slope of the tangent to the TP curve) rises up to point G′, becomes zero at I′, and is negative thereafter. When the AP_L curve rises, the MP_L is above it; when the AP_L falls, the MP_L is below it; and when AP_L is highest, $MP_L = AP_L$.

ical law, not a proposition of economics. It postulates that as more units of a variable input are used with a fixed amount of other inputs, after a point, a smaller and smaller return will accrue to each additional unit of the variable input. In other words, the marginal (physical) product of the variable input eventually declines. This occurs because each additional unit of the variable input has less and less of the fixed inputs with which to work. Eventually, too much of the variable input is used with the fixed inputs, and so the marginal product of the variable input declines.

In Figure 7-2, the law of diminishing returns for labor begins to operate past point G' (i.e., when more than $1.5L$ are applied to one acre of land). Further additions of labor will eventually lead to zero and then to negative MP_L. Note that to observe the law of diminishing returns, at least one input (here, land) must be held constant. Technology is also assumed to remain unchanged. It should also be noted that when less than $1.5L$ is employed, labor is used too sparsely in the cultivation of one acre of land and the MP_L rises. Had land been kept constant at two acres instead of one, the TP, AP_L, and MP_L curves would retain their general shape but would all be higher, since each unit of labor would have more land to work with (see Section 7-3b).

The relationship between the AP and the MP curves can be used to define the three stages of production as follows. The range from the origin to the point where the AP is maximum is **stage I of production** for the variable input. **Stage II of production** proceeds from the point where the AP of the variable input is maximum to the point where the MP of that input is zero. The range over which the MP is negative is **stage III of production** for the variable input. In Figure 7-2, stage I for labor extends up to $2.5L$ (i.e., up to point H'); stage II extends from $2.5L$ to $4.5L$ (i.e., from point H' to point I'); stage III extends beyond $4.5L$ (i.e., beyond point I', in the range where MP_L is negative).

The rational producer would not operate in stage III of labor, even if labor time were free, because the MP_L is negative. That is, adding one additional unit of labor in stage III of labor actually causes output to decline. This means that a greater output or TP could be produced by using *less* labor! Thus, the rational producer will not produce in stage III of labor. Similarly, he or she will not produce in stage I for labor because (as shown in more advanced texts) this corresponds to stage III of land (where the MP of land is negative).[5] Thus, the rational producer will operate in stage II where the MP of both factors is positive but declining. The precise point within stage II at which the rational producer operates will depend on the prices of inputs and output. This is examined in Chapter 10, where we

---

[5] Stage I of labor corresponds to stage III for land only under constant returns to scale. This is the case where output changes in the same proportion as the change in all inputs (see Section 7-5). As we will see in Chapter 8, average costs of production decrease over stage I of labor and so it pays for the producer to use more labor until he or she is in stage II of labor.

discuss profit maximization by the firm. Sometimes a production function exhibits diminishing returns from the very start and reflects only stage II of production (see Example 7-1).

Example 7-1   Diminishing Returns in Potato Production

The Facts: Table 7-2 presents the results of an actual experiment conducted on a farm in Maine between 1927 and 1941. The output (*TP*) of potatoes (in bushels per year) results from applying various quantities of fertilizer (in 500-lb. units) on one acre of land (with labor and capital held constant).

Comment: The *AP* and the *MP* of fertilizer decline after the initial application of fertilizer and the *MP* remains positive. Thus, only stage II of production for fertilizer is observed. This type of production function is often encountered in empirical work and is discussed in greater detail in Chapter 9. (The student should plot the *TP*, *AP*, and *MP* quantities given by Table 7-2 and compare the shape of the resulting curves with those of Figures 7-1 and 7-2).

7-3

Production With Two Variable Inputs

In this section, we examine production theory with two variable inputs by introducing isoquants. We will also show how to derive total product curves from an isoquant map, thus highlighting the relationship between production with one and two variable inputs. We will then examine the shape of isoquants in Section 7-4.

TABLE 7-2   Total, Average, and Marginal Product of Fertilizer in the Cultivation of Potatoes on One Acre of Land (Bushels per Year)

Fertilizer (In 500-lb. Units)	Output or Total Product	Average Product of Fertilizer	Marginal Product of Fertilizer
0	0	. . .	. . .
1	103	103.0	103
2	174	87.0	71
3	223	74.3	49
4	257	64.3	34
5	281	56.2	24
6	298	49.7	17
7	308	44.0	10

Source: E.O. Heady, *Economics of Agricultural Production and Resource Use* (Englewood Cliffs, N.J.: Prentice-Hall, 1952), p. 36.

7-3a Definition of Isoquants

An **isoquant** shows the various combinations of two inputs (say, labor and capital) that can be used to produce a specific level of output. A higher isoquant refers to a larger output, while a lower isoquant refers to a smaller output. If the two variable inputs (labor and capital) are the only inputs used in production, we are in the long run. If the two variable inputs are used with other fixed inputs (say, land), we would still be in the short run.

Table 7-3 gives a hypothetical production function, which shows the outputs (the Q's) that can be produced with various combinations of labor (L) and capital (K). For example, the table shows that 12 units of output (i.e., $12Q$) can be produced with 1 unit of labor (i.e., $1L$) and 5 units of capital (i.e., $5K$) or with $1L$ and $4K$.[6] Table 7-3 also shows that $12Q$ can also be produced with $3L$ and $1K$ or with $6L$ and $1K$. On the other hand, the table indicates that 26 units of output ($26Q$) could be produced with $2L$ and $5K$, $2L$ and $4K$, $3L$ and $2K$, and $6L$ and $2K$. From the table we can also determine the various combinations of L and K to produce $34Q$ and $38Q$. Note that to produce a greater output, more labor, more capital, or both more labor and capital are required.

Plotting the various combinations of labor and capital that can be used to produce 12, 26, 34, and 38 units of output gives the isoquant for each of these levels of output shown in Figure 7-3. The figure shows that 12 units of output (the lowest isoquant shown) can be produced with 1 unit of labor ($1L$) and 5 units of capital ($5K$). This defines point J. Twelve units of output can also be produced with $1L$ and $4K$ (point M), $3L$ and $1K$ (point C), and $6L$ and $1K$ (point F). Joining these points with a smooth curve, we obtain the isoquant for 12 units of output. Similarly, by plotting the various combinations of labor and capital that can be used to produce 26 units of output ($2L$ and $5K$, $2L$ and $4K$, $3L$ and $2K$, and $6L$ and $2K$) and joining the resulting points by a smooth curve we get the isoquant for $26Q$ in Figure 7-3. The isoquant for $34Q$ and $38Q$ in the figure can be similarly derived from the data in Table 7-3.

TABLE 7-3   Production Function with Two Variable Inputs

Capital	(K)		1	2	3	4	5	6	
		6	10	22	29	(34)	(38)	39	
		5	(12)	(26)	(34)	(38)	40	(38)	
		4	(12)	(26)	(34)	(38)	(38)	(34)	Q (Outputs)
		3	10	22	31	34	34	30	
		2	7	17	(26)	28	28	(26)	
↑		1	3	8	(12)	14	14	(12)	
K		0	1	2	3	4	5	6	
		L →					Labor	(L)	

[6] Of course, since inputs are not free, a firm would prefer to produce $12Q$ with $1L$ and $4K$ rather than with $1L$ and $5K$.

FIGURE 7-3.
Isoquants

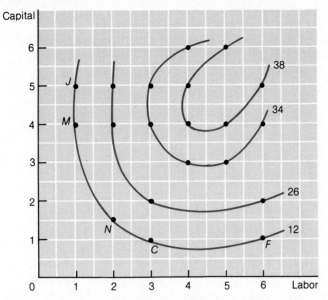

An isoquant shows the various combinations of two inputs that can be used to produce a specific level of output. Thus, 12 units of output can be produced with 1L and
5K (point J), 1L and 4K (point M), 2L and 1.5K (point N), 3L and 1K (point C), or 6L
and 1K (point F). Higher isoquants refer to higher levels of output. The above isoquants are obtained from the data in Table 7–3.

7-3b Derivation of Total Product Curves from the Isoquant Map

By drawing a horizontal line across an isoquant map at the level at which
the input measured along the vertical axis is fixed, we can generate the
total product curve for the variable input measured along the horizontal
axis. For example, by starting with the isoquant map of Figure 7-3 and
keeping capital constant at $K = 4$, we can derive the total product curve of
labor for $K = 4$. This corresponds to the higher of the two TP curves in the
bottom panel of Figure 7-4. Thus, from point M (1L and 4K) on the isoquant
for 12Q in the top panel, we obtain point M' on the TP curve for $K = 4$ in
the bottom panel. From point V (2L and 4K) on the isoquant for 26Q in the
top panel we derive point V' on the TP curve for $K = 4$ in the bottom panel,
and so on. This is equivalent to reading across the row for $K = 4$ in Table
7-3.

With capital held constant at the lower level of $K = 1$, we generate the
lower total product curve in the bottom panel of Figure 7-4. This is equivalent to reading across the row for $K = 1$ in Table 7-3. Note that when
capital is held constant at a smaller level, the TP curve for labor is lower
since each unit of labor has less capital to work with.

207

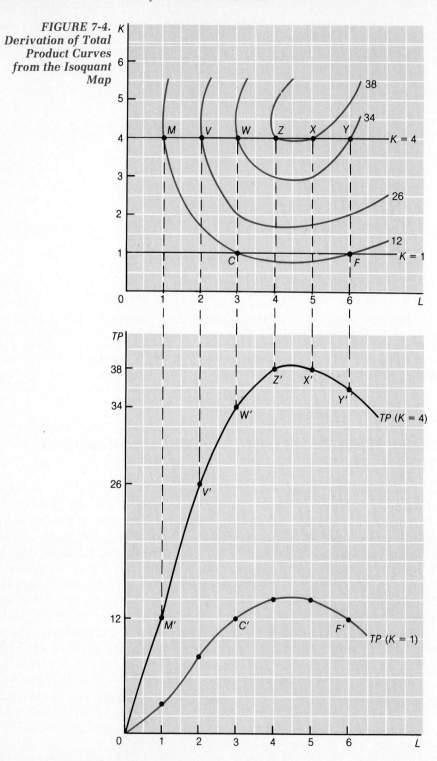

FIGURE 7-4.
*Derivation of Total
Product Curves
from the Isoquant
Map*

If, instead, we held the quantity of labor constant and changed the quantity of capital used, we would derive the *TP* curve for capital. This can be obtained by drawing a vertical line on the isoquant map at the level at which labor is held constant. This is equivalent to reading up the appropriate column of Table 7-3. The higher the level at which labor is held constant, the higher is the total product curve of capital. From a given total product curve we could then derive the corresponding average and marginal product curves, as shown in the bottom panel of Figure 7-2. Thus, Table 7-3 and Figure 7-3 could provide information about the long run as well as the short run, depending on whether labor and capital are the only two inputs and both are variable (the long run), or whether labor and capital are used with other fixed inputs (such as land), or either labor or capital is fixed (the short run).

7-4

The Shape of Isoquants

In this section we examine the characteristics of isoquants, define the economic region of production, and consider the special cases where commodities can only be produced with fixed input combinations. We will see that the shape of isoquants plays as important a role in production theory as the shape of indifference curves plays in consumption theory.

7-4a Characteristics of Isoquants

The characteristics of isoquants are crucial for understanding production theory with two variable inputs. Isoquants are similar to indifference curves. However, while an indifference curve shows the various combinations of two commodities that provide the consumer equal satisfaction (measured ordinally), an isoquant shows the various combinations of two

---

By keeping capital constant at K = 4 in the top panel, we can derive the higher of the two total product curves in the bottom panel. Thus, from point M (1L and 4K) on the isoquant for 12Q in the top panel, we obtain point M′ on the TP curve for K = 4 in the bottom panel. From point V (2L and 4K) in the top panel we derive point V′ in the bottom panel, and so on. With capital constant at K = 1 (i.e., reading across the row for K = 1 in Table 7–3), we get the lower total product curve in the bottom panel.

FIGURE 7-5.
Characteristics of
Isoquants

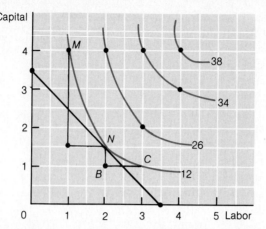

FIGURE 7-5.
Characteristics of
Isoquants

Isoquants are negatively sloped in the economically relevant range, convex to the origin, and do not intersect. The absolute value of the slope of the isoquant is called the marginal rate of technical substitution (MRTS). Between point M and point N on the isoquant for 12 units of output (12Q), $MRTS_{LK} = 2.5$. Between point N and point C, $MRTS_{LK} = \frac{1}{2}$. The MRTS at any point on an isoquant is given by the absolute slope of the tangent to the isoquant at that point. Thus, at point N on the isoquant for 12Q, $MRTS_{LK} = 1$. The $MRTS_{LK}$ is also equal to MP_L/MP_K.

inputs that give the same level of output (measured cardinally, or in actual units of the commodity).[7]

Isoquants have the same general characteristics of indifference curves. That is, they are negatively sloped in the economically relevant range, convex to the origin, and do not intersect. These properties are shown in Figure 7-5.[8] The nonintersecting property of isoquants can easily be explained. Intersecting isoquants would mean that two different levels of output of the same commodity could be produced with the identical input combination (i.e., at the point where the isoquants intersect). This is impossible under our assumption that the most efficient production techniques are always used.

Isoquants are negatively sloped in the economically relevant range. This means that if the firm wants to reduce the quantity of capital used in production, it must increase the quantity of labor in order to continue to produce the same level of output (i.e., remain on the same isoquant). For example, starting at point *M* (1L and 4K) on the isoquant for 12 units of output (12Q), the firm could reduce the quantity of capital by 2.5K by adding 1L in production and reach point N on the same isoquant (see Figure 7-5). Thus, the slope of the isoquant between points *M* and N is −2.5K/1L. The slope between N and C is −½.

[7] Compare Figure 7-5 to Figure 3-2.

[8] The positively sloped portions of the isoquants have been omitted in Figure 7-5 because they are irrelevant. The reason for this is discussed in Section 7-3c.

The absolute value of the slope of the isoquant is called the **marginal rate of technical substitution (MRTS).** This is analogous to the marginal rate of substitution of one good for another in consumption, which is given by the absolute value of the slope of an indifference curve. For a movement down along an isoquant, the marginal rate of technical substitution of labor for capital ($MRTS_{LK}$) is given by $-\Delta K/\Delta L$. It measures the amount of capital that the firm can give up by using one additional unit of labor and still remain on the same isoquant. Because of the reduction in K, $MRTS_{LK}$ is negative. However, we multiply by -1 and express $MRTS_{LK}$ as a positive value. Thus, the $MRTS_{LK}$ between points M and N on the isoquant for $12Q$ is 2.5. Similarly, the $MRTS_{LK}$ between points N and C is ½. The $MRTS_{LK}$ at any point on an isoquant is given by the absolute value of the slope of the isoquant at that point. Thus, the $MRTS_{LK}$ at point N is 1 (the absolute value of the slope of the tangent to the isoquant at point N; see Figure 7-5).

The $MRTS_{LK}$ is also equal to MP_L/MP_K. To prove this, we begin by remembering that all points on an isoquant refer to the same level of output. Thus, for a movement down a given isoquant, the gain in output from using more labor must be equal to the loss in output from using less capital. Specifically, the increase in the quantity of labor used (ΔL) times the marginal product of labor (MP_L) must equal the reduction in the amount of capital used ($-\Delta K$) times the marginal product of capital (MP_K). That is,

$$(\Delta L)(MP_L) = -(\Delta K)(MP_K) \tag{7-3}$$

so that

$$MP_L/MP_K = -\Delta K/\Delta L = MRTS_{LK} \tag{7-4}$$

Thus, $MRTS_{LK}$ is equal to the absolute value of the slope of the isoquant and to the ratio of the marginal productivities.

While we know that the absolute value of the slope of the isoquant or $MRTS_{LK}$ equals the ratio of MP_L to MP_K, we cannot infer from that the actual value of MP_L and MP_K. For example, at point N on the isoquant for $12Q$ in Figure 7-5, we know that $MRTS_{LK} = -\Delta K/\Delta L = MP_L/MP_K = 1$ (so that $MP_L = MP_K$) but we do not know what the actual (common) value of MP_L and MP_K is. Similarly, we know that between points N and C on the isoquant for $12Q$, $MRTS_{LK} = -\Delta K/\Delta L = MP_L/MP_K = $ ½ (so that $MP_L = \frac{1}{2}MP_K$) but we do not know what the actual value of either marginal product is. However, they can be calculated from Figure 7-5.

For example, we can find the value of MP_L and MP_K between points N and C on the isoquant for $12Q$ in Figure 7-5 by comparing point N (2L, 1.5K) and point C (3L, 1K) referring to $12Q$ to point B (2L, 1K) referring to $8Q$ (see Table 7-3). The rightward movement from point B to point C keeps capital constant at $1K$ and increases labor by $1L$, and it results in an increase in output of $4Q$ (from $8Q$ to $12Q$). Thus, $MP_L = 4$. On the other hand, the upward movement from point B to point N keeps labor constant at $2L$ and increases capital by $\frac{1}{2}K$, and it also results in an increase in output of $4Q$. Thus, the $MP_K = 8$. With $MP_L = 4$ and $MP_K = 8$, $MP_L/MP_K = \frac{4}{8} = \frac{1}{2} = MRTS_{LK}$, as found earlier.

Within the economically relevant range, isoquants are not only negatively sloped but also convex to the origin. That is, as we move down along an isoquant, the absolute value of its slope or $MRTS_{LK}$ declines and the isoquant is convex (see Figure 7-5). The reason for this can best be explained by separating the movement down along an isoquant (say, from point N to point C along the isoquant for $12Q$ in Figure 7-5) into its two components: the movement to the right (from point B to point C) and the movement downward (from point N to point B). The increase in L with constant K (the movement from point B to point C) will lead to a decline in the MP_L since we are in stage II of production. In addition, the reduction in K (the movement from point N to point B), by itself, will cause the entire MP_L curve to shift down. Thus, MP_L declines for both reasons. On the other hand, by using less K and more L, the MP_K rises.[9] With the MP_L declining and the MP_K rising as we move down along an isoquant, the $MRTS_{LK} = MP_L/MP_K$ will fall and the isoquant is convex to the origin.[10]

7-4b Economic Region of Production

The firm would not operate on the positively sloped portion of an isoquant because it could produce the same level of output with less capital and less labor. For example, the firm would not produce $34Q$ at point P in Figure 7-6 because it could produce $34Q$ by using the smaller quantity of labor and capital indicated by point R. Similarly, the firm would not produce $34Q$ at point S because it could produce $34Q$ at point T with less L and K. Since inputs are not free, the firm would not want to produce in the positively sloped range of isoquants.

Ridge lines separate the relevant (i.e., the negatively sloped) from the irrelevant (or the positively sloped) portions of the isoquants. In Figure 7-6, ridge line ORU joins points on the various isoquants where the isoquants have zero slope (and thus zero $MRTS_{LK}$). The isoquants are negatively sloped to the left of this ridge line and positively sloped to the right. This means that starting, for example, at point R on the isoquant for $34Q$, if the firm used more labor it would also have to use more capital to remain on the same isoquant (compare point P to point R on the isoquant for $34Q$). Starting from point R, if the firm used more labor with the same amount of capital, the level of output would fall (i.e., the firm would fall back to a lower isoquant; see the dashed horizontal line at $K = 2.8$ in Figure 7-6). The same is true at all other points on ridge line ORU. Therefore, the MP_L

[9] The reasoning is exactly the opposite as for the decline in MP_L.

[10] For a mathematical presentation of indifference curves and their characteristics using rudimentary calculus, see Section A7 of the Mathematical Appendix.

212

FIGURE 7-6.
The Economic
Region of
Production

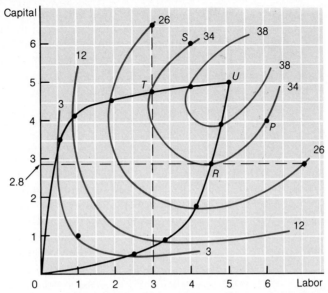

Ridge lines define the economic region of production. This is the region within the ridge lines where isoquants are negatively sloped. Isoquants are positively sloped to the right of ridge line ORU and to the left of or above ridge line OTU. The firm would never produce at a point such as P or S in the positively sloped portion of the iso-quant because it could produce the same output with less of both inputs. At all points on ridge line ORU, $MP_L = MRTS_{LK} = 0$. At all points on ridge line OTU, MP_K is zero and $MRTS_{LK}$ is infinite.

must be negative to the right of this ridge line. This corresponds to stage III of production for labor. Note that points on ridge line *ORU* specify the minimum quantity of capital required to produce the levels of output indicated by the various isoquants. Note also that at all points on this ridge line, $MRTS_{LK} = MP_L/MP_K = 0/MP_K = 0$.

On the other hand, ridge line *OTU* joins points where the isoquants have infinite slope (and thus infinite $MRTS_{LK}$). The isoquants are negatively sloped to the right of this ridge line and positively sloped to the left. This means that starting, for example, at point *T* on the isoquant for 34Q, if the firm used more capital it would also have to use more labor to remain on the same isoquant (compare point S to point T on the isoquant for 34Q). Starting at point *T*, if the firm used more capital with the same quantity of labor, the level of output would fall (i.e., the firm would fall back to a lower isoquant; see the dashed vertical line at *L* = 3 in Figure 7-6). The same is true at all other points on ridge line *OTU*. Therefore, the MP_K must be negative to the left of or above this ridge line. This corresponds to stage III of production for capital. Note that points on ridge line *OTU* indicate the minimum quantity of labor required to produce the levels of output indicated by the various isoquants. Note also that at all points on this ridge line, $MRTS_{LK} = MP_L/MP_K = MP_L/0 = $ infinity.

Thus, we conclude that the negatively sloped portion of the isoquants

213

within the ridge lines represents the economic region of production. This refers to stage II of production for labor and capital, where the MP_L and the MP_K are both positive but declining. Producers will never want to operate outside this region. As a result, from this point on, whenever we will draw isoquants, we usually show only their negatively sloped portion. Indeed, some special types of production functions have isoquants without positively sloped portions.

7-4c Fixed-Proportions Production Functions

So far, we have drawn isoquants as smooth curves, and this indicates that there are many different (really, an infinite number of) input combinations that can be used to produce any output level. There are cases, however, where inputs can only be combined in fixed proportions in production. In such a case, there would be no possibility of input substitution in production and the isoquants would be at right angle or L-shaped.

For example, Figure 7-7 shows that 10 units of output (10Q) can only be produced at point A with 2L and 1K. Employing more labor will not change output since $MP_L = 0$ (the horizontal portion of the isoquant). Similarly, using more capital will not change output since $MP_K = 0$ (the vertical portion of the isoquant). Here, there is no possibility of substituting L for K in production and the $MRTS_{LK} = 0$. Production would only take place at the constant capital-labor ratio of $K/L = \frac{1}{2}$. A larger output can only be produced by increasing both labor and capital in the same proportion. For example, 20Q can be produced at point B by using 4L and 2K at the constant K/L ratio of $\frac{1}{2}$. Similarly, 30Q can only be produced at point C with 6L and 3K and $K/L = \frac{1}{2}$.

In the real world, some substitution of inputs in production is usually possible. The degree to which this is possible can be gathered from the curvature of the isoquants. In general, the smaller is the curvature of the isoquants, the more easily inputs can be substituted for each other in production. On the other hand, the greater the curvature (i.e., the closer are isoquants to right angle or L-shape), the more difficult is substitution. To be able to easily substitute inputs in production is extremely important in the real world. For example, if petroleum had good substitutes, users could easily have switched to alternative energy sources when petroleum prices rose sharply in the fall of 1973. Their energy bill would then not have risen very much. As it was, good substitutes were not readily available (certainly not in the short run), and so most energy users faced sharply higher energy costs. An example of real-world isoquants showing a fair degree of substitutability between inputs is given in Example 7-2.

Example 7-2 Isoquants in Corn Production

The Facts: Figure 7-8 shows four isoquants of corn obtained from an empirically estimated production function in Iowa in 1953. The variable inputs

214

FIGURE 7-7.
Fixed-Proportions
Production
Functions

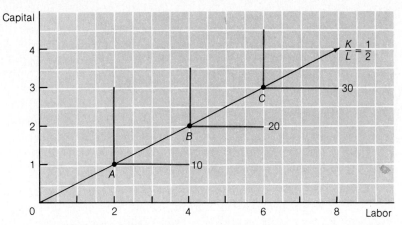

When isoquants are at right angle or L-shaped, inputs must be used in fixed proportions in production. Thus, 10 units of output (10Q) can only be produced at point A
with 2L and 1K. Using more labor or capital would not change output because MP_L
$= MP_K = 0$. 20Q can only be produced with 4L and 2K (point B), and 30Q only with
6L and 3K (point C). Thus, output can only be produced at the constant or fixed
capital-labor ratio or proportion of $K/L = \frac{1}{2}$.

FIGURE 7-8.
Isoquants for Corn

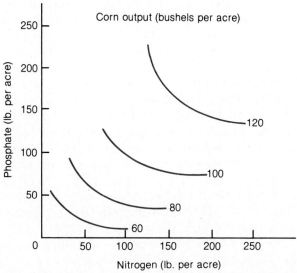

The four isoquants of corn shown were obtained from an empirically estimated production function in Iowa in 1953. The variable inputs were pounds of two fertilizers,
nitrogen and phosphate, applied per acre. The output was corn in bushels per acre.

215

were pounds of two fertilizers, nitrogen and phosphate, applied per acre. The output was corn in bushels per acre.

Comment: The small curvature of the corn isoquants in Figure 7-8 indicates that the two fertilizers can be substituted rather easily for each other in the production of corn. It should also be noted that the corn isoquants shown do not have positively sloped portions (it is not that we have not drawn them). That is, the special type of production function estimated for corn exhibits only stage II of production, just as the production function for potato examined in Example 7-1. This type of production function is often used in the empirical work and will be examined in detail in Chapter 9.

Source: H.O. Heady, "An Econometric Investigation of the Technology of Agricultural Production Functions," *Econometrica,* April 1957, p. 253.

7-5

Constant, Increasing, and Decreasing Returns to Scale

The word "scale" refers to the long-run situation, where all inputs are changed in the same proportion. The result might be constant, increasing, or decreasing returns. **Constant returns to scale** refers to the situation where output changes by the *same* proportion as inputs. For example, if all inputs are increased by 10 per cent, output also rises by 10 per cent. If all inputs are doubled, output also doubles. **Increasing returns to scale** refers to the case where output changes by a *larger* proportion than inputs. For example, if all inputs are increased by 10 per cent, output increases by more than 10 per cent. If all inputs are doubled, output more than doubles. Another name for increasing returns to scale is economies of scale. Finally, with **decreasing returns to scale,** output changes by a *smaller* proportion than inputs. Thus, increasing all inputs by 10 per cent increases output by less than 10 per cent, and doubling all inputs, less than doubles output.

Constant, increasing, and decreasing returns to scale can be shown by the spacing of the isoquants in Figure 7-9. The left panel shows constant returns to scale. Here, doubling inputs from $3L$ and $3K$ to $6L$ and $6K$ doubles output from 100 (point A along ray OD) to 200 (point B). Tripling inputs from $3L$ and $3K$ to $9L$ and $9K$ triples output from 100 (point A) to 300 (point C). Thus, $OA = AB = BC$ along ray OD and we have constant returns to scale. The middle panel shows increasing returns to scale. Here, output can be doubled or tripled by less than doubling or tripling the quantity of inputs. Thus, $OA > AB > BC$ along ray OD and the isoquants are compressed closer together. Finally, the right panel shows decreasing returns to scale. In this case, in order to double and triple output we must more

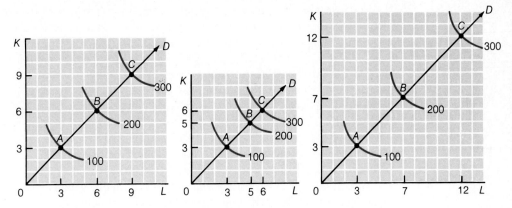

FIGURE 7-9. Constant, Increasing, and Decreasing Returns to Scale

The left panel shows constant returns to scale. Here, doubling inputs from 3L and 3K to 6L and 6K doubles output from 100 (point A along ray OD) to 200 (point B). Tripling inputs to 9L and 9K triples output to 300 (point C). Thus, OA = AB = BC along ray OD. The middle panel shows increasing returns to scale. Here, output can be doubled or tripled by less than doubling or tripling the quantity of inputs. Thus, OA > AB > BC and the isoquants become closer together. The right panel shows decreasing returns to scale. Here, output changes proportionately less than labor and capital and OA < AB < BC.

than double and triple the quantity of inputs. Thus, $OA < AB < BC$ and the isoquants move farther and farther apart. Note that in all three panels, the capital-labor ratio remains constant at $K/L = 1$ along ray OD.

Constant returns to scale make sense. We would expect two similar workers using identical machines to produce twice as much output as one worker using one machine. Similarly, we would expect the output of two identical plants employing an equal number of workers of equal skill to produce double the output of a single plant. However, increasing and decreasing returns to scale are also possible.

Increasing returns to scale arise because, as the scale of operation increases, a greater division of labor and specialization can take place and more specialized and productive machinery can be used. With a large scale of operation, each worker can be assigned to perform only one repetitive task rather than numerous ones. Workers become more proficient in the performance of the single task and avoid the time lost in moving from one machine to another. The result is higher productivity and increasing returns to scale. At higher scales of operation, more specialized and productive machinery can also be used. For example, using a conveyor belt to unload a small truck may not be justified, but it greatly increases efficiency in unloading a whole train or ship. In addition, some physical properties of equipment and machinery also lead to increasing returns to scale. Thus, doubling the diameter of a pipeline more than doubles the flow, doubling the weight of a ship more than doubles its capacity to transport cargo, and so on. Firms also need fewer supervisors, fewer spare parts, and smaller inventories per unit of output as the scale of operation increases.

Decreasing returns to scale arise primarily because, as the scale of operation increases, it becomes ever more difficult to manage the firm effectively and coordinate the various operations and divisions of the firm. The channels of communications become more complex, and the number of meetings, the paper work, and telephone bills increase more than proportionately to the increase in the scale of operation. All of this makes it increasingly difficult to ensure that the managers' directives and guidelines are properly carried out. Thus, efficiency decreases. Decreasing returns to scale must be clearly distinguished from diminishing returns. *Decreasing returns to scale* refers to the long-run situation when all inputs are variable. On the other hand, *diminishing returns* refers to the short-run situation where at least one input is fixed. Diminishing returns in the short run is consistent with constant, increasing, or decreasing returns to scale in the long run.

In the real world, the forces for increasing and decreasing returns to scale often operate side by side. The forces for increasing returns to scale usually prevail at small scales of operation. The tendency for increasing returns to scale may be balanced by the tendency for decreasing returns to scale at intermediate scales of operation. Eventually, the forces for increasing returns to scale may be overcome by the forces for decreasing returns to scale at very large scales of operation. Whether this is true for a particular industry can only be determined empirically. This point will be discussed in Chapter 8. In the real world, most industries seem to exhibit near constant returns to scale (see Example 7-3).

Example 7-3 **Returns to Scale in U.S. Manufacturing Industries**

The Facts: Table 7-4 reports the estimated returns to scale in U.S. manufacturing industries in 1957. A value of 1 refers to constant returns to scale, a value greater than 1 refers to increasing returns to scale, and a value smaller than 1 to decreasing returns to scale. The table shows that for a doubling of (i.e., with a 100 per cent increase in) all inputs, output would rise by 111 per cent in the furniture industry, by 109 per cent in chemicals, but only by 95 per cent in petroleum (the last entry in the second column of the table).

Comment: According to the data in the above table, only textiles exhibit exactly constant returns to scale. Most other industries, however, exhibit close-to-constant returns to scale. A discussion of the methods used to estimate production functions and returns to scale in a particular industry is presented in Chapter 9.

218

TABLE 7-4   Estimated Returns to Scale in U.S. Manufacturing in 1957

Industry	Returns to Scale	Industry	Returns to Scale
Furniture	1.11	Leather	1.04
Chemicals	1.09	Electrical machinery	1.03
Printing	1.08	Nonelectrical machinery	1.02
Food, beverages	1.07	Transport equipment	1.02
Rubber, plastics	1.06	Textiles	1.00
Instruments	1.04	Paper pulp	0.98
Lumber	1.04	Primary metals	0.96
Apparel	1.04	Petroleum	0.95

Source: J. Moroney, "Cobb-Doublas Production Functions and Returns to Scale in U.S. Manufacturing Industry," *Western Economic Journal*, Dec. 1967, pp. 39–51.

7-6

Applications

In this section, we present some uses and applications of the tools of analysis developed in this chapter. In Application 1, we use our tools to analyze the very important relationship between population, technology, and diminishing returns over time. This represents a long-standing interest of economists since at least the time of Malthus. The other applications deal with the ability to substitute time for gasoline in automobile transportation and energy for capital in manufacturing production, and with economies and diseconomies of scale and the optimum size of tankers. These uses and applications clearly demonstrate the great importance and relevance of the tools of analysis introduced in this chapter.

Application 1: Population, Technology, and Diminishing Returns

In the early 19th century, Malthus and other classical economists predicted that population growth in the face of given land and other nonhuman resources could doom mankind to a subsistence standard of living. That is, rapid population growth could reduce the average and the marginal product of labor sufficiently to keep humanity always near starvation. This gloomy prediction earned for economics the label of the "dismal science."

These predictions have not proved correct, at least for the United States and other industrial nations of the world, where standards of living are much higher than a century or two ago. The reasons for the sharply increased standard of living are (1) the quantity of capital, land, and minerals used in production have vastly increased since the beginning of the 19th century; (2) population growth has slowed down considerably in the industrial nations; and (3) most importantly, very significant improvements in technology have greatly increased productivity.

We can use Figure 7-10 to show changes in standards of living over time. In the figure, the vertical axis measures the average (physical) product of labor or the average real per capita output or income for the entire economy. The horizontal axis measures population. With a constant labor-to-population ratio, a growing population also refers to a growing labor force. If land, capital, and technology remained constant, the growth in population and labor force would lead, after a point, to diminishing average and marginal returns to labor. In the figure, we use only the average product of labor curve since we are interested in the *average* real per capita income or standard of living.

An increase in population and labor force only would be indicated by a movement down along a given average product of labor curve such as AP_1 and the average standard of living would decline. Over time, however, the quantity of capital and land used in production also increases and technology improves. As a result, the average product of labor curve shifts up to AP_2 and AP_3. Thus, we may have a growth path such as AB along which the standard of living improves or a growth path such as AC along which the standard of living falls.

Contrary to Malthus' dismal predictions, standards of living have increased over the past century throughout most of the world. Malthus inappropriately applied a short-run law (the law of diminishing returns) to the long run and came up with the wrong prediction! There are fears, however, today that increases in the quantity of capital and land and improvements in technology in poor countries may not be sufficiently large to over-

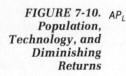

FIGURE 7-10.
Population,
Technology, and
Diminishing
Returns

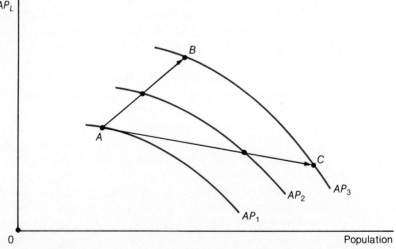

The vertical axis measures the average product of labor or standard of living and the horizontal axis measures population or labor force. With constant land, capital, and technology, the growth in population would lead, after a point, to diminishing AP and MP of labor, as down along the AP₁ curve. With increases in capital and land and improvements in technology, the AP_L curve shifts up to AP₂ and AP₃. Over time, we may then have a growth path such as AB along which the standard of living increases or AC along which the standard of living falls.

220

come the tendency for diminishing returns due to very rapid population growth.

Application 2: Speed Limit and Gasoline Consumption

Higher automobile speed reduces the driving time to cover a given distance but reduces gas mileage and thus increases gasoline consumption. The trade-off between traveling time and gasoline consumption can be represented by an isoquant such as the one in Figure 7-11. In the figure, the vertical axis measures hours of traveling time while the horizontal axis measures gallons of gasoline consumed. Gasoline and travel time are thus the inputs into the production of automobile transportation. The isoquant in the figure refers to 600 miles of automobile transportation.

At 50 miles per hour (mph), the 600 miles can be covered in 12 hours and with 16 gallons of gasoline at 37.5 miles per gallon (point A). At 60 mph, the 600 miles can be covered in 10 hours and with 20 gallons of gasoline at 30 miles per gallon (point B). Driving at 60 mph saves 2 hours of travel time (one scarce resource) but increases gasoline consumption by 4 gallons (another scarce resource). Thus, the trade-off or marginal rate of technical substitution (MRTS) of gasoline for travel time between point A and point B on the isoquant in Figure 7-11 is ½. At 66.7 mph (assuming that the speed limit is above it), the 600 miles can be covered in 9 hours and 30 gallons of gasoline at 20 miles per gallon (point C). Thus, the MRTS of gasoline for travel time between points B and C is ⅒.

In order to determine the most economical (i.e., the least cost) combina-

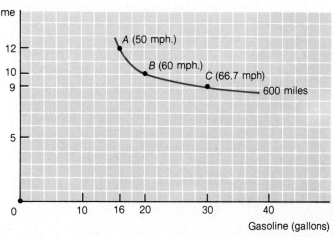

FIGURE 7-11.
Speed Limit and
Gasoline
Consumption

Higher automobile speed reduces both driving time and gas mileage and thus increases gasoline consumption. The trade-off between traveling time and gasoline consumption can be represented by an isoquant. Thus, at 50 mph, 600 miles can be covered in 12 hours and with 16 gallons of gasoline (point A). At 60 mph, the 600 miles can be covered in 10 hours and with 20 gallons of gasoline (point B). At 66.7 mph, it can be covered in 9 hours and 30 gallons (point C).

tion of gasoline and travel time to cover the 600 miles, we need to know the price of gasoline and the value of labor time to the individual. This is addressed in the next chapter, where we take up costs of production. If the price of gasoline were to increase, the individual would want to substitute traveling time for gasoline (i.e., drive at a lower speed so as to increase gas mileage and save gasoline) to minimize the cost of traveling the 600 miles. This, too, will be examined in greater detail in the next chapter. Note that there is also a trade-off between travel speed and safety (i.e., lower speeds increase travel time but save lives).

Application 3: Energy and Capital Substitution in Production

Many empirical studies seem to indicate that capital and energy were complements rather than substitutes in production in the United States during the 1970s. That is, more sophisticated and productive capital equipment required more energy to operate. Thus, the sharp increase in petroleum prices during the 1970s not only led producers to economize on the use of energy but also resulted in their using less capital per worker in production. Producers postponed or canceled the introduction of new and more productive but energy-inefficient capital equipment, and also withdrew from production some of the older and less energy-efficient equipment. The result was that the K/L ratio in the American economy declined and this has been used as one explanation for the decline in the growth of labor productivity during the 1970s.[11]

In the long run, however, the increase in the price of energy is likely to stimulate the development of more energy-efficient capital equipment. For example, the new Boeing 757 aircraft was developed as a result of the sharp increase in energy prices and is more energy-efficient than the older aircrafts that it is replacing (such as the Boeing 727 and the DC 9). Similarly, the increasing scarcity of other natural resources has led to greater conservation efforts and to the discovery of new resources and new uses for other more abundant resources. For example, the scarcity of bauxite (the raw material to produce aluminum) and the high energy cost to transform bauxite into aluminum has led to the substitution of plastic for aluminum in many uses. Thus, while in the short run, capital, natural resources, and energy may be complements in many uses, in the long run, they are likely to be substitutes. As we will see in the next chapter, the ability to substitute cheaper for more expensive inputs in production is extremely important to keep production costs as low as possible and increase standards of living.

---

[11] For a more detailed and advanced discussion of energy capital substitution in U.S. manufacturing production, see E. R. Berndt and D. O. Wood, "Technology, Prices and the Derived Demand for Energy," *The Review of Economics and Statistics*, August, 1975.

Application 4: Economies and Diseconomies of Scale and the Optimal Size of Tankers

During the postwar period, the size of oil tankers increased by leaps and bounds until they reached 500,000 tons in the early 1970s. The reason was that the hauling operation of tankers is subject to large economies of scale (i.e., their ability to transport cargo increases proportionately more than the weight of the ship). This is similar to the large economies of scale achieved by gas or oil pipelines, where doubling the diameter of the pipeline more than doubles its flow capacity. At the same time, the handling operation (such as loading and unloading) is subject to strong diseconomies of scale (i.e., increasing the size of the tanker increases the cost of handling cargo more than proportionately). Thus, the sizeable economies of scale in the hauling of cargo must be balanced against the serious diseconomies of scale in the handling operation. The former exceeded the latter until the tank size of about 500,000 tons, but was overwhelmed thereafter. Thus, tank capacity was increased up to that tonnage in the early 1970s, but not more.

However, the sharp increase in petroleum prices and reduced oil consumption in the late 1970s, as well as the altered supply patterns, reduced the optimal size of tankers. This made many of the largest tankers uneconomical to operate, and many of them were left idle. In 1980, Chevron decided to "downsize" four of its tankers from 200,000 to 150,000 tons to make them more economical to operate and to make them accessible to shallower harbors or to harbors with limited cargo and handling facilities. This involved cutting each tanker in half, removing about 100 feet from their middle section, and rewelding the two parts of the tanker together. This was like "removing the center leaf of a dining room table and shoving the table back together again."[12]

Summary

1. Production refers to the transformation of resources or inputs into outputs of goods and services. A firm is an organization that combines and organizes resources for the purpose of producing goods and services for sale at a profit. In general, the aim of firms is to maximize profits. Profits refer to the revenue of the firm from the sale of the output after all costs have been deducted. Inputs can be broadly classified into labor, capital, and land, and into fixed and variable. Entrepreneurship refers to the introduction of new technologies and products to exploit perceived profit opportunities. The time period during which at least one input is fixed is called the short run. In the long run, all inputs are variable.

2. The production function is a unique relationship between inputs and output. It can be represented by a table, graph, or equation showing the max-

[12] The New York Times, July 18, 1980, p. D1. A more detailed and advanced discussion of economies and diseconomies of scale in the operation of cargo ships is found in J. O. Jansson and D. Shneerson, "Economies of Scale of General Cargo Ships," The Review of Economics and Statistics, May 1978.

imum output or total product (*TP*) of a commodity that can be produced per time period with each set of inputs. Average product (*AP*) is total product divided by the quantity of the variable input used. Marginal product (*MP*) is the change in total output per-unit change in the variable input. The *MP* is above the *AP* when *AP* is rising, *MP* is below *AP* when *AP* is falling, and *MP* = *AP* when *AP* is maximum. The declining portion of the *MP* curve reflects the law of diminishing returns. The range over which *AP* rises is stage I of production for the variable input. Stage II covers the range from maximum *AP* to where the *MP* of the input is zero. Stage III covers the range over which the *MP* of the variable input is negative.

3. An isoquant shows the various combinations of two inputs that can be used to produce a specific level of output. From the isoquant map, we can generate the total product curve of each input by holding the quantity of the other input constant.

4. Isoquants are negatively sloped in the economically relevant range, convex to the origin, and do not intersect. The absolute value of the slope of the isoquant is called the marginal rate of technical substitution (*MRTS*). This equals the ratio of the marginal product of the two inputs. As we move down along an isoquant the absolute value of its slope or *MRTS* declines and the isoquant is convex. Ridge lines separate the relevant (i.e., the negatively sloped) from the irrelevant (or positively sloped) portions of the isoquants. With right-angled or L-shaped isoquants, inputs can only be combined in fixed proportions in production.

5. Constant, increasing, and decreasing returns to scale refer to the situation where output changes, respectively, by the same, by a larger, and by a smaller proportion than do inputs. These can be shown by the spacing of isoquants. Increasing returns to scale arise because of specialization and division of labor and from using specialized machinery. Decreasing returns to scale arise primarily because as the scale of operation increases, it becomes more and more difficult to manage the firm and coordinate its operations and divisions effectively. In the real world, most industries seem to exhibit near-constant returns to scale.

6. Over time, population growth leads to diminishing returns but this can be overcome by the increase in the other inputs and by improvements in technology. The isoquant can be used to demonstrate the alternative ways in which any set of resources may be used. For example, it can be used to show the trade-off between travel time and gasoline consumption (since higher speeds result in lower gas mileage). Capital and natural resources are likely to be complements to energy in the short run but substitutes in the long run. Up to a certain size of tankers, economies of scale in hauling cargo exceed diseconomies of scale in handling cargo. Afterwards, diseconomies of scale prevail, making it uneconomical to construct and operate larger tankers.

Glossary

Production The transformation of resources or inputs into outputs of goods and services.

Firm An organization that combines and organizes resources for the purpose of producing goods and services for sale at a profit.

Inputs The resources or factors of production used to produce goods and services.

Entrepreneurship The introduction of new technologies and products to exploit perceived profit opportunities.

Fixed inputs The resources that cannot be varied or can be varied only with excessive cost during the time period under consideration.

Variable inputs The resources that can be varied easily and on short notice during the time period under consideration.

Short run The time periods when at least one input is fixed.

Long run The time period when all inputs can be varied.

Production function The unique relationship between inputs and output represented by a table, graph, or equation showing the maximum output of a commodity that can be produced per period of time with each set of inputs.

Total product (*TP*) Total output.

Average product (*AP*) The total product divided by the quantity of the variable input used.

Marginal product (*MP*) The change in total product per-unit change in the variable input used.

Law of diminishing returns After a point, the marginal product of the variable input declines.

Stage I of production The range of increasing average product.

Stage II of production The range from maximum average product to zero marginal product.

Stage III of production The range over which marginal product is negative.

Isoquant A curve showing the various combinations of two inputs that can be used to produce a specific level of output.

Marginal rate of technical substitution (*MRTS*) The absolute value of the slope of the isoquant. It also equals the ratio of the marginal product of the two inputs.

Ridge lines The lines that separate the relevant (i.e., the negatively sloped) from the irrelevant (or the positively sloped) portions of the isoquants.

Constant returns to scale Output changes in the same proportion as inputs.

Increasing returns to scale Output changes by a larger proportion than inputs.

Decreasing returns to scale Output changes by a smaller proportion than inputs.

Questions for Review

1. (a) What is production?
   (b) What is the definition of a firm? What is the reason for its existence?
   (c) What do firms seek to maximize? What are some related goals of some firms?
   (d) What are inputs? Fixed inputs? Variable inputs? What is entrepreneurship? What is meant by the short run? By the long run?

2. What is meant by the following:
   (a) Production function?
   (b) Total product?
   (c) Average product?
   (d) Marginal product?

3. (a) What is the shape of the total product curve? Why?
   (b) How can the average and the marginal product be derived graphically?
   (c) What is the relationship between the average and the marginal product?

4. (a) What is the law of diminishing returns?
   (b) How is the law of diminishing returns reflected in the shape of the total product curve? In the shape of the marginal product curve?
   (c) What is stage I, II, and III of production?
   (d) What is the relationship between diminishing returns and the stages of production?

5. (a) What do isoquants show?
   (b) Does an isoquant refer to the short or to the long run? Why?
   (c) How can the total product curve of the variable input be derived from the isoquant map?

6. (a) What are the characteristics of isoquants?
   (b) In what way are isoquants similar to indifference curves?
   (c) In what way are isoquants different from indifference curves?
   (d) Why can't isoquants intersect?

7. (a) What is the marginal rate of technical substitution?
   (b) What is the geometric interpretation of the marginal rate of technical substitution?
   (c) Which property of isoquants reflects declining marginal rate of technical substitution?

8. (a) What are ridge lines? What is their function?
   (b) To which stage of production does the region within the ridge lines refer?
   (c) Suppose capital is measured along the vertical axis and labor along the horizontal axis. To which stage of production for labor does the region below the lower ridge line refer? The region above the top ridge line?
   (d) What is the shape of the isoquants when inputs can only be combined in fixed proportions in production?

9. With respect to constant returns to scale, indicate
   (a) its meaning.
   (b) how it can be shown by isoquants.

(c) why it arises.

(d) how prevalent it is in the real world.

10. With regard to increasing and decreasing returns to scale, indicate

(a) their meaning.

(b) how they can be shown by isoquants.

(c) why they arise.

(d) how prevalent they are in the real world.

11. (a) What are the forces that can overwhelm the tendency for diminishing returns in the standard of living in the real world in the long run?

(b) What did Malthus predict? Why was he wrong?

(c) What do we mean when we say that there is a trade-off between travel time and gasoline consumption?

12. (a) Are capital and energy complements or substitutes?

(b) How did the relationship between capital and energy in production affect labor productivity in the United States in the 1970s?

(c) Can economies and diseconomies of scale operate simultaneously?

Problems

1. From the following production function, showing the bushels of corn raised on one acre of land by varying the amount of labor employed (in man-years),

Labor	1	2	3	4	5	6
Output	8	20	30	34	34	30

(a) derive the average and the marginal product of labor.

(b) plot the total, the average, and the marginal product curves.

2. Plot again the total product curve of Problem 1 on the assumption that labor time is infinitesimally divisible, and derive graphically the corresponding average and marginal product curves.

★3. (a) On the *same set of axes* redraw the total, the average, and the marginal product curves of Problem 2 and indicate the three stages of production for labor.

(b) Where on the total product and on the marginal product of labor curves does the law of diminishing returns begin to operate? What gives rise to the law of diminishing returns?

4. From the following production function,

Production Function with Two Variable Inputs

Capital	(K)	6		6	18	25	30	30	25	
		5		8	20	30	34	34	30	
		4		8	20	30	34	34	30	Q
		3		6	18	25	30	30	25	
		2		4	13	20	25	25	20	
	↑	1		1	5	7	8	8	7	
	K									
		0		1	2	3	4	5	6	
			L →				Labor		(L)	

(a) derive the isoquants for 8 units of output (8Q), 20Q, 25Q, 30Q, and 34Q.

(b) what is the relationship between the above table and the table in Problem 1?

5. From the isoquant map of Problem 4a, derive

(a) the total product curve for labor when the quantity of capital is held fixed at $K = 4$.

(b) the average and the marginal product curves for labor from the total product curve of part (a).

6. (a) From Problem 4, redraw the isoquant for 20 units of output (20Q) and show how to measure the marginal rate of technical substitution of labor for capital (i.e.,

226

$MRTS_{LK}$) between the point where 2 units of labor and 4 units of capital (i.e., $2L$ and $4K$) are used (call this point M) and the point where ($3L$, $2K$) are used (call this point N). What is the $MRTS_{LK}$ at point N? At point C ($4L$, $1.5K$)?

(b) Find the value of the MP_L and MP_K for a movement from point N on the isoquant for $20Q$ and point N' ($4L$, $2K$) and N'' ($3L$, $3K$) on the isoquant for $25Q$, and show that $MRTS_{LK} = MP_L/MP_K$.

(c) Explain why the $MRTS_{LK}$ falls as we move down along the isoquant.

7. (a) On the isoquant map of Problem 4, draw the ridge lines.

(b) Explain why a firm would neve produce below the lower ridge line or above the top ridge line.

★8. On the same set of axes draw two isoquants, one indicating that the two inputs must be combined in fixed proportions in production, and the other showing that inputs are perfect substitutes for each other.

9. Does the production function of Problem 4 exhibit constant, increasing, or decreasing returns to scale? Explain.

★10. Suppose that the production function for a commodity is given by

$$Q = 10\sqrt{LK}$$

where Q is the quantity of output, L is the quantity of labor, and K is the quantity of capital.

(a) Indicate whether this production function exhibits constant, increasing, or decreasing returns to scale.

(b) Does the above production function exhibit diminishing returns? If so, when does the law of diminishing returns begin to operate? Could we ever get negative returns?

★11. Indicate whether each of the following statements is true or false and give the reason.

(a) The quantity of fertile land is fixed in the real world.

(b) A student preparing for an examination should not study after reaching diminishing returns.

(c) If large and small firms operate in the same industry, we must have constant returns to scale.

12. If the price of gasoline is $1.50 per gallon and travel time is worth $6 per hour to the individual, determine at which speed the cost of traveling the 600 miles is minimum in Figure 7-11.

Supplementary Readings

For a problem-solving approach to the topics discussed in this chapter, see

Dominick Salvatore, *Microeconomic Theory,* 2nd ed. (New York: McGraw-Hill, 1983), Chapter 7.

On the law of diminishing returns, see

John M. Clark, "Diminishing Returns," *Encyclopedia of Social Sciences,* Vol. 5 (New York: Macmillan, 1931), pp. 144–146.

John M. Cassels, "On the Law of Variable Proportions," in *Explorations in Economics* (New York: McGraw-Hill, 1936), pp. 223–236. Reprinted in *Readings in the Theory of Income Distribution* (Philadelphia: Blakinston, 1951), pp. 103–118.

Fritz Machlup, "On the Meaning of the Marginal Product," in *Explorations in Economics* (New York: McGraw-Hill, 1936), pp. 250–263. Reprinted in *Readings in the Theory of Income Distribution* (Philadelphia: Blakinston, 1951), pp. 158–174.

For production theory in general, see

Paul H. Douglas, "Are there Laws of Production," *American Economic Review,* March 1948.

C. E. Ferguson, *The Neoclassical Theory of Production and Distribution* (London: Cambridge University Press, 1969), Chapters 1–6.

Chapter 8

Costs of Production

8-1   The Nature of Production Costs

8-2   Optimal Combination of Inputs

8-3   Theory of Cost in the Short Run

8-4   Long-Run Theory of Costs

8-5   The Shape of the Long-Run Average Cost Curve

8-6   Applications

Examples

8-1   The Cost of Attending College

8-2   The Average and Marginal Cost of Corn

8-3   Long-Run Average Cost Curve in Electricity Generation

8-4   Long-Run Average Cost Estimates for Selected U.S. Industries

Applications

Application 1:   Derivation of the Total Variable Cost Curve from the Total Product Curve

Application 2:   The Least-Cost Combination of Gasoline and Driving Time for a Trip

Application 3:   Cost Reductions from the Short Run to the Long Run

Application 4:   Input Substitution in Production

Application 5:   Input Prices and the Average and Marginal Cost Curves

---

Preview Questions

What is the relationship between production theory and costs of production?

What do costs of production include?

What is the least-cost input combination in production?

What do short-run cost curves measure? What is their usefulness?

What do long-run cost curves measure? What is their usefulness?

What is the relationship between short-run and long-run cost curves?

What is the relationship between economies of scale and costs of production?

Are decreasing costs consistent with large and small firms in the same industry?

What is the relationship between costs and profit maximization?

In this chapter we examine the costs of production of the firm and their relationship to production theory (discussed in Chapter 7). The short-run and long-run cost curves of the firm derived in this chapter will be utilized in Part IV of the text (Chapters 10–13) to determine the profit-maximizing level of output of the firm under various market structures.

The chapter begins by examining the nature of costs of production. These include explicit, implicit, and opportunity costs, as well as private and social costs. Then we go on to discuss the optimal combination of inputs. We define isocost lines, the least-cost input combination, and examine how firms minimize costs of production in the short run and in the long run. Subsequently, we derive the short-run and long-run, total and per-unit cost curves of the firm and examine their shapes and relationship. Finally, we present some important applications of cost theory. These applications, together with the real-world examples in the theory sections, highlight the importance and relevance of the analysis of costs presented in this chapter.

8-1

The Nature of Production Costs

From the firm's production function (showing the input combinations that the firm can use to produce various levels of output) and the price of inputs, we can derive the firm's cost functions. These show the minimim costs that the firm would incur in producing various levels of output. For simplicity, we assume that the firm is too small to affect the prices of the inputs it uses. Thus, the prices of inputs remain constant regardless of the quantity demanded by the firm. (The determination of input prices when the firm does and does not affect input prices is discussed in Part V, Chapters 14–16).

In economics, costs include explicit and implicit costs. **Explicit costs** are the actual out-of-pocket expenditures of the firm to purchase or hire the inputs it requires in production. These expenditures include the wages to hire labor, interest on borrowed capital, rent on land and buildings, and the expenditures on raw and semifinished materials. **Implicit costs,** on the other hand, refer to the value of the inputs owned and used by the firm in its own production processes. The value of these owned inputs must be imputed or estimated from what these inputs could earn in their best alternative use.

Implicit costs include the maximum wages that the entrepreneur could earn in working for someone else in a similar capacity (say, as the manager of another firm), and the highest return that the firm could obtain from investing its capital elsewhere and renting out its land and other inputs to others. The inputs owned and used by the firm in its own production processes are not free to the firm, even though the firm can use them without any actual or explicit expenditures. Their implicit cost is what these same inputs could earn in their best alternative use outside the firm. Accountants traditionally include only actual expenditures in costs, while economists always include both explicit and implicit costs.[1]

The cost to a firm in using any input is what the input could earn in its best alternative use (outside the firm). This is true for inputs purchased or hired by the firm as well as for inputs owned and used by the firm in its own production. For example, a firm must pay wages of $20,000 per year to one of its employees if that is the amount the worker would earn in his or her best alternative occupation in another firm. If this firm attempted to pay less, the worker would simply seek employment in the other firm. Similarly, if the entrepreneur could earn more in managing another firm than in directing his or her own firm, it would not make much economic sense to continue to be self-employed.[2] Thus, for a firm to retain any input for its own use, it must pay what the input could earn in its best alternative use or employment. This is the **alternative** or **opportunity cost doctrine.** Similarly, the cost of attending college includes not only the explicit cost of tuition, books, and so on, but also the foregone earnings of not working (see Example 8-1).

---

[1] For tax purposes, the accountants' definition of costs, which include only explicit costs, is usually used. However, in economics, we must always consider both explicit and implicit costs.

[2] Unless this individual valued the freedom associated with being self-employed more than the extra income in managing a similar firm for someone else.

Costs are also classified into private and social. **Private costs** are the explicit and the implicit opportunity costs incurred by *individuals and firms* in the process of producing goods and services. **Social costs** are the costs incurred by *society* as a whole. Social costs are higher than private costs when firms are able to escape some of the economic costs of production. For example, a firm dumping untreated waste into the air imposes a cost on society (in the form of higher cleaning bills, more breathing ailments, and so on) that is not reflected in the costs of the firm. Private costs can be made equal to social costs by public regulation requiring the firm to install antipollution equipment. In this and subsequent chapters, we will be primarily concerned with private costs. Social costs will be examined in detail in Chapter 19.

Example 8-1   The Cost of Attending School

The Facts: Table 8-1 reports the annual explicit and implicit cost of attending a private college during the 1985–86 academic year. Explicit costs include tuition, room, meals, and books and supplies. Implicit costs include the student's foregone earnings by attending college rather than entering the labor force. It also includes the foregone interest on half of the explicit costs, if they have to be paid at the beginning of each semester (since these funds could have been lent at the going interest rate).

Comment: The annual implicit costs of attending college are higher than the explicit costs. Attending a public college is cheaper only to the extent that tuition for state residents in many states is about $1,000 (so that the total costs of attending a public college are about $14,425). For out-of-state residents, the annual cost of attending a public college may be close to $16,000 or $17,000. Of course, these costs would be lower if the student continued to live at home while attending college. The annual total cost of

TABLE 8-1   Annual Cost of Attending a Private College

Explicit Costs		
Tuition	$5,500	
Room	1,300	
Meal Plan	1,350	
Books and Supplies	350	
Subtotal		$8,500
Implicit Costs		
Foregone Earnings	$10,000	
Foregone Interest ($4,250 at 10%)	425	
Subtotal		$10,425
Total Costs		$18,925

Source: Admission Office, Fordham University.

231

attending an Ivy League College is more than $25,000, since tuition alone exceeds $10,000 per year.

Source: "Ahead: Another Big Jump in College Tuition," *U.S. News & World Report*, April 8, 1985, pp. 60–61.

8-2

Optimal Combination of Inputs

Since cost functions and cost curves provide the minimum cost of producing various levels of output, we must examine the process of cost minimization by the firm. This involves defining isocost lines and the optimal combination of inputs in production. We will then examine how the firm minimizes costs of production in the short run and in the long run.

8-2a Isocost Lines

Suppose that a firm uses only labor and capital in production. Then the total cost (TC) of the firm for the use of a specific quantity of labor and capital is equal to the price of labor (w or wage rate) times the quantity of labor hired (L), plus the price of capital (r or rental price of capital) times the quantity of capital rented (K). If the firm owns the capital, r is the rent foregone from not renting out the capital (such as machinery) to others. The total cost of the firm can thus be expressed as

$$TC = wL + rK \tag{8-1}$$

That is, the total cost (TC) is equal to the amount that the firm spends on labor (wL) plus the amount that the firm spends on capital (rK).

Given the wage rate of labor (w), the rental price of capital (r), and a particular total cost (TC), we can define an **isocost line** or equal-cost line. This shows the various combinations of labor and capital that the firm can hire or rent for the given total cost. For example, for $TC_1 = \$80$, $w = \$10$, and $r = \$10$, the firm could either hire 8L or rent 8K, or any combination of L and K shown on isocost line RS in the left panel of Figure 8-1. For each unit of capital the firm gives up, it can hire one more unit of labor. Thus, the slope of isocost line RS is −1.

By subtracting wL from both sides of Equation (8-1) and then dividing by r, we get the general equation of an isocost line in the following more useful form:

$$K = TC/r - (w/r)L \tag{8-2}$$

The first term on the right-hand side of Equation (8-2) is the vertical or Y-intercept of the isocost line, while −w/r is the slope. Thus, for $TC_1 = \$80$ and $w = r = \$10$, the vertical or Y-intercept is $TC_1/r = \$80/\$10 = 8K$,

232

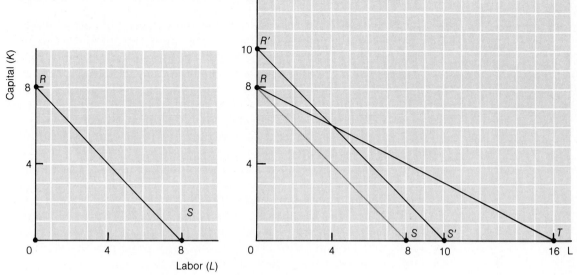

FIGURE 8-1. Isocost Lines

With capital measured along the vertical axis, for TC_1 = $80 and w = r = $10, the Y- intercept of the isocost line is TC_1/r = $80/$10 = 8K and the slope is $-w/r$ = $-$10/$10 = -1. This gives budget line RS in the left and right panels. With TC_2 = $100 and unchanged w = r = $10, we have isocost line R'S', with Y-intercept of TC_2/r = $100/$10 = 10K and slope of $-w/r$ = $-$10/$10 = -1 in the right panel. With TC_1 = $80 and r = $10 but w = $5, we have isocost line RT with slope of $-\frac{1}{2}$.

and the slope is $-w/r$ = $-$10/$10 = -1 (see isocost line RS in the left panel of Figure 8-1).

A different total cost will define a different but parallel isocost line, while a different relative price of an input will define an isocost line with a different slope. For example, an increase in total expenditure to TC_2 = $100 with unchanged w = r = $10 will generate isocost line R'S' in the right panel of Figure 8-1. The vertical or Y-intercept of isocost line R'S' is equal to TC_2/r = $100/K = $10 = 10K and its slope is $-w/r$ = $-$10/$10 = -1. With TC_1 = $80 and r = $10 but w = $5, we have isocost line RT with slope of $-\frac{1}{2}$.

Note the symmetry between the isocost line and the budget line. In Section 3-3 we define the *budget line* as showing the various combinations of two commodities that a consumer could purchase with his or her given money income. The *isocost line* shows the various combinations of two inputs that a firm can hire at a given total cost. However, while an individual's income is usually given and fixed over a specific period of time (so that we usually deal with only one budget line), a firm's total costs of production vary with output (so that we have a whole family of isocost lines).[3]

---

[3] A consumer's budget line can also change over a given period of time because consumers can save or borrow as well as vary the hours worked and type of job. However, these possibilities are usually not considered in order to keep the analysis simple.

8-2b Least-Cost Input Combination

In order to minimize the cost of producing a given level of output, the firm must produce at the point where an isocost line is tangent to the isoquant. For example, the left panel of Figure 8-2 shows that the minimum cost of producing 4 units of output (4Q) is $80 (isocost line RS). This is the lowest isocost line that will allow the firm to reach the isoquant for 4Q. The firm must produce at point D and use 4L (at the cost of wL = $40) and 4K (at the cost of rK = $40). This is the least-cost input combination. Any other input combination results in higher total costs for the firm to produce 4 units of output (i.e., to reach isoquant 4Q).

Minimizing the cost of producing a given level of output is equivalent to maximizing the output for a given cost outlay. The right panel of Figure 8-2 shows that the maximum output or highest isoquant that the firm could reach at the total cost of $80 (i.e., with isocost line RS) is the isoquant for 4Q. Thus, the condition for cost minimization is equivalent to the condition for output maximization. For both, the firm must produce where an isoquant and an isocost are tangent (point D in both panels of Figure 8-2). The concept of output maximization for a given cost outlay for a producer is completely analogous to the concept of consumer utility maximization for a given budget constraint, which was discussed in Section 3-4.

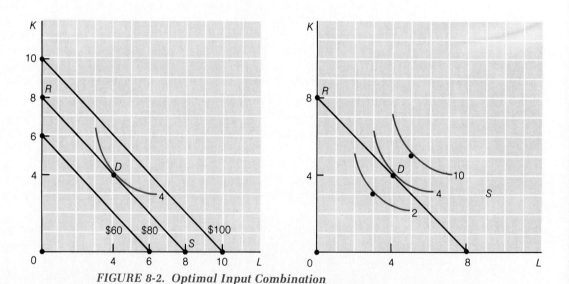

FIGURE 8-2. *Optimal Input Combination*

The optimal input combination is the one at which the firm minimizes costs or maximizes output. This occurs where an isoquant is tangent to an isocost line. The left panel shows that RS is the lowest isocost with which the firm can reach isoquant 4Q. The firm minimizes the cost of producing 4 units of output at point D by using 4L and 4K at a total cost of $80. The right panel shows that isoquant 4Q is the highest one that the firm can reach with isocost line RS. Thus, the firm maximizes output with a total cost of $80 by producing at point D and using 4L and 4K.

At the point of tangency, the (absolute) slope of the isoquant or marginal rate of technical substitution of labor for capital is equal to the (absolute) slope of the isocost line. That is,

$$MRTS_{LK} = w/r \tag{8-3}$$

Since the $MRTS_{LK} = MP_L/MP_K$, we can rewrite the **least-cost input combination** as

$$MP_L/MP_K = w/r \tag{8-3A}$$

Cross multiplying, we get

$$MP_L/w = MP_K/r \tag{8-3B}$$

Equation (8-3B) indicates that to minimize production costs (or maximize output for a given total cost), the extra output or marginal product per dollar spent on labor must be equal to the marginal product per dollar spent on capital. If $MP_L = 5$, $MP_K = 4$, and $w = r$, the firm would not be maximizing output or minimizing costs since it is getting more extra output for a dollar spent on labor than on capital. To maximize output or minimize costs, the firm would have to hire more labor and rent less capital. As the firm does this, the MP_L declines and the MP_K increases (since the firm is in stage II of production for L and K). The process would have to continue until Condition (8-3B) held. If w were higher than r, the MP_L would have to be proportionately higher than the MP_K for Condition (8-3B) to hold.

The same general condition would have to hold to minimize production costs, no matter how many inputs the firm uses. That is, the MP per dollar spent on each input would have to be the same for all inputs. Another way of stating this is that, for costs to be minimized, an additional unit of output should cost the same whether it is produced with more labor or more capital.[4]

8-2c Cost Minimization in the Long and Short Runs

We have seen in the left panel of Figure 8-2 that the minimum cost of producing 4 units of output (4Q) is $80 when the firm uses 4 units of labor (4L) at $10 per unit and 4 units of capital (4K) at $10 per unit (point D, where the isoquant for 4Q is tangent to the isocost for $80). This is repeated in Figure 8-3. Figure 8-3 also shows that in the long run (when both L and K can be varied), the firm can produce 10Q with 5L and 5K at the *minimum* total cost of $100 (point H, where the isoquant for 10Q is tangent to the isocost for $100). Points D and H can also be interpreted as the points of

---

[4] For a mathematical presentation of cost minimization using rudimentary calculus, see Section A8 of the Mathematical Appendix.

maximum output for cost outlays of $80 and $100, respectively. Note that this production function exhibits strong economies of scale (i.e., 4L and 4K produce 4Q, while 5L and 5K produce 10Q!).

If capital were fixed at 4K (in the short run), the *minimum cost* of producing 10Q would be higher or $110 because the firm would have to use 7L and 4K (point V, where the isoquant for 4Q crosses the isocost for $110). Thus, the minimum cost of producing a given level of output is lower in the long run when both L and K are variable than in the short run when only L is variable. Note that at point V, the $MRTS_{LK} < w/r$. This means that the rate at which L can be substituted for K *in production* is smaller than the rate at which L can be substituted for K *in the market*. Thus, total costs can be reduced in the long run by using less labor and more capital in production. But this is impossible in the short run.

In the next section, we derive short-run cost curves. These show the minimum cost of producing the various levels of output when at least one input (here, capital) is fixed. Costs are minimized in the sense discussed above. In the section following the next, we derive long-run cost curves. These show the minimum cost (in the sense discussed above) of producing various levels of output when all inputs are variable.

8-3

Theory of Cost in the Short Run

In this section we examine the theory of cost in the short run. We first define fixed, variable, and total costs, and draw these total cost curves. We then define average fixed cost, average variable cost, average total cost, and marginal cost, and draw these per-unit cost curves. Finally, we show how per-unit cost curves can be derived graphically from the corresponding total cost curves.

8-3a Total Costs

In the short run, some inputs are fixed and some are variable, and this leads to fixed and variable costs. **Total fixed costs (*TFC*)** are the total obligations of the firm per time period for all fixed inputs. These include payments for renting the plant and equipment (or the depreciation on plant and equipment if the firm owns them), most kinds of insurance, property taxes, and some salaries (such as those of top management which are fixed by contract and must be paid over the life of the contract whether the firm produces or not). **Total variable costs (*TVC*)** are the total obligations of the firm per time period for all the variable inputs of the firm. These include payments for raw materials, fuels, most types of labor, excise taxes, and so on. **Total costs (*TC*)** equal TFC plus TVC.

Within the limits imposed by the given plant, the firm can vary its output

FIGURE 8-3.
Long-Run and Short-
Run Cost
Minimization

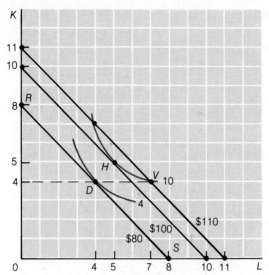

Starting from point D, the firm minimizes the long-run cost of producing 10Q at point H, where isoquant 10Q is tangent to the isocost line for $100 and the firm uses 5L and 5K. If capital is fixed at 4K, the firm minimizes the short-run cost of producing 10Q by using 7L and 4K (point V, where the isoquant for 10Q crosses the isocost line for $110).

in the short run by varying the quantity of the variable inputs used per period of time. This gives rise to TFC, TVC, and TC schedules and curves. These show, respectively, the *minimum* fixed, variable, and total costs of producing the various levels of output in the short run. In defining these cost schedules and curves, all inputs are valued at their opportunity cost, which includes both explicit and implicit costs.

Table 8-2 presents hypothetical TFC, TVC, and TC schedules. These schedules are then plotted in Figure 8-4. From Table 8-2, we see that TFC are $30 regardless of the level of output. This is reflected in Figure 8-4 in the horizontal TFC curve at the level of $30. TVC are zero when output is zero and rise as output rises. The shape of the TVC curve follows directly from the law of diminishing returns. Up to point W' (the point of inflection),

TABLE 8-2   Fixed, Variable, and Total Costs

Quantity of Output	Total Fixed Costs	Total Variable Costs	Total Costs
0	$30	$ 0	$ 30
1	30	20	50
2	30	30	60
3	30	45	75
4	30	80	110
5	30	145	175

237

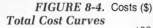

FIGURE 8-4.
Total Cost Curves

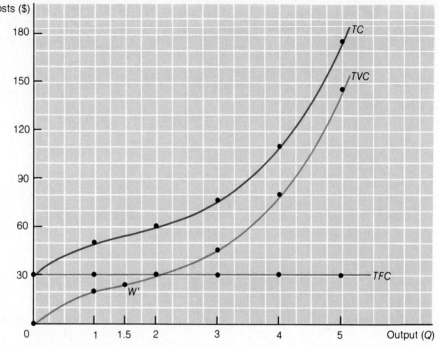

Total fixed costs (TFC) are the total obligations of the firm per time period for all fixed inputs. With TFC = $30, the TFC curve is horizontal at the level of $30 regardless of the level of output. Total variable costs (TVC) are the total obligations of the firm per time period for all the variable inputs used by the firm. TVC are zero when output is zero and rise as output rises. Past point W', the law of diminishing returns operates and the TVC curve faces upward or rises at an increasing rate. Total costs (TC) equal TFC plus TVC. Thus, the TC curve has the same shape as the TVC curve but is $30 above it at each output level.

the firm uses so little of the variable inputs with the fixed inputs that the law of diminishing returns is not yet operating. As a result, the *TVC* curve faces downward or rises at a decreasing rate. Past point *W'* (i.e., for output levels greater than 1.5), the law of diminishing returns operates and the *TVC* curve faces upward or rises at an increasing rate. (The relationship between the shape of the *TVC* curve and the law of diminishing returns will be clarified in Application 1). Since *TC = TFC + TVC*, the *TC* curve has the same shape as the *TVC* curve but is $30 (the *TFC*) above it at each output level.

8-3b Per-Unit Costs

From total costs we can derive per-unit costs. These are even more important in the short-run analysis of the firm. **Average fixed cost (*AFC*)** equals total fixed costs divided by output. **Average variable cost (*AVC*)** equals total variable costs divided by output. **Average total cost (*ATC*)** equals total costs divided by output. *ATC* also equals *AFC* plus *AVC*. **Marginal cost (MC)** equals the change in *TC* or in *TVC* per unit change in output.

Table 8-3 presents the per-unit cost schedules derived from the corresponding total cost schedules of Table 8-2. The *AFC* values given in column 5 are obtained by dividing the *TFC* values in column 2 by the quantity of output in column 1. *AVC* (column 6) equals *TVC* (column 3) divided by output (column 1). *ATC* (column 7) equals *TC* (column 4) divided by output (column 1). *ATC* also equals *AFC* plus *AVC*. *MC* (column 8) is given by the change in *TVC* (column 3) or in *TC* (column 4) per unit change in output (column 1). Thus, *MC* does not depend on *TFC*.

The per-unit cost schedules given in Table 8-3 are plotted in Figure 8-5. Note that *MC* is plotted *between* the various levels of output. From Table 8-3 and Figure 8-5, we see that the *AFC* curve falls continuously, while the *AVC*, *ATC*, and *MC* curves first fall and then rise (i.e., they are U-shaped). Since the vertical distance between the *ATC* and the *AVC* curve equals *AFC*, a separate *AFC* curve is superfluous and can be omitted from the figure.

The reason the *AVC* curve is U-shaped can be explained as follows. With labor as the only variable input in the short run, *TVC* for any output level (*Q*) equals the wage rate (*w*) times the quantity of labor (*L*) used. Then,

$$\text{AVC} = \frac{TVC}{Q} = \frac{wL}{Q} = \frac{w}{Q/L} = \frac{w}{AP_L} \tag{8-4}$$

With *w* constant and from our knowledge (from Section 7-2) that the average physical product of labor (AP_L or Q_L) usually rises first, reaches a maximum, and then falls, it follows that the *AVC* curve first falls, reaches a minimum, and then rises. Thus, the *AVC* curve is the monetized mirror image, reciprocal, or "dual" of the AP_L curve. Since the *AVC* curve is U-shaped, the *ATC* curve is also U-shaped. The *ATC* curve continues to fall after the *AVC* curve begins to rise because, for a while, the decline in *AFC* exceeds the rise in *AVC* (see Figure 8-5).

TABLE 8-3   Total and Per-Unit Costs

Quantity of Output (1)	Total Fixed Costs (2)	Total Variable Costs (3)	Total Cost (4)	Average Fixed Cost (5)	Average Variable Cost (6)	Average Total Cost (7)	Marginal Cost (8)
1	$30	$ 20	$ 50	$30	$20	$50	$20
2	30	30	60	15	15	30	10
3	30	45	75	10	15	25	15
4	30	80	110	7.50	20	27.50	35
5	30	145	175	6	29	35	65

239

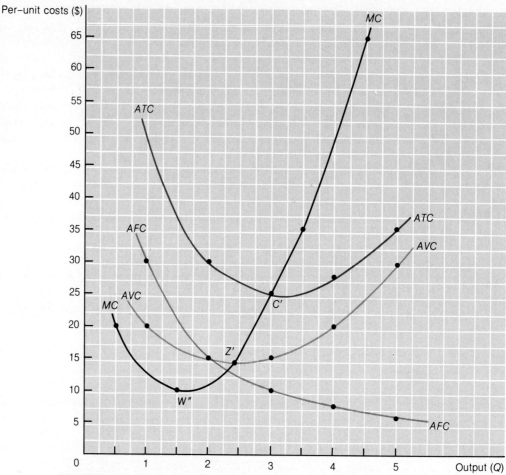

FIGURE 8-5. Per-Unit Cost Curves

Average fixed cost (AFC) equals TFC/Q. Average variable cost (AVC) equals TVC/ Q. Average total cost (ATC) equals TC/Q. Marginal cost (MC) equals the change in TC or in TVC per unit change in Q. MC is plotted between the various output levels. The AFC curve falls continuously, while the AVC, ATC, and MC curves are U- shaped. The AVC falls when the AP of the variable input rises, and AVC rises when the AP falls. MC and MP are similarly related. The ATC curve falls as long as the decline in AFC exceeds the rise in AVC. The rising portion of the MC curve intersects from below the AVC and the ATC curves at their lowest point.

The U-shape of the MC curve can similarly be explained as follows:

$$\text{MC} = \frac{\Delta \text{TVC}}{\Delta Q} = \frac{\Delta(wL)}{\Delta Q} = \frac{w(\Delta L)}{\Delta Q} = \frac{w}{\Delta Q/\Delta L} = \frac{w}{\text{MP}_L} \tag{8-5}$$

Since the marginal product of labor (MP_L or $\Delta Q/\Delta L$) first rises, reaches a maximum, and then falls, it follows that the MC curve first falls, reaches a

240

minimum, and then rises. Thus, the rising portion of the *MC* curve reflects the operation of the law of diminishing returns.

Note that the *MC* curve reaches its minimum point at a smaller level of output than the *AVC* and the *ATC* curves, and it intersects from below the *AVC* and the *ATC* curves at their lowest point (see Figure 8-5). The reason is that for average costs to fall, the marginal cost must be lower. For average costs to rise, the marginal cost must be higher. Also, for average costs neither to fall nor rise (i.e., to be at their lowest point), the marginal cost must be equal to them. While the *AVC*, *ATC*, and *MC* curves are U-shaped, they sometimes have a fairly flat bottom (see Example 8-2).

8-3c The Geometry of Per-Unit Cost Curves

The shape of the per-unit cost curves is determined by the shape of the corresponding total cost curves. The *AFC*, the *AVC*, and the *ATC* are given, respectively, by the slope of a line from the origin to the *TFC*, the *TVC*, and the *TC* curves, while the *MC* is given by the slope of the *TC* and the *TVC* curves. This is similar to the derivation of the average and the marginal product curves from the total product curve in Section 7-2b.

Panel A of Figure 8-6 shows that the *AFC* for one unit of output (*Q*) is equal to the slope of the line (ray) from the origin to $Q = 1$ on the *TFC* curve. This is \$30/1 or \$30. At $Q = 2$, $AFC = \$30/2 = \$15$. At $Q = 3$, $AFC = \$30/3 = \$10$, and so on. Note that since *TFC* are constant, *AFC* falls continuously as output rises. Thus, the *AFC* curve is a rectangular hyperbola. Panel B shows that the *AVC* at 1 and 4 units of output is given by the slope of ray *OY*, which is \$20. Note that the slope of a ray from the origin to the *TVC* curve falls up to point *Z* (where the ray from the origin is tangent to the *TVC* curve) and then rises. Thus, the *AVC* curve falls up to point *Z'* (i.e., up to $Q = 2.5$) and rises thereafter. Panel C shows that the *ATC* at $Q = 3$ is \$25 (the slope of ray *OC*). Note that the slope of a ray from the origin to the *TC* curve falls up to point *C* (where the ray from the origin is tangent to the *TC* curve) and then rises. Thus, the *ATC* curve falls up to point *C'* (i.e., up to $Q = 3$) and rises thereafter.

Panel D shows that the slope of the *TC* and *TVC* curves falls up to point *W* and *W'* (the point of inflection) on the *TC* and the *TVC* curves, respectively, and then rises. Thus, the *MC* curve falls up to point *W''* and rises thereafter. At point *Z*, the *MC* and the *AVC* are both equal to the slope of ray *OZ*. This is \$35/2.5 or \$14 and equals the lowest *AVC*. At point *C*, the *MC* and the *ATC* are both equal to the slope of ray *OC*. This is \$75/3 or \$25 and equals the lowest *ATC*.

Example 8-2 The Average and Marginal Cost of Corn

The Facts: Figure 8-7 shows the actual estimated *AVC*, *ATC*, and *MC* per bushel of corn raised on central Iowa farms in 1971.

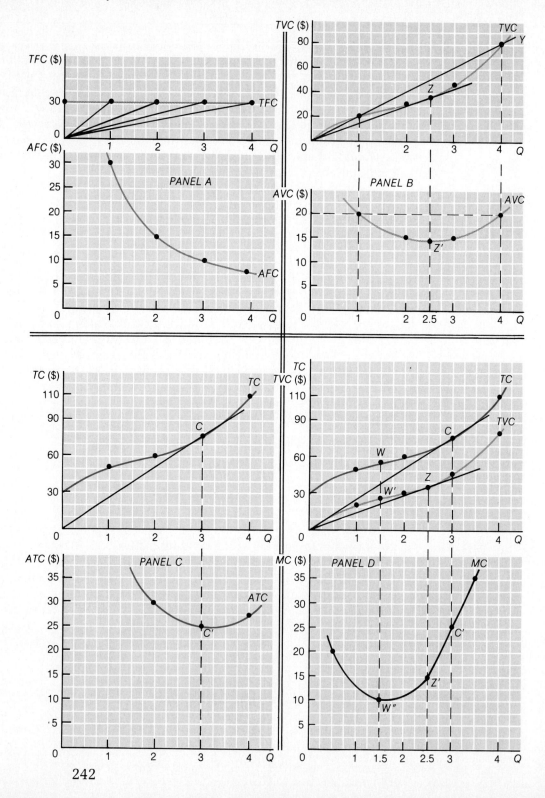

FIGURE 8-6. Graphical Derivation of Per-Unit Cost Curves

AFC, AVC, and ATC are given, respectively, by the slope of a line from the origin to
the TFC, the TVC, and the TC curves, while MC is given by the slope of the TC or
TVC curves. In panel A, the slope of a ray from the origin to the TFC curve (the AFC
falls continuously. In panel B, the slope of a ray from the origin to the TVC curve
(the AVC) falls up to point Z and rises thereafter. In panel C, the slope of a ray from
the origin to the TC curve (the ATC) falls up to point C and rises thereafter. Panel D
shows that the slope of the TC and TVC curves (the MC) falls up to point W and
W', respectively, and then rises.

Comments: The per-unit cost curves in the figure have the same general
shape as the typical curves examined earlier, but with flatter bottoms. Note
that once MC starts rising, it does so very rapidly. This is true not only in
raising corn but also in many other cases. For example, traveling costs (in
terms of travel time) rise very steeply during peak hours on highways. Similarly, landing costs (in terms of landing time) at airports also rise rapidly
during peak hours (3–5 P.M.).

Sources: D. Suits, "Agriculture," in W. Adams, *The Structure of the American Economy*, 5th ed. (New York: Macmillan, 1977), p. 17. A. Carlin and R.
Park, "Marginal Cost Pricing of Airport Runway Capacity," *American Economic Review*, June 1970, pp. 310–319.

FIGURE 8-7.
Estimated Average
and Marginal Costs
of Corn

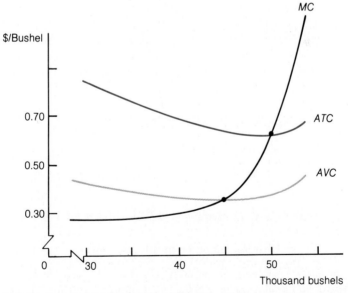

The figure shows actual estimated AVC, ATC, and MC per bushel of corn raised on
central Iowa farms in 1971. The per-unit cost curves in the figure have the same general shape as the typical curves examined earlier, but with flatter bottoms. Note that
once MC starts rising, it does so very rapidly.

8-4

Long-Run Theory of Costs

In this section we examine the theory of costs in the long run. We first define the firm's expansion path and, from it, derive the firm's long-run total cost curve. Then we derive the firm's long-run average cost curve. Finally, we show the relationship between the firm's short-run and long-run cost curves.

8-4a Expansion Path and the Long-Run Total Cost Curve

With constant input prices and higher total cost outlays by the firm, isocost lines will be higher and parallel. By then joining the origin with the points of tangency of isoquants and the isocost lines, we derive the firm's **expansion path**. For example, in the top panel of Figure 8-8, the expansion path of the firm is line $OBDFHJN$. Note that in this case, the expansion path is a straight line, and this indicates a constant capital-labor ratio (K/L) for all output levels. At the tangency points, the slope of the isoquants is equal to the slope of the isocost lines. That is, $MRTS_{LK} = MP_L/MP_K = w/r$, and $MP_L/w = MP_K/r$. Thus, points along the expansion path show the least-cost input combinations to produce various levels of output in the long run.

From the expansion path, we can derive the **long-run total cost (LTC)** curve of the firm. This shows the minimum long-run total costs of producing various levels of output. For example, point B in the top panel of Figure 8-8 indicates that the minimum total cost of producing two units of output ($2Q$) is $60 ($30 to purchase $3L$ and $30 to purchase $3K$). This gives point B' in the bottom panel of Figure 8-8, where the vertical axis measures total costs and the horizontal axis measures output. From point D in the top panel, we get point D' in the bottom panel. Other points on the LTC curve are similarly obtained. Note that the LTC curve starts at the origin since in the long run there are no fixed costs.

FIGURE 8-8. Derivation of the Expansion Path and the Long-Run Total Cost Curve

The expansion path of the firm is line OBDFHJN in the top panel. It is obtained by joining the origin with the points of tangency of isoquants with the isocost lines and with input prices constant. Points along the expansion path show the least-cost input combinations to produce various output levels in the long run. The long-run total cost curve in the bottom panel is derived from the expansion path. For example, point B' on the LTC curve is derived from point B on the expansion path. The LTC curve shows the minimum long-run total costs of producing various levels of output when the firm can build any desired scale of plant.

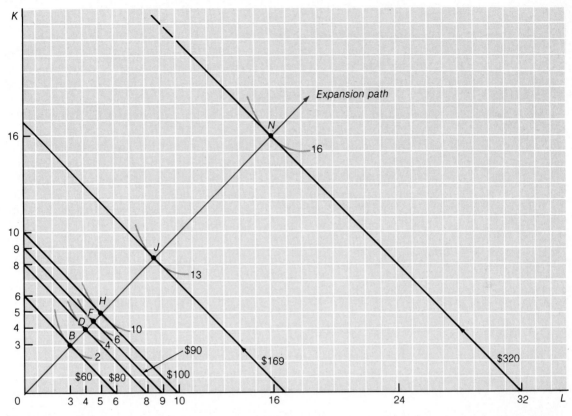

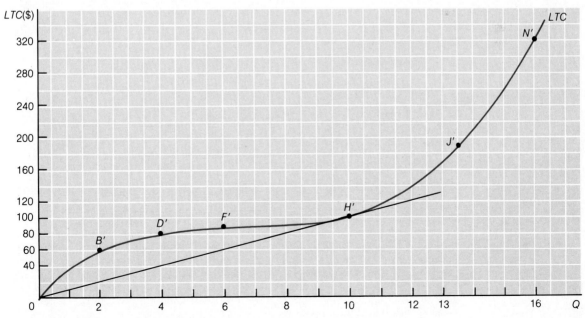

8-4b Derivation of the Long-Run Average Cost Curve

The **long-run average cost (*LAC*)** curve is derived from the *LTC* curve in the same way as the short-run average total cost (*SATC*) curve is derived from the short-run total cost (*STC*) curve. For example, in Figure 8-9, the *LAC* for two units of output (2*Q*) is obtained by dividing the *LTC* of $60 (point *B'* on the *LTC* curve in the bottom panel of Figure 8-8) by 2. This is the slope of the ray from the origin to point *B'* on the *LTC* curve and is plotted as point *B* in Figure 8-9. Other points on the *LAC* curve are similarly obtained. Note that the slope of a line from the origin to the *LTC* curve falls up to point *H'* (in the bottom panel of Figure 8-8) and then rises. Thus, the *LAC* curve in Figure 8-9 falls up to point *H* (10*Q*) and rises thereafter. However, while the U-shape of the *SATC* curve is explained by the law of diminishing returns, the U-shape of the *LAC* curve depends on the operation of increasing, constant, and decreasing returns to scale, respectively, as explained in Section 8-5.

Figure 8-9 also shows that the *LAC* curve is tangent to various *SATC* curves. Each *SATC* curve represents the plant to be used to produce a par-

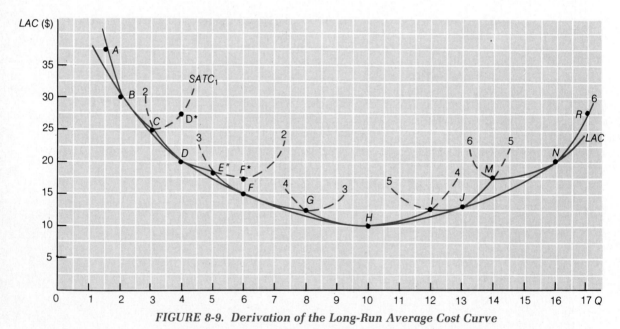

FIGURE 8-9. Derivation of the Long-Run Average Cost Curve

The LAC of $30 for two units of output (point B) is given by the slope of the line from the origin to point B' on the LTC curve (in the bottom panel of Figure 8-8). Other points on the LAC curve are similarly obtained. The slope of a ray from the origin to the LTC curve falls up to point H' (in the bottom panel of Figure 8-8) and then rises. Thus, the LAC curve falls up to point H and rises thereafter. The LAC curve is tangent to the SATC curves, each representing the plant size to produce a particular level of output at minimum cost.

ticular level of output at minimum cost. The *LAC* curve is then the tangent to these *SATC* curves and shows the minimum cost of producing each level of output. For example, the lowest *LAC* (of $30) to produce two units of output results when the firm operates plant 1 at point *B* on *SATC1* curve. The lowest *LAC* (of $20) to produce 4 units of output results when the firm operates plant 2 at point *D* on its *SATC2* curve. Four units of output could also be produced by the firm operating plant 1 at point *D** on its *SATC1* curve (see the figure). However, this would not represent the lowest cost of producing 4*Q* in the long run. Other points on the *LAC* curve are similarly obtained. Thus, the *LAC* curve shows the minimum per-unit cost of producing any level of output *when the firm can build any desired scale of plant.* Note that the *LAC* to produce 3*Q* is the same for plant 1 and plant 2 (point *C*).

With only six plant sizes, the *LAC* curve would be *ABCDE"FGHIJMNR* (the solid portion of the *SATC* curves). With the infinite or very large number of plant sizes that the firm could build in the long run, the *LAC* curve would be the smooth curve passing through points *BDFHJN* (that is, the "kink" at points *C*, *E"*, *G*, *I*, and *M* would be eliminated by having many plant sizes). Mathematically, the *LAC* curve is the "envelope" to the *SATC* curves.

The long run is often referred to as the **planning horizon.** In the long run, the firm has the time to build the plant that minimizes the cost of producing any anticipated level of output. Once the plant has been built, the firm operates in the short run. Thus, the firm plans in the long run and operates in the short run.

8-4c Relationship Between Short- and Long-Run Cost Curves

The relationship between the *long-run* total and per-unit cost curves is generally the same as between the *short-run* total and per-unit cost curves. There is also a unique relationship between the *LTC* and *STC* curves and between the long-run and the short-run per-unit cost curves. These are shown in Figure 8-10.

The top panel of Figure 8-10 shows the *LTC* curve of the bottom panel of Figure 8-8 and the *STC* curve of Figure 8-4.[5] The bottom panel of Figure 8-10 shows the *LAC* curve of Figure 8-9 and the *SATC* and the *SMC* curves of Figure 8-5. As previously pointed out, the *LAC* is given by the slope of a ray from the origin to the *LTC* curve. Thus, the *LAC* curve falls up to point *H* and rises thereafter.

The **long-run marginal cost (*LMC*)** curve is given by the slope of the *LTC* curve. From the top panel of Figure 8-10, we see that the slope of the *LTC* curve (the *LMC*) falls up to $Q = 7$ (the point of inflection) and rises there-

---

[5] It should be noted that an infinite number of *STC* curves could be drawn in the top panel of Figure 8-10—one for each quantity of the fixed input or *TFC*.

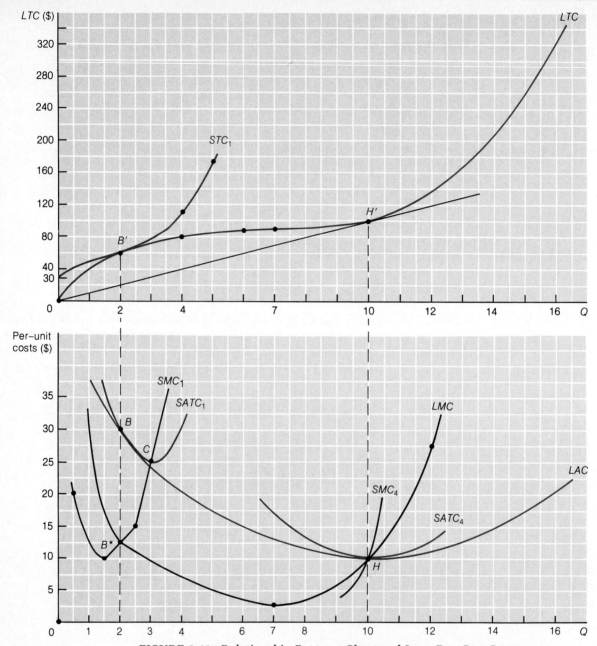

FIGURE 8-10. Relationship Between Short and Long-Run Cost Curves.

The top panel shows the LTC curve of Figure 8-8 and the STC curve of Figure 8-4. The bottom panel shows the LAC curve of Figure 8-9 and the SATC and the SMC curves of Figure 8-5. The long-run marginal cost (LMC) is given by the slope of the LTC curve. This falls up to Q = 7 (the point of inflection) and rises thereafter. SATC = LAC at point B because STC = LTC at point B'. Also, SMC = LMC at point B* because the slope of the LTC and STC curves are equal at point B'. At the lowest point on the LAC curve (i.e., at point H), LAC = LMC = SATC = SMC.

248

after. Also, the slope of the *LTC* curve (the *LMC*) is smaller than the slope of a ray from the origin to the *LTC* curve (the *LAC*) up to point *H'* and larger thereafter. At point *H*, *LMC* = *LAC*. Note that the *LMC* curve intersects from below the *LAC* curve at the lowest point of the latter. The *LMC* is $30 at *Q* = 1 because *LTC* increases from 0 to $60 when output rises from zero (the origin) to 2 units. Thus, the change in *LTC* per unit change in output (the *LMC*) is $60/2 = $30. *LMC* is $10 at *Q* = 3 because *LTC* increases from $60 to $80 for a 2-unit increase in output (from *Q* = 2 to *Q* = 4). The other *LMC* values shown in Figure 8-10 are obtained in the same way.

The *SATC* = *LAC* at point *B* (in the bottom panel of Figure 8-10) because *STC* = *LTC* at point *B'* in the top panel. Also, *SMC* = *LMC* at point *B** in the bottom panel because the slope of the *LTC* and *STC* curves are equal at point *B'* in the top panel. Also note that at the lowest point on the *LAC* curve (i.e., at point *H*), *LAC* = *LMC* = *SATC* = *SMC*. The reason for this is that the STC_4 curve (not shown in the top panel) is tangent to the *LTC* curve at point *H'*.

Example 8-3 Long-Run Average Cost Curve in Electricity Generation

The Facts: Figure 8-11 shows the actual estimated *LAC* curve for a sample of 114 firms generating electricity in the United States in 1970.

Comment: The lowest point on the *LAC* curve is at the output level of about 30 billion kilowatt hours. However, the *LAC* curve is nearly L-shaped (the reason and significance of this are explained next).

FIGURE 8-11.
Long-Run Average
Cost Curve in
Electricity
Generation

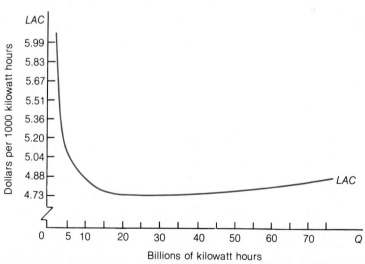

The figure shows the actual estimated LAC curve for a sample of 114 firms generating electricity in the United States in 1970. The lowest point on the LAC curve is at the output level of about 30 billion kilowatt hours. However, the LAC curve is nearly L-shaped.

249

Source: L. Christensen and W. Green, "Economies of Scale in U.S. Electric Power Generation," *Journal of Political Economy*, August 1976, p. 674.

8-5

The Shape of the Long-Run Average Cost Curve

In Figures 8-9 and 8-10, the *LAC* curve has been drawn as U-shaped, just like the *SATC* curve. However, the reason for this similarity is entirely different. The *SATC* curve turns upward when the rise in *AVC* (resulting from the operation of the law of diminishing returns) exceeds the decline in *AFC* (see Figure 8-5 and the discussion relating to it). However, in the long run, all inputs are variable (i.e., there are no fixed inputs) and so the law of diminishing returns is not applicable. The U-shape of the *LAC* curve depends instead on increasing and decreasing returns to scale. That is, as output expands from very low levels, increasing returns to scale prevail and cause the *LAC* curve to fall. However, as output continues to expand, the forces for decreasing returns to scale eventually begin to overtake the forces for increasing returns to scale and the *LAC* curve begins to rise.

As seen in Section 7-4, increasing returns to scale means that output rises proportionately more than inputs, and so the cost per unit of output falls if input prices remain constant. On the other hand, decreasing returns to scale means that output rises proportionately less than inputs, and so the cost per unit of output rises if input prices remain constant. Therefore, decreasing *LAC* and increasing returns to scale are two sides of the same coin. Similarly, increasing *LAC* and decreasing returns to scale are equivalent. When the forces for increasing returns to scale are just balanced by the forces for decreasing returns to scale, we have constant returns to scale and the *LAC* curve is horizontal.

Empirical studies seem to indicate that in many industries the *LAC* curve has a very shallow bottom or is nearly L-shaped, as in Figure 8-11. This means that economies of scale are rather quickly exhausted, and constant or near-constant returns to scale prevail over a considerable range of output. This permits relatively small and large firms to co-exist in the same industry (see Example 8-4).

Were increasing returns to scale to prevail over a very large range of output, large (and more efficient) firms would drive smaller firms out of business. In an extreme case, only one firm could most efficiently satisfy the entire market demand for the commodity. This is usually referred to as a "natural monopoly." In such cases, the government allows only one firm to operate in the market, but the firm is subject to regulation. Examples are provided by public utilities (such as electricity, telephone, and so on). This topic is discussed in detail in Chapter 11. On the other hand, the reason we do not often observe steeply rising *LAC* in the real world is that firms may generally know when their *LAC* would begin to rise rapidly and avoid expanding output in that range.

Example 8-4 **Long-Run Average Cost Estimates for Selected U.S. Industries**

The Facts: Table 8-4 shows the long-run average cost for small firms as a percentage of the long-run average cost of large firms in six U.S. industries.

Comment: The table shows that the *LAC* of small hospitals is 29 per cent higher than for large hospitals. Aside from hospitals, the *LAC* of small firms is not much different from the *LAC* of large firms in the same industry. These results are consistent with the widespread near-constant returns to scale reported in Table 7-4 in Example 7-3. Note that small trucking firms seem to have a small cost advantage over their large counterparts.

Source: H. Cohen, "Hospital Cost Curves with Emphasis on Measuring Patient Care Output," in H. Klarman (ed.), *Empirical Studies in Health Economics* (Baltimore: Johns Hopkins Press, 1970), pp. 279–293. F. Bell and N. Murphy, *Costs in Commercial Banking* (Boston: Federal Reserve Bank of Boston, Research Report No. 41, 1968). L. Christensen and W. Greene, "Economies of Scale in U.S. Electric Power Generation," *Journal of Political Economy*, August 1976, p. 674. G. Eads, M. Nerlove, and W. Raduchel, "A Long-Run Cost Function for the Local Service Airline Industry," *The Review of Economics and Statistics*, August 1969, pp. 258–270. Z. Griliches, "Cost Allocation in Railroad Regulation," *The Bell Journal of Economics and Management Science*, Spring 1972, pp. 26–41. R. Koenker, "Optimal Scale and the Size Distribution of American Trucking Firms," *Journal of Transport Economics and Policy*, January 1977, 54–67.

8-6

Applications

In this section we examine a number of important applications of the tools of analysis developed in the chapter. These demonstrate the great usefulness of the theory presented in this chapter in analyzing the process by which the firm minimizes production costs.

TABLE 8-4 *LAC* of Small Firms as a Percentage of *LAC* of Large Firms

Industry	Percentage
Hospitals	129
Commercial banking	
Demand Deposits	116
Installment loans	102
Electric power	112
Airline (local service)	100
Railroads	100
Trucking	95

Application 1: Derivation of the Total Variable Cost Curve from the Total Product Curve

The top panel of Figure 8-12 reproduces the total product (TP) curve of Figure 7-2. With labor (L) as the only variable input and with the constant wage rate of $10, the total variable cost (TVC) of producing various quantities of output is given by $TVC = \$10L$ (the lower horizontal scale in the top panel). If we now transpose the axes and plot TVC on the vertical axis and output on the horizontal axis, we obtain the TVC curve shown in the bottom panel of Figure 8-12. Thus, the shape of the TVC curve is determined by the shape of the TP curve.

Note that the slope of the TP curve (or MP_L) rises up to point G (the point of inflection) in the top panel and then declines. On the other hand, the slope of the TVC curve (the MC) falls up to point G' (the point of inflection) in the bottom panel and then rises. At points G and G', the law of diminishing returns begins to operate. The MC is the monetized mirror image or dial of the MP_L. That is, MC falls when MP_L rises, MC is minimum when MP_L is highest, and MC rises when MP_L falls. The same inverse relationship exists between the AVC and the AP_L. Note also that the TVC curve is dashed above point I' in the bottom panel since no firm would want to incur higher TVC to produce smaller outputs.

Application 2: The Least-Cost Combination of Gasoline and Driving Time for a Trip

Figure 8-13 repeats the isoquant of Figure 7-11 showing the various combinations of gasoline consumption and driving time required to cover 600 miles. If the price of gasoline is $1.50 per gallon and the opportunity cost of driving time is $6.00 per hour, the minimum total cost of the trip is $90. This is given by point B, where the isocost line is tangent to the isoquant. Thus, to minimize traveling costs, the individual would have to drive 10 hours at 60 mph and use 20 gallons of gasoline. The individual would spend $30 on gasoline (20 gallons at $1.50 per gallon) and incur an opportunity cost of $60 for the travel time (10 hours of driving at $6.00 per hour).

If the government set the speed limit at 50 mph, the trip would require 16 gallons of gasoline and 12 hours of driving time (point A). The total cost of the trip would then be $24 for the gasoline (16 gallons at $1.50 per gallon) plus $72 for the driving time (12 hours at $6 per hour), or $96.

Application 3: Cost Reductions from the Short Run to the Long Run

Figure 8-14 (an extension of Figure 8-3) shows that with capital fixed at 4K in the short run, the firm would incur a total cost of $110 to produce 10Q (point V). At point V, $MRTS_{LK} < w/r$. In the long run, the firm could reduce the total cost of producing 10Q from $110 to $100 by substituting K for L in production until it reaches point H. Similarly, with capital fixed at 4K in the short run, the firm would incur a total cost of $65 to produce 2Q (point X). At point X, $MRTS_{LK} > w/r$. In the long run, the firm could reduce the total cost of producing 2Q from $65 to $60 by substituting L for K in pro-

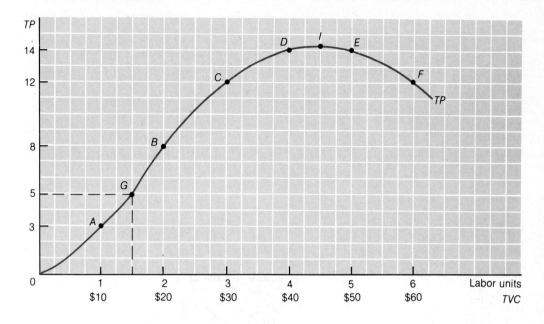

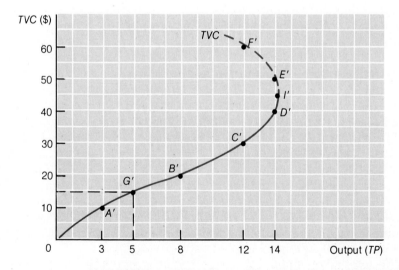

FIGURE 8-12. Derivation of the TVC Curve from the TP Curve

The top panel reproduces the TP curve of Figure 7-2. With labor (L) as the only variable input, and with the constant wage rate of $10, TVC = $10L (the lower horizontal scale in the top panel). If we now transpose the axes and plot TVC on the vertical axis and output on the horizontal axis, we obtain the TVC curve shown in the bottom panel. At points G and G', the law of diminishing returns begins to operate.

253

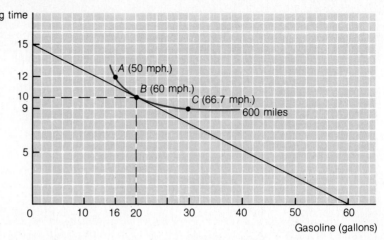

FIGURE 8-13.
The Minimum Cost
of a Trip

The figure repeats the isoquant of Figure 7-11 showing the various combinations of gasoline consumption and driving time required to cover 600 miles. If the price of gasoline is $1.50 per gallon and the opportunity cost of driving is $6 per hour, the minimum cost of the trip is $90 (point B). The individual spends $30 on gasoline (20 gallons at $1.50 per gallon) and $60 in driving time (10 hours at $6 per hour). With a speed limit of 50 mph, the trip would require 16 gallons of gasoline and 12 hours of driving time (point A) at a total cost of $96.

duction until it reaches point B. Thus, total costs are usually smaller in the long run than in the short run. Note, however, that the total costs of producing 4Q could not be reduced in the long run if the firm was already at point D in the short run.

Application 4: Input Substitution in Production

Figure 8-15 shows that with $TC = \$140$ and $w = r = \$10$, the firm minimizes the cost of producing 10Q by using 7K and 7L (point A, where isocost line FG is tangent to isoquant 10Q). At point A, $K/L = 1$.

If r remains at $10 but w falls to $5, the isocost line becomes FH and the firm can reach an isoquant higher than 10Q with $TC = \$140$. The firm can now reach isoquant 10Q with $TC = \$100$. This is given by isocost F'H', which is parallel to FH (i.e., $w/r = \frac{1}{2}$ for both) and is tangent to isoquant 10Q at point B. At point B, $K/L = \frac{1}{2}$. Thus, with a reduction in w (and constant r), a lower TC is required to produce a given level of output. To minimize production costs, the firm will have to substitute L for K in production, so that K/L declines.

The ease with which the firm can substitute L for K in production depends on the shape of the isoquant. The flatter is the isoquant, the easier it is to substitute L for K in production. On the other hand, if the isoquant is at a right angle or L-shaped (as in Figure 7-7), no input substitution is possible (i.e., $MRTS_{LK} = 0$). In such a case, K/L will then always be constant regardless of input prices.

254

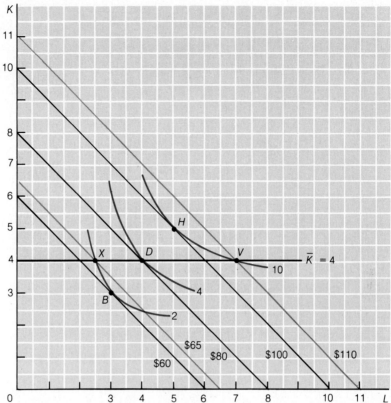

FIGURE 8-14.
Cost Reductions
from the Short Run
to the Long Run

With capital fixed at 4K, the firm would incur TC = $110 to produce 10Q (point V). At point V, $MRTS_{LK}$ < w/r. In the long run, the firm would reduce the TC of producing 10Q from $110 to $100 by substituting K for L in production until it reaches point H. Similarly, with capital fixed at 4K, the firm would incur TC = $65 to produce 2Q (point X). At point X, $MRTS_{LK}$ > w/r. In the long run, the firm would reduce the TC of producing 2Q from $65 to $60 by substituting L for K in production until it reaches point B.

Application 5: Input Prices and the Average and Marginal Cost Curves

In deriving the firm's cost curves, input prices are kept constant. Per-unit costs differ at different levels of output because the physical productivity of inputs varies as output varies. If input prices do change, the AC and the MC curves of the firm will shift—up if input prices rise and down if input prices fall.[6]

For example, point B in Figure 8-15 shows that 10Q is produced at TC = $100 when w = $5, so that AC = $10. With w = $10, the production of 10Q requires TC = $140 (point A in Figure 8-15) so that AC′ = $14. This is shown in Figure 8-16 by point B′ and A′ on average cost curves AC and

---

[6] The AC and MC curves shift in the opposite direction when the price of an inferior input changes.

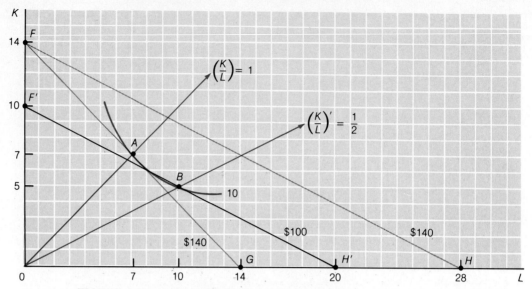

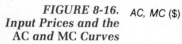

FIGURE 8-15. Input Substitution in Production

With TC = $140 and w = r = $10, the firm minimizes the cost of producing 10Q by using 7K and 7L (point A, where isocost FG is tangent to isoquant 10Q). At point A, K/L = 1. If r remains at $10 but w falls to $5, the firm can reach isoquant 10Q with TC = $100. The least-cost combination of L and K is then given by point B, where isocost F'H' is tangent to isoquant 10Q. At point B, K/L = ½.

FIGURE 8-16. Input Prices and the AC and MC Curves

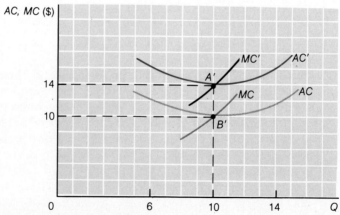

Point B' on curve AC shows that with w = $5, AC = $10 for Q = 10 (from point B in Figure 8-15). Point A' on curve AC' shows that with w = $10, AC = $14 for Q = 10 (from point A in Figure 8-15). Thus, an increase in w from $5 to $10 shifts AC and MC up to AC' and MC'.

AC', respectively. Note that the marginal cost curve will also shift up from MC to MC' when w rises. For simplicity, we assume that the firm produces at the lowest point on its average cost curve before and after the increase in w.

Summary

1. In economics, costs include explicit and implicit costs. Explicit costs are the actual expenditures of the firm to purchase or hire inputs. Implicit costs refer to the value (imputed from their best alternative use) of the inputs owned and used by the firm. The cost to a firm in using any input (whether owned or hired) is what the input could earn in its best alternative use. This is the alternative or opportunity cost doctrine. Costs are also classified into private and social. Private costs are those incurred by individuals and firms, while social costs are those incurred by society as a whole.

2. Given the wage rate of labor (w), the rental price of capital (r), and a particular total cost (TC), we can define the isocost line. This shows the various combinations of L and K that the firm can hire. With K plotted along the vertical axis, the Y-intercept of the isocost line is TC/r and its slope is $-w/r$. In order to minimize production costs or maximize output, the firm must produce where an isoquant is tangent to an isocost line. There, $MRTS_{LK} = w/r$ and $MP_L/w = MP_K/r$. This means the MP per dollar spent on L must be equal to the MP per dollar spent on K. The minimum cost of producing a given level of output is usually lower in the long run than in the short run.

3. In the short run we have fixed, variable, and total costs. Total fixed costs (TFC) plus total variable costs (TVC) equal total costs (TC). The shape of the TVC curve follows directly from the law of diminishing returns. Average fixed cost (AFC) equals TFC/Q, where Q is output. Average variable cost (AVC) equals TVC/Q. Average total cost (ATC) equals TC/Q. $ATC = AFC + AVC$ also. Marginal cost (MC) equals the change in TC or in TVC per-unit change in output. The AVC, ATC, and MC curves first fall and then rise (i.e., they are U-shaped). AVC and MC move inversely to the AP_L and the MP_L, respectively. The AVC and the ATC are given, respectively, by the slope of a line from the origin to the TVC and to the TC curves, while the MC is given by the slope of the TC and the TVC curves.

4. The expansion path joins the origin with the points of tangency of isoquants and isocost lines with input prices held constant. It shows the least-cost input combination to produce various output levels. From the expansion path, we can derive the long-run total cost (LTC) curve. This shows the minimum long-run total costs of producing various levels of output when the firm can build any desired plant. The long-run average cost (LAC) equals LTC/Q. The LAC curve is tangent to the short-run average cost curves. The long-run marginal cost (LMC) equals $\Delta LTC/\Delta Q$. The relationship between the LAC and LMC curves and their derivation from the LTC curve is similar to that of the short run. When $LTC = STC$, $LAC = SATC$ and $LMC = SMC$. The firm plans in the long run and operates in the short run.

5. The U-shape of the long-run average cost curve of the firm results from the operation of increasing, constant, and decreasing returns to scale, respectively. Empirical studies seem to indicate that in many industries the LAC curve has a very shallow bottom or is nearly L-shaped. This means that economies of scale are quickly exhausted, and constant or near-constant returns to scale prevail over a considerable range of output. This permits relatively small and large firms to coexist in the same industry.

6. The TVC curve can be derived from the TP curve. Total costs are usually smaller in the long run than in the short run. A change in the price of an input will change the total costs of producing a given level of output and will lead to input substitution to minimize production costs. The AC and the MC curves shift up with an increase in input prices and down with a decrease in input prices.

Glossary

Explicit costs   The actual expenditures of the firm to purchase or hire inputs.

Implicit costs   The value of the inputs owned and used by the firm; value is imputed from the best alternative use of the inputs.

Alternative or **opportunity cost doctrine**   The doctrine that postulates that the cost to a firm in using any input (whether owned or hired) is what the input could earn in its best alternative use.

Private costs   The costs incurred by individuals and firms.

Social costs   The costs incurred by society as a whole.

Isocost line   It shows the various combinations of two inputs that the firm can hire with a given total cost outlay.

Least-cost input combination   The condition where the marginal product per dollar spent on each input is equal. Graphically, it is the point where an isoquant is tangent to an isocost line.

Total fixed costs (TFC)   The total obligations of the firm per time period for all fixed inputs.

Total variable costs (TVC)   The total obligations of the firm per time period for all the variable inputs the firm uses.

Total costs (TC)   TFC plus TVC.

Average fixed cost (AFC)   Total fixed costs divided by output.

Average variable cost (AVC)   Total variable costs divided by output.

Average total cost (ATC)   Total costs divided by output. Also equals $AFC + AVC$.

Marginal cost (MC)   The change in TC or in TVC per unit change in output.

Expansion path   The line joining the origin with the points of tangency of isoquants and isocost lines with input prices held constant. It shows the least-cost input combination to produce various output levels.

Long-run total cost (LTC)   The minimum total costs of producing various levels of output when the firm can build any desired scale of plant.

Long-run average cost (LAC)   The minimum per-unit cost of producing any level of output when the firm can build any desired scale of plant. It equals long-run total cost divided by output.

Planning horizon   The time period when the firm can build any desired scale of plant; the long run.

Long-run marginal cost (LMC)   The change in long-run total costs per-unit change in output; the slope of the LTC curve.

Questions for Review

1. What is the definition of
   (a) explicit costs?
   (b) implicit costs?
   (c) private costs?
   (d) social costs?
2. (a) How are implicit costs calculated?
   (b) What does the opportunity cost doctrine postulate?
   (c) What is the relationship between explicit and implicit costs, on the one hand, and opportunity costs, on the other?
3. (a) What does an isocost line measure?
   (b) What is the general equation for an isocost line when capital is plotted on the vertical axis and labor along the horizontal axis?
   (c) How does an isocost line change if only total outlays or costs change?

   (d) How does an isocost line change if only one input price changes?
4. (a) What is the graphical condition for a firm to minimize production costs?
   (b) What is the graphical condition for a firm to maximize output?
   (c) Should the firm use more labor or more capital if the marginal product per dollar spent on labor exceeds the marginal product per dollar spent on capital?
   (d) Can minimum production costs be lower in the long run than in the short run? How?
5. (a) What are fixed, variable, and total costs?
   (b) Do fixed and variable costs refer to the short run or to the long run?
   (c) What is the shape of the fixed, variable, and total cost curves?

(d) Why do fixed, variable, and total cost curves have the shape they do?

6. (a) What are average fixed costs (AFC), average variable costs (AVC), average total costs (ATC), and marginal costs (MC)?

(b) What is the general shape of the AFC, AVC, ATC, and MC curves?

(c) Why is an explicit AFC curve not generally needed?

7. (a) What explains the shape of the AVC and the MC curves?

(b) Why does the ATC curve reach its lowest point after the AVC curve?

(c) Why does the MC curve intersect the AVC and the ATC curves at their lowest point?

(d) How can the AFC, AVC, ATC, and the MC curves be derived geometrically?

8. (a) How is an expansion path derived? What does it show?

(b) How can the long-run total cost (LTC) curve be derived from the expansion path?

(c) What does the LTC curve of the firm show?

9. (a) What does the long-run average cost (LAC) curve of the firm show?

(b) How can the LAC curve of the firm be derived from its LTC curve?

(c) How can the LAC curve of the firm be derived from the short-run average total cost (SATC) curves of the firm?

(d) What is the planning horizon? What is its relationship to the long run and the short run?

10. (a) How can the long-run marginal cost (LMC) curve of the firm be derived? What does it show?

(b) What is the relationship between the LAC and the LMC curves?

(c) What is the relationship between the LTC and STC curves?

(d) What is the relationship between the LAC and the SAC curves? Between the LMC and the SMC curves?

11. (a) On what does the U-shape of the LAC curve depend?

(b) Are the reasons for the U-shape of the LAC and the SATC curves similar?

(c) What shape of the LAC curve has been found in many empirical studies?

(d) What does the shape of the LAC found in many empirical studies mean for the survival of small firms in an industry?

12. (a) How can the TVC curve be derived from the TP curve?

(b) Why are total costs usually lower in the long run than in the short run?

(c) What determines the degree of input substitution in production when the price of an input changes?

(d) What is the effect of an increase in the price of an input on the firm's AC and MC curves?

Problems

★1. A woman working in a large duplicating (photocopying) establishment for $15,000 per year decides to open a small duplicating place of her own. She runs the operation by herself without hired help and invests no money of her own. She rents the premises for $10,000 per year and the machines for $30,000 per year. She spends $15,000 per year on supplies (paper, ink, envelopes), electricity, telephone, and so on. During the year her gross earnings are $65,000.

(a) How much are the explicit costs of this business?

(b) How much are the implicit costs?

(c) Should this woman remain in business after the year, if she is indifferent between working for herself or for others in a similar capacity?

2. Suppose that the marginal product of the last worker employed by a firm is 30 units of output per day and the daily wage that the firm must pay is $20, while the marginal product of the last machine rented by the firm is 80 units of output per day and the daily rental price of the machine is $40.

(a) Why is this firm not maximizing output or minimizing costs in the long run?

(b) How can the firm maximize output or minimize costs?

3. With reference to Figure 8-3, answer the following questions.
   (a) If capital were fixed at 5 units, what would be the minimum cost of producing 10 units of output in the short run?
   (b) If capital were variable but labor fixed at 4 units, what would be the minimum cost of producing 10 units of output?
4. (a) Plot the total fixed cost (TFC) curve, the total variable costs (TVC) curve, and the total costs (TC) curve given in the following table.
   (b) Explain the reason for the shape of the cost curves in part (a).

Quantity of Output	Total Variable Costs	Total Costs
0	0	$ 30
1	$ 20	50
2	30	60
3	48	78
4	90	120
5	170	200

5. (a) Derive the average fixed costs (AFC), the average variable costs (AVC), the average total costs (ATC), and the marginal costs (MC) from the total cost schedules given in the table of Problem 4.
   (b) Plot the AVC, ATC, and MC curves of part (a) on a graph and explain the reason for their shape. How are AFC reflected in the figure?
   (c) How can the AFC, AVC, ATC, and MC curves be derived geometrically?
★6. Electrical utility companies usually operate their most modern and efficient equipment around the clock and use their older and less efficient equipment only to meet periods of peak electricity demand.
   (a) What does this imply for the short-run marginal cost of these firms?
   (b) Why do these firms not replace all of their older with newer equipment in the long run?
7. (a) Suppose that $w = \$10$ and $r = \$10$ and the least-cost input combination is 3L and 3K to produce 2 units of output (2Q), 4L and

4K to produce 4Q, 4.5L and 4.5K to produce 6Q, 5L and 5K to produce 8Q, 7.5L and 7.5K for 10Q, and 12L and 12K for 12Q. Draw the isocost lines, the isoquants, and the expansion path of the firm.
   (b) From the expansion path of part (a), derive the long-run total cost curve of the firm.
   (c) Redraw your figure of part (b) and on it draw the STC curve of Problem 4a, the STC curve tangent to the LTC curve at $Q = 8$, and the STC curve tangent to the LTC curve at $Q = 12$.
8. (a) From the LTC curve of the firm of Problem 7b, derive the LAC and the LMC curves of the firm.
   (b) Redraw the figure of part (a) and on the same figure draw the ATC and the MC curves of Problem 5b. Also draw the ATC curve that forms the lowest point of the LAC curve at $Q = 8$ and the corresponding SMC curve. On the same figure, draw the ATC curve that is tangent to the LAC curve at $Q = 12$ and the corresponding SMC curve.
★9. (a) Under what condition would the LTC curve be a positively sloped straight line through the origin?
   (b) What would then be the shape of the LAC and the LMC curves?
   (c) Would this be consistent with U-shaped STC curves?
   (d) Draw a figure showing your answer to parts (a) to (c).
10. Derive the total variable cost curve of the firm from the total product curve of Problem 7.1b on the assumption that the price of labor time or the wage rate (w) is $20. What is the relationship between the two curves?
11. If the price of nitrogen fertilizer was $1.00 per pound and the price of phosphate was $0.60 per pound and the corn farmer had $150 to spend on fertilizers,
   (a) What is the maximum quantity of corn that he or she could produce?
   (b) How much nitrogen and phosphate should the farmer use?
★12. Starting at the least-cost input combination shown by point A in Figure 8-15,
   (a) calculate the minimum cost of producing

10Q if the isoquant had been L-shaped with origin at point *A* and *w* fell to $5.

(b) draw the figure for part (a).

(c) in what way and why is your result different from that in Application 4?

Supplementary Readings

For a problem-solving approach to the topics discussed in this chapter, see

Dominick Salvatore, *Microeconomic Theory,* 2nd ed. (New York: McGraw-Hill, 1983), Chapter 7 (Sections 7-7 to 7-11) and Chapter 8.

An excellent presentation of the material covered in this chapter is found in

George J. Stigler, *The Theory of Price* (New York: Macmillan, 1966), Chapters 6, 8, and 9.

The classic article on cost curves is

Jacob Viner, "Cost Curves and Supply Curves," in *Readings in Price Theory,* American Economic Association (Homewood, Ill.: Irwin, 1952), Chapter 10.

Extensions of Production and Cost Theory

Chapter 9

9-1 The Cobb-Douglas Production Function

9-2 The Elasticity of Substitution

9-3 Technological Progress

9-4 Linear Programming: The Basic Concepts

9-5 Linear Programming: A More Complete Picture

9-6 Applications

Examples

9-1 Output Elasticity of Labor and Capital in U.S. Manufacturing

9-2 Technological Progress and Productivity Growth in the U.S.

9-3 Linear Programming in the Petroleum Industry

Applications

Application 1: Short-Run Total and Per-Unit Cost Curves for the Cobb-Douglas Production Function

Application 2: Long-Run Total and Per-Unit Cost Curves for the Cobb-Douglas Production Function

Application 3: Technological Progress and the Distribution of Income

Application 4: The Dual Problem and Shadow Prices

Preview Questions

What is the Cobb-Douglas production function? How is it estimated?

What is the elasticity of substitution? What is its usefulness?

What is technological progress? What are its different types?

How can technological progress be shown graphically?

What is linear programming? What is its usefulness?

What is the relationship between linear programming and production theory?

On what do changes in the distribution of income over time depend?

What is the meaning and importance of shadow prices?

This chapter extends traditional production and cost theory in some important directions. We begin by examining the Cobb-Douglas production function. This is the simplest and most widely used production function in empirical work today. Then we discuss the elasticity of substitution of inputs in production. The ability to substitute cheaper inputs for more expensive ones is crucial to keep production costs down. We then go on to examine the meaning and measurement of technological progress. This is responsible for the greater part of the increase in the standard of living in industrial nations. As such, technological progress is certainly of great interest to economists and significantly affects us all. Subsequently, we deal with linear programming. This is a very useful and powerful technique with many important applications in production and commercial decisions by modern corporations and in government activities.

Finally, we present some important applications of the tools of analysis introduced in the chapter. While the chapter itself stresses extensions of production theory, the applications represent, for the most part, extensions of cost theory. These applications, as well as the examples presented in the chapter, clearly demonstrate the importance of the extensions of traditional production and cost theory presented. As for Chapter 6, the topics in this chapter are somewhat more advanced than those presented in the other chapters, but the extra effort will be amply rewarded.

9-1

The Cobb-Douglas Production Function

In this section, we present the Cobb-Douglas production function. We begin with the formula. This is followed by a simple illustration. Next, we consider the methods available to empirically estimate the Cobb-Douglas production function and some of the difficulties involved. Finally, we will present some empirical results.

9-1a The Formula

The formula for the **Cobb-Douglas production function** is

$$Q = AL^\alpha K^\beta \tag{9-1}$$

where Q = output in physical units
L = quantity of labor
K = quantity of capital

A, α (alpha), and β (beta) are positive parameters estimated in each case from the data. The parameter A refers to technology. The more advanced the technology, the greater is the value of A. The parameter α refers to the percentage increase in Q for a 1 per cent increase in L, while holding K constant. Thus, α is the **output elasticity of labor.** For example, if $\alpha = 0.7$, this means that a 1 per cent increase in the quantity of labor used (while holding the quantity of capital constant) leads to 0.7 per cent increase in output. Thus, the output elasticity of labor (α) is 0.7 per cent. Similarly, the parameter β refers to the percentage increase in Q for a 1 per cent increase in K, while holding L constant. Thus, β is the **output elasticity of capital.** For example, if $\beta = 0.3$, this means that a 1 per cent increase in K, while holding L constant, leads to a 0.3 per cent increase in Q. Thus, the output elasticity of K (β) is 0.3 per cent.

In the above example, $\alpha + \beta = 0.7 + 0.3 = 1$. Thus, we have constant returns to scale. That is, a 1 per cent increase in both L and K leads to a 1 per cent increase in Q. Specifically, a 1 per cent increase in L, by itself, leads to a 0.7 per cent increase in Q, and a 1 per cent increase in K, by itself, leads to a 0.3 per cent increase in Q. Thus, with an increase of both L and K by 1 per cent, Q increases by a total of 1 per cent also and we have constant returns to scale. Another name for constant returns to scale is **homogeneous of degree 1** or **linearly homogeneous.**

On the other hand, if $\alpha + \beta > 1$, we have increasing returns to scale. That is, a 1 per cent increase in L and K leads to a greater than a 1 per cent increase in Q. For example, if $\alpha = 0.8$ and $\beta = 0.3$, a 1 per cent increase in L and K leads to a $0.8 + 0.3 = 1.1$ per cent increase in Q. Finally, if $\alpha + \beta < 1$, we have decreasing returns to scale (i.e., an increase in L and K by 1 per cent leads to an increase in Q of less than 1 per cent).

9-1b Illustration

Suppose $A = 10$, $\alpha = \beta = \frac{1}{2}$, and $\overline{K} = 4$ and is held constant (so that we are dealing with the short run). By substituting these values into Equation

(9-1), we get

$$Q = 10L^{1/2}4^{1/2} = 10\sqrt{4}\ \sqrt{L} = 20\sqrt{L} \qquad (9\text{-}1A)$$

By then substituting alternative quantities of L used in production into Equation (9-1A), we derive the total product (TP) schedule, and from it, the average product of labor (AP_L) and the marginal product of labor (MP_L) schedules. The results are given in Table 9-1.

Plotting the TP, the AP_L, and the MP_L schedules of Table 9-1 and Figure 9-1, we see that the Cobb-Douglas production function exhibits only stage II of production. That is, the AP_L and the MP_L decline from the very start (i.e., the law of diminishing returns begins to operate with the first unit of L used) and the MP_L never becomes negative. Note that the MP_L is plotted between the various quantities of labor used. The AP_L and the MP_L are functions of or depend only on the K/L ratio. That is, they remain the same regardless of how much L and K are used in production as long as the K/L ratio remains the same (as along any given ray from the origin—see Problem 2 with answer provided in the back of the book).

In the long run, both L and K are variable. Thus,

$$Q = 10L^{1/2}K^{1/2} = 10\sqrt{L}\ \sqrt{K} = 10\sqrt{LK} \qquad (9\text{-}1B)$$

Since $\alpha + \beta = 0.5 + 0.5 = 1$ in this case, we have constant returns to scale. This is shown in Table 9-2. Here, output grows at the same rate as the rate of increase in both inputs. For example, doubling the quantity of labor and capital used, from 1 to 2 units, doubles output from 10 to 20 units. Increasing L and K by 50 per cent, from 2 to 3 units, increases Q by 50 per cent from 20 to 30 units, and so on.

We can also define the isoquants for this Cobb-Douglas production function. For example, the isoquant for $50Q$ can be defined by substituting 50 for Q in Equation (9-1B). By then substituting various quantities of labor into the resulting equation, we get the corresponding quantities of capital required to produce the $50Q$. That is,

TABLE 9-1   Total, Average, and Marginal Product of Labor

L	TP	AP_L	MP_L
0	0	. . .	. . .
1	20.00	20.00	20.00
2	28.28	14.14	8.28
3	34.64	11.55	6.36
4	40.00	10.00	5.36
5	44.72	8.94	4.72

$$50 = 10\sqrt{LK}$$
$$5 = \sqrt{LK}$$
$$25 = LK$$
$$25/L = K$$

(9-1C)

Thus, if $L = 10$, $K = 2.5$; if $L = 5$, $K = 5$; if $L = 2.5$, $K = 10$, and so on. Other isoquants can be similarly derived. Isoquants are parallel along any ray from the origin and are equally spaced to reflect constant returns to scale. If, in addition, the wage rate (w) equals the rental price of capital (r), the slope of the isocost lines is $w/r = -1$, and the expansion path is a straight line through the origin with $K/L = 1$. This is shown in Figure 9-2.

FIGURE 9-1. Total, Average, and Marginal Product of Labor for the Cobb-Douglas Production Function

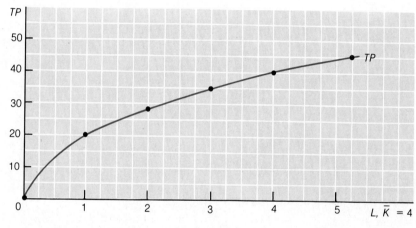

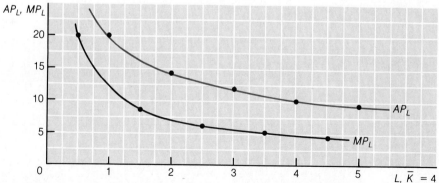

The figure shows the TP, the AP_L, and the MP_L schedules given in Table 9-1. From the figure, we see that the Cobb-Douglas production function exhibits only stage II of production. That is, the AP_L and the MP_L decline from the very start and the MP_L never becomes negative. Note that the MP_L is plotted between the various quantities of labor used and capital is held constant at $\bar{K} = 4$.

TABLE 9-2 Production in the Long Run

L	K	$10\sqrt{(L)(K)}$	Q
0	0	$10\sqrt{(0)(0)}$	0
1	1	$10\sqrt{(1)(1)}$	10
2	2	$10\sqrt{(2)(2)}$	20
3	3	$10\sqrt{(3)(3)}$	30
4	4	$10\sqrt{(4)(4)}$	40
5	5	$10\sqrt{(5)(5)}$	50

FIGURE 9-2.
The Expansion Path
for the Cobb-
Douglas

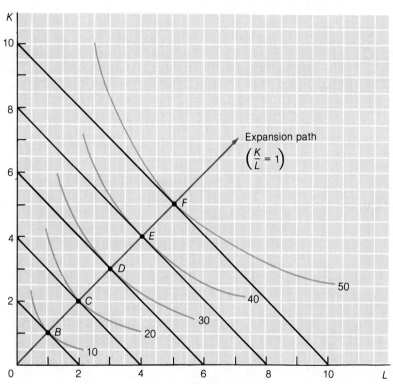

If $\alpha = \beta = \frac{1}{2}$ so that $\alpha + \beta = 1$, the Cobb-Douglas exhibits constant returns to scale. We can define any particular isoquant by substituting various quantities of labor into equation (9-1B) and obtaining the corresponding quantities of capital required to produce the specified level of output. Isoquants are parallel along any ray from the origin and are equally spaced to reflect constant returns to scale. If $w = r$, the slope of the isocost lines is $w/r = -1$ and the expansion path is a straight line through the origin with $K/L = 1$.

9-1c Empirical Estimation

One method of estimating the parameters of the Cobb-Douglas production function (i.e., A, α, and β) applies statistical (i.e., regression) analysis to *time series data* on the inputs used and the output produced.[1] For example, the researcher may collect data on the number of automobiles produced by an automaker in each year from 1950 to 1986 and on the quantity of labor and capital used in each year to produce the automobiles. The data are usually transformed into natural logarithms (indicated by the symbol "ln") and the regression analysis is conducted on the transformed data. The form of the estimated Cobb-Douglas production function is then

$$\ln Q = \ln A + \alpha \ln L + \beta \ln K \tag{9-1D}$$

The researcher thus obtains an estimate of the value of $\ln A$, α, and β.[2] Of primary interest to the researcher is the value of α and β.[3]

Another method of estimating the value of A, α, and β is by regression analysis using *cross-section data*. In this case, the researcher collects data for a given year (or other time unit) for each of many producers or firms in a particular industry on the quantity of labor and capital used and the output produced. That is, instead of collecting data for one firm over many years (time series), the researcher now collects data for a given year for many firms in the same industry (cross section). As in the previous case, the researcher usually first transforms the data into natural logarithms and then estimates Equation (9-1D) by regression analysis to obtain the values of parameters A, α, and β. Once again the researcher is primarily interested in the value of α and β. Table 9-3 in Example 9-1 that follows presents the values of α and β estimated for various U.S. manufacturing industries for the year 1957.[4]

Input-output relationships can also be obtained from engineering studies. All of these methods (i.e., regression analysis using time series or cross-section data and engineering studies) face difficulties. One of these is that we must assume that the best production techniques are used by all firms at all times. Due to a lack of information or erroneous decisions, this may not be the case. Another difficulty arises in the measurement of the capital input, since machinery and equipment are of different types, ages (vintage), and productivities. A further shortcoming characteristic of engineering

---

[1] For a general discussion of regression analysis, see Section 6-6.

[2] The value of parameter A can then be obtained by finding the antilog of $\ln A$.

[3] In Cobb-Douglas time series estimates, technological progress must also be accounted for. This is usually accomplished by including time (t) as an additional explanatory variable in Equation (9-1D).

[4] Data for many firms in each of the various U.S. manufacturing industries for the year 1957 were used to estimate the value of α and β for each industry. Thus, these are cross-section estimates.

studies is that they typically cover only some production activities of the firm. Despite these and other problems, numerous studies have been conducted over the years using these different approaches. They have provided very useful information on production for the entire economy and for various industries.

Example 9-1 Output Elasticity of Labor and Capital in U.S. Manufacturing

The Facts: Table 9-3 reports the estimated output elasticities of labor (α) and capital (β) for various U.S. manufacturing industries in 1957. A value of $\alpha = 0.90$ for furniture means that a 1 per cent increase in the quantity of labor used (holding K constant) results in a 0.90 per cent increase in the quantity prdouced of furniture. A value of $\beta = 0.21$ means that a 1 per cent increase in K (holding L constant) increases Q by 0.21 per cent. Increasing both L and K by 1 per cent increases Q by $0.90 + 0.21 = 1.11$ per cent. This means that the production of furniture is subject to increasing returns to scale.

Comment: The values of α and β reported in the above table were estimated by regression analysis using cross-section data for many firms in each industry for the year 1957. The value of α ranges from 0.51 for food and beverages to 0.96 for leather. This is the output elasticity of production and nonproduction workers combined. The value of β ranges from 0.08 for

TABLE 9-3 Estimated Output Elasticity of Labor (α) and Capital (β) in U.S. Manufacturing in 1957

Industry	α	β	$\alpha + \beta$
Furniture	0.90	0.21	1.11
Chemicals	0.89	0.20	1.09
Printing	0.62	0.46	1.08
Food, beverages	0.51	0.56	1.07
Rubber, plastics	0.58	0.48	1.06
Instruments	0.84	0.20	1.04
Lumber	0.65	0.39	1.04
Apparel	0.91	0.13	1.04
Leather	0.96	0.08	1.04
Electrical machinery	0.66	0.37	1.03
Nonelectrical machinery	0.62	0.40	1.02
Transport equipment	0.79	0.23	1.02
Textiles	0.88	0.12	1.00
Paper pulp	0.56	0.42	0.98
Primary metals	0.59	0.37	0.96
Petroleum	0.64	0.31	0.95

Source: J. Moroney, "Cobb-Douglas Production Functions and Returns to Scale in U.S. Manufacturing Industry," *Western Economic Journal,* December 1967, pp. 39–51.

leather to 0.56 for food and beverages. Note that most industries exhibit close-to-constant returns to scale (i.e., the value of $\alpha + \beta$ is close to 1).[5]

9-2

The Elasticity of Substitution

The elasticity of substitution measures the degree by which a cheaper input can be substituted for more expensive ones in production. This is very important for the firm to be able to keep costs as low as possible. For example, if petroleum had good substitutes (i.e., if the elasticity of substitution between petroleum and other inputs were very high), users could easily have switched to alternative energy sources when petroleum prices rose sharply in the fall of 1973. Their energy bill would then not have risen very much. As it was, good substitutes were not readily available (certainly not in the short run), and so most energy users faced sharply higher energy costs.

As explained in Section 7-4c, the degree to which inputs can be substituted in production can be gathered from the curvature of the isoquants. In general, the smaller is the curvature of the isoquants, the more easily inputs can be substituted for each other in production. On the other hand, the greater the curvature (i.e., the closer are isoquants to right angle or L-shape), the more difficult substitution is. A more precise measure of the degree by which one input can be substituted for another in production is given by the elasticity of substitution.

The **elasticity of substitution of labor for capital (e_{LK})** is equal to the relative percentage change in the K/L ratio over the relative percentage change in the $MRTS_{LK}$. That is,

$$e_{LK} = \frac{\Delta(K/L)/(K/L)}{\Delta(MRTS_{LK})/(MRTS_{LK})} \tag{9-2}$$

where $\Delta(K/L)$ is the change in the K to L ratio, K/L is the original K to L ratio, $\Delta MRTS_{LK}$ is the change in the absolute value of the slope of the isoquant, and $MRTS_{LK}$ is the original absolute value of the slope of the isoquant. Thus, e_{LK} depends on the slope and location of the isoquant, just as the price elasticity of demand (η) depends on the slope and location of the demand curve (see Section 2-2c).

---

[5] The Cobb-Douglas production function can be extended to deal with more than two inputs, say, labor, capital, and raw material (see Problem 4b). At this point, we could also derive the short-run and the long-run total and per-unit cost curves for the Cobb-Douglas production function. However, for the sake of continuity, we go on to present other extensions of production theory and leave these extensions of cost theory for Section 9-6 on applications. The interested student, however, could go to Applications 1 and 2 now.

For the Cobb-Douglas production function, $e_{LK} = 1$. That is, the relative percentage change in the K/L ratio (the numerator of the elasticity of substitution formula) is equal to the relative percentage change in the $MRTS_{LK}$ (the denominator of the elasticity of substitution formula), so that $e_{LK} = 1$. For example, for a movement from point F to point G on isoquant $50Q$ for the Cobb-Douglas production function in Figure 9-3 (the same as in Figure 9-2), we get $K/L = 1$, $\Delta(K/L) = \frac{1}{4} - 1 = -\frac{3}{4}$, $MRTS_{LK} = 1$, $\Delta(MRTS_{LK}) = \frac{1}{4} - 1 = -\frac{3}{4}$. Substituting these values into Formula (9-2), we obtain

$$e_{LK} = \frac{(-\frac{3}{4})/1}{(-\frac{3}{4})/1} = 1$$

If the researcher knows or suspects with his or her knowledge of the industry that e_{LK} is not equal or close to 1, it would be inappropriate to use the Cobb-Douglas production function. He or she would then have to utilize other more advanced types of production functions that allow e_{LK} to assume values other than 1. Comparisons among different industries based on the value of their e_{LK} could then profitably be made. For example, if the

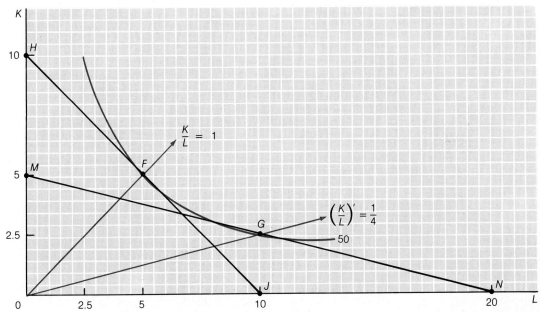

FIGURE 9-3.   The Elasticity of Substitution for the Cobb-Douglas Production Function

The degree by which a firm can substitute L for K in production depends on the shape and location of the isoquant and can be measured by the elasticity of substitution of L for K (e_{LK}) [Formula (9-2)]. For the Cobb-Douglas production function, $e_{LK} = 1$. For example, to measure e_{LK} for a movement from point F to point G on isoquant 50Q in the figure, we substitute the following values into formula (9-2): $K/L = 1$; $\Delta (K/L) = \frac{1}{4} - 1 = -3/4$; $MRTS_{LK} = 1$; $\Delta MRTS_{LK} = \frac{1}{4} - 1 = -3/4$. This gives $e_{LK} = 1$.

rental price of capital (r) rises relative to the wage rate (w), firms in those industries facing higher e_{LK} are in a better position to keep costs from rising very much (by substituting L for K in production) than firms facing a low e_{LK}.

9-3

Technological Progress

Until now we have implicitly assumed a given technology. However, over time, **technological progress** takes place. This refers to increases in the productivity of inputs so that a given output can be produced with a smaller quantity of inputs.[6] Technological progress can thus be shown by a shift of the isoquants toward the origin.

Technological progress can be classified as **neutral, capital-using,** or **labor-using,** depending on whether the MP_K increases, respectively, at the same, higher, or lower rate than the MP_L, at a given K/L ratio. These outcomes can be seen in Figure 9-4.

The left panel shows neutral technological progress. Since the MP_K and the MP_L increase at the same rate, MP_L/MP_K (equals $MRTS_{LK}$ or slope of the isoquant) remains constant at points E and E' along the $K/L = 1$ ray. Now $50Q$ can be produced with $3L$ and $3K$ instead of $5L$ and $5K$.

The middle panel shows capital-using technological progress. Here, the MP_K increases proportionately more than the MP_L, so that the absolute value of the slope of the isoquant (i.e., MP_L/MP_K) declines as it shifts toward the origin along the $K/L = 1$ ray. With constant w/r, this would lead the firm to substitute K for L in production so that K/L would rise (see Problem 6, with the answer provided in the back of the book).

The right panel shows labor-using technological progress. This is the opposite of capital-using technological progress. That is, with labor-using technological progress, the MP_K increases proportionately less than the MP_L, so that the absolute value of the slope of the isoquant increases as it shifts toward the origin along the $K/L = 1$ ray. With constant w/r, this would lead the firm to substitute L for K in production so that K/L would fall (see Problem 6).

K-using technological progress is often called K-deepening or L-saving technological progress because it leads to a higher K/L ratio. Similarly, L-using technological progress is often called L-deepening or K-saving because it lowers the K/L ratio. The type of technological progress taking place is an important determinant of the relative share of output going to L and K over time (see Application 3).

---

[6] This also means that a larger output can be produced with the same quantity of inputs. However, in the diagrammatic presentation that follows, we show technological progress by the former effect (i.e., by a given output being produced with a smaller quantity of inputs).

272

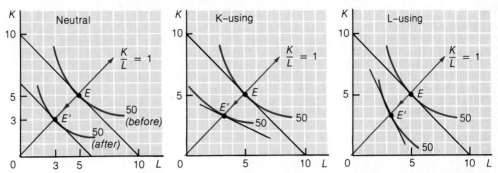

FIGURE 9-4.   *Neutral, Capital-Using, and Labor-Using Technological Progress*
*Since neutral technological progress increases the MP_K and the MP_L in the same pro-
portion, MP_L/MP_K (equals $MRTS_{LK}$ or the absolute value of the slope of the isoquant)
remains constant at point E and E' along the K/L = 1 ray (see the left panel). Now
50Q can be produced with 3L and 3K instead of 5L and 5K. Since capital-using technological progress increases the MP_K proportionately more than the MP_L, the absolute value of the slope of the isoquant declines as it shifts toward the origin along the
K/L = 1 ray (the middle panel). Labor-using technological progress is the opposite
of capital-using technological progress and is shown in the right panel.*

Example 9-2 Technological Progress and Productivity Growth in the U.S.

The Facts: Table 9-4 reports the annual percentage growth in total factor
productivity and in labor productivity in the U.S. private business sector
over time. The growth in total factor productivity approximates the rate of
technological progress. The growth in labor productivity is defined as the
change in output per hour of work. The data are adjusted for the effect of
the business cycle.

Comment: The growth in total factor productivity and in labor productivity
slowed down considerably from the early postwar period to the early
1980s. Several explanations have been advanced for this decline in productivity growth. One is based on the sharp increase in energy prices and
the resultant inflation. Another blames increased government environmental and safety regulations. Other explanations run in terms of lagging

**TABLE 9-4   Productivity Growth in the U.S. Private Sector, 1948–1982 (Annual
Percentage Growth Rate)**

Growth	1948–57	1957–68	1968–73	1973–76	1977–82
Total productivity	1.90	1.85	1.50	0.34	· · ·
Labor productivity	3.30	3.17	2.14	1.03	0.60

Source: E. Denison, *Accounting for Slower Economic Growth: The United States in the 1970's* (Washington,
D.C.: The Brookings Institution, 1979), and U.S. Department of Labor, Bureau of Labor Statistics.

research and development efforts and an eroded work ethic. There is no agreement on the relative importance of these explanations. In the mid-1980s, the growth in productivity has increased from the low points reached in the latter part of the 1970s and early 1980s. Technological progress during the mid-1980s is particularly rapid in computers, plastics, and medicine.

9-4

Linear Programming: The Basic Concepts

In this section we begin our discussion of linear programming. As mentioned in the chapter introduction, linear programming is a very useful and powerful technique often used by large corporations and government agencies to analyze very complex production, commercial, and other activities. Since linear programming is a rather complex technique, we begin by providing a general introduction to the topic and presenting some of its basic concepts in this section. This will lay the groundwork for Section 9-5, where we examine how linear programming is actually carried out.

9-4a Introduction to Linear Programming

Linear programming is a mathematical technique for solving maximization and minimization problems where the constraints and the function to be optimized can be represented by straight lines. Linear programming is an important development in the theory of the firm and has wide applicability. Its usefulness arises because firms almost invariably face more than one constraint (with only one constraint, the problem can more easily be solved with the traditional methods presented in the previous chapters).

Specifically, we saw in Chapter 8 how the firm maximizes output given its isocost line. The isocost line was the single constraint faced by the firm in trying to reach the highest isoquant. For optimization problems of this nature where there is a single constraint, the techniques presented earlier are both simple and adequate. However, in the real world, firms often face more than one constraint. For example, the firm may not be able to hire some labor with special skills or expand its plant and obtain some sophisticated equipment within the time period under consideration. Thus, the firm may face many constraints as it tries to maximize output or minimize costs. In cases such as these, it would be extremely difficult or impossible to solve optimization problems by traditional methods. This is when linear programming becomes essential.

Linear programming was developed by the Russian mathematician L. V. Kantorovich in 1939 and extended by the American mathematician G. B. Dantzig in 1947. The acceptance and usefulness of linear programming has been greatly enhanced by the advent of powerful computers since the tech-

274

nique often requires vast calculations. In 1984, N. Karmarkar of AT&T Bell Laboratories announced a significant theoretical breakthrough that makes it possible for linear programming problems to be solved much faster than with the approach used until now and provides the solution to some problems previously considered too complex to be solved even with the most powerful computers.

Linear programming is based on the assumption of constant input and output prices, constant returns to scale, and the existence of several technologically fixed input combinations with which to produce a particular commodity. These assumptions are necessary in order to reduce the problem to a linear one (i.e., one in which the function to be optimized and the constraints faced by the firm can be represented by straight lines). For example, the assumption of constant input prices results in the isocost being a straight line (as shown in Chapter 8). The assumption of constant returns to scale ensures that the long-run average cost curve (LAC) is horizontal, and the existence of several technologically fixed input combinations with which to produce a given commodity results in isoquants that are not smooth curves (as we have drawn them so far) but instead are made up of straight line segments (as shown next).

9-4b Some Basic Linear Programming Concepts

We now present some basic linear programming concepts and illustrate them graphically. As pointed out above, one of the basic assumptions of linear programming is that a particular commodity can be produced with a number of technologically fixed input combinations. Each of these technologically fixed input combinations is called a **process** or **activity** and can be represented in input space by a straight line ray from the origin.

For example, the top left panel of Figure 9-5 shows that a particular commodity can be produced with three different processes: process 1 with $K/L = 3$, process 2 with $K/L = 1$, and process 3 with $K/L = \frac{1}{3}$. Each of these processes is represented by the ray from the origin with slope equal to the particular K/L ratio that can be used to produce the commodity (see the figure). Process 1 is shown by the ray from the origin with slope of 3, which refers to the ratio of 3 to 1 with which capital and labor can be combined to produce the commodity. Process 2 is shown by the ray from the origin with slope of 1, which indicates that K and L can also be combined in the ratio of $1K$ to $1L$ to produce the commodity. Finally, process 3 is shown by the ray of slope $\frac{1}{3}$, representing the third method by which K and L can be combined to produce the commodity (i.e., in the ratio of $1K$ to $3L$).[7]

By joining points of equal output on the rays or processes available to

---

[7] In the real world, many more processes may be available to produce a particular commodity. These are determined by the production engineer and depend on the available technology. However, in order to simplify the graphical analysis, we assume that only the above three processes are available to produce the commodity under consideration.

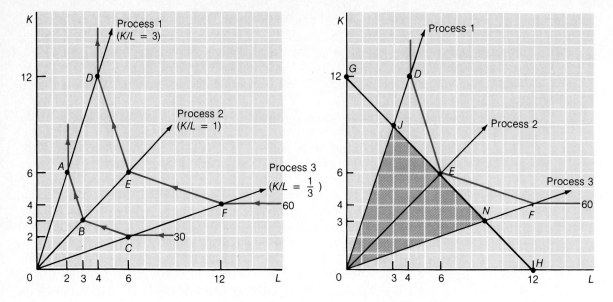

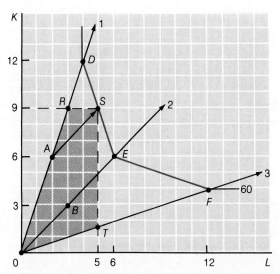

FIGURE 9-5. Processes, Isoquants, Feasible Region, and Optimal Solution

The top left panel shows process 1 with K/L = 3, process 2 with K/L = 1, and process 3 with K/L = 1/3. By joining points A, B, and C we get the isoquant for 30Q. With twice the amount of inputs, we get isoquant 60Q. With isocost GH in the top right panel, the feasible area is shaded triangle OJN and the optimal solution is at point E. In the bottom panel the firm faces no cost constraint but has available only 5L and 9K. The feasible solutions are represented by the shaded area ORST. The maximum output is 60Q at point S. To reach point S, the firm will have to produce 30Q with process 1 (OA) and 30Q with process 2 (OB = AS).

produce the commodity, we define the isoquant for the particular level of output of the commodity. These isoquants will be made up of straight line segments and will have kinks rather than being smooth (as we have drawn them so far). For example, suppose that the output of 30 units of the commodity in the left panel of Figure 9-5 can be produced with process 1 at point A (i.e., by using 2L and 6K), with process 2 at point B (by using 3L and 3K), or with process 3 at point C (with 6L and 2K). By joining these points we get the isoquant for 30Q. Note that the isoquant is not smooth but has kinks at points A, B, and C.[8] Furthermore, since we have constant returns to scale, the isoquant for twice as much output is determined by using twice as much of each input with each process. This defines the isoquant for 60Q with kinks at points D (4L, 12K), E (6L, 6K), and F (12L, 4K) in the top left panel. Note that corresponding segments on the isoquant for 30Q and 60Q are parallel.

If the firm faced only one constraint, such as isocost line GH in the top right panel of Figure 9-5, the area of attainable or **feasible solutions** is then represented by shaded triangle OJN. That is, the firm can purchase any combination of labor and capital on or below isocost line GH, but since no production process is available to the firm that is more capital intensive than process 1 (i.e., which involves a K/L higher than 1) or less capital intensive than process 3 (i.e., with K/L smaller than 1/3), the area of attainable or feasible solutions is restricted to the shaded area OJN. As it can be seen from the top right panel, the best or **optimal solution** is then at point E, where the area of feasible solutions reaches the 60Q isoquant (the highest possible). Thus, the firm produces the 60 units of output with process 2 by using 6L and 6K.

The bottom panel of Figure 9-5 extends the analysis to the case where the firm faces no *cost* constraint but has available only 5L and 9K. That is, the firm does not face isocost line GH or any other one but there are no more than 5L and 9K available for the firm to purchase within the period of time considered.[9] The area of feasible solutions is then given by shaded area ORST in the figure. That is, only those combinations given by shaded area ORST are relevant, given that only 5L and 9K *and* that only production processes 1, 2, and 3 are available. The maximum output that the firm can produce is then 60Q given at point S. The isoquant for 60Q is the highest that the firm can reach with the constraints it faces. To reach point S, the

---

[8] The greater is the number of processes available to produce a particular commodity, the more its isoquants will approach the smooth shape that we have assumed so far. Some commodities such as textiles can be produced with many different techniques, some of which are very capital-intensive (and are used in K-abundant industrial countries) while some others are very labor-intensive (and are used mostly in K-poor countries). Other commodities, such as petroleum extraction, can only be produced with few processes. This depends on the available technology.

[9] Of course, if the period of time considered is extended, more labor with the required skills can be trained and more of the specialized capital can be built.

firm will have to produce 30Q with process 1 (OA) and 30Q with process 2 (OB = AS).[10]

Note that when the firm faced the single isocost constraint (GH in the top right panel of Figure 9-5), the firm used only one process (process 2) to reach the optimum. When the firm faced two constraints (the bottom panel), the firm required two processes to reach the optimum. From this, we can generalize and conclude that to reach the optimal solution a firm will require *no more* processes than the number of constraints that the firm faces. Sometimes fewer processes will do. For example, if the firm could use no more than 4L and 12K, the optimum would be at point D (60Q) and this is reached with process 1 alone (see the bottom panel of Figure 9-5).

A final point can be made about the top right panel of Figure 9-5. Even if w/r increased (so that isocost line GH would become steeper), the optimal solution would remain at point E as long as the GH constraint line remained flatter than segment DE on the isoquant for 60Q. If w/r rose so that the GH constraint line coincided with segment DE, the firm could reach isoquant 60Q with process 1, process 2, or any combination of process 1 and process 2 that would allow the firm to reach a point on segment DE between points D and E. If w/r rose still further, the firm would reach the optimal solution (maximum output) at point D (see the top right panel of Figure 9-5).

To summarize, we can say that each of the technologically fixed input combinations with which a particular commodity can be produced is called a process or activity. Each process or activity can be represented by a straight line ray from the origin into input space. By joining points of equal output on these rays or processes, we define the isoquant for the particular level of output of the commodity. These isoquants will be made up of straight-line segments and have kinks rather than being smooth. A point on an isoquant that is not on a ray or process can be reached by the appropriate combination of the two adjacent processes. By then adding the linear constraints of the problem, we can solve the linear programming problem graphically. The above concepts will be extended presently and used to illustrate how an actual linear programming problem can be set up and solved.

9-5

Linear Programming: A More Complete Picture

In this section, we make use of the basic linear programming concepts introduced in the previous section and outline the steps to be followed in

---

[10] OA and OB are called vectors. Thus, the above is an example of vector analysis, whereby vector OJ (not shown in the bottom panel of Figure 9-5) is equal to the sum of vectors OA and OB. Also to be noted is that in this case half of the output is produced with process 1 and the other half with process 2. But this is only by coincidence.

solving a linear programming problem graphically. We will then illustrate the linear programming solution for a profit maximization and a cost minimization problem.

9-5a Solution of Linear Programming Problems

The function to be optimized in linear programming is called the **objective function.** This usually refers to profit maximization or cost minimization. In linear programming problems, constraints are given by inequalities (called **inequality constraints**). The reason is that the firm often can use up to, but no more than, specified quantities of some inputs, or the firm must meet some minimum requirement. These inequality constraints are often called **technical constraints.** In addition, there are **nonnegative constraints** on the solution to indicate that the firm cannot produce a negative output or use a negative quantity of any input.

In what follows, we outline the steps to follow in order to solve a linear programming problem graphically. The explanation of each step is provided in the process of performing each operation indicated in the outline for the specific examples that will be presented in Sections 9-5b and 9-5c.

To solve a linear programming problem graphically, we proceed as follows:

1. Express the objective function as an equation and the constraints as inequalities.
2. Graph the inequality constraints and define the area of feasible solutions.
3. Graph the objective function as a series of isoprofit (i.e., equal profit) or isocost lines, one for each level of profit or costs, respectively.
4. Find the optimal solution at the extreme point or corner of the region of feasible solutions that touches the highest isoprofit line or lowest isocost line. This represents the optimal solution subject to the constraints faced.

9-5b Illustration of Profit Maximization

In this section we follow the steps outlined above to show how a linear programming maximization problem can be solved. The problem is as follows. Suppose that a firm produces two commodities: X and Y. Each unit of commodity X requires $1L$, $0.5K$, and zero R (raw material) to produce. On the other hand, each unit of commodity Y requires $1L$, $1K$, and $0.5R$. The firm can use no more than $9L$, $6K$, and $2.5R$. The firm earns \$20 on each unit of X it sells and \$30 on each unit of commodity Y. The question we want to answer is how much of commodity X and how much of commodity Y the firm should produce to maximize its total profit.[11]

---

[11] Note that even though this is a very simple problem, we would find it very difficult to solve it with the traditional method presented in Chapter 8.

To solve this linear programming problem graphically, we follow the steps outlined above.

1. The objective function and the inequality constraints of the problem are

objective function: $\pi = \$20X + \$30Y$ where π = total profits
L constraint: $1X +\ 1Y \le 9$
K constraint: $0.5X +\ 1Y \le 6$ technical constraints
R constraint: $OX + 0.5Y \le 2.5$
nonnegative constraints: $X, Y \ge 0$

Specifically, since the firm earns a profit of $20 on each unit of X sold and $30 on each unit of Y sold, its profit function (π) is equal to $20 times the units of X sold plus $30 times the units of Y sold. The L constraint indicates that 1L (required to produce each unit of commodity X) times the quantity of X plus 1L (required to produce each unit of commodity Y) times the quantity of Y must be equal to or smaller than the 9L that the firm can use. The K constraint indicates that 0.5K (required to produce each X) times the quantity of X plus 1K (to produce each unit of Y) times the quantity of Y must be equal to or smaller than the 6K that the firm can use. The R constraint indicates that the 0.5R required to produce each unit of Y times the quantity of Y must be equal to or smaller than 2.5R. Note input R is not required to produce commodity X. The nonnegative constraints are required to preclude negative values for the solution.

2. If we now treat each of the technical constraints as an equation (rather than as an inequality) and solve for Y, we get

$Y = 9 - X$ from the L constraint
$Y = 6 - \frac{1}{2}X$ from the K constraint
$Y\ = 5$ from the R constraint

Each technical constraint is given by all the points on or *below* the relevant constraint line plotted in the top panel of Figure 9-6. The X and Y axes give the nonnegative constraints. The area of feasible solutions is then given by shaded area $OABCD$ in the top panel.

3. Solving the profit function for Y, we get

$$Y = \frac{\pi}{30} - \frac{2}{3}X$$

For each profit level (π) that we specify, we get a particular isoprofit line with slope of $-\frac{2}{3}$ (the profit ratio). Three such isoprofit lines (the dashed lines) are shown in the bottom panel of Figure 9-6.

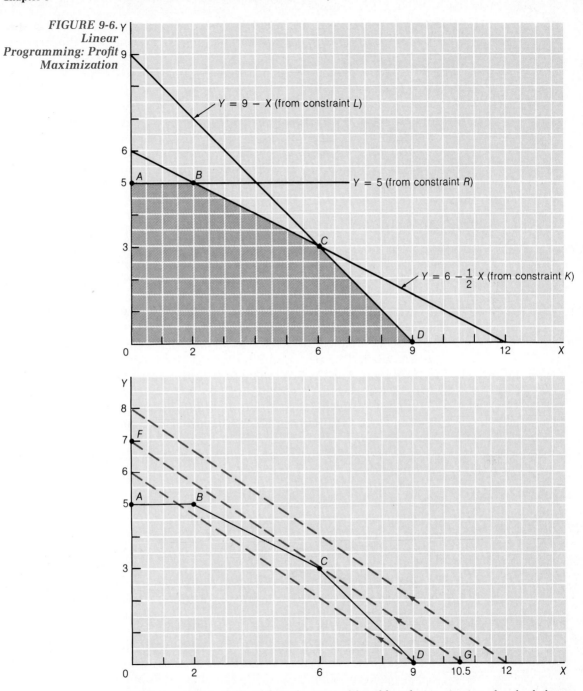

FIGURE 9-6.
*Linear
Programming: Profit
Maximization*

With constraints L, K, and R, the area of feasible solutions is given by shaded area OABCD in the top panel. The bottom panel shows that the highest isoprofit line the firm can reach is FG at point C (6X, 3Y). With a profit of $20 per unit of X and $30 per unit of Y, the total profits are maximized at $210.

281

4. The firm maximizes profit at point C ($6X$ and $3Y$), where the area of feasible solutions touches isoprofit line FG (the highest the firm can reach). At point C,

$$\pi = (\$20)(6) + (\$30)(3) = \$210$$

Profits at point C ($210) are higher than at point A ($150), point B ($190), point D ($180), or at any other point on or inside the area of feasible solutions.[12] Note that in this case, only constraints L and K are binding. That is, the firm utilizes all of the $9L$ and $6K$ but not all of the $5R$ available to it.

9-5c Illustration of Cost Minimization

In this section we follow the steps outlined in Section 9-5a to show how a linear programming minimization problem can be solved. The problem is as follows. Suppose that the manager of a college dining hall is required to prepare meals that satisfy the minimum daily requirement of basic nutrients A, B, and C. Suppose that the minimum daily requirement has been established at $18A$, $14B$, and $18C$. The manager can use two basic foods (say, meat and fish) in the preparation of meals. Meat (food X) contains $1A$, $1B$, and $2C$ per pound. Fish (food Y) contains $2A$, $1B$, and $1C$ per pound. The price of X is \$2 per pound, while the price of Y is \$3 per pound. The manager wants to provide meals that fulfill the minimum daily requirement of nutrients A, B, and C at the least possible cost.

We can solve this linear programming problem graphically as follows:

1. The objective function to be minimized is $TC = \$2X + \$3Y$, subject to constraints:

constraint A:	$1X + 2Y \geq 18$
constraint B:	$1X + 1Y \geq 14$
constraint C:	$2X + 1Y \geq 18$
nonnegative constraints:	$X, \quad Y \geq 0$

Specifically, since the price of food X is \$2 per pound while the price of food Y is \$3 per pound, the total cost function that the firm seeks to minimize is $TC = \$2X + \$3Y$. Constraint A indicates that $1A$ (found in each unit of food X) times the quantity of X plus $2A$ (found in each unit of food Y) times the quantity of Y must be equal to or *larger* than the $18A$ minimum requirement that the manager must satisfy. Similarly, since each unit of foods X and Y contains 1 unit of nutrient B and meals

---

[12] The profit of \$150 at point A is obtained from $\pi = (\$30)(5)$. The profit of \$190 at point B is obtained from $\pi = (\$20)(2) + (\$30)(5)$, and at point D, by $\pi = (\$20)(9) = \$180$.

must provide a minimum of 14B, constraint B is given by $1X + 1Y = 14$. On the other hand, since each unit of X contains 2C and each unit of Y contains 1C, and meals must provide a minimum of 18C, constraint C is $2X + 1Y = 18$. Note that the technical constraints are now expressed in the form of "equal to or larger than" since the minimum daily requirements must be fulfilled but can be exceeded. Finally, the nonnegative constraints are required to preclude negative values for the solution.

2. Expressing each of the technical constraints as an equation and solving for Y, we get

$$Y = \;\;\;9 - \tfrac{1}{2}X \quad \text{from } A$$
$$Y = 14 - \;\;\;X \quad \text{from } B$$
$$Y = 18 - 2X \quad \text{from } C$$

Each of the technical constraints is given by all the points on or *above* the particular constraint line in the top panel of Figure 9-7. The area of feasible solutions is the shaded area above DEFG. All points in the shaded area simultaneously satisfy all the technical and nonnegative constraints.

3. Solving the objective function for Y, we get

$$Y = \frac{TC}{3} - \frac{2}{3}X$$

For each level of TC, we get a specific isocost line with slope of $-\tfrac{2}{3}$ $(-P_x/P_y)$. Three such isocost lines (the dashed lines) are shown in the bottom panel of Figure 9-7.

4. The manager minimizes TC at point F (10X and 4Y), where the area of feasible solutions touches isocost line HJ (the lowest isocost line that allows the manager to meet the daily nutritional requirements for the students). At point F, the manager minimizes the total cost per student at

$$TC = (\$2)(10) + (\$3)(4) = \$32$$

TC at point F ($32) are lower than at point D ($54), point E ($38), point G ($36), or at any other point on or above the area of feasible solutions.[13] Note that in this case only constraints A and B are binding. If P_x rose to $3 (so that P_x/P_y increased from $\tfrac{2}{3}$ to 1), the isocost line would coincide with segment FE of the area of feasible solutions. In that case, the minimum TC ($42) is given by any point on FE. For any value of P_x/P_y above 1 but lower than 2, TC would be minimized at point E.

---

[13] At point D, $TC = (\$3)(18) = \$54$; at point E, $TC = (\$2)(4) + (\$3)(10) = \$38$; at point G, $TC = (\$2)(18) = \$36$.

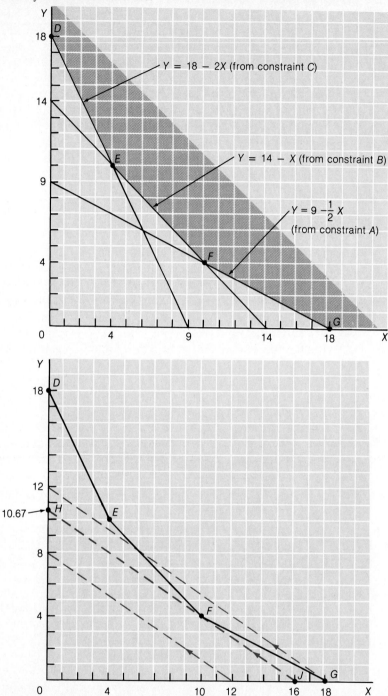

FIGURE 9-7.
Linear Programming: Cost Minimization

With constraints A, B, and C, the area of feasible solutions is given by shaded area DEFG in the top panel. The bottom panel shows that the lowest isocost line the manager can reach is HJ at point F (10X, 4Y). With a price of $2 per unit of X and $3 per unit of Y, total costs are mimimized at $32.

In the real world, firms often use many inputs, produce many commodities, and face numerous constraints. These many-variable, multiconstraint problems are beyond the scope of the graphical approach. They are solved by computers. Computers quickly compare the value of the objective function at various corners of the area of feasible solutions and choose the extreme point or corner that optimizes the objective function. This is referred to as the extreme-point theorem and the method of solution is called the **simplex method.**[14]

Example 9-3 Linear Programming in the Petroleum Industry

The Facts: One of the first successful applications of linear programming has been in the petroleum industry. Large petroleum firms engage in exploration, extraction, refining, and marketing of petroleum products. Each phase can be and has been approached as a linear programming problem. In each phase, the firm seeks to optimize an objective function, such as maximizing the chance of finding petroleum deposits, minimizing extraction and production costs, and maximizing profits from sales. Each phase is subject to certain constraints, such as the availability of funds, technical personnel, specialized capital equipment in exploration and extraction, refining capacity, transportation, and marketing outlets in the other phases. For example, in refining, more than 10 chemically distinct blending stocks (semirefined oils) are mixed together to produce gasoline of various knock ratings, vapor pressures, sulfur contents, etc. The firm wants to minimize the cost of producing the various types of gasoline subject to the availability of the blending stocks, refining capacity, transportation network, contract requirements, and so on. The problem is too complicated for graphical analysis but is easily solved by linear programming. The technique is also essential for determining the proper "mix" of the various activities or phases of the firm.

Comment: There are many other problems which lend themselves and are being solved by linear programming techniques. Some of these are (1) the selection of the least-cost route to ship commodities from plants in different locations to warehouses in other locations, and from there, to different markets (this is the so-called "transportation problem"); (2) the selection of the best combination of operating schedules, payload, cruising altitude, speed, seating configuration, and so on, for an airline in order to maximize profits; (3) the best combination of logs, plywood, and paper that a forest-product company can produce from given supplies of logs and milling capacity; (4) the distribution of a given advertising budget among TV, radio, magazines, newspapers, billboards, and other methods to minimize the cost of reaching a specific number of consumers in a particular socio-eco-

---

[14] It is on this traditional method of finding the optimal solution to linear programming problems that Dr. Karmarkar of Bell Lab greatly improved upon.

nomic group; (5) the best routing of millions of telephone calls over long distances, the best combination of cattle to produce milk of a given quality, the best combination of securities for banks to hold in their portfolios, and so on.

Source: A. Charnes, W. Cooper, and B. Mellon, "Blending Aviation Gasoline," *Econometrica,* April 1952; A. Manne, *Scheduling of Petroleum Refinery Operations* (Cambridge, Mass.: Harvard University Press, 1956).

9-6

Applications

In this section we examine a number of important applications of the tools of analysis developed in the chapter. They are, for the most part, extensions of cost theory. We examine the short-run and the long-run total and per-unit cost curves for the Cobb-Douglas production function, the effect of technological change on the distribution of income, and the measurement and usefulness of so-called shadow prices.

Application 1: Short-Run Total and Per-Unit Cost Curves for the Cobb-Douglas Production Function

With K constant at $K = 4$ and if $r = \$10$, the total fixed costs (*TFC*) of the firm are

$$TFC = rK = (\$10)(4) = \$40$$

Furthermore, starting from the Cobb-Douglas production function of Equation (9-1a), we get

$$Q = 20\sqrt{L}$$
$$\sqrt{L} = Q/20$$
$$L = Q^2/400$$

If $w = \$10$, the total variable costs of the firm (*TVC*) are

$$TVC = wL = \$10Q^2/400 = Q^2/40$$

Thus, the short-run total cost of the firm is

$$STC = TFC + TVC = \$40 + Q^2/40$$

From the last equation, we can (by substituting values for Q) derive the *STC* schedule given in Table 9-5, and from that, the *ATC* and the *SMC* schedules. For example, when $Q = 10$, $STC = \$40 + {}^{100}\!/_{40} = \$42.50$ and

TABLE 9-5   *STC*, *ATC*, and *SMC* Schedules for the Cobb-Douglas Production Function

Q	STC	ATC = STC/Q	ΔSTC	MC = ΔSTC/ΔQ
10	$ 42.50	$4.25		
20	50.00	2.50	$ 7.50	$0.75
30	62.50	2.08	12.50	1.25
40	80.00	2.00	17.50	1.75
50	102.50	2.05	22.50	2.25
60	130.00	2.17	27.50	2.75
70	162.50	2.32	32.50	3.25
80	200.00	2.50	37.50	3.75

$ATC = STC/Q = \$42.50/10 = \$4.25$ (the first row of the table). When $Q = 20$, $STC = \$40 + {}^{400}\!/_{40} = \$50$, so that $ATC = \$50/20 = \$2.50$ and $MC = \Delta STC/\Delta Q = (\$50 - \$42.50)/10 = \$0.75$ (the second row of the table). The other *STC*, *ATC*, and *MC* values in Table 9-5 are similarly obtained.

The *STC*, *ATC*, and *MC* values in Table 9-5 are plotted in Figure 9-8. Note that the *STC* curve (in the top panel) faces upward and the *MC* curve (in the bottom panel) rises from the very beginning because the law of diminishing returns operates from the start.[15] That is, the *STC* curve does not first face down (so that *MC* declines) and then faces up (so that *MC* rises) as in panel *D* of Figure 8-6, but it faces up and the *MC* curve rises (so that the law of diminishing returns begins to operate) from the very beginning. Thus, the Cobb-Douglas production function is a special or simpler case of the more general production function discussed in Chapter 7.[16] Furthermore, only when 4*L* is used with 4*K* are we on the expansion path (point *E* in Figure 9-2).[17]

Application 2: Long-Run Total and Per-Unit Cost Curves for the Cobb-Douglas Production Function

As we have seen in Section 8-4, the long-run total cost (*LTC*) is given by

$$LTC = wL + rK$$

and can be derived from the expansion path of the firm and the price of the inputs. For example, from the expansion path of Figure 9-2 and the assumption that $w = r = \$10$, we can derive the *LTC* curve in the left panel of Figure 9-9 with slope equal to 2, and from it, the horizontal and coincidental $LAC = LMC = \$2$ curves in the right panel.

---

[15] As usual, the *MC* values are plotted between the various levels of output in the bottom panel of Figure 9-8. Note that in this case, the *MC* curve is a straight line through the origin.

[16] It is as if the *STC* curve in panel *D* of Figure 8-6 started (i.e., its vertical axis was drawn) to the right of point *Z*.

[17] That is, using different quantities of *L* with $K = 4$ to produce outputs other than 40 units will result in higher short-run than long-run costs (see Section 8-2c).

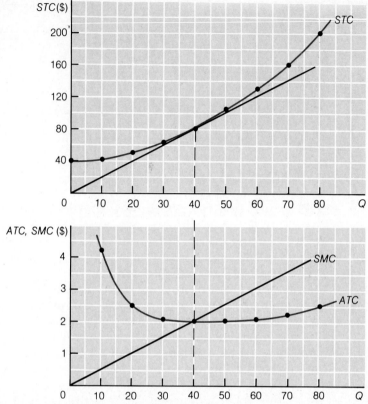

The top panel shows the STC curve and the bottom panel shows the ATC and the SMC curves from Table 9-5. The STC curve faces upward and MC rises from the very beginning because the law of diminishing returns operates from the start. Also, only when 4L is used with 4K are we on the expansion path (point E in Figure 9-2).

For example at point B on the expansion path in Figure 9-2 at which the firm produces 10Q with 1L and 1K, $LTC = (\$10)(1) + (\$10)(1) = \$20$ (point B' on the LTC curve in the left panel of Figure 9-9). At point C in Figure 9-2 at which the firm produces 20Q with 2L and 2K, $LTC = (\$10)(2) + (\$10)(2) = \$40$ (point C' on the LTC curve in the left panel of Figure 9-9). The other points on the LTC curve can be similarly obtained. Since the expansion path of Figure 9-2 exhibits constant returns throughout, the LTC curve in the left panel of Figure 9-4 is a straight line through the origin and increases at the same rate as the increase in output. For example, the LTC doubles when output is doubled.

From the LTC curve in the left panel of Figure 9-9, we can then derive the corresponding LAC and LMC curves in the right panel. Since the LTC curve in the left panel is a straight line through the origin, the slope of a ray from the origin to any point on the LTC curve (the LAC) is equal to the slope of the LTC curve at any point (the LMC) and is constant at the value

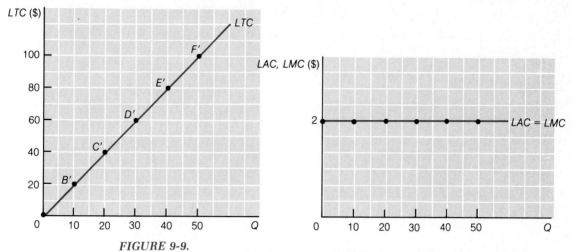

FIGURE 9-9.
LTC, LAC, *and the* LMC *Curves for the Cobb-Douglas Production Function*

From the expansion path of Figure 9-2 (showing constant returns to scale) and the assumption that w = r = $10, we get the straight line through the origin LTC curve with slope equal to 2 (the left panel). The corresponding LAC and LMC curves are horizontal and coincidental at LAC = LMC = $2 (the right panel).

of $2. Thus, $LAC = LMC = \$2$ at every level of output and the LAC and LMC curves are horizontal and coincide at the value of $2 in the right panel of Figure 9-9. Thus, costs and returns are constant for the Cobb-Douglas production function of Section 9-1.

Application 3: Technological Progress and the Distribution of Income

If we let w be the average wage rate, r the average rental price of capital, L the total quantity of labor employed in the economy, K the total quantity of capital, P the general price index, and Q the general quantity index, then

$$PQ = NNP \text{ (Net National Product)}, \tag{9-3}$$
$$wL/PQ = \text{relative share of NNP going to } L \tag{9-4}$$
$$rK/PQ = \text{relative share of NNP going to } K \tag{9-5}$$
$$wL/rK = \text{ratio of relative shares of NNP going to } L \text{ and } K \tag{9-6}$$

Ratio (9-6) can be rewritten $(w/r)(L/K)$. Thus, the relative share of NNP going to L increases if w/r or L/K rises. Since neutral technological progress leaves K/L (and L/K) unchanged, the ratio of the relative shares of NNP going to L and K (i.e., wL/rK) remains unchanged if w/r also does not change. Since K-using technological progress leads to higher K/L (and lower L/K), wL/rK falls at unchanged w/r. Finally, since L-using technological progress leads to lower K/L (and higher L/K), wL/rK rises at unchanged w/r.

However, w/r is likely to change over time, especially in the case of non-

289

neutral technological progress, and this must also be considered in determining the effect of technological progress on the distribution of income. Thus, what happens to the relative share of NNP going to L and K depends on the type of technological progress taking place and on the change in w/r over time. In addition, since various commodities are produced with different K/L ratios, relative commodity prices also change when w/r and K/L change, and this also affects the relative share of NNP going to L and K.

In the real world, the share of NNP going to L has remained fairly constant at about 75 per cent over long periods of time (i.e., over the past several decades) and in most industrial nations of the world. This is in the face of tremendous technological changes that, on balance, have been K-using, and changes in w/r and K/L. The reason for the constancy in the share of NNP going to L and K over time and in many nations in the face of great technological and other changes has yet to be satisfactorily explained.

Application 4: The Dual Problem and Shadow Prices

Every linear programming or **primal problem** has a corresponding **dual problem.** A profit-maximization primal problem has a cost-minimization dual problem, and vice versa. The dual of a profit maximization problem provides the **shadow price** or marginal valuation of the inputs to the firm. Specifically, the shadow price of an input is determined by the increase in the total profits resulting from using one additional unit of the input. This is the maximum price the firm would pay for one additional unit of the input. If an input is not fully utilized or is a **slack variable,** increasing its quantity will not change the total profits of the firm, and so the shadow price of the input is zero. Such an input is not a bottleneck or an *effective* constraint on production.

For example, if the L constraint in the profit-maximization problem of Figure 9-6 were increased by one unit, from 9 to 10 units, the area of feasible solutions would be $OABC'D'$ in the top panel of Figure 9-10, and the optimal solution would be at point C' (8X and 2Y) in the bottom panel. The total profits of the firm would then rise from ($20)(6) + ($30)(3) = $210 at point C to ($20)(8) + ($30)(2) = $220 at point C' (see the bottom panel of Figure 9-10). Thus, the shadow price of L is $10. That is, the firm should hire an additional unit of L only if the wage rate is less than and up to $10. Since K was also fully utilized at point C in Figure 9-6, its shadow price is also positive (can you find its value?). Finally, since at point C in Figure 9-6, input R is a slack variable, its shadow price is zero.

Shadow prices are used by a number of large corporations with many divisions and decentralized management to price correctly the output of one division that is the input of another division in order to maximize total profits for the entire corporation. Shadow prices can also be used by governments to price appropriately some government services. Shadow prices are also very useful for planning in developing countries where the market system often does not function properly (i.e., input and output prices do not truly reflect their relative scarcity).

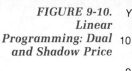

FIGURE 9-10.
Linear
Programming: Dual
and Shadow Price

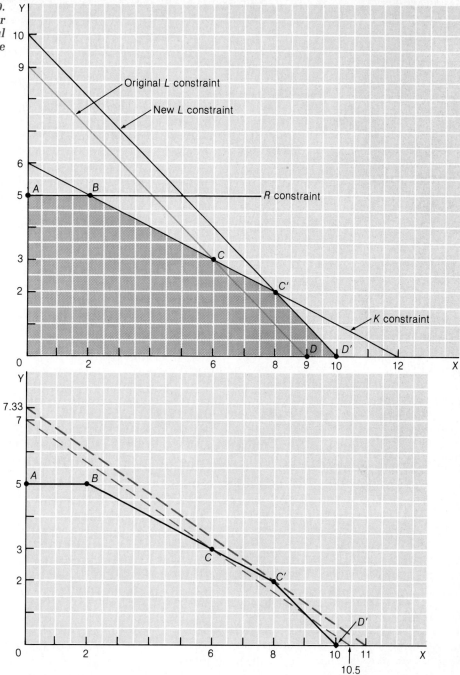

If the L constraint in the profit-maximization problem of Figure 9-6 were increased by one unit, from 9 to 10 units, the area of feasible solution would be OABC′D′ in the top panel, and the optimal solution would be at point C′ (8X and 2Y) in the bottom panel. The total profits of the firm would then rise from $210 at point C to ($20)(8) + ($30)(2) = $220 at point C′. Thus, the shadow price of L, which is the difference between these two profit levels, is $10.

Summary

1. The Cobb-Douglas production function is given by $Q = AL^\alpha K^\beta$, where Q refers to output, L to labor, K to capital, and A, α, and β are positive parameters estimated in each case from the data. Parameter A refers to technology, α is the output elasticity of labor, and β is the output elasticity of capital. If $\alpha + \beta = 1$, we have constant returns to scale. If $\alpha + \beta > 1$, we have increasing returns to scale, and if $\alpha + \beta < 1$, we have decreasing returns to scale. The Cobb-Douglas production function shows only stage II of production and its expansion path is a straight line through the origin. It can be estimated with time series, cross-section, or engineering data.

2. The elasticity of substitution measures the degree by which a cheaper input can be substituted for more expensive ones in production. It is very important for the firm to be able to keep costs as low as possible. The elasticity of substitution of labor for capital (e_{LK}) is equal to the relative percentage change in the K/L ratio over the relative percentage change in the $MRTS_{LK}$. For the Cobb-Douglas production function, $e_{LK} = 1$. For many industries, e_{LK} is far different from 1 and so the Cobb-Douglas function is not the appropriate production function to use in these industries.

3. Technological progress refers to increases in the productivity of inputs and can be shown by a shift of the isoquants toward the origin. Technological progress can be classified as neutral, capital-using, or labor-using, depending on whether the MP_K increases, respectively, at the same, higher, or a lower rate than the MP_L, at a given K/L ratio. Thus, the absolute slope of the isoquant remains the same, decreases, or increases (as the isoquant shifts toward the origin at constant K/L), depending on whether technological progress is, respectively, neutral, K-using, or L-using.

4. Linear programming is a mathematical technique for solving maximization and minimization problems where the constraints and the function to be optimized are straight lines. The technologically fixed input combinations available to produce a commodity are called processes. These can be represented by rays from the origin in input space. By joining points of equal output on these rays, we define an isoquant. Points not on a process or ray can be reached by combining two adjacent processes. By also considering the linear constraints of the problem, we can define the area of feasible solutions and determine the optimal solution. The firm requires no more processes than the number of constraints it faces to reach the optimal solution.

5. The function optimized in linear programming is called the objective function. This usually refers to profit maximization or cost minimization. To solve a linear programming problem graphically, we (1) express the objective function as an equation and the constraints as inequalities; (2) graph the inequality constraints and define the area of feasible solutions; (3) graph the objective function as a series of isoprofit or isocost lines; and (4) find the optimal solution at the extreme point or corner of the region of feasible solutions that touches the highest isoprofit line or lowest isocost line. Problems with more than two variables are solved by computers with the simplex method (until now).

6. For a Cobb-Douglas production function exhibiting constant returns to scale, SMC rises from the very beginning while $LAC = LMC$ and are constant at every output level. Technological progress leaves the relative share of NNP going to L unchanged, lowers it, or increases it, depending on whether technological progress is, respectively, neutral, K-using, or L-using. However, changes in w/r and K/L must also be considered. Every linear programming problem or primal has a corresponding dual. The dual of profit maximization is cost minimization, and vice versa. The dual of a profit maximization problem gives the shadow price or marginal valuation of inputs to the firm. The shadow price of an input that is not fully utilized (i.e., a slack variable) is zero.

Glossary

Cobb-Douglas production function The relationship between inputs and output expressed by $Q = AL^{\alpha}K^{\beta}$, where Q is output, L is labor, K is capital, and A, α, and β are positive parameters estimated from the data.

Output elasticity of labor The percentage increase in output resulting from a 1 per cent incrase in the quantity of capital used. For the Cobb-Douglas production function, this is given by the exponent of L.

Output elasticity of capital The percentage increase in output resulting from a 1 per cent increase in the quantity of capital used. For the Cobb-Douglas production function, this is given by the exponent of K.

Homogeneous of degree 1 In production, it refers to constant returns to scale.

Linearly homogeneous In production, it refers to homogeneous of degree 1 or constant returns to scale.

Elasticity of substitution of L for K (e_{LK}) The percentage change in the K/L ratio over the percentage change in the $MRTS_{LK}$. For the Cobb-Douglas production function, $e_{LK} = 1$.

Technological progress It refers to increases in the productivity of inputs and can be shown by a shift of the isoquants toward the origin. It is classified as neutral, capital-using, or labor-using.

Neutral technological progress The type of technological progress that increases the MP_K in the same proportion as the MP_L and leaves the slope of the isoquant unchanged as it shifts toward the origin at a given K/L ratio.

Capital-using technological progress The type of technological progress that increases the MP_K proportionately more than the MP_L and reduces the absolute slope of the isoquant as it shifts toward the origin at a given K/L ratio.

Labor-using technological progress The type of technological progress that increases the MP_K proportionately less than the MP_L and increases the absolute slope of the isoquant as it shifts toward the origin at a given K/L ratio.

Linear programming A mathematical technique for solving maximization and minimization problems where the constraints and the objective function to be optimized can be represented by straight lines.

Process or activity A technologically fixed input combination that can be used to produce a commodity. It is depicted by a ray from the origin into input space.

Feasible solutions All the solutions that are possible with the given constraints.

Optimal solution The best of the feasible solutions.

Objective function The function to be optimized in linear programming.

Inequality constraints Limitations on the use of some inputs or certain minimum requirements that must be met.

Technical constraints All except the nonnegative constraints in a linear programming problem.

Nonnegative constraints Limits that preclude negative values for the solution of a linear programming problem.

Simplex method A mathematical technique for solving linear programming problems.

Primal problem The original maximization (e.g., profit) or minimization (e.g., cost) linear programming problem.

Dual problem The inverse of the primal linear programming problem.

Shadow price The marginal valuation of an input or output to the firm.

Slack variable An input or other quantity that is not fully utilized.

Questions for Review

1. (a) What is the equation of the Cobb-Douglas production function?
   (b) What is the meaning of each term in the equation of the Cobb-Douglas production function?
   (c) When does the Cobb-Douglas production

function show constant, increasing, or decreasing returns to scale?

(d) What is the meaning of homogeneous of degree 1 and linearly homogeneous in production theory?

2. (a) What is the shape of the TP, AP_L, and MP_L curves for the Cobb-Douglas production function?

(b) Why are the TP, the AP_L, and the MP_L curves shaped as they are?

(c) What stage(s) of production does the Cobb-Douglas production function show?

(d) What is the shape of the expansion path for a Cobb-Douglas production function?

3. (a) How can a Cobb-Douglas production function be estimated?

(b) What difficulties are faced in estimating the parameters of the Cobb-Douglas production function?

(c) What is the range of the estimated values for α? For β?

(d) How can the Cobb-Douglas production function be extended to deal with more than two inputs?

4. (a) What does the elasticity of substitution measure?

(b) What is the formula for the elasticity of substitution of L for K?

(c) What is the value of e_{LK} for the Cobb-Douglas production function?

(d) What is the shape of the isoquants when $e_{LK} = 0$?

5. What is meant by the following and how can each be shown graphically?

(a) Technological progress?

(b) Neutral technological progress?

(c) Capital-using technological progress?

(d) Labor-using technological progress?

6. What is

(a) linear programming?

(b) a process or activity?

(c) a feasible solution?

(d) the optimal solution?

7. With regard to linear programming, indicate

(a) the assumption on which it rests.

(b) its usefulness as compared to the traditional theory of the firm.

(c) its limitations

8. With regard to linear programming, indicate

(a) how isoquants are derived.

(b) in what way the isoquants of linear programming differ from the isoquants of traditional production theory.

(c) how the area of feasible solutions is derived.

(d) how the optimal solution is found.

9. What is

(a) the objective function?

(b) an inequality constraint?

(c) a technical constraint?

(d) the simplex method?

10. For a Cobb-Douglas production function,

(a) what is the shape of the STC, ATC, and SMC curves?

(b) what is the reason for the shape of the STC, ATC, and SMC curves?

(c) what is the shape of the LTC, LAC, and LMC curves if $\alpha + \beta = 1$? Why?

11. (a) What is meant by the ratio of the share of NNP going to L and K?

(b) How does neutral technological progress affect the relative share of NNP going to L and K?

(c) How does capital-using technological progress affect the relative share of NNP going to L and K? What about labor-using technological progress?

(d) On what factors other than the type of technological change do variations in the relative share of NNP going to L and K depend? How have these relative shares changed over time?

12. What is a

(a) primal problem?

(b) dual problem?

(c) shadow price?

(d) slack variable?

Problems

1. Assuming that $A = 10$, $\alpha = \beta = \frac{1}{2}$, and $K = 9$ and is constant,

(a) derive the TP, the AP_L, and the MP_L schedules.

(b) plot the schedules of part (a).

(c) with regard to the figure in part (b), indicate where the law of diminishing returns begins to operate? Where is stage II of production? What is the output elasticity of L and K?

★2. Given that $\beta = 1 - \alpha$, prove that

(a) the AP_L is a function of or depends only on the K/L ratio.

(b) given that $MP_L = AL^{\alpha-1}K^{1-\alpha}$, show that the MP_L is a function only of K/L.

3. With regard to the Cobb-Douglas production function of Problem 9-1,

(a) derive the isoquant for $40Q$.

(b) draw the isoquant for $10Q, 20Q, 30Q, 40Q$, and $50Q$ and the expansion path on the assumption that $w = r = \$10$.

4. (a) Suppose $A = 10$ and $\alpha = \beta = 1$, and $w = r = \$10$. Derive the isoquant for $40Q$ and for $90Q$ and the expansion path of the firm.

(b) Suppose that three inputs (L, K, and R or raw materials) are required to produce a commodity. What is the form of the Cobb-Douglas production function in this case? (Use γ, the Greek letter gamma, as the exponent of the R variable.) If $\alpha = 0.6$, $\beta = 0.3$, and $\gamma = 0.2$, by how much does output increase by doubling only L? By doubling only K? By doubling only R? By doubling L, K, and R?

5. For the isoquant for $90Q$ in Problem 4(b), find the elasticity of substitution of L for K for a movement from $w/r = -1$ to $w/r = \frac{1}{4}$.

★6. Repeat Figure 9-4 and show on it the effect of each type of technological progress on the K/L ratio *at constant relative input prices* (w/r).

7. (a) With reference to the top right panel of Figure 9-5, define the feasible solutions and show the optimal solution if $w/r = 2$. What if $w/r = 3$? If $w/r = 4$? Show each of your answers by a graph.

(b) With reference to the bottom panel of Figure 9-5, indicate the area of feasible solutions and the optimal solution if the firm had no cost constraint but could use no more than $4K$. What if the firm could use no more than $9L$ and $5K$? No more than $6K$? Answer each part of the question with a graph.

★8. Suppose that a firm produces two commodities: X and Y. Each unit of X requires $1A$, $1B$, and $1D$ to produce, and each unit of Y requires $2A$, $0.5B$, and $1C$. The firm can use no more than $12A$, $6B$, $5C$, and $5D$. The firm earns $\$10$ on each unit of X and Y it sells. How much of commodity X and Y should the firm produce to maximize its total profit?

9. Suppose that a chicken farmer wants to feed chickens the minimum daily requirement of basic nutrient A, B. and C. Suppose that this has been established at $28A$, $18B$, and $15C$. Each pound of feed grain X contains $1A$, $1B$ and $\frac{3}{4}C$, and each pound of feed grain Y contains $4A$, $1.5B$, and $1C$. The price of feed grain X and Y is $\$1$ per pound. What is the least-cost quantity of feed grain X and feed grain Y that the chicken farmer should use to fulfill the minimum daily requirement of nutrient A, B, and C for the chickens?

10. Assuming that $A = 10$, $\alpha = \beta = \frac{1}{2}$, and $w = r = \$10$, and K is constant at $K = 9$,

(a) derive the TP, AP_L, and MP_L, and plot them.

(b) plot the LTC, LAC, and the LMC of the firm.

11. Suppose L-using technological progress raises w/r. What are the additional forces that must be considered in order to determine what will happen to the relative share of NNP going to L and K?

★12. For the cost-minimization problem in Figure 9-7,

(a) find the shadow price of nutrient B.

(b) what is the shadow price of nutrient C?

Supplementary Readings

For a problem-solving approach to the topics discussed in this chapter, see

Dominick Salvatore, *Microeconomic Theory*, 2nd ed. (New York: McGraw-Hill, 1983), Chapter 9.

The original paper that introduced the Cobb-Douglas production function is

C. W. Cobb and Paul H. Douglas, "A Theory of Production," *American Economic Review*, March 1928.

An advanced discussion of the estimation of production and cost functions is found in

A. A. Walters, "Production and Cost Functions," *Econometrica*, January 1963.

Jack Johnston, *Statistical Cost Analysis* (New York: McGraw-Hill, 1960).

For the classification of technological progress and its measurement, see

John R. Hicks, *The Theory of Wages* (London: Macmillan, 1932).

Murray Brown, *On the Theory and Measurement of Technological Change* (New York: Cambridge University Press, 1968).

A clear and simple exposition of linear programming is found in

William J. Baumol, "Activity Analysis in One Lesson," *American Economic Review*, December 1958.

Robert Dorfman, "Mathematical, or Linear, Programming: A Nonmathematical Exposition," *American Economic Review*, December 1953.

For a more complete and difficult presentation of linear programming, see

Robert Dorfman, P. Samuelson, and R. Solow, *Linear Programming and Economic Analysis* (New York: McGraw-Hill, 1958).

Theory of the Firm and Market Structure

FOUR

Part Four (Chapters 10–13) presents the theory of the firm and market structure. It brings together the theory of consumer behavior and demand (from Part Two) and the theory of production and costs (from Part Three) to analyze how price and output are determined under various types of market organization. Chapter 10 shows how price and output are determined under perfect competition. Chapter 11 shows price and output determination under pure monopoly. Chapter 12 does the same for monopolistic competition, and Chapter 13 does so for oligopoly. As in previous parts of the text, the presentation of the theory in this part is reinforced with many real-world examples and important applications.

Price and Output under Perfect Competition

10-1 Market Structure: Perfect Competition

10-2 Price Determination in the Market Period

10-3 Short-Run Equilibrium of the Firm

10-4 Short-Run Supply Curve and Equilibrium

10-5 Long-Run Equilibrium of the Firm and Industry

10-6 Constant, Increasing, and Decreasing Cost Industries

10-7 Applications

Examples

10-1 Competition in the Stock Market

10-2 Fish Auctions

10-3 The Supply of Shale Oil

10-4 The Russian Wheat Deal

10-5 Long-Run Adjustment in the U.S. Cotton Textile Industry

Applications

Application 1: Allocation Over Time

Application 2: Effect of Rent Control on the Industry and Firm

Application 3: Effect of an Excise Tax on the Industry and Firm

Application 4: Medicare and Medicaid and the Price of Medical Services

Application 5: Change in Demand and the Allocation of Inputs

Chapter 10

Preview Questions

What are the different types of market structure?

What is meant by perfect competition in economics?

In everyday usage?

How is the price of a commodity determined when the supply of the commodity is fixed?

When would the firm remain in business in the short run even if incurring a loss?

How is the short-run supply curve of the firm and industry determined?

What is the function of the short-run industry supply curve?

When are the industry and the firm in long-run equilibrium?

What is meant by constant, increasing, and decreasing cost industries?

In this chapter we bring together the theory of consumer behavior and demand (from Part II) and the theory of production and costs (from Part III) to analyze how price and output are determined under perfect competition. As explained in Chapter 1, the analysis of how price and output are determined in the market is a primary aim of microeconomic theory.

The chapter begins by identifying the various types of market structure and defining perfect competition. It then goes on to examine price determination in the market period, or the very short run, when the supply of the commodity is fixed. Subsequently, we examine how the firm determines its best level of output in the short run at various commodity prices. In the process, we derive the short-run supply curve of the firm and industry, and show how the interaction of the industry demand and supply curves determines the equilibrium price of the commodity. This was already demonstrated in Chapter 2, but now we know what lies behind the market demand and supply curves and how they are derived.

From the analysis of the market period and the short run we go on to examine the long-run equilibrium of the firm and define constant, increasing, and decreasing cost industries. Finally, we present several important applications of the perfectly competitive model. Some of these represent extensions to the firm of industry-wide applications presented in Section 2-6. These applications, together with the several real-world examples presented in the theory sections, highlight the great importance and relevance of the analytical tools developed in this chapter.

10-1

Market Structure: Perfect Competition

In economics, we usually identify four different types of market structure. These are perfect competition, monopoly, monopolistic competition, and oligopoly. In this chapter we examine perfect competition. The other three types of market organization are examined in the next three chapters: monopoly in Chapter 11, monopolistic competition in Chapter 12, and oligopoly in Chapter 13.

Perfect competition refers to the type of market organization in which (1) there are many buyers and sellers of a commodity, each too small to affect the price of the commodity; (2) the commodity is homogeneous; (3) there is perfect mobility of resources; and (4) economic agents have perfect knowledge of market conditions (i.e., prices and costs). Let us now examine in detail the meaning of each of the four aspects of the definition.

First, in perfect competition, there are many buyers and sellers of the commodity, each of which is too small (or behaves as if he or she is too small) in relation to the market to have a perceptible effect on the price of the commodity. Under perfect competition, the equilibrium price and quantity of the commodity is determined at the intersection of the market demand and supply curves of the commodity. The equilibrium will not be affected perceptibly if only one or a few consumers or producers change the quantity demanded or supplied of the commodity.

Second, the commodity is *homogeneous*, identical, or perfectly standardized, so that the output of each producer is indistinguishable from the output of others. An example of this might be grade A winter wheat. Thus, buyers are indifferent as to the output of which producer they purchase.

Third, resources are perfectly mobile. This means that resources or inputs are free to move (i.e., they can move at zero cost) among the various industries and locations within the market in response to monetary incentives. Firms can enter or leave the industry in the long run without much difficulty. That is, there are no artificial barriers (such as patents) or natural barriers (such as huge capital requirements) to entry into and exit from the industry.

Fourth, consumers, firms, and resource owners have perfect knowledge of all relevant prices and costs in the market. This ensures that the same price prevails in each part of the market for the commodity and for the inputs required in the production of the commodity.

Needless to say, these conditions have seldom if ever existed in any market. The closest we might come today to a perfectly competitive market is the stock market (see Example 10-1). Another example, might be U.S. agriculture at the turn of the century, when millions of small farmers raised wheat. Despite this, the perfectly competitive model is extremely useful to analyze market situations that approximate perfect competition. More importantly, the perfectly competitive model provides the point of reference or standard against which to measure the economic cost or *ineffi-ciency* of departures from perfect competition. These departures can take the form of monopoly, monopolistic competition, or oligopoly. In the case of monopoly, there is a *single* seller of a commodity for which there are no good substitutes. Under monopolistic competition, there are many sellers of a *differentiated* commodity.[1] In oligopoly, there are *few* sellers of a homogeneous or differentiated commodity.

Note that the economist's definition of perfect competition is diametrically opposite to the everyday usage of the term. In economics, the term perfect competition stresses the *impersonality* of the market. One producer does not care and is not affected by what other producers are doing. The output of all producers is identical, and an individual producer can sell any quantity of the commodity at the given price without any need to advertise. On the other hand, in everyday usage, the term competition stresses the notion of *rivalry* among producers or sellers of the commodity. For example, GM managers speak of the fierce competition that their firm faces from other domestic and foreign auto producers with regard to style, mileage per gallon, price, and so on. Because of this, GM mounts very elaborate and costly advertising campaigns to convince consumers of the superiority of its vehicles. However, this is not what the economist means by competition.

Under perfect competition, the firm is a *price taker* and can sell any quantity of the commodity at the given market price. If the firm raised its price by the slightest amount, it would lose all of its customers. On the other hand, there is no reason for the firm to reduce the commodity price since the firm can sell any quantity of the commodity at the given market price. Thus, the perfectly competitive firm faces a horizontal or infinitely elastic demand curve (as in Figure 5-7) at the price determined at the intersection of the market demand and supply curves for the commodity (as in Figure 2-5).

Example 10-1 Competition in the Stock Market

The Facts: The market for stocks traded on the major stock exchanges is as close as we come today to a perfectly competitive market of buyers and sellers. In most cases, the price of the stock is determined by the demand and supply of the stock, and the individual buyer and seller of the stock has no perceptible effect on price (i.e., he or she is a price taker). All stocks within each company category are more or less homogeneous. The frequency with which a particular type of stock is bought and sold is evidence that resources are mobile. Finally, information on prices and quantities traded is readily available. In general, the price of a stock reflects knowledge of the present and expected future net income stream from the stock.

---

[1] An example of a differentiated commodity is the different brand names of the same commodity.

301

Comment: The price of a stock at any point in time usually reflects (though seldom, if ever, perfectly) all the publicly known information about the stock. This is known as the *efficient-market hypothesis.* Information about greater profitability of a company will be reflected, rather quickly, by a higher price of its stock (as those who first learn of the increased current or expected profitability purchase the stock). On the other hand, expectations of lower profitability will result in a decline in the price of the stock (as those who first learn of the reduced profitability sell the stock). Funds flow into stocks, and resources into uses where the rate of return, corrected for risk, is highest. Thus, stock prices provide the signals for the efficient allocation of investments in the economy. An example of perfect competition in production is provided by wheat farming in nineteenth century America.

Sources: Understanding the New York Stock Exchange (New York: The New York Stock Exchange, 1985).

10-2

Price Determination in the Market Period

The **market period,** or the very short run, refers to the period of time during which the market supply of a commodity is fixed. This may be a day, a week, a month, or longer, depending on the industry. For example, if milk is delivered every morning to New York City, and no other deliveries can be arranged for the rest of the day, the market period is one day. For wheat, the market period extends from one harvest to the next. For Michelangelo's paintings, the length of the market period is infinite since their supply is fixed forever.

During the market period, costs of production are irrelevant in the determination of price, and the entire stock of a perishable commodity is put up for sale at whatever price it can fetch. Thus, with perfect competition among buyers and sellers, demand alone determines price, while supply alone determines quantity in the market period. This is shown in Figure 10-1.

In the figure, S is the fixed or zero-elastic market supply curve for 350 units of the commodity. With D as the market demand curve, the equilibrium price is $35. Only at this price the quantity demanded equals the quantity supplied and the market clears. At higher prices, there will be unsold quantities, and this will cause the price to fall to the equilibrium level. For example, at the price of $40, only 300 units would be demanded (see the figure); hence, the quantity supplied would exceed the quantity demanded and the commodity price would fall. On the other hand, at lower than the equilibrium price, the quantity demanded exceeds the quantity supplied, and the price will be bid up to $35. For example, at the

FIGURE 10-1.
Price Determination
in the Market
Period

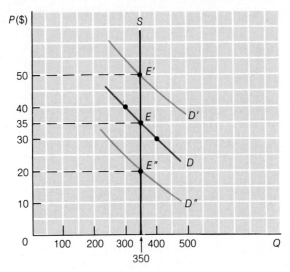

With the quantity supplied fixed at 350, the market supply curve of the commodity is S. With D as the market demand curve, the equilibrium price is $35. At prices higher than $35, there will be unsold quantities, and this will cause the price to fall to the equilibrium level. At prices below $35, the quantity demanded exceeds the quantity supplied, and the price will be bid up to $35. With D' as the demand curve, P = $50. With D", P = $20.

price of $30, 400 units of the commodity would be demanded; hence the quantity demanded would exceed the quantity supplied and the price would be bid up to $35 (the equilibrium price at which the quantity demanded equals the quantity supplied). With D' as the demand curve, $P = \$50$. With D'', $P = \$20$.

Example 10-2 **Fish Auctions**

The Facts: A good example of the market period is provided by the auction of a perishable commodity such as fresh fish. The entire catch must be sold quickly in the wholesale market at whatever price it can fetch. Given the market demand for fresh fish, the price will be higher on those days when few boats go out because of bad weather (and the catch is small). Auction participants must know the exact quantity of the commodity available for sale to avoid overpaying. Realizing this, fishermen in some Far Eastern markets unload only part of the catch at first to make it look small (so that prices will be bid higher). Buyers counter this connivance with informers to learn the exact size of the catch before bidding. The result is usually a price at or near the equilibrium price that clears the market.

Comment: The function of price is to ration the available supply of the commodity among potential buyers *and* over the length of time of the mar-

303

ket period (see Application 1). For fresh fish the market period is one day if boats go out every day.

Source: R. Cassady, *Auctions and Auctioneering* (Berkeley: University of California Press, 1967).

10-3

Short-Run Equilibrium of the Firm

While analysis of the market period is interesting, we are primarily interested in the short run and in the long run, when the quantity produced and sold of the commodity can be varied. In this section, we examine the determination of output by the firm in the short run. We will first do so with the total approach and then with the marginal approach. Finally, we will focus on the process of profit maximization or loss minimization by the firm.

10-3a Total Approach

We have seen in Section 7-1 that profit maximization provides the framework for the analysis of the firm. The equilibrium output of the firm is the one that maximizes the total profits of the firm. Total profits equal total revenue minus total costs. Thus, total profits are maximized when the positive difference between total revenue and total costs is largest. This is shown in Figure 10-2.

The short-run total cost (STC) curve in the top panel of Figure 10-2 is the one of Figure 8-4. The vertical intercept ($30) gives the fixed costs of the firm. Within the limits imposed by the given plant, the firm can vary its output by varying the quantity of the variable inputs it uses. This generates the STC curve of the firm. The STC curve shows the minimum total costs of producing the various levels of output in the short run. Past point W, the law of diminishing returns begins to operate and the STC curve faces upward or rises at an increasing rate (see Section 8-3).

The total revenue curve is a straight line through the origin because the firm can sell any quantity of the commodity at the given price (determined at the intersection of the market demand and supply curves of the commodity). With $P = \$35$, the total revenue (TR) of the firm is $35 if the firm sells one unit of output. The $TR = \$70$ if the firm sells two units of output, $TR = \$105$ with $Q = 3$, $TR = \$140$ with $Q = 4$, and so on. Put more succinctly, $TR = (\$35)(Q)$. Thus, the TR of the firm is a straight line through the origin with slope equal to the commodity price of $35 (see the top panel of Figure 10-2).

At zero output, $TR = 0$ while $STC = \$30$. Thus, the firm incurs a total loss of $30 equal to its fixed costs. This gives the negative intercept of $(-)\$30$ of the total profit curve in the bottom panel. At $Q = 1$, $TR = \$35$ and $STC = \$50$, so that total profits are $-\$15$. At $Q = 1.5$, $TR = STC =$

FIGURE 10-2.
Short-Run
Equilibrium of the
Firm: Total
Approach

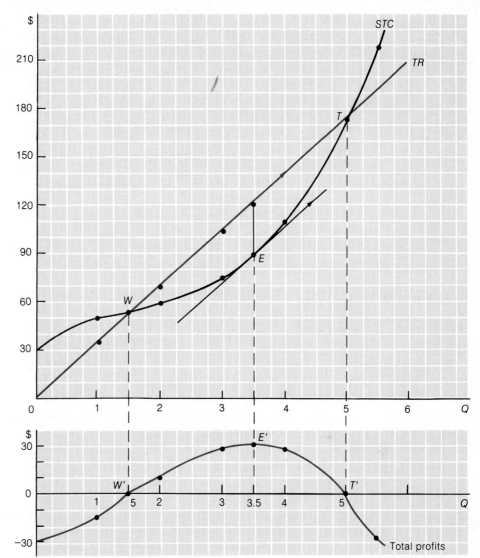

The STC curve in the top panel is that of Figure 8-4. The TR curve is a straight line through the origin with slope of P = $35. At Q = 0, TR = 0 and STC = $30, so that total profits are −$30 and equal the firm's TFC (see the bottom panel). At Q= 1, TR = $35 and STC = $50, so that total profits are −$15. At Q = 1.5, TR = STC = $52.50, and total profits are zero. This is the break-even point. Between Q= 1.5 and Q = 5, TR exceeds STC and the firm earns (positive) economic profits. Total profits are greatest at $31.50 when Q = 3.5 (and the TR and the STC curves are parallel). At Q = 5, TR = STC = $175 so that total profits are zero (points T and T'). At Q greater than 5, TR is smaller than STC and the firm incurs a loss.

$52.50 (point W in the top panel), and total profits are zero (point W' in the bottom panel). This is called the **break-even point.** Between $Q = 1.5$ and $Q = 5$, TR exceeds STC and the firm earns a profit. Total profits equal the positive difference between TR and STC. Total profits are largest at $31.50 when $Q = 3.5$ (i.e., where the TR and the STC curves are parallel and the total profit curve has zero slope). At Q smaller than 3.5, say, $Q = 3$, TR = $105 and STC = $75, so that total profits are $30. At $Q = 4$, TR = $140, STC = $110, and total profits are again $30. At $Q = 5$, TR = STC = $175, so that total profits are zero (points T and T', respectively). At Q greater than 5, TR is smaller than STC and the firm incurs a loss. Thus, the level of output at which the firm maximizes total profits is $Q = 3.5$ (point E and E' in the top and bottom panels, respectively). Figure 10-2 is summarized in Table 10-1.[2]

10-3b Marginal Approach

While the total approach to determine the equilibrium output of the firm is useful, the marginal approach is even more valuable and more widely used. This approach is shown in Figure 10-3. In the figure, the demand curve facing the firm (d) is horizontal or infinitely elastic at the given price of $P = 35. That is, the perfectly competitive firm is a price taker and can sell any quantity of the commodity at $P = 35. Since marginal revenue (MR) is the change in total revenue per-unit change in output, and price (P) is constant, then $P = MR$ (see Section 5-5). For example, with $P = 35 and $Q = 1$, TR = $35. With $P = 35 and $Q = 2$, TR = $70. Thus, the change in TR per-unit change in output (the slope of the TR curve or marginal revenue) is $MR = P = 35 (see Figure 10-3).

The short-run marginal cost (MC) and the average total cost (ATC) curves of the firm in Figure 10-3 are those of Figure 8-5 (and derived from the STC curve of Figures 8-4 and 10-2). The $MC = \Delta STC/\Delta Q$, while $ATC = STC/Q$. As explained earlier, total profits are maximized where the TR and the STC curves are parallel and their slopes are equal. Since the slope of the TR curve is $MR = P$ and the slope of the STC curve is MC, this implies that when total profits are maximum, $P = MR = MC$. Furthermore, since the STC curve faces upward where profits are maximum, the MC curve must be rising. Thus, the firm is in short-run equilibrium or maximizes total profits by producing the output where $P = MR = MC$, and MC is rising.

For example, the best level of output for the firm in Figure 10-3 is $Q = 3.5$ (point E), and this is the same result as with the total approach. At

---

[2] When the firm has no knowledge of the exact shape of its STC curve it uses a break-even chart to determine the minimum sales volume to avoid losses (see Problem 4, with answer in the back of the book). For a mathematical presentation of profit maximization using rudimentary calculus, see Section A9 of the Mathematical Appendix.

TABLE 10-1   Total Revenue, Total Costs, and Total Profits

Quantity of Output	Price	Total Revenue	Total Costs	Total Profits
0	$35	$ 0	$30	$−30
1	35	35	50	−15
1.5	35	52.50	52.50	0
2	35	70	60	+10
3	35	105	75	+30
*3.5	35	122.50	91	+31.50
4	35	140	110	+30
5	35	175	175	0
5.5	35	192.50	220	−27.50

*Output at which firm maximizes total profits.

FIGURE 10-3.
Short-Run
Equilibrium of the
Firm: Marginal
Approach

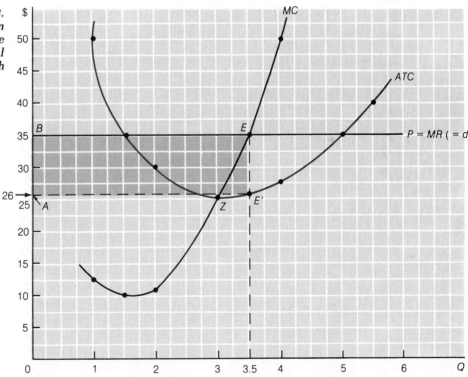

The demand curve facing the firm (d) is horizontal or infinitely elastic at the given price of P = $35. Since P is constant, marginal revenue (MR) equals P. The firm maximizes total profits where P = MR = MC, and MC is rising. This occurs at Q = 3.5 (point E). At Q = 3.5, P = $35 and ATC = $26. Therefore, profit per unit is $9 (EE'), and total profits are $31.50 (shaded rectangle EE'AB).

307

$Q = 3.5$, $P = \$35$ and $ATC = \$26$. Therefore, profit per unit is \$9 (EE' in the figure), and total profits are ($\$9)(3.5) = \$31.50$ (shaded rectangle $EE'AB$). Until point E, MR exceeds MC and so the firm earns higher profits by expanding output. On the other hand, past point E, MC exceeds MR and the firm earns higher profits by *reducing* output. This leaves point E as the profit-maximizing level of output. Note that at point E, P or $MR = MC$ and MC is rising and the conditions for profit maximization are fulfilled.

Also note that at $Q = 3$, $P = \$35$, and $ATC = \$25$, and profit per unit is largest at that point (\$10). The firm, however, seeks to maximize total profits, not profit per unit, and this occurs at $Q = 3.5$, where total profits are \$31.50, as opposed to \$30 at $Q = 3$. The total profits of the firm at various levels of output with $P = \$35$ are summarized in Table 10-2. The MR, MC, and ATC values given in the table are read off Figure 10-3 *at* various output levels. For example, at $Q = 1$, $MR = \$35$, $MC = \$12.50$, and $ATC = \$50$. At $Q = 2$, $MR = \$35$, $MC = \$11$, and $ATC = \$30$, and so on.

10-3c Profit Maximization or Loss Minimization

We have seen above that the best or optimum level of output of the firm is given at the point where P (or MR) equals MC, and MC is rising. At this level of output, however, the firm can either make a profit (as in Figure 10-3), break even, or incur a loss. In Figure 10-3, P was higher than the ATC at the best level of output, and the firm made a profit. If P were smaller than the ATC at the best level of output, the firm would incur a loss. However, as long as P exceeds the average *variable* cost (AVC), it pays for the firm to continue to produce because by doing so it would *minimize its losses*. That is, the excess of P over the AVC can be used to partially cover the fixed costs of the firm. Were the firm to shut down, it would incur a greater loss equal to its total fixed costs. This is shown in Figure 10-4.

In the figure, the MC and the ATC curves are the same as in Figure 10-3. Figure 10-4 also includes the AVC curve of the firm (from Figure 8-

TABLE 10-2   Profit Maximization for the Perfectly Competitive Firm: Per-Unit Approach

Q	$P = MR$	MC	ATC	Profit Per Unit	Total Profits	Relationship between MR and MC
1	\$35	\$12.50	\$50	\$$-15$	\$$-15$	
1.50	35	10	35	0	0	$MR > MC$
2	35	11	30	$+5$	$+10$	
3	35	25	25	$+10$	$+30$	
*3.50	35	35	26	$+9$	$+31.50$	$MR = MC$
4	35	50	27.50	$+750$	$+30$	
5	35		35	0	0	$MR < MC$
5.5	35		40	-5	-27.50	

*Output at which firm maximizes total profits.

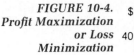

FIGURE 10-4.
Profit Maximization
or Loss
Minimization

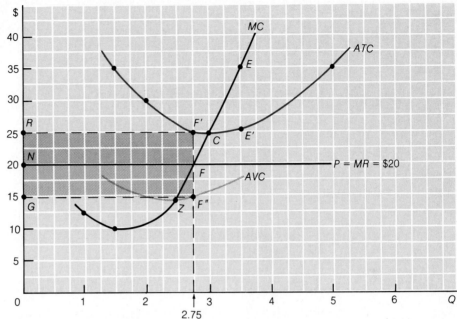

At P = $20, the best level of output of the firm is 2.75 units (point F, where P = MR = MC, and MC is rising). At Q = 2.75, average total cost (ATC) exceeds P and the firm will incur a loss of F'F (about $5.50) per unit, and a total loss of F'FNR (about $15, given by the area of the cross-hatched rectangle). If, however, the firm were to shut down, it would incur the greater loss of $30 equal to its total fixed costs (the area of the larger rectangle F'F"GR). The shutdown point (Z) is at P = AVC.

5). In Figure 10-4, we assume that $P = MR = \$20$. The best level of output of the firm is then 2.75 units, given at point F, where $P = MR = MC = \$20$, and MC is rising. At $Q = 2.75$, ATC exceeds P and the firm incurs a loss equal to $F'F$ (about $5.50) per unit, and a total loss of $F'FNR$ (about $15, given by the area of the cross-hatched rectangle). Were the firm to shut down, it would incur the greater loss of $30 (its total fixed costs, given by the area of the larger rectangle $F'F''GR$).

Put in another way, by continuing to produce $Q = 2.75$ at $P = \$20$, the firm will cover FF'' (about $5.50) of its fixed costs per unit and $FF''GN$ (about $15, the shaded area) of its total fixed costs. Thus, it pays for the firm to stay in business, even though it incurs a loss. That is, by remaining in business, the firm will incur losses that are smaller than its total fixed costs (which would be the firm's losses by shutting down). Only if P were smaller than the AVC at the best level of output would the firm minimize losses by going out of business. By doing so, the firm would limit its losses to an amount no larger than its total fixed costs. Finally, if $P = AVC$, the firm would be indifferent between producing or going out of business because in either case it would incur a loss equal to its total fixed costs.

309

The point where $P = AVC$ (point Z in the figure) is called the **shutdown point**.[3]

10-4

Short-Run Supply Curve and Equilibrium

In this section we derive the short-run supply curve of a perfectly competitive firm and industry. We will then show how the equilibrium price of the commodity is determined at the intersection of the market demand and supply curves for the commodity. This is the price at which the perfectly competitive firm can sell any quantity of the commodity.

10-4a Short-Run Supply Curve of the Firm and Industry

We have seen so far that a perfectly competitive firm always produces at the point where $P = MC$ and MC is rising, and this is so as long as $P > AVC$. As a result, the rising portion of the firm's MC curve above the AVC curve is the firm's short-run supply curve of the commodity. This is shown in the left panel of Figure 10-5.

The left panel of Figure 10-5 reproduces the firm's MC curve above point Z (the shutdown point) from Figure 10-4. This is the perfectly competitive firm's short-run supply curve (s) because it shows the quantity of the commodity that the firm would supply in the short run at various prices. For example, the firm supplies 3 units of the commodity at the price of $25 (point C in the left panel). The reason is that at $P = \$25$, $P = MR = MC = \$25$, and MC is rising. At $P = \$35$, the firm supplies 3.5 units of the commodity (point E), while at $P = \$50$, it supplies 4 units (point T). The firm will supply no output at prices below the shutdown point (point Z in the figure). Thus, the rising portion of the firm's MC curve above the shutdown point is the firm's short-run supply curve of the commodity (s in the left panel of Figure 10-5). It shows the quantity of the commodity that the firm would supply in the short run at various prices.

The horizontal summation of the supply curves of all firms in the industry then gives the industry short-run supply curve for the commodity. This is given by the $\Sigma MC = S$ curve in the right panel of Figure 10-5, where the symbol Σ refers to the "summation of." The perfectly competitive industry's short-run supply curve in the right panel is based on the assumption that there are 100 identical firms in the industry (and input prices do not vary with industry output). For example, at $P = \$25$, each firm supplies 3

---

[3] Since $STC = TVC + TFC$ and total profits equal $TR - STC$, when $P = AVC$, $TR = TVC$, so that the firm's total losses would equal its TFC whether it produces or shuts down. Thus, point Z at which $P = AVC$ (and $TR = TVC$) is the firm's shutdown point.

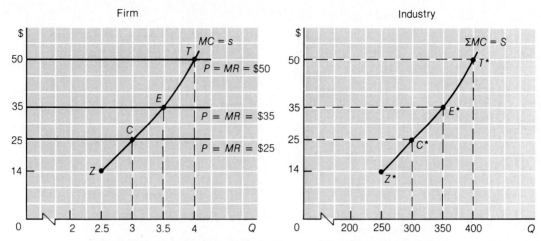

FIGURE 10-5. Short-Run Supply Curve of the Firm and Industry

The left panel reproduces the firm's MC curve above point Z (the shutdown point) from Figure 10-4. This is the perfectly competitive firm's short-run supply curve s. For example, at P = \$25, Q = 3 (point C); at P = \$35, Q = 3.5 (point E); at P = \$50, Q = 4 (point T). The right panel shows the industry's short-run supply curve on the assumption that there are 100 identical firms in the industry and input prices are constant. This is given by the ΣMC = S curve. Thus, at P = \$25, Q = 300 (point C*); at P \$35, Q = 350 (point E*); at P = \$50, Q = 400 (point T*).

units of the commodity (point C in the left panel) and the entire industry supplies 300 units (point C* in the right panel). At P = \$35, each firm supplies 3.5 units (point E) and the industry supplies 350 units (point E*). At P = \$50, Q = 4 for the firm (point T) and Q = 400 for the industry (point T*). Note that no output of the commodity is produced at prices below P = \$14 (points Z and Z' in the figure).[4]

The derivation of the perfectly competitive industry short-run supply curve of the commodity as the horizontal summation of each firm's short-run supply curve is based on the assumption that input prices are constant regardless of the quantity of inputs that each firm and the industry demand. That is, it is based on the assumption that the firm is able to hire a greater quantity of the inputs (to produce the larger output) at constant input prices. If input prices were to rise as firms demanded more of the inputs, the industry supply curve would be steeper or less elastic than indicated in the right panel of Figure 10-5. An increase in the commodity price will then result in a smaller increase in the quantity supplied of the commodity (see Problem 7, with answer in the back of the book).

---

[4] Point Z in the left panel of Figure 10-5 corresponds to point Z' in Figure 8-5 and in panels B and D of Figure 8-6.

Example 10-3 The Supply of Shale Oil

The Facts: In a 1978 study, Ericsson and Morgan estimated (from engineering studies) that the industry supply curve of shale oil (often called "synthetic fuel") was as shown in Figure 10-6. This indicates that it would not be economical to produce oil from shale at prices below $10 per barrel. The quantity of oil supplied, in million barrels per day, would be 2 at the price of $10 per barrel, 6 at the price of $16 per barrel, and 16 at $18 per barrel. The maximum that would be supplied at any price would be about 16 million barrels per day. This compared with a consumption of about 18 million barrels per day in the U.S. in 1978 (of which over 3 million were imported at the price of about $13 per barrel).

Comment: In 1980, Congress created the Synthetic Fuel Corporation to stimulate the production of oil from shale and reduce American dependence on imported petroleum. The original plan called for the production of one-half million barrels of oil from shale per day by 1987. By the end of 1984, $3 billion of federal subsidies had been spent on four projects. However, because of large cost overruns, the cost of producing synthetic oil was sharply revised upward in 1984 to be double the price of $28 per barrel for imported oil. This led Exxon, one of the cosponsors of the project, to withdraw from the project in 1982, and placed the future of the entire shale oil project into question.

Source: N. Ericsson and P. Morgan, "The Economic Feasibility of Shale Oil: An Activity Analysis," *Bell Journal of Economics,* August 1978; "Exxon

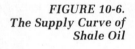

FIGURE 10-6.
The Supply Curve of
Shale Oil

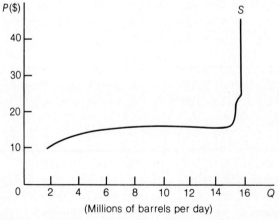

(Millions of barrels per day)

The supply curve for shale oil (estimated from engineering studies) shows that it would not be economical to produce oil from shale at prices below $10 per barrel. At $10 per barrel, about 2 million barrels of oil per day would be supplied, while at $16 per barrel, about 6 million barrels would be supplied. About 15 million barrels would be supplied at $18 per barrel. The maximum that would be supplied at any price would be about 16 million barrels per day.

Abandons Shale Oil Project," *The New York Times*, May 3, 1982, p. 1, and "Any Hope for Synfuel Plan?" *U.S. News and World Report*, November 5, 1984, p. 46.

10-4b Short-Run Equilibrium of the Industry and Firm

In Section 5-1, we showed how the market demand curve for a commodity was derived from the horizontal summation of the demand curves of all the individual consumers of the commodity in the market. We have now shown how to derive the industry or market supply curve of the commodity. In a perfectly competitive market, the equilibrium price of the commodity is determined at the intersection of the market demand curve and the market supply curve of the commodity. This was already explained in Section 2-4. Thus, we have traveled a complete circle and returned to the point of departure. We now know, however, what lies behind the market demand curve and the market supply curve of the commodity and how they are derived (i.e., we no longer simply assume that these curves are given, as in Chapter 2).

Given the price of the commodity, the perfectly competitive firm can sell any quantity of the commodity at that price. As noted earlier, the firm will produce at the point where P or $MR = MC$, provided that MC is rising and $P \geq AVC$. This is shown in Figure 10-7.

The *right* panel of Figure 10-7 shows the short-run market supply curve S (from Figure 10-5) and hypothetical market demand curve D for the commodity. These curves intersect at point E^*, and result in the equilibrium

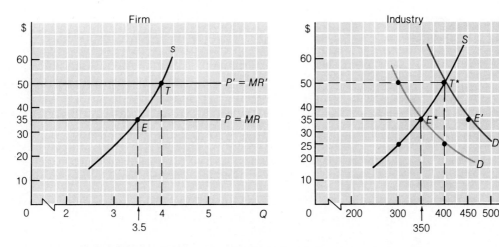

FIGURE 10-7. *Short-Run Equilibrium of the Firm and Industry*
With S (from Figure 10-5) and D in the right panel, P= \$35 and Q= 350 (point E*), and the perfectly competitive firm would produce 3.5 units (point E in the left panel, as in Figure 10-3). If D shifted up to D', P= \$50 and Q= 400 (point T*) and the firm would produce 4 units of ouptut (point T in the left panel).

313

price of \$35 and the equilibrium quantity of 350 units. At P = \$25, the quantity demanded (400 units) exceeds the quantity supplied (300 units), and the resulting shortage will drive the commodity price up to P = \$35. On the other hand, at P = \$50, the quantity supplied (400 units) exceeds the quantity demanded (300 units), and the resulting surplus will drive the price down to P = \$35. The left panel shows that at P = \$35, the perfectly competitive firm will produce 3.5 units (point E, as in Figure 10-3). Note that each firm produces $\frac{1}{100}$ of the total industry or market output.[5]

If the market demand curve then shifted up to D' (for example, as a result of an increase in consumers' incomes), there would be a shortage of 100 units of the commodity at P = \$35 (E^*E' in the right panel of Figure 10-7). This would cause the equilibrium price to rise to \$50 and the equilibrium quantity to 400 units (point T^*). Then, at P = \$50, the perfectly competitive firm maximizes profits at point T by producing 4 units of output (see the left panel). This is based on the assumption that there are 100 identical firms in the perfectly competitive industry and that input prices remain constant.[6]

Example 10-4 The Russian Wheat Deal

The Facts: In July of 1982, the Soviet Union announced that it would purchase 400 million bushels of winter wheat from the U.S. This was approximately one quarter of the total U.S. annual production. With the short-run supply curve for winter wheat fairly price inelastic, the increased demand for American wheat led to a sharp rise in the price of wheat in the U.S., from about \$1.60 per bushel at the end of June of 1982 to about \$2.25 by the end of September.

Comment: The size of the Russian wheat deal caught many farmers by surprise and angered those who had sold their wheat just before the wheat deal was announced. The increase in demand for American wheat led to an increase in the price of wheat, exactly as predicted by our model (see the right panel of Figure 10-7). Furthermore, since the supply curve for American (winter) wheat was fairly price inelastic, the price increase was sharp. In the face of continued difficulties in Russian agriculture and in the expectation of continued purchases of American wheat by the Soviet Union and high wheat prices in the U.S., American farmers increased their wheat output in 1983 and 1984 (also as predicted by our model).

Source: B. Luttrell, "Grain Export Agreements," *Federal Reserve Bank of St. Louis Review*, August/September 1981.

---

[5] For a mathematical presentation of how equilibrium is determined in a perfectly competitive industry using rudimentary calculus, see Section A10 of the Mathematical Appendix.

[6] The case where the quantity supplied of the commodity reponds with a lag to a change in its price is analyzed by the cobweb model. This is examined graphically in Application 4 of Chapter 2 and mathematically in Section A11 of the Mathematical Appendix.

10-5

Long-Run Equilibrium of the Firm and Industry

Having analyzed how equilibrium is reached in the market period and in the short run, we can now go on to examine adjustment in the long run. In this section, we analyze how the perfectly competitive firm and industry reach equilibrium in the long run. This will set the stage for the analysis of constant, increasing, and decreasing cost industries in Section 10-6.

10-5a Long-Run Equilibrium of the Firm

In the long run, all inputs are variable and the firm can build the most efficient plant to produce the best or most profitable level of output. The *best (i.e., the profit-maximizing) level of output* of the firm in the long run is the one at which price or marginal revenue equals long-run marginal cost. The *most efficient plant* is the one that allows the firm to produce the best level of output at the lowest possible cost. This is the plant represented by the *SATC* curve tangent to the *LAC* curve of the firm at the best level of output, as shown in Figure 10-8.[7]

The *LAC* curve in Figure 10-8 is the one of Figure 8-9, and the $SATC_1$ curve is that of Figures 8-5, 8-9, and 10-3. At $P = MR = \$35$ in Figure 10-8, the firm is in *short-run* equilibrium at point E by producing 3.5 units of output. The firm makes a profit of \$9 per unit (vertical distance EE') and \$31.50 in total (as in Figure 10-3).

In the long run, the firm can increase its profits significantly by producing at point J', where P or $MR = LMC$ (and LMC is rising). The firm should build plant $SATC_5$ and operate it at point J (at $SATC = \$13$). Plant $SATC_5$ is the best plant (i.e., the one which allows the firm to produce the best level of output at the lowest $SATC$). In the long run, the firm will make profits of \$22 ($J'J$) per unit and \$286 in total (\$22 times 13 units of output). This compares with total profits of \$31.50 in the short run. Note that when the firm is in long-run equilibrium, it will also be in short-run equilibrium since P or $MR = SMC = LMC$ (see point J' in the figure). This analysis assumes that input prices are constant.

10-5b Long-Run Equilibrium of the Industry and Firm

While the firm would be in long-run equilibrium at point J' in Figure 10-8, the industry would not. This is because the large profits that this and other firms earn at point J' will attract more firms to the industry. As new firms enter the industry (since entry is free and resources are mobile), aggregate

---

[7] Since in the long run all costs are variable, the firm must at least cover all of its costs to remain in business in the long run.

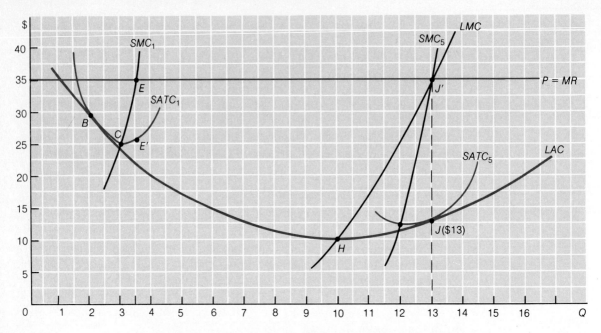

FIGURE 10-8.   Long-Run Equilibrium of the Firm
At P = MR = $35, the firm is in short-run equilibrium at point E (as in Figure 10-3). In the long run, the firm can increase its profits by producing at point J′, where P or MR = LMC (and LMC is rising) and operating plant SATC$_5$ at point J. In the long run, the firm will make profits of $22 (J′J) per unit and $286 in total ($22 times 13 units of output). Since at point J′, P = MR = SMC = LMC, the firm is also in short-run equilibrium.

output expands. This will shift the short-run industry supply curve to the right until it intersects the market demand curve at the commodity price at which all firms make zero economic profits (i.e., they earn only a normal return) in the long run. Then, and only then, will the industry (and the firm) be in equilibrium. In fact, the building of the best plant by the firm and the entrance of new firms into the industry will take place simultaneously in the long run. The final result (equilibrium) is shown in Figure 10-9.

In the figure, the industry (in the right panel) and the firm (in the left panel) are in long-run equilibrium at point H, where $P = MR = LMC = SMC = LAC = SATC = \$10.$[8] The firm produces at the lowest point on its LAC curve (operating optimal plant $SATC_4$ at point H) and earns zero economic profits. Zero economic profit means that the owner of the firm receives only a normal return on his or her investment when the industry

---

[8] Note that the supply curve labeled S in the right panel of Figure 10-9 is larger than the supply curve S in the right panel of Figure 10-7 since more firms have entered the industry in the long run and industry output is larger.

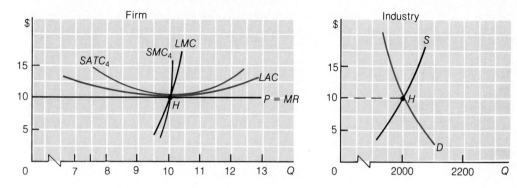

FIGURE 10-9.   Long-run Equilibrium of the Industry and Firm
*The industry (in the right panel) and the firm (in the left panel) are in long-run equi-
librium at point H, where P = MR = SMC = LMC = SATC = LAC = $10. The firm
produces at the lowest point on its LAC curve (operating optimal plant SATC₄ at
point H) and earns zero profits. Competition in the input markets as well as in the
commodity market will result in all firms having the identical lowest LAC and earning zero profits when the industry is in the long-run equilibrium.*

and firm are in long-run equilibrium. That is, the owner receives a return
on the capital invested in the firm equal only to the amount that he or she
would earn by investing the capital in a similarly risky venture. If the
owner manages the firm, zero economic profits also includes what he or
she would earn in the best *alternative* occupation (i.e., managing a similar
firm for someone else). Thus, zero profits in economics means that the total
revenues of the firm just covers all costs (explicit and implicit).[9]

Note that when the perfectly competitive industry is in long-run equilibrium, the firm not only earns zero profits but produces at the lowest point
on its *LAC* curve (point *H* in the left panel of Figure 10-9). Thus, resources
are used most efficiently to produce the goods and services most desired
by society at the minimum cost. Since firms also earn zero profits, consumers purchase the commodity at the lowest possible price ($10 at point *H*
in the figure). In this sense, perfect competition is the most efficient form
of market organization. This is to be contrasted to the situation under
imperfect competition (discussed in the next three chapters), where we
will see that producers seldom, if ever, produce at the lowest point on their
LAC curve, and they charge a price that also usually includes a profit
margin.

We have seen so far that when a perfectly competitive firm earns (economic) profits, in the long run more firms will enter the industry and this

---

[9] As pointed out in Section 10-1, the meaning of profit in economics is to be distinguished
clearly from the everyday use of the term (which considers implicit costs as part of profits).
In economics, profits always refer only to the excess of total revenue over total costs, and total
costs include both explicit and implicit costs (see Section 8-1). In short, in economics, profits
mean above-normal returns.

will lower the commodity price until all firms just break even (i.e., earn zero profits). On the other hand, if the perfectly competitive firm incurs a loss in the short run and would continue to incur a loss in the long run even by constructing the best plant, some firms would leave the industry. This would shift the industry supply curve to the left until it intersected the industry demand curve at the (higher) commodity price at which the remaining firms made zero economic profits but incurred no losses. The final result would be as shown in Figure 10-9, except that there would now be fewer firms in the industry and the industry output would be smaller. As it is, Figure 10-9 indicates that if all firms had identical cost curves, there would be 200 identical firms in the industry when in long-run equilibrium. Each firm would produce 10 units of output and break even.

It should be noted that perfectly competitive firms need not have identical cost curves (although we assume so for simplicity), but the *minimum point* on their *LAC* curves must occur at the same cost per unit. If some firms had more productive inputs and, thus, lower average costs than other firms in the industry, the more productive inputs would be able to extract from their employer higher rewards (payments) commensurate to their higher productivity, under the threat of leaving to work for others. As a result, their *LAC* curves would shift upward until the lowest point on the *LAC* curve of all firms is the same. Thus, competition in the input markets as well as in the commodity market will result in all firms having identical (minimum) average costs and zero economic profits when the industry is in the long run equilibrium.

Example 10-5   Long-Run Adjustment in the U.S. Cotton Textile Industry

The Facts: In studying the U.S. cotton textile industry, Lloyd Reynolds found that this industry was closer to perfect competition than any other U.S. manufacturing industry during the interwar period. The product was nearly homogeneous, there were many buyers and sellers of cotton cloth, each too small to affect its price, and entry into and exit from the industry was relatively easy. Reynolds found that the rate of return on investments in the textile industry was about 6 per cent in the South and 1 per cent in the North (due to higher costs for labor and raw cotton in the North). These returns compared to an average rate of return of about 8 per cent for all manufacturing industries in the U.S. As a result, many textile firms went out of business in the long run and capacity declined by more than 33 per cent from 1925 to 1938. The decline was more rapid in the North than in the South.

Comment: The decline in capacity in the U.S. cotton textile industry was as predicted by the perfectly competitive model. According to the model, firms would leave an industry in the long run until remaining firms break even (or returns on investment in the industry rise to the average for other industries). Also as predicted by the model, most textile firms going out of business were in the North, where returns were much lower than in the South.

Source: L. Reynolds, "Competition in the Textile Industry," in W. Adams and T. Traywick, Eds., *Readings in Economics* (New York: Macmillan, 1948).

10-6

Constant, Increasing, and Decreasing Cost Industries

In the previous section we examined how a perfectly competitive industry and firm reach equilibrium in the long run. Starting from a position of long-run equilibrium, we now examine how the perfectly competitive industry and firm adjust in the long run to an increase in the market demand for the commodity. This allows us to define constant, increasing, and decreasing cost industries and analyze their behavior graphically.

10-6a Constant Cost Industries

Starting from the long-run equilibrium condition of the industry and the firm (point H) in Figure 10-9, if the market demand curve for the commodity increases, the equilibrium price will rise in the short run and firms earn economic profits (i.e., they receive above-normal returns). This will attract more firms into the industry, and the short-run industry or market supply curve of the commodity increases (shifts to the right). If input prices remain constant (as more inputs are demanded by the expanding industry), the new long-run equilibrium price for the commodity will be the same as before the increase in demand and supply. Then, the long-run industry supply curve (*LS*) for the commodity is horizontal at the minimum *LAC*. This is a **constant cost industry** and is shown in Figure 10-10.

In Figure 10-10, point H in the right and left panels show the long-run equilibrium position of the perfectly competitive industry and firm, respectively (as in Figure 10-9), before the increase in demand (*D*) and supply (*S*). The increase in *D* to *D'* results in the short-run equilibrium price of \$20 (point H' in the right panel). At $P = \$20$, each of the 200 identical firms in the industry will produce $Q = 10.5$ (given by point H' in the left panel at which $P = SMC_4 = \$20$) for a total industry output of 2,100 units.

Since each firm earns profits at $P = \$20$ (see the left panel), more firms enter the industry in the long run, shifting S to the right. If input prices remain constant, S shifts to S', reestablishing the original equilibrium price of \$10 (point H'' in the right panel). At $P = \$10$, each firm produces at the lowest point on its *LAC* and earns zero economic profit (point H in the left panel). By joining points H and H'' in the right panel, we derive the long-

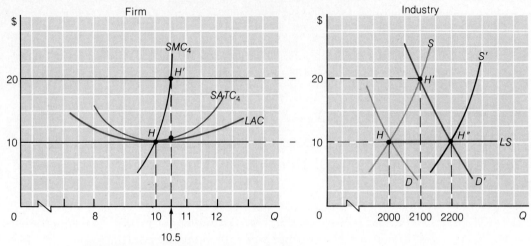

FIGURE 10-10. Constant Cost Industry

Point H is the original long-run equilibrium point of the industry and firm. An increase in D to D' results in P = $20 and all firms earn economic profits. As more firms enter the industry, S shifts to S' and P = $10 if input prices remain constant. By joining points H and H" in the right panel, we derive horizontal long-run supply curve LS for the (constant cost) industry.

run supply curve of the industry (LS). Since LS is horizontal, this is a constant cost industry (with 220 identical firms producing a total output of 2,200 units).

Constant costs are more likely to result in industries that utilize general rather than specialized inputs and that account for only a small fraction of the total quantity demanded of the inputs in the economy. Then, the industry may be able to hire a greater quantity of the general inputs it uses without driving input prices upward.

10-6b Increasing Cost Industries

If input prices *rise* as more inputs are demanded by an expanding industry, the long-run industry supply curve for the commodity will be positively sloped and we have an **increasing cost industry.** This means that greater outputs of the commodity per time period will be supplied in the long run only at higher commodity prices (see Figure 10-11).

Starting from point *H* in the right and left panels of Figure 10-11, the increase in *D* to *D'* results in *P* = $20 (point *H'* in the right panel), at which all firms earn economic profits (point *H'* in the left panel). More firms enter the industry in the long run, and more inputs are demanded as industry output expands. So far, this is identical to Figure 10-10. If input prices now rise, each firm's per-unit cost curves shift up (as explained in Application 5 and chapter 8), and S shifts to the right to S' so as to establish equilibrium

320

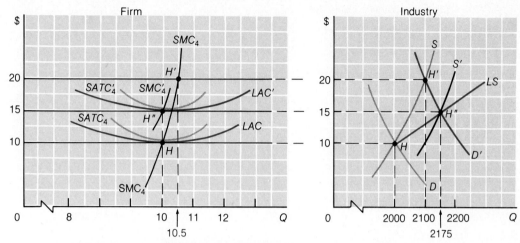

FIGURE 10-11. Increasing Cost Industry

Point H is the original long-run equilibrium point of the industry and firm. An increase in D to D' results in P= $20 and all firms earn economic profits. As more firms enter the industry, S shifts to S' and P= $15 if input prices rise. By joining points H and H " in the right panel, we derive positively sloped long-run supply curve LS for the (increasing cost) industry.

P = minimum LAC' = $15 (see point H'' in both panels of Figure 10-11). All profits are squeezed out as costs rise and price falls. By joining points H and H'' in the right panel, we get the long-run industry supply curve (LS). Since LS is positively sloped, the industry is an increasing cost industry (with 217.5 or 218 identical firms).

Increasing costs are more likely to result in industries that utilize some specialized input such as labor with unique skills (e.g., highly trained lab technicians to conduct experiments in genetics) or custom-made machinery to perform very special tasks (e.g., oil drilling platforms). Then, the industry may have to pay higher prices to bring forth a greater supply of the specialized inputs it requires and we have an increasing cost industry.

10-6c Decreasing Cost Industries

If input prices *fall* as more inputs are demanded by an expanding industry, the long-run industry supply curve for the commodity will be negatively sloped and we have a **decreasing cost industry.** This means that greater outputs of the commodity per time period will be supplied in the long run at lower commodity prices (see Figure 10-12).

The movement from point H to point H' in both panels of Figure 10-12 is the same as in Figures 10-10 and 10-11. Since at point H' firms earn profits, more firms enter the industry in the long run. Industry output expands,

321

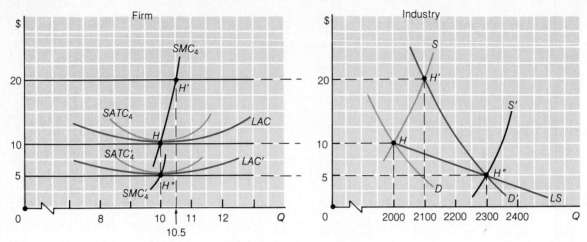

FIGURE 10-12. Decreasing Cost Industry

Points H and H′ are the same as in the preceeding two figures. Starting from point H′, as more firms enter the industry, S shifts to S′ and P = $5 if input prices fall. By joining points H and H ″ in the right panel, we derive the negatively sloped long-run supply curve LS for the (decreasing cost) industry.

and more inputs are demanded. If input prices fall, each firm's per-unit cost curves shift down, and S shifts to the right to S′ so as to establish equilibrium P = minimum LAC′ = $5 (point H″ in both panels). By joining points H and H″ in the right panel, we derive LS, the industry long-run supply curve. Since LS is negatively sloped, we have a decreasing cost industry (with 230 identical firms).

Decreasing costs may result when the expansion of an industry leads to (1) the establishment of technical institutes to train labor for skills required by the industry at a lower cost than firms in the industry do; (2) the setting up of enterprises to supply some equipment used by the industry and that was previously constructed by the firms in the industry for themselves at higher cost; (3) the exploitation of some cheaper natural resource that the industry can substitute for more expensive resources but which was not feasible to exploit when the demand for the natural resource was smaller.

In the real world, we have examples of constant, increasing, and decreasing cost industries. In fact, a particular industry could exhibit constant, increasing, or decreasing costs over different time periods and at various levels of demand.[10] It should also be noted that the shifts in firms' per-unit cost curves in the left panel of Figures 10-11 and 10-12 were vertical (so that the lowest point on both the LAC and LAC′ curves occurred at Q =

---

[10] Of the three cases, increasing cost industries may be, perhaps, somewhat more common than the other two cases.

10). This is the case if the price of all inputs change in the same proportion. Otherwise, per-unit cost curves would also shift to the right or to the left.

The *downward shift* in the firm's per-unit cost curves (due to a fall in input prices) as the *industry expands* is called **external economy,** while the *upward shift* in the firm's per-unit cost curves (due to an increase in input prices) as the *industry expands* is called **external diseconomy.** These are to be clearly distinguished from economies or diseconomies of scale, which are *internal* to the firm and refer instead to a downward or an upward *movement along* a given *LAC* curve (as the firm expands output and builds larger scales of plants). The assumption here is that as only a single firm expands output, input prices remain constant. External economies and diseconomies will be examined in detail in Chapter 19.

10-7

Applications

In this section, we examine a number of important applications of the tools of analysis developed in this chapter. These include the allocation of a given supply of a commodity over time, and the effect of (1) rent control and excise taxes on the industry and firm, (2) medicare and medicaid on the price of medical services, and (3) changes in the demand for commodities on the allocation of inputs in production. These applications as well as the numerous examples provided in the text clearly demonstrate the great usefulness of the tools of analysis presented in this chapter.

Application 1: Allocation Over Time
Prices not only ration the available supply of a commodity among potential buyers of the commodity, but also ration it over the time of the market period. For example, the price of wheat is not so low right after harvest that most of the wheat available is sold long before the next harvest. At the same time, the price of wheat is usually not so high during the year that large quantities of wheat are left unsold by the next harvest or must be sold at very low prices. In general, the price of wheat is lowest immediately after harvest and rises over the year sufficiently to just cover the opportunity cost of holding the wheat, plus the cost of insurance and the risk of unexpected price changes. In the real world, this is accomplished by speculators operating in the futures market for the commodity. In this market, wheat can be purchased and sold for future delivery at a predetermined price.

For example, suppose that the market period is one year and the demand in each of the three four-month periods of the year is given by *D* in Figure 10-13. Since sellers have the option of selling the total quantity of the commodity available for the year during any of the three four-month periods, the supply curve for the first four-month period is not vertical, but is pos-

FIGURE 10-13.
Allocation Over
Time

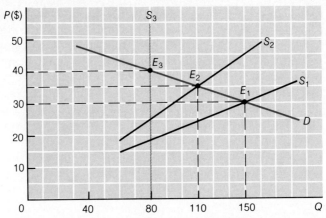

itively sloped (S_1 in the figure).[11] With D and S_1, $P = \$30$ and $Q = 150$ in the first period. The supply curve for the second four-month period is S_2. Supply curve S_2 is above S_1 because sellers require higher prices to be induced to hold over part of the commodity to the second period. Also, S_2 is less elastic than S_1 because sellers have fewer options (i.e., two periods instead of three during which) to dispose of the quantities of the commodity they hold. With D and S_2, $P = \$35$ and $Q = 110$.

In the third four-month period, the supply is S_3 and is vertical since the remaining quantity of the commodity must be sold in this period (i.e., before the next harvest when the price will be much lower). Thus, with D and S_3, $P = \$40$ and $Q = 80$. It should be noted, however, that the process will occur exactly as described only if sellers and/or speculators correctly anticipate the market for each of the three four-month periods. If sellers hold over too much of the commodity for the last period, price may fall below that in earlier periods. When correct, speculative activity will smooth out the price of the commodity over the time of the market period. The explanation is basically the same for generally rising prices of exhaustible (i.e., nonreplenishable) natural resources, such as minerals, over time (see Chapter 16).

[11] That is, the higher is the price of the commodity during the first four-month period, the greater is the proportion of the total yearly supply of the commodity that sellers are willing to sell during the first four-month period. However, since they need not sell the entire yearly supply of the commodity during this first four-month period, S_1 is not vertical.

Application 2: Effect of Rent Control on the Industry and Firm

When the demand for a commodity or service (say rental housing) rises, we expect the quantity supplied to increase in the short run and to increase even more in the long run. However, if rents are not allowed to rise because of rent control, a shortage of apartments for rent will result. We have already discussed this in Chapter 2 (see Application 1). We now amplify that discussion to include the long-run, as well as the short-run, response of an individual firm and the industry to an increase in the demand for rental apartments in the face of rent control.

In the *right* panel of Figure 10-14, the market demand curve for rental apartments (D) intersects both the short-run market supply curve (S) and the long-run supply curve (LS) at point H. Thus, the equilibrium rent is $500 per month and the equilibrium quantity is 2.4 million apartments, and both the industry (the right panel) and the typical firm (the left panel) are in long-run (and, hence, also in short-run) equilibrium at point H.

If now D shifts up to D′, the industry (in the right panel) and the firm (in the left panel) will be in short-run equilibrium at point H′ at the rent of $700, in the absence of rent control.[12] Since this and other firms make prof-

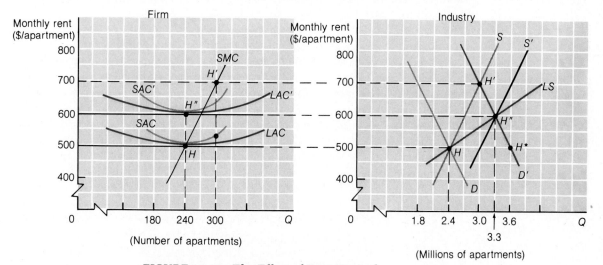

FIGURE 10-14. The Effect of Rent Control

The industry and the firm are originally in short- and long-run equilibrium at the rent of $500 (point H, where D intersects S and LS). When D shifts up to D′, they are in short-run equilibrium at point H′ at the rent of $700. Since firms make profits (point H′ in the left panel), more firms enter the industry in the long-run, shifting S to the right to S′ (if the industry is an increasing cost industry). The new long-run equilibrium will occur at point H″ for the industry and firm at the rent of $600. With D′ and rent control at $500, there would be a demand for 3.6 million rental apartments and a resulting shortage of 1.2 million apartments (HH* in the right panel).

---

[12] When D shifts up to D′, the perfectly competitive firm is in short-run equilibrium at point H′ because that is where P = SMC = $700.

its (see point H' in the left panel), more firms enter the industry in the long run, shifting S to the right to S' (in the right panel), if the industry is an increasing cost industry. The new long-run equilibrium will occur at point H'' for the industry (in the right panel) and for the firm (in the left panel) at the rent of $600.

However, with rent control at $500, there would be no short-run or long-run supply response to the increase in demand. With D', consumers would demand 3.6 million apartments for rent (H^* in the right panel), as opposed to 2.4 million available (point H), leaving a shortage of 1.2 million apartments (HH^* in the right panel) at the controlled rent of $500. While the firm seems to remain at point H in the left panel after the increase in demand under rent control, many distortions occur in the housing market, as explained in Application 1 in chapter 2. One result is that owners of rent-controlled apartments attempt to cut maintenance and repairs to reduce costs. Another is that fewer rental apartments will be constructed. Still another result is a black market for rental apartments.

Distortions result in other controlled markets as well. It is for this reason that Congress adopted a program of "phased deregulation" for natural gas in 1979. Deregulation, however, has created its own problems, as discussed in Chapters 12 and 13.

Application 3: Effect of an Excise Tax on the Industry and Firm

An excise tax is a tax on each unit of the commodity. If collected from sellers, the tax would cause the supply curve to shift upward by the amount of the tax, since sellers require that much more per unit to supply each amount of the commodity. The result will be that consumers will purchase a smaller quantity at a higher price, while sellers receive a smaller net price after payment of the tax. The effect of an excise tax was already discussed in Chapter 2 (see application 3). We now elaborate on that discussion to include the long-run as well as the short-run response of an individual firm and the industry to the imposition of an excise tax collected from sellers.

In Figure 10-15, point H is the original long-run and short-run equilibrium of the industry and firm (as in Figures 10-9 to 10-12). If now a tax of $4 per unit is imposed on sellers of the commodity, S and LS shift up by that amount to S' and LS', respectively (point H^* in the right panel). The immediate effect of the tax is to shift the firm's per-unit cost curves up to $SATC'$, SMC', and LAC' in the left panel. In the short run, the equilibrium price is $12 (point H', where D and S' intersect in the right panel) and each of the 200 firms in the industry produces 9.5 units of the commodity (point H', where $P = SMC' = \$12$ in the left panel) for a total industry output of 1,900. At $P = \$12$, each firm incurs a loss in the short run because $P < SATC'$ at $Q = 9.5$.

In the long run, some firms leave the industry and S' shifts to the left until $P = \$13$ and $Q = 1,850$ (point H'', where D intersects S'' and LS' in the right panel). Since this is an increasing cost industry, input prices *fall*

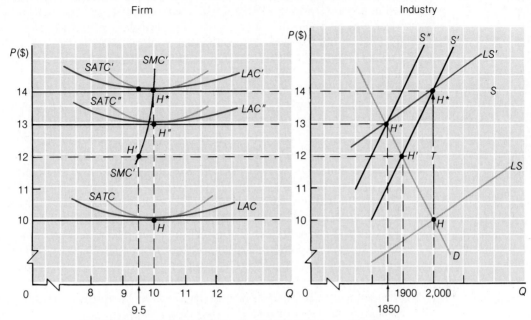

FIGURE 10-15. The Effect of a Per-Unit Tax on Producers

Starting from point H, if a $4 per-unit tax is imposed on sellers, S and LS shift up to S′ and LS′ (point H* in the right panel) and the firm's cost curves shift up to SATC′, SMC′, LAC. In the short run, P = $12 (point H′, where D and S′ intersect) and each firm produces where P = SMC′ = $12 and incurs a loss. In the long run, some firms leave the industry until P = $13 (point H″, where D intersects S″ and LS′). Input prices fall, shifting the firm's per-unit cost curves down to SATC″, SMC″, and LAC″. Each of 185 firms now produces 10 units and earns zero profit.

(as the *decrease* in industry output *reduces* input demand). This shifts the firm's per-unit cost curves down to *SATC″*, *SMC″*, and *LAC″* in the left panel. There will now be 185 firms left in the industry, each producing 10 units of the commodity (point *H″* in the left panel) and earning zero economic profit.

    Thus, in the long run, $3 of the $4 per-unit tax falls on consumers (in the form of higher prices) and $1 falls on input owners (in the form of lower input prices). Each firm earns zero profit at the original (point *H*) and at the new long-run equilibrium point (*H″*). Given the market supply curve of the commodity, the more inelastic is the market demand curve, the greater is the incidence of the tax on consumers. The analysis for a per-unit subsidy to each firm is the exact opposite (see Problem 11).

Application 4: Medicare and Medicaid and the Price of Medical Services
Medicare is a government program that covers most of the medical expenses of the elderly, while Medicaid covers practically all medical expenses of the poor. Both programs were enacted in 1965. The effect of

Medicare and Medicaid on the price and quantity of medical services consumed by people not covered by either program is analyzed in Figure 10-
16. For simplicity, we assume that all medical costs of the elderly and the
poor are covered by the programs and all medical services take the form of
doctors' visits.

In the figure, D_c is the demand curve of medical services of the elderly
and the poor *before the subsidy* or coverage under Medicare and Medicaid,
while D_n is the demand curve of the rest of the population. $D_c + D_n = D_t$.
The intersection of D_t and S (point E) defines the equilibrium price of $15
per visit (and a total of 900 million visits) for the to-be covered group and
for the noncovered group. At $P = \$15$, the elderly and the poor purchase
200 million doctor's visits per year, while the rest of the population consumes 700 million visits per year, for a total of 900 million visits for the
entire population.

When the government covers the entire cost of the doctors' visits of the
elderly and the poor, their demand curve becomes D'_c. This is vertical at
the quantity purchased at zero price. That is, the covered group will
demand 400 million visits per year regardless of price. $D'_c + D_n = D'_t$. The
intersection of D'_t and S (point E') defines the new equilibrium price of $20
for the noncovered group. The noncovered group now pays a higher price
than before ($20 per visit instead of $15) and consumes a smaller quantity
of medical services as read off D_n (600 million instead of the previous 700

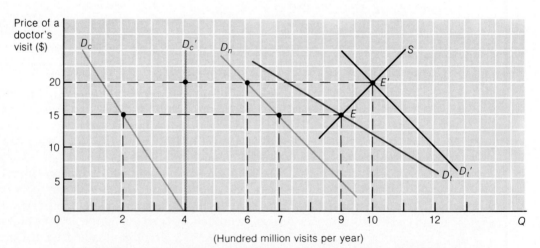

FIGURE 10–16. Medicare and Medicaid and the Price of Medical Services
D_c *is the demand curve of medical services of the elderly and the poor before the
subsidy, while* D_n *is the demand curve of the rest of the population.* $D_c + D_n = D_t$.
With D_t *and S, P = \$15 (point E). The to-be covered group purchases 200 million visits
and others 700 million. When the government covers the entire cost of the doctors'
visits of the elderly and the poor, their demand curve becomes* D'_c. $D'_c + D_n = D'_t$.
Then P = \$20 and Q = 6 million (point E') for the noncovered group.

million visits per year). The nonsubsidized group also pays the taxes to pay for the subsidy; the covered group, as well as doctors, receive the benefits.

Although the market for medical services is not perfectly competitive (and much more complex than assumed above), the conclusion of the foregoing analysis has been broadly borne out by the events that followed the adoption of Medicare and Medicaid. Thus, the perfectly competitive model can also be useful (i.e., provide a first approximation) in the analysis of markets that depart from perfect competition.

Application 5: Change in Demand and the Allocation of Inputs

Suppose that from a condition of long-run equilibrium, the demand for wheat rises while the demand for corn falls, as a result of a change in tastes. In the market period (i.e., between harvests), the supply of each commodity is fixed and the price of wheat rises while the price of corn falls. Wheat farmers earn a profit while corn farmers incur losses (but continue to produce as long as they cover variable costs).

In the short run, wheat farmers demand more variable inputs to raise more wheat, thereby bidding up the prices of their variable inputs. On the other hand, the prices of the variable inputs used by corn farmers tend to fall as they demand fewer inputs to produce less corn. There is a reallocation of variable inputs in the short run from corn to wheat production. In the short run, the quantity supplied of wheat rises and the price falls compared with the market period. On the other hand, the quantity supplied of corn falls and its price rises, compared with the market period.

In the long-run, wheat farmers increase their scale of operation and more farmers begin to cultivate wheat. The opposite is true for corn. As the supply of wheat rises in the long run, the price of wheat falls from the short-run level. At the same time, input prices may rise, as still more inputs are demanded by wheat farmers in the long run. If input prices do rise, there will be a double squeeze on the profits of wheat farmers, as their costs rise and the price of wheat falls. This continues until all wheat farmers earn zero profits in the long run. The exact opposite happens in corn production. At this point, the reallocation of inputs comes to an end, and both wheat and corn farmers are once again in long-run equilibrium (see Problem 12, with answer at the end of the text). More will be said on this in Chapter 14, when we discuss input markets.

Summary

1. Economists identify four different types of market organization: perfect competition, monopoly, monopolistic competition, and oligopoly. In a perfectly competitive market, no buyer or seller affects (or behaves as if he or she affects) the price of a commodity, all units of the commodity are homogeneous or identical, resources are mobile, and knowledge of the market is perfect. This definition stresses the impersonality of the market rather than rivalry, which is emphasized in the colloquial usage of the term. The perfectly competitive model is useful in markets that

approximate perfect competition and to evaluate inefficiency in other markets.

2. The market period, or the very short run, refers to the period of time during which the market supply of a commodity is fixed. During the market period, costs of production are irrelevant in the determination of the price of a perishable commodity and the entire supply of the commodity is put up for sale at whatever price it can fetch. Thus, demand alone determines price (while supply alone determines quantity).

3. The TR of a perfectly competitive firm is a straight line through the origin with slope of MR = P. The best or profit-maximizing level of output is that which maximizes total profits. This occurs where the positive difference between TR and STC is greatest. The same result is obtained where P or $MR = MC$ and MC is rising, provided that $P = AVC$. If P is smaller than ATC at the best level of output, the firm will incur a loss. As long as P exceeds AVC, it pays for the firm to continue to produce because it covers all variable costs and part of its fixed costs. If the firm were to shut down, it would incur a loss equal to its total fixed costs. The shutdown point is where $P = AVC$.

4. The rising portion of the firm's MC curve above the AVC curve (the shutdown point) is the firm's short-run supply curve of the commodity. The industry short-run supply curve is the horizontal summation of the firms' short-run supply curves. The equilibrium price is at the intersection of the market demand and supply curves of the commodity. The firm will then produce the output at which P or $MR = MC$, and MC is rising (as long as P exceeds AVC). With an increase in demand, the equilibrium price will rise and firms will expand their output. If input prices rise, the MC curve of each firm shifts up and so the short-run supply curve of each firm and of the industry are less elastic.

5. In the long run, the industry and the firm are in long-run equilibrium where $P = MR = SMC = LMC = SATC = LAC$. Each firm operates at the lowest point on its LAC curve and earns zero profits. Competition in the input markets as well as in the commodity market will result in all firms having identical average costs and zero profits when the industry is in long-run equilibrium.

6. One of three possible cases can result as industry output expands and more inputs are demanded. If input prices remain constant, the industry long-run supply curve is horizontal and we have a constant cost industry. If input prices rise (external diseconomy), the industry long-run supply curve is positively sloped and we have an increasing cost industry. This may be more common than the other two cases. If input prices fall (external economy), the industry long-run supply curve is negatively sloped and we have a decreasing cost industry.

7. Prices ration the available supply of a commodity among potential buyers and over the time of the market period. Rent control prevents a supply response to an increase in demand and leads to a shortage of apartments for rent. In an increasing cost industry, part of a per-unit tax is paid by consumers and part by input owners. Medicare and Medicaid increase the price and reduce the quantity of medical services consumed by the noncovered population. Variable inputs in the short run and all inputs in the long run are reallocated to reach equilibrium.

Glossary

Perfectly competitive market A market where no buyer or seller affects (or behaves as if he or she affects) the price of a commodity; all units of the commodity are homogeneous or identical, resources are mobile, and knowledge of the market is perfect.

Market period The time period during which the market supply of a commodity is fixed. Also called the very short run.

Break-even point The point where total revenues equal total costs, and profits are zero.

Shutdown point The output level at which price equals average variable cost, and losses equal total fixed costs, whether the firm produces or not. Also, the lowest point on the AVC curve at which $MC = AVC$.

Constant cost industry An industry with a horizontal long-run supply curve (a minimum LAC).

It results if input prices remain constant as industry output expands.

Increasing cost industry   An industry with a positively sloped long-run supply curve. It results if input prices rise as industry output expands.

Decreasing cost industry   An industry with a negatively sloped long-run supply curve. It results if input prices fall as industry output expands.

External economy   A downward shift in all firms' per-unit cost curves resulting from a decline in input prices as the industry expands.

External diseconomy   An upward shift in all firms' per-unit cost curves resulting from an increase in input prices as the industry expands.

Questions for Review

1. (a) What are the four different types of market organization?
   (b) When is a market perfectly competitive?
   (c) How does the economist's definition of competition diverge from the everyday usage of the term?
   (d) What is the usefulness of the perfectly competitive model?

2. (a) What is the market period?
   (b) How long is the market period?
   (c) How is the equilibrium price determined in the market period?

3. (a) What is the shape of the total revenue curve of a perfectly competitive firm?
   (b) What does the slope of the total revenue curve of the firm measure?
   (c) What other total curve is required to determine the best level of output of the firm?
   (d) How is the firm's best level of output determined with total curves?

4. (a) What is the shape of the marginal revenue curve of a perfectly competitive firm? Why?
   (b) How is the firm's best level of output determined using the marginal revenue curve?
   (c) What determines whether the firm earns a profit or incurs a loss at the best level of output?
   (d) Should the firm shut down if it incurs a loss in the short run?

5. If at the best level of output,
   (a) price equals average total cost, will the firm make a profit? Should the firm continue to produce?
   (b) price is lower than average total cost but higher than average variable cost, will the firm make a profit or a loss? Should the firm continue to produce? Why?

   (c) price equals average variable cost, will the firm continue to produce? Why?
   (d) price exceeds average variable cost, what should the firm do? Why?

6. (a) Where is the shutdown point of a firm?
   (b) What is the short-run supply curve of a perfectly competitive firm?
   (c) How is the short-run supply curve of a perfectly competitive industry determined?
   (d) Would the short-run supply curve of a perfectly competitive firm and industry be more or less elastic if input prices rise?

7. (a) If the perfectly competitive firm is in long-run equilibrium, must the industry also be in long-run equilibrium? Why?
   (b) If the perfectly competitive industry is in long-run equilibrium, must each competitive firm also be in long-run equilibrium? Why?
   (c) If the perfectly competitive firm is in short-run equilibrium, must it also be in long-run equilibrium? Why?
   (d) If the perfectly competitive firm is in long-run equilibrium must it also be in short-run equilibrium? Why?

8. (a) What is the best level of output for the perfectly competitive firm when the industry is in long-run equilibrium?
   (b) What is the best scale of plant for the perfectly competitive firm when the industry is in long-run equilibrium?
   (c) In what way is perfect competition the most efficient form of market organization?
   (d) Why must all perfectly competitive firms earn zero economic profits when the industry is in long-run equilibrium?

9. (a) What are constant, increasing, and decreasing cost industries?
   (b) How are constant, increasing, and decreasing cost industries related to input prices?
   (c) What is an external economy?
   (d) What is an external diseconomy?
10. (a) How do external economies differ from increasing returns to scale?
    (b) How do external diseconomies differ from decreasing returns to scale?
    (c) Do we have a constant, an increasing, or a decreasing cost industry in the absence of external economies and external diseconomies?
11. (a) How do prices ration the available supply of a commodity over the time of the market period?
    (b) If the controlled rent is set below the equilibrium rent, will a shortage or surplus of rental housing result?
    (c) What are some of the other results of rent control?
12. (a) What is the incidence of a per-unit tax in an increasing cost industry in the long run?
    (b) What is the effect of Medicare and Medicaid on the price and quantity of medical services consumed by the noncovered population?
    (c) How are inputs reallocated to reach short-run and long-run equilibrium?

Problems

★1. Suppose that the market demand function of a perfectly competitive industry is given by $QD = 4,750 - 50P$ and the market supply function is given by $QS = 1,750 + 50P$, and P is expressed in dollars.
   (a) Find the market equilibrium price.
   (b) Find the quantity demanded and supplied in the market at

   $P = \$50, \$40, \$30, \$20, \$10.$

   (c) Draw the market demand curve, the market supply curve, and the demand curve for one of 100 identical perfectly competitive firms in this industry.
   (d) Write the equation of the demand curve of the firm.
2. (a) If the market supply function of a commodity is $QS = 3,250$, are we in the market period, the short run, or the long run?
   (b) If the market demand function is $QD = 4,750 - 50P$ and P is expressed in dollars, what is the market equilibrium price (P)?
   (c) If the market demand increases to $QD' = 5,350 - 50P$, what is the equilibrium price?
   (d) If the market demand decreases to $QD'' = 4,150 - 50P$, what is the equilibrium price?
   (e) Draw a figure showing parts (b), (c), and (d) of this problem.

3. Using the STC schedule provided in the table for Problem 4a in Chapter 8 and $P = \$26$ for a perfectly competitive firm,
   (a) draw a figure similar to Figure 10-2 and determine the best level of output of the firm.
   (b) construct a table similar to Table 10-1 showing TR, STC, and total profits at each level of output.
★4. Suppose that a perfectly competitive firm has no knowledge of the exact shape of its STC curve. It knows that its total fixed costs are $200 and it assumes that its average variable costs are constant at $5.
   (a) If the firm can sell any amount of the commodity at the price of $10 per unit, draw a figure and determine the sales volume at which the firm breaks even.
   (b) How can an increase in the price of the commodity, in the total fixed costs of the firm, and in average variable costs be shown in the figure of part (a)?
   (c) What is an important shortcoming of this analysis?
5. Using the per-unit cost schedules derived from the table for Problem 4a in Chapter 8 and $P = \$26$,
   (a) draw a figure similar to Figure 10-3 and show the best level of output of the firm.
   (b) construct a table similar to Table 10-2

showing P, MR, ATC, and MC at each level of output.

6. For your figure in Problem 5a, determine the best level of output, the profit or loss per unit, total profit or losses, and whether the firm should continue to produce or not at
   (a) $P = \$42$.
   (b) $P = \$18$.
   (c) $P = \$12.50$.

7. Graph the quantity supplied (Q) at various prices (P by firms 1, 2, and 3 given below, and derive the industry supply curve on the assumption that the industry is composed only of these three firms and input prices are constant.

Price and Quantity Supplied by Firms 1, 2, and 3

P	Q1	Q2	Q3
$1	0	0	0
2	20	0	0
3	40	10	10
4	60	20	20

★8. Starting from Figure 10-5, suppose that as each of the 100 identical firms in the perfectly competitive industry increases output (as a result of an increase in the market price of the commodity), input prices rise, causing the SMC curve of each firm to shift upward by $15. Draw a figure showing the original and the new MC curve, and the quantity supplied by each firm and by the industry as a whole at the original price of $P = \$35$ and at $P = \$50$. On the same figure show the supply curve of each firm and of the industry.

9. (a) For the perfectly competitive firm of Problem 5, draw a figure similar to Figure 10-8 showing short-run and long-run equilibrium on the assumption that the firm, but not the industry, is in long-run equilibrium. Assume $P = \$30$, the lowest $LAC = \$12.50$ at $Q = 8$, the best level of output is $Q = 10$, and $LAC = \$15$ with $SATC_5$ and $SMC_5 = LMC = \$30$ when the firm, but not the industry, is in long-run equilibrium.

   (b) Draw a figure similar to Figure 10-9 for the firm of part (a) showing the long-run equilibrium point for the firm and the industry.

10. Starting from point H in both panels of Figure 10-14, draw a figure similar to Figure 10-14, but assuming that the government imposes a rent ceiling of $400 and the industry is an increasing cost industry.

11. (a) Starting from long-run equilibrium point H in Figure 10-15, analyze the effect of a subsidy of $8 on each unit of the commodity produced to all producers of the commodity.

    (b) Who are the beneficiaries of the per-unit subsidy? What form does the benefit take?

★12. Starting from long-run equilibrium in a perfectly competitive increasing-cost industry, show on one diagram the effect on price and quantity of an increase in demand in the market period, in the short run, and in the long run.

Supplementary Readings

For a problem-solving approach to the topics discussed in this chapter, see

Dominick Salvatore, *Microeconomic Theory*, 2nd ed. (New York: McGraw-Hill, 1983), Chapter 10.

Important readings on the perfectly competitive model are

Alfred Marshall, *Principles of Economics*, 9th ed. (London: Macmillan, 1920), Book V, Chapter V.

George J. Stigler, "Perfect Competition, Historically Contemplated," *Journal of Political Economy*, February 1957.

Chapter 11

Price and Output under Pure Monopoly

11-1 Pure Monopoly

11-2 Short-Run Equilibrium Price and Output

11-3 Long-Run Equilibrium Price and Output

11-4 Multiplant Monopolist

11-5 Price Discrimination

11-6 Applications

Examples

11-1 Barriers to Entry and Monopoly in Aluminum Production

11-2 The Market Value of Monopoly Profits

11-3 The Social Cost of Monopoly in the United States

11-4 Price Discrimination in the Pricing of Electricity

Applications

Application 1: Per-Unit Tax: Perfect Competition and Monopoly Compared

Application 2: Regulating Monopoly Price

Application 3: Regulation of Natural Monopolies

Application 4: Price Discrimination and the Existence of the Industry

Application 5: Conflict Between Publishers and Authors

Preview Questions

What is monopoly?

What is the shape of the demand curve facing a monopolist?

Will a monopolist always earn profits in the short run?

Can we derive a monopolist's supply curve from its marginal cost curve?

Will a monopolist earn profits in the long run?

Will a monopolist produce at the lowest point on its long-run average cost curve?

How should a monopolist allocate production among various plants?

How can a monopolist increase total profits by price discrimination?

How can the government regulate monopoly?

In this chapter we bring together the theory of consumer behavior and demand (from Part II) and the theory of production and costs (from Part III) to analyze how price and output are determined under pure monopoly. Monopoly is the opposite extreme from perfect competition in the spectrum or range of market organizations. The monopoly model is useful to analyze cases that approximate monopoly, and it provides insights into the operation of other imperfectly competitive markets (i.e., monopolistic competition and oligopoly).

The chapter begins by defining pure monopoly, examining the sources of monopoly, and defining the demand curve facing a monopolist. It then goes on to examine the determination of price and output in the short run and in the long run, and comparing the long-run equilibrium of the monopolist with that of a perfectly competitive firm and industry. Subsequently, we extend the monopoly model to examine how a monopolist (1) should allocate production among its various plants to minimize production costs and (2) can increase total profits by charging different prices for different quantities and in different markets. Finally, we present many important applications of the pure monopoly model. As in previous chapters, these applications, together with the several real-world examples presented in the theory sections, highlight the importance and relevance of the analytical tools developed in the chapter.

335

11-1

Pure Monopoly

In this section, we first define the meaning of pure monopoly and examine the sources of monopoly power, and then examine the shape of the demand and marginal revenue curves facing the monopolist, and compare them to those of a perfectly competitive firm.

11-1a Definition and Sources of Monopoly

Pure monopoly is the form of market organization in which a *single firm* sells a commodity for which there are *no close substitutes*. Thus, the monopolist represents the industry and faces the industry's negatively sloped demand curve for the commodity. As opposed to a perfectly competitive firm, a monopolist can earn profits in the long run because *entry into the industry is blocked* or very difficult. Thus, monopoly is at the opposite extreme from perfect competition in the spectrum or range of market organizations. While the perfect competitor is a price taker and has no control over the price of the commodity it sells, the monopolist has complete control over price.

Monopoly can arise from several causes. *First*, a firm may own or control the entire supply of a raw material required in the production of a commodity, or the firm may possess some unique managerial talent. For example, until World War II, the Aluminum Company of America (Alcoa) controlled practically the entire supply of bauxite (the basic raw material necessary for the production of aluminum) and had almost a complete monopoly in the production of aluminum in the United States (see Example 11-1).

Second, a firm may own a patent for the exclusive right to produce a commodity or to use a particular production process. Patents are granted by the government for 17 years as an incentive to inventors.[1] It is argued that if an invention could be copied freely (thus leaving little, if any, reward for the inventor), the flow of inventions and technical progress would be greatly reduced. Examples of monopolies based on patents in the postwar period are the Xerox corporation for copying machines and Polaroid for instant cameras. An alternative to patents might be for the government to financially reward the inventor directly and allow inventions to be freely used. However, it is often difficult to determine the value of an invention: government archives are full of patents that found no commercial use.

Third, economies of scale may operate (i.e., the long-run average cost

---

[1] As opposed to copyrights, patents are not renewable. Improvement patents are available, however.

curve may fall) over a sufficiently large range of outputs as to leave a single firm supplying the entire market. Such a firm is called a **natural monopoly.** Examples of natural monopolies are public utilities (electrical, water, gas, telephone, and transportation companies).[2] To have more than one firm supplying electricity, water, gas, telephone, and transportation services in a given market would lead to overlapping distribution systems and much higher per-unit costs. In cases such as these, the government usually allows a single firm to operate in the market subject to some form of government regulation. For example, electricity rates are set so as to leave the local electrical company only a "normal rate of return" (say 10 per cent) in its investment (see Application 3).

Fourth, some monopolies are created by government franchise itself. An example of this is the post office (which many believe is *not* a natural monopoly). In addition, licenses are often required by local governments to start a radio or television station, to open a liquor store, to operate a taxi, to be a plumber, a barber, a funeral director, and so on. The purpose of these licenses is to ensure minimum standards of competency. Nevertheless, since the number of licenses issued (e.g., the number of taxi medallions issued in most metropolitan areas) is often restricted by the regulatory agency, licenses also protect present license holders from *new* competition (i.e., confer monopoly power to them as a group). In most cases, local governments turn the regulatory function (such as the issuance of licenses) over to the professional association involved. Examples are the medical and bar associations.

Aside from the few cases mentioned above and for public utilities, pure monopoly is rare in the United States today and attempts to monopolize the market is forbidden by our antitrust laws.[3] Nevertheless, the pure monopoly model is very useful to analyze situations that approach pure monopoly and for other types of imperfectly competitive markets (i.e., monopolistic competition and oligopoly).

Also, a monopolist does not have unlimited market power but faces many forms of direct and indirect competition. On a general level, a monopolist competes for the consumers' dollars with the sellers of all other commodities in the market. Furthermore, while *close* substitutes do not exist for the particular commodity supplied by the monopolist, imperfect substitutes are likely to exist. For example, while duPont was the only producer of cellophane in the late 1940s (see Application 5 in Chapter 5), duPont faced a great deal of competition from the producers of all other

---

[2] In view of the recent divestiture and restructuring of AT&T, only local telephone companies are natural monopolies. Electrical, water, gas, local telephone, and companies providing transportation services are organized as public utilities because they are natural monopolies.

[3] It should be noted that "monopoly" per se is not illegal; only "monopolizing" or "attempting to monopolize the market" are illegal under U.S. antitrust laws (Section 2, Sherman Antitrust Act, 1890).

flexible plastic materials (waxed paper, aluminum foil, and so on). Finally, the market power of the monopolist (or the would-be monopolist) is sharply curtailed by fear of government antitrust prosecution and by the threat of potential competitors.

Example 11-1 Barriers to Entry and Monopoly in Aluminum Production

The Facts: The Aluminum Company of America (Alcoa) provides a classic example of how a monopoly was created and maintained for almost 50 years. The monopoly was created in the late nineteenth century when Alcoa acquired a patent on the method to remove oxygen from bauxite to obtain aluminum. This patent expired in 1906, but in 1903, Alcoa had patented another more efficient method to produce aluminum. This patent expired in 1909. By that time, Alcoa had signed long-term contracts with producers of bauxite prohibiting them from selling bauxite to any other American firm. At the same time, Alcoa entered into agreements with foreign producers of aluminum not to export aluminum into each other's market. Alcoa even went as far as purchasing electricity only from those power companies that agreed not to sell energy for the production of aluminum to any other firm. In 1912, the courts invalidated all of these contracts and agreements. Nevertheless, Alcoa retained monopoly power by always expanding productive capacity in anticipation of any increase in demand and by pricing aluminum in such a way as to discourage new entrants. The monopoly was finally broken after World War II, when Alcoa was not allowed to purchase government-financed aluminum plants built during the war. This is how Reynolds and Kaiser aluminum came into existence.

Comment: An association of all the producers of a commodity can also operate as a monopoly. This is known as a cartel (discussed in Chapter 13). For example, South Africa produces 80 per cent of the world's uncut diamonds (the remainder coming from the Soviet Union) and mine owners use de Beers as their sole export agent. De Beers restricts the quantity of diamonds it puts on the world market, thus keeping diamond prices high. Another cartel, which was highly successful from the fall of 1973 to the early 1980s, is OPEC (the Organization of Petroleum Exporting Countries). While monopolistic behavior (such as price fixing) are illegal under our antitrust laws, "tacit collusion" or implicit cooperation among the producers of a commodity is difficult to eradicate (see Chapter 13).

Sources: R. Lanzilotti, "The Aluminum Industry," in W. Adams, Ed., *The Structure of American Industry* (New York: Macmillan, 1961); and "How de Beers Dominates the Diamonds," *The Economist*, February 23, 1980, pp. 101–102.

11-1b The Monopolist's Demand Curve

Since a monopolist is the sole seller of a commodity for which there are no close substitutes, the monopolist faces the negatively sloped industry demand curve for the commodity. That is, while the perfectly competitive firm is a price taker and faces a demand curve that is horizontal or infinitely elastic at the price determined by the intersection of the industry or market demand and supply curves for the commodity, the monopolist *is* the industry and, thus, it faces the negatively sloped industry demand curve for the commodity. This means that in order to sell more units of the commodity, the monopolist must lower the commodity price. As a result, marginal revenue (defined as the change in total revenue per-unit change in the quantity sold) is smaller than price, and the monopolist's marginal revenue curve lies below his demand curve (see Section 5-5).[4] This is shown in Table 11-1 and Figure 11-1.

The first two columns of Table 11-1 give a hypothetical market demand schedule for the commodity faced by a monopolist. Note that in order to sell more of the commodity, the monopolist must lower the commodity price. Price times quantity gives total revenue (the third column of the table). The change in total revenue per-unit change in the quantity of the commodity sold gives the marginal revenue (the fourth column). For example, at $P = \$8$, the monopolist sells one unit of the commodity, so $TR = \$8$. To sell 2 units of the commodity, the monopolist must lower price to $7 on both units of the commodity. TR is then $14. The change in TR resulting from selling the additional unit of the commodity is then $MR = \$14 - \$8 = \$6$. This equals the price of $7 for the second unit of commodity sold minus the $1 reduction in price (from $8 to $7) on the first unit (since to sell two units of the commodity, the monopolist must lower the price of the commodity to $7 for both units).

The information contained in Table 11-1 is plotted in Figure 11-1. Since MR is defined as the change in TR per-unit change in Q, the MR revenue values are plotted at the midpoint of each quantity interval. Note that the MR curve starts at the same point on the vertical axis as the demand curve and at every point bisects (i.e., cuts in half) the distance between D and the vertical or price axis.[5] The MR is positive when D is elastic (i.e., in the top segment of the demand curve) because an increase in Q increases TR. $MR = 0$ when D is unitary elastic (i.e., at the geometric midpoint of D) because an increase in Q leaves TR unchanged (at its maximum level). MR is negative when D is inelastic (i.e., the bottom segment of D) because an increase in Q reduces TR (see Figure 11-1 and Section 5-5).

This is to be contrasted with the case of a perfectly competitive firm

---

[4] At this point, the student should review the material in Section 5-5.

[5] This is true only when, as in this case, the demand curve that the monopolist faces is a negatively sloped straight line.

TABLE 11-1 Hypothetical Demand, Total Revenue, and Marginal Revenue Faced by a Monopolist

P	Q	TR	MR
$9	0	$ 0	. . .
8	1	8	$ 8
7	2	14	6
6	3	18	4
5	4	20	2
4	5	20	0
3	6	18	−2
2	7	14	−4
1	8	8	−6
0	9	0	−8

(examined in Chapter 10), which faced a horizontal or infinitely elastic demand curve for the commodity at the price determined at the intersection of the market demand and supply curves for the commodity. Since the perfect competitor is a price taker and can sell any quantity of the commodity at the given price, price equals marginal revenue, and the demand and marginal revenue curves are horizontal and coincide.

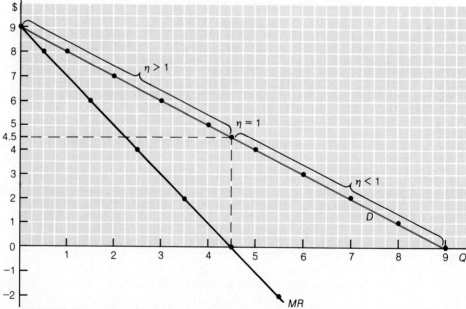

FIGURE 11-1. Hypothetical Demand and Marginal Revenue Curves of a Monopolist

Since D is negatively sloped, MR is lower than P. The MR values are plotted at the midpoint of each quantity interval. The MR curve starts at the same point as the D curve and at every point bisects the distance between D and the vertical axis. MR is positive when D is elastic. MR = 0 when D is unitary elastic and TR is maximum. MR is negative when D is inelastic.

The relationship between price, marginal revenue, and elasticity (η) can be examined with Formula (5-6) introduced in Section 5-5:

$$MR = P(1 - 1/\eta) \tag{5-6}$$

Using the formula, we see that since $\eta = \infty$ for the perfect competitor, $MR = P$ always. That is, $MR = P(1 - 1/\infty) = P(1 - 0) = P$. Since $\eta < \infty$ (i.e., since the demand curve is not infinitely elastic) for the monopolist, $MR < P$. That is, for any value of η smaller than infinity, MR will be smaller than P, and the MR curve will be below the market demand curve. Furthermore, we can see from the formula that when $\eta = 1$, $MR = 0$; when $\eta > 1$, $MR > 0$; and when $\eta < 1$, $MR < 0$. Since $MR < 0$ when $\eta < 1$, the monopolist can increase its TR by selling a *smaller* qunatity of the commodity. Thus, the monopolist would never operate over the inelastic portion of the demand curve. By reducing output, the monopolist would increase total revenue, reduce total costs, and thus increase total profits.

11-2

Short-Run Equilibrium Price and Output

In this section we examine the determination of price and output by a monopolist in the short run. We will first do so with the total approach and then with the marginal approach. We will also show that a monopolist, like a perfect competitor, can incur losses in the short run. Finally, we will demonstrate that, unlike the case of the perfectly competitive firm, the monopolist's short-run supply curve cannot be derived from its short-run marginal cost curve.

11-2a Total Approach

As with the perfectly competitive firm, profit maximization provides the framework for the analysis of monopoly. The equilibrium price and output of a monopolist are the ones which maximize its total profits. Total profits equal total revenue minus total costs. Total revenue is given by price times quantity. The total costs of the monopolist are similar to those discussed in Chapter 8 and need not differ from those of the perfectly competitive firm (if the monopolist does not affect input prices). Thus, the basic difference between monopoly and perfect competition lies on the demand side rather than on the production or cost side.

Table 11-2 gives the total revenue (TR), the short-run total costs (STC), and the total profits of a monopolist in the short run at various levels of output.

The total revenue schedule is that of Table 11-1. As usual, a short-run total costs rise slowly at first and then more rapidly (when the law of

TABLE 11-2 Total Revenue, Short-Run Total Costs, and Total Profits

Q	P	TR	STC	Total Profits
0	$9	$ 0	$ 6	$ −6
1	8	8	10	−2
2	7	14	12	2
*3	6	18	13.50	4.50
4	5	20	19	1
5	4	20	30	−10
6	3	18	48	−30

*Output at which firm maximizes total profits.

diminishing returns begins to operate). The best or optimum level of output for the monopolist in the short run is where total profits are maximized. For the monopolist of Table 11-2, this is at 3 units of output per time period. At this level of output, the monopolist charges the price of $6 and earns the maximum total profit of $4.50 per time period.

The data of Table 11-2 are plotted in Figure 11-2. The top panel shows that, unlike the case of a perfectly competitive firm, the monopolist's TR curve is not a straight line, but has the shape of an inverted U. The reason is that the monopolist must lower the price to sell additional units of the commodity. The monopolist's STC faces upward or increases at an increasing rate past $Q = 2$ because of diminishing returns.

Total profits are maximized at $Q = 3$, where the positive difference between the TR and the STC curves is greatest ($4.50). This is the point where the TR and the STC curves are parallel (see the top panel) and the total profits curve reaches its highest point (see the bottom panel). Total profits are positive between $Q = 1.5$ and $Q = 4.1$ and negative at other output levels. At $Q = 0$, $TR = 0$, while $STC = 6. Thus, by going out of business, the monopolist would incur the total loss of $6, which equals its total fixed costs. Note that the monopolist maximizes total profits at an output level smaller than the one at which TR is maximum (i.e., at $Q = 3$ rather than at $Q = 4.1$—see Figure 11-2).

11-2b Marginal Approach

While the total approach to determine the equilibrium price and output of the monopolist is useful, the marginal approach is even more valuable and widely used. According to the marginal approach, a monopolist maximizes total profits by producing the level of output at which *marginal revenue equals marginal cost*. The difference between the commodity price and the monopolist's average total cost at the best or optimum level of output then gives the profit per unit. Profit per unit times output gives total profits. Thus, to be able to use the marginal approach and in order to determine

FIGURE 11-2.
Short-Run
Equilibrium of the
Monopolist: Total
Approach

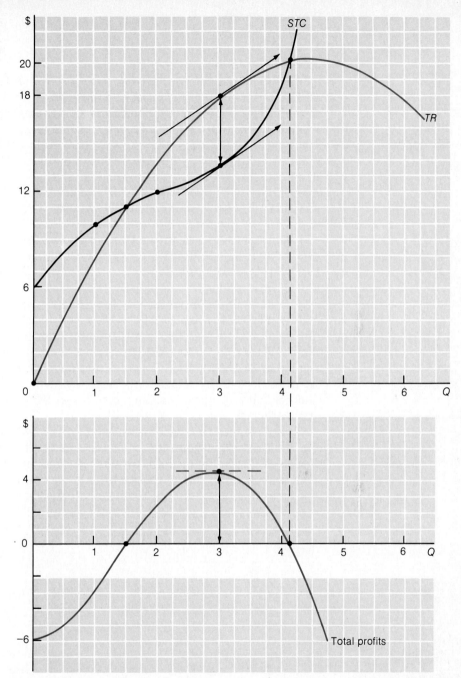

The monopolist's TR curve has the shape of an inverted U because the monopolist must lower the commodity price to sell additional units. The STC has the usual shape. Total profits are maximized at Q = 3, where the positive difference between TR and STC is greatest ($4.50). This is the point where the TR and the STC curves are parallel (see the top panel) and the total profit curve is highest (see the bottom panel). Total profits are positive between Q = 1.5 and Q = 4.1, and negative at other output levels. At Q = 0, total loss is $6 and equals total fixed costs.

the level of total profits, we must calculate the marginal cost and the average total cost of the monopolist.[6]

From the monopolist's short-run total cost schedule given in Table 11-2, we can derive the marginal cost and the average total cost schedules given in Table 11-3. Marginal cost equals the change in short-run total costs per-unit change in output. That is, $MC = \Delta STC/\Delta Q$. For example, at $Q = 1$, $STC = \$10$, while at $Q = 2$, $STC = \$12$. Therefore, $SMC = (\$12 - \$10)/1 = \$2$. The other SMC values in Table 11-3 are similarly obtained. On the other hand, average total costs equal short-run total costs divided by the level of output. That is, $ATC = STC/Q$. For example, at $Q = 1$, $STC = \$10$, and so $ATC = \$10/1 = \$10$. At $Q = 2$, $STC = \$12$, and so $ATC = \$12/2 = \$6$.

By plotting the monopolist's D and MR schedules of Table 11-1 and the MC and ATC schedules of Table 11-3 on the same set of axes, we get Figure 11-3. Note that MR and MC are plotted *between* the various levels of output, while D and ATC are plotted *at* the various output levels. In Figure 11-3, the best or optimum level of output of the monopolist is 3 units. This is given by point G, where $MR = MC$. At $Q = 3$, $P = \$6$ (point A on the demand curve), while $ATC = \$4.50$ (point B on the ATC curve). Thus, the monopolist earns $\$1.50$ (AB) per unit of output sold and $\$4.50$ in total (shaded area $ABCF$ in the figure). Note that at point G, the MC curve cuts the MR curve from below. This is always true for profit maximization, whether the MC curve is rising or falling at the point of intersection (see Application 3).

At outputs smaller than 3 units, MR exceeds MC (see the figure). Therefore, by expanding output, the monopolist would be adding more to TR than to STC, and total profits would rise. On the other hand, at outputs larger than 3 units, MC exceeds MR. A *reduction* in output would reduce STC more than TR and total profits would also rise. Thus, the monopolist

TABLE 11-3 Short-Run Total Cost, Marginal Cost, and Average Total Cost

Q	STC	MC	ATC
0	$ 6	. . .	. . .
1	10	$ 4	$10
2	12	2	6
3	13.50	1.50	4.50
4	19	4.50	4.75
5	30	11	6
6	48	18	8

[6] Since we already know the monopolist's MR (see Figure 11-1), all we need to calculate now is the monopolist's marginal cost in order to determine the best or profit-maximizing level of output. This is given at the point where $MR = MC$. The average total cost is only required to measure the monopolist's profit at the best level of output.

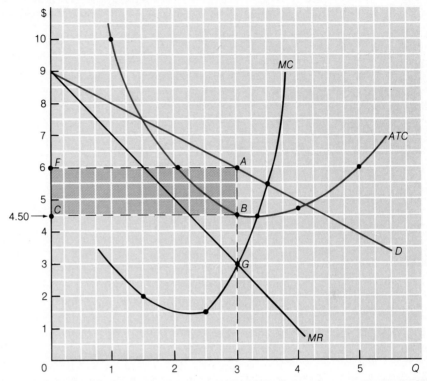

FIGURE 11-3.
Short-Run
Equilibrium of the
Monopolist:
Marginal Approach

The best or optimum level of output of the monopolist is 3 units. This is given by point G, where MR= MC (and the MC curve intersects the MR curve from below). At Q= 3, P= \$6 (point A on the demand curve), ATC = \$4.50 (point B on the ATC curve), and the monopolist earns \$1.50 (AB) per unit of output sold and \$4.50 in total (shaded area ABCF). At Q< 3, MR>MC and total profits rise by increasing Q. At Q> 3, MC> MR and total profits rise by reducing Q.

must produce where $MR = MC$ (in this case 3 units of output) in order to maximize total profits. This is the same result as obtained earlier by the total approach.

Table 11-4 summarizes the marginal approach numerically. Note that the MR and the MC values given in the table are read off Figure 11-3 at various output levels, just as P and ATC. For example, at $Q = 3$, $P = \$6$, $ATC = \$4.50$, and $MR = MC = \$3$. Table 11-4 shows that the monopolist maximizes total profits (equal to \$4.50) at $Q = 3$, where $MR = MC = \$3$ (as shown in Figure 11-3).

11-2c Profit Maximization or Loss Minimization

As for the perfect competitor, the monopolist can earn a profit, break even, or incur a loss in the short run. The monopolist will remain in business in the short run (minimizing losses) as long as price exceeds the average variable cost at the best or optimum level of output. Were the monopolist to

TABLE 11-4   Profit Maximization for the Monopolist: Marginal Approach

Q	P	ATC	Profit Per Unit	Total Profits	MR	MC	Relationship of MR to MC
1	$8	$10	$−2	$ −2	$ 7	$ 3 ⎫	MR > MC
2	7	6	1	2	5	1.50 ⎭	
*3	6	4.50	1.50	4.50	3	3	MR = MC
4	5	4.75	0.25	1	1	8 ⎫	MR < MC
5	4	6	−2	−10	−1	15 ⎭	

*Output at which firm maximizes total profits.

shut down, it would incur the higher loss equal to its total fixed costs (TFC).

To show this, assume that, for whatever reason, the monopolist's demand curve shifts down from its level in Figure 11-3 while its costs curves remain unchanged so that $ATC > P$ at the best level of output. The monopolist will now incur losses at the best level of output. To determine whether the monopolist will minimize losses by remaining in business, we now need to calculate the monopolist's average variable costs. Average variable costs (AVC) equal total variable costs (TVC) divided by output (Q). We can obtain the monopolist's total variable costs by subtracting its total fixed costs from its short-run *total* costs. That is, $TVC = STC − TFC$.

The monopolist's TVC and AVC are calculated in Table 11-5 from the STC of Tables 11-2 and 11-3. Specifically, since $STC = \$6$ at $Q = 0$ in Table 11-5, $TFC = \$6$. The TVC schedule is then obtained by subtracting TFC from STC at various output levels, and AVC is calculated by TVC/Q. For example, at $Q = 1$, $TVC = STC − TFC = \$10 − \$6 = \$4$ and $AVC = TVC/Q = \$4/1 = \$4$. At $Q = 2$, $TVC = \$12 − \$6 = \$6$ and $AVC = \$6/2 = \$3$. The other TVC and AVC values in Table 11-5 are calculated in a similar way.

In Figure 11-4, the MC and the ATC curves are those of Figure 11-3, and the AVC curve is obtained by plotting the AVC schedule given in Table 11-5. These per-unit *cost* curves are unchanged from Figure 11-3. The monopolist, however, now faces lower demand curve D' with marginal rev-

TABLE 11-5 Short-Run Total Cost, Total Variable Costs, and Average Variable Costs

Q	STC	TFC	TVC	AVC
0	$ 6	$6	$ 0	. . .
1	10	6	4	$4
2	12	6	6	3
3	13.50	6	7.50	2.50
4	19	6	13	3.25

FIGURE 11-4.
Profit Maximization
or Loss
Minimization

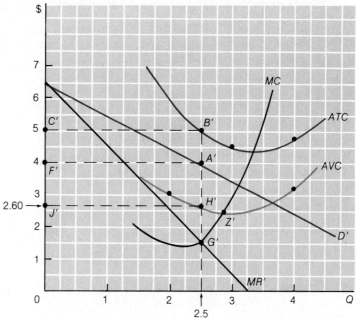

With D', the best or optimum level of output of the monopolist is Q= 2.5 (given by point G', where MR= MC and the MC curve intersects the MR curve from below). At Q= 2.5, ATC> P and the firm incurs a loss of $1 (B'A') per unit and $2.50 in total (the area of rectangle B'A'F'C'). If, however, the firm were to shut down, it would incur the greater loss of $6 equal to its total fixed costs (the area of rectangle B'H'J'C'). The shutdown point (Z') is at P= AVC.

enue curve MR'. The best or optimum level of output of the monopolist is now 2.5 units. This is given by point G', where MR' = MC (and the MC curve intersects the MR' curve from below in Figure 11-4). At Q = 2.5, P = $4 (point A' on demand curve D') and ATC = $5 (point B' on the ATC curve). Thus, the monopolist incurs a loss of $1 (B'A') per unit of output sold and $2.50 in total (the area of rectangle B'A'F'C').

At Q = 2.5, AVC = $2.60 (point H' on the AVC curve). Since price ($4) exceeds average variable costs ($2.60) at the best level of output (2.5 units), the monopolist covers $1.40 (A'H') of its fixed costs per unit and $3.50 (the area of rectangle A'H'J'F') of its total fixed costs. If the monopolist were to shut down, it would incur the greater loss of $6 (its total fixed costs, given by the area of rectangle B'H'J'C'). Only if P were smaller than AVC at the best level of output would the monopolist minimize total losses by going out of business (and incurring a loss equal only to its total fixed costs). At P = AVC, the monopolist would be indifferent between producing or going out of business because in either case it would incur a loss equal to its total fixed costs. Thus, the point where P = AVC (point Z' in the figure) is the monopolist's shutdown point.

11-2d Short-Run Marginal Cost and Supply

While the rising portion of the marginal cost curve over the average variable cost curve (the shutdown point) is a perfect competitor's short-run supply curve (when input prices are constant), this is not the case for the monopolist. The reason is that the monopolist could supply the same quantity of a commodity at different prices depending on the price elasticity of demand. Thus, for the monopolist there is no unique relationship between price and quantity supplied, or no supply curve.

This is shown in Figure 11-5, where *D* is the original demand curve and *D″* is an *alternative* and less elastic demand curve facing the monopolist. In the figure, *MR* is the marginal revenue curve for demand curve *D*, while

FIGURE 11-5.
Short-Run Marginal
Cost and Supply

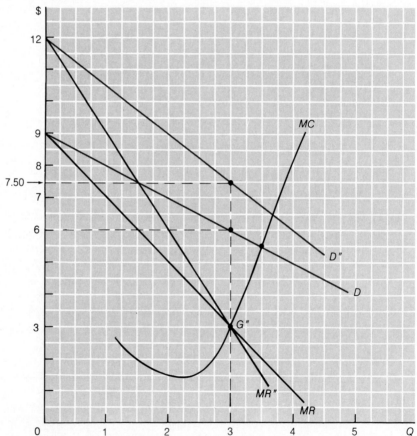

D is the original demand curve and D″ is an alternative and less elastic demand curve facing the monopolist. Since the MC curve intersects the MR and MR″ curves from below at point G″, the best level of output is 3 units whether the monopolist faces D or D″. However, with D, the monopolist charges P = $6, while with D″, it would charge P = $7.50. Thus, under monopoly, there is no unique relationship between price and output (i.e., the supply curve is undefined).

MR'' is the marginal revenue curve for demand curve D''. Since the MC curve intersects the MR and MR'' curves from below at the same point (point G''), the best level of output is 3 units whether the monopolist faces D or D''. However, with D, the monopolist would sell the 3 units of output at $P = \$6$ (as in Figure 11-3), while with D'', the monopolist would sell the 3 units of output at $P = \$7.50$ (see Figure 11-5). Thus, the same quantity (i.e., $Q = 3$) can be supplied at two different prices (i.e., at $P = \$6$ or $P = \$7.50$) depending on the price elasticity of demand (i.e., depending on whether the monopolist faced demand curve D or D''). Therefore, under monopoly, costs are related to the quantity supplied of the commodity, but there is no unique relationship between price and output (i.e., we cannot derive the monopolist's supply curve from its MC curve). Note that the monopolist would charge a higher price if he faces the less elastic demand curve (i.e., D'').

11-3

Long-Run Equilibrium Price and Output

In this section, we analyze the behavior of the monopolist in the long run and compare it with the behavior of a perfectly competitive firm and industry. We will also measure the welfare costs of monopoly.

11-3a Profit Maximization in the Long Run

In the long run, all inputs are variable and the monopolist can build the most efficient plant to produce the best level of output. The best or profit-maximizing level of output is given by the point where the monopolist's *long-run marginal cost* curve intersects the marginal revenue curve from below. The most efficient plant is the one that allows the monopolist to produce the best level of output at the lowest possible cost. This is the plant represented by the $SATC$ curve tangent to the LAC curve at the best level of output. As before, we assume that the monopolist does not affect input prices.

Figure 11-6 shows that the monopolist maximizes profits in the long run by producing $Q = 4$; this is given by point M, where the LMC curve intersects the MR curve from below. The monopolist should build plant $SATC_2$ and operate it at point N with $SATC = \$3.5$. Plant $SATC_2$ is the most efficient plant (i.e., the one that allows the monopolist to produce $Q = 4$ at the lowest $SATC$). In the long run, the monopolist will charge $P = \$5$ (point R), and earn a profit of $\$1.50$ (RN) per unit and $\$6$ in total (as opposed to $\$4.50$ in the short run).

While profits will attract additional firms into the perfectly competitive industry until all firms just break even in the long run, the monopolist can continue to earn profits in the long run because of blocked entry. However,

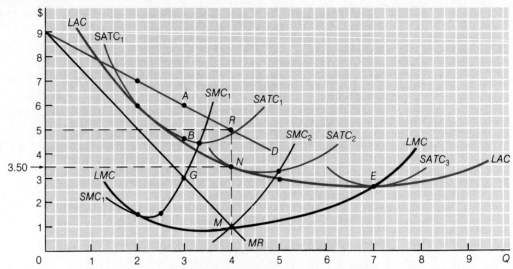

FIGURE 11-6. Long-Run Equilibrium of the Monopolist

In the long run, the monopolist maximizes profits by producing at point M(Q = 4), where the LMC curve intersects the MR curve from below. The monopolist should build plant $SATC_2$ and operate it at point N at SATC = \$3.50. The monopolist will earn a profit of \$1.50 (RN) per unit and \$6 in total (as opposed to \$4.50 in the short run).

the value of these long-run profits will be capitalized into the market value of the firm. Thus, it is the original owner of the monopoly that directly benefits from the monopoly power. A purchaser of the firm would have to pay a price that reflected the present (discounted) value of the monopoly profits, and so he would only break even in the long run. That is, monopoly profits become part of the opportunity costs of the original monopolist (see Example 11-2).

Note also that the monopolist, as opposed to a perfectly competitive firm, does not produce at the lowest point on its *LAC* curve (see Figure 11-6). Only if the monopolist's *MR* curve happened to go through the lowest point on its *LAC* would this be the case (see Problem 7). Furthermore, a monopolist may earn long-run profits. Thus, as compared with a perfectly competitive firm when the industry is in long-run equilibrium (see Section 10-5b), monopoly is inefficient because the monopolist is not likely to produce at the lowest point on its *LAC* curve and consumers are likely to pay a price that also usually includes a profit margin. These social costs of monopoly are measured in Section 11-3b for a perfectly competitive industry that faces constant returns to scale and is subsequently monopolized.

Example 11-2   The Market Value of Monopoly Profits

The Facts: In order to operate a taxicab in most municipalities (cities) in the United States, a "medallion" or license is needed. Municipalities are not issuing any more medallions, thus conferring monopoly power (the ability to earn economic profits) on the original medallion owners. The value of owning a medallion is given by the present (discounted) value of the future stream of earnings resulting from the ownership rights to the monopoly. This process is called *capitalization*. For example, the purchase price of a medallion in New York City was about $84,000 in 1985 (when there were 11,787 medallions). The price of a medallion was lower in other American cities to reflect the lower earning power of the medallion in other cities. Similarly, the price of a seat on the New York Stock Exchange (giving the right to purchase and sell stock on the Exchange) reached $625,000 in 1929, reflecting the very large trading activity and brokerage profits just before the market crashed in October of that year. The price of a "seat" was $49,000 in 1945, $135,000 in 1960, $130,000 in 1970, $225,000 in 1980, and $375,000 in 1984, as trading activity and brokerage profits surged in 1984.

Comment: The monopoly power of taxicab license owners arose because of government restrictions on the number of licenses issued. Were municipalities to freely grant a license to the asking, the price of the license would drop to zero. Similarly, if any one could freely trade on the New York Stock Exchange, a seat would have zero price. Note also that only the original owner benefits from the monopoly rights. A buyer of the rights would have to pay a price that fully reflected the future stream of earnings from the monopoly power, and so the buyer would only break even in the long run. The only way to prevent windfall gains to the original owners of the monopoly rights is for the government to auction off the licenses when they are first issued.

Sources: D. Adelman, "New York's Taxi Industry Thriving on Some Controversial Economics," *The New York Times*, March 13, 1980, pp. A1, B8. The price of the medallion in 1985 was provided by the Taxi and Limousine Commission. *The New York Stock Exchange Fact Book* (New York: The New York Stock Exchange, 1976), pp. 58, 82. The average price of a seat for 1980 and 1984 was obtained from the *The Stock Exchange Weekly*.

11-3b Comparison with Perfect Competition: The Social Cost of Monopoly

In order to measure the long-run social cost of monopoly, we assume that a perfectly competitive industry operating under constant returns to scale is suddenly monopolized and the market demand and cost curves remain unchanged. We will see that in that case output will be smaller and price will be higher than under perfect competition. In addition, there will be a redistribution of income from consumers to the monopolist and a welfare loss due to less efficient resource use. These are shown in Figure 11-7.

In Figure 11-7, *D* is the perfectly competitive industry market demand curve and *LS* is the perfectly competitive industry long-run supply curve

FIGURE 11-7.
The Social Cost of
Monopoly

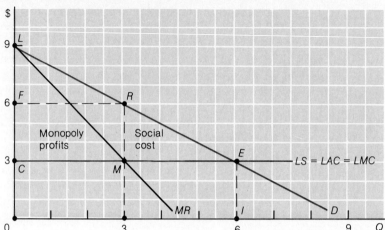

With perfect competition, D is the market demand curve and LS is the supply curve
under constant costs. Equilibrium is at point E, where D intersects LS, and Q = 6
and P = $3. When the perfectly competitive industry is monopolized, the LS curve
becomes the monopolist's LAC and LMC curve. Equilibrium is at point M, where MR
= LMC. At point M, Q = 3, P = $6, total profits are RMCF, and REM is the social
cost to society due to the less efficient resource use under monopoly.

under constant costs. The long-run perfectly competitive equilibrium is at
point E, where D intersects LS. At point E, Q = 6 and P = $3. Consumers
collectively would be willing to pay LEIO ($36) for 6 units of the commod-
ity, but need only pay EIOC ($18). Thus, the consumers' surplus is LEC or
$18 (see Application 2 in Chapter 4).

   When the perfectly competitive industry is monopolized, the LS curve
becomes the monopolist's LAC and LMC curves (the monopolist would
simply operate the plants of the previously perfectly competitive firms).[7]
The best level of output for the monopolist in the long run is then given by
point M, where MR = LMC. Thus, with monopoly, Q = 3, P = $6, and the
monopolist will earn total profits equal to RMCF ($9). The consumers' sur-
plus is now only LRF ($4.50), down from LEC ($18) under perfect competition. Of the RECF ($13.50) reduction in the consumers' surplus, RMCF
($9) represents a redistribution of income from consumers to the monopo-
list in the form of profits and REM ($4.50) is the social cost to society due
to the less efficient resource use under monopoly.

   Specifically, monopoly profits are not a net loss to society as a whole

---

   [7] Specifically, a perfectly-competitive, constant-cost industry in long-run equilibrium has
a horizontal LS curve at the minimum LAC of the individual firms (see Figure 10-10). A
monopolist taking over the industry could change output by changing the number of plants
previously operated by the independent firms at minimum LAC (where LAC = LMC). Thus,
the horizontal LS supply curve of the competitive industry is the LAC and LMC curves of the
monopolized industry. They show the constant LAC and LMC at which the monopolist can
change output.

since they represent simply a redistribution of income from consumers of the commodity to the monopolist producer. This redistribution is "bad" only to the extent that society "values" the welfare of consumers more than that of the monopolist. As we will see later, all of the monopolist's profits could be taxed away and redistributed to consumers of the commodity. On the other hand, the area of welfare triangle *REM* represents a true welfare or deadweight loss to society as a whole, which is inherent to monopoly and which society cannot avoid under monopoly. We now want to examine exactly how this welfare loss arises.

Welfare triangle *REM* arises because the monopolist artificially restricts the output of the commodity so that some resources flow into the production of other commodities society values less. Specifically, consumers pay $P = \$6$ for the third unit of the commodity produced by the monopolist. This is a measure of the social value of this unit of the commodity to consumers. The marginal cost (*MC*) to produce this unit of the commodity, however, is only $3. This means that society foregoes one unit of the monopolized commodity valued at $6 for a unit of another commodity valued at $3. Thus, some of society's resources are used to produce less valuable commodities under monopoly. Since under perfect competition, production takes place at point *E*, where $P = LMC$ (see Figure 11-7), welfare triangle *REM* represents the social cost or welfare loss from the less efficient use of society's resources under monopoly.

Example 11-3 The Social Cost of Monopoly in the United States

The Facts: In 1954, Harberger measured the area of the welfare triangle (*REM* in Figure 11-7) in each manufacturing industry in the United States on the assumption that the marginal cost was constant and that the price elasticity of the demand curve was 1. He found that the total social cost of monopoly was only about one tenth of 1 per cent of gross national product (*GNP*). With some refinements of the estimating method, Scherer found that the social welfare loss from monopoly was between 0.5 per cent and 2 per cent of *GNP*, and most likely to be about 1 per cent. The reason for these relatively low estimates is that there are few firms in the American economy which earn huge profits. In fact, Siegfried and Tiemann found that 44 per cent of the total welfare loss due to monopoly power in the United States in 1963 came from the auto industry; the remainder of the loss was mostly due to a few other industries such as petroleum refining, plastics, and drugs.

Comment: There are other losses resulting from monopoly power that are not included in the above measure. One is that, in the absence of competition, monopolists do not keep their costs as low as possible. Another is that monopolists waste a lot of resources (from society's point of view) lobbying, engaging in legal battles, and in advertising in the attempt to create and retain the monopoly power, and to avoid antitrust prosecution. These

353

are sometimes referred to as the social costs of "rent seeking." In fact, some economists believe that these other social costs of monopoly are larger than those measured by the welfare triangle. The charge that monopolists suppress inventions (for example, the introduction of a longer-lasting light bulb that costs the same to produce) is not correct, however. It is true that consumers would purchase fewer such light bulbs, but they would also be willing to pay a higher price for them, and this can lead to higher profits for the monopolist. The monopolist would then have an incentive to introduce rather than to suppress the invention. Only when the monopolist is not successful in patenting an invention that would lead to a loss of monopoly power should the monopolist seek to suppress the invention. The real issue here, however, is whether perfect competition would lead to more inventions than monopoly (see Application 5 in Chapter 18).

Source: A. Harberger, "Monopoly and Resource Allocation," *American Economic Review,* May 1954. F. Scherer, *Industrial Market Structure and Economic Performance* (Chicago: Rand McNally, 1980). J. Siegfried and T. Tiemann, "The Welfare Cost of Monopoly: An Interindustry Analysis," *Economic Inquiry,* June 1974. For the social costs of rent seeking, see W. Rogerson, "The Social Costs of Monopoly and Regulation: A Game-Theoretic Analysis," *Bell Journal of Economics* (now *The Random Journal of Economics*), Autumn 1982.

11-4

Multiplant Monopolist

So far, the discussion has been based on the implicit assumption that the monopolist operated a single plant. This is not always or even usually the case. In this section, we examine how a multiplant monopolist should distribute its best level of output among its various plants, both in the short run and in the long run, in order to minimize its costs of production and maximize profits.

11-4a Short-Run Equilibrium

A multiplant monopolist will minimize the total cost of producing the best level of output in the short run when the marginal cost of the last unit of the commodity produced in each plant is equal to the marginal revenue from selling the combined output. This is shown in Figure 11-8, which refers to a two-plant monopolist.

The left and center panels of Figure 11-8 show the SMC curve of each of the two plants operated by the monopolist. The *horizontal* summation of SMC_1 and SMC_2 yields ΣSMC in the right panel. The ΣSMC curve shows the monopolist's minimum SMC of producing each additional unit of the

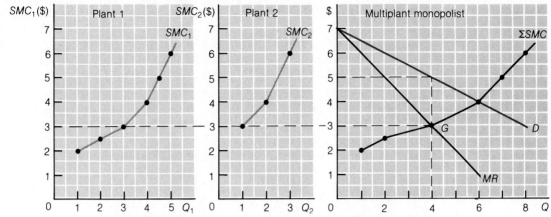

FIGURE 11-8. Short-Run Equilibrium of the Multiplant Monopolist

The SMC curve of each of two plants of a monopolist are SMC_1 and SMC_2 in the left and center panel, respectively. The horizontal summation of SMC_1 and SMC_2 yields ΣSMC in the right panel. ΣSMC shows the monopolist's minimum SMC of producing each additional unit of the commodity. The best level of output is $Q = 4$, given by point G, where the ΣSMC curve intersects the MR curve from below. To minimize STC, the monopolist should produce 3 units of the commodity in plant 1 and 1 unit in plant 2 so that $SMC_1 = SMC_2 = \Sigma SMC = MR = \$3$.

commodity. Thus, the monopolist should produce the first and second unit of the commodity in plant 1 (at a SMC of $2 and $2.50, respectively), the third and fourth unit in plant 1 and plant 2 (one unit in each plant, at SMC = $3), and so on.

If the monopolist were to produce all four units of the commodity in plant 1, it would incur a SMC = $4 for the fourth unit (instead of a SMC = $3 with plant 2). Thus, the monopolist should produce three units of the commodity in plant 1 and one unit in plant 2. By adding the three units of the commodity produced in plant 1 and the one unit produced in plant 2, we get point G on the ΣSMC curve in the right panel of Figure 11-8. Thus, the ΣSMC curve in the right panel is obtained from the horizontal summation of the SMC_1 and SMC_2 curves in the left and center panel, respectively. The ΣSMC shows the monopolist's minimum SMC of producing each additional unit of the commodity.

The best level of output of this monopolist is 4 units of the commodity and is given by point G, where the ΣSMC curve intersects the MR curve from below. The monopolist should produce 3 units of the commodity in plant 1 and 1 unit of the commodity in plant 2 so that $SMC_1 = SMC_2 = \Sigma SMC = MR = \$3$ (see the figure). This minimizes the total cost of producing the best level of output of four units at $10.50 ($2 + $2.50 + $3 + $3) in the short run. If the monopolist were to produce all four units in plant 1, it would incur a STC = $11.50 ($2 + $2.50 + $3 + $4). The STC would be even higher if the monopolist produced all 4 units in plant 2 (see the center panel of the figure).

355

Whether the monopolist earns a profit, breaks even, or incurs a loss by producing 3 units of the commodity in plant 1 and 1 unit of the commodity in plant 2 depends on the value of the $SATC$ at $Q = 4$. Even if the monopolist were to incur a loss at its best level of output, it would stay in business in the short run as long as $P > AVC$ (see Section 11-2c).

11-4b Long-Run Equilibrium

In the long run, a monopolist can build as many identical plants of optimal size (i.e., plants whose $SATC$ curve from the lowest point of the LAC curve) as required to produce the best level of output. This is shown in Figure 11-9. The left panel shows one of the plants of the monopolist. The monopolist will operate this plant at point E', where $SATC_1 = SMC_1 = LAC_1 = LMC_1 = \$1$ and $Q = 3$. To produce larger outputs, the monopolist will build additional identical plants and run them at the optimal rate of output of $Q = 3$. If input prices remain constant, the LMC curve of the monopolist is horizontal at $LAC = LMC = \$1$ (see the right panel).

The best level of output of the monopolist in the long run is then given by point E, where $LMC = MR = \$1$ in the right panel. At point E, $Q = 6$, $P = \$4$, $LAC = \$1$, and the monopolist earns a profit of \$3 per unit and \$18 in total. The monopolist will produce 3 units of output in each of two identical plants (point E' in the left panel). If the best level of output is not a multiple of three, the monopolist will either have to run some plants at outputs greater than 3 units or build and run an extra plant at less than 3 units of output.

If input prices rise when the multiplant monopolist builds additional plants to increase output, then the LAC curve of each plant shifts up (as in Figure 10-11) and the LMC curve of the monopolist will be upward-sloping.

11-5

Price Discrimination

In this section we examine various types of price discrimination. **Price discrimination** refers to the charging of different prices, for different quantities of a commodity or in different markets, which are not justified by cost differences. By practicing price discrimination, the monopolist can increase its total revenue and profits. We will first examine the charging of different prices by the monopolist for different quantities sold, and then the charging of different prices in different markets.

11-5a Charging Different Prices for Different Quantities

If a monopolist could sell each unit of the commodity separately and charge the highest price each consumer would be willing to pay for the commod-

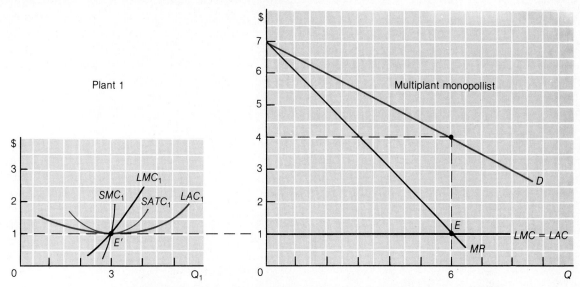

FIGURE 11-9. Long-Run Equilibrium of the Multiplant Monopolist
The left panel shows one of the plants of the monopolist. The monopolist will operate this plant at point E', where LAC₁ = LMC₁ = $1 and Q = 3. To produce larger outputs, the monopolist will build additional identical plants and run them at Q = 3. If input prices remain constant, the LMC curve of the monopolist is horizontal at LMC = $1 (see the right panel). The best level of output is at point E, where LMC = MR = $1. At point E, Q = 6, P = $4, LAC = $1, the monopolist earns a total profit $18, and operates two plants.

ity rather than go without it, the monopolist would be able to extract the entire consumers' surplus from consumers. This is called **first degree** or **perfect price discrimination.**

For example, in Figure 11-10, the consumer would be willing to pay *LRZO* ($22.50) for three units of the commodity. Since he or she only pays *RZOF* ($18), this consumer's surplus is *LRF* ($4.50). If the monopolist, however, charged $8.50 for the first unit (the highest price that this consumer would pay rather than forego entirely the consumption of the commodity), $7.50 for the second unit of the commodity, and $6.50 for the third unit, then the monopolist would receive $22.50 (the sum of the areas of the rectangles above the first three units of the commodity), thereby extracting the entire consumer's surplus from this consumer. The result would be the same if the monopolist made an all-or-nothing offer to the consumer either to purchase all three units of the commodity for $22.50 or none at all.

However, to be able to practice first degree price discrimination, the monopolist must know the exact shape of each consumer's demand curve and be able to charge the highest price that each and every consumer would pay for each unit of the commodity. Even if this were possible, it would probably be prohibitively expensive to carry out. Thus, first degree price discrimination is not very common in the real world.

357

FIGURE 11-10.
First and Second
Degree Price
Discrimination

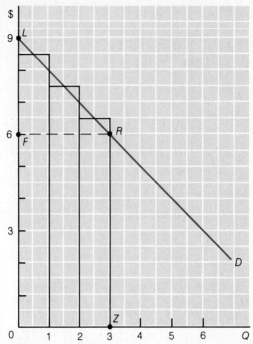

Since the consumer is willing to pay $22.50 for 3 units of the commodity, but only pays $18, this consumer's surplus is $4.50. If the monopolist charged $8.50 for the first unit, $7.50 for the second, and $6.50 for the third, it would receive $22.50, thus extracting the entire consumer's surplus. This is first degree price discrimination. If the monopolist set P = $7 for the first 2 units and P = $6 for additional units, he would sell 3 units and extract $2 of the consumer's surplus. This is second degree price discrimination.

More practical and common is **second degree** or **multipart price discrimination.** This refers to the charging of a uniform price per unit for a specific quantity of the commodity, a lower price per unit for an additional batch or block of the commodity, and so on. By doing so, the monopolist will be able to extract part, but not all, of the consumers' surplus. For example, in Figure 11-10, the monopolist could set the price of $7 per unit on the first 2 units of the commodity, and a price of $6 on additional units of the commodity. The monopolist would then sell 3 units of the commodity to this individual for $20 and extract $2 from the total consumer's surplus of $4.50. Second degree price discrimination is often practiced by public utilities such as electrical power companies (see Example 11-4).

11-5b Charging Different Prices in Different Markets

The charging of a different price in different markets is called **third degree price discrimination.** For simplicity, we will assume that there are only two markets. To maximize profits, the monopolist must produce the best level of output and sell that output in the two markets in such a way that the marginal revenue of the last unit sold in each market is the same. This will require the monopolist to sell the commodity at a higher price in the market with the less elastic demand.

In Figure 11-11, D_1 is the market demand curve in the first market (with MR_1 as the corresponding marginal revenue curve) and D_2 is the market demand curve in the second market (with corresponding MR_2 curve). By summing horizontally the MR_1 and MR_2 curves we get the ΣMR curve. We sum horizontally the MR_1 and the MR_2 curves because the monopolist obtains extra revenue from selling the commodity in both markets. Note that until $Q = 2.5$, the ΣMR curve coincides with the MR_1 curve. The best level of output for the monopolist is 7 units, given where the LMC curve intersects the MR curve from below. To maximize total profits the monop-

FIGURE 11-11.
Third Degree Price
Discrimination

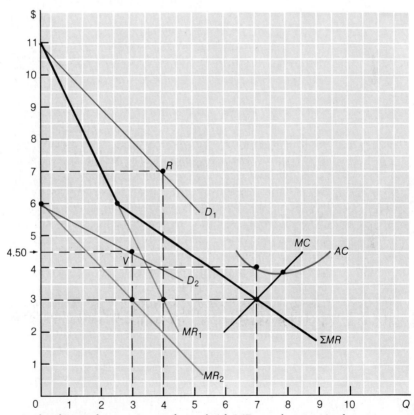

D_1 is the demand curve in market 1 (with MR_1 as the marginal revenue curve) and D_2 and MR_2 refer to market 2. By summing horizontally the MR_1 and MR_2 curves we get the ΣMR curve. The best level of output is 7 units, given where the LMC curve intersects the ΣMR curve from below. To maximize total profits the monopolist should sell $Q = 4$ at $P = \$7$ in market 1 and $Q = 3$ at $P = \$4.50$ in market 2, so that $MR_1 = MR_2 = LMC = \$3$. Note that the price is higher in market 1, where demand is less elastic. TR $= \$41.50$ ($\$28$ from market 1 and $\$13.50$ from market 2). With TC $= \$28$ (seven units at LAC $= \$4$), total profits are $\$13.50$.

olist should sell 4 units of the commodity in market 1 and the remaining 3 units in market 2 so that $MR_1 = MR_2 = \Sigma MR = LMC = \$3$ (see the figure). If the MR for the last unit of the commodity sold in one market were different from the MR of the last unit sold in the other market, the monopolist could increase his total revenue and profits by redistributing sales from the market with the lower MR to the market with the higher MR until $MR_1 = MR_2$.

The monopolist should charge $P = \$7$ for each of the 4 units of the commodity sold in market 1 (point R on D_1) and $P = \$4.50$ for each of the 3 units of the commodity in market 2 (point V on D_2). Note that the price is higher in market 1, where demand is less elastic. The total revenue of the monopolist would be $41.50 ($28 from selling 4 units of the commodity at $P = \$7$ in market 1 plus $13.50 from selling 3 units of the commodity at $P = \$4.50$ in market 2). With total costs of $28 (7 units at $LAC = \$4$), the monopolist earns a profit of $13.50 (the total revenue of $41.50 minus the total costs of $28). Any other output or distribution of sales between the two markets would lead to lower total profits for the monopolist. This type of analysis is valid for the long run as well as the short run.[8]

In order for a firm to be able to practice third degree price discrimination, three conditions must be met. First, the firm must have some monopoly power (i.e., the firm must not be a price taker). Second, the firm must be able to keep the two markets separate. Third, the price elasticity of demand for the commodity or service must be different in the two markets. All three conditions are met in the sale of electricity. For example, electrical power companies can set prices (subject to government regulation). The market for the industrial use of electricity is kept separate from that of household use by meters installed in each production plant and home. The price elasticity of demand for electricity for industrial use is higher than for household use because industrial users have better substitutes and more choices available (such as generating their own electricity) than households. Thus, electrical power companies usually charge lower prices to industrial users than to households.

Note that without market power the firm would be a price taker and could not practice any form of price discrimination. If the firm were unable to keep the markets separate, users in the lower-priced market could purchase more of the service than they needed and resell some of it in the higher-priced market (thus underselling the original supplier of the service). Finally, if the price elasticity of demand were the same in both markets, the best that the firm could do is to charge the same price in both markets.

---

[8] If the monopolist knows the price elasticity of demand for the commodity in the two markets, he can determine the price to charge in each market to maximize total profits by utilizing Formula (5-6). See Problem 10, with answer at the end of the book. For a mathematical presentation of price discrimination using rudimentary calculus, see Section A12 of the Mathematical Appendix.

There are many other examples of third degree price discrimination. Some of these are (1) the lower fees that doctors usually charge low-income people than high-income people for basically identical services; (2) the lower prices that airlines, trains, and cinemas usually charge children and the elderly than other adults; (3) the lower postal rates for third-class mail than for equally heavy first-class mail; (4) the lower prices that producers usually charge abroad than at home for the same commodity, and so on.

Third degree price discrimination is more likely to occur in service industries than in manufacturing industries because it is more difficult (often impossible) for a consumer to purchase a service in the low-price market and resell it at a higher price in the other market (thus undermining the monopolist's differential pricing in the two markets). For example, a low-income person could not possibly resell a doctor's visit at a higher fee to a high-income person. On the other hand, if an elderly person were charged a lower price for an automobile, he or she could certainly resell it at a higher price to other people. Note also that it is not clear that the charging of $0.95 for two bars of soap and $0.50 for one bar by a supermarket is price discrimination since the supermarket saves on clerks' time in marking the merchandise and on cashiers' time in ringing up customers' bills.

Example 11-4   Price Discrimination in the Pricing of Electricity

The Facts: Table 11-6 shows the price per KWH (kilowatt-hour) that Con Edison charged residential and commercial users for various quantities of electricity consumed in New York City in 1984 during winter and summer months. Since Con Edison charged different rates for different categories of customers (i.e., residential and commercial) and for different quantities of electricity purchased, it is clear that Con Edison practiced both second and third degree price discrimination.

TABLE 11-6   Electricity Rates (Cents per KWH)

	KWH	Cents/KWH	KWH	Cents/KWH
Residential Rates (Single Residence)				
Winter	0–250	13.28	Above 250	12.76
Summer	0–250	13.28	Above 250	14.76
Commercial Rates (Small Business)				
Winter	0–900	15.39	Above 900	14.28
Summer	0–900	16.89	Above 900	15.78
Commercial Rates (Large Business)				
Winter & Summer	0–15,000	17.30	Above 15,000	6.74

Source: Con Edison, New York City.

Comment: While some price differences are based on cost differences of supplying various quantities or blocks of electricity (quantity discounts) to residential and commercial users, other price differences reflect price discrimination. One type of price difference that is not price discrimination is *peak-load pricing.* This refers to the charging of higher prices during peak times (such as during summer months) to reflect the higher costs of generating electricity at peak times when older and less efficient equipment has to be brought into operation to meet peak demand. In short, price differences are discriminatory only if they are not based on cost differences.

11-6

Applications

In this section, we examine a number of important applications of the tools of analysis developed in this chapter. These include a comparison of the effect of a per-unit tax on a monopolist and on a perfect competitor, the regulation of monopoly price and natural monopolies, showing that some commodities could only be supplied with price discrimination, and the behind-the-scene conflict between publishers and authors. These applications serve to highlight the importance and relevance of the tools introduced in this chapter.

Application 1: Per-Unit Tax: Perfect Competition and Monopoly Compared

One additional way to compare monopoly with perfect competition is with respect to the incidence of a per-unit tax. A per-unit excise tax (such as on cigarettes, gasoline, and liquor) will be entirely on consumers if the industry is perfectly competitive and will fall only partly on consumers under monopoly, if both the monopolist and the perfectly competitive industry operate under constant costs.[9] For simplicity we assume that the perfectly competitive industry and the monopolist face the same demand and cost conditions. Thus, S in Figure 11-12 refers to the long-run supply curve of the perfectly competitive industry and to the $LAC = LMC$ curve of the monopolist under constant cost.

Before the imposition of the per-unit tax, the perfectly competitive industry operates at point E, where D and S intersect, so that $Q = 6$ and $P = \$3$. If a tax of \$2 per unit is imposed, S shifts up by \$2 to S'. The per-

---

[9] The fact that a per-unit excise tax falls entirely on consumers under perfect competition but falls only partly on consumers with monopoly does not mean, however, that monopoly is "better" than perfect competition. When all inefficiencies associated with monopoly are considered, perfect competition leads to a higher level of social welfare than monopoly. Furthermore, the incidence of a per-unit tax is entirely on consumers only if the perfectly competitive industry operates under constant cost.

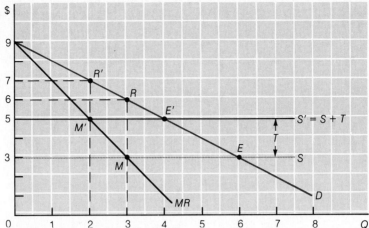

FIGURE 11-12.
Per-Unit Tax:
Perfect Competition
and Monopoly
Compared

Before the per-unit tax, the perfectly competitive industry operates at point E, where D and S intersect, so that Q= 6 and P= $3. With a $2 per unit tax, S shifts up to S', and Q= 4 and P= $5, so the tax falls entirely on consumers. Before the tax, the monopolist is in equilibrium at point M. Q= 3, P= $6, and the monopolist earns a profit of $3 (RM) per unit and $9 in total. With a tax of $2 per unit, Q= 2, P= $7, and half of the per-unit tax falls on the monopolist.

fectly competitive industry would then operate at point E', where D and S' intersect, so that Q = 4 and P = $5. Thus, when the industry is perfectly competitive and operates under constant costs, the entire amount of the per-unit tax ($2 in this case) falls on consumers in the form of higher prices (so that P = $5 instead of $3).

The case is different under monopoly. Before the imposition of the tax, the monopolist operates at point M, where MR and S (the LMC = LAC of the monopolist) intersect. Q = 3, P = $6 (point R), LAC = $3, and the monopolist earns a profit of $3 (RM) per unit and $9 in total. If the same tax of $2 per unit is imposed on the monopolist, S shifts up to S' (= LMC' = LMC + 2 = LAC' = LAC + 2). The monopolist would then operate at point M', where MR and S' intersect. At point M', Q = 2, P = $7 (point R'), LAC' = $5, and the monopolist earns $2 per unit (R'M') and $4 in total. Thus, with monopoly, the price to consumers rises by only $1 (one half of the per-unit tax). The remaining half of the tax falls on the monopolist, so that it now only earns a profit of $2, rather than $3, per unit. Note also that with the tax, the decline in output under monopoly is half that with perfect competition (i.e., output falls from 6 to 4 units with perfect competition, but only from 3 to 2 units under monopoly).

Application 2: Regulating Monopoly Price
One way for the government to regulate a monopoly is to set a price below the price that the monopolist would charge in the absence of regulation. This leads to a larger output and lower profits for the monopolist, as shown in Figure 11-13.

363

FIGURE 11-13.
Regulating
Monopoly Price

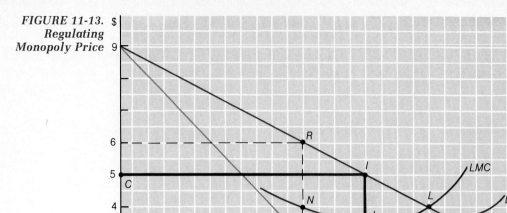

In the absence of regulation, Q = 3, P = $6, LAC = $4, and profits are $2 per unit
(RN) and $6 in total. If the government set the maximum price at P = $5, the demand
curve becomes CID and the MR curve is CIKW. Then, Q = 4, P = $5, LAC = $3.60,
and profits are $1.40 per unit (IJ), and $5.60 in total.

The figure shows that, in the absence of regulation, the best level of output of the monopolist is given by point M, where the LMC curve intersects the MR curve from below. Thus, $Q = 3$, $P = \$6$ (point R), $LAC = \$4$ (point N), and profits are \$2 per unit (RN) and \$6 in total.

If the government now set the maximum price that the monopolist could charge at $P = \$5$, the demand curve facing the monopolist would become CID (see the figure). Thus, the monopolist's demand curve would be horizontal until $Q = 4$ (since the monopolist cannot charge a price higher than \$5) and would resume its usual downward shape at $Q > 4$ (since the monopolist can charge prices lower than \$5). As a result, the monopolist's MR curve is also horizontal and coincides with the demand curve until point I, and resumes its usual downward shape when the demand curve does. That is, the monopolist's MR curve becomes $CIKW$. Note that the MR curve has a discontinuous (vertical) section at point I, where the demand curve has a kink.

With price set at $P = \$5$, the best level of output of the monopolist is given by point J', where $LMC = MR$. Thus, $Q = 4$, $P = \$5$ (point I), $LAC = \$3.60$ (point J), and profits are \$1.40 per unit and \$5.60 in total. Price is lower, output is larger, and the monopolist's profits are lower than without regulation.

If the government set the maximum price at point L, where the LMC curve intersects the D curve (so that $P = LMC = \$4$), the best level of output of the monopolist would be 5 units (see the figure). The monopolist would then earn a profit of $0.50 per unit and $2.50 in total. If the government, in an effort to eliminate all monopoly profits, were to set the lower price (about $3.50) given by point I, where the monopolist's LAC curve intersects the D curve, a shortage of the commodity (and a black market) would arise. This is because consumers would demand nearly 5.5 units of the commodity while the monopolist would only produce about 4.5 units (given by the point where $P = LMC$ at about $3.50 in the figure).

Application 3: Regulation of Natural Monopolies

As defined in Section 11-1, natural monopoly refers to the case where a single firm can most efficiently supply the entire market with a commodity or service. This arises when the LAC curve is declining at the point where it intersects the market demand curve. Examples of natural monopolies are public utilities (electrical, water, gas, local telephone, and transportation companies). In cases such as these, the government usually allows a single firm to operate but sets the maximum price that the firm can charge for the service. For example, electricity rates are usually set so as to leave the local electrical company only a "fair" or normal rate of return (say 10 per cent) on investment. This is shown in Figure 11-14.

In the absence of regulation, the monopolist of Figure 11-14 would produce at point M, where the LMC curve intersects the MR curve from below. At point M, $Q = 4$, $P = \$5$, $LAC = \$4.50$, and the monopolist would earn a profit of $0.50 per unit ($RN$) and $2 in total. Note that at point M' (i.e., at $Q = \frac{1}{2}$) the LMC curve intersects the MR curve *from above*, but this is not the best level of output since the firm would incur a large loss at that point (at $Q = \frac{1}{2}$, $LAC > P$; see the figure).

If the state regulatory commission set the price at $P = LAC = \$3.50$ (point H) for the service, the firm would break even (i.e., would earn only a normal return on its investment) in the long run. This, however, would result in a welfare loss *to society as a whole* since the price of the last unit of the commodity produced by the monopolist (i.e., the 5.5 unit) exceeds the LMC of producing that unit. That is, society pays a price for the last unit of the commodity that exceeds the LMC of producing it (see the figure). The welfare loss *to society* or social cost of setting $P = \$3.50$ at which $P = LAC$ is equal to $(0.5)(1.5)(1.5) = \$1.13$ (the area of shaded triangle $HJ'K$). The only way to avoid this *social loss* is for the commission to set $P = LMC = \$2$ (point J' in the figure). But that would result in a loss of $1 ($JJ'$) per unit and $7 in total *to the public utility company*. In that case, the public utility company would not supply the service in the long run without a

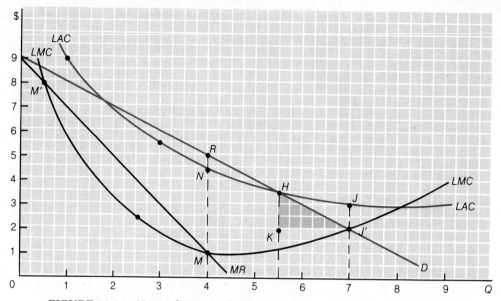

FIGURE 11-14. Natural Monopoly Regulation
*If the regulatory commission set P = LAC = $3.50 (point H), the firm will break even
in the long run. This, however, would result in a welfare loss to society or social cost
equal to $1.13 (the area of shaded triangle HJ'K), since only at point J' is P = LMC.
This could be avoided if the commission set P = LMC = $2. However, that would
result in a loss of $1 per unit and $7 in total for the firm, and the service would not
be supplied in the long run without a subsidy.*

subsidy. In general, regulatory commissions set $P = LAC$ (point H in the
figure), at which a public utility company breaks even.[10]

Another difficulty faced by regulatory commissions is to determine the
value of the plant or investment on which to allow a normal return. Should
it be the original cost of the investment or the replacement cost? More
often than not regulatory commissions decide on the former. Finally, regulatory commissions must be alert because usually regulated public utility
companies, having been guaranteed a normal rate of return *after all costs*
are included, have no incentive to keep costs down. For example, management may decide on salaries for themselves higher than their opportunity
cost, have luxurious offices, and large expense accounts. The firm will also
have a tendency to overinvest (i.e., to use too much capital and too little
labor), reduce the quality of service, and show little interest in the development and introduction of cost-saving technology.

Application 4: Price Discrimination and the Existence of the Industry
Sometimes price discrimination is necessary for an industry to exist. For

---

[10] Sometimes, regulators allow the public utility company to practice second degree price
discrimination or use multipart pricing of some kind (see Section 11-5a) to ensure that the
company's total revenue equals total costs.

example, in Figure 11-15, D_1 is the demand curve for the commodity for one group of consumers (i.e., in market 1), while D_2 is the demand curve for another group (market 2). The horizontal summation of D_1 and D_2 yields D_T (ABC). Since the LAC curve is above D_T at every level of output, the commodity or service would not be supplied in the long run in the absence of price discrimination or a subsidy.

With third degree price discrimination (to the extent that the two markets can be kept separate), the firm could sell 1 unit of the commodity at $P = \$4$ in market 1 and sell 3 units of the commodity at $P = \$1.50$ in market 2. The total output would then be 4 units sold at the (weighted) average price of $2.13 which equals the LAC of producing 4 units in the long run (point F in the figure).[11]

Application 5: Conflict Between Publishers and Authors

Authors receive royalties. These are a fixed percentage (ranging from 10 per cent to 15 per cent) of the total revenue from the sale of the book. A conflict usually arises between the publisher and the author in the pricing

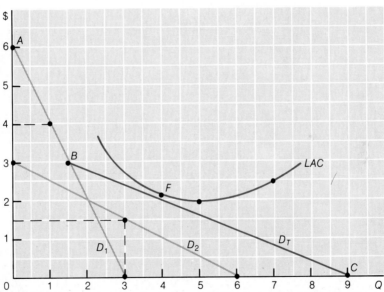

FIGURE 11-15.
Price Discrimination and the Existence of an Industry

The demand curve is D_1 in market 1 and D_2 in market 2. The horizontal summation of D_1 and D_2 gives D_T (ABC). Since the LAC curve is above D_T at every output level, the commodity or service would not be supplied in the long run without price discrimination or a subsidy. With third degree price discrimination, the firm could sell $Q = 1$ at $P = \$4$ in market 1 and sell $Q = 3$ at $P = \$1.50$ in market 2 and break even (since at point F, the weighted average $P = \$2.13$ equals LAC).

[11] The weighted average price of $2.13 is obtained by $[(1)(\$4) + (3)(\$1.50)]/4 = \$8.50/4$. The sale of $Q = 1$ in market 1 and $Q = 3$ in market 2 was obtained from inspection of the figure. This is the only output and distribution of sales (in whole units of the commodity) between the two markets by which this firm covers all costs.

of a book. The reason is that once the author has written a book, he or she incurs no (marginal) cost of printing additional copies. Thus, he or she would like the publisher to operate where $MR = MC = 0$. This is where demand is unitary elastic and total revenue and royalties are maximum (see Section 11-1). The publisher, however, incurs the cost of the paper and the cost of printing additional copies of the book, and he produces where $MR = MC > 0$ (i.e., in the elastic or upper range of the demand curve). Thus, the publisher sets a higher price and sells a smaller quantity than the author would like. This is shown in Figure 11-16.

In Figure 11-16, D is the market demand curve for the book and MR is the corresponding MR curve. If we assume that the publisher incurs a total fixed cost of \$60,000 and a constant $MC = \$10$ of producing each additional copy of the book, we get the publisher's $SATC$ and SMC curves shown in

FIGURE 11-16.
Pricing Conflict
Between Publishers
and Authors

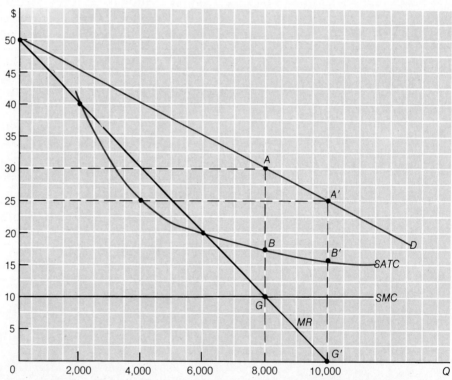

D is the market demand curve for a book. The SATC and SMC curves refer to the publisher. The best level of output is 8,000 copies (point G, where SMC = MR). The publisher sets P = \$30 and earns a profit of \$12.50 (AB) per unit and \$100,000 in total. With 12 per cent of gross sales, the author receives \$28,800 (12 per cent of 8,000 times \$30). With SMC = 0, the author would prefer P = \$25, at which Q = 10,000 (point A'). This would give the author \$30,000 (12 per cent of TR = \$250,000). The publisher, however, would only earn a profit of \$9 per copy (A'B') and \$90,000 in total.

[12] Note that the author's SMC curve coincides with the horizontal axis.

the figure. The best level of output for the publisher is 8,000 copies (given by point G, where $MR = SMC$). The publisher sets $P = \$30$ and earns a profit of $12.50 ($AB$) per unit and $100,000 in total. If royalties are 12 per cent of sales, the author receives \$28,800 (12 per cent of 8,000 times \$30).

The author, however, prefers $P = \$25$, at which $Q = 10,000$ (given by point G', where $MR = SMC = 0$).[12] This would give the author \$30,000 (12 per cent of $TR = \$250,000$). But at $Q = 10,000$, the publisher earns a profit of only \$9 per copy ($A'B'$) and \$90,000 in total (as compared with \$100,000 at $P = \$30$). Thus, a pricing conflict arises between the publisher and the author. Of course, this is not the only source of friction between them. Since the author does not incur any marginal cost, the author would like the publisher to use the best type of paper for the book, elaborate cover design, and multicolor diagrams. The only bargaining power the author has is the threat to write for another publisher.

Summary

1. A monopolist is a firm selling a commodity for which there are no close substitutes. Thus, the monopolist faces the industry's negatively sloped demand curve for the commodity, and marginal revenue is smaller than price. Monopoly can be based on control of the entire supply of a required raw material, a patent or government franchise, or declining long-run average costs over a sufficiently large range of outputs so as to leave a single firm supplying the entire market. In the real world, there are usually many forces that limit the monopolist's market power.

2. The best level of output of the monopolist in the short run is the one that maximizes total profits. This occurs where the positive difference between TR and STC is greatest. The same result is obtained where the MC curve intersects the MR curve from below. If P is smaller than ATC, the monopolist will incur a loss in the short run. However, if P exceeds AVC, it pays for the monopolist to continue to produce because it covers part of its fixed costs. There is no unique relationship between price and output or supply curve for the monopolist.

3. The best or profit-maximizing level of output of the monopolist in the long run is given by the point where the LMC curve intersects the MR curve from below. The best plant is the one whose $SATC$ curve is tangent to the LAC at the best level of output. The monopolist can make

long-run profits because of restricted entry and does not usually produce at the lowest point on the LAC curve. The long-run profits of the monopolist will be capitalized into the market value of the firm and benefit only the original owner of the monopoly. As compared with perfect competition, monopoly restricts output, results in a higher price, redistributes income from consumers to the monopolist, and leads to less efficient use of society's resources.

4. A multiplant monopolist minimizes the total cost of producing the best level of output in the short run when the marginal cost of the last unit of the commodity produced in each plant is equal to the marginal revenue from selling the combined output. In the long run, a monopolist can build as many identical plants of optimal size (i.e., plants whose $SATC$ curve form the lowest point of the LAC curve) as required to produce the best level of output.

5. Under first degree price discrimination, the monopolist sells each unit of the commodity separately and charges the highest price that each consumer is willing to pay rather than go without it. By doing so, the monopolist extracts the entire consumers' surplus. More practical and common is second degree price discrimination. This refers to the charging of a lower price per unit of output for each additional batch or block of the commodity. By doing so, the monopolist

will be able to extract part of the consumers' surplus. Third degree price discrimination refers to the charging of a higher price for a commodity in the market with the less elastic demand in such a way as to equalize the MR of the last unit of the commodity sold in the two markets. To be able to do this, the firm must have some control over prices, it must be able to keep the two markets separate, and the price elasticity of demand must be different in the two markets.

6. A per-unit excise tax will fall on consumers in its entirety under perfect competition, but only in part under monopoly under constant costs. By setting price below the monopoly price, regulatory commissions can induce a monopolist to produce a larger output and have lower profits. Regulatory commissions usually set $P = LAC$ for public utilities, but this leads to some welfare loss for society. Price discrimination may be necessary to permit the existence of an industry. Authors generally prefer lower book prices than publishers are likely to set.

Glossary

Pure Monopoly   The form of market organization in which there is a single seller of a commodity for which there are no close substitutes.

Natural monopoly   The case of declining long-run average costs over a sufficiently large range of outputs so as to leave a single firm supplying the entire market.

Price discrimination   The charging of different prices (for different quantities of a commodity or in different markets) that are not justified by cost differences.

First degree price discrimination   The charging of the highest price for each unit of a commodity that each consumer is willing to pay rather than go without it.

Second degree price discrimination   The charging of a lower price for each additional batch or block of the commodity.

Third degree price discrimination   The charging of a higher price for a commodity in the market with the less elastic demand in such a way as to equalize the MR of the last unit of the commodity sold in the two markets.

Questions for Review

1. (a) What is pure monopoly?
   (b) In what ways does pure monopoly differ from perfect competition?
   (c) What are the bases for pure monopoly?
   (d) Is pure monopoly very common in the real world?
   (e) What forces limit the monopolist's market power in the real world?
2. (a) What is the shape of the demand curve facing a pure monopolist?
   (b) How is the marginal revenue curve of a monopolist facing a straight-line demand curve derived?
   (c) Is MR larger, equal, or smaller than zero over the elastic range of a monopolist's demand curve?
   (d) Why would a firm never operate over the inelastic range of its demand curve?

3. (a) What is the shape of the total revenue curve for the monopolist?
   (b) How does the shape of the total revenue curve of the monopolist differ from that of the perfect competitor? What is the reason for the difference?
   (c) How is the best level of output of the monopolist determined by the total approach?
   (d) Why doesn't the monopolist produce where total revenue is maximum?
4. (a) How is the best level of output of the monopolist determined by the marginal approach?
   (b) How can we determine if the monopolist earns a profit, breaks even, or incurs a loss in the short run?

(c) Should the monopolist shut down if he incurs a loss in the short run? Why?

5. (a) Where is the shutdown point of the monopolist in the short run?
   (b) Can we define the monopolist's short-run supply curve from his marginal cost curve? Why?
   (c) Will the monopolist sell a given quantity of output at a higher price in the market with the more elastic or less elastic demand curve?

6. (a) What is the best level of output of the monopolist in the long run?
   (b) What is the best scale of plant of the monopolist in the long run?
   (c) How do long-run monopoly profits affect the market value of the firm?
   (d) Does the monopolist produce at the lowest point on its long-run average cost curve when in long-run equilibrium?

7. Answer the following with reference to Figure 11-7.
   (a) How much are consumers willing to pay for the monopolist's output? How much do they actually pay without price discrimination?
   (b) How much is the consumers' surplus?
   (c) How much are the monopolist's costs of production?
   (d) How large are the monopolist's profits?
   (e) What is the welfare cost or deadweight loss of monopoly? How does it arise?

8. (a) How can we obtain the SMC curve of a multiplant monopolist?
   (b) Where is the best level of output of a multiplant monopolist in the short run?
   (c) How should a multiplant monopolist distribute the production of its best level of output among its various plants in order to minimize its short-run total costs?

(d) How will a multiplant monopolist minimize the cost of producing its best level of output in the long run?

9. (a) What is price discrimination?
   (b) What is first degree price discrimination? How frequently does this occur?
   (c) What is second degree price discrimination? How frequently does this occur?
   (d) What is third degree price discrimination? What are some examples?

10. With third degree price discrimination,
    (a) what must be true of the MR in each market?
    (b) in which market will the firm charge a higher price: in the market with the less elastic or more elastic demand?
    (c) what are the conditions that must hold in order to practice it?
    (d) why are these conditions necessary?

11. (a) Can a monopolist shift the entire amount of a per-unit tax on consumers?
    (b) Assuming that everything else is the same, does a per-unit tax reduce output more under monopoly or under perfect competition?
    (c) How can price regulation induce a monopolist to produce a larger output and have lower profits?

12. (a) What price do regulatory commissions usually set for public utilities? How does this lead to some welfare loss for society?
    (b) Under what condition would price discrimination be necessary for an industry to exist?
    (c) Why is there a conflict between the publisher and the author on the pricing of a book?

Problems

1. Given that the demand function of a monopolist is $Q = \frac{1}{6}(55 - P)$:
   (a) derive the monopolist's demand and marginal revenue schedules from $P = \$55$ to $P = \$20$, at \$5 intervals.

   (b) On the same set of axes, plot the monopolist's demand and marginal revenue curves, and show the range over which D is elastic and inelastic, and the point where D is unitary elastic.

(c) Using the formula relating marginal revenue, price, and elasticity, find the price elasticity of demand at $P = \$40$.

2. Using the TC schedule of Table 8-2 and the demand schedule of Problem 1,
   (a) construct a table similar to Table 11-2 showing TR, STC, and total profits at each level of output and indicate by an asterisk the best level of output of the monopolist.
   (b) draw a figure similar to Figure 11-2 and determine the best level of output of the monopolist.

3. Using the per-unit cost curves of Figure 8-5 and the demand and marginal revenue curves from Problem 1(b):
   (a) draw a figure similar to Figure 11-3 and show the best level of output of the firm.
   (b) From your figure in part (a), construct a table similar to Table 11-4 showing P, ATC, profit per unit, total profits, MR, and MC at each level of output.

★4. Suppose the demand curve facing the monopolist changes to $Q' = \frac{1}{6}(30 - P)$, while cost curves remain unchanged.
   (a) Draw a figure similar to Figure 11-4 showing the best level of output.
   (b) Does the monopolist make a profit, break even, or incur a loss at the best level of output? Should the monopolist go out of business? Why? Where is the monopolist's shutdown point?

5. Suppose that the monopolist has unchanged cost curves but faces two alternative demand functions:

$$Q = \frac{1}{6}(55 - P) \text{ and } Q'' = \frac{1}{6}(45 - P)$$

   (a) Draw a figure similar to Figure 11-5 showing the best level of output with each demand function.
   (b) Which of the two demand functions is more elastic? Where is the monopolist's supply curve?

6. Starting with the cost curves of Figure 8-10 and the demand and marginal revenue curves of Problem 1, draw a SATC curve (label it $SATC_2'$) and its associated SMC curve (label it SMC_2') showing that the monopolist is in long-run equilibrium at $Q = 5$.

★7. Draw two figures and label the best level of output as Q^* and label per-unit profit as AB for a monopolist that
   (a) produces at the lowest point on its LAC curve.
   (b) overutilizes a plant larger than the one that forms the lowest point on its LAC curve.

8. Given that the market demand function facing a two-plant monopolist is $Q = 20 - 2P$ and the short-run marginal cost for plant 1 and plant 2 at various levels of output are:

Q	0	1	2	3	4
SMC_1 ($)	$\cdots$	2	4	6	8
SMC_2 ($)	$\cdots$	2.50	3.50	4.50	5.50

Draw a figure showing D, MR, SMC_1, SMC_2 and ΣMC schedules of this monopolist. What is the best level of output of the monopolist? How much should the monopolist produce in plant 1 and how much in plant 2?

9. Given the following demand curve of a consumer for a monopolist's product:

$$Q = 14 - 2P$$

   (a) Find the total revenue of the monopolist when he sells 6 units of the commodity without practicing any form of price discrimination. What is the value of the consumer's surplus?
   (b) What would be the total revenue of the monopolist if he practiced first degree price discrimination? How much would be the consumer's surplus in this case?
   (c) Answer part (a) if the monopolist charged $P = \$5.50$ for the first 3 units of the commodity and $P = \$4$ for the next 3 units. What type of price discrimination is this?

★10. With reference to Figure 11-11, prove using Formula (5-6) that if the monopolist charges $P = \$4.50$ in market 2, he must charge $P = \$7$ in market 1 in order to maximize total profits with third degree price discrimination.

11. Draw a figure showing how a regulatory commission could induce the monopolist of Figure 11-3 to behave as a perfect competitor in the short run by setting the appropriate price.

★12. Starting from Table 11-3 and Figure 11-3,

construct a table and draw a figure showing

(a) how a lump-sum tax can be used to eliminate all of the monopolist's profits.

(b) what would happen if the government imposed a per-unit tax of $2.50.

Supplementary Readings

For a problem-solving approach to the topics discussed in this chapter, see

Dominick Salvatore, *Microeconomic Theory,* 2nd ed. (New York: McGraw-Hill, 1983), Chapter 11.

Important readings on the pure monopoly model are

Alfred Marshall, *Principles of Economics,* 9th ed. (London: Macmillan, 1920), Book V, Chapter XIV.

Joan Robinson, *The Economics of Imperfect Competition* (London: Macmillan, 1933), pp. 47–82.

John R. Hicks, "Annual Survey of Economic Theory: The Theory of Monopoly," *Econometrica,* 1935. Reprinted in J. Stigler and K. Boulding, *Readings in Price Theory* (Chicago: Irwin, 1952).

Edwin Mansfield, *Monopoly Power and Economic Performance* (New York: Norton, 1978).

For regulation of monopoly, see

Alfred E. Khan, *The Economics of Regulation: Principles and Institutions* (New York: Wiley, 1970).

George J. Stigler, "The Theory of Economic Regulation," *The Bell Journal of Economics and Management Science,* 1971.

Price and Output under Monopolistic Competition

12-1 Monopolistic Competition

12-2 Short-Run Equilibrium Price and Output

12-3 Long-Run Equilibrium Price and Output

12-4 Product Variation and Selling Expenses

12-5 Evaluation of Monopolistic Competition

12-6 Applications

Examples

12-1 The New York City Restaurant "Industry"

12-2 Breakfast Cereals: A Market That Seems, But Is Not, Monopolistically Competitive

12-3 Advertisers Are Taking on Competitors by Name

12-4 Advertising and the Price of Eyeglasses and Legal Services

Applications

Application 1: The Use of Coupons by Monopolistic Competitors

Application 2: Price Dispersion in Monopolistic Competition

Application 3: Monopolistic Competition with Blocked Entry

Application 4: Consumers' Tastes and Excess Capacity

Application 5: Does Advertising Create False Needs?

Chapter 12

Preview Questions

What is monopolistic competition?

What are the competitive and the monopolistic elements in monopolistic competition?

Will a monopolistic competitor earn profits in the long run?

Will a monopolistic competitor produce at the lowest long-run average cost?

What is meant by excess capacity in monopolistic competition?

How does a monopolistic competitor decide on the degree of product variation?

Why do monopolistic competitors advertise?

How much advertising will a monopolistic competitor do?

Does advertising create false needs?

In this chapter we bring together the theory of consumer behavior and demand (from Part II) and the theory of production and costs (from Part III) to analyze how prices and output are determined under monopolistic competition. Monopolistic competition falls between the two extremes of perfect competition and pure monopoly in the spectrum or range of market organizations and, as such, it contains elements of both. The theory of monopolistic competition has fallen somewhat in popularity among economists in recent years. Yet, this model contains some important insights, such as product variation and selling expenses, which are also applicable to oligopolistic markets (discussed in Chapter 13).

The chapter begins by defining monopolistic competition and the demand curves facing a monopolistic competitor. It then goes on to examine the determination of price and output in the short run and in the long run. Subsequently, we examine product variation and selling expenses. This is followed by a comparison of long-run equilibrium under monopolistic competition and perfect competition, and an evaluation of the theory of monopolistic competition as a whole. Finally, we present some applications of the monopolistically competitive model. These applications, together with the several real-world examples presented in the theory sections of the chapter, demonstrate the relevance of the analytical tools developed in the chapter.

Monopolistic Competition

In this section, we examine the nature of monopolistic competition, identify its monopolistic and perfectly competitive elements, and define the two types of demand curves faced by each monopolistically competitive firm.

12-1a The Nature of Monopolistic Competition

In Chapter 10 we defined perfect competition as the form of market organization in which there are many sellers of a homogeneous product. In Chapter 11 we defined pure monopoly as the single seller of a commodity for which there are no close substitutes. Between these two extreme forms of market organization lies **monopolistic competition.** This refers to the case where there are many sellers of a heterogeneous or differentiated product, and entry into or exit from the industry is rather easy in the long run.

Differentiated products are products that are similar but not identical. The similarity of differentiated products arises from the fact that they satisfy the same basic consumption needs. Examples are the numerous brands of breakfast cereals, toothpaste, cigarettes, detergents, cold medicines, and so on, on the market today. The differentiation may be real (as in the case of the various breakfast cereals with greatly different nutritional and sugar contents) or imaginary (as in the case of the different brands of aspirin, all of which contain the same ingredients). Product differentiation may also be based entirely on some sellers being more or less conveniently located or on the kind of service they provide (i.e., more or less friendly).

As the name implies, monopolistic competition is a blend of competition and monopoly. The competitive element arises from the fact that there are many sellers of the differentiated product, each of which is too small to affect the other sellers. Firms can also enter and leave a monopolistically competitive industry rather easily in the long run. The monopolistic element arises from **product differentiation.** That is, since the product of each seller is similar but not identical, each seller has a monopoly power over the *specific* product it sells. This monopoly power, however, is severely limited by the existence of close substitutes. Thus, if a seller of a particular brand of aspirin charged a price more than a few pennies higher than competitive brands, it would lose a great deal of its sales.

Monopolistic competition is most common in the retail and service sectors of the economy. On the national level, clothing, cotton textiles, and food processing are industries that come closest to monopolistic competition. On the local level, the best examples of monopolistic competition are the numerous gasoline stations, barber shops, grocery stores, drug stores, newspaper stands, restaurants, pizza parlors, liquor stores, and so on, all located near one another. Each of these businesses has some monopoly power over its competitors due to the uniqueness of its product, better location, slightly lower prices, better service, a greater range of products, and so on. Yet, this market power is very limited due to the availability of close substitutes.

Because each firm produces a somewhat different product under monopolistic competition, we cannot define the industry (which refers to the producers of an *identical* product). Chamberlin, who introduced the theory of monopolistic competition in the early 1930s, sought to overcome this difficulty by lumping all the sellers of *similar* products into a **product group.** For simplicity, we will continue to use the term "industry" in this chapter but in this broader sense (i.e., to refer to all the sellers of the differentiated products in a product group). However, because of product differentiation, we cannot derive the industry demand and supply curves as we did under perfect competition, and we do not have a single equilibrium price for the differentiated product, but a cluster of prices. Thus, our graphical analysis will have to be confined to the "typical" or "representative" firm rather than to the industry.

The analysis is greatly simplified if we also assume (as Chamberlin did) that all firms in the "industry" or product group face identical demand and cost curves. This is a rather strong assumption since we would expect firms producing somewhat different (i.e., differentiated) products to also face somewhat different cost and demand curves. Nevertheless, making such an assumption will greatly simplify the analysis. Under monopolistic competition, firms can affect the volume of their sales by changing the product price, by changing the characteristics of the product, or by varying their selling expenses (such as advertising). In this chapter, we will deal with each of these choice-related variables.

Example 12-1   The New York City Restaurant "Industry"

The Facts: The restaurant "industry" in any city has all the characteristics of monopolistic competition. For example, there are literally thousands of restaurants in New York City providing a very great variety of foods and type of service. The variety of cuisines range from Chinese, French, and Italian to Indian, Korean, Lebanese, and many others. Some restaurants are very luxurious and expensive, while others are very simple and inexpensive. Some provide entertainment, while others do not. Some are located in the theater district, some in the financial district, and some in residential areas of the city. In one small block in mid-Manhattan, the author counted 20 restaurants: 5 Italian, 4 French, 3 Chinese, and 1 each serving Argentinian, Brazilian, Greek, Indian, Japanese, Korean, Mexican, Pakistani, and Spanish food. In a recent issue of a New York magazine, more than 319 *Manhattan* restaurants of all types were advertised, of which 84 provided some type of entertainment, and this is only a small minority of the restaurants located in Manhattan. Entry into the restaurant industry is also relatively easy, as evidenced by the fact that hundreds of new restaurants open (and about an equal number close) in Manhattan during each year.

Comment: Since the services offered by each restaurant are somewhat unique and information is imperfect, restaurants find it useful to advertise in order to inform consumers of their existence, location, and menu, and to increase demand by claiming superiority over all other restaurants in a given class. The claim of being the "best French restaurant in town" occurs so many times in these ads that no one takes that claim seriously. This is to be contrasted to a perfectly competitive market where all firms sell identical products, knowledge is assumed to be perfect, and each firm can sell any quantity of the commodity it wishes at the market price. Thus, there is no reason for perfectly competitive firms to advertise. Note also that the restaurant "industry" is local rather than national. People will normally not travel to another city simply to patronize a particular restaurant, no matter how superior they might think it is.

Source: New Yorker, March 1984.

12-1b Demand Curves Under Monopolistic Competition

Each firm under monopolistic competition faces two demand curves. One is very elastic, on the assumption that when the firm changes its price, the other firms in the industry or product group do not change theirs. This "subjective" demand curve arises because each firm *believes* that others will not follow its price changes. The other is much less elastic, on the assumption that all firms in the "industry" raise or lower their price simultaneously (so that each firm only retains a constant share of the market). This is called a **proportional demand curve.** For example, with 100 identical firms in the market, each faces a demand curve that is 1/100 of the market demand curve. This proportional or "objective" demand curve arises because firms, being in a similar situation, all have the same incentive to change prices, more or less, by the same amount. These two types of demand curves are shown in Figure 12-1.

In Figure 12-1, d is the demand curve of a representative firm on the assumption that when the firm changes its price, the other firms selling the differentiated product do not change theirs. Thus, starting at point A, if only this firm lowered its price from $P = \$9$ to $P = \$7$, its sales would increase from 2 to 6 units. This is shown by a movement from point A to point B along demand curve d. Demand curve d is very elastic because this firm would attract many customers from the other firms by lowering its price. On the other hand, if only this firm raised its price, it would lose a great deal of customers.

However, if (as we have assumed) all firms in the industry face identical demand and cost curves, all firms believe that they can increase their sales significantly by lowering their price. But when they do, each firm retains only its share of the market. This is shown by proportional demand curve

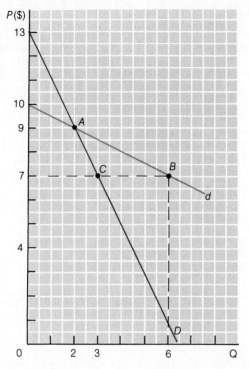

Starting from point A, a reduction in price from $9 to $7 increases the sales of the firm from 2 to 6 units if only this firm lowers its price (a movement from point A to point B along demand curve d), but it increases sales only from 2 to 3 units if all firms lowered their price simultaneously (a movement from point A to point C along proportional demand curve D).

D in Figure 12-1. Thus, starting at point A, a reduction in price from P = $9 to P = $7 increases the sales of the representative firm from 2 to 3 units only when all firms lower their price (charge the same price). This is shown by a movement from point A to point C along proportional demand curve D. Thus, D is less elastic than d.

12-2

Short-Run Equilibrium Price and Output

Since a monopolistic competitor believes that the other firms in the industry will not match any of its price changes, the firm thinks that it faces a highly elastic demand curve (d in Figure 12-1) for the differentiated product it sells. Since demand curve d is negatively sloped, the corresponding marginal revenue curve is also negatively sloped and lies below the demand curve (except at its vertical or price intercept). As in the case of monopoly, the best or optimum level of output for the monopolistically competitive firm in the short run is given by the point where the firm's MC curve intersects its MR curve from below (provided that the price of the commodity at this level of output is equal to or greater than the average variable cost). The process by which the monopolistically competitive firm reaches short-run equilibrium is much more complex, however, than for the perfectly competitive firm and the monopolist.[1] This is shown in Figure 12-2.

Suppose that the monopolistically competitive firm originally sells $Q = 2$ at $P = \$9$ (point A, where the d and the D curves intersect in the left panel of Figure 12-2). Since the firm believes to be operating on the d curve, the marginal revenue curve corresponding to this demand curve (i.e., mr) is also drawn in the figure. Furthermore, the figure shows the MC curve of the firm. Since at $Q = 2$, $mr > MC$, this is not the best level of output. The best level of output of the firm in the short run is given by point G, where the MC curve intersects the mr curve from below. That is, the firm should charge $P = \$7$ and sell $Q = 6$ (point B on the d curve in the left panel of Figure 12-2).

However, since all firms in the industry face identical demand and cost curves, they will all find it profitable to lower their prices to $P = \$7$. As a result, our representative firm does not move from point A to point B along the d curve, as anticipated, but from point A to point C along proportional demand curve D (see the left panel of the figure). *The result is that demand curve d slides down demand curve D from point A to point C.* This gives demand curve d' (and its corresponding mr' curve) in the middle panel. The reason the new demand curve d' intersects demand curve D at point C (i.e., at $P = \$7$) is that demand curve d' shows how much our representative firm believes it can sell at $P = \$7$ if all other firms keep their price constant at $P = \$7$ (rather than at $P = \$9$). Note that under monopolistic competition, firms change their prices *not as a reaction* to price changes by other firms in the industry, but because all firms face the same basic conditions. Therefore, what is profitable for one firm to do is also profitable for all firms to do. Thus, all firms lower their prices from $9 to $7, and this results in our representative firm facing demand curve d' in the middle panel rather than demand curve d in the left panel.

The process is now repeated from point C in the middle panel. That is, at point C, $mr' > MC$ and it pays for the firm to expand output. The best level of output of the firm in the short run is given by point G', where the MC curve intersects the mr' curve from below. Thus, the firm should charge $P = \$6$ and sell $Q = 5$ (point F on d' in the middle panel). However, since all firms in the industry face identical demand and cost curves, they

[1] This greater difficulty, in relation to the understanding gained from the analysis, is one reason that the monopolistic competitive model has fallen somewhat into disfavor. We present this model, nevertheless, because it does provide some useful insights (which are also applicable to the discussion of oligopoly presented in Chapter 13).

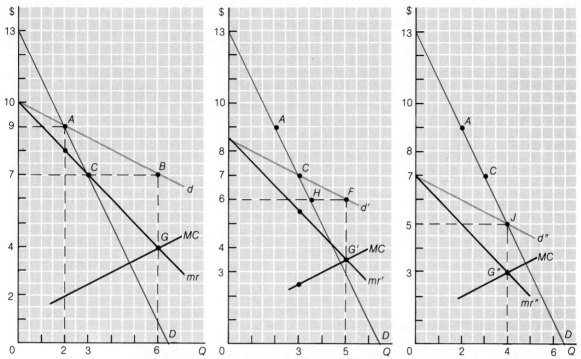

FIGURE 12-2. Short-Run Equilibrium of a Monopolistically Competitive Firm
The firm is originally at point A in the left panel. Since the firm believes that d is its relevant demand curve, it lowers price to $7 in order to sell 6 units and maximize profits (point G, where MC = mr). Since all firms do the same, the firm moves to point C on D instead, and d shifts down to d' (see the middle panel). To maximize profits, the firm now charges P = $6 to sell Q = 5 (given by point G', where mr' = MC). Once again, all firms do the same and the firm moves instead to point H. The process continues until Q = 4, at which mr'' = MC and d and D intersect (see the right panel).

will all find it profitable to lower their prices to P = $6. As a result, our representative firm does not move from point C to point F along d' as anticipated, but from point C to point H along D (see the middle panel). The result (not shown in the figure) is that demand curve d' slides down proportional demand curve D from point C to point H. This process continues until our representative firm faces demand curve d'' (and its corresponding mr'' curve) in the right panel. The reason why this is the final result is explained next.

In the right panel, the best level of output of the firm is given by point G'', where the MC curve of the firm intersects the mr'' curve from below. Thus, the firm should charge a price of P = $5 and sell Q = 4 (point J on d''). Since point J is now also on D (i.e., the d'' and the D demand curves intersect at point J), there is no further incentive for the firm to change its price and output. That is, this and the other firms in the monopolistically competitive industry are now in short-run equilibrium, since they can no longer increase their total profits by changing output. At point J, the representative firm will sell 4 units of output and charge a price of $5 (as long as P exceeds AVC at Q = 4).

As in the case of perfect competition and monopoly, the monopolistically competitive firm can earn a profit, break even, or incur a loss in the short run. To determine which is the case, we need the average total cost (ATC) curve (not shown in Figure 12-2). If P > ATC at Q = 4 (the best level of output), the firm earns a profit per unit equal to the positive difference between P and ATC. If P = ATC at Q = 4, the firm breaks even. If P < ATC, the firm incurs a loss per unit equal to the excess of ATC over P, but it will remain in business (thereby minimizing total losses) as long as P > AVC. If P = AVC (the shutdown point), the firm is indifferent between remaining in business or going out of business (since in either case, it would incur a loss equal to its total fixed costs). Finally, if P < AVC, the firm will minimize its short-run losses (equal to its total fixed costs) by going out of business.

12-3

Long-Run Equilibrium Price and Output

As in perfect competition, firms in a monopolistically competitive industry can change their scale of plant and enter or leave the industry in the long run without much difficulty. If firms earned profits in the short run, more firms will enter the industry in the long run. This reduces the firm's market share and shifts demand curves D and d to the left until all profits are eliminated. The opposite occurs when firms incur short-run losses. This is shown in Figure 12-3.

In the left panel of Figure 12-3, point J on demand curve D is the short-run equilibrium point of the representative firm (as in the right panel of Figure 12-2). Since at point J, P > LAC, this and other firms in the industry earn short-run profits, and so more firms enter the industry in the long run. This shifts demand curves D and d'' (the latter not shown in the figure) to the left as each firm's market share declines.

The process continues until (1) demand curve d* is tangent to the LAC curve (so that this and other firms break even) and (2) proportional demand curve D* intersects demand curve d* at the point where d* is tangent to the LAC curve (so that there is no incentive for this and other firms to change price and output). Thus, the firm charges P = $3 and sells Q = 3 when in long-run equilibrium (point R in the left panel of Figure 12-3). Point R is directly above point M, where the firm's LMC curve intersects its mr* curve from below, as required for long-run equilibrium. To minimize production costs in the long run, the firm constructs the scale of plant represented by the SATC curve (not shown in the figure) that is tangent to the LAC curve at point R.

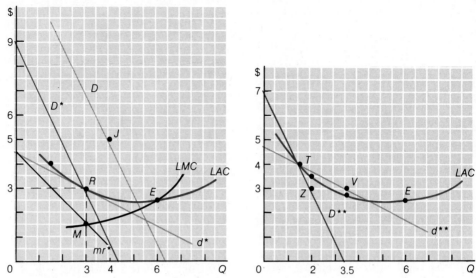

FIGURE 12-3. Long-Run Equilibrium of a Monopolistically Competitive Firm
Since at point J in the left panel, P> LAC, this and other firms earn short-run profits. More firms enter the industry in the long run until D and d" (the latter not shown) shift down to D* and d*. Thus, the firm is in long-run equilibrium at point R with P = \$3 and Q = 3. At point R, d* is tangent to the LAC curve (so that P = LAC) and D* intersects d* at the tangency point (so that there is no tendency for the firm to change price). In the right panel, the firm breaks even at point T because P = LAC. But the firm is not in long-run equilibrium because it believes that it can earn profits by lowering price to \$3 and move to point V on d*. Since all firms lower price to P = \$3, the firm moves instead to point Z on D* and incurs long-run losses.

The concept of long-run equilibrium for a monopolistically competitive firm is clarified by examining why point T in the right panel of Figure 12-3 *is not* a point of long-run equilibrium, and comparing point T to point R in the left panel which *is* a point of long-run equilibrium. Note that in both panels of Figure 12-3, the *LAC* is the same. At point T in the right panel, the firm breaks even because P = *LAC*. However, since demand curve d^{**} is not tangent to, but intersects, the *LAC* curve at point T, the firm is not in long-run equilibrium. That is, the firm believes that by lowering price from P = \$4 to, say, P = \$3, it will move along demand curve d^{**} to point V and earn a profit of \$0.30 per unit and \$1.05 in total (on Q = 3.5 sold).[2]

Yet, other firms face identical demand and cost curves, and they too will lower their prices to \$3. The result is that the firm does not move along demand curve d^{**}, as it anticipated, but it moves instead along the proportional demand curve D^{**} from point T to point Z (see the right panel of

---

[2] The profit of \$0.30 per unit is obtained by subtracting *LAC* = \$2.70 from P = \$3 (point V on d^{**}) at Q = 3.5 in the right panel of Figure 12-3.

Figure 12-3). At point Z, the firm incurs a long-run loss of $0.50 per unit and $1 in total. This is given by the excess of the LAC over $P = \$3$ at $Q = 2$. The firm will similarly incur long-run losses at any other price. The firm does not even think that it can return to point T and break even (see the answer to Problem 7 in the back of the book). The only way for the firm to avoid long-run losses now is for some firms to leave the industry, and thus increase the market share of the remaining firms. The process will continue until demand curves D^{**} and d^{**} (in the right panel of Figure 12-3) shift up to D^* and d^* (as in the left panel) so that the firm is in long-run equilibrium at point R and breaks even.[3]

Throughout our discussion, we implicitly assumed that as firms enter or leave the industry in the long run, input prices do not change (so that the firm's cost curves do not shift). In addition, we have also implicitly assumed that firms do not change their expenditures on product differentiation and advertising. These topics are discussed in the next section.

Example 12-2 **Breakfast Cereals: An Industry That Seems, But Is Not, Monopolistically Competitive**

The Facts: The market for breakfast cereals in the United States may seem to be monopolistically competitive. After all, there are more than 100 different brands of breakfast cereals on the market today covering all possible degrees of sweetness, crunchiness, fiber content, and so on. New brands are frequently introduced and some taken off the market, and producers vigorously advertise their product. Nevertheless, this market is not monopolistically competitive. The reason is that most of the breakfast cereals are produced by a few large companies. Specifically, the four largest firms (Kelloggs, General Mills, General Foods, and Quaker) account for about 90 per cent of total sales, and the largest 8 firms account for 98 per cent of the market. In addition, entry into the industry is not easy, as evidenced by the fact that over the past 15 years, only a handful of new firms were able to enter this market. This was despite the fact that the industry was highly profitable and had long-run rates of returns significantly higher than in other manufacturing sectors. Thus, the market for breakfast cereals is oligopolistic (few producers of a homogeneous or differentiated product—see Chapter 13) rather than monopolistically competitive.

Comment: In 1972, the Federal Trade Commission (FTC) charged that the four largest firms producing breakfast cereals had erected strong barriers to entry. The FTC argued that vigorous advertising and the proliferation of brands by the four largest producers covered all possible forms of product variation and left no room for new entrants. In 1981, however, a new

---

[3] Once again, note how much more complex the analysis is here as compared with the long-run analysis of the perfectly competitive firm and the monopolist.

administration in Washington decided that the economic and legal basis of the case against the top four cereal manufacturers was not sound, and dropped the case.

Source: Special Report Series: Concentration Ratios in Manufacturing, U.S. Government Printing Office, 1975. "F.T.C. Staff is Rebuffed on Cereals," *The New York Times*, September 11, 1981, IV, pp. 1, 6.

12-4

Product Variation and Selling Expenses

In this section, we examine two crucial features of monopolistically competitive markets: product variation and selling expenses. Under monopolistic competition, firms can change not only the product price but also some of the characteristics of the product, and they can also increase their advertising expenses in order to increase sales and profits. Product variation and selling expenses are sometimes referred to as "nonprice competition."

12-4a Product Variation

Under monopolistic competition, a firm can change some of the characteristics of its product to make it more appealing to consumers. For example, producers may reduce the amount of sugar in breakfast cereals and the caloric content of beer in order to make these products more appealing to today's weight-conscious consumers. The firm may also design a more attractive and functional (and perhaps reusable) container for the product. Thus, plastic bottles are replacing glass bottles because they are lighter and unbreakable. Through **product variation,** producers can attempt to increase the demand for their product and make the demand curve less elastic so as to reap larger (short-run) profits. This is to be contrasted to the case in perfectly competitive markets, where the output of all producers is homogeneous and product variation is not possible. For example, grade A winter wheat produced by one farmer is identical with that produced by other farmers, and no variation is possible. Once product differentiation becomes possible, we are no longer in perfect competition.

Product variation can increase the firm's sales and profits, but it also leads to additional costs. That is, the firm incurs some costs to develop variants of the product, to test consumers' reaction, and to introduce the variants of the product. Thus, product variation is another choice variable (besides price changes) of the firm under monopolistic competition. The firm should compare the marginal or extra revenue resulting from product variation with the marginal or extra cost involved in introducing it. Spe-

385

cifically, the firm should vary its product as long as the *MR* from the product variation exceeds *MC* and until *MR* = *MC*.[4] However, while this may increase sales and profits in the short run, the firm will return to a break-even position in the long run.

In terms of the left panel of Figure 12-3, the successful introduction of product variation by the firm will shift up the firm's demand curves D^* and d^* as well as its *LAC* and *LMC* curves. In long-run equilibrium, however, the relationship among these curves must be the same as at point *R*. That is, at the firm's best long-run level of output (given by the point where the firm's *LMC* curve intersects its *mr* curve from below) *d* must be tangent to the *LAC* curve and *D* must intersect *d* and the *LAC* curve at the point of tangency. Price and output will be higher, but the firm once again breaks even (i.e., earns zero economic profits) when in long-run equilibrium. Note that depending on the amount of product variation, the demand and cost curves will shift by different amounts, and so will the price and output of the firm. But, in long-run equilibrium, the firm will always be in a situation such as point *R* in the left panel of Figure 12-3.

12-4b Selling Expenses

A firm under monopolistic competition can also increase its selling expenses in order to increase its sales. **Selling expenses** are all those expenditures that the firm incurs to advertise its product, to increase its sales force, to provide more and better servicing of the product, and to otherwise induce consumers to purchase the product. As in the case of product variation, a firm should increase its selling expenses as long as the *MR* received from them exceeds *MC*, and until *MR* = *MC*.[5] Again as in the case of product variation, an increase in selling expenses (when successful) will shift up the firm's demand curves, but it will also shift up its cost curves. This can lead to short-run profits, but at long-run equilibrium the firm only breaks even. This is shown in Figure 12-4.

In Figure 12-4, the *LAC* curve is that of Figure 12-3, and point *R* is the original long-run equilibrium point (as in the left panel of Figure 12-3) *before* the firm increases its selling expenses. The *LAC** curve arises when the firm increases its selling expenses. Note that the vertical distance between the *LAC** and the *LAC* curves increases on the (realistic) assumption that to sell larger quantities of the product requires larger selling expenses per unit. Larger selling expenses also lead (when successful) to higher demand curves D^{**} and d^{**} (as compared with D^* and d^* in the left panel of Figure 12-3).

---

[4] It should be noted that marginal revenue and marginal costs refer, respectively, to the extra revenue and the extra cost that result from changes in *quantity*. Here, marginal revenue and marginal cost are used instead to measure, respectively, the extra revenue and the extra cost that result from *product variation* and from *quality* changes.

[5] Marginal revenue and marginal costs are used here to refer, respectively, to the extra revenue and the extra cost of changing selling expenses rather than quantity.

FIGURE 12-4.
Long-Run
Equilibrium of the
Firm with Selling
Costs

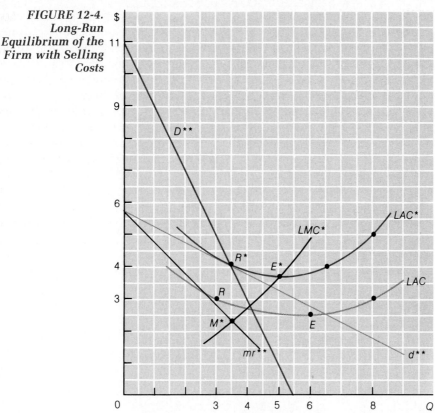

The LAC* curve arises when the firm increases its selling expenses. The vertical distance between the LAC* and the LAC curves increases on the (realistic) assumption that to sell larger quantities of the product requires larger selling expenses per unit. Larger selling expenses also lead (when successful) to higher demand curves D** and d**. The firm is in long-run equilibrium at point R*, where d** is tangent to the LAC* curve and D** intersects d** at that point. At point R*, the firm breaks even.

Larger selling expenses can lead to larger short-run profits for the firm. At long-run equilibrium, however, the firm just breaks even. This is given by point R^* in Figure 12-4. Thus, the firm charges $P = \$4$ and sells $Q = 3.5$ when in long-run equilibrium. Note that at the best level of output, the firm's LMC^* curve intersects from below its mr^{**} curve (point M^*). In addition at point R^*, d^{**} is tangent to the LAC^* curve, and the D^{**} curve intersects the d^{**} and the LAC^* curves at that point. Note also that at point R^*, the firm charges a higher price and sells a greater quantity than before the increase in selling expenses (compare point R^* with point R), but the firm will nevertheless earn zero economic profits in the long run. If all firms in the industry increase their selling expenses, each firm may retain no more than its share of an increasing market.

Selling expenses are similar to transaction costs. **Transaction costs** are

387

those costs that arise in order to facilitate a business transaction. Most transaction costs arise from the existence, and represent the fee or earnings, of middlemen. In the real world, middlemen help bring buyers and sellers together, provide price and quality information, and insure prompt payment. For these services, middlemen receive a fraction of the price of the commodity. An example of this is the difference between the higher price that retailers charge their customers and the price that retailers pay the suppliers of the product. Note that the higher is the fee or earnings of the middlemen (and hence the price of the commodity), the smaller is the quantity sold of the commodity. In the limit, a sufficiently high fee could end all trade in the commodity. This has occurred in the used-clothing business, where the selling price is so high relative to the price at which second-hand clothes can be sold that most used clothes are either donated to charitable organizations or thrown away in the United States at the present time.

Example 12-3   **Advertisers Are Taking on Competitors by Name**

The Facts: Until a few years ago, advertisers on television and in magazines praised the superior qualities of their product as compared with "brand X." Today, "brand X" has all but disappeared from advertisings, as advertisers have taken off their gloves and have become more personal by mentioning their competitors' products by name. This became possible in 1981 when the National Association of Broadcasters abolished its guidelines against making disparaging remarks against competitors' products. The change was welcomed by the Federal Trade Commission on grounds that it might increase competition and lead to better-quality products and lower prices. Taking on competitors by name, though less sportsmanlike and possibly resulting in legal suits, seems to be very effective. This is how Centrum vitamins displaced the market leader, Theragram-M. After months of advertising that Centrum were more complete vitamins than Theragramn-M, the effort paid off. Similarly, by stressing that the Commodore 64 had more memory than both the IBM and the Apple personal computers and cost about one third of the price, Commodore was able to expand its market share of personal computers in 1982. Burger King sales began to soar when it began to attack McDonald's by name, and so did the revenues of Airborne Freight after it began to name Federal Express in its advertising. (Note, however, that some of these industries may be oligopolistic rather than monopolistically competitive.)

Comment: When a firm's sales fall as a result of its product being constantly named as being inferior to that of a competitor, the firm is likely to react with competitive advertisements of its own. Sometimes, these competitive advertisements provide information of potential importance to consumers (e.g., that hamburgers are broiled at a particular chain of fast-food restaurants as opposed to being fried as at a competitive chain; that a particular

388

soft drink does not contain caffeine, while a competitor's does; that certain foods contain Nutrasweet rather than saccharin, etc.). Most competitive advertisements, however, are likely to have little, if any, informational value and lead only to waste and higher costs. Yet, as long as firms believe in the effectiveness of removing the cover from "brand X" in their advertisements, they are likely to continue to do so.

Source: "Advertisers Remove the Cover from Brand X," *U.S. News and World Report,* December 19, 1983, pp. 75–76.

12-5

Evaluation of Monopolistic Competition

In this section, we compare the efficiency and welfare effects of monopolistic competition with those of perfect competition and evaluate the usefulness of the monopolistically competitive model.

12-5a Comparison with Perfect Competition

As mentioned in Chapter 10, the perfectly competitive model is useful not only in the analysis of those industries that approximate perfect competition, but as a standard of reference or yardstick to measure the efficiency and welfare costs to society from departures from perfect competition. While these comparisons are not as straightforward as they might seem (and some economists actually object to them), there are several things we can say when we compare the monopolistically competitive model with the perfectly competitive model.

First, the monopolistically competitive firm will produce a smaller than the ideal output and utilize a smaller than the ideal plant when in long-run equilibrium. The **ideal output** is the output at which the LAC is minimum, and the **ideal plant** is the one with the $SATC$ curve tangent to the lowest point on the LAC curve. This is shown in Figure 12-5.

The d^*, mr^*, LAC, and the LMC curves in Figure 12-5 are those of Figure 12-3 (but doubled in size for clarity). Figure 12-5 also shows that the monopolistically competitive firm utilizes plant $SATC_1$ at its long-run equilibrium point R as compared with plant $SATC_2$ that a perfectly competitive firm (with the same LAC curve) would use at point E when in long-run equilibrium. This arises because the monopolistically competitive firm faces a negatively sloped demand. Both the monopolistically competitive firm and the perfect competitor, however, earn zero economic profits when in long-run equilibrium.

From the figure we see that the monopolistically competitive firm produces $Q = 3$ rather than the ideal output of $Q = 6$, and utilizes plant $SATC_1$, which is smaller than ideal plant $SATC_2$ when in long-run equilib-

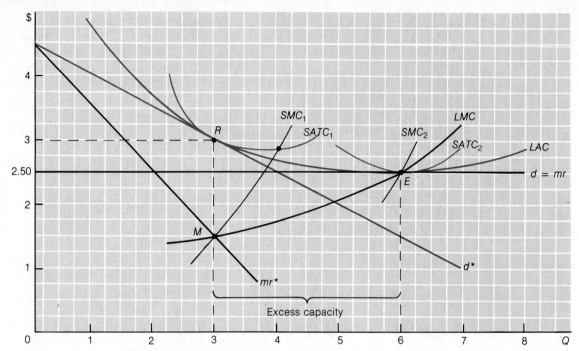

FIGURE 12-5. Comparison of Monopolistic Competition with Perfect Competition

The d*, mr*, LAC, and the LMC curves are those of Figure 12-3. The monopolistically competitive firm utilizes plant SATC₁ at its long-run equilibrium point R as compared with plant SATC₂ that a perfectly competitive firm (with the same LAC curve) would use at point E when in long-run equilibrium. The difference between the ideal output of 6 units (point E) and the actual output of 3 units (point R) measures the excess capacity under monopolistic competition. However, this can be regarded as the "cost" of product differentiation.

rium. The difference between the ideal output and the actual output when the monopolistically competitive firm is in long-run equilibrium (3 units in Figure 12-5) is called **excess capacity.** This allows more firms to exist under monopolistic competition than if the industry were perfectly competitive. Evidence of this is the "overcrowding" of gasoline stations, barber shops, restaurants, grocery stores, etc., each idle a great deal of the time.

Second, from Figure 12-5 we see that the long-run equilibrium price of the commodity is $P = \$3$ under monopolistic competition as opposed to $2.50 if the industry were perfectly competitive. Also, $P > LMC$ under monopolistic competition, while $P = MR = LMC$ under perfect competition. While the excess of price over long-run marginal cost could be regarded as a measure of the inefficiency associated with monopolistic competition (see Application 3 in Chapter 11), Chamberlin regarded this as the "cost" of product differentiation. It is the price that society pays for the variety of products available under monopolistic competition. The more elastic is the demand curve facing the monopolistic competitor, the smaller

390

is the difference in price or "cost" associated with monopolistic competition, and the more the industry approaches perfect competition (see Figure 12-5).

Third, while some of the selling expenses, particularly advertising, may be competitive and excessive, and only add to costs, at least some advertising is informative and may actually lead to lower product prices (see Example 12-4). The same can be said for product variation. That is, while some product variation under monopolistic competition may be excessive (and may in fact confuse consumers), some of it is very useful since it satisfies the consumers' thirst for variety. At present, we cannot say how much of the expenditures on advertising and product variation is useful and how much is simply competitive and wasteful. Different people are also likely to have a different opinion.

Example 12-4 Advertising and the Price of Eyeglasses and Legal Services

The Facts: In a study using 1963 data, Benham found that the average price of eyeglasses was $37.48 in North Carolina (a state with very strong restrictions on advertising by optometrists and opticians), $24.68 (in states with less stringent restrictions on advertising by optometrists and opticians than in North Carolina), and $17.98 in Texas and the District of Columbia (where there was no restriction on advertising). Benham attributed the much lower price of eyeglasses in Texas and the District of Columbia to the competition resulting from advertising. In 1978, the Federal Trade Commission (FTC) ruled that restrictions on eyeglasses advertising by professional societies of opticians and optometrists were illegal. This resulted in a widespread decline in the average price of eyeglasses in states which had previously forbidden such advertising. The FTC also found that consumers were *not* more likely to get the wrong eyeglass prescription where advertising was allowed (and prices were lower than the national average) than where advertising was not allowed (and prices were higher than the national average). The decision on eyeglass advertising followed a 1977 U.S. Supreme Court ruling that allowed lawyers to advertise. This also resulted in a sharp drop in practically all types of legal fees. For example soon after the Supreme Court ruling, the price of an uncontested divorce dropped from $350 to $150 in Phoenix, Arizona (where the case originated).

Comment: From the above, it seems that informative advertising can lead to more competition and lower product prices. This may even occur for doctors' fees. For example, in 1979, the FTC told the American Medical Association to end its ban on advertising fees and services by doctors, and in 1980 a federal appeals court actually opened the way for this. When it occurs, we are likely to see a decline in doctors' fees.

Sources: L. Benham, "The Effect of Advertising on the Price of Eye Glasses," *Journal of Law and Economics,* October 1972. "Lawyers Are Facing Surge in Competition as Courts Drop Curbs," *The Wall Street Journal,* October 18, 1978, pp. 1, 21. "FTC Tells American Medical Association to End its Curbs on Doctors' Advertising," *The Wall Street Journal,* October 25, 1979, p. 23.

12-5b Evaluation of the Theory of Monopolistic Competition

The theory of monopolistic competition faces several serious shortcomings. First, the concept of the product group is extremely ambiguous. There is likely to be a great deal of disagreement as to precisely which products and firms to include in a particular product group. For example, should individually wrapped moist paper tissues such as Wash 'n Dri be included with other paper tissues or with soaps? Should dental floss be included with toothpaste? What about water picks? Are housing in a city slum and suburban mansions part of the same product group?

Second, and related to the above, the original main attraction of the theory of monopolistic competition was thought to be that it more closely describes the real world, where there are many firms selling differentiated products. As pointed out in Section 1-4, however, an economic theory cannot be judged by how closely it describes the real world, but rather by its ability to accurately explain and predict economic events. The theory of perfect competition has at least as much (and some economists would say more) explanatory power as the theory of monopolistic competition, even in markets characterized by many firms selling differentiated products.

Third, many markets which at first sight seem to be monopolistically competitive, are in fact oligopolistic on closer examination. Thus, in Example 12-3 we found that, though there are over 100 different brands of breakfast cereals on the market today, most of these are produced by four large firms. The same is true for producers of toothpaste, cigarettes, detergents, and many other products. These markets are oligopolistic rather than monopolistically competitive and are discussed in Chapter 13.

Fourth, it is rather strange that monopolistically competitive firms do not learn from experience that they generally cannot increase their share of the market by lowering their price, and so they pathetically continue to do so on their way to their zero-profit long-run equilibrium. However, the moment we admit of the possibility that the firm realizes this, we would no longer be in a monopolistically competitive market. Finally, as pointed out in Sections 12-2 and 12-3, the theory of monopolistic competition is much more complex than the theory of perfect competition.

In conclusion, we can say that while the introduction of the theory of monopolistic competition was regarded as a significant theoretical breakthrough at the time Chamberlin introduced it over forty years ago, today many economists have grown somewhat disenchanted with it. The theory, however, is still an integral part of microeconomic theory and this is the reason that it is included in this and other microeconomic texts. The importance of the theory of monopolistic competition today may be primarily for its shortcomings and for the hope that it will stimulate the development of a more useful theory to deal with the "gray area" between perfect competition, on one extreme, and pure monopoly on the other.

12-6

Applications

In this section, we examine a number of important applications of the tools of analysis developed in this chapter. We examine the use of coupons in monopolistically competitive markets, the degree of price dispersion, the case of monopolistic competition with blocked entry, the relationship between consumers' tastes and excess capacity, and the question of whether advertising creates false needs.

Application 1: The Use of Coupons by Monopolistic Competitors
Cents-off coupons is a form of price discrimination practiced by monopolistically competitive firms. It is made possible by the slight degree of monopoly power that such firms have because of product differentiation. That is, since high income people place a greater value (opportunity cost) on their time than low income people, they are less willing to shop around for lower prices, and seek and clip coupons from newspapers and magazines in order to save few pennies on purchases. In short, their demand curve for the product is less price elastic than the demand curve of lower income people.

According to the theory of third degree price discrimination (discussed in Section 11-5), a firm that has some monopoly power and control over prices would increase its total profits by charging a higher price in the market where the demand for its product is less elastic than in the market where demand is more elastic. The monopolistically competitive firm achieves this by using cents-off coupons. Thus, high income people have a less elastic demand and end up paying higher prices than low income people since the former do not bother to use cents-off coupons. Since the degree of monopoly power is very slight, however, the price that higher income people pay for the firm's product is only slightly higher than the price paid for the same product by lower income people.

Thus, we see how the theory of monopolistic competition can explain the widespread use of coupons in markets where there are many firms selling a differentiated product. Another example might be tipping at restaurants by higher income people in order to be seated immediately (and avoid incurring the high opportunity cost of their waiting time).

Application 2: Price Dispersion in Monopolistic Competition
We have seen that under monopolistic competition, there is a cluster of prices rather than a single price for the differentiated product. Yet, only

part of the observed price dispersion is due to product differentiation; another part is due to lack of information. Gathering price information can lead to benefits (for example, finding a service station with a lower gasoline price), but it also involves a cost for the search (mostly in the form of search time). The marginal benefit or revenue of the search declines (i.e., the MR curve is negatively sloped) because the more is the time already spent on the search, the smaller is the probability of finding still lower prices and, even when found, the smaller the price advantage is likely to be.

On the other hand, the greater is the amount of time already spent on the search, the greater is the marginal cost of further search (i.e., the MC curve is positively sloped). The reason for this is that the cost of the leisure time foregone becomes higher. As for other purchases, an individual should increase his or her search effort as long as the MR exceeds the MC of further search, and until $MR = MC$.[6]

We can go further and say that an increase in the level of education of the consumer will shift up his or her MR curve from the search. The reason is that more education is expected to lead to more efficient search. Similarly, an increase in the quantity of a commodity that a consumer purchases will also shift up his or her MR curve of the search, because the benefit of a lower price per unit will be multiplied by the larger quantity purchased. On the other hand, an increase in the consumer's income will shift up his or her MC curve because of the increase in the opportunity cost of search time for this consumer.

From the above, we can conclude that price dispersion in monopolistically competitive markets is only in part based on product differentiation. Some of it is due to lack of information. Price dispersion is inversely related to the amount of search effort undertaken by consumers. Furthermore, price dispersion decreases with rising education, quantity purchased, and incomes. These predictions are generally confirmed by empirical studies.

Application 3: Monopolistic Competition with Blocked Entry

In monopolistic competition, entry is usually easy, and firms can enter and leave the industry without much difficulty in the long run. For example, it does not usually take much money or technical training to open a gasoline station, a small grocery store, a fast-food restaurant, or a barber shop. Sometimes, however, a trade association of producers of a particular commodity or service may have enough influence in local government as to induce it to pass legislation blocking entry. For example, we have seen in Example 11-2 that the taxi owners association has convinced many municipalities not to issue any more licenses (medallions). Even more impressive has been the American Medical Association's ability to restrict the number of students admitted to medical schools (and so the number of doctors) in

---

[6] Note that MR and MC are here expressed in terms of time rather than quantity.

the United States over the past several decades. Blocked or restricted entry has allowed individuals and firms to earn long-run profits. This is shown in Figure 12-6.

In Figure 12-6, the *LAC* and the *LMC* curves are the same as in the left panel of Figure 12-3. With blocked or restricted entry, demand curve D' and d' (in Figure 12-6) are higher than D^* and d^* (in the left panel of Figure 12-3) with free entry. As a result, the monopolistically competitive firm earns profits (since P is higher than the *LAC*) at long-run equilibrium point R', instead of breaking even at point R with free entry (see Figure 12-6 and the left panel of Figure 12-3). With blocked or restricted entry, however, the monopoly model is more appropriate and simpler for analysis (except that it cannot deal with product differentiation).

Application 4: Consumers' Tastes and Excess Capacity

We have seen earlier that monopolistically competitive firms produce less than the ideal output in plants smaller than the ideal plant, and this leads

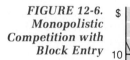

FIGURE 12-6. Monopolistic Competition with Block Entry

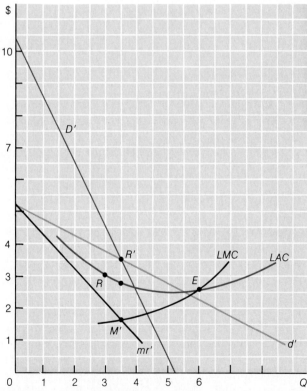

The LAC and the LMC curves are the same as in the left panel of Figure 12-3. With blocked or restricted entry, demand curve D' and d' are higher than D* and d* (in the left panel of Figure 12-3) with free entry. As a result, the firm earns profits (since P is higher than the LAC) at long-run equilibrium point R'.

to excess capacity and overcrowding. According to many economists, the term "excess capacity" implies that it is unwanted by consumers and that it *unnecessarily* leads to higher costs and prices. According to these same economists, this is not true. They point out that consumers do prefer many businesses to operate with unused capacity so as to avoid long waits in buying a service such as getting a haircut, fill up on gasoline, check out at a grocery store, eat at a restaurant, and so on.[7] Since businesses that charge a bit more but serve customers with a minimum of delay are not driven out of business by competitors that charge less but subject customers to long delays, this means that consumers prefer it this way (i.e., are willing to pay a slightly higher price to avoid waiting).

Since consumers do prefer the convenience of easy accessibility and are willing to pay a slightly higher price for this "luxury," the so-called "excess capacity" is really an inventory of unused capacity available to consumers in the form of reduced waiting time. Another way of looking at this is that a great deal of unused capacity is the price that consumers willingly pay for being able to choose the variant of the product which best suits their fancy and pocketbook. Of course, if we all wanted exactly the same haircut (or did not care), the price of a haircut would be lower, but this is not what consumers want. In short, the unused capacity usually found in monopolistic markets is wanted and desired by consumers as evidenced by the fact that they are willing to pay for it. Therefore, calling the inventory of unused capacity "excess capacity" is misleading. According to some economists, there is no such thing as excess capacity.

Application 5: Does Advertising Create False Needs?

As noted previously, some advertisements are informative. They serve to let consumers know of the existence of a particular product, its uses, and price. This type of advertising serves the useful function of informing consumers, improving the functioning of markets, and actually leading to lower prices (see Example 12-4). Some type of advertising, however, is competitive and persuasive. This simply repeats the same slogan (which often contains no informational value) time after time to implant the product name in the consumers' subconscious. This is the type of advertising that, according to some, seeks to create false needs, such as to wear a particular type of jeans, to drink a particular type of soft drink, to smoke a particular brand of cigarettes, and so on.

How successful are these persuasive advertisements is an open question. However, since many firms continue to spend billions of dollars annually on this type of advertising, they must be convinced that it is useful in creating new needs and inducing consumers to purchase the particular product being advertised. To the extent that this advertising is successful in creating false needs, it wastes some of the society's resources. These are

---

[7] This is analogous to "unused capacity" in a home, where a bathroom is used only a small fraction of the time, and a guest room is only seldom used.

also likely to be the most offensive type of advertisements (at least to some people). This is not to say that the more informative advertisements are immune to being offensive. One only needs to mention the concentration at dinner time of television commercial about hemorrhoids, "irregularity," and many others, to be convinced of this.

In the final analysis, most advertising seeks to do both, inform and persuade. As expected, this is an area where there is a great deal of disagreement and controversy. A particular advertisement may be offensive to some individuals and informative to others. Still other individuals may be completely indifferent. Today, about 2 per cent of the national product of the United States is spent on advertising. Of this, only about one fifth is spent on TV advertising, but it is against this type of advertising that the most vehement criticism is directed. Most other advertising, in newspapers, magazines, trade journals, yellow pages, direct mail, and even radio is generally informative and useful.

Summary

1. Monopolistic competition is the form of market organization characterized by many firms selling a differentiated product. Thus, instead of the industry we have a product group and the graphical analysis is confined to the "typical" or "representative" firm. Monopolistic competition is most common in the retail and service sectors of our economy. Each firm faces a very elastic demand curve (on the assumption that only this firm changes its price) and a less elastic or proportional demand curve (on the assumption that all firms in the "industry" change their prices simultaneously). These demand curves are represented, respectively, by d and D.

2. Under monopolistic competition, each firm believes that it operates on its very elastic demand curve d. Since d is negatively sloped, so is the corresponding MR curve. As in monopoly, the optimum short-run level of output for the monopolistically competitive firm is given by the point where the firm's MC curve intersects its MR curve from below, and the two demand curves (d and D) faced by the firm intersect at the price the firm charges. In the short run, the monopolistically competitive firm can earn profits, break even, or incur losses, but the firm will remain in business only if $P > AVC$.

3. As in perfect competition, firms in a monopolistically competitive industry can change their scale of plant and enter or leave the industry in the long run. If firms earn profits in the short run, more firms will enter the industry in the long run. This reduces the firm's market share and shifts the demand curves faced by the firm to the left until all profits are eliminated. The firm is in long-run equilibrium where its LMC curve intersects the mr curve from below. At long-run equilibrium, d is tangent to the LAC curve and proportional demand curve D intersects demand curve d at the point where d is tangent to the LAC curve.

4. Under monopolistic competition, firms can change not only the product price but also some of the characteristics of the product, and they can increase their selling expenses (such as advertising) in order to increase sales and profits. These forms of nonprice competition should be continued as long as the MR from nonprice competition exceeds MC and until the point where MR = MC. Product variation and selling expenses will shift up the demand and cost curves of the firm and can lead to short-run profits, but in long-run equilibrium the firm will only break even. Transaction costs are similar to selling expenses.

5. A monopolistically competitive firm in long-run equilibrium will produce a smaller output and charge a higher price than if the firm were per-

fectly competitive and faced the same *LAC* curve. The difference in the output is called excess capacity. This can be regarded as the cost of product differentiation. Some advertising and product variation is clearly useful, while some is excessive and wasteful. The theory of monopolistic competition is attacked on the grounds that the concept of the product group is very ambiguous and its predictive power is inferior to that of the perfectly competitive model.

6. Cents-off coupons are an example of third degree price discrimination in monopolistically compet-

itive markets. Price dispersion is due to product differentiation and lack of information. Price dispersion is inversely related to the amount of search effort by consumers. It diminishes with increases in education, the volume of purchases, and consumers' incomes. With entry blocked, monopolistically competitive firms can earn long-run profits. Excess capacity is really an inventory of unused capacity demanded by consumers to avoid waiting time. Most advertising is informative and persuasive.

Glossary

Monopolistic competition The form of market organization characterized by many sellers of a differentiated product.

Differentiated product Products that are similar, but not identical.

Product group The sellers of a differentiated product.

Proportional demand curve The constant share of the market demand curve faced by monopolistically competitive firms.

Ideal output The output at which the long-run average cost (*LAC*) is minimum.

Ideal plant The plant with the short-run average

total cost (*SATC*) curve tangent to the lowest point on the *LAC* curve.

Product variation Changes in some of the characteristics of differentiated products.

Selling expenses Expenditures (such as advertising) that the firm incurs to induce consumers to purchase more of the product.

Transaction costs The costs (such as the earnings of middlemen) required to facilitate transactions.

Excess capacity The difference between the ideal output and the actual output when the monopolistically competitive firm is in long-run equilibrium.

Questions for Review

1. (a) What is monopolistic competition?
   (b) What is the competitive element in monopolistic competition?
   (c) What is the monopolistic element in monopolistic competition?
   (d) What is product differentiation?
   (e) What is a product group? How does this compare to an industry?

2. (a) On what assumption is based the very elastic demand curve faced by a monopolistically competitive firm?
   (b) What is a "proportional demand curve"?
   (c) On what assumption is the proportional demand curve based?

3. (a) Does a firm under monopolistic competition believe it is on its proportional demand

   curve (*D*) or on its more elastic demand curve (*d*)?
   (b) Why does demand curve *d* slide down demand curve *D* in the process of reaching short-run equilibrium by a monopolistically competitive firm?
   (c) What is the general condition for short-run profit maximization for a monopolistically competitive firm?
   (d) What is the relationship between demand curves *d* and *D* when the firm is in short-run equilibrium?

4. (a) Will a firm under monopolistic competition earn profits, break even, or incur losses when in short-run equilibrium?
   (b) Will a monopolistically competitive firm

remain in business in the short run if it incurs losses at its best level of output?

(c) Where is the shutdown point for the monopolistically competitive firm?

5. (a) What happens in the long run if firms in a monopolistically competitive industry earn short-run profits?

(b) What effect will short-run profits have on the firm's proportional demand curve in the long run?

(c) What effect will short-run profits have on demand curve d of the firm in the long run?

6. When a monopolistically competitive firm is in long-run equilibrium, what is the relationship between

(a) the d and the LAC curves?

(b) the d and the D curves?

(c) the LMC and the mr curves?

7. (a) What are the choice-related variables of a firm under monopolistic competition?

(b) What is nonprice competition?

(c) What is product variation? Selling expenses? Transaction costs?

8. (a) How much should a firm spend on product variation and selling expenses?

(b) What effect will product variation and selling expenses have on the firm's demand and cost curves?

(c) What effect will product variation and selling expenses have on the firm's short-run and long-run equilibrium point?

9. (a) What is the ideal output?

(b) What is the ideal plant?

(c) What is excess capacity?

(d) What is the relationship between product differentiation and excess capacity?

10. (a) What is the usefulness of advertising?

(b) What is the usefulness of product variation?

(c) How much advertising and product variation is useful? How much is wasteful?

(d) Will advertising lead to higher or lower prices for the product?

11. (a) In what way is the concept of the product group ambiguous?

(b) What was thought to be a major advantage of the theory of monopolistic competition when it was first introduced?

(c) What are some disadvantages of the theory of monopolistic competition?

(d) Why do we continue to study the theory of monopolistic competition?

12. (a) In what way is cents-off coupons an example of third degree price discrimination in monopolistically competitive markets?

(b) What causes price dispersion? What factors cause it to diminish? To increase?

(c) Under what conditions can a monopolistically competitive firm earn long-run profits?

(d) What useful function does excess capacity serve?

(e) What are the pros and cons of advertising?

Problems

1. (a) Plot demand function $D = 8 - P$ and $d = 26 - 4P$ facing a monopolistically competitive firm.

(b) Explain the function (purpose) of each demand curve.

2. (a) Draw again the figure for Problem 1a and draw on it the mr curve of the firm corresponding to demand curve d. On the same figure, plot the MC curve of the firm if the $MC = 2 + \frac{1}{4}Q$.

(b) What price does the firm believe it should charge to maximize short-run profits?

(c) Why will the firm not be maximizing short-run profits at that price?

★3. Draw a figure showing the short-run equilibrium point for the monopolistically competitive firm of Problem 2.

4. If at the best level of output, $ATC = \$6$ and $AVC = \$3$ for the monopolistically competitive firm of Problem 3,

(a) How much profit or loss per unit and in total will the monopolistically competitive firm make?

(b) Will the firm produce or not? Why?

★5. Can the short-run supply curve of a monopolistically competitive firm be derived? Why?

6. Draw a figure for the firm of Problem 3 show-

ing that when in long-run equilibrium the firm charges $P = \$3$ and sells $Q = 2$.

★7. Starting at point Z on demand curve D^* in the right panel of Figure 12-3, explain why the monopolistically competitive firm does not believe that it can return to point T in the long run and break even.

8. Draw a figure showing that a monopolistically competitive firm
   (a) incurs economic losses in the short run, but remains in business.
   (b) breaks even when in long-run equilibrium.
   (c) breaks even in the long run even after it introduces a successful product variation.

9. Many firms under monopolistic competition set their advertising budgets at a fixed percentage of their anticipated sales. Does this mean that these firms behave in a nonmaximizing way? Explain.

10. What would happen if a monopolistically competitive firm produced the ideal output with the ideal plant when in long-run equilibrium?

★11. Excess capacity is inversely related to the price elasticity of demand faced by a monopolistically competitive firm. True or False? Explain.

12. (a) How much profit will the monopolistically competitive firm of Figure 12-6 earn in the long-run with blocked entry?
    (b) What adjustment can the firm of Figure 12-6 make in the long run?
    (c) Under what unusual situation would a monopolistically competitive firm produce the ideal output with the ideal scale of plant when in long-run equilibrium?

Supplementary Readings

For a problem-solving approach to the topics discussed in this chapter, see

Dominick Salvatore, *Microeconomic Theory,* 2nd ed. (New York: McGraw-Hill, 1983), Sections 12-1–12-3.

The ground-breaking works on monopolistic competition are

Edward H. Chamberlin, *The Theory of Monopolistic Competition* (Cambridge, Mass.: Harvard University Press, 1933).

Joan Robinson, *The Theory of Imperfect Competition* (London: Macmillan, 1933).

On product variation and selling expenses, see

James E. Meade, "The Optimal Balance Between Economies of Scale and Variety of Products: Studies in Impact," *Economica,* August 1974.

Richard L. Schmalensee, *The Economics of Advertising* (Amsterdam: North-Holland, 1972).

For an evaluation of the theory of monopolistic competition, see

Robert E. Kuenne, Ed., *Monopolistic Competition Theory: Studies in Impact* (New York: John Wiley, 1967).

George J. Stigler, *Five Lectures on Economic Problems* (New York: Macmillan, 1949).

Price and Output Under Oligopoly

Chapter 13

13-1   Oligopoly: Definition and Sources

13-2   No Rivalry Recognized: the Cournot and the Edgeworth Models

13-3   Rivalry Recognized: the Chamberlin and the Kinked-Demand Curve Models

13-4   Theory of Games and Oligopolistic Behavior

13-5   Collusion: Cartels, Price Leadership Models, and Antitrust Laws

13-6   Long-run Adjustments and Efficiency Implications

13-7   Applications

Examples

13-1   Concentration Ratios in the United States

13-2   The Organization of Petroleum Exporting Countries (OPEC)

13-3   The Electrical Conspiracy

13-4   Price Leadership in the Steel Industry

13-5   The Cost of Automobile Model Changes

Applications

Application 1:   Limit Pricing

Application 2:   Sales Maximization Model

Application 3:   Managerial Theories of the Firm

Application 4:   Cost-Plus Pricing

Application 5:   Product Differentiation and the Hotelling Paradox

---

Preview Questions

What is oligopoly?

What is the distinguishing feature of oligopoly?

What is the relationship between concentration ratios and oligopoly?

What is the usefulness of oligopoly models in which rivalry is not recognized?

What is the usefulness of game theory to oligopoly theory?

What is the incentive for oligopolistic firms to collude?

How can a cartel induce oligopolistic firms to operate as a monopoly?

What form other than cartel can collusion take?

What are the advantages and disadvantages of oligopoly?

In this last chapter of Part IV on the theory of the firm and markets, we bring together the theory of consumer behavior and demand (from part II) and the theory of production and costs (from Part III) to analyze how prices and output are determined under oligopoly.

We begin the chapter by defining oligopoly and by examining its sources. We then present many different models of oligopolistic behavior. We start with the simplest and most naive of the oligopolistic models in which firms do not recognize their interdependence or rivalry. We then move on to more realistic models where oligopolistic firms do recognize their interdependence. This is clearly brought out in models where oligopolists behave as players in a game and use strategic behavior as in warfare. Finally, we examine still more realistic models where firms not only recognize their interdependence but also attempt to improve their situation and profitability by collusion. These are the cartel and price-leadership models.

After the various oligopoly models have been presented, we examine the long-run efficiency implications of oligopoly as compared with other types of market structure. The last section of the chapter presents many important applications and extensions of the oligopoly models. While the theory of oligopoly leaves much to be desired, these applications and the many real-world examples presented in the theory sections highlight the importance and relevance of the analytical tools developed in this chapter.

13-1

Oligopoly: Definition and Sources

In Chapter 10 we defined perfect competition as the form of market organization in which there are many sellers of a homogeneous product. In Chapter 11 we said that monopoly is the single seller of a product. In Chapter 12 we then defined monopolistic competition as the market organization in which there are many sellers of a differentiated product. Between perfect competition and monopolistic competition on the one hand, and monopoly on the other, lies **oligopoly.** This refers to few sellers of a homogeneous or differentiated product. If there are only two sellers, we have a **duopoly.** If the product is homogeneous we have a **pure oligopoly,** and if the product is differentiated we have a **differentiated oligopoly.** While entry into an oligopolistic industry is possible, it is not easy (as evidenced by the fewness of firms in the industry).

Oligopoly is the most prevalent form of market organization in the manufacturing sector of the United States and other industrial countries. Some oligopolistic industries in the United States are automobiles, electrical equipment, breakfast cereals, cigarettes, primary aluminum, steel, soap and detergents, beer brewing, and many others. Some of these products (such as primary aluminum and steel) are homogeneous. Others (such as automobiles, breakfast cereals, cigarettes, and soap and detergents) are differentiated. For simplicity, we will deal mostly with pure oligopolies (where products are homogeneous) in this chapter.

Since there are only a few firms selling a homogeneous or differentiated product in oligopolistic markets, the actions of each firm affect the other firms in the industry, and vice versa. For example, if General Motors sharply reduced the price of its Oldsmobile Cutlass Supreme model, it would very likely take many customers away from Ford's Tiempo and Chrysler's Dodge 400. As a result, it is likely that Ford and Chrysler would respond with price cuts of their own. Since this might lead to a ruinous price war, producers of automobiles and other products in oligopolistic markets usually prefer to compete on the basis of product differentiation and advertising. Yet even here, if Chrysler mounted a major advertising campaign, G.M. and Ford would soon be likely to respond in kind.

In short, the distinguishing characteristic of oligopoly is the interdependence or rivalry among firms. This is the natural result of fewness. That is, in deciding on its pricing, product characteristics, advertising, and other policies, each firm must consider the possible reaction of competitors. Since competitors can react in many different ways, we do not have a single oligopoly model, but many. Each particular behavioral response of competitors assumed leads to a different oligopoly model. In this chapter, we will present some of the most important of these models. The existence of many different and often conflicting models, however, points to the rather unsatisfactory state of oligopoly theory. This is unfortunate because oligopoly (as mentioned above) is the most prevalent form of market organization in the manufacturing sector of industrial countries today.

The sources of oligopoly are generally the same as for monopoly. That is, oligopoly may arise because (1) economics of scale may operate over a sufficiently large range of outputs as to leave only a few firms supplying the entire market (as, for example, in the automobile industry), (2) only a few firms may own or control the entire supply of a raw material required in the production of a commodity, (3) a few firms may own a patent for the exclusive right to produce a commodity or to use a particular production process, and finally, (4) only a few firms may be allowed to operate in a market by government franchise.

The degree by which a particular industry is dominated by a few large firms is measured by the **concentration ratio.** This gives the percentage of total industry sales of 4, 8, and 20 largest firms in the industry (see Example 13-1). An industry in which the 4-firm concentration ratio is close to 100 percent is clearly oligopolistic in nature, and industries where this ratio is higher than 50 per cent or 60 percent are also likely to be oligopolistic.

Example 13-1   Concentration Ratios in the United States

The Facts: Table 13-1 presents the 4-firm and the 8-firm concentration ratios for various industries in the United States in 1977.

Comment: Concentration ratios must be used with caution since they may underestimate or overestimate the true market power of the largest firms in a market. For example, the four largest firms in the cement industry

TABLE 13-1   Concentration Ratios in the United States, 1977

Industry	4-Firm Ratio	8-Firm Ratio
Motor vehicles	93	99
Electric lamps	90	95
Breakfast cereals	89	98
Household refrigerators	82	98
Primary aluminum	76	93
Tires	70	88
Roasted coffee	61	73
Aircraft	59	81
Soaps and detergents	59	71
Steel Mills	45	65
Electronic computing equipment	44	55
Cheese	35	48
Cement	24	41
Book publishing	17	30
Men's clothing	12	22
Women's dresses	8	12

Source: U.S. Bureau of the Census, 1977 Census of Manufactures, *Concentration Ratios in Manufacturing* (Washington, D.C.: U.S. Government Printing Office, 1981).

supply only 24 per cent of the (national) market, but because of the very high costs of transporting cement, only two or three firms may actually compete in many local markets. On the other hand, the high concentration ratio in the United States automobile industry overestimates the market power of U.S. auto manufacturers because of automobile imports. How broadly or narrowly a product is defined is also very important. Thus, the concentration ratio in the computer industry as a whole is higher than in the personal-computer segment of the market. On the other hand, the high concentration in the market for breakfast cereals exaggerates the market power of the largest firms in this market because of the availability of close substitutes (such as eggs, muffins, or peanuts).

13-2

No Rivalry Recognized: The Cournot and the Edgeworth Models

In this section we examine the Cournot and the Edgeworth models. These are the two earliest and most naive oligopoly models. In these models, the oligopolists never recognize their interdependence or rivalry. As such, these models are quite unrealistic. Nevertheless, they do serve to highlight the interdependence that exists among oligopolistic firms, and they are the forerunners of the more realistic models discussed in subsequent sections.

13-2a The Cournot Model

The first of the oligopoly models was introduced by the French economist Augustin Cournot nearly one hundred and fifty years ago.[1] For simplicity Cournot assumed that there were only two firms (duopoly) selling identical spring water. Consumers came to the springs with their own containers, so that the marginal cost of production was zero for the two firms. With these assumptions, the analysis is greatly simplified without losing the essence of the model.[2]

The basic behavioral assumption made in the **Cournot model** is that each firm, while trying to maximize profits, assumes that the other duopolist holds its *output* constant at the existing level. The result is a cycle of moves and countermoves by the duopolists until each sells ⅓ of the total industry output (if the industry is organized along perfectly competitive lines). This is shown in Figure 13-1.

---

[1] A. Cournot, *Recerces sur les Principes Mathematiques de la Theorie des Richess* (Paris: 1838). English translation by N. Bacon, *Researches into the Mathematical Principles of the Theory of Wealth* (New York: Macmillan, 1897).

[2] The model, however, can be extended to deal with more than two firms and nonzero marginal costs.

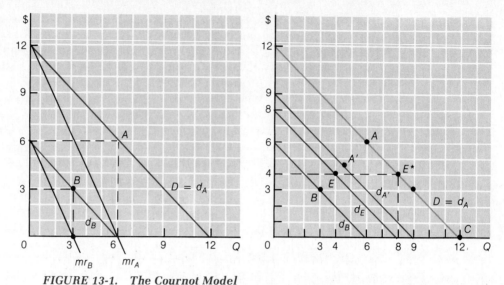

FIGURE 13-1.   The Cournot Model
In the left panel, D is the market demand curve for spring water. The marginal cost of production is assumed to be zero. When only firm A is in the market, $D = d_A$ and the firm maximizes profits by selling Q = 6 at P = \$6 (point A, given by mr_A = MC = 0). When firm B enters the market, it will face d_B (given by D minus 6 units). Firm B maximizes profits by selling Q = 3 at P = \$3 (point B, the midpoint of d_B at which mr_B = MC = 0). Duopolist A now faces d_A, (given by D minus 3 in the right panel) and maximizes profits by selling Q = 4.5 at P = \$4.50 (point A'). The process continues until each duopolist is at point E on d_E and sells Q = 4 at P = \$4.

In the left panel of Figure 13-1, D is the market demand curve for spring water. Initially, suppose that firm A is the only firm in the market, and thus, it faces the total market demand curve. That is, $D = d_A$. The marginal revenue curve of firm A is then mr_A (see the figure). Since the marginal cost is zero, the MC curve coincides with the horizontal axis. Under these circumstances, firm A maximizes total profits where mr_A = MC = 0. Firm A sells 6 units of spring water at P = \$6 so that its total revenue (TR) is \$36 (point A in the left panel). This is the monopoly solution. Note that point A is the midpoint of demand curve $D = d_A$, at which price elasticity is 1 and TR is maximum (see Section 5.5). With total costs equal to zero, total profits equal TR = \$36.

Next, assume that firm B enters the market, and believes that firm A will continue to sell 6 units. Then the demand curve that firm B faces is the market demand curve D minus the 6 units sold by firm A, or d_B in the left panel. The marginal revenue curve of firm B is then mr_B. Firm B maximizes total profits where mr_B = MC = 0. Therefore, firm B sells 3 units at P = \$3 (point B, the midpoint of d_B). This is also shown in the right panel of Figure 13-1. Starting from point B on d_B in the right panel, and assuming that firm B continues to sell 3 units, firm A reacts and faces $d_{A'}$, given by D minus 3. Firm A will then maximize profits by selling 4.5 units at P = \$4.5 (point

A', the midpoint of $d_{A'}$, at which $mr_{A'} = MC = 0$). Firm B now reacts once again and maximizes profits on its new demand curve, which is obtained by subtracting the 4.5 units supplied by firm A from market demand D (see Problem 1, with answer in the back of the book).

The process continues until each duopolist faces demand curve d_E and maximizes profits by selling 4 units at $P = \$4$ (point E). This is equilibrium because whichever firm faces demand curve d_E and reaches point E first, the other will also face demand curve d_E (given by $D - 4$) and will also maximize profits at point E. With each duopolist selling 4 units, a combined total of 8 units will be sold in the market at $P = \$4$ (point E^* on D). If the market had been organized along perfectly competitive lines, sales would have been 12 units given by point C, where market demand curve D intercepts the horizontal axis. At point C, $P = MR = LMC = LAC = 0$ and all the perfectly competitive firms would break even when in long-run equilibrium.

Thus, the duopolists supply 1/3 or 4 units each (and 2/3 or 8 units together) of the total perfectly competitive market quantity of 12 units. With three oligopolists, each would supply 1/4 (i.e., 3 units) of the perfectly competitive market of 12 units and 3/4 (i.e., 9 units) in total. Note that when $Q = 9$, $P = \$3$ on market demand curve D. Thus, as the number of firms increases, the total combined output of all the firms together increases and price falls. As more firms enter, the market will eventually no longer be oligopolistic. In the limit, with many firms, total output will approach 12 units and price will approach zero (the perfectly competitive solution)[3]

13-2b The Edgeworth Model

The **Edgeworth model** arose from the criticism that the French mathematician Joseph Bertrand raised in 1883 against the Cournot model.[4] Bertrand suggested that it might be more appropriate to assume that each duopolist kept its *price* rather than its output unchanged. Some years later, the English economist F. Edgeworth picked up this suggestion, and developed a duopoly model of his own.[5]

Specifically, Edgeworth assumed with Cournot that there were two firms selling identical spring water under conditions of zero marginal cost. However, as opposed to Cournot, Edgeworth adopted Bertrand's behavioral assumption that each duopolist, in trying to maximize profits, assumed that the other kept its price constant. Edgeworth made the additional assump-

---

[3] It should be noted that the Cournot solution results only when the rather special behavioral assumptions of the model hold.

[4] J. Bertrand, "Theorie Mathematique de la Richesse Sociale," *Journal des Savantes*, 1883.

[5] F. Edgeworth, "La Teoria Pura del Monopolio," *Giornale degli Economisti*, 1897. The article was reprinted in English as "The Pure Theory of Monopoly," in F. Edgeworth, *Papers Relating to Political Economy* (London: Macmillan, 1925).

tion that because of production limitations each duopolist could not satisfy the entire market by itself. With these assumptions, Edgeworth developed a model in which price fluctuated between the monopoly price and the maximum output price of each duopolist. Thus, in the Edgeworth model there is no stable equilibrium as in the Cournot model. This is shown in Figure 13-2.

In Figure 13-2, duopolist A faces demand curve d_A and duopolist B faces identical demand curve d_B (measured from the origin to the left). Each duopolist cannot produce more than 5 units. If duopolist A enters the market first, duopolist A maximizes profits by selling 3 units at $P = \$3$ (point A). Point A is the midpoint of d_A and is given by $mr_A = MC = 0$ (not shown in the figure). Duopolist B now enters the market and, by setting its price slightly below $P = \$3$ charged by duopolist A, sells the maximum output of 5 units (point B) and captures most of A's market (because the product is homogeneous). Duopolist B will not capture all of A's market because of its output limitation. Having lost most of its market, duopolist A reacts by lowering its price below that charged by firm B, and itself captures most of the market (point A'). The process continues until each firm sells its maximum output of 5 units at $P = \$1$ (points A* and B*, respectively).

At this point, one of the duopolists, say duopolist A, realizes that it can

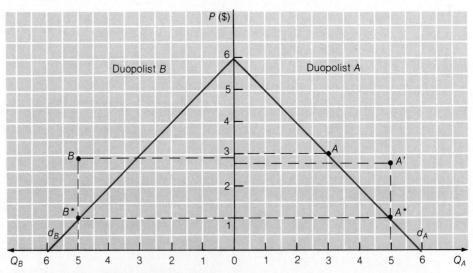

FIGURE 13-2.   The Edgworth Model
Duopolist A and B face demand curve d_A and d_B, respectively. The commodity is homogeneous, $MC = 0$, and each firm cannot produce more than $Q = 5$. Duopolist A enters the market first and maximizes profits by selling $Q = 3$ at $P = \$3$ (point A). Duopolist B, assuming that A keeps price constant, sets price slightly below $P = \$3$ and captures most of the A's market (point B). Duopolist A reacts, sets price lower than B's price, and captures most of the market (point A'). B reacts and the process continues until $Q = 5$ and $P = \$1$ for each firm. However, A or B now realizes that it can increase profits with $P = \$3$, and the cycle is repeated.

increase profits by returning to the monopoly price of $P = \$3$. Since duopolist B is already selling its maximum output of 5 units (point B^*), duopolist A is confident that it can sell 3 units at $P = \$3$ and increase (and maximize) its TR and total profits at point A. Duopolist B, however, will not keep its price at $P = \$1$ as assumed by duopolist A. That is, B realizes that by charging a price slightly less than $3, it can sell its maximum output of 5 units at this high price (point B) and considerably increase its profits. A reacts and the entire cycle is repeated. Thus, in the Edgeworth model, price fluctuates between $P = \$3$ and $P = \$1$, and quantity fluctuates between $Q = 3$ to $Q = 5$, indefinitely.[6]

The problem with the Cournot and the Edgeworth models is that the duopolists never recognize their interdependence and never learn from their experience. This is indeed very unrealistic. In addition, Edgeworth assumes that each duopolist has fixed production capacity, while in most cases production can be expanded in the long run. Thus, these naive models cannot possibly be used to analyze the real-world behavior of oligopolists. Their main usefulness is that they forcefully show the interdependence among firms in oligopolistic markets and represent the point of departure for the more realistic models examined in the following sections.

13-3

Rivalry Recognized: The Chamberlin and the Kinked-Demand Curve Models

We now consider two other oligopoly models, the Chamberlin model and the kinked-demand curve model, in which the oligopolists do recognize their interdependence or rivalry. Although these models also face many shortcomings, by removing the major objection to the Cournot and Edgeworth models, they represent a step forward in the direction of greater realism and usefulness.

13-3a The Chamberlin Model

In 1933, Chamberlin extended the Cournot model and gave us the more realistic duopoly model that bears his name.[7] Chamberlin started with the same basic assumptions as Cournot, but he assumed further that the duopolists do recognize their interdependence. The result is that without any formal agreement or collusion, the duopolists set the monopoly price and

---

[6] As for the Cournot's model, the result of the Edgeworth's model arises only if the special behavioral assumptions of that model hold.

[7] E. Chamberlain, *The Theory of Monopolistic Competition* (Cambridge, Mass.: Harvard University Press, 1933).

share equally in the monopoly output and profits. This is shown in Figure 13-3.

In Figure 13-3, D is the total market demand curve for spring water supplied at zero marginal cost by duopolists A and B. If duopolist A is the first to enter the market, it will maximize profits by selling the monopoly output of 6 units at the monopoly price of $6 (point A on $D = d_A$, as in Figure 13-1). Next, duopolist B enters the market, and taking A's output as constant, sells 3 units at $P = \$3$ (point B on d_B). So far this is identical with the Cournot model.

At this point, the **Chamberlin model** departs from the Cournot model. Specifically, the duopolists now recognize their interdependence and realize that the best they can do is to share equally in the monopoly output and sell at the monopoly price. Thus, duopolist A will voluntarily and without collusion reduce its output from 6 to 3 units and charge $P = \$6$. Duopolist B will keep its output at 3 units and will also charge $P = \$6$ (point B' in the figure). With total costs equal to zero, each duopolist will have TR and profits of $18 (obtained from $Q = 3$ times $P = \$6$) as compared with $16 (obtained from $Q = 4$ times $P = \$4$) in the Cournot model.

Note that the solution of the Chamberlin model is stable and it is reached without agreement or collusion. Price is also quite stable. How prevalent this noncollusive and sophisticated type of behavior occurs in the real world is difficult to determine.

FIGURE 13-3.
The Chamberlin
Model

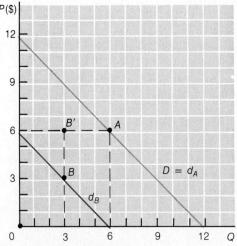

D is the market demand curve for spring water supplied at MC= 0 by duopolists A and B. If duopolist A is the first to enter the market, it will maximize profits by selling Q= 6 at P= $6 (point A on D= d$_A$). Next, duopolist B enters the market, and taking A's output as constant, sells Q= 3 at P= $3 (point B on d$_B$). Each duopolist now recognizes its interdependence, and without collusion, sells Q= 3 at P= $6 and shares equally in the monopoly profits.

13-3b The Kinked-Demand Curve Model

Another model where the oligopolists recognize their interdependence but act without collusion is the **kinked-demand curve model,** introduced by Paul Sweezy in 1939.[8] With his model, Sweezy attempted to explain the price rigidity that is often observed in some oligopolistic markets.

Sweezy postulated that if an oligopolist raised its price, it would lose most of its customers since the other firms in the industry would not match the price increase. On the other hand, an oligopolist could not increase its share of the market by lowering its price since its competitors would immediately match the price reduction. As a result, according to Sweezy, oligopolists face a demand curve that is highly elastic for price increases and less elastic for price reductions. That is, the demand curve faced by oligopolists has a kink at the established price and, because of this, oligopolists tend to keep prices constant even in the face of changed costs and demand conditions. This is shown in Figure 13-4.

In Figure 13-4, the demand curve facing the oligopolist is d or HBC and has a "kink" at the prevailing price of $8 and $Q = 4$ (point B). The demand curve is much more elastic above than below the kink on the assumption that competitors will not match price increases but quickly match price cuts.[9] Thus, the oligopolist's marginal revenue curve is mr or $HJKFG$. Segment HJ of the mr curve corresponds to segment HB of the demand curve, and segment FG of the mr curve corresponds to segment BC of the demand curve (see the figure). The kink at point B on the demand curve results in discontinuity JF in the mr curve.

With SMC as the short-run marginal cost curve, the oligopolist will maximize profits by selling 4 units of output at $P = \$8$ (given by point K, where the SMC curve intersects the discontinuous segment of the mr curve). Any shift in the oligopolist's SMC curve that falls within the discontinuous segment of the mr curve will leave the oligopolist's price and output unchanged. That is, the oligopolist's best level of output will continue to be 4 units and price $8 for any shift in the SMC curve up to SMC' or down to SMC'' (see the figure). Only if the SMC curve shifts above the SMC' curve will the oligopolist raise price, and only if the SMC curve shifts below the SMC'' curve will the oligopolist lower price (see Problem 3). Similarly, a rightward or leftward shift in the demand curve will induce the oligopolist to increase or decrease output, respectively, but to keep price unchanged if the kink remains at the same level (see Problem 4, with answer in the back of the book).

[8] P. Sweezy, "Demand under Conditions of Oligopoly," *Journal of Political Economy,* August 1939, pp. 568–573.

[9] That is, since competitors do not match price increases, the quantity demanded from the oligopolist that increases price *falls a great deal.* On the other hand, since competitors quickly match price reductions, the quantity demanded from the oligopolist that cuts price *does not increase very much.* This makes the demand curve faced by an oligopolist more elastic for price increases than for price reductions.

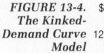

FIGURE 13-4.
The Kinked-
Demand Curve
Model

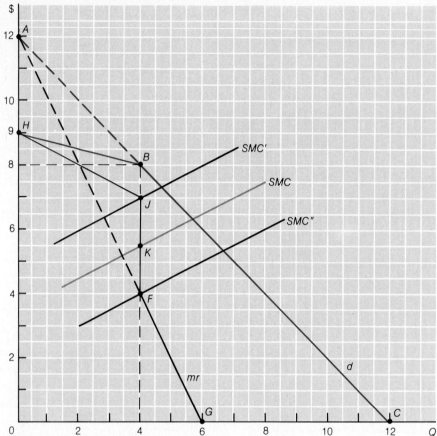

The demand curve facing the oligopolist is d or HBC and has a "kink" at the prevailing price of $8 and Q= 4 (point B), on the assumption that competitors match
price cuts but not price increases. The marginal revenue curve is mr or HJKFG. The
oligopolist maximized profits by selling Q= 4 and P= $8 (given by point K, where
the SMC curve intersects the discontinous segment of the mr curve). Any shift
between SMC′ and SMC″ will leave price and output unchanged.

When the kinked-demand curve model was first introduced, it was
hailed by some economists as a general theory of oligopoly. Yet, the model
failed to live up to its expectations. For example, Stigler found no evidence
that oligopolists were reluctant to match price increases as readily as price
reductions, and thus he seriously questioned the existence of the kink.[10]
The same was found by other researchers in other oligopolistic industries.
Even more serious is the criticism that while the kinked-demand curve
model can *rationalize* the existence of rigid prices where they occur, it can-

[10] G. Stigler, "The Kinky Oligopoly Demand Curve and Rigid Prices," *Journal of Political
Economy*, October 1947, pp. 432–449.

not *explain* at what price the kink occurs in the first place. Since one of the major aims of microeconomic theory is to explain how prices are determined, this theory is, at best, incomplete.

13-4

Theory of Games and Oligopolistic Behavior[11]

Since oligopolists must consider the reactions of the other firms in the industry to their own action, the behavior of oligopolists has been likened to that of the players in a game and to the strategic behavior of warring factions. This crucial aspect of oligopolistic behavior is captured in a novel approach to oligopoly called game theory. Game theory was introduced by John von Neumann and Oskar Morgenstern in 1944, and it was soon hailed as a breakthrough in the study of oligopoly.[12] In general, **game theory** is concerned with the choice of the optimum strategy in conflict situations. Specifically, game theory can help an oligopolist choose the course of action (for example, the best price to charge) that maximizes its benefit or profits after considering all possible reactions of its competitors.

13-4a Zero-Sum Games

The simplest type of game theory is a two-person zero-sum game. For example, suppose that an industry is composed of two firms, A and B. Each duopolist has a choice of various strategies regarding the price to charge, the degree of product differentiation, the amount to spend on advertising, and so on. Thus, it might be possible for firm A to increase its share of the market by 1 per cent (at the expense of firm B) by increasing its expenditures on advertising, if firm B kept its advertising expenditurs unchanged. However, if firm B also increased its advertising expenditures, firm A may not gain any market share. On the other hand, if A increased its price and B did not match it, firm A might lose 2 per cent of the market to firm B. Games of this nature, where the gains of one firm equal the losses of the other (so that total gains plus total losses sum to zero) are called **zero-sum games.** These are the simplest types of games, and we now concentrate on these.

For each strategy adopted by firm A there are usually a number of strategies (reactions) open to firm B. The outcome or **payoff** of each *combination* of strategies will then take the form (in our example) of a percentage gain (+) or loss (−) of market share by firm A. Of course, the gain in market

---

[11] This section can be omitted without loss of continuity.

[12] J. von Neumann and O. Morgenstern, *Theory of Games and Economic Behavior* (Princeton, N.J.: Princeton University Press, 1944).

share by firm A equals the loss of market share by firm B, and vice versa. A zero payoff means that each firm retains its share of the market. For example, suppose that firm A has two possible strategies open to it (A1 and A2), while firm B has three strategies (B1, B2, B3) to choose from. For each of the two strategies available to firm A, firm B can respond with one of the three possible strategies. Thus, we have a **payoff matrix** with 6 (2 × 3) possible *combinations*, as shown in Table 13-2. By convention, the payoff matrix reflects firm A's perspective and is known to both firms.

Table 13-2 shows that each of the two strategies open to firm A is associated with one of three possible payoffs or outcomes depending on firm B's response, as indicated along a row of the table. For example, strategy A1 by firm A can be associated with strategy (response) B1, B2, or B3 by firm B (the first row of the table). Specifically, if firm B responds with strategy B1 to strategy A1 by firm A, firm A will gain 1 per cent in market share from market B (the first entry in the first row of the table). If, instead, firm B responds to A1 with strategy B2, firm A gains zero market share (and thus B suffers no loss in market share). This is given by the second entry in the first row of the table. Finally, with strategies A1 and B3, firm A gains 2 per cent of the market at the expense of firm B. With strategies A2 and B1 (A2B1) firm A *loses* 2 percent of the market to firm B (the first entry in the second row of the table), and so on.

The last column of the table shows the *minimum* payoff to firm A in each row. For example, the smallest gain in market share associated with A1 (row 1) is zero. This occurs when firm B responds with strategy B2 to A1. Similarly, the minimum payoff for strategy A2 involves a 2 per cent loss in market share by firm A to firm B. This results when firm B responds with strategy B1 to A2. The crucial question facing firm A now is which of the two strategies is best, in view of the known possible responses by firm B.

Firm A knows that firm B will always respond with the strategy that *minimizes A's gain* because that is the strategy that *minimizes B's loss*. Thus, firm A will adopt a **maximin strategy.** That is, A will choose the strategy that maximizes its minimum gain, in view of B's response. For example, if firm A adopts strategy A1, it knows that firm B will choose B2 because that minimizes A's gain (B's losses). This involves no market gain or loss for both A and B. If firm A chose strategy A2, firm B would choose B1 so that

TABLE 13-2 Matrix of Firm A's Gain (+) and Loss (−) of Market Share (in Percentages)

			Firm B		
		B1	B2	B3	Row Minimum
Firm A	A1	1	0	2	0
	A2	−2	−1	0	−2
Column Maximum		1	0	2	0 = 0

firm A would lose 2 per cent of the market to firm B. Thus, A1 is the best or **dominant strategy** open to firm A. This is the maximum of the row minima, or maximin. Note that each payoff in the first row is larger than the corresponding payoff in the second row, and so firm A would never choose strategy A2.

Let us now shift attention to firm B. Since firm B knows that firm A will always choose strategy A1, firm B will adopt strategy B2 to minimize A's gains (B's losses). Thus, B adopts a **minimax strategy.** That is, B will minimize the column maxima (shown in the last row of the table). When firm B adopts strategy B2, firm A gains zero market share, as opposed to a 1 per cent and 2 per cent gain with B1 and B3, respectively (see the table). Thus, while A adopts a maximin strategy (maximizes the row minimum), B adopts a minimax strategy (minimizes the column maximum).

But in our example, the maximum of the row minima coincides with the minimum of the column maxima. The payoff of each is zero (shown by the bottom lower corner entry of the table). Each firm chooses a unique or **pure strategy** (firm A chooses A1 and firm B chooses B2), and neither firm can accomplish more. Examples of this might be the canceling effects of advertising by rivals in the cigarette industry or automobiles style changes. Games of this type where the maximin behavior of A coincides with the minimax behavior of B are said to be **strictly determined.** The solution of a strictly determined game (A1B2 in our example) is called a **saddle point.** All games that are strictly determined have a saddle point, but (as we will show next) not all games are strictly determined.

13-4b Mixed Strategies

Not all games are strictly determined or have a saddle point. That is, in some games, the row minima does not coincide with the column maxima. For example, suppose that two individuals (A and B) play a coin-matching game, whereby if both individuals present a head (H) or a tail (T), individual A wins a dollar from individual B. If one individual presents a head and the other presents a tail or vice versa (i.e., if the coins do not match), individual B wins a dollar. The payoff matrix is then given by Table 13-3.

This coin-matching game is not strictly determined and has no saddle point since the row minima (−$1) is not equal to the column maxima ($1). In this game, if individual A presents a head every time, individual B will eventually always present a tail and B would win every time. If A presents T every time, B will eventually always present H and, again, B wins every time. On the other hand, if A knows what B is going to do, A will win every time by matching B's coin. In such cases, the best that each individual can do is to adopt a **mixed strategy,** rather than a pure strategy, and present H and T half of the time but at random. One way to do this is to toss a coin and present the result. With such a random behavior, each individual will win approximately half of the time and thus break even in the long run. This is the best that each individual can do.

415

TABLE 13-3   Matrix of Individual A Gain (+) and Loss (−1) of $1

		Individual B		Row Minimum
		H	T	
Individual A	H	$1	−$1	−$1
	T	−$1	$1	−$1
Column Maximum		$1	$1	$1 = −$1

In games requiring mixed strategies, advance knowledge of the opponents' plans would give a player a crucial advantage. Thus, secrecy and random behavior become essential in nonstrictly determined games. It is for this reason that professors usually choose quiz questions at random from a book, border patrols frequently change their routine, top government officials frequently change their detailed travel plans for security reasons, and top management tries to keep their firm's marketing strategy secret as long as possible. Von Neumann and Morgenstern proved that when each player adopts the optimal mixed strategy, a stable solution can always be found in the sense that no player can further improve his or her position. However, a stable solution depends on the assumption that each player knows and assigns the same probability to each pair of payoffs. This is seldom, if ever, true in the real world.

13-4c Nonzero Sum Games

Not all games are zero sum. For example, in voluntary exchange both parties gain (see Application 3 in Chapter 4). Thus, voluntary exchange is an example of a positive-sum game. Negative-sum games are also possible in which both parties lose (an example might be war). Oligopoly itself is one of the best examples of a nonzero sum game. Table 13-4 gives an example of a nonzero (positive) sum game.

In Table 13-4, firm A has a choice of two possible strategies: charging a low price or a high price, and so does firm B. Thus, there are four possible combinations of strategies. A low or a high price by firm A can be associated with a low or a high price by firm B. The first number for each of the four combinations of strategies in Table 13-4 is the payoff of firm A and the second number is the payoff of firm B.

For example, if both firms charge a low price, each will earn $1 million profit. If firm A charges a low price while firm B charges a high price, firm A earns a profit of $3 million and firm B incurs a loss of $1 million. On the other hand, if firm A charges a high price while firm B charges a low price, firm A incurs a loss of $1 million and firm B earns profits of $3 million. Finally, if both firms charge a high price, each firm earns a $2 million profit. Note that the sum of the payoffs for each of the four combinations of strategies by the two firms is positive rather than zero, and so we have a non-

416

TABLE 13-4 Payoff Matrix for a Nonzero Sum Game (Profits in Millions of Dollars)

		Firm B	
		Low Price	High Price
Firm A	Low Price	1, 1	3, −1
	High Price	−1, 3	2, 2

zero (positive) sum game. The usual question now is which of the two strategies open to firm A and B is best from each firm's point of view.

The low-price strategy by firm A is better than (i.e., dominant over) the high-price strategy for firm A because no matter how firm B responds, firm A earns a higher profit. That is, when firm A charges a low price, it will earn $1 million if firm B responds with a low price and $3 million if firm B responds with a high price. On the other hand, if firm A charged a high price, it would suffer a loss of $1 million if firm B responded with a low price and earn a profit of only $2 million if firm B responded with a high price. Thus, firm A charges a low price.

Then, the best that firm B can do is to also charge a low price (and also earn a profit of $1 million). If firm B responded with a high price, it would incur a loss of $1 million. Thus, firm B also charges a low price. This is a strictly determined **nonzero sum game** with the saddle point occurring when each firm charges a low price and earns a $1 million profit. Note that in this game both firms adopt a maximin strategy. Firm A maximizes the row minima of its "winnings" charges a low price, while firm B maximizes the column minima of its "winnings" and also charges a low price. Note also that this is a *noncooperative* game. By colluding, both firms can charge a high price and increase their profits to $2 million (see the collusion models of oligopoly, discussed in Section 13-5).

13-4d The Prisoners' Dilemma

A two-person, nonzero (and nonconstant) sum game where the *payoffs are negative* is given by the **prisoners' dilemma**. This can be explained with the following example.

Two suspects are arrested for robbery and if convicted, they could each receive a maximum sentence of 10 years imprisonment. However, unless one or both suspects confess, the evidence is such that they can only be convicted of possessing stolen goods, which carries a maximum sentence of 1 year in prison. Each suspect is interrogated separately and no communication is allowed between the two suspects. The District Attorney promises each suspect that by confessing, he or she will go free while the other suspect (who does not confess) will receive the full 10-year sentence. If both suspects confess, each gets a reduced sentence of 5 years imprisonment. If neither suspect confesses, each will receive a 1-year jail sen-

TABLE 13-5   Negative Payoff Matrix for Suspect A and Suspect B (Years of Detention)

		Suspect B	
		Confess	Don't Confess
Suspect A	Confess	5, 5	0, 10
	Don't Confess	10, 0	1, 1

tence. The (negative) payoff matrix in terms of years of detention is given by Table 13-5.

From Table 13-5, we see that confessing is the best strategy for suspect A no matter what suspect B does. The reason for this is that if suspect B also confesses, suspect A receives a 5-year jail sentence. If suspect B does not confess, suspect A goes free. On the other hand, if suspect A does not confess and suspect B does, suspect A gets the full 10-year sentence. If suspect B does not confess either, each gets only a 1-year jail sentence. That is, suspect A gets 5 years or goes free by confessing, as opposed to 10 years or 1 year by not confessing. Thus, suspect A confesses. The same is true for suspect B. That is, by confessing suspect B gets either a 5-year sentence or goes free, as opposed to 10 years or 1 year by not confessing. Thus, the dominant strategy is to expect the worst (a confession) from the other suspect, and so both suspects confess (maximin).[13]

An important economic application of this is given by the fact that when one oligopolist (say, a cigarette manufacturer) introduces a new advertising campaign in an attempt to increase its market share, its rivals are likely to retaliate in kind and launch an advertising campaign of their own. The result may be that these rival advertisements will cancel each other out and only add to the oligopolists' costs (a negative payoff). Yet, no firm would then reduce its advertising expenditures unilaterally. Thus, when cigarette advertising on television was banned, all tobacco companies benefited by spending less on advertising (see Problem 7, with answer at the end of the text). Another interesting illustration of the prisoners' dilemma is in the analysis of auto style changes.[14]

Game theory faces some serious criticisms. First, many economists feel that the essential maximin-minimax principle is too conservative. This assumes that each player decides on his or her course of action on the assumption that the rival always chooses the most damaging strategy from

---

[13] Only if the two suspects could communicate with each other would neither one confess and receive only a 1-year (rather than a 5-year) sentence. Another way by which this non-cooperative game can become a cooperative game (where neither suspect confesses, so that each gets only a 1-year jail sentence) is if both suspects fear being killed for confessing by other implicated criminals still at large.

[14] See, H. Bierman and R. Tollison, "Styling Changes and the 'Prisoner's Dilemma'," *Antitrust Law and Economics Review*, Fall 1970, pp. 95–100.

the former's point of view. That is, each player takes the best of the worst possible situations. Many economists question this assumption as overly pessimistic. But if the worst situation does not arise, the course of action chosen by the first player will not be his or her best. Second, oligopolists often adopt a more dynamic behavior and spend considerble effort to improve the worst possible situation. Third, the theory in its present stage can only be used to deal with simple (essentially one-move) duopoly problems, and it provides only some insights into the more complex oligopoly problems encountered in the real world (which involve more than two players and a sequence of moves, as in bridge and poker). Nevertheless, although it did not fully meet expectations, game theory has added a new and useful dimension to the analysis of oligopoly.

13-5

Collusion: Cartels, Price Leadership Models, and Antitrust Laws

In the oligopoly models examined until now, oligopolists did not collude. However, in view of the interdependence in oligopolistic markets, there is a natural tendency to collude. With **collusion**, oligopolistic firms can avoid behavior that is detrimental to their general interest (for example, price wars) and adopt policies that increase their profits. Collusion can be overt (i.e., explicit), as in a centralized cartel, or tacit (i.e., implicit) as in price leadership models. In this section we examine oligopolistic models with collusion and provide several real-world examples. We also discuss briefly the antitrust laws forbidding collusion.

13-5a The Centralized Cartel

A **cartel** is a formal organization of producers of a commodity. Its purpose is to coordinate the policies of the member firms so as to increase profits. Cartels are illegal in the United States under the provision of the Sherman Antitrust Act passed in 1890 (see Section 13-5d) but not in some other nations. There are many types of cartels. At one extreme is the **centralized cartel.** This sets the monopoly price for the commodity, allocates the monopoly output among the member firms, and determines how the monopoly profits are to be shared. The centralized cartel is shown in Figure 13-5.

In Figure 13-5, D is the total market demand curve and MR is the corresponding marginal revenue curve for a homogeneous commodity produced by, say, four firms that have formed a centralized cartel. The ΣSMC curve for the cartel is obtained by summing horizontally the SMC curve of the four firms on the assumption that input prices remain constant. The cen-

419

FIGURE 13-5.
Centralized Cartel

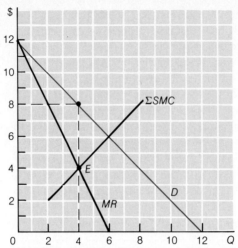

D is the market demand curve and MR is the corresponding marginal revenue curve for a homogeneous commodity produced by the four firms in a centralized cartel. The ΣSMC curve for the cartel is obtained by summing horizontally the four firms' SMC curves on the assumption that input prices are constant. The centralized authority will set P= $8 and Q= 4 (given by point E, where the ΣSMC curve intersects the MR curve from below). This is the monopoly solution.

tralized authority will set $P = \$8$ and sell $Q = 4$ (given by point E, where the ΣSMC curve intersects the MR curve from below). This is the monopoly solution. To minimize production costs, the centralized authority will have to allocate output among the four firms in such a way that the SMC of the last unit produced by each firm are equal. If the SMC of one firm were higher than for the other firms, the total costs of the cartel as a whole can be reduced by shifting some production from the firm with higher SMC to the other firms until the SMC of the last unit produced by all firms are equal. The cartel will also have to decide on the distribution of profits.

If all firms are of the same size and have identical cost curves, then it is very likely that each firm will be allocated the same output and will share equally in the profits generated by the cartel. In Figure 13-5, each firm would be allocated 1 unit of output. The result would be the same if a monopolist acquired the four firms and operated them as a multiplant monopolist. If the firms in the cartel are of different size and have different costs, it will be more difficult to agree on the share of output and profits. Then the allocation of output is likely to be based on past output, present capacity, and bargaining ability of each firm, rather than on the equalization of the SMC of the last unit of output produced by all member firms. Sometimes the market is divided among the firms in the industry as indicated in the next subsection.

Cartels often fail. There are several reasons for this. First, it is very difficult to organize all the producers of a commodity if there are more than a few of them. Second, as pointed out above, it is difficult to reach agree-

420

ment among the member firms on how to allocate output and profits when firms face different cost curves. Third, there is a strong incentive for each firm to remain outside the cartel or cheat on the cartel by selling more than its quota. Fourth, monopoly profits are likely to attract other firms into the industry and undermine the cartel agreement.

While cartels are illegal in the United States, many trade associations and professional associations perform many of the functions usually associated with cartels. Some cartellike associations are in fact sanctioned by the government. An example of this is the American Medical Association, which, by rigidly restricting the number of students admitted to medical schools and forbidding advertising by physicians (until recently), has been able to ensure very high doctors' fees and incomes. Another example is the New York Taxi and Limousine Commission, which restricts the number of taxis licensed, thus conferring monopoly profits to the original owners of the "medallions" (see Example 11-2). The best example of a successful international cartel (until recently) is OPEC (the Organization of Petroleum Exporting Countries).

Example 13-2 The Organizaton of Petroleum Exporting Countries (OPEC)

The Facts: In 1960 the governments of Iran, Iraq, Kuwait, Saudi Arabia, and Venezuela met in Baghdad and formed OPEC, the Organization of Petroleum Exporting Countries. By 1980, eight more nations joined (Algeria, Ecuador, Gabon, Indonesia, Libya, Nigeria, Qatar, and the United Arab Emirates). For the first ten years, OPEC had little, if any, market power, and petroleum prices were low and declined in real terms. However, as a result of the embargo of oil exports by Arab nations during the Arab-Israeli War in the fall of 1973, the price of petroleum rose from about $2.50 per barrel to over $12 per barrel. Another price shock occurred during the Iranian revolution in 1979–1980 when petroleum prices reached the all-time high of almost $40 per barrel. These prices increases led to lower settings on thermostats, a shift toward smaller cars, and other conservation measures; these also stimulated petroleum exploration and production in new fields, resulted in a huge transfer of purchasing power in favor of petroleum-exporting nations, and plunged the world into a deep recession. It is often asserted that OPEC was able to sharply increase prices and profits for its members by restricting supply and behaving as a cartel.

Comment: That OPEC has some market power and resembles a cartel is undeniable. However, OPEC is far from being a centralized cartel. Though member nations meet regularly to set prices, they seldom succeed in agreeing on a common price. In general, the densely populated members of OPEC such as Indonesia, Iran, and Nigeria have little petroleum reserves and would like to charge the highest possible price to maximize short-run profits. The sparsely populated members such as Saudi Arabia, Libya, and Kuwait, which happen to have the largest petroleum reserves, prefer lower

421

prices to discourage the development of substitutes and to maximize long-run profits. OPEC members have generally been unable to agree on the allocation of production among member nations or prevent price discounts by some of its members. As a result, OPEC may operate more as a price leadership model by the dominant supplier (Saudi Arabia) than as a cartel. High petroleum prices have also stimulated petroleum production and export by non-OPEC members (Mexico, the U.K., and Norway), so that OPEC exports are now less than 40 per cent of all petroleum sold on the international market, down from over 60 per cent a decade earlier. Today (1985), petroleum prices are below $30 per barrel and still falling.

Source: "Power of OPEC Beginning to Fall," *New York Times*, April 14, 1983, pp. 1, 16. "The Collapse of World Oil Prices," *Business Week*, March 7, 1983, pp. 92–94. "OPEC Discord Thwarts Bid for a Pricing Accord," *The New York Times*, January 29, 1985, p. D10.

13-5b Market-Sharing Cartel

The difficulties encountered by the members of a centralized cartel (such as agreeing on the price to charge, allocating output and profits among members, and avoiding cheating) make a market-sharing cartel more likely to occur. In a **market-sharing cartel** the member firms agree only on how to share the market. Each firm then agrees to operate only in one area or region, and not to encroach on the others' territories. An example is the agreement in the early part of this century between duPont (American) and Imperial Chemical (English) for the former to have exclusive selling rights for their products in North America (except for British colonies) and the latter in the British Empire. Under certain simplifying assumptions, a market-sharing cartel can also result in the monopoly solution. This is shown in Figure 13-6.

In Figure 13-6, we assume that there are two identical firms selling a homogeneous product and deciding to share the market equally. D is the total market demand for the commodity. Then, d is the half-share demand curve of each firm and mr is the corresponding marginal revenue curve. If each firm has the same SMC curve as shown in the figure, each will sell two units of output at $P = \$8$ (given by point E', at which $mr = SMC$). Thus, the duopolists together will sell the monopolist output of 4 units at $P = \$8$ (see the figure). In the real world there may be more than two firms, each may have different cost curves, and the market may not be shared equally. Then, we are not likely to have the neat monopoly solution shown above. The firm with greater capacity or operting in an inferior territory may demand a greater share of the market. The result will then depend on bargaining, and the possibility of incursions into each other's territory cannot be excluded.

The firms in a market-sharing cartel can also operate in the same geographical area by deciding which is to fill each particular contract. These

FIGURE 13-6.
Market-Sharing
Cartel

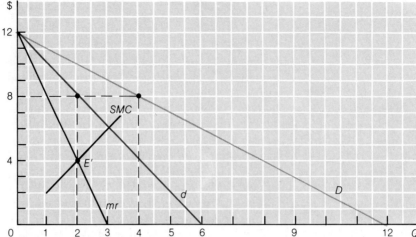

D is the total market demand for a homogeneous commodity, d is the half-share demand curve of each firm, and mr is the corresponding marginal revenue curve. If each duopolist also has the same SMC curve shown in the figure, each will sell two units of output at P = $8 (given by point E', at which mr = SMC). Thus, the duopolists together will sell the monopolist output of 4 units at P = $8.

market-sharing cartels are likely to be very unstable due to cheating (as the following example clearly demonstrates). Some loose market-sharing cartels are sanctioned by law. For example, local medical and bar associations essentially set the fees that doctors and lawyers are to charge. Similarly, many states had *fair trade laws* (until they became illegal in the mid-1970s), which allowed manufacturers to set the price that each retailer was to charge for the product. The market was then shared by means other than price.

Example 13-3 The Electrical Conspiracy

The Facts: In 1961, General Electric, Westinghouse, and a number of smaller companies producing electrical equipment pleaded guilty to violations of antitrust laws for price fixing and dividing up the market. The companies were fined a total of $2 million and were required to pay millions of dollars in damages to customers, seven of their executives were sent to jail, and twenty three others received suspended sentences. The equipment involved was capacitors, circuit breakers, electric meters, generators, insulators, switchgear, transformers, and other products sold to electric power companies, government agencies, and other industrial firms. The conspiracy took place from 1956 to 1959 and worked as follows. The executives of these companies would meet at conventions or trade associations, or would write or call one another to decide which of them would submit the lowest (sealed) bid on a particular contract. During the late

423

1950s, these companies split hundreds of millions of dollars in annual sales this way.

Comment: The executives involved in the conspiracy knew perfectly well that what they were doing was illegal. During the trial, evidence was introduced indicating that most of the meetings and communciations were secretive, code words were used, executives would not register at hotels under their company's name, letters were sent without return addresses and using only first names. In spite of this (and as predicted by economic theory), the agreements did not last very long; some lasted less than a week. The problem was that in order to get business in a period of over-capacity, some companies submitted the lowest bid when they had agreed that some other firm was to do so. During the trial, the defendants argued that the profitability of the firms involved was less during than before the alleged conspiracy. They were, nevertheless, found guilty because, whether successful or not, the prosecution proved that a conspiracy had in fact taken place.

Source: "The Incredible Electrical Conspiracy," *Fortune,* April 1961, p. 132 and May 1961, p. 161.

13-5c Price Leadership

One way by which firms in an oligopolistic market can make necessary price adjustments without fear of starting a price war and without overt collusion is by **price leadership.** Here, the firm generally recognized as the price leader starts the price change and the other firms in the industry quickly follow. The price leader is usually the dominant or largest firm in the industry. Sometimes, it is the low-cost firm (see Problem 10, with answer in the back of the book) or any other firm (called the **barometric firm**) recognized as the true interpreter or barometer of changes in demand and cost conditions in the industry warranting a price change. Then, an orderly price change is accomplished by other firms following the leader.

In the price leadership model by the dominant firm, the dominant firm sets the price for the commodity that maximizes its profits, allows all the other (small) firms in the industry to sell all they want at that price, and then it comes in to fill the market. Thus, the small firms in the industry behave as perfect competitors or price takers, and the dominant firm acts as the residual supplier of the commodity. This is shown in Figure 13-7.

In the figure, D $(ABCFG)$ is the market demand curve for the homogeneous commodity sold in the oligopolist market. Curve ΣSMC_s is the (horizontal) summation of the marginal cost curves of all the small firms in the industry. Since the small firms in the industry can sell all they want at the industry price set by the dominant firm (i.e., they are price takers), they behave as perfect competitors and always produce at the point where $P = \Sigma SMC$. Thus, the ΣSMC curve (above the average variable cost of the small firms) represents the short-run supply curve of the commodity for all

FIGURE 13-7.
Price Leadership by
the Dominant Firm

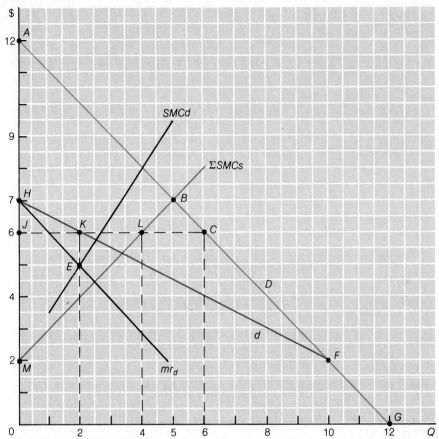

D (ABCFG) is the market demand curve and ΣSMC_s is the marginal cost curve of all
the small firms in the industry. Since the small firms can sell all they want at the
price set by the dominant firm, they behave as perfect competitors and produce
where $P = \Sigma SMC_s$. The horizontal distance between D and ΣSMC_s curves then gives
the (residual) quantity supplied by the dominant firm at each price. Thus, the
demand curve of the dominant firm (d) is HKFG, and the corresponding marginal
revenue curve is mr_d. With SMC_d, the dominant firm will set $P = \$6$ (given by point
E, where $mr_d = SMC_d$) to maximize its profits. At $P = \$6$, the small firms will supply
4 units of the commodity and the dominant firm JK = LC or 2 units.

the small firms in the industry as a group (on the assumption that input
prices remain constant).

The horizontal distance between D and ΣSMC_s at each price then gives
the (residual) quantity of the commodity demanded from and supplied by
the dominant firm at each price. For example, if the dominant firm set
$P = \$7$, the small firms in the industry together supply HB or 5 units of the
commodity, leaving nothing to be supplied by the dominant firm. This
gives the vertical intercept (point H) on the demand curve of the dominant
firm (d). If the dominant firm set $P = \$6$, the small firms in the industry

425

supply JL or 4 units of the commodity, leaving 2 units ($LC = JK$) to be supplied by the dominant firm (point K on the d curve). Finally, if the dominant firm set $P = \$2$, the small firms together supply zero units of the commodity (point M), leaving the entire market quantity demanded of MF or 10 units to be supplied by the dominant firm. Thus, the demand curve of the dominant firm is d or $HKFG$.

With demand curve d, the marginal revenue curve of the dominant firm is mr_d (bisects the distance from the vertical axis to the d curve). If the short-run marginal cost curve of the dominant firm is SMC_d, the dominant firm will set $P = \$6$ (given by point E, where $mr_d = SMC_d$) to maximize its profits. Note that the industry price set by the dominant firm is determined on the demand curve of the dominant firm (d), not on the market demand curve (D). At $P = \$6$, the small firms together will supply JL or 4 units of the commodity (see the figure). The dominant firm will then come in to fill the market by selling $JK = LC$ or 2 units of the commodity at $P = \$6$ which it set.

Among the firms that operated as price leaders are Alcoa (in aluminum), American Tobacco, American Can, Chase Manhattan Bank (in setting the prime rate), General Motors, Goodyear Tire and Rubber, Gulf Oil, Kellogg (in breakfast cereals), U.S. Steel, and so on. Many of these industries are characterized by more than one large firm, and the role of the price leader has sometimes changed from one large firm to another. For example, Reynolds has also behaved at times as the price leader in tobacco products. Continental Can, Bethlehem and National Steel, and General Mills (in the breakfast cereals market) also behaved as the price leaders in their respective markets during some periods of time. Finally, note that one important advantage of price leadership is that it can be accomplished informally by tacit collusion, which is much more difficult to prove than overt or explicit collusion.

Example 13-4 Price Leadership in the Steel Industry

The Facts: On April 6, 1962, U.S. Steel announced a price increase of \$6 per ton of steel. Within two days, the other large steel producers matched the price increase. On April 11, before the small steel producers increased their price, President John F. Kennedy called a news conference at which he charged that the increase in the price of steel was unjustified, calling it an irresponsible act against the public interest. President Kennedy pointed out that profit margins in the steel industry were "normal" and that wage increases had been matched by productivity increases, and so no price increase was justified. President Kennedy threatened that the Department of Justice and the Federal Trade Commission would examine how the price increase by U.S. Steel was so quickly matched by the other large steel producers and what legislative action might be needed to protect the public interest. On April 13, U.S. Steel and the other large steel producers, while defending the need to raise steel prices, rescinded their price increase.

426

Their decision was based on the threat of prosecution for price fixing under antitrust laws, loss of market share to the small steel producers (which, under the circumstances, could not be expected to raise their prices), and loss of defense contracts.

Comment: U.S. Steel was obviously the price leader in 1962. Had President Kennedy not acted so quickly, the small steel producers would soon have followed the lead of U.S. Steel and other large steel producers and increased their prices as well. Under attack was tacit or implicit price collusion in a situation where cost conditions did not seem to justify the price increase.

Source: "President Assails Steel for Irresponsible Rise in Price and Contempt for Nation," *The New York Times*, April 12, 1961, pp. 1–2.

13-5d Oligopoly and Antitrust Laws

According to Section I of the **Sherman Antitrust Act** passed in 1890: "Every contract, combination . . . , or conspiracy in restraint of trade or commerce among the several states, or with foreign nations, is hereby declared to be illegal" in the United States. This does not make oligopoly, as such, illegal. What is illegal is collusion (i.e., formal or informal agreements or arrangements in restraint of trade). These refer to all types of cartels, but also to informal understandings to share the market, price fixing, and price leadership. What the courts have *not* ruled as illegal is **conscious parallelism,** or the adoption of similar policies by oligopolists in view of their recognized interdependence. Specifically, the courts have ruled that parallel business behavior does not, in and of itself, constitute proof of collusion or an offense under the Sherman Antitrust Act.

The most difficult part of applying Section I of the Sherman Antitrust Act is to prove tacit or informal collusion. Sometimes the case is clear-cut. For example, in 1936, the U.S. Department of the Navy received 31 closed bids to supply a batch of steel, and all of which quoted a price of $20,727.26. Also in 1936, the U.S. Engineer's Office received 11 closed bids to supply 6,000 barrels of cement, each quoting a price of $3.286854 per barrel! The probability of identical prices, down to the sixth decimal, occurring without some form of collusion is practically zero.

Section II of the Sherman Antitrust Act makes attempts to monopolize the market illegal. This, too, has sometimes been difficult to prove. For example, in 1982, after 13 years of litigation, 104,400 trial transcript pages, and over $25 million in cost to the government alone, the giant antitrust case against IBM was dismissed as "without merit." However, also in 1982, the Justice Department settled its antitrust case against the American Telephone and Telegraph Company (AT&T), with AT&T agreeing to divest itself or give up its 22 local telephone companies. Perhaps the most significant effect of the antitrust laws is in deterring collusion rather than in fighting it after it occurs.

427

13-6

Long-Run Adjustments and Efficiency Implications

Most of the analysis of oligopoly until this point has referred to the short run. In this section we analyze the long-run adjustments and efficiency implications of oligopoly. We examine the long-run plant adjustments of existing firms and the entry prospects of other firms into the industry, we discuss nonprice competition, and examine the long-run welfare effects of oligopoly.

13-6a Long-Run Adjustments

As in other forms of market organization, oligopolistic firms can build the best plant to produce their anticipated best level of output in the long run. However, in view of the uncertainty generally surrounding oligopolistic industries, it is even more difficult than under other forms of market organization for firms to determine their best level of output and plant in the long run. An oligopolist would leave the industry in the long run if it would incur a loss even after building the best scale of plant. On the other hand, if existing firms earn profits, more firms will seek to enter the industry in the long run and, unless entry is blocked or somehow restricted, industry output will expand until industry profits fall to zero. There may then be so many firms in the industry that the actions of each no longer affects the others. In that case the industry would no longer be oligopolistic.

For an industry to remain oligopolistic in the long run, entry must be somewhat restricted. This may result from many reasons, some natural and some artificial. These are generally the same barriers that led to the existence of the oligopoly in the first place. One of the most important natural barriers to entry is the smallness of the market in relation to the optimum size of the firm. For example, only three of four firms can most efficiently supply the entire national market for automobiles. Potential entrants know that by entering this market they would probably face huge losses and possibly also impose losses on the other established auto makers (see Problem 12).

Another important natural barrier to entry in oligopolistic markets is the usually huge investment and specialized inputs required (as, for example, to enter the automobile, steel, aluminum, and similar industries). Many artificial barriers to entry may also exist. These include control over the source of an essential raw material (such as bauxite to produce aluminum) by the few firms already in the industry, unwillingness of existing firms to license potential competitors to use an essential industrial process on which they hold a patent, and the inability to obtain a government franchise (for example, to run a bus line or a taxi fleet). Still another artificial barrier to entry is **limit pricing,** whereby existing firms charge a price low enough to discourage entry into the industry.[15] By doing so, they voluntarily sacrifice some short-run profits in order to maximize their profits in the long run (see Application 1).

13-6b Nonprice Competition

All the models discussed in this chapter, with the exception of the Edgeworth model, predict sticky or infrequent price changes in oligopolistic markets. This conforms to what is often observed in the real world. To be sure, costly price wars do sometimes erupt as a result of miscalculations on the part of one of the oligopolists, but they usually last only short periods. It is to avoid the possibility of starting a price war that oligopolists prefer to leave price unchanged, and compete instead on the basis of **nonprice competition** (advertising and product differentiation). Only when demand and cost conditions make a price change absolutely essential will oligopolists change prices. An orderly price change is then usually accomplished by price leadership.

As pointed out in Section 12-4, a firm may use advertising to try to increase (i.e., to shift to the right) the demand curve for its product. If successful, the firm will then be able to sell a greater quantity of the product at an unchanged price. The problem is that other firms, upon losing sales, are likely to retaliate and also increase their advertising expenditures. The result may be simply to increase all firms' costs, with each firm retaining more or less its share of the market and earning less profits. Thus, as indicated earlier, when the government banned cigarette advertising on television, all tobacco companies benefited by spending less on advertising—a step that each firm alone was not willing to take before the ban. While some advertising provides useful information to consumers on new or improved products and uses, a great deal does not. Examples might be the huge advertising expenditures (running in the hundreds of millions of dollars per year) of beer producers, auto makers, and others.

The same is generally true for product differentiation. That is, producers often differentiate their product in order to increase sales, but this usually leads to retaliation and higher costs and prices. Sometimes product changes are simply cosmetic (as, for example, the yearly automobile model changes). Other changes may truly improve the product as, for example, when a new and longer-lasting razor blade is introduced at the same price. Some product differentiation is introduced to better serve particular segments of the market. For example, the Chevrolet Impala is a somewhat cheaper version of the Chevrolet Caprice. Advertising, product differentiation, and market segmentation can be combined in many different ways and used with still other forms of nonprice competition in oligopolistic markets.

[15] See, J. Bain, *Industrial Organization*, rev. ed. (New York: John Wiley, 1967). Perhaps, more than an artificial barrier to entry, limit pricing is a practice that is designed to exploit barriers that do exist (e.g., economies of scale).

13-6c Welfare Effects

We now turn to some of the long-run welfare effects of oligopoly. First, as in the case of monopoly and monopolistic competition, oligopolists usually do not produce at the lowest point on their *LAC* curve. This would only occur by sheer coincidence if the oligopolist's *MR* curve intersected the *LAC* curve at the lowest point of the latter. Only under perfect competition will firms *always* produce at the lowest point on the *LAC* curve. Oligopoly, however, often results because of the smallness of the market in relation to the optimum size of the firm, and so it does not make much sense to compare oligopoly to perfect competition. Automobiles, steel, aluminum, and many other products could only be produced at prohibitive costs under perfectly competitive conditions.

Second, as in the case of monopoly, oligopolists can earn long-run profits, and so price can exceed *LAC*. This is to be contrasted to the case of perfect competition and monopolistic competition where $P = LAC$ in the long run. However, some economists believe that oligopolists utilize a great deal of their profits for research and development (R&D) to produce new and better products, and to find cheaper production methods. These are the primary sources of growth in modern economies. These same economists point out that monopolists do not have as much incentive to engage in research and development, and perfect competitors and monopolistic competitors are too small, and do not have the resources to do so on a large scale.

Third, as in imperfect competition in general, $P > LMC$ under oligopoly and so there is underallocation of resources to the industry. Specifically, since the demand curve facing oligopolists is negatively sloped, $P > MR$. Thus, at the best level of output (given by the point where the *LMC* intersects the firm's *MR* curve from below) $P > LMC$. This means that society

TABLE 13-6   The Cost of Automobile Model Changes, 1950–1960 (in Millions of Dollars)

Year	Direct Costs	Retooling Costs	Gasoline Costs	Total Costs	Total Costs per Car in Dollars
1950	−27	20	13	6	1
1951	267	45	36	348	65
1952	460	82	102	644	148
1953	436	246	161	844	138
1954	1,072	264	240	1,576	362
1955	2,425	469	372	3,266	527
1956	3,040	336	590	3,966	630
1957	4,048	772	806	5,626	905
1958	2,354	626	949	3,924	922
1959	3,675	532	1,147	5,354	962
1960	3,456	537	1,346	5,339	888

Source: F. Fisher, Z. Griliches, and C. Kaysen, "The Cost of Automobile Model Changes since 1949," *The Journal of Political Economy*, October 1962.

values an additional unit of the commodity more than the marginal cost of producing it. But again, $P = LMC$ only under perfect competition and economies of scale may make perfect competition not feasible.

Fourth, while some advertising and product differentiation are useful because they provide information and satisfy the consumers' tastes for diversity, they are likely to be pushed beyond what is socially desirable in oligopolistic markets. However, exactly how much advertising and product differentiation is socially desirable is an unsettled question (see Example 13-5).

Turning to oligopoly theory itself, we now see why we said at the beginning of the chapter that there is no general theory of oligopoly. In this chapter, we have examined a number of oligopoly models, all of which are somewhat incomplete and unsatisfactory. This is unfortunate as oligopoly is the most prevalent form of market organization in production in all modern economies.

Example 13-5 The Cost of Automobile Model Changes

The Facts: Table 13-6 gives the estimated cost of automobile model changes in total and per car from 1950 to 1960. The cost of model changes include direct costs (which refer to the extra cost of building the larger, heavier, and more powerful cars with automatic transmission, power steering, power brakes, and other options), retooling costs (which refer to the costs of making the required changes in capital equipment), and the gasoline costs (the extra gasoline consumed by the newer and bigger cars). The last column of the table gives the cost per car of the yearly model change. In many years, these equalled about ¼ of the price of a new car.

Comment: Since consumers generally could purchase an automobile with only the previous year's options, but generally chose to have the new options as they were introduced into the new models, we can infer that most of the cost of model changes were wanted by consumers and did not represent a waste of resources. However, the demand for some of the new options may have been created by advertising and may not have represented true needs.

13-7

Applications

In this section we discuss some important applications of the theory presented in the chapter. These include limit pricing, an examination of the sales maximization model, managerial theories of the firm, cost-plus pricing, and the Hotelling paradox. Some of these are, perhaps, more truly extensions rather than applications of the topics presented in the chapter.

They do, however, clearly indicate the usefulness and applicability of the theory presented in this chapter.

Application 1: Limit Pricing

Limit pricing has been defined earlier as the charging of a price low enough to discourage entry into the industry. By doing so, existing firms voluntarily sacrifice some short-run profits in order to maximize their profits in the long run. We can show this with Figure 13-8.

In the left panel of Figure 13-8, D is the total market demand curve for the commodity. Suppose that existing firms are already selling 4 units of the commodity at $P = \$8$ (point A). The entrance of a new firm would increase industry output and cause price to fall. That is, a potential entrant assumes that it faces the segment of demand curve D to the right of point A. Subtracting the 4 units of the commodity supplied by existing firms from the market demand curve (D) gives the potential entrant's demand curve (d_2). If existing firms were selling instead 6 units of the commodity at $P = \$6$ (point B), the potential entrant's demand curve would be d_1.

For simplicity we assume that per-unit costs of existing firms and for the potential entrant are constant. We also assume (quite realistically) that the per-unit costs of the potential entrant are somewhat higher than for the established firms. These are shown in the right panel of Figure 13-8, where

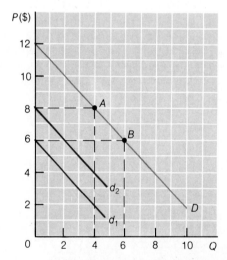
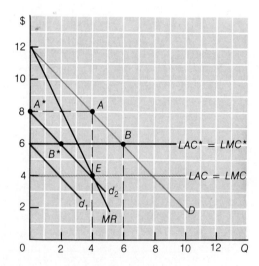

FIGURE 13-8. Limit Pricing
In the left panel, D is the total market demand curve for the commodity. The demand curve of a potential entrant is d_2 if existing firms sell $Q = 4$, and d_1 if they sell $Q = 6$. In the right panel, the LAC = LMC curve refers to the constant costs of the established firms, while LAC* = LMC* refers to the constant and higher costs of the potential entrant. Existing firms maximize profits by selling $Q = 4$ at $P = \$8$ (given by point E, at which MR = LMC). The demand curve facing the potential entrant is then d_2 and it could earn profits. To discourage entrance, existing firms can set price at \$6 so that d_1 lies everwhere below LAC*.

the horizontal $LAC = LMC$ curve refers to the constant costs of the established firms and the horizontal $LAC^* = LMC^*$ curve refers to the constant and higher costs of the potential entrant.

Existing firms maximize profits by selling $Q = 4$ at $P = \$8$ (given by point E, at which $LMC = MR$) and earn profits of AE or $\$4$ per unit and $\$16$ in total. The demand curve facing the potential entrant is then d_2. Since over the range A^*B^* of d_2, $P > LAC^*$, the potential entrant would find it profitable to enter the industry. However, this would increase industry output and lower price so that the profits of existing firms would fall. To avoid this, existing firms may choose to sell $Q = 6$ at $P = \$6$ so that the demand curve facing the potential entrant is d_1. Since d_1 lies everywhere below the LAC^* curve, the potential entrant would incur losses at all output levels and would not enter the industry. Therefore, $P = \$6$ is the entry-limit price. This is the highest price that existing firms can charge without inducing entry. By setting the limit price, existing firms sacrifice some profits in the short run in order to maximize their profits in the long run.

Note that existing firms may only charge the limit price when they believe entry is imminent and set their profit-maximizing price of $P = \$8$ at other times. Sometimes existing firms, faced with the entry of another firm, may voluntarily reduce their output to accommodate the new entrant and avoid a price reduction. Finally, note that limit pricing assumes some form of collusion (such as price leadership) on the part of existing firms.[16]

Application 2: Sales Maximization Model

Until now we have assumed that firms generally seek to maximize profits. William Baumol and other economists have pointed out that incentives to managers are often more closely related to sales than to profits.[17] For example, the highest salaries are paid to the managers of the largest corporations rather than to the managers of the most profitable ones. In addition, bank credit is more readily available to large and growing firms than to small ones. As a result, Baumol and others postulated that modern corporations seek to maximize sales revenue subject to a minimum profit constraint. That is, after an appropriate rate of profit has been earned to satisfy stockholders, firms seek to maximize their sales revenue even if that necessarily means somewhat lower profits.

We can examine the sales maximization model with Figure 13-9. In the figure, TR refers to total revenue, TC refers to total costs, and TP refers to total profits. $TP = TR - TC$. TP are maximized at $\$35$ when $Q = 4$, at which the positive distance between TR and TC is greatest (and the slopes of the two curves are equal). TR is maximum at $\$100$ when $Q = 6$ and the

---

[16] For more dynamic theories of limit pricing that predict that the limit price will be above the existing firms' LAC, see R. T. Masson and J. Shaanan, "Stochastic-Dynamic Limiting Pricing: An Empirical Test," *The Review of Economics and Statistics*, August 1982, pp. 413–422.

[17] W. Baumol, *Business Behavior, Value, and Growth* (New York: Macmillan, 1959).

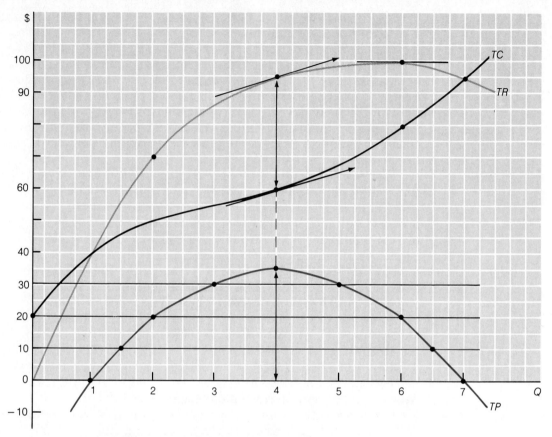

FIGURE 13-9. *Sales Maximization Model*
TR *refers to total revenue,* TC *refers to total costs, and* TP *refers to total profits.*
TP = TR − TC. TP *are maximized at $35 when* Q = 4. TR *is maximum at $100 when*
Q = 6. *If the firm had to earn a profit of at least $10, the firm would produce 6 units*
of output and maximize TR *at $100. In this case, the profit constraint is not operative*
since TP = $20. *The result is the same if the profit constraint was $20. But if the profit*
constraint was $30, the largest TR = $98 *at* Q = 5.

TR curve has zero slope.[18] At this point, TP = $20. If the firm had to earn
a profit of at least $10 to satisfy its minimum profit constraint, the firm
would produce 6 units of output and maximize TR at $100. In this case, the
profit constraint is not operative since the TP of $20 exceeds the required
profit of $10. The result is the same if the profit constraint was $20. But if
the profit constraint was $30, the largest sales revenue that the firm could
achieve (while satisfying the profit constraint) would be about $98 at
Q = 5; here, the profit constraint would be binding. If the firm wanted to

---

[18] Note that total sales or TR are maximized when MR = 0 (as opposed to profit maximization, which is given by the point at which MC = MR).

maximize profits, it would have to produce 4 units of output, at which $TR = \$95$ and $TP = \$35$.

Several things need to be mentioned with respect to the above model. First, the profit constraint is usually expressed as a *rate* of profit or return on investment. But given the value of the investment (i.e., the value of the firm), the minimum rate of profit can easily be transformed into a minimum *dollar* value of profits per year. Second, the minimum rate of profit will vary from industry to industry and is higher during periods of high demand than during recessions. Third, if the minimum profit constraint had been $40 in the above figure, no output or revenue level would satisfy the profit constraint. Managers will then try to come as close as possible to the profit target by producing $Q = 4$, thus maximizing profits. Hence, the profit-maximizing model is a special case of the revenue-maximization model. Fourth, output is usually larger and price lower with sales than with profit maximization. Fifth, empirical evidence on the sales-maximization model is mixed and inconclusive.

Application 3: Managerial Theories of the Firm

Managerial theories of the firm postulate multiple goals for the modern corporation, where ownership is divorced from management. That is, after achieving "satisfactory" rather than maximum profits, the large modern corporation is said to seek to maximize sales or growth, maintain or increase its market share, maintain a large staff of executives with lavish offices, minimize uncertainty, create and maintain a good public image as a desirable member of the community, and so on. However, Herbert Simon, Richard Cyert and James March pointed out that because of the complexity of the oligopoly environment, uncertainty and lack of adequate data, the large modern corporation is not able to maximize anything; it can only strive for some "satisfactory" goals in terms of revenue, profits, growth, market share, and so on.[19] Simon called this **satisficing behavior.** That is, the large modern corporation is not a maximizing, but rather a satisficing, organization.

While managerial theories of the firm do stress some relevant aspects of the operation of modern corporations, they do not provide, according to many economists, a satisfactory alternative to profit maximization as the basic goal of the firm. For one thing, some of the multiple goals of the firm postulated by managerial theories may conflict and are much too general to be tested. Second, many of the multiple goals, such as to maximize growth, can truly be regarded as indirect ways to earn and increase profits in the long run. Third, satisficing behavior is not necessarily inconsistent with profit maximization. Presumably with more and better data and search procedures, the large corporation can find ways to improve its per-

---

[19] H. Simon, *Administrative Behavior* (New York: Free Press, 1976); R. Cyert and J. March, *A Behavioral Theory of the Firm* (Englewood Cliffs, N.J.: Prentice-Hall, 1963).

formance. In that case, the corporation will choose the option with the highest expected payoff. For all of these reasons, we retain the profit-maximizing assumption in the study of microeconomics. It is from this vantage point that the behavior of the firm can be studied most fruitfully.

Application 4: Cost-Plus Pricing

In the real world, firms generally lack the information to set the price that maximizes their profits (given by the point where the firm's MC curve intersects its MR curve from below). Therefore, firms adopt **cost-plus pricing.** Here, the firm estimates the average cost for a "normal" output level (usually between two thirds and three quarters of capacity output) and then adds a certain percentage or **markup** over cost to determine the price of the commodity. The markup varies depending on the industry and the conditions of demand. For example, the markup was about 20 per cent in the steel industry in general but was higher for products facing less elastic demand or in periods of high demand.

Cost-plus pricing is fairly common in oligopolistic industries and, under certain conditions, it is not inconsistent with profit maximization. That is, because of lack of adequate data, firms cannot generally follow the $MR = MC$ rule to maximize profits. However, to the extent that the markup is varied inversely with the elasticity of demand of a product, it leads to a price that is approximately the profit-maximizing price. This can be shown as follows:

$$m = \frac{P - AC}{P} \tag{13-1}$$

where m is the markup over cost expressed as a percent of price, P is price, and AC is average cost.

Solving for P, we get

$$
\begin{aligned}
mP &= P - AC \\
mP - P &= -AC \\
-mP + P &= AC \\
P(1 - m) &= AC \\
P &= \frac{AC}{1 - m}
\end{aligned}
\tag{13-2}
$$

From section 5-5c we know that

$$MR = P(1 - 1/\eta) \tag{13-3}$$

where MR is marginal revenue, P is price, and η is the price elasticity of demand.

436

Solving for P we get

$$P = \frac{MR}{1 - 1/\eta}$$

Since profits are maximized where $MR = MC$, we can substitute MC for MR in the above formula and get

$$P = \frac{MC}{1 - 1/\eta}$$

To the extent that the firm's MC are constant over a wide range of outputs, $MC = AC$. Substituting AC for MC in the above formula, we get

$$P = \frac{AC}{1 - 1/\eta} \tag{13-4}$$

Formula (13-4) for profit maximization equals Formula (13-2) for the markup, if $1/\eta = m$. Thus, the firm will maximize profits if its markup is inversely related to the price elasticity of demand for the commodity. For example, when $\eta = 2$, m should be ½ or 50 per cent for profit maximization. For $\eta = 4$, $m = $ ¼ or 25 per cent. This means that if $AC = \$75$, P should equal \$100 (so that the markup is 25 per cent of price) to maximize profits.

Cyert and March found that firms in the retailing sector adjusted prices on the basis of feedback from the market, and did reduce the markup and price when the demand for a product declined and became more elastic. Thus, using cost-plus pricing with a markup that varies inversely with elasticity is consistent with profit maximization. In any event, those firms that choose a markup and price that is not near the profit-maximizing price are less likely to grow and may go out of business in the long run, as compared to firms that choose the appropriate markup. Cost-plus pricing is one of many *rules of thumb* that firms are forced to use in the real world because of inadequate data.

Application 5: Product Differentiation and the Hotelling Paradox
To the extent that product differentiation is possible, this offers still another way by which oligopolists can compete with one another. Product differentation refers to all the characteristics, real or imagined, of the product. These include the product performance, appearance, brand name, the conditions of the sale, and so on. One way to differentiate the product is to build a new store closer to potential buyers and thus gain an advantage over competitors based on lower costs of transportation and time spent to purchase the commodity.

Panel (a) in Figure 13-10 shows 15 (15 hundred, 15 thousand, or 15 million) customers uniformly located along a straight road from west (W) to east (E). Suppose that there are only two producers selling a homogeneous

437

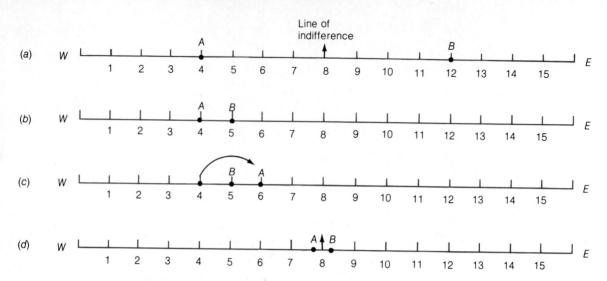

FIGURE 13-10.   The Hotelling Paradox

Panel a shows 15 customers uniformly located along a straight road from west (W)
to east (E). If there are only two producers selling a homogeneous product at the same
price, total transporation costs would be minimum if firm A located at 4 and firm B
at 12. Then, customers 1 through 7 would buy from firm A and 9 through 15 would
buy from B. Customer 8 is indifferent between buying from A or B. But if firm A was
at 4, it would pay for firm B to locate at 5 (see panel b). However, firm A would then
relocate to 6 (see panel c). The process would continue until firms A and B locate at
8 very close to each other (see panel d).

product at the same price, customers buy the product only once in a given
time period, and they cannot pool trips. The total transportation cost of all
the customers would be minimized if the two firms were located symmet-
rically at the quartile point on the road, with firm A at the location of consumer 4 and firm B at the location of consumer 12. Then, customers 1
through 7 would buy from firm A, and customers 9 through 15 would buy
from firm B. Customer 8, being equally distant from firm A and firm B, is
indifferent between buying from A or B.

If the transportation cost between any two adjacent locations were $1,
the total transportation cost for all customers is $28. This is obtained as
follows: customers 4 and 12 would incur no transportation cost; customers
3, 5, 11, and 13 would incur transportation cost of $1 each for a total of $4;
customers 2, 6, 10, and 14 would spend $2 on transportation for a total of
$8; customers 1, 7, 9, and 15 would spend $3 each for a total of $12; cus-
tomer 8 could buy from firm A or B and incur a transportation cost of $4.
The total transportation cost of $28 for all customers represents the small-
est transportation cost. However, as we will show next, firm A and B will
not choose location 4 and 12, respectively.

If firm A were located at 4, it would pay for firm B to locate at 5 (as shown
in panel b) because by doing so, firm B would have customers 5 through
15, leaving only customers 1 through 4 to firm A. However, if relocation

costs were zero, firm A would relocate to 6 and have customers 6 through 15, leaving only customers 1 through 5 to firm B (see panel c). The process would continue until firm A would locate at 8 on the left side of the line of indifference and firm B would locate very close to A on the right side of the line of indifference (see panel d). Then firm A will have customers 1 through 7, firm B will have customers 9 through 15, and customer 8 will be indifferent as between buying from firm A or B. In this case the total transportation costs for all the customers is $56 (can you see why?) and much larger than if A were to locate at 4 and B at 12. However, the firms will not locate there.

The above analysis has much greater applicability than might be thought at first sight. Product differentation need not be in terms of distance, but rather in terms of any characteristics of the product. It can be in terms of alcoholic content of beer, fiber content of breakfast cereals, or even the platform of the Democratic and Republican parties. The above analysis explains why competition often results in products that are hardly differentiated, as each firm attempts to produce products as close as possible to those of competitors and with characteristics close to the center of the spectrum of consumers' tastes.

The costs to society in terms of consumer dissatisfaction in being unable to get products that closely match his or her tastes is much greater when products are so much alike. For example, if customers were spread evenly in their preferences for beer with alcoholic content from 1 per cent to 15 per cent, but most of the beers on the market have about 8% alcoholic content, the total dissatisfaction of society as a whole is greater than if one beer had a 4 per cent alcoholic content and another had 12 per cent. Then, no customer would have to be more than 3 percentage points away from his or her preferred beer in terms of alcoholic content. **Hotelling paradox** refers to the fact that competition often results in products that are too similar to maximize society's satisfaction.[20]

Note that with three firms, no stable equilibrium could be reached if customers were located along a straight line (as in Figure 13-10) because then one firm would always be boxed in between the other two and would always jump over the firm on either side. Then the firm remaining in the middle would do the same, and this would go on indefinitely. The problem would be resolved if buyers were located uniformly around a ring. In that case, equilibrium will be reached when each firm locates one third of the way from the other two firms around the ring.

Summary

1. Oligopoly is the market organization where there are only a few firms selling a homogeneous or differentiated product. If there are two firms, we have a duopoly. If the product is homoge-

[20] H. Hotelling, "Stability in Competition," *Economic Journal*, March 1929, pp. 41–57.

neous, we have a pure oligopoly; otherwise, we have a differentiated oligopoly. Since there are few firms in oligopolistic markets, the action of each firm affects the others, and vice versa. This interdependence among firms is the most distinguishing characteristic of oligopolistic markets. Some indication of market power is given by the concentration ratio.

2. Cournot assumed that two firms sold identical spring water produced at zero marginal cost. Each duopolist, in its attempt to maximize profits, assumes the other will keep output constant at the existing level. The result is a sequence of moves and countermoves until each duopolist sells 1/3 of the total output that would be sold if the market were perfectly competitive. In the Edgeworth model, each duopolist faces an output limitation and assumes that the other keeps its price constant. The result is that price and output oscillate between the monopoly and the maximum output levels. Both models are extremely naive.

3. In the Chamberlin model, the duopolists, recognizing their interdependence but without collusion, set the monopoly price and share equally in the monopoly output and profits. In the kinked-demand or Sweezy model, it is assumed that oligopolists match the price reductions, but not the price increases of competitors. Thus, the demand curve has a kink at the prevailing price. Oligopolists maintain the price as long as the SMC curve intersects the discontinuous segment of the MR curve. Empirical studies do not support the existence of the kink and the model does not explain how the price is set in the first place.

4. Game theory deals with the choice of the optimum strategy in conflict situations. Games in which the gains of one player equal the losses of the other are called zero-sum games. A payoff matrix gives the outcome of all the possible combinations of strategies by two players. In game theory, each player assumes that the other always adopts the most damaging strategy from the former's point of view. Thus, one player adopts a maximin strategy (i.e., maximizes the minimum gain open to it) and the other adopts a minimax strategy (i.e., minimizes the maximum gain open to the first player). Games in which maximin equals minimax are said to be strictly determined. The solution is called the saddle point. When maximin does not equal minimax, the best that each player can do is to adopt a mixed strategy. When the sum of the payoffs is not equal to zero, we have a nonzero sum game. The prisoners' dilemma is an example of a nonconstant sum game with negative payoffs. To date, game theory can only be applied to simple duopoly problems.

5. A centralized cartel is a formal organization of suppliers of a commodity that sets the price and allocates output and profits among its members so as to increase their joint profits. A market-sharing cartel is an organization of suppliers of a commodity that overtly or tacitly divides the market among its members. Cartels can result in the monopoly solution but are unstable and often fail. A looser form of collusion is price leadership by the dominant, the low-cost, or the barometric firm. Under price leadership by the dominant firm, the small firms are allowed to sell all they want at the price set by the dominant firm, and then the dominant firm comes in to fill the market. The Sherman Antitrust Act prohibits all contracts and combinations in restraints of trade, and all attempts to monopolize the market.

6. In the long run, oligopolistic firms can build their best scale of plant and firms can leave the industry. However, entry has to be blocked or restricted if the industry is to remain oligopolistic. There can be several natural and artificial barriers to entry. Oligopolists seldom change prices for fear of starting a price war, and prefer instead to compete on the basis of advertising and product differentiation. In oligopolistic markets, production does not usually take place at the lowest point on the LAC curve, $P > LAC$, $P > LMC$, and too much may be spent on advertising and product differentiation. However, oligopoly may result from the limitation of the market, and it may lead to more research and development.

7. Limit pricing refers to the charging by existing firms of a sufficiently low price to discourage entry into the industry. The sales maximization model postulates that firms maximize sales revenue subject to a profit constraint. Managerial theories of the firm postulate multiple goals for the firm (such as maximization of sales, growth, and so on) after attaining "satisfactory," rather than maximum, profits. Cost-plus pricing refers

to the setting of a price equal to average cost plus a markup. The Hotelling paradox refers to the fact that competition often results in products that are too similar to maximize society's satisfaction.

Glossary

Oligopoly   The form of market organization in which there are few firms selling a homogeneous or differentiated product.

Duopoly   An oligopoly of two firms.

Pure oligopoly   An oligopoly in which the product of the firms in the industry is homogeneous.

Differentiated oligopoly   An oligopoly where the product is differentiated.

Concentration ratio   The percentage of total industry sales of the 4, 8, and 20 largest firms in the industry.

Cournot model   The oligopoly model where each firm assumes that the other keeps output constant. With two firms, each will sell 1/3 of the perfectly competitive output.

Edgeworth model   The duopoly model where each firm assumes that the other keeps price constant and faces an output limitation. The result is that price and output fluctuate between the monopoly and the maximum output level.

Chamberlin model   The duopoly model where each firm, recognizing their interdependence but without collusion, sets the monopoly price and shares equally in the monopoly output and profits.

Kinked-demand curve model   The model that seeks to explain price rigidity by postulating a demand curve with a kink at the prevailing price.

Game theory   A method of choosing the optimum strategy in conflict situations.

Zero-sum game   Games in which the gains of one player equal the losses of the other player.

Payoff   The outcome or result of a combination of strategies by the two players of a game.

Payoff matrix   The table showing the outcome of all the possible combinations of strategies by two players.

Maximin strategy   The strategy of maximizing the minimum payoff in game theory.

Dominant strategy   The strategy with the highest payoff.

Minimax strategy   The strategy of minimizing the maximum payoff of the rival player in game theory.

Pure strategy   The single best strategy in game theory.

Strictly determined game   Game in which maximin equals minimax.

Saddle point   The solution or outcome of a strictly determined game.

Mixed strategy   The best strategy for each player in a nonstrictly determined game.

Nonzero sum game   A game in which the sum of the payoffs for each combination of strategies is not equal to zero.

Prisoners' dilemma   A nonconstant sum game with negative payoffs.

Collusion   A formal or informal agreement among the suppliers of a commodity to restrict competition.

Cartel   An organization of suppliers of a commodity aimed at restricting competition and increasing profits.

Centralized cartel   A formal agreement of the suppliers of a commodity that sets the price and allocates output and profits among its members so as to increase joint profits. It can result in the monopoly solution.

Market-sharing cartel   An organization of suppliers of a commodity that overtly or tacitly divides the market among its members.

Price leadership   The form of market collusion in oligopolistic markets whereby the firm that serves as the price leader initiates a price change and the other firms in the industry soon match it.

Sherman Antitrust Act   It prohibits all contracts, and combinations in restraints of trade, and all attempts to monopolize the market.

Conscious parallelism   The adoption of similar policies by oligopolists in view of their recognized interdependence.

Barometric firm   An oligopolistic firm that is recognized as a true interpreter or barometer of changes in demand and cost conditions warranting a price change in the industry.

Limit pricing The charging of a sufficiently low price by existing firms to discourage entry into the industry.

Nonprice competition Competition based on advertising and product differentiation rather than on price.

Managerial theories of the firm They postulate multiple goals for the firm (such as maximization of sales, growth, and so on) after attaining "satisfactory," rather than maximum, profits.

Cost-plus pricing The setting of a price equal to average cost plus a markup.

Satisficing behavior The goal of modern corporations to achieve "satisfactory" results in terms of revenue, profits, growth, market share, and so on, rather than profit maximization.

Markup The percentage over average cost in cost-plus pricing.

Hotelling paradox The observation that competition often results in products that are too similar to maximize society's satisfaction.

Questions for Review

1. (a) What is an oligopoly? A duopoly?
   (b) What is a pure oligopoly? A differentiated oligopoly?
   (c) What is the distinguishing characteristic of oligopoly in relation to the other forms of market organization?
   (d) In which sector of the United States economy is oligopoly most prevalent?
2. Answer the following questions for the Cournot model.
   (a) What is the basic behavioral assumption of the model?
   (b) Is the assumption of duopoly and zero marginal cost essential?
   (c) What is the final equilibrium solution?
3. (a) What is the basic behavioral assumption in the Edgeworth model?
   (b) What other assumption does Edgeworth make?
   (c) How does the outcome of the Edgeworth model differ from the Cournot model?
   (d) What are the major shortcomings of the Edgeworth and the Cournot models? Why do we study them?
4. (a) What is the basic behavioral assumption of the Chamberlin model?
   (b) In what way is the outcome of the Chamberlin model different from those of the Cournot and Edgeworth models?
   (c) In what way is the Chamberlin model superior to the Cournot and Edgeworth models?
5. Answer the following questions for the kinked-demand curve model.

(a) What alleged pricing behavior of oligopolists does the model seek to explain?
   (b) How does the model explain the pricing behavior of oligopolists?
   (c) What criticisms does the model face?
6. What is
   (a) game theory?
   (b) payoff?
   (c) payoff matrix?
   (d) strictly determined game?
   (e) saddle point?
   (f) nonzero sum game?
7. What is
   (a) maximin strategy?
   (b) minimax strategy?
   (c) dominant strategy?
   (d) pure strategy?
   (e) mixed strategy?
   (f) the prisoners' paradox?
8. What is
   (a) collusion?
   (b) a cartel?
   (c) a centralized cartel?
   (d) a market-sharing cartel?
9. (a) How can cartels achieve the monopoly solution?
   (b) Why are cartels unstable and often fail?
   (c) Why do we study cartels if they are illegal in the United States?
   (d) In what ways does OPEC resemble a cartel? In what way does it not?
10. (a) What is price leadership?
    (b) What is a barometric firm?

(c) Which firm is the price leader?
(d) How does price leadership by the dominant firm take place?
(e) What is the Sherman Antitrust Act? Conscious parallelism?
11. (a) What long-run adjustments can take place in an oligopolistic industry?
(b) What are some of the barriers to entry into oligopolistic markets?
(c) Why do oligopolists prefer nonprice competition? To what does this refer?

(d) What are some of the advantages and disadvantages of oligopoly?
12. What is (are)
(a) limit pricing?
(b) the sales maximization model?
(c) managerial theories of the firm? Satisficing behavior?
(d) cost-plus pricing?
(e) the Hotelling paradox?

Problems

1. Draw a figure on graph paper combining the left and right panels of Figure 13-1 and showing demand curve $d_{B'}$.
2. How would the outcome of the Edgeworth model differ if we do not assume that the duopolists face an output limitation?
3. Draw a figure showing the best level of output and price for the oligopolist of Figure 13-4 if
(a) its SMC curve shifts up by $3.50 or down by $4.
(b) the government sets a price ceiling of $8.
(c) the government sets a price ceiling of $7.
★4. Draw a figure showing the best level of output and price for the oligopolist of Figure 13-4 if the demand curve it faces shifts
(a) up by $0.50 but the kink remains at P = $8.
(b) down by $0.50 but the kink remains at P = $8 and the SMC curve shifts down to SMC'.
5. Find the solution for the game with the following payoff matrix.

lowing payoff matrix.

Matrix of Firm A's Gain (+) and Loss (−) of Market Share (in Percentages)

		Firm B			
		B1	B2	B3	B4
Firm A	A1	1	−3	2	3
	A2	5	6	4	5
	A3	−2	−1	0	1

★6. How would the outcome of the game of Table 13-2 differ if we interchanged the payoff of 0 and −1 in the second column of the table?
★7. Given the following payoff matrix of firm A and firm B with low and high advertising expenditures (in millions of dollars of net profits after subtracting the advertising expenses), determine the best strategy for each firm. In the payoff matrix, the first number for each combination of strategies refers to firm A and the second number refers to firm B.

Payoff Matrix (Profits in Millions of Dollars)

		Firm B	
		Low Advertising	High Advertising
Firm A	Low Advertising	2, 3	0, 6
	High Advertising	4, 0	1, 2

8. Assume that (1) the four identical firms in a purely oligopolistic industry form a centralized cartel; (2) the total market demand function facing the cartel is $QD = 20 - 2P$ and P is given in dollars; and (3) each firm's SMC function is given by $\$\frac{1}{4}Q$ and input prices are

443

constant. Find (a) the best level of output and price for this centralized cartel; (b) how much should each firm produce if the cartel wants to minimize production costs? (c) How much profits will the cartel make if the average total cost of each firm at the best level of output is $4?

9. Redraw Figure 13-6 and show on it the MR and the ΣSMC curves for the cartel as a whole. How is the best level of output and price for the cartel as a whole determined? On the same figure, draw the $SATC$ curve of one of the duopolists if $SATC = \$6$ at $Q = 2$ and $Q = 4$. How much profit does each duopolist earn?

★10. Start with Figure 13-6 where the duopolists share equally the market for a homogeneous product.

(a) Draw a figure such that duopolist 1's short-run marginal cost (SMC_1) is as shown in Figure 13-6 and duopolist 2's short-run marginal cost is given by $SMC_2 = 6 + 2Q$. What quantity of the commodity will each duopolist produce? What price would each like to charge? What is the actual result likely to be?

(b) If $SATC_1 = \$5$ at $Q = 2$ and $SATC_2 = \$8$ at $Q = 1$, how much profit will each duopolist earn?

11. Assume that (1) in a purely oligopolistic industry, there is one dominant firm and 10 small identical firms; (2) the market demand curve for the commodity is $Q = 20 - 2P$, where P is given in dollars; (3) $SMC_d = 1.5 + Q/2$, while $SMC_s = 1 + Q/4$; and (4) input prices remain constant. Based on the above assumptions,

(a) draw a figure similar to Figure 13-7 showing the market demand curve, SMC_d, SMC_s, and the demand curve that the dominant firm faces.

(b) what price will the dominant firm set? How much will the small firms supply together? How much will the dominant firm supply?

12. Draw a figure showing that when two identical firms share the market equally for a homogeneous product they both earn profits, but if a third identical firm entered the industry, they would all face losses. How is this related to the existence of oligopoly?

Supplementary Readings

For a problem-solving approach to the topics covered in this chapter, see

Dominick Salvatore, *Microeconomic Theory,* 2nd ed. (New York: McGraw-Hill, 1983), Sections 12.4–12.12.

Other excellent presentations of the topics covered in this chapter are found in

William J. Fellner, *Competition Among the Few: Oligopoly and Similar Market Structures* (New York: Knopf, 1949).

F. M. Scherer, *Industrial Market Structure and Economic Performance,* 2nd ed. (Chicago: Rand McNally, 1980).

For a more recent discussion of game theory see

Martin Shubik, *Strategy and Market Structure* (New York: John Wiley, 1959).

Managerial theories of the firm are also discussed in

A. D. H. Kaplan, J. Dirlam, and R. Lanzillotti, *Pricing in Big Business: A Case Approach* (Washington, D.C.: Brookings Institution, 1958).

Darius W. Gaskins, "Dynamic Limit Pricing: Optimal Pricing under Threat of Entry," *Journal of Economic Theory,* No. 3, 1971, pp. 306–322.

Pricing and Employment of Inputs

FIVE

Part Five (Chapters 14–16) presents the theory of input-pricing and employment. Until this point, input prices were assumed to be given. In this part we examine how input prices and the level of their employment are determined in the market. Chapter 14 examines input pricing and employment under perfect competition in the output and input markets. Chapter 15 deals with input pricing and employment under imperfect competition in the output and/or input markets. Chapter 16 presents interest and capital theory; that is, it deals with choices in the allocation of inputs over time. As in previous parts of the text, the presentation of the theory is reinforced with many real-world examples and important applications.

Chapter 14

Input Price and Employment Under Perfect Competition

14-1 Profit Maximization and Optimal Input Employment

14-2 The Demand Curve of a Firm for an Input

14-3 The Market Demand Curve for an Input and Its Elasticity

14-4 The Supply Curve of an Input

14-5 Pricing and Employment of an Input

14-6 Economic Rent

14-7 Applications

Examples

14-1 The Wage Elasticity of the Demand for Labor

14-2 The Supply Curve of Physicians' Services

14-3 The Glut of Lawyers

14-4 Economic Rent and the Cost of the Military Draft

Applications

Application 1: Substitution and Income Effects of a Change in the Wage Rate

Application 2: Overtime Pay and the Supply of Labor Services

Application 3: Wage Differentials

Application 4: The Effect of Minimum Wages

Application 5: The Negative Income Tax

Preview Questions

Why do firms demand inputs?

How does a firm determine how much of an input to hire?

How can the market demand curve of an input be derived?

How does an individual decide between work and leisure?

What does the market supply of an input show?

How is the price of an input determined?

What are the reasons for wage differences?

What is the effect of minimum wages?

What is a negative income tax?

In Part III (Chapters 7–9) we examined how firms combine inputs to minimize production costs on the assumption of given input prices. In Part IV (Chapters 10–13) we dealt with the product market and examined the pricing and output of consumers' goods, again, on the assumption of given input prices. We now turn our attention to the input market and examine the pricing and employment of inputs. In terms of the circular flow diagram of Figure 1-1, we are shifting attention from the top portion or loops of the diagram dealing with the product market to the bottom loops dealing with the input market. In the top loops, individuals demand goods and services supplied by firms. In the bottom loops, the roles are reversed with firms demanding the inputs supplied in part by individuals, and paying wages, rents, and interests to input owners.

The pricing and employment of inputs determines the distribution of income among people. Some people have higher incomes than others because they own more highly priced or greater quantities of inputs. For example, a physicians' income is generally higher than the income of a teacher because physicians' services are more highly priced. Similarly, the income of some families is very high because of their ownership of stocks and land. Individuals and families with larger incomes have more money votes and can claim a greater portion of society's output than lower-income individuals and families. Thus, the pricing and employment of inputs is crucial to our understanding of the workings of the economic system.

In many ways the determination of input prices and employment is similar to the pricing and output of commodities. That is, the price and employment of an input is generally determined by the interaction of the forces of market demand and supply of the input. Yet, there several important qualifications. *First*, while consumers demand commodities because of the utility or satisfaction they receive in consuming the commodities,

447

firms demand inputs in order to produce the goods and services demanded by society. That is, the demand for an input is a derived demand; it is derived from the demand of the final commodity that the input is used in producing. *Second*, while consumers demand commodities, firms demand the *services* of inputs. That is, firms demand the *flow* of input services (e.g., labor time), not the stock of the inputs themselves. The same is generally true for the other inputs. *Third*, the analysis in this and in the next chapter deals with inputs generally. That is, it refers to all types of labor, capital, raw materials, and land inputs. However, since the various types of labor receive more than three quarters of the national income, the discussion is couched in terms of labor.

We begin the chapter with a summary discussion of profit maximization and optimal input employment. Then, we derive the demand curve of an input by a firm. By adding the demand curve for the input by all firms, we get the market demand curve for the input. This is followed by a discussion of an individual's decision between work and leisure, and of the market supply curve of an input in general. We will then show how the interaction of the market demand and supply of an input determines its price and employment under perfect competition (the case of imperfect competition is examined in the next chapter). A discussion of rent and quasirent follows. Finally, we present many important applications and extensions of the theory.

14-1

Profit Maximization and Optimal Input Employment

In this section we bring together and summarize the discussion of Chapters 7, 8, and 10 on the conditions for profit maximization and optimal input employment by firms operating under perfect competition. This will be the first step in the derivation of the demand curve for an input by a firm.

In Section 8-2b, we saw that the least-cost input combination of a firm was given by Equation (8-3B), repeated below as (14-1):

$$MP_L/w = MP_K/r \tag{14-1}$$

where MP refers to the marginal (physical) product, L refers to labor, K to capital, w to wages or the price of labor time, and r to the interest rate or the rental price of capital. Equation (14-1) indicates that to minimize production costs, the extra output or marginal product per dollar spent on labor must be equal to the marginal product per dollar spent on capital. If $MP_L = 5$, $MP_K = 4$, and $w = r$, the firm would not be minimizing costs since it is getting more extra output for a dollar spent on labor than on capital. To minimize costs, the firm would have to hire more labor and rent less capital. As the firm does this, the MP_L declines and the MP_K increases (because the firm operates in stage II of production). The process would have to continue until Condition (14-1) held. If w were higher than r, the MP_L would have to be proportionately higher than the MP_K for Condition (14-1) to hold. The same general condition would have to hold to minimize production costs, no matter how many inputs the firm uses. That is, the MP per dollar spent on each input would have to be the same for all inputs.

Going one step further, we can show that the reciprocal of each term (ratio) in Equation (14-1) equals the marginal cost (MC) of the firm to produce an additional unit of output. That is,

$$w/MP_L = r/MP_K = MC \tag{14-2}$$

Consider labor first. The wage rate (w) is the addition to the total costs of the firm from hiring one additional unit of labor, while MP_L is the resulting increase in the total output, of the commodity of the firm. Thus, w/MP_L gives the changes in total costs (in terms of labor) per unit increase in output. This is the definition of marginal cost. That is, $w/MP_L = MC$.[1] For example, if the hourly wage is \$10 and the firm produces five additional units of the commodity with an additional hour of labor time, the marginal cost per unit of output is \$2 ($w/MP_L = \$10/5 = \$2 = MC$). The same is true for capital. That is, $r/MP_K = MC$.[2]

To maximize profits, the firm must use the optimal or least-cost input combination to produce the *best level of output*. We saw in Section 10-3 that the best level of output for a perfectly competitive firm is the output at which marginal cost equals marginal revenues (MR) or price (P).[3] Thus, it follows that to maximize profits

$$w/MP_L = r/MP_K = MC = MR = P \tag{14-3}$$

By cross multiplication and rearrangement of the the terms, we get Equations (14-4) and (14-5):

$$MP_L \cdot MR = w \quad \text{or} \quad MP_L \cdot P = w \tag{14-4}$$
$$MP_K \cdot MR = r \quad \text{or} \quad MP_K \cdot P = r \tag{14-5}$$

Thus, the profit-maximizing rule is that the firm should hire labor until the

---

[1] Specifically,

$$\frac{w}{MP_L} = \frac{\Delta TC/\Delta L}{\Delta Q/\Delta L} = \frac{\Delta TC}{\Delta L} \cdot \frac{\Delta L}{\Delta Q} = \frac{\Delta TC}{\Delta Q} = MC$$

[2] Specifically,

$$\frac{r}{MP_K} = \frac{\Delta TC/\Delta K}{\Delta Q/\Delta K} = \frac{\Delta TC}{\Delta K} \cdot \frac{\Delta K}{\Delta Q} = \frac{\Delta TC}{\Delta Q} = MC$$

[3] Remember that with perfect competition in the commodity market, $MR = P$.

marginal product of labor times the firm's marginal revenue or price of the commodity equals the wage rate. Similarly, the firm should rent capital until the marginal product of capital times the firm's marginal revenue or price of the commodity is equal to the interest rate. To maximize profits, the same rule would have to hold for all inputs that the firm uses. In the next section we will see that this provides the basis for the firm's demand curve for an input.[4]

14-2

The Demand Curve of a Firm for an Input

In this section we build on the discussion of the last section and derive the demand curve of a firm for an input: first, when the input is the only variable input, and then when the input is one of two or more variable inputs.

14-2a The Demand Curve of a Firm for One Variable Input

We have stated earlier that a firm demands an input in order to produce a commodity demanded by consumers. Thus, the demand for an input is a **derived demand,** that is, derived from the demand of the final commodities that the input is used in producing. The demand for an input by a firm shows the quantities of the input that the firm would hire at various alternative input prices. We begin by assuming that only one input is variable (i.e., the amount used of the other inputs is fixed and cannot be changed). This assumption is relaxed in the next subsection.

A profit maximizing firm will hire an input as long as the income from the sale of the extra output produced by the input is larger than the extra cost of hiring the input. The extra income is given by the marginal product of the input times the marginal revenue of the firm. Since the firm is a perfect competitor in the product market, its marginal revenue equals the price of the commodity. The extra income earned by the firm is called the **value of the marginal product (*VMP*)** and is equal to the marginal product of the input times the marginal revenue of the firm or the product price. That is,

$$VMP = MP \cdot MR \quad \text{or} \quad VMP = MP \cdot P \tag{14-6}$$

If the variable input is labor, we have

$$VMP_L = MP_L \cdot MR \quad \text{or} \quad VMP_L = MP_L \cdot P \tag{14-6A}$$

---

[4] For a mathematical presentation of how much of an input a perfectly competitive firm in the commodity and input markets should hire to maximize profits using rudimentary calculus, see Section A13 of the Mathematical Appendix.

Thus, the VMP_L is the left-hand side of Equation (14-4). Similarly, the VMP_K is the left-hand side of Equation (14-5).

The extra cost of hiring an input is equal to the price of the input if the firm is also a perfect competitor in the input market. Perfect competition in the input market means that the firm demanding the input is too small, by itself, to affect the price of the input. In other words, each firm can hire any amount of the input (service) at the given market price for the input. Thus, the firm faces a horizontal or infinitely elastic *supply* curve for the input it purchases. For example, if the input is labor, this means that the firm can hire any quantity of labor time at the given wage rate. Thus, a profit maximizing firm should hire labor as long as the value of the marginal product of labor exceeds the wage rate and until $VMP_L = w$, as indicated by Equation (14-4).

The actual derivation of a firm's demand schedule for labor when labor is the only variable input (i.e., when capital and other inputs are fixed) is shown with Table 14-1. In Table 14-1, L refers to the number of workers hired by the firm per day. Q_x is the total output of commodity X produced by the firm by hiring various numbers of workers. The MP_L is the marginal or extra output generated by each additional worker hired. The MP_L is obtained by the change in Q_x per unit change in L. Note that the law of diminishing returns begins to operate with the hiring of the second worker. P_x refers to the price of the final commodity, which is constant (at $10) because the firm is a perfect competitor in the product market. The value of the marginal product of labor (VMP_L) is obtained by multiplying the MP_L by P_x.[5] Note that the VMP_L declines as more workers are hired because the MP_L declines (due to diminishing returns). The last column gives the daily wage rate (w) that the firm must pay to hire each worker. Since the firm is also a perfect competitor in the labor market, w is constant (at $40 per day) and gives the increase in the firm's total costs (the marginal expense) of hiring each additional worker.

Looking at Table 14-1, we see that the first worker contributes $120 to the firm's revenue (i.e., $VMP_L = \$120$) while the firm incurs a cost of only $40 to hire this worker. Thus, it pays for the firm to hire the first worker. The VMP_L of the second worker falls to $100 (because of diminishing returns), but this still greatly exceeds the daily wage of $40 that the firm must pay the second (and all) worker(s). According to Equation (14-4), the profit maximizing firm should hire workers until the $VMP_L = w$. Thus, this firm should hire five workers, at which $VMP_L = w = \$40$. The firm will not hire the sixth worker because he or she will contribute only $20 to the firm's total revenue while adding $40 to its total costs.

Thus, the VMP_L schedule gives the firm's demand schedule for labor. It indicates the number of workers that the firm would hire at various wage

---

[5] Note also that
$$VMP_L = MP_L \cdot MR = \frac{\Delta Q}{\Delta L} \cdot \frac{\Delta TR}{\Delta Q} = \frac{\Delta TR}{\Delta L}$$

TABLE 14-1 The Value of the Marginal Product of Labor and the Firm's Demand Schedule for Labor

L	Q_x	MP_L	P_x	VMP_L	w
0	0	$\cdots$	$10	$\cdots$	$40
1	12	12	10	$120	40
2	22	10	10	100	40
3	30	8	10	80	40
4	36	6	10	60	40
5	40	4	10	40	40
6	42	2	10	20	40

rates. For example, if w = $120 per day, the firm would hire only one worker per day. If w = $100, the firm would hire two workers. At w = $80, the firm would hire three workers. At w = $40, L = 5, and so on. If we plotted the the VMP_L values of Table 14-1 on the vertical axis and L on the horizontal axis, we would get the firm's negatively sloped demand *curve* for labor when labor is the only variable input. This is shown next.

14-2b The Demand Curve of a Firm for One of Several Variable Inputs

We have seen above that the declining VMP_L schedule given in Table 14-1 gives the firm's demand schedule for labor in the short run when labor is the only variable input. This is shown by the negatively sloped VMP_L curve in Figure 14-1 (on the assumption that labor is infinitesimally divisible or that workers can be hired for any part of a day). The VMP_L or demand of labor curve when labor is the only variable input shows that the firm will hire three workers at w = $80 (point A in Figure 14-1) and five workers at w = $40 (point B).

However, when labor is not the only variable input (i.e., when the firm can also change the quantity of capital and other inputs), the firm's demand curve for labor can be derived from the VMP_L curve, but it is not the VMP_L curve itself. Figure 14-1 shows the derivation of the demand curve for labor by a firm when both labor and capital are variable. As a first step, recall that at w = $80, the profit maximizing firm would hire three workers (point A on the VMP_L curve in Figure 14-1). This gives the first point on the firm's demand curve for labor when only labor is variable and when both labor and capital are variable. When the daily wage rate falls from w = $80 to w = $40, the firm does not move to point B on the given VMP_L curve and hire five workers (as shown before) if labor is not the only variable input.

To get another point on the firm's demand curve for labor when both labor and capital are variable, we should realize that labor and capital are usually **complementary inputs** in the sense that when the firm hires more

FIGURE 14-1.
*The Demand Curve
of the Labor by a
Firm with Labor
and Capital
Variable*

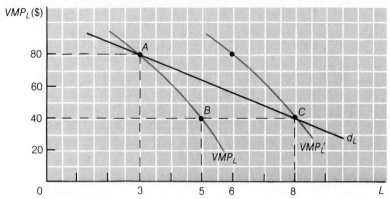

At $w = \$80$, the firm will employ three workers per day (point A on the VMP_L curve).
At $w = \$40$, the firm would employ five workers if labor were the only variable input
(point B on the VMP_L curve). However, since capital is also variable and complementary to labor, as the firm hires more labor, the VMP_K shifts to the right and the
firm also employs more capital (not shown in the figure). But as the firm employs
more capital, the VMP_L curve shifts to the right to VMP'_L and the firm employs eight
workers per day at $w = \$40$ (point C on the VMP'_L). By joining point A and point C,
we derive d_L (the firm's demand curve for labor).

labor it will also employ more capital (e.g., rent more machinery). For
example, when the firm hires more computer programmers, it will usually
also pay for the firm to rent more computer terminals, and vice versa.
Recall also that the VMP_L curve is drawn on the assumption that the quantity of capital used is fixed at a given level. Similarly, the VMP_K curve is
drawn on the assumption of a given amount of labor being used. If the
quantity of labor used with various amounts of capital increases (because
of a reduction in wages), the entire VMP_K curve will shift outward or to the
right. The reason for this is that with a greater amount of labor, each unit
of capital will produce more output (see Section 7-3b). Given the
(unchanged) rental price of capital or interest rate, the profit maximizing
firm will then want to expand its use of capital.

But the increase in the quantity of capital used by the firm will, in turn,
shift the entire VMP_L curve outward or to the right because each worker
will have more capital with which to work (and produce more output).
This is shown by the VMP'_L in Figure 14-1. Thus, when the daily wage rate
falls to $w = \$40$, the profit maximizing firm will hire eight workers (point
C on the VMP'_L curve) rather than five workers (point B on the VMP_L curve).
Thus, point C is another point on the firm's demand curve for labor when
labor and capital are both variable. Other points can be similarly obtained.
Joining point A and point C gives the firm's demand curve for labor (d_L in
Figure 14-1) when labor and capital are both variable and complementary.

To summarize, when $w = \$80$, the firm will hire three workers (point A
in Figure 14-1). Point A is a point on the firm's demand curve for labor,
whether or not labor is the only variable input. When the wage rate falls

to $w = \$40$, the firm will hire five workers (point B on the VMP_L curve) if labor is the only variable input. Thus, the VMP_L curve gives the firm's demand curve for labor when labor is the only variable input. If capital is also variable and complementary to labor, as the firm hires more labor because of the reduction in the wage rate, the VMP_K curve (not shown in Figure 14-1) shifts to the right and the firm uses more capital at the unchanged interest rate. However, as the firm uses more capital, its VMP_L curve shifts outward or to the right to VMP_L' and the firm hires not just five workers (point B on the VMP_L curve), but eight workers (point C on the VMP_L' curve). The reason is that only by hiring eight workers will $VMP_L' = w = \$40$. Joining points A and C gives the demand curve for labor of the firm d_L (see the figure) when labor and capital are both variable and complementary.

If capital or other inputs were substitutes of labor, the increase in the quantity of labor used by the firm as a result of a reduction in the wage rate will cause the VMP curves of these other inputs to shift to the *left* (as the utilization of more labor substitutes for, or replaces, some of these other inputs). This, in turn, will cause the VMP_L curve to shift outward and to the right as in Figure 14-1. Thus, whether other inputs are complements or substitutes of labor, the VMP_L shifts outward and to the right when the wage rate falls (and the price of these other inputs remains unchanged). As a result, the firm will hire more labor than indicated on its original VMP_L curve at the lower wage rate (see Figure 14-1).

Thus, the d_L curve is negatively sloped and generally more elastic than the VMP_L curve in the long run when all inputs are variable (whether the other inputs are complements or substitutes of labor, or both). In general, the better the complement and substitute inputs available for labor, the greater the outward shift of the VMP_L curve as a result of a decline in the wage rate, and the more elastic is d_L. The negative slope of d_L curve means that when the wage rate falls, the profit maximizing firm will hire more workers. The same is generally true for other inputs. That is, as the price of any input falls, the firm will hire more units of the input (i.e., the demand curve of the input by the firm is negatively sloped).

14-3

The Market Demand Curve for an Input and Its Elasticity

In this section we examine how to derive the market demand curve for an input from the individual firm's demand curves for the input. The determination of the market demand curve for an input is important because the equilibrium price of the input is determined at the intersection of the market demand and supply curves of the input under perfect competition.

After deriving the market demand curve for an input, we will discuss the determinants of the price elasticity of the demand for the input.

14-3a The Market Demand Curve for an Input

The market demand curve for an input is derived from the individual firm's demand curves for the input. While the process is similar to the derivation of the market demand curve for a commodity, the market demand curve for an input is not simply the horizontal summation of the individual firm's demand curves for the input. The reason is that when the price of an input falls, not only this firm but all other firms will employ more of this and other (complementary) inputs, as explained in Section 14-2b. Thus, the output of the *commodity* increases and its price falls. Since the VMP of an input is equal to the MP of the input times the commodity price, the reduction in the commodity price will cause each firm's VMP and demand curves of the input to shift down or to the left. The market demand curve for an input is then derived by the horizontal summation of the individual firm's demand curves for the input *after the effect of the reduction in the commodity price has been considered.* This is shown in Figure 14-2.

In the left panel of Figure 14-2, d_L is the individual firm's demand curve for labor time derived in Figure 14-1. The d_L curve was derived from the VMP_L of the firm, which itself depended on the marginal product of labor (i.e., MP_L) and the commodity price of $P_x = \$10$. The d_L curve shows that at the wage rate of $w = \$80$ per day the firm would hire three workers per day (point A on d_L). If there were 100 identical firms demanding labor, all

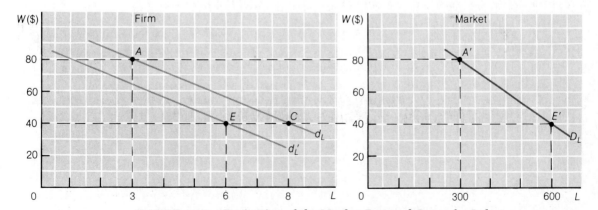

FIGURE 14-2. Derivation of the Market Demand Curve for Labor
In the left panel, d_L is the firm's demand curve for labor derived in Figure 14-1. At $w = \$80$ the firm hires three workers (point A on D_L). One hundred identical firms employ 300 workers (point A' in the right panel). Point A' is one point on the market demand curve for labor. When w falls to $w = \$40$, all firms employ more labor, the output of the commodity rises, and its price falls. Then d_L shifts to the left to d'_L, so that at $w = \$40$ the firm hires 6L (point E on d'_L), and all firms together will employ 600L(point E' in the right panel). By joining points A' and E', we get D_L.

firms together would employ 300 workers at $w = \$80$ (point A' in the right panel of Figure 14-2). Point A' is then one point on the market demand curve for labor.

When the wage rate falls to $w = \$40$, the firm would employ eight workers per day (point C on d_L). However, when we consider that all firms will be employing more labor (and capital) when the wage rate falls, they will produce more of the commodity, and the commodity price falls. The reduction in the commodity price will cause a leftward shift in d_L, say to d_L' in the left panel, so that when the wage rate falls to $w = \$40$, the firm will not hire eight workers per day but six workers (point E on d_L'). With 100 identical firms in the market, all firms together will employ 600 workers (point E' in the right panel). By joining points A' and E' in the right panel, we get the market demand curve for labor, D_L. Note that D_L is less elastic than if it were obtained by the straightforward horizontal summation of the d_L curves.

14-3b Determinants of the Price Elasticity of Demand for an Input

In Section 2-2c we defined the price elasticity of demand for a commodity as the percentage change in the quantity demanded of the commodity resulting from a given percentage change in its price. The price elasticity of demand for an input can similarly be defined as the percentage change in the quantity demanded of the input resulting from a given percentage change in its price. The greater the percentage change in quantity resulting from a given percentage change in price, the greater is the price elasticity of demand. For example, if 2 per cent more workers are employed as a result of 1 per cent reduction in the wage rate, the price (wage) elasticity of the market demand for labor is 2. If the quantity demanded of labor increased by only ½ per cent, the wage elasticity of labor would be ½.

The determinants of the price elasticity of demand for an input are generally the same as the determinants of the price elasticity of demand for a commodity (discussed in Section 5-2c). *First*, the price elasticity of demand for an input is larger the closer and the greater are the number of available substitutes for the input. For example, the price elasticity of demand for copper is greater than the price elasticity of demand for chromium (a metallic element used in alloys and in electroplating) because copper has better and more substitutes (silver, aluminum, fiber glass) than chromium. Thus, the same percentage change in the price of copper and chromium elicits a larger percentage change in the quantity demanded of copper than of chromium.

Second, since the demand for an input is derived from the demand of the final commodity produced with the input, the price elasticity of demand for the input is greater the larger is the price elasticity of demand of the commodity. The reason is that (as we have seen in the previous section) a reduction in the price of an input results in a reduction in the price of the final commodity produced with the input. The more elastic the demand for the final commodity, the greater is the increase in the quantity demanded of the commodity, and so the greater is the quantity demanded of the input used in the production of the commodity. For example, if the wage rate falls, the price of new homes also declines. If the price elasticity of demand for new homes is very high, then a price reduction for new homes increases very much the quantity demanded of new homes, and greatly increases the demand for labor and other inputs going into the production of new homes.

Third, the price elasticity of demand for an input, say aluminum, is greater the larger the price elasticity of *supply* of other inputs for which aluminum is a very good substitute in production. The reason is as follows. A reduction in the price of aluminum will lead producers to substitute aluminum for these other inputs. This is the same as the first reason discussed above, but it is not the end of the story. If the supply curve of these other inputs is very elastic, the reduction (i.e, leftward shift) in their demand curve will not result in a large decline in their price, and so the original increase in the quantity demanded of aluminum as a result of a reduction in its price will persist. This makes the demand curve for aluminum price elastic (if aluminum is a good substitute for these other inputs). Had the supply of these other inputs been inelastic, a reduction in their demand would have reduced their price very much, and checked the increase in the quantity demanded (and the price elasticity of demand) for aluminum.

Fourth, the price elasticity of demand for an input is *lower* the smaller the percentage of the total cost contributed by the input. For example, if the percentage of the total cost of the firm going to an input is only 1 per cent, a doubling of the price of the input will only increase the total costs of the firm by 1 per cent. In that case, a firm is then not likely to make great efforts to economize on the use of the input. Therefore, the price elasticity of an input on which the firm spends only a small percentage of its costs is likely to be low. However, this is usually, but not always, the case.

Finally, the price elasticity of an input is greater the longer the period of time allowed for the adjustment to the change in the input price. For example, an increase in the wage of unskilled labor may not reduce their employment very much in the short run because the firm must operate the given plant built to take advantage of the low wage of unskilled labor. However, in the long run, the firm can build a plant using more capital-intensive production techniques to save on the use of the now more expensive unskilled labor. Thus, the reduction in the employment (and the wage elasticity of the demand) of unskilled labor is likely to be greater in the long run than in the short run. In Figure 14-1, the d_L curve (which is the firm's demand curve for labor when labor and other inputs are variable) is more elastic than the VMP_L curve (which is the firm's short-run demand curve for labor when labor is the only variable input).

Example 14-1 The Wage Elasticity of the Demand for Labor

The Facts: Table 14-2 presents the wage elasticity of labor in some U.S. manufacturing industries. These are measured by the percentage change in the number of man-hours of labor demanded divided by the percentage change in the hourly wages of production workers. The wage elasticities have not been premultiplied by -1 (as in Section 2-3c) in order to clearly show the inverse relationship between wages and employment. These wage elasticities range from -0.51 in the food industry to -2.37 in the fabricated metals industry.

Comments: According to the figures in Table 14-1, a 10 per cent increase in the hourly wage of production workers in the U.S. food manufacturing industry reduces the number of man-hours of production workers demanded by 5.1 per cent. In the fabricated metals industry, a 10 per cent increase in wages reduces the quantity demanded of labor by 23.7 per cent. Thus, the ability to substitute other inputs for labor is much greater in the fabricated metals industry than in the food industry. An explanation of the reason for these large differences would require a detailed knowledge of the various industries.

14-4

The Supply Curve of an Input

In this section, we first derive an individual's supply curve of labor. Then, we examine the substitution and the income effects of a wage increase. Finally, we discuss the market supply curve of an input in general, and the market supply of labor in particular. In the next section we will use the market supply curve presented in this section and the market demand

TABLE 14-2 Wage Elasticity of Production Workers in Some U.S. Manufacturing Industries

Industry	Wage Elasticity
Food	-0.51
Chemicals	-0.65
Petroleum	-1.53
Instruments	-1.69
Stone, clay, glass	-1.97
Electrical machinery	-2.14
Fabricated metals	-2.37

Source: R. Waud, "Man-Hour Behavior in U.S. Manufacturing: A Neoclassical Interpretation," *Journal of Political Economy*, May/June 1968.

curve derived in Section 14-3b to determine the equilibrium price of an input (the wage rate).

14-4a The Supply of Labor by an Individual

The short-run supply curve of an input (like the supply curve of a final commodity) is generally positively sloped, indicating that a greater quantity of the input is supplied per unit of time at higher input prices. For example, if the price of iron ore rises, mining firms will supply more iron ore per time period. The same is true for an **intermediate good** such as steel (produced with iron ore) and itself used as an input in the production of many final commodities such as automobiles. That is, steel producers will supply more steel at higher steel prices. However, while natural resources (such as iron ore) and intermediate goods (such as steel) are supplied by firms and their supply curves are generally positively sloped, labor is supplied by individuals and their supply curve may be backward bending. That is, after some wage rate, higher wage rates may result in individuals demanding more leisure time and supplying fewer *hours* of work per day. This is shown in Figure 14-3.

The left panel of Figure 14-3 is used to derive the backward-bending supply curve of labor of an individual shown in the right panel. The movement from left to right on the horizontal axis of the figure in the left panel measures hours of leisure time for the individual (the top scale at the bottom of the figure). Subtracting hours of leisure from the 24 hours of the day, we get the hours worked by the individual per day (the bottom scale in the left panel). Hours of leisure plus hours of work always equal 24. On the other hand, the vertical axis in the left panel measures money income.

Indifference curves U_1, U_2, U_3, and U_4 in the left panel show the trade-off between leisure and income for the individual. They are similar to the individual's indifference curves between two commodities, discussed in Section 3-2. For example, the individual is indifferent between 14 hours of leisure (10 hours of work) and a daily income of $60 (point M on U_2) on the one hand, and 16 hours of leisure (8 hours of work) and a daily income of $40 (point E on U_2) on the other. Thus, the individual is willing to give up $20 of income to increase his or her leisure time by 2 hours. Indifference curves U_3 and U_4 provide more utility or satisfaction to the individual than U_2, and U_2 provides more utility or satisfaction than U_1.

Given the wage rate, we can easily define the budget line of the individual. When the individual takes all 24 hours in leisure (i.e., works zero hours), the individual's income is zero regardless of the wage rate. Thus, any budget line of the individual starts at this point on the horizontal axis in the left panel. On the other hand, if the individual worked 24 hours per day, his or her income would be $60 if the wage rate were $2.50 (the lowest budget line), his or her income would be $120 if $w = $5 (the second budget line), $180 if $w = $7.50 (the third budget line), and $240 if $w = $10 (the highest budget line). Note that the wage rate is given by the absolute value

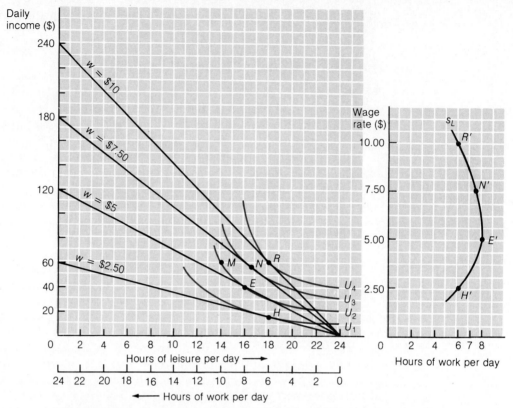

FIGURE 14-3.   Derivation of an Individual's Supply Curve of Labor
In the left panel, U_1, U_2, U_3, and U_4 show the trade-off between leisure and income for the individual, while the straight budget lines show the trade-off between leisure and income in the market. The absolute slope of the budget lines gives the wage rate. The individual maximizes satisfaction at point H (with 18 hours of leisure per day and a daily income of $15) on U_1 with w = $2.50, at point E (with 16 hours of leisure and income of $40) on U_2 with w = $5, and so on. By plotting hours of work per day at various wage rates, we get the individual's backward-bending supply curve of labor (s_L) in the right panel.

of the slope of the budget line. Thus, w = $60/24 hrs = $2.50/hour for the lowest budget line, w = $120/24 hrs = $5 for the second budget line, w = $180/24 hrs = $7.50 for the third budget line, and w = $240/24 hrs = $10 for the highest budget line. These budget lines are similar to the individual's budget lines derived in Section 3-3.

As shown in Section 3-5, an individual maximizes utility or satisfaction by reaching the highest indifference curve possible with his or her budget line. Thus, if the wage rate is $2.50, the individual will take 18 hours in leisure (i.e., works 6 hours) and earn an income of $17.50 per day (point H on U_1 in the left panel of Figure 14-3). This gives point H' on the individual's supply curve of labor (s_L) in the right panel. With w = $5, the individual takes 16 hours of leisure (i.e., works 8 hours) and earns an income of \$40 per day (point E on U_2 in the left panel). This gives point E' on s_L in the right panel. At $w = \$7.50$, the individual chooses 16.5 hours of leisure (works 7.5 hours) and has an income of \$56.25 per day (point N on U_3 and N' on s_L). Finally, at $w = \$10$, the individual chooses 18 hours of leisure (works 6 hours) and has an income of \$60 per day (point R on U_4 and R' on s_L).

Note that the individual's supply curve of labor (s_L in the right panel of Figure 14-3) is positively sloped until the wage rate of \$5, and it bends backward at higher wage rates. Thus, the individual works *more* hours (i.e., takes less leisure) until the wage rate of \$5 per hour and works *fewer* hours (i.e., takes more leisure) at higher wage rates.

14-4b The Substitution and the Income Effects of a Wage Increase

The reason that an individual's supply curve of labor is backward bending can be explained by separating the substitution from the income effect of the wage increase. That is, an increase in wages (just like an increase in a commodity price) gives rise to a substitution and an income effect. In the case of an increase in a commodity price, the substitution and the income effects work in the same direction (to reduce the quantity demanded of the commodity). On the other hand, in the case of an increase in the wage rate, the substitution and the income effects operate in opposite directions, and (as explained next) this causes the individual's supply curve of labor to be backward bending.

According to the substitution effect, an increase in the wage rate leads an individual to work more (i.e., to substitute work for leisure). That is, as the wage rate rises, the price of leisure increases and the individual takes less leisure (i.e., works more). Thus, the substitution effect of the wage increase always operates to make the individual's supply curve of labor *positively* sloped. However, an increase in the wage rate also raises the individual's income, and with a rise in income, the individual demands more of every normal good, including leisure (i.e., supplies fewer hours of work). Thus, the income effect of a wage increase always operates to make the individual's supply curve *negatively* sloped.

The substitution and income effects operate over the entire length of the individual's supply curve of labor. Until the wage rate of $w = \$5$ in Figure 14-3, the substitution effect overwhelms the opposite income effect and the individual works more (i.e., his or her supply curve of labor is positively sloped). At $w = \$5$, the substitution effect is balanced by the income effect and s_L is vertical (point E' in the figure). At wage rates higher than $w = \$5$, the (positive) substitution effect is overwhelmed by the (negative) income effect and s_L bends backward. Note that theory does not tell us at what wage rate the bend occurs. It only says that at some sufficiently high wage rate this is likely to occur. Since individuals' tastes differ, the wage rate at which an individual supply curve of labor bends backward is likely to differ from individual to individual.

Also note that while the substitution effect is usually greater than the income effect for a *commodity*, this is not the case for labor. The reason is that a consumer spends his or her income on many commodities so that an increase in the price of any one commodity is not going to greatly reduce his or her real income (i.e., the income effect is small in relation to the substitution effect). On the other hand, since most individuals' incomes come primarily from wages, an increase in wages will greatly affect the individuals' incomes (so that the income effect may overwhelm the opposite substitution effect). At the wage rate at which this occurs, s_L will bend backward. The separation of the substitution and the income effect of a wage increase is shown graphically in Application 1.

It might be argued that individuals do not have a choice of the number of hours they work per day, and so the above analysis is not relevant. Yet, this is not entirely true. For example, an individual may choose to work any number of hours on a part-time basis, may choose an occupation that requires six or seven hours of work per day instead of eight, an occupation that allows more or less vacation time, and may or may not accept to work overtime (see Application 2), and so on. All that is required for the above analysis to be relevant is for *some* occupations to require different hours of work per day and/or some flexibility in hours of work.

Note that as workers' wages and incomes have risen over time, the average workweek (and the length of the average workday) has declined from 10 hours per day for six days per week at the turn of the century to 8 hours per day for five days per week, or even slightly less today. However, the trend toward fewer hours of work per day and per week seems to come to an end or to have considerably slowed down over the past half a century. Thus, the substitution and income effect of higher wages must have been more or less in balance in recent decades. Over the same period of time, however, the participation rate (i.e., the percentage of the population in the labor force) has increased.

14-4c The Market Supply Curve for an Input

The market supply curve for an input is obtained from the straightforward horizontal summation of the supply curve of individual suppliers of the input, just as in the case of the supply curve of a final commodity (see Section 10-4). In the case of inputs of natural resources and intermediate goods, which are supplied by firms, the short-run market supply curve of the input is generally positively sloped (as is the firm's supply curve). The market supply curve of labor is usually also positively sloped, but it may bend backward at very high wages (see Example 14-2).

Figure 14-4 shows a hypothetical market supply curve of labor (S_L) measuring the *number* of workers on the horizontal axis and the *daily* wage rate on the vertical axis. It shows that at the wage of $20 per day, 400 people

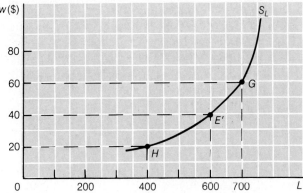

*FIGURE 14-4.
The Market Supply
Curve of Labor*

Market supply curve of labor S_L shows that at the wage of $20 per day, 400 people
are willing to work in this market (point H). At w = $40 per day, 600 people are
willing to work (point E'). At w = $60, 700 are willing to work (point G), and so on.
S_L is positively sloped over the range of daily wages shown but becomes less elastic
at high wage rates (and may eventually bend backward at still higher wage rates).

are willing to work in this market (point *H*). At *w* = $40 per day, 600 people
are willing to work (point *E'*). At *w* = $60, 700 are willing to work (point
G), and so on. Note that S_L is positively sloped over the range of daily wages
shown in the figure but becomes less elastic at high wage rates (and may
eventually bend backward at still higher wage rates).

The shape of S_L is also the net result of two opposing forces. Higher daily
wages will, on the one hand, induce some individuals to enter the labor
market (to take advantage of the higher wages), but it will also result in
some individuals to leave the job market as their spouse's wages and
income rise. Note that the supply curve of labor is less likely to be backward bending for a particular industry than for the economy as a whole
since workers can always be attracted to an industry from other industries
by raising wages sufficiently.

Example 14-2   The Supply Curve of Physicians' Services

The Facts: One specific labor market where the supply curve of labor services seems to be backward bending is the market for physicians' services.
Martin Feldstein found that the price elasticity of supply of physicians' services in the United States was between −0.67 and −0.91 over the 1948–
1966 period. This means that a 10 per cent increase in the price of physicians' services results in a *reduction* in the quantity supplied of services of
between 6.7 per cent and 9.1 per cent. Thus, according to Feldstein's
results, the sharp increase in the fees for physicians' services in recent
years actually resulted in a reduction in the quantity of services supplied.
Feldstein also confirmed the results of previous studies, which indicated
that doctors charged higher fees to richer than to poorer patients.

463

Comment: The enactment of Medicare (a subsidiary of the medical care for the elderly) and Medicaid (a subsidy of the medical care for the poor) in 1965, as well as the increased insurance coverage for physicians' bills, greatly increased the ability of broad segments of the population to pay for medical services. This greater ability to pay may have been an important contributor to the sharp rise in medical fees and to the reduction in the quantity supplied of physicians' services.

Source: M. Feldstein, "The Rising Price of Physicians' Services," *The Review of Economics and Statistics,* May 1970.

14-5

Pricing and Employment of an Input

Just as in the case of a final commodity, the equilibrium price and employment of an input is given at the intersection of the market demand and the market supply curve of the input in a perfectly competitive market. This is shown in Figure 14-5 for labor.

In Figure 14-5, D_L is the market demand curve for labor (from the right panel of Figure 14-2), while S_L is the market supply curve of labor (from Figure 14-4). The intersection of D_L and S_L at point E' gives the equilibrium (daily) wage of $40 and level of employment of 600 workers per day. At the lower wage rate of $20 per day, firms would like to employ 800 workers per day but only half that number are willing to work; thus, there is a shortage of 400 workers per day (*HJ* in the figure) and the wage rate rises.

FIGURE 14-5.
Determination of
the Equilibrium
Wage Rate and
Level of
Employment

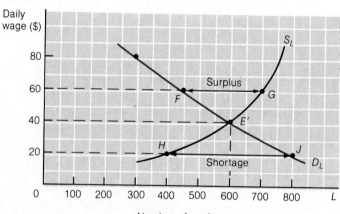

D_L is the market demand curve for labor (from the right panel of figure 14-2), while S_L is the market supply curve for labor (from Figure 14-4). The intersection of D_L and S_L at point E' gives the equilibrium (daily) wage rate of $40 and the equilibrium level of employment of 600 workers per day.

At the high wage of $60 per day, 700 workers are willing to work but firms would like to employ only 450; there is a surplus of 250 workers (*FG*) and the wage rate falls. Only at *w* = $40 is the number of workers who are willing to work equal to the number of workers that firms want to employ (600), and the market is in equilibrium.

Note that at the equilibrium daily wage of $40, each of the 100 identical firms in the market will employ 6 workers per day (point *E* on d_L' in the left panel of Figure 14-2). In a perfectly competitive input market, each firm is too small to perceptibly affect the wage rate (i.e., the firm can employ any number of workers per day at the equilibrium market wage rate of $40 per day). Another way of saying this is that the firm faces a horizontal or infinitely elastic supply curve of labor at the given wage rate. Since the price of an input equals the value of its marginal product (*VMP*), the theory of input pricing and employment has been called the **marginal productivity theory.**

Finally, note that we have implicitly assumed that all units of the input are identical (have the same productivity) and receive the same price. In the case of labor, the wages of all workers would be the same only if all occupations were equally attractive (or unattractive), if all workers had identical qualifications and productivity, and if there was no interference with the operation of the market. These topics are discussed in Application 3.

Example 14-3 The Glut of Lawyers

The Facts: There are 650,000 licensed lawyers in the U.S. today. Their number doubled in just a decade and is expected to grow to 1 million by 1990. While some increase in the number of lawyers is justified by population growth, the proliferation of laws and regulations, and the greater propensity on the part of citizens to bring legal action, 70 per cent of the members of the American Bar Association believe that the boom has gotten out of hand and that something must be done to limit their number. As predicted by economic theory, the larger increase in the supply relative to the demand of law services resulted in a reduction in the price of many law services, such as for uncontested divorces, wills, small personal injury cases, and for nonbusiness bankruptcy cases. (It is primarily in large *corporate* disputes that costs are rising sharply and multimillion dollar fees are becoming the rule rather than the exception.) Competition for business has resulted in attorneys setting up legal clinics, often in drugstores and shopping malls, to handle simple cases at cut-rate prices. Lawyers' search for business has also been blamed by some for the rash of law suits in recent years. In search for business, lawyers have also increasingly turned to advertising since 1977, when the U.S. Supreme Court abolished state prohibitions against it.

Comment: A similar situation may be developing in the medical profession.

By the end of the decade, the Graduate Medical Education National Advisory Committee predicts that there will be 63,000 doctors "too many" for the needs of the population. To be sure, a "shortage" of psychiatrists (especially child psychiatrists) is developing, but a major "surplus" of surgeons, obstetricians, pediatricians, cardiologists, and diagnostic radiologists is expected. While doctors are not unemployed (so that the use of the term "surplus" by the mass media is not appropriate), some are having trouble getting enough patients and are recommending more unnecessary treatment. Economic theory predicts that, under these circumstances, a completely free market would result in lower (or less rapidly rising) prices for medical services.

Source: "A Glut of Lawyers—Impact on U.S.," *U.S. News and World Report*, December 19, 1983, pp. 59–61, and "For Doctors, Too, It's a Surplus," *U.S. News and World Report*, December 19, 1983, pp. 62–64.

14-6

Economic Rent

Economic rent differs from the everyday meaning of the term rent, which is a payment made to lease an apartment, an automobile, or any other durable asset. Economic rent originally referred only to the payment made to landowners to lease their land (which was assumed to be in fixed supply). Today, **economic rent** is defined as that portion of the payment to the supplier of any input (not just land) that is in excess of the minimum amount necessary to retain the input in its present use. If the market supply of an input is fixed, demand alone determines the input price and all of the payment made to the input is rent. If the market supply of an input is positively sloped, only the area above the supply curve and below the price of the input represents rent. This is shown in Figure 14-6.

In the left panel of Figure 14-6, the market supply of the input, say, land, is fixed at 600 acres (i.e., S is vertical). If the market demand curve is D, the (rental) price is $40 per acre (point E) and the entire payment of $24,000 ($40 times 600) per month made to the owners of land is economic rent. If the market demand were D', the rental price would be $60 (point E') and rent is $36,000 per month. If the market demand for the input were D'', the rental price would be $20 (point E'') and rent is $12,000 per month. Note that regardless of the level of demand and price, the same quantity of land will be supplied per month, even at an infinitesimally small rental price. Thus, all of the payments made to the landowners represent economic rent. This is true not only for land but for any input in fixed supply. For example, since the supply of Picasso paintings is fixed, they will be supplied (sold) at whatever price (including the retention price of present owners) they can fetch. Therefore, all payments made to purchase Picassos represent economic rent.

FIGURE 14-6.
The Measurement of
Economic Rent

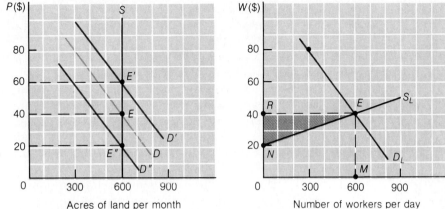

In the left panel, 600 acres of land are supplied per month regardless of the rental price. With D, the price is $40 (point E) and the entire payment of $24,000 ($40 times 600) is rent. With D', P = $60 (point E') and rent is $36,000. With D'', P = $20 and rent is $12,000. In the right panel, S_L is positively sloped. With D_L, w = $40 and 600 workers are employed (point E). Shaded area ENR = $6,000 represents economic rent or a payment that is not needed to retain the 600 workers in the particular industry.

In the right panel, the supply of the input, say, labor, to an industry is positively sloped. This means that higher daily wages will induce more individuals to work in the industry. The equilibrium wage of $40 is determined at the intersection of D_L and S_L (point E in the figure, at which 600 workers are employed). Each of the 600 (identical) workers receive a wage of $40 per day. Yet, one worker could be found who would work for a wage of only $20, and 300 workers would be willing to work at a daily wage of $30 each (see the S_L curve in the left panel). Thus, the shaded area above the supply curve and below the equilibrium wage of $40 represents economic rent. It is the workers' excess earnings over their next-best employment. That is, the 600 workers receive a total wage of $24,000 (the area of rectangle EMOR), but they only need be paid EMON to be retained in the industry. Therefore, the area of shaded triangle ENR ($6,000) represents economic rent or the payment that need not be made by the particular industry to retain 600 workers in the long run.

Note that even land may not be fixed in supply to any industry since some land could be bid away from other uses. Land may not even be fixed for the economy as a whole, since over time, land can be augmented through reclamation and drainage, and be depleted through erosion and loss of fertility. Thus, the payment to lease land, too, may be only partly rent. In general, the more inelastic is the supply curve of an input to the industry, the greater is the proportion of economic rent. In the extreme case, the supply curve is vertical and all the payment to the input is rent. The importance of this is that rent could all be taxed away without reducing the quantity supplied of the input. This is an excellent tax since it does not discourage work or reduce the supply of labor (or other inputs) even in the long run. Note that economic rent is analogous to the concept of consumer surplus (see Application 2 in chapter 4). Consumer surplus is the difference between what a *consumer* is willing to pay for a given quantity of a commodity and what he or she actually pays for it. Economic rent is the excess payment that an *input owner* receives and the minimum he or she requires to continue to keep the input in its present use.

While all or some of the payment made by an industry to the suppliers of an input is rent, all payments made by an *individual firm* to employ an input is a *cost* to the firm, which the firm must pay in order to retain the use of the input. If the firm tried to pay less than the market price for the input, the firm would be unable to retain any unit of the input. For example, if a firm tried to employ workers at less than the $40 daily wage prevailing in the market, the firm will lose all of its workers to other firms. Finally, note that any payment made to *temporarily* fixed inputs is sometimes called *quasirent*. Thus, the return to fixed inputs in the short run are quasirents (see Problem 8). These payments need not be made in order for these fixed inputs to be supplied in the short run. In the long run, however, all inputs are variable, and unless they receive a price equal to their next-best alternative, they will not be supplied. To the extent that they receive more than this, the inputs receive economic rent. In long-run perfectly competitive equilibrium, all inputs receive the value of their marginal product and the firm breaks even.

Example 14-4 Economic Rent and the Cost of the Military Draft

The Facts: Figure 14-7 gives the summarized and simplified supply curve (S) of military personnel estimated by Walter Oi for the United States for the year 1965. It shows that to induce the enlistment of 472,000 soldiers (as required by the U.S. government in 1965) into an all-voluntary army, a yearly wage of $5,900 would have had to be paid per enlistee for a total yearly cost of $2.78 billion ($5900 times 472,000) given by area $OGEF$ in the figure. As it was, only $2,500 was paid per enlistee per year. At this low pay, only 263,000 were "true" volunteers (point B in the Figure). Another 153,700 were "reluctant" volunteers, in the sense that they volunteered only to avoid being drafted into the army. The yearly wage would have to be $4,700 per enlistee for these reluctant volunteers to be true volunteers (point C). With the actual low yearly wage of $2,500 per enlistee, 55,300 had to be drafted to reach the required number of 472,000 enlistees.

We have seen above that to get 472,000 enlistees as true volunteers, the yearly wage would have had to be $5,900 per enlistee (point E) for a total cost of $2.78 billion ($OGEF$). By paying only $2,500 per enlistee, the budgetary cost was instead $1.18 billion ($OHJF$) per year, at a total *budgetary saving* of $1.6 billion per year ($HGEJ$). This, however, was not a true savings from the point of view of society as a whole since an explicit tax on all individuals (to finance the government budget) was simply replaced by an

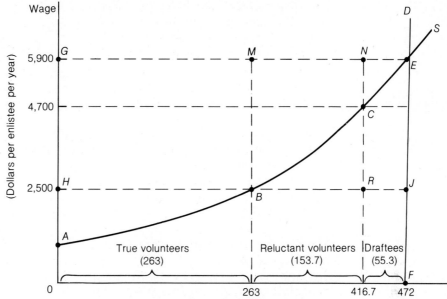

FIGURE 14-7.
Economic Rent and
the Cost of the
Military Draft

To get 472,000 true volunteers in the military, the yearly wage would have had to be $5,900 per enlistee (point E) at a total cost of $2.78 billion (OGEF). By paying only $2,500 per enlistee, the budgetary cost was instead $1.18 billion (OHJF) per year, at a total budgetary saving of $1.6 billion (HGEJ). The true volunteers as a group, however, lost HGMB out of their total rent of AGMB. Reluctant volunteers lost BMNC in rent and BCR in alternatives forgone. The draftees lost CNE of rent and RCEJ in other earnings.

implicit tax on enlistees. The true volunteers as a group lost *HGMB* out of their total rent of *AGMB*. Reluctant volunteers lost *BMNC* in rent and *BCR* in payments that they would have required to be true volunteers. The draftees lost *CNE* of rent and *RCEJ* in payments that they would require to be true volunteers. Thus, the budgetary savings of the government was matched by the total implicit tax on the enlistees as a group.

Comment: The move to an all-volunteer army was actually made in 1973. As civilian wages rise over time, the wages per enlistee would also have to increase in order to attract and retain the required number of enlistees as (true) volunteers. The wage per enlistee would also have to rise if an increase in the size of the all-voluntary army were sought. On the other hand, an increase in the rate of unemployment in the economy would reduce the cost of an all-voluntary army by reducing opportunities for civilian employment. Note that the move toward an all-voluntary army eliminated the losses resulting from some individuals taking lower-paying but draft-exempt jobs, going or remaining in college to escape the draft, illegal draft evasion, and so on.

469

Source: W. Oi, "The Economic Cost of the Draft," *American Economic Review*, May 1967, pp. 39–62.

14-7

Applications

In this section we discuss some important applications of the theory presented in the chapter. They include the separation of the substitution from the income effect of a change in wages, the analysis of overtime pay, the cause of wage differentials, the effect of minimum wages, and the negative income tax. These applications clearly indicate the usefulness and applicability of the theory presented in this chapter.

Application 1: Substitution and Income Effects of a Change in the Wage Rate

We have seen in Section 14-4b that an increase in wages gives rise to a substitution and an income effect. That is, when the wage rate rises, on the one hand, the individual tends to substitute work for leisure (since the price of leisure has increased). On the other hand, the increase in income resulting from the wage rise leads the individual to demand more of every normal good, including leisure (i.e, to work fewer hours). We can separate the substitution from the income effect as in Section 4-3a. This is shown in Figure 14-8.

The movement from point E to point R in Figure 14-8 is the combined substitution and income effects of the wage increase from \$5 to \$10 (as in Figure 14-3). The substitution effect can be isolated by drawing the hypothetical budget line that is tangent to U_2 at point M and with slope reflecting the higher wage of \$10. Since the consumer is on original indifference curve U_2, his or her income is the same as before the wage rise, and the movement along U_2 from point M to point E measures the substitution effect. By itself, it shows that when w rises from \$5 to \$10, the individual reduces leisure time from 16 to 12 hours (i.e., increases hours of work from 8 to 12 per day). Then, the shift from point M on U_2 to point R on U_4 is the income effect of the wage increase. In this case, the increase in wages raises the individual's income by \$50 (\$240–\$190; see the vertical axis of the figure). By itself, the income effect leads the individual to increase leisure from 12 to 18 hours (i.e., to work 6 hours less). The net result is that the individual increases leisure (works less) by two hours per day (ER).

Application 2: Overtime Pay and the Supply of Labor Services

The hourly wage of many workers increases after a specified number of hours worked per day. This is called **overtime pay.** Figure 14-9 shows the additional number of hours worked per day by an individual as a result of overtime pay.

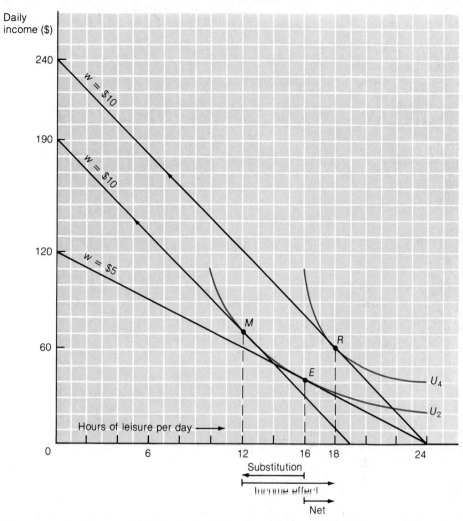

FIGURE 14-8.
Separation of the
Substitution from
the Income Effect of
a Wage Rise

The movement from point E to point R is the combined substitution and income effects of the wage increase from $5 to $10 (as in Figure 14-3). We can isolate the substitution effect by shifting the highest budget line down parallel to itself until it is tangent to indifference curve U_2 at point M. The movement along U_2 from point M to point E measures the substitution effect of the wage increase. The shift from point M on U_2 to point R on U_4 is the income effect.

Initially, at the wage rate of $5 per hour, the individual demands 16 hours of leisure (works 8 hours per day) and earns an income of $40 (point E on U_2, as in Figures 14-3 and 14-8). With an overtime pay of $20 per hour (the slope of ET in Figure 14-9), the individual can be induced to work two additional hours per day and have a total income of $80 per day (point T on higher indifference curve U_3). Thus, the substitution effect (which encourages work) exceeds the income effect (which discourages work) and the individual works more hours with overtime pay.

471

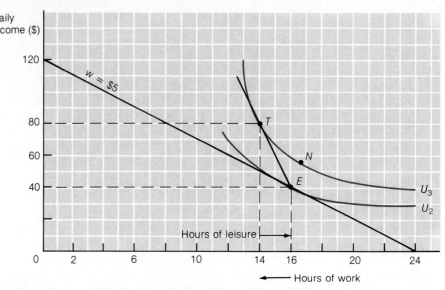

FIGURE 14-9.
Overtime Pay and
the Supply of Labor
Services

Initially, at w = $5, the individual demands 16 hours of leisure (works 8 hours per day) and earns an income of $40 (point E on U_2, as in Figures 14-3 and 14-8). With overtime pay of w = $20 per hour (the slope of ET), the individual will work two additional hours per day and have a total income of $80 (point T on U_3).

Application 3: Wage Differentials

Up to this point we have generally assumed that all occupations are equally attractive and that all units of an input, say, labor, are homogeneous (i.e., have the same training and productivity), so that the wages of all workers were the same. If all jobs and workers were identical, wage differences could not persist among occupations or regions of a country under perfect competition. Workers would leave lower-wage occupations and regions for higher-wage occupations and regions until all wage differentials disappeared (see Problem 11, with answer at the end of this book).

In the real world, jobs differ in attractiveness, workers have different qualifications and trainings, and markets may not be perfectly competitive. All of these can result in different wages for different occupations and for workers with different training and abilities. More formally, wages differ among different jobs and categories of workers because of (1) equalizing differentials, (2) the existence of noncompeting groups, and (3) imperfect competition. We will now briefly examine each of these.

Equalizing wage differentials are wage differences that compensate workers for the nonmonetary differences among jobs. While some jobs (such as garbage collection and being a porter in a hotel) may require equal qualifications, one job (garbage collection) may be more unpleasant than another (being a porter). Hence, the more unpleasant job must pay a higher wage in order to attract and retain workers in it. These wage differentials equalize or compensate for the nonmonetary differences among jobs and

472

will persist in time. In the real world, many wage differences are of this type.

For example, policemen's salaries are usually higher than firemen's salaries because of the alleged greater risk in being a policeman. Similarly, construction work generally pays more than garbage collection because of less job security in the former. Note that a particular individual may prefer being a policeman or a construction worker even if the salary were the same as (or lower than) that of a fireman or garbage collector, respectively. But it is the intersection of the market demand and supply curves of labor for each occupation that determines the equilibrium wage in the occupation and the equalizing wage differentials among occupations that require the same general level of qualifications and training.

Noncompeting groups are occupations requiring different capacities, skills, education and training, and, therefore, receiving different wages. That is, labor in some occupations is not in direct competition with labor in some other occupations. For example, physicians form one noncompeting group not in direct competition with lawyers (which form another noncompeting group). Other noncompeting groups are engineers, accountants, musicians, electricians, and so on. Engineers and electricians belong to different noncompeting groups because, although engineers could probably work easily as electricians, engineers' productivity and wages are so much higher when working as engineers than as electricians that they form a separate noncompeting group. On the other hand, electricians do not have the training and may not have the ability to be engineers.

Each noncompeting group has a particular wage structure as determined by the intersection of its demand and supply curves. Note that some mobility among noncompeting groups is possible (as, for example, when an electrician becomes an engineer by attending college at night), and this possibility is greater in the long run than in the short run. However, mobility among noncompeting groups is limited, even in the long run, especially if based on innate ability (e.g., not everyone can be a brain surgeon or an accomplished violinist).

An imperfect labor market can also result in wage differences for identical jobs requiring the same ability and level of training. A labor market is imperfect if workers lack information on wages and job opportunities in other occupations, if they are unwilling to move to other jobs and occupations, or if there are labor unions and large employers able to affect wages. These topics will be explored in detail in the next chapter.

Application 4: The Effect of Minimum Wages

In 1938, Congress passed the Fair Labor Standard Act, which established a minimum wage of $0.25 per hour. By 1981, the federal minimum wage had risen to $3.35 per hour (which is the rate still prevailing today, 1985). Coverage was also extended over the years, so that today 85 per cent of all workers in the United States are covered. Since skilled workers generally have wages well above the minimum wage, they are not affected by it.

Thus, most of the effect of minimum wages is on unskilled workers. We can analyze the effect of the minimum wage on unskilled workers (assuming for the moment that all unskilled workers are identical) with the aid of Figure 14-10.

In Figure 14-10, D_L is the market demand curve, while S_L is the market supply curve for unskilled workers. In a perfectly competitive labor market, the equilibrium wage would be $2.00 per hour ($16 per day with an 8 hour workday) and the equilibrium level of employment would be 4.5 million workers (point E in the figure). The imposition of a federal minimum wage of $3.35 per hour would result in firms hiring only 4 million workers (point M on D_L) as opposed to the 5 million workers (point N on S_L) willing to work at this minimum wage. Thus, the minimum wage would lead to a total **unemployment gap** of 1 million workers (MN). This is composed of the half million additional workers who would like to work at the minimum wage (the movement from point E to point N on the S_L curve) plus the **disemployment effect** of another half million workers as firms employ fewer workers at the above-equilibrium minimum wage (the movement from point E to point M on the D_L curve). While the minimum wage benefits those unskilled workers who remain employed, some unskilled workers

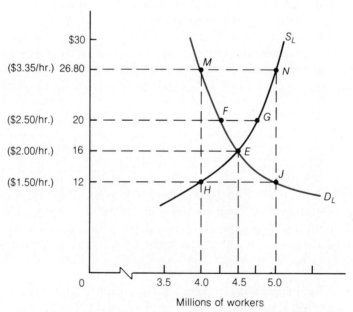

FIGURE 14-10.
The Effect of
Minimum Wages

D_L *is the market demand curve, while* S_L *is the market supply curve for unskilled workers. The equilibrium wage is $2.00 per hour at which 4.5 million workers are employed (point E). A minimum wage of $3.35 results in 4 million workers employed as opposed to 5 million willing to work, leaving an unemployment gap of 1 million workers (MN). The disemployment effect is a half million workers (the movement from point E to point M on* D_L*).*

would lose their jobs, and still more would like to work but cannot find employment.

Empirical studies have confirmed the notion that raising the minimum wage leads to disemployment and to an even greater unemployment gap. This is particularly true for teenagers in general, and black teenagers in particular. The unemployment rate of teenagers (generally the least skilled in the labor force) relative to other age groups has increased after each increase in the minimum wage and now (mid-1984) stands at near 20 per cent (16 per cent for white teenagers and 43 per cent for black teenagers). This is more than double the corresponding rates for workers in other age categories. Aware of the adverse effect of the minimum wage on teenage employment, the National Conference of Black Mayors endorsed in May 1984 a Reagan Administration proposal for the subminimum wage of $2.50 for teenagers. It was estimated that this would create 500,000 additional jobs (FG in Figure 14-10) and substantially cut teenage unemployment.[6]

There are other ways by which the imposition or the raising of a minimum wage rate can harm the very people it is supposed to help. An increase in the minimum wage may lead some employers to reduce or cut other fringe benefits (such as some health benefits, free or subsidized meals, free uniforms, and so on). Some employers may suspend apprenticeships and on-the-job training for unskilled workers that they were hiring at wages below the minimum wage. The harmful effect of a rise in the minimum wage is even greater in the long run when employers have a greater opportunity to substitute more capital-intensive production techniques for unskilled labor. Today many economists believe that there are better ways to help low-wage workers. Perhaps the most promising is to provide training to increase their productivity.[7]

Application 5: The Negative Income Tax

The **negative income tax (NIT)** is a type of welfare program involving cash transfers to low-income families. Many economists have urged that the U.S. replace its numerous and uncoordinated welfare programs with an NIT. With an NIT, the higher is the family income, the smaller is the amount of the transfer.

For example, suppose that the minimum yearly family income is set at $12,500 ($50 per day) and no family is allowed to fall below that income. This is called the **minimal income maintenance** and is given by horizontal line DF in Figure 14-11. A family earning no income at all will receive a transfer or subsidy of $50 per day, as shown by point F in the figure. A family earning $30 per day (point H) would receive a transfer or subsidy of $35 per day (HG) so that the family would have a total income of $65 per day (point G). *This is equivalent to the government continuing to give a sub-*

---

[6] Some people believe that the figure of 500,000 additional jobs was created for political reasons without much economic or statistical justification.

[7] For a discussion of the effect of minimum wages, see F. Welch, *Minimum Wages: Issues and Evidence* (Washington, D.C.: American Enterprise Institute, 1978).

FIGURE 14-11.
The Negative Income
Tax and Work Effort

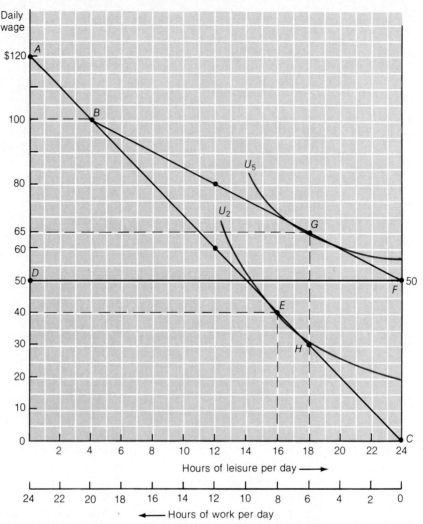

In the absence of the NIT, the family maximizes utility at point E, where its indifference curve U_2 in tangent to budget line CA. The family supplies 8 hours of work per
day at a daily wage of $40. With a NIT providing the minimal income maintenance
level of $50 per day and the marginal tax rate of 50 per cent, the family's budget line
becomes FBA and the family will be at point G on U_5. The family's income is now
$65 per day ($30 earned plus the $35 subsidy) and the family supplies only 6 hours
of work per day.

sidy of $50 per day and taxing at the rate of 50 per cent (i.e., taxing away
half of) the family's earned income of $30 per day. (Disregard, for now, the
family's leisure-income indifference curves shown in the figure).

A family earning $60 per day would receive a transfer or subsidy of $20
per day, so that the family would have a total income of $80 per day (see
the figure). *This is equivalent to the government continuing to give a subsidy*

of $50 per day and taxing at the rate of 50 per cent (i.e., taxing away half of) the family's earned income of $60 per day. At the family's income of $100 per day, the net subsidy would be zero. This is equivalent to the government continuing to give the subsidy of $50 but imposing a 50 per cent tax and collecting $50 in taxes, which is equal to half of the family's earned income of $100 per day. This is called the **break-even income.** Above this income ($100 per day of $25,000 per year), the family pays (positive) taxes.

Thus, the dollar amount of aid given to the family declines as the family's earned income rises. This is given by the declining vertical distance between lines *FB* and *CB* in the figure as the family works more hours and earns higher incomes (a movement toward the left in the figure). Note that the absolute slope of lines *CA* or *CB* is $5 and equals the hourly wage earned by the family. The absolute slope of *FB* is $2.50, or half that of *CB*. The ratio of the two slopes ($2.50/$5.00 = 0.5) gives the **benefit reduction rate** or marginal tax rate of 50 per cent. Since the family's total income exceeds its earned income (for earned incomes below $100 per day), taxes are negative. Hence, the name negative income tax.

An important question with regard to an NIT is its effect on work effort or incentives. This can be analyzed by examining the leisure-income indifference curves of the family shown in Figure 14-10. In the absence of the NIT, the family maximizes utility at point *E*, where its indifference curve U_2 is tangent to budget line *CA*. The family (say, the head as the only working member of the family) supplies 8 hours of work per day at a daily wage of $40. With an NIT providing the minimal income maintenance of $50 per day and the marginal tax rate of 50 per cent, the family's budget line becomes *FBA* and the family will be at point *G* on U_4. The total family's income is now $65 per day ($30 earned plus the $35 subsidy) and the family supplies only 6 hours of work. The NIT increased the family's income and amount of leisure.

The reduction in work effort with the NIT results from the income and substitution effects. The income effect arises because when the family's income rises (with the NIT), the family will demand more of every normal good, including leisure (i.e., supply less labor). The higher the minimal income maintenance level, the greater is the reduction in work effort. In the case of the NIT, the substitution effect *reinforces* the income effect. That is, imposing a marginal tax on earned income further discourages work. The higher the marginal tax rate (it is 50 per cent in our example), the greater is the substitution of leisure for work (i.e, the smaller is the work effort). However, had the government guaranteed the minimum wage of $50 per day without the NIT, the family would have stopped working altogether (see Problem 14-12a with answer at the end of the text). Sometimes, an NIT will cause the family to take a smaller income than without the NIT and more leisure (see Problem 12b).

Between 1968 and 1980, the U.S. Office of Economic Opportunity conducted four large experiments to test the effect of an NIT on work effort. The last, largest, and the most reliable of these experiments was conducted on a random sample of 4,800 low-income families in Seattle and Denver. The experiment lasted five years, the minimal income maintenance was equal to the official poverty line, and the marginal tax rate was 50 per cent. The results of the NIT experiments showed moderate reduction in work effort. Husbands reduced the number of hours worked by 5.3 per cent; wives, by nearly 14.6 per cent; and female family heads, by nearly 12 per cent. The reduction in work effort might have been even less had the program been permanent. As such, the NIT compares favorably with other welfare programs (such as minimum wages) that face even greater negative side effects. The estimated annual cost of implementing a national income-maintenance program is about $10 billion.[8]

Summary

1. To maximize profits a firm must produce the best level of output with the least-cost input combination. The optimal or least-cost input combination is the one at which the marginal product per dollar spent on each input is the same. The ratio of the input price to the marginal product of the input gives the marginal cost of the commodity. The best level of output of the commodity of a perfectly competitive firm is the output at which the firm's marginal cost equals its marginal revenue or price.

2. A profit maximizing firm will employ an input only as long as it adds more to its total revenue than to its total cost. If only one input is variable and the firm is a perfect competitor in the product and input markets, the firm's demand curve for the input (d) is given by the value of the marginal product (VMP) curve of the input. The VMP equals the marginal product (MP) of the input times the commodity price. With more than one variable input, the input price falls, the demand curve for the input is obtained by points on different VMP curves of the input and will be more elastic than the VMP curves. A firm will employ an input until the input's VMP on its demand curve equals the input price.

3. When the price of an input falls, all firms will hire more of the input and produce more of the final commodity. This will reduce the commodity price and shift the individual firm's demand curves for the input to the left. This has to be taken into account in summing the individual firm's demand curves for the input to obtain the market demand curve. The price elasticity of demand for an input is greater (1) the more and better are the available substitutes for the input, (2) the more elastic is the demand for the final commodity made with the input, (3) the more elastic is the supply of other inputs, and (4) the longer is the period of time under consideration.

4. The market supply curve of an input is obtained by the straightforward horizontal summation of the supply curves of the individual suppliers of the input. While natural resources and intermediate goods are supplied by firms and their supply curves are generally positively sloped, labor is supplied by individuals and their supply curves may be backward bending. That is, as the wage rate rises, eventually the substitution effect (which, by itself, leads individuals to substitute work for leisure) may be overwhelmed by the opposite income effect, so that the individual's supply curve of labor bends backward. The market supply curve of labor is usually positively

    [8] For a discussion of the negative income tax and the supply of labor, see R. Ferber and W. Hirsh, "Social Experimentation and Economic Policy: A Survey," *Journal of Economic Literature*, December 1978, pp. 1379–1414, and P. Robbins and R. West, "Labor Supply Response to the Seattle and Denver Income Maintenance Experiments," in *The Seattle and Denver Income Maintenance Experiment* (Washington, D.C.: U.S. Government Printing Office, 1983).

sloped, but it may bend backward at very high wages.

5. Under perfect competition, the equilibrium price and the level of employment of an input are determined at the intersection of the market demand curve and the market supply curve of the input. Each firm can then employ any quantity of the input at the given market price of the input. Since each firm employs an input until the value of its marginal product equals its price, this theory is usually referred to as the marginal productivity theory. If all inputs were identical (and all occupations equally attractive for labor), all units of the same input would have the same price.

6. Economic rent is that portion of the payment made to the supplier of an input that is in excess of the minimum amount necessary to retain the input in its present employment. When the supply of an input is fixed, demand alone determines its price and all the payment made to the input is rent. When the market supply curve of an input is positively sloped, the area above the supply curve and below the input price is rent. The return or payment to inputs that are fixed in the short run are sometimes called quasirents.

7. By correcting for the income effect of an input-price change, we can graphically isolate the substitution effect as a movement along a consumer leisure-income indifference curve. The same type of analysis can also be used to show the additional number of hours an individual is willing to work per day with overtime pay. Wage differentials can be equalizing, and they can be based on the existence of noncompeting groups and imperfect competition. Minimum wages lead to a disemployment effect and to an even greater unemployment gap. The negative income tax (NIT) is a type of welfare program involving declining cash transfers to low-income families as the family's earned income rises. Experiments indicate that an NIT has a moderate negative effect on work effort.

Glossary

Derived demand   The demand of an input that arises from the demand for the final commodities that the input is used in producing.

Complementary inputs   Inputs related to one another in such a way that an increase in the employment of one input raises the marginal product of the other input.

Intermediate good   The output of a firm or industry that is the input of another firm or industry producing final commodities.

Marginal productivity theory   The theory according to which each input is paid a price equal to its marginal productivity.

Economic rent   That portion of a payment made to the supplier of an input that is in excess of what is necessary to retain the input in its present employment in the long run.

Quasirent   The return or payment to inputs that are fixed in the short run (i.e., $TR - TVC$).

Overtime pay   The higher hourly wage of many workers for working additional hours after the regular workday.

Equalizing wage differentials   Wage differences that compensate workers for the nonmonetary differences among jobs.

Noncompeting groups   Occupations requiring different capacities, skills, education and training, and, therefore, receiving different wages.

Unemployment gap   The excess in the quantity supplied over the quantity demanded of labor at above equilibrium wages.

Disemployment effect   The reduction in the number of workers employed as a result of an increase in the wage rate (as with the imposition of an effective minimum wage).

Negative income tax (NIT)   A type of welfare program involving declining cash transfers to low-income families as the family's earned income rises.

Minimal income maintenance   The transfer or subsidy going to families that have no other income under a negative income tax program.

Break-even income   The family income at which

the transfer or subsidy under a negative income tax program is zero.

Benefit reduction rate The marginal tax rate on earned income under a negative income tax program.

Questions for Review

1. (a) What is the function of input prices in the operation of a free enterprise system?
   (b) What is meant by the price of an input?
   (c) How is the determination of input prices similar to the determination of commodity prices?
   (d) How is the determination of input prices different from the determination of commodity prices?

2. (a) What is the optimal or least-cost input combination for a firm?
   (b) How is the marginal cost of a commodity defined in terms of the least-cost input combination of the firm?
   (c) What is the best level of output of the firm?
   (d) What is the condition for profit maximization for a firm?

3. (a) How is the demand for an input a derived demand?
   (b) What is the value of the marginal product of an input?
   (c) Why is the value of the marginal product curve of a firm negatively sloped?
   (d) Under what condition does the value of the marginal product of an input represent the firm's demand curve for the input?
   (e) When is a firm a perfect competitor in the input market?

4. (a) When are two inputs complements? Substitutes?
   (b) What happens to the value of the marginal product curve of an input if the *price* of a complementary input falls? If the price of a substitute input falls?
   (c) What happens to the value of the marginal product curve of an input if the *amount* employed of a complementary input rises? If the amount employed of a substitute input declines?
   (d) How is the firm's demand curve of an input derived when there are other variable inputs?

5. (a) Why does the market price of a commodity fall with a reduction in the price of an input used in the production of the commodity?
   (b) What effect will a reduction in the commodity price have on the demand curve for an input by a firm?
   (c) How is the market demand curve for an input derived?
   (d) What are the determinants of the price elasticity of demand for an input?

6. Answer the following questions with respect to the left panel of Figure 14-3.
   (a) What do the indifference curves show?
   (b) What do the budget lines show?
   (c) What do the slopes of the budget lines show?
   (d) At what points does the individual maximize satisfaction? Why?

7. Answer the following questions with regard to the individual's supply curve for labor shown in the right panel of Figure 14-3.
   (a) Why is s_L positively sloped until point E'?
   (b) Why is S_L vertical at point E'?
   (c) Why is s_L negatively sloped above point E'?
   (d) How can the individuals' supply curve of labor be used to determine the market supply curve of labor? What is the shape of the latter?

8. (a) How is the equilibrium price of an input determined under perfect competition?
   (b) What happens if the price of an input is above the equilibrium price? Below the equilibrium price?
   (c) What does the marginal productivity theory postulate?

9. (a) What is economic rent?
   (b) To what input does economic rent refer?
   (c) What is the amount of economic rent when the supply of an input is fixed?
   (d) What is the amount of economic rent when the supply curve of the input is positively sloped?

10. (a) What is quasirent?
    (b) Does quasirent refer to the long run or to the short run?
    (c) How is quasirent measured?
    (d) If total revenue equals total variable costs, how much is quasirent?
11. (a) How can the substitution effect of a wage increase be measured graphically?
    (b) How can the income effect of a wage increase be isolated?
    (c) What is the relationship between the substitution and the income effect of a wage increase and the shape of an individual's supply curve of labor?
    (d) How can the effect of overtime pay on the individual's supply of labor be analyzed?
12. (a) What are equalizing wage differentials? Noncompeting groups?
    (b) What are the causes of wage differences in different occupations?
    (c) What is the effect of minimum wages?
    (d) What is a negative income tax? What is its effect on work effort?

Problems

1. (a) Express in terms of Equation (14-1) the condition for a firm utilizing too much labor or too little capital to minimize production costs. What is the graphical interpretation of this?
   (b) What is the graphical interpretataion of a firm utilizing the least-cost input combination but with its marginal cost exceeding its MR?
   (c) Express in terms of Equation (14-3) the condition for a firm minimizing the cost of producing an output that is too small to maximize profits. What is the graphical interpretation of this?
2. Given is the following production function of a firm, where L is the number of workers hired per day (the only variable input) and Q_x is the quantity of the commodity produced per day, and the constant commodity price of $P_x = \$5$ is assumed.

L	0	1	2	3	4	5
Q_x	0	10	18	24	28	30

   (a) Find the value of the marginal product of labor and plot it.
   (b) How many workers per day will the firm hire if the wage rate is $50 per day? $40? $30? $20? $10? What is the firm's demand curve for labor?
3. Assume that (1) labor is infinitesimally divisible (i.e., workers can be hired for any part of the day) in the production function of the previous problem; (2) both labor and capital are variable and complementary; and (3) when the wage rate falls from $40 per day to $20 per day, the firm's value of the marginal product curve shifts to the right by two labor units. Derive the demand curve for labor of this firm. How many workers will the firm hire per day at the wage rate of $20 per day?
4. Derive the market demand curve for labor if there are 100 firms identical to the firm of Problem 3 demanding labor and each individual firm's demand curve for labor shifts to the left by one unit when the wage rate falls from $w = \$40$ to $w = \$20$ per day.
★5. Assume that (1) U_1, U_2, U_3, and U_4 given in the following table are the indifference curves of an individual, where H refers to hours of leisure per day and Y to the daily income, and (2) the wage rate rises from $1 per hour of work, to $2, $3, and then to $4.

U_1		U_2		U_3		U_4	
H	Y	H	Y	H	Y	H	Y
10	20	10	32	12	40	14	48
16	8	14	20	15	27	17	28
24	4	24	12	24	16	24	20

   (a) Derive the individual's supply curve of labor.
   (b) Why is the individual's supply curve of labor backward bending?
6. Given that the market demand curve is the

one derived in Problem 3 and that 400 individuals will work at $w = \$10$, 500 at $w = \$20$, and 600 at $w = \$30$, determine the equilibrium wage rate and the level of employment. What would happen if $w = \$10$? If $w = \$30$?

7. Given the industry demand function for labor, $D_L = 800 - 15w$, where w is given in dollars per day, draw a figure showing the equilibrium wage and find the amount of economic rent if the supply function of labor to the industry is $S_L = 500$, $S'_L = 25w$, or $S''_L = 50w - 500$.

8. Draw a figure for a perfectly competitive firm in the product and input markets and label the price at which quasirent is (1) negative as P_1; (2) zero as P_2; (3) smaller than total fixed costs as P_3; (4) equal to total fixed costs as P_4; and (5) exceeds total fixed costs as P_5. (Hint: See Figure 10-4.)

★9. Separate the substitution from the income effect of an increase in wages from $w = \$2$ to $w = \$4$ in Problem 5.

10. Starting with your answer to Problem 5 (also provided at the end of the book), draw a figure showing how many additional hours the individual will work and his or her total income (1) starting from $w = \$1$ and overtime $w = \$4$ and (2) starting from $w = \$2$ and overtime $w = \$10$.

★11. Assuming (1) homogeneous labor, (2) identical jobs, (3) perfect competition, and (4) perfect labor mobility with no mobility costs, draw a graph showing how a difference in wages between two occupations or regions will be eliminated.

★12. Draw a figure similar to Figure 14-10 showing that
(a) if the family was guaranteed a daily income of $50 with the NIT, the family would reach a higher indifference curve by not working at all.
(b) with an income higher than the minimal income maintenance level of $50 per day before the NIT, the family's income may be lower than with the NIT.

Supplementary Readings

For a problem-solving approach to the topics covered in this chapter, see

Dominick Salvatore, *Microeconomic Theory,* 2nd ed. (New York: McGraw-Hill, 1983), Sections 13.1–13.8.

Some of the original works on which the material of this chapter is based are

George J. Stigler, *Production and Distribution Theories* (New York: Macmillan, 1941).

John R. Hicks, *Value and Capital* (Oxford: The Claredon Press, 1946), Chapter 7.
American Economic Association, *Readings in the Theory of Income Distribution* (New York: Blakiston, 1946).

On the theory of wages and employment, see

John R. Hicks, *The Theory of Wages* (New York: Macmillan, 1932).
Allan M. Cartter, *Theory of Wages and Employment* (Homewood, Ill.: Irwin, 1959), pp. 11–74.

Input Price and Employment Under Imperfect Competition

15-1   Profit Maximization and Optimal Input Employment

15-2   The Demand Curve of a Firm for an Input

15-3   The Market Demand Curve, and Input Price and Employment

15-4   Monopsony

15-5   Monopsony Pricing and Employment of One Variable Input

15-6   Monopsony Pricing and Employment of Several Variable Inputs

15-7   Applications

Examples

15-1   The Dynamics of the Engineers' Shortage

15-2   Occupational Licensing, Mobility, and Imperfect Labor Markets

15-3   Monopsonistic Exploitation in Major League Baseball

15-4   Imperfect Competition in the Labor Market and the Pay of Top Executives

Applications

Application 1:   Regulation of Monopsony

Application 2:   Bilateral Monopoly

Application 3:   The Effect of Labor Unions on Wages

Application 4:   The Goals of Labor Unions

Application 5:   The Economics of Discrimination in Employment

Chapter 15

Preview Questions

How much of an input does a firm demand when the product market is imperfectly competitive?

How is the price of an input determined when the product market is imperfectly competitive?

What is meant by imperfect competition in the input market?

What is the marginal expense or cost of an input?

How much of an input does a firm demand when the input market is imperfectly competitive?

What is bilateral monopoly?

What is the effect of labor unions on wages?

What are the goals of labor unions?

How can discrimination in employment be analyzed?

In the previous chapter, we analyzed the pricing and employment of inputs when the firm was a perfect competitor in both the product and input markets. In this chapter we extend the discussion to the pricing and employment of inputs when the firm is (1) an imperfect competitor in the product market but a perfect competitor in the input market and (2) an imperfect competitor in both the product and input markets. As in Chapter 14, the analysis deals with all inputs in general but will be geared toward labor because of the greater importance of labor.

The presentation in this chapter will proceed along the same general lines as in the previous chapter. We begin the chapter with a summary discussion of profit maximization and optimal input employment under imperfect competition in the product market. Then, we derive the demand curve for an input by a firm and by the market as a whole, and show how the interaction of the forces of demand and supply determines the price and employment of the input under imperfect competition in the product market but perfect competition in the input market. We next turn to the case of imperfect competition in input markets and examine the pricing and employment of an input when only that input is variable and when all inputs are variable. Finally, we present several important applications of the theory.

15-1

Profit Maximization and Optimal Input Employment

In this section we extend the discussion of profit maximization and optimal input employment of Section 14-1 to the case where the firm is an imperfect competitor in the product market but is still a perfect competitor in the input markets. A firm that is an imperfect competitor in the product market (a monopolist, an oligopolist, or a monopolistic competitor) faces a negatively sloped demand curve for the commodity it sells and its marginal revenue is smaller than the commodity price. Such a firm, however, can still be one of many firms hiring inputs. That is, the firm can still be a perfect competitor in the input markets, so that it can hire any quantity of an input at the given market price of the input. This is the case we examine in this and in the next two sections of this chapter.

We have seen in Section 14-1 that to maximize profits, a firm must use the optimal or least-cost input combination to produce the best level of output. The profit maximizing condition was given by Equation (14-3), repeated below as (15-1):

$$w/MP_L = r/MP_K = MC = MR \tag{15-1}$$

where w is the wage rate, r is the rental price of capital, MP is the marginal (physical) product, L refers to labor time, K refers to capital, MC is the marginal cost of the firm, and MR is its marginal revenue. The only difference between Equations (14-3) and (15-1) is that Equation (14-3) and the discussion in Section 14-1 referred to the case where the firm was a perfect competitor both in the product and input markets. Thus, the marginal revenue of the firm equaled the product price (P). Since the firm is now an imperfect competitor in the product market, $MR < P$ and Equation (15-1) is the relevant condition for profit maximization.

By cross multiplying and rearranging the terms of Equation (15-1), we get Equations (15-2) and (15-3):

$$MP_L \cdot MR = w \tag{15-2}$$
$$MP_K \cdot MR = r \tag{15-3}$$

Thus, the profit maximizing rule is that the firm should hire labor until the marginal product of labor times the firm's marginal revenue from the sale of the commodity equals the wage rate. Similarly, the firm should rent capital until the marginal product of capital times the firm's marginal revenue equals the rental price of capital. To maximize profits, the same rule would have to hold for all inputs that the firm uses. The condition is the same as when the firm is a perfect competitor in the product market, except that in

485

that case, $MR = P$. In the next section we will see that Equation (15-2) provides the basis for the derivation of the firm's demand curve for labor.

15-2

The Demand Curve of a Firm for an Input

We now extend the discussion of the last section and derive the demand curve of a firm for an input, first when the input is the only variable input, and then when the input is one of two or more variable inputs.

15-2a The Demand Curve of a Firm for One Variable Input

We have seen in Section 14-2a that a profit maximizing firm will hire more units of a variable input as long as the income from the sale of the extra output produced by the input is larger than the extra cost of hiring the input. When the firm is an imperfect competitor (say, a monopolist) in the product market, the extra income earned by the firm is called the **marginal revenue product (MRP)** *and is equal to the marginal product of the input times the marginal revenue of the firm. That is,*

$$MRP = MP \cdot MR \tag{15-4}$$

If the variable input is labor, we have

$$MRP_L = MP_L \cdot MR \tag{15-4A}$$

Thus, the MRP_L is the left-hand side of Equation (15-2). Similarly, the MRP_K is the left-hand side of Equation (15-3). Note that when the firm is a perfect competitor in the product market, the firm's marginal revenue equals the product price (i.e., $MR = P$) and the marginal revenue product equals the value of the marginal product (i.e., $MRP = VMP$). Since we are now dealing with a firm that is an imperfect competitor in the product market and $MR < P$, $MRP < VMP$.

Because the firm is a perfect competitor in the input market (i.e., faces a horizontal or infinitely elastic supply curve of the input), the extra cost of hiring each additional unit of the variable input is equal to the price of the input. If the variable input is labor, a profit maximizing firm should hire labor as long as the marginal revenue product of labor exceeds the wage rate and until $MRP_L = w$, as indicated by Equation (15-2).

The actual derivation of a firm's demand schedule for labor when labor is the only variable input (i.e., when capital and other inputs are fixed) and the firm is an imperfect competitor (monopolist) in the product market but a perfect competitor in the labor market is shown with Table 15-1. In Table 15-1, L refers to the number of workers hired by the firm per day. Q_x is the

TABLE 15-1 The Marginal Revenue Product of Labor and the Firm's Demand Schedule for Labor

L	Q_x	MP_L	P_x	TR_x	MRP_L	w
1	12	12	$13	$156	$\cdots$	$40
2	22	10	12	264	$108	40
3	30	8	11	330	66	40
4	37	7	10	370	40	40
5	43	6	9	387	17	40
6	48	5	8	376	-9	40

total output of commodity X produced by the firm by hiring various numbers of workers. The MP_L is the marginal or extra output generated by each additional worker hired. The MP_L is obtained by the change in Q_x per unit change in L. Note that the law of diminishing returns begins to operate with the hiring of the second worker. P_x refers to the price for the final commodity and it declines because the firm is an imperfect competitor (monopolist) in the product market. Total revenue (TR_x) is obtained by multiplying P_x by Q_x. The marginal revenue product of labor (MRP_L) is then given by the change in the firm's total revenue by selling the output of commodity X that results from the hiring of an additional worker. More briefly, $MRP_L = \Delta TR_x/\Delta L$. This is the same as MP_L times MR_x (not given in the table; see Problem 3, with answer at the end of the text). The MRP_L declines because both the MP_L and MR_x decline. That is, as the firm hires more labor and produces more units of the commodity, the MP_L declines (because of diminishing returns) and MR_x also declines (because the firm must lower the commodity price to sell more units of the commodity). The last column of Table 15-1 gives the daily wage rate (w) that the firm must pay to hire each worker. Since the firm is a perfect competitor in the labor market, w is constant (at $40 per day) and is equal to the increase in the firm's total costs (the marginal expense) of hiring each additional worker.

Looking at Table 15-1, we see that the second worker contributes $108 extra revenue to the firm (i.e., $MRP_L = \$108$) while the firm incurs a cost of only $40 to hire this worker. Thus, it pays for the firm to hire the second worker. (Since the MRP of the first worker is even greater than the MRP of the second worker, the firm should certainly hire the first worker.) The MRP of the third worker falls to $66, but this still exceeds the daily wage of $40 that the firm must pay each worker. Thus, the firm should also hire the third worker. According to Equation (15-2), the profit maximizing firm should hire workers until the $MRP_L = w$. Thus, this firm should hire four workers, at which $MRP_L = w = \$40$. The firm will not hire the fifth worker because he or she will contribute only $17 to the firm's total revenue while adding $40 to its total costs.

Thus, the MRP_L schedule gives the firm's demand schedule for labor. It indicates the number of workers that the firm would hire at various wage

rates. For example, if $w = \$108$ per day, the firm would hire only two work-
ers per day. If $w = \$66$, the firm would hire three workers. At $w = \$40$,
$L = 4$, and so on. If we plotted the MRP_L values of Table 15-1 on the vertical
axis and L on the horizontal axis, we would get the firm's negatively sloped
demand curve for labor when labor is the only variable input. This is
shown next.

Note that since the firm is a monopolist in the product market, the MRP_L
is smaller than the VMP_L and the MRP_L curve lies below the VMP_L curve.
As a result, the firm hires less labor and produces less of the commodity
than if the firm were a perfect competitor in the product market. Joan Robinson called the excess of the VMP_L over the MRP_L at the point where
$MRP_L = w$ (the level of employment) **monopolistic exploitation.**[1] Yet, this
emotionally laden term is somewhat misleading since the firm does not
pocket the difference between the VMP_L and the MRP_L (see Problem 3, with
answer at the end of the text). That is, the last worker hired receives the
entire increase in the total revenue of the firm (the MRP) that he or she
contributes.

15-2b The Demand Curve of a Firm for One of Several Variable Inputs

We have seen above that the declining MRP_L schedule given in Table 15-1
gives the firm's demand schedule for labor in the short run when labor is
the only variable input. This is shown by the negatively sloped MRP_L curve
in Figure 15-1 (on the assumption that labor is infinitesimally divisible or
that workers can be hired for any part of a day). The MRP_L or demand of
labor curve when labor is the only variable input shows that the firm will
hire three workers at $w = \$66$ (point A in Figure 15-1) and four workers at
$w = \$40$ (point B).

When labor is not the only variable input (i.e., when the firm can also
change the quantity of capital and other inputs), the firm's demand curve
for labor can be derived from the MRP_L curve, but it is not the MRP_L curve
itself. The derivation is basically the same as explained in Section 14-2b
and is shown in Figure 15-1. That is, as the wage rate falls and the firm
hires more labor (i.e., moves down its MRP_L curve), the MRP curve of
inputs that are complements to labor shifts to the right and the MRP curve
of inputs that are substitutes for labor shifts to the left (exactly as explained
in Section 14-2b). Both of these shifts cause the MRP_L to shift to the right,
say, from MRP_L to MRP'_L in Figure 15-1. Thus, when the daily wage falls
from $66 to $40, the firm will increase the number of workers hired from
three (point A on the MRP'_L curve) to six (point C on the MRP'_L curve) rather
than to four (point B on the original MRP_L curve). By joining points A and

---

[1] J. Robinson, *The Economics of Imperfect Competition* (London: Macmillan, 1933), Chapter
25.

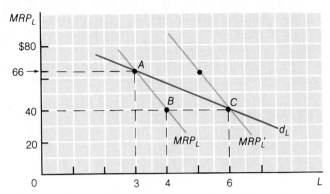

FIGURE 15-1.
The Demand Curve
for Labor of a
Monopolist with All
Inputs Variable

As the wage rate falls and the firm hires more labor (i.e., moves down its MRP$_L$ curve), the MRP curve of inputs that are complements to labor shifts to the right and the MRP curve of inputs that are substitutes for labor shifts to the left. Both of these shifts cause the MRP$_L$ curve to shift to the right to MRP'$_L$. Thus, when the daily wage falls from $66 to $40, the firm increases the number of workers hired from three (point A on the MRP$_L$ curve) to six (point C on the MRP'$_L$ curve). By joining points A and C, we get the firm's demand curve for labor (d$_L$).

C, we get the firm's demand curve for labor (d$_L$ in Figure 15-1) when other inputs besides labor are variable.

Note that the d$_L$ curve is negatively sloped and generally more elastic than the MRP$_L$ curve in the long run, when all inputs are variable. In general, the better the complementary and substitute inputs available for labor are, the greater is the outward shift of the MRP$_L$ curve as a result of a decline in the wage rate, and the more elastic d$_L$ is.

15-3

The Market Demand Curve, and Input Price and Employment

The market demand curve for an input is derived from the individual firm's demand curves for the input. If all the firms using the input are monopolists in their respective product markets, the market demand for the input is derived by the straightforward horizontal summation of the individual firms' demand curves for the input. The reason is that the reduction in the commodity price (as each monopolist produces and sells more of its commodity by hiring more inputs) has already been considered or incorporated in full into the calculation of the MRP of the input.

The case is different when a commodity market is composed of oligopolists and monopolistic competitors. That is, when all the oligopolists or monopolistic competitors in a product market hire more inputs and produce more of the commodity, the commodity price will decline. This decline in the price of the commodity causes a downward shift in each firm's demand curve for labor, exactly the same as when firms are perfect competitors in the product market (see Section 14-3a). It is by adding the quantity demanded of each input on these downward shifting demand curves of the input of each firm that the market demand curve is obtained. The process is identical to that shown in Figure 14-2 in Section 14-3a, and so it is not repeated here (see Problem 6).

The equilibrium price and employment of an input is then given at the intersection of the market demand and the market supply curves of the input, as described in Section 14-5. When all firms are perfect competitors in the input market, each firm can hire any quantity of the input at the given market price of the input. Each firm will then hire the input until the *MRP* of the input on their demand curve for the input equals the input price.

If, for whatever reason, the market demand curve for the input rises (i.e., shifts up) from the equilibrium position, the market price and employment of the input will also increase until a new equilibrium point is reached. This usually does not occur instantaneously. During the adjustment period, there will be a temporary shortage of the input (see Example 15-1).

Example 15-1 The Dynamics of the Engineers' Shortage

The Facts: During the late 1950s and early 1960s a shortage of engineers existed in the United States, which might have endangered winning the "space race." This can be analyzed with the aid of Figure 15-2. The inter-

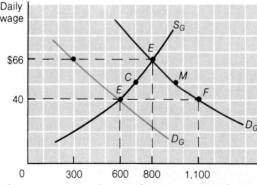

FIGURE 15-2.
The Dynamics of the
Engineers' Shortage

The intersection of D_G and S_G at point E determines the equilibrium daily wage of $40 for engineers. There are 600,000 engineers employed and there is no shortage. If D_G shifts up to D'_G, a temporary shortage of 500,000 (EF) results at w = $40 and wages rise. As this occurs, the shortage is somewhat alleviated. At w = $50, the shortage declines to 250,000 (CM). Only after the wage rises to $66 and enough new engineers are trained is the temporary shortage eliminated and new equilibrium point E' reached.

490

section of the hypothetical market demand curve for engineers D_G and the market supply curve of engineers S_G at point E determines the equilibrium daily wage of $40 for engineers. At $w = \$40$, the 600,000 engineers employed matches the number of engineers demanded and there is no shortage. In the late 1950s and early 1960s, the demand for engineers unexpectedly increased (i.e., shifted up, say, to D_G') because of the space race. At the original equilibrium wage rate of $w = \$40$, there is a shortage of 500,000 (EF) engineers and engineers' wages rise. As this occurs, employers economize on the use of engineers and more students enter engineering studies. Thus, the shortage is somewhat alleviated. For example, at $w = \$50$, the shortage declines to 250,000 (CM). Only after several years as wages rise to $66 and enough new engineers are trained is the shortage eliminated and new equilibrium point E' reached with 800,000 engineers employed. If, within this time, the demand for engineers increases again, a new temporary shortage emerges. During the 1970s, the opposite occurred and there was a temporary surplus of engineers.

Comment: The above is an example of dynamic analysis. This considers the time path whereby one equilibrium position evolves into another. Had the adjustment to the upward shift in D_G in Figure 15-2 been instantaneous (as in comparative static analysis), no temporary shortage or surplus would have arisen.

Source: K. Arrow and W. Capron, "Dynamic Shortages and Price Rises: The Engineer-Scientist Case," *Quarterly Journal of Economics,* May 1959.

15-4

Monopsony

Until this point we have assumed that the firm is a perfect competitor in the input market. This means that the firm faces an infinitely elastic or horizontal supply curve of the input and that the firm can hire any quantity of the input at the given market price of the input. We now examine the case where the firm is an imperfect competitor in the input market. When there is a single firm hiring an input, we have a **monopsony.** Thus, while monopoly refers to the single seller of a commodity, monopsony refers to the single buyer of an input. As such, the monopsonist faces the (usually) positively sloped *market* supply curve of the input. This means that to hire more units of the input, the monopsonist must pay a higher price per unit of the input.

An example of monopsony is provided by the "company towns" in nineteenth century America, where a mining or textile firm was practically the sole employer of labor in many isolated communities. A present day example of monopsony might be an automaker, which is the sole buyer of some specialized automobile component or part, such as radiators, from a number of small local firms set up exclusively to supply these components or parts to the large firm (the automaker).

Monopsony arises when an input is specialized and thus much more productive to a particular firm or use than to any other firm or use. This allows the firm (in which the input is more productive) to pay a much higher price for the input than other firms and so become a monopsonist. Monopsony can also result from lack of geographical and occupational mobililty. For example, people often become emotionally attached to a given locality because of family ties, friends, and so on, and are unwilling to move to other areas. Also, people may lack the information, the money, or the qualifications to move to other areas or occupations. Thus, monopsony can be overcome by providing information about job opportunities elsewhere, by helping to pay for moving expenses, and by providing training for other occupations.

We have said above that the monopsonist faces the usually positively sloped market supply curve of the input, so that it must pay a higher price to hire more units of the input. However, as all units of the input must be paid the same price, the monopsonist will have to pay a higher price, not only for the additional units, but for all units of the input it hires. As a result, the **marginal expense for the input** exceeds the input price. This is shown in Table 15-2 for labor.

In Table 15-2, w is the daily wage rate that a monopsonist must pay to hire various number of workers (L). Thus, the first two columns of the table give the market supply schedule of labor faced by the monopsonist. TE_L is the total expense incurred by the monopsonist to hire various number of workers and is obtained by multiplying L by w. ME_L is the marginal expense of labor and gives the extra cost that the monopsonist faces to hire each additional worker. That is, $ME_L = \Delta TE_L/\Delta L$.

Note that $ME_L > w$. For example, the monopsonist can hire one worker at the wage rate of $10 for a total expense of $10. To hire the second worker, the monopsonist must increase the wage rate from $10 to $20 and incur a total expense of $40. Thus, the increase in the total expense (i.e., the marginal expense) to hire the second worker is $30 and exceeds the wage rate of $20 that the monopsonist must pay for each of the two workers.

TABLE 15-2 Marginal Expense of Labor

L	w	TE_L	ME_L
1	$10	$ 10	. . .
2	20	40	$30
3	30	90	50
4	40	160	70
5	50	250	90

FIGURE 15-3.
A Monopsonist's
Supply and
Marginal Expense
of Labor Curves

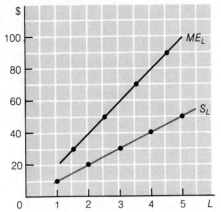

S_L is the positively sloped market supply curve of labor faced by the monopsonist (from columns 1 and 2 of Table 15-2) and ME_L is the marginal expense of labor curve (from the first and the last columns of Table 15-2). The ME_L values are plotted between the various units of L used, and the ME_L curve is everywhere above the S_L curve.

Figure 15-3 gives the positively sloped market supply curve of labor (S_L) faced by the monopsonist (from columns 1 and 2 of Table 15-2) and the marginal expense of labor curve (ME_L, from the first and the last columns of Table 15-2). Since the ME_L measures the changes in TE_L per unit change in L used, the ME_L values given in Table 15-2 are plotted between the various units of labor hired. Note also that the ME_L curve is everywhere above the S_L curve. Similarly, a firm that is the single renter of a particular type of specialized capital (i.e., a monopsonist in the capital market) faces the positively sloped market supply curve of capital, so that the firm's marginal expense of capital (ME_K) curve is above the supply curve of capital (S_K).[2]

While our discussion has been exclusively in terms of monopsony, there are other forms of imperfect competition in input markets. Just as we have monopoly, oligopoly, and monopolistic competition in product markets, so we can have monopsony, oligopsony, and monopsonistic competition in input markets. **Oligopsony** refers to the case where there are only a few firms hiring a homogeneous or differentiated input. **Monopsonistic competition** refers to the case where there are many firms hiring a differentiated input. As for the monopsonist, oligopsonists and monopsonistic competitors must also pay higher prices to hire more units of an input, and so the marginal expense for the input exceeds the input price for them also.

Finally, note that when the firm is a perfect competitor in the input mar-

[2] In Section A14 of the Mathematical Appendix, we derive an important relationship among input price, marginal expense, and the price elasticity of input supply. This is analogous to the relationship among commodity price, marginal revenue, and the price elasticity of commodity demand derived in Section 5-5c.

493

ket, the marginal expense of the input is equal to the input price, and the marginal expense curve of the input is horizontal and coincides with the supply curve of the input that the firm faces. That is, since the firm hires such a small quantity of the input, the supply curve of the input that the firm faces is infinitely elastic, even though the market supply curve of the input is positively sloped. For example, if $w = \$10$ no matter how many workers a firm hires, then $ME_L = w = \$10$ and the ME_L curve is horizontal at $w = \$10$ and coincides with s_L curve (the supply curve of labor faced by the firm).

Example 15-2 Occupational Licensing, Mobility, and Imperfect Labor Markets

The Facts: Many states do not recognize the occupational license obtained in other states to practice law and dentistry in the state. Invariably, these nonreciprocity regulations are the result of lobbying on the part of the professions involved as a way of restricting the possible competition that would arise from an inflow of professionals from other states. Pashigian estimated that, with reciprocity, interstate migration would increase by 5 per cent for lawyers and from 3 to 4 per cent for dentists, over a 5-year period. Reciprocity would thus eliminate one source of imperfection in these labor markets. On theoretical grounds, we would expect that the income of professionals in states without reciprocity agreements would be higher than in states with reciprocity. In fact, Shepard found that the fees and income of dentists in the 35 states that have no reciprocity agreements are 12–15 per cent higher than in states with reciprocity.

Comment: If all states adopted reciprocity agreements, some lawyers and dentists in states with lower fees and incomes would migrate to those states with higher fees and income. This would reduce (and in the limit eliminate) all interstate differences in fees and incomes and increase the degree of competition in these labor markets.

Source: B. Pashigian, "Occupational Licensing and the Interstate Mobility of Professionals," *Journal of Law and Economics*, April 1979, and L. Shepard, "Licensing Restrictions and the Cost of Dental Care," *Journal of Law and Economics*, October 1978.

15-5

Monopsony Pricing and Employment of One Variable Input

As pointed out in Section 14-2a, a firm using only one variable input maximizes profits by hiring more units of the input until the extra revenue from the sale of the commodity equals the extra cost of hiring the input.

This is a general condition and applies whether the firm is a perfect or imperfect competitor in the product and/or input market. If the variable input is labor and the firm is a monopsonist in the labor market, the monopsonist maximizes its total profits by hiring labor until the marginal revenue product of labor equals the marginal expense of labor. That is, the monopsonist should hire labor until Equation (15-5) or, equivalently, Equation (15-5A) holds:

$$MRP_L = ME_L \qquad\qquad (15\text{-}5)$$
$$MP_L \cdot MR = ME_L \qquad\qquad (15\text{-}5A)$$

The wage rate paid by the monopsonist is then given by the corresponding point on the market supply curve of labor (S_L). This is shown in Figure 15-4.

In Figure 15-4, the S_L and the ME_L curves are those of Figure 15-3. With the firm's MRP_L curve shown in Figure 15-4, the monopsonist maximizes profits by hiring three workers (given by point E, at which the MRP_L curve intersects the ME_L curve and $MRP_L = ME_L = \$60$). To prove this, consider that the second worker adds $80 (point A) to the monopsonist's total revenue but only $40 (point A') to its total costs. Thus, the monopsonist's profits rise (by $AA' = \$40$) by hiring the second worker. On the other hand, the monopsonist would not hire the fourth worker because he or she would add more to total cost ($80, given by point B) than to total revenue ($40, given by point B'), so that the monopsonist's total profits would fall by $40 ($BB'$ in the figure). Only at $L = 3$, $MRP_L = ME_L = \$60$ (point E) and the monopsonist maximizes total profits.

FIGURE 15-4.
Optimal
Employment of
Labor and the Wage
Rate Paid by a
Monopsonist

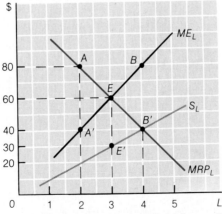

The S_L and the ME_L curves are those of Figure 15-3. With MRP_L, the monopsonist maximizes profits by hiring three workers (given by point E, at which the MRP_L curve intersects the ME_L curve and $MRP_L = ME_L = \$60$). The monopsonist then pays w = $30 to each worker (given by point E' on S_L). The excess of MRP_L over w ($EE' = \$30$) at L = 3 is called monopsonistic exploitation.

Figure 15-4 also shows that to hire three workers, the monopsonist must pay the wage of $30. This is given by point E' on the S_L curve at $L = 3$. Thus, the intersection of the MRP_L and ME_L curves gives only the profit maximizing number of workers that the firm should hire. The wage rate is then given by the amount that the firm must pay each worker, and this is given by the point on the market supply curve of labor at the level of employment. Note that $MRP_L = \$60$ (point E) exceeds $w = \$30$ (point E') at $L = 3$.

Joan Robinson called the excess of the marginal revenue product of the variable input over the input price ($EE' = \$30$ at $L = 3$ in Figure 15-4) **monopsonistic exploitation.**[3] It arises because the monopsonist produces where the $MRP_L = ME_L$ in order to maximize profits. Since the S_L curve is positively sloped, the ME_L curve is above it, and $ME_L > w$. The more inelastic the market supply curve is that the monopsonist faces, the greater is the degree of monopsonistic exploitation. If the firm in Figure 15-4 had been a perfect competitor in the labor market, it would have hired four workers (given by point B', at which $MRP_L = ME_L = w = \$40$). As we have seen above, the monopsonist maximizes total profits by restricting output and employment, and by hiring only three workers (point E). In Application 1, we will see how government regulation and/or union power can reduce or eliminate monopsonistic exploitation.

Example 15-3 Monopsonistic Exploitation in Major League Baseball

The Facts: Table 15-3 gives the net marginal revenue product (MRP) and the salary of mediocre, average, and star hitters and pitchers in major league baseball calculated by Scully for the year 1969. Scully found that the team's winning record increased attendance and revenues, and that a team's performance depended primarily on the "slugging average" for hit-

TABLE 15-3 **Net Marginal Revenue Product and Salaries in Major League Baseball, 1969 Average**

Type of Player	Quality of Player	Net *MRP*	Salary
Hitters	Mediocre	$-32,300	$15,200
	Average	129,500	28,000
	Star	313,900	47,700
Pitchers	Mediocre	$-13,400	$13,700
	Average	159,900	31,800
	Star	397,000	61,000

Source: G. Scully, "Pay and Performance in Major League Baseball," *American Economic Review*, December 1974, p. 928.

[3] J. Robinson, *The Economics of Imperfect Competition* (London: Macmillan, 1933), Chapter 26.

ters and on the ratio of "strikeouts to walks" for pitchers. Using these data, Scully calculated the net *MRP* or extra gate revenues and broadcast receipts resulting from each type of player's performance after subtracting the player's development cost. In 1969, development costs were as high as $300,000 per player. Table 15-3 shows that for mediocre players, the net *MRP* was negative (−$32,300 for hitters and −$13,400 for pitchers). Of course, the team's scouts and managers could not precisely foresee which players would turn out to be mediocre, average, or star. The table also shows the average players' salaries in each category.

Mediocre players reduced the team's profits. Average players received salaries far lower than their net *MRP*. Star players received salaries that were more than 6 times lower than their net *MRP*. Thus, monopsonistic exploitation was large for average players and very large for star players. On the other hand, mediocre players exploited their team! Note that even though star players received very large salaries (for 1969), they contributed so much more to the team's revenue (after subtracting the cost for their development) and they were greatly "exploited" by their teams. This exploitation was made possible by the "reserve clause," under which the player became the exclusive property of the team that first signed him on. Aside from being traded, a player could only play for the team for whatever salary the team offered. Thus, the reserve clause practically eliminated all competition in hiring and remuneration and essentially established a cartel of employers (teams) for major league baseball players. As such, the cartel behaved much like a monopsonist and exploited players.

Comment: In 1975, the reserve clause was substantially weakened. Players could declare themselves "free agents" and negotiate their salaries and the team for which they would play. As anticipated, competition resulted in startling increases in players' salaries and sharply reduced the monopsonistic power of baseball clubs. Today, salaries of one-million dollars per year for star players are not uncommon.

15-6

Monopsony Pricing and Employment of Several Variable Inputs

We have seen in Section 15-5 that when labor is the only variable input, a monopsonist maximizes profits by hiring labor until the marginal revenue product of labor equals the marginal expense of labor. This was given by Equation (15-5) and (15-5A). The same condition holds when there is more than one variable input. That is, the monopsonist maximizes profits by hiring each input until the marginal revenue product of the input equals the marginal expense of hiring it. With labor and capital as the variable inputs, the monopsonist should hire labor and capital until equations (15-5A) and (15-5B) hold:

$$MP_L \cdot MR = ME_L \qquad \text{(15-5A)}$$
$$MP_K \cdot MR = ME_K \qquad \text{(15-5B)}$$

Dividing both sides of Equations (15-5A) and (15-5B) by MP_L and MP_K, respectively, and combining the results we get (15-6)

$$ME_L/MP_L = ME_K/MP_K = MR \qquad \text{(15-6)}$$

This is identical to Equation (15-1), except that w has been replaced by the ME_L and r has been replaced by the ME_K to reflect the fact that the firm is now a monopsonist in the labor and capital markets, and it must pay a higher wage and rental price to hire more labor and rent more capital, respectively. That is, the optimal input combination is now given by Equation (15-7) rather than by Equation (14-2) and each ratio in Equation (15-7) equals the MC of the firm:

$$ME_L/MP_L = ME_K/MP_K \qquad \text{(15-7)}$$

For example, if ME_L/MP_L is smaller than ME_K/MP_K, the monopsonist would not be minimizing production costs. The monopsonist can reduce the cost of producing any level of output by substituting labor for capital in production. As the monopsonist hires more labor, ME_L rises and MP_L declines, so that ME_L/MP_L rises. As the monopsonist rents less capital, ME_K falls and MP_K rises, so that ME_K/MP_K falls. To minimize the cost of producing any level of output, the monopsonist should continue to substitute labor for capital in production until Equation (15-7) holds.

Note that the ME_L/MP_L and ME_K/MP_K measure the extra cost (in terms of labor and capital, respectively) to produce an extra unit of the commodity. This is the marginal cost of the firm. For example, if $ME_L = \$10$ and $MP_L = 5$, the marginal cost of the firm is $ME_L/MP_L = \$10/5 = \$2$. This means that it costs the monopsonist \$2 extra to hire the additional labor to produce one extra unit of the commodity. The same is true for capital. That is, $ME_K/MP_K = MC$ or the marginal cost of the firm (in terms of capital). The best level of output is then given by the point where $MC = MR$ [see Equation (15-6)].

Example 15-4 Imperfect Competition in the Labor Market and the Pay of Top Executives

The Facts: Table 15-4 gives the earnings of the 12 highest-paid executives in the United States in 1983. Their earnings ranged from over \$2.1 million

TABLE 15-4   Earnings of the Ten Highest-Paid Executives in 1983, in Millions of Dollars

Executive, Position, Company	Salary	Bonus	Total
1. Barry Diller, vice president Gulf & Western	$0.55	$1.57	$2.12
2. John Gutfreund, cochairman Philbro-Salomon	2.11	—	2.11
3. David Tendler, cochairman Philbro-Salomon	2.08	—	2.08
4. Henry Kaufman, vice president Philbro-Salomon	1.95	—	1.95
5. Richard Schmeelk, vice president Philbro-Salomon	1.95	—	1.95
6. Thomas Strauss, vice president Philbro-Salomon	1.95	—	1.95
7. Peter Buchanan, president First Boston	1.72	—	1.72
8. Rawleigh Warner, chairman Mobil	1.64	—	1.64
9. Alvin Shoemaker, chairman First Boston	1.60	—	1.60
10. Rober Fomon, chairman E.F. Hutton	1.50	—	1.50
11. Roger Smith, chairman General Motors	0.63	0.87	1.50
12. Benjamin Biaggini, chairman Southern Pacific	0.48	1.00	1.48

Source: "Growing Furor Over Pay of Top Executives," *U.S. News and World Report*, May 21, 1984, pp. 79–81.

for Barry Diller, the vice president of Gulf & Western to $1.48 million for Benjamin Biaggini, the chairman of Southern Pacific. The question is "are these executives worth to their employer the huge salaries and bonuses that they are paid?." One answer is that since firms voluntarily pay these salaries and bonuses, the marginal revenue product of these top executives must be at least as high. However, the committee of board of directors that decides the salaries of the top officials of the company usually look at the pay scale of the top executives of other companies of similar size. This probably results in the relatively poor performers getting too much and top performers getting too little. It should also be noted that some of these top executives can set their own salaries.

Comment: Many workers and their union called the huge salaries and bonuses received by some top executives during 1983 "obscene," especially in view of the fact that many union workers, such as autoworkers, had to accept pay cuts during 1983, allegedly to save their company from possible bankruptcy. This was not forgotten by the union leaders during the subsequent wage negotiations.

Applications

In this section we discuss some important applications of the theory presented in the chapter. These include the regulation of monopsony, bilateral monopoly, the effect of unions on wages, the goals of labor unions, and discrimination in employment. These applications clearly indicate the usefulness and applicability of the theory presented in this chapter.

Application 1: Regulation of Monopsony

By setting a minimum price for an input at the point where the marginal revenue product curve of the input intersects the market supply curve of the input, the monopsonist can be made to behave as a perfect competitor in the input market, and monopsonistic exploitation is eliminated. If the input is labor, the minimum wage that would eliminate labor exploitation can be set by the government or negotiated by the union. This is shown in Figure 15-5.

In the absence of a minimum wage, the monopsonist of Figure 15-5 hires three workers (given by point E, where the MRP_L curve intersects the ME_L curve) and the daily wage is $30 (point E' on S_L), exactly as explained in Section 15-5 and Figure 15-4. Monopsonistic exploitation of labor is given by the excess of the MRP_L over w at $L = 3$ and is equal to $30 per worker ($EE'$ in the figure). If the daily wage is set at $40 (point B' in the figure, at which the MRP_L curve intersects S_L), $CB'F$ becomes the new supply of labor curve facing the monopsonist. The new ME_L curve is then $CB'BG$, with the

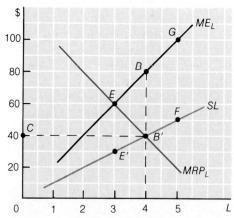

FIGURE 15-5.
Regulation of
Monopsony

By setting $w = 40, $CB'F$ becomes the new supply of labor curve facing the monopsonist. The new ME_L curve is then $CB'BG$, with the vertical or discontinuous portion directly above and caused by the kink (at point B') on the new S_L curve. To maximize total profits, the monopsonist now hires four workers (given by point B', at which the MRP_L curve intersects the new ME_L curve) and $w = MRP_L = 40 (so that monopsonistic exploitation is zero).

vertical or discontinuous portion directly above and caused by the kink (at point B') on the new S_L curve.

To maximize total profits when the minimum wage of $40 is imposed, the monopsonist hires four workers (given by point B', at which the MRP_L curve intersects the new ME_L curve) and $w = MRP_L = \$40$. Thus, the monopsonist behaves as a perfect competitor in the input market (operates at point B', where the MRP_L curve intersects S_L) and the monopsonistic exploitation of labor is entirely eliminated. With a daily wage between $30 and $40, the monopsonist will hire three or four workers per day and only part of the labor exploitation is eliminated. Setting a wage above $40 will eliminate all labor exploitation but the monopsonist will hire fewer than four workers (see Problem 9, with answer at the end of the text).

Application 2: Bilateral Monopoly

Bilateral monopoly is said to exist when the single buyer of a product or input (the monopsonist) faces the single seller of the product or input (the monopolist). While this is a rare occurrence in the real world, it is approximated by the "one-mill town" facing the union of all the town's workers, and (until recently) by Western Electric as the sole producer of telephone equipment facing AT&T as the sole buyer of telephone equipment.

In bilateral monopoly, price and output are indeterminate, in the sense that they cannot be established by the profit maximizing marginal calculations employed by economists; rather, they are determined by the relative bargaining strength of the monopsonist buyer and the monopolist seller of the product or input. This is shown in Figure 15-6.

In the figure, D is the monopsonist's demand (MRP) curve for the product or input. Curve D is also the market demand curve faced by the monopolist seller of the product or input. Then MR is the corresponding marginal revenue curve of the monopolist. If the monopolist's marginal cost curve is as shown in the figure, the monopolist will maximize profits by selling 5 units of the product (given by point B', where its MC curve intersects its MR curve from below) at the price of $15 per unit (point B on its D curve).

To determine the monopsonist's profit maximizing purchase of the product, we must realize that the monopolist's marginal cost curve is the supply curve of the product that the monopsonist faces. It shows the price at which the monopsonist can purchase various quantities of the product. Thus, the monopsonist's marginal expense curve for the product is higher, as indicated by the ME curve in the figure. To maximize profits, the monopsonist must buy 4 units of the product [given by point E, at which the monopsonist demand $(D$ or $MRP)$ curve intersects its ME of the product curve] and pay the price of $8 (given by point E' on the supply curve of the product that the monopsonist faces).

Thus, to maximize profits, the monopolist seller of the product wants to sell $Q = 5$ at $P = \$15$, while the monopsonist buyer of the product wants to purchase $Q = 4$ at $P = \$8$. The solution is indeterminate and depends on the relative bargaining strength of the two firms. All we can say is that

501

FIGURE 15-6.
Bilateral Monopoly

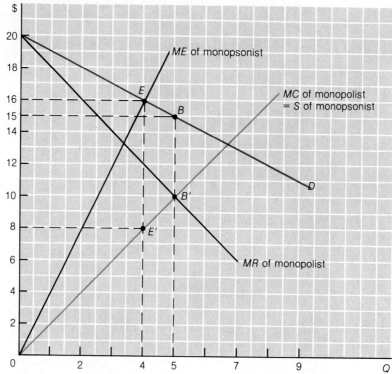

D is the monopsonist's demand (MRP) curve for the product or input that the monopolist seller faces. MR is the monopolist's marginal revenue curve. The monopolist
maximizes profits at Q = 5 (given by point B', where MC = MR) at P = $15 (point
B on the D curve). The monopolist's MC curve is the supply curve of the product that
the monopsonist faces, and ME is its marginal expense curve. The monopsonist maximizes profits at Q = 4 (given by point E, where MRP = ME) and P = $8 (given by
point E' on the supply curve that the monopsonist faces). The solution is indeterminate and will be within area E'B'BE.

the level of output and sales of the product will be between 4 and 5 units
and the price will be between $8 and $16 (i.e., the solution will be within
area E'B'BE). The greater the relative bargaining strength of the monopolist
seller of the product, the closer output will be to 5 units and price to $15.
The greater the relative bargaining strength of the monopsonist buyer of
the product, the closer the purchase of the product will be to 4 units and
the price to $8.

Application 3: The Effect of Labor Unions on Wages
A **labor union** is an organization of workers that seeks to increase the
wages and the general welfare of union workers through collective bargaining with employers. The Wagner Act passed in 1935 prohibited firms
from interfering with the workers' rights to form unions. Union membership as a percentage of the nonagricultural labor force of the U.S. peaked

at 35.5 per cent in 1947, but it has declined to 23 per cent in 1980 and 18.8 per cent in 1984.

A labor union can try to increase the wages of its members by (1) restricting the supply of union labor that employers must hire, (2) bargaining for an above-equilibrium wage, or (3) increasing the demand for union labor. These are shown in Figure 15-7. In each of the three panels in the figure, the intersection of the market demand curve for labor (D_L) and market supply curve of labor (S_L) at point E determines the equilibrium wage rate of $40 and the equilibrium level of employment of 600 workers in the absence of the union.

The left panel shows that if the union can reduce the supply of union labor that employers must hire from S_L to S_L', the equilibrium daily wage will rise to $66, at which 300 workers are hired (point F, where S_L' intersects D_L). The union can restrict the number of union members by high initiation fees and by long apprenticeship periods. The center panel shows that the union can achieve the wage of $66 through bargaining with employers. The result is the same as if the government set the minimum wage of $66. Note that at $w = \$66$, 800 workers would like to work but only 300 find employment. Thus, there is an unemployment gap of 500 workers (FG in the center panel), 300 of which represent the disemployment effect (see Application 4 in chapter 14).

Finally, the right panel of Figure 15-6 shows that by shifting D_L up to D_L', the union can increase wages to $66 and employment to 800 workers (given by point G, where D_L' intersects S_L). The union can increase the demand for union labor by advertising to buy "union labels" and by lob-

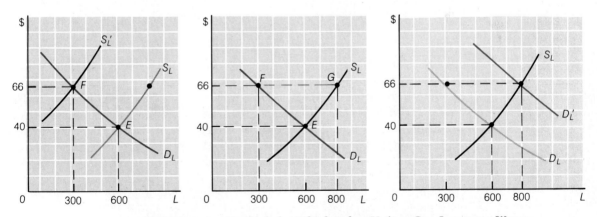

FIGURE 15-7. Methods by Which Labor Unions Can Increases Wages
The union can increase wages from $40 to $66 by reducing the supply of union labor from S_L to S'_L (the left panel), by bargaining with employers for $w = \$66$ (the center panel), or by increasing the demand for union labor from D_L to D'_L (the right panel). Employment falls from 600 workers to 300 workers with the first two methods (the left and center panels) and increases to 800 workers with the last method (the most difficult to accomplish).

bying to restrict imports. Thus, trying to increase union wages by increasing the demand for union labor is the most advantageous method to raise wages from the point of view of union labor because it also increases employment. This, however, is also the most difficult for unions to accomplish.

There is a great deal of disagreement regarding the amount by which labor unions have increased the wages of their members. To be sure, unionized workers do receive, on the average, about 33 per cent higher wages than nonunionized workers. At least to some extent, this is due to the fact that unionized labor is generally more skilled than nonunion labor and is employed in more efficient large-scale industries, and received higher wages even before unionization. On the other hand, wage differences between union and nonunion labor underestimate the effectiveness of labor unions in raising wages because nonunionized firms tend to increase wages when union wages rise in order to retain their workers and avoid unionization. Empirical studies seem to indicate that labor unions have been able to increase union wages by 6–15 per cent over what they would have been in the absence of unions.

In their actual negotiations with management, labor unions usually "demand" higher wage increases than they really expect in order to leave room for bargaining. The wage increases in a few major industries, such as the automobile and steel industries, often set the pattern for the wage demands in other industries. Union wage demands are also likely to be larger in periods of high profits and employment than in recessionary periods. In the final analysis, the actual wage settlement in a particular industry or firm depends on the relative bargaining strength of the union and the employer, along the lines of the bilateral monopoly model. Labor unions also seem to have reduced wages differentials among union workers of different skills and among different regions of the country.[4]

Application 4: The Goals of Labor Unions

In the previous discussion, it was implicitly assumed that labor unions seek to increase the wages of their members. Yet, as we have seen in the left and center panels of Figure 15-6, this reduces the level of employment of union labor. Thus, labor unions are likely to take into account the effect of wage increases on employment. Some of the goals of labor unions are to (1) ensure that all of its members are employed, (2) maximize the wages of union labor, subject to the condition that a minimum number of its members be employed, and (3) maximize the aggregate income of its members. These conflicting goals are analyzed with Figure 15-8.

In the figure D_L is the hypothetical demand curve for union labor. If the union has a membership of 900 and wants all of its members to be employed, it will want the wage of $20 (point A on D_L). If, instead, the union

---

[4] For a discussion of labor unions and their effect on wages, see H. Lewis, *Unionism and Relative Wages in the United States* (Chicago: University of Chicago Press, 1963) and J. Dunlop, *Wage Determination under Trade Unionism* (New York: August Kelley, 1966).

FIGURE 15-8.
The Goals of Labor
Unions

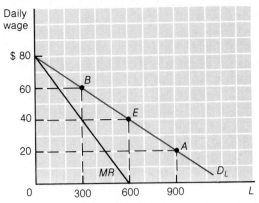

D_L is the hypothetical demand curve for union labor. If the union wants all of its 900 members to be employed, it will want the wage of $20 (point A on D_L). If the union seeks to maximize the aggregate income of its members, it will want w = $40 (point E). At point E, MR = 0 and the total wage bill of union labor is maximum. If the union wants to maximize wages with a minimum of 300 members employed, it should bargain for w = $60 (point B).

seeks to maximize the aggregate income of its members, it will want the wage of $40 (point E). At point E, MR = 0 and the total revenue (i.e., the total wage bill of union labor) is maximum (see Section 11-1a). Finally, if the union wants to maximize wages with a minimum of 300 members employed, it should bargain for the daily wage rate of $60 (point B). Note that with objective 2 and 3, a considerable number of union labor remains unemployed and the question of who works and who does not raises a difficult problem for the union. In these cases, seniority is likely to play an important role.

The above are but three possible goals of unions. Other important union goals are job security and fringe benefits (such as pensions, vacations, insurance coverage, and better working conditions in general). Fringe benefits are particularly attractive because they are often nontaxable (see Application 4 in chapter 3). Another union objective is for its leadership to remain in office. Note also that by bargaining with management for higher wages, the union can also reduce or eliminate monopsonistic exploitation (see Application 1).[5]

Application 5: The Economics of Discrimination in Employment

Discrimination in employment can take many forms, but in this section we will consider only discrimination between male and female workers of equal productivity and its effect on their wages and employment. This is shown in Figure 15-9, where S_F and S_M are the supply curves of female and male labor to a particular industry, respectively; S_L is the total supply of

---

[5] For a discussion of the goals of labor unions, see R. Ehrenberg and R. Smith, *Modern Labor Economics* (Glenview, Ill.: Scott Foresman, 1982).

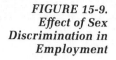

FIGURE 15-9.
Effect of Sex
Discrimination in
Employment

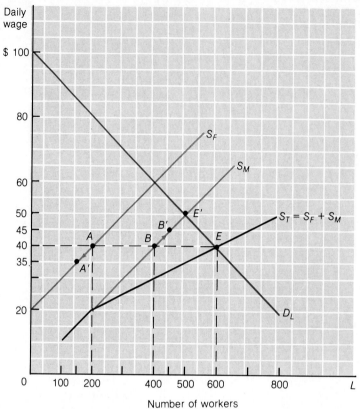

Number of workers

Without discrimination, w = $40 for males and females (given by point E, at which
S_L *intersects* D_L*) and 200 females (point A) and 400 males (point B) are employed. If*
employers refused to hire females, 500 males would be hired at w = $50 (point E',
where S_M *intersects* D_L*). Females would have to find employment in other industries,*
and this would depress wages for all workers in these other industries. With a less
extreme form of discrimination, employers may hire females if their wage is, say, $10
less than for males of the same productivity. Employers would then hire 150 females
at w = $35 (point A') and 450 males at w = $45 (point B').

female and male labor; and D_L is the total demand for labor by the industry.
The figure shows that in the absence of sex discrimination, the equilibrium
wage is $40 for males and females (given by point E, at which S_L intersects
D_L) and 200 females (point A) and 400 males (point B) are employed.

However, if employers in the industry refused to hire females, the supply curve of labor to the industry would be only S_M and 500 male workers
would be hired at w = $50 (point E', where S_M intersects D_L). No females
would now be hired by the industry. Females would have to find employment in other industries which do not practice sex discrimination, and this
would depress wages for all workers in these other industries. Thus, the
gains of male workers from sex discrimination in the industry come at the

expense of workers (both males and females) in other industries where there is no sex discrimination.

With a less extreme form of sex discrimination against females, employers in the industry may prefer to hire males over females at the same wage rate, but the employer's "taste for discrimination" is not absolute and can be overcome by a sufficiently lower wage for female labor than for male labor. For example, employers may also hire females if the wage of female workers is, say, $10 less than for male workers of the same productivity. Compared with the no-discrimination case, employers hire more males (and their wages rise) and fewer females (and their wages fall) until the male-female wage difference is $10. In Figure 15-9, employers hire 150 females at $w = \$35$ (point A') and 450 males at $w = \$45$ (point B'), as compared with 200 females and 400 males at $40 (points A and B, respectively) without discrimination. Once again, males gain at the expense of females and other employees of this and other industries. The gain is larger the greater is the employers' taste for discrimination in the industry.

If only some employers in the industry discriminated against females, they would employ only male workers while nondiscriminating employers would employ mostly females. If there are enough nondiscriminating employers in the industry to employ all the female workers, no male-female wage differences need arise in the industry. Even if all employers in the industry discriminated against females so that female wages tended to be lower than the wages of male workers, more firms would enter the industry (attracted by the lower female wages) and this, once again, would tend to eliminate sex-based wage differences in the industry. Note that discrimination may also be practiced by employees and by customers. Empirical studies[6] seem to indicate that from one half to three quarters of the male-female and white-black wage differences are due to differences in productivity based on different levels of education, training, age, hours of work, region of employment, and so on. Whether and to what extent the remaining difference is due to discrimination or to other still-unmeasured productivity factors has not yet been settled.

Summary

1. A firm that is an imperfect competitor in the product market but a perfect competitor in the input market will maximize profits by hiring any input until the marginal product of the input times the firm's marginal revenue from the commodity equals the price of the input.

2. If only one input is variable and the firm is a monopolist in the product market but a perfect competitor in the input market, the firm's demand curve for the input is given by the marginal revenue product (MRP) curve of the input. MRP equals the marginal product (MP) of the

[6] See G. Becker, *The Economics of Discrimination*, 2nd ed. (Chicago: University of Chicago Press, 1971), and R. Ehrenberg and R. Smith, *Modern Labor Economics* (Glenview, Ill.: Scott Foresman, 1982), Chapter 14.

input times the marginal revenue (MR) from the commodity. The excess of an input's VMP over MRP at the level of utilization of the input is called monopolistic exploitation. When all inputs are variable, the demand curve of an input is obtained by points on different MRP curves of the input and will be more elastic than the MRP curves. A perfect competitor in an input market will employ the input until the input's MRP on its demand curve equals the input price.

3. When all firms hiring an input are monopolists in their respective product markets, the market demand curve of the input is obtained by the straightforward horizontal summation of all the firms' demand curves for the input. On the other hand, when the firms are oligopolists or monopolistic competitors in the product market, the market demand curve of the input is derived as in Section 14-3a. The equilibrium price and employment of the input is then determined at the intersection of the market demand and the market supply curve of the input.

4. Monopsony refers to the case where there is a single buyer of an input. The monopsonist faces the positively sloped market supply curve of the input so that its marginal expense for the input exceeds the price of the input. Oligopsonists and monopsonistic competitors must also pay higher prices to hire more units of an input. Monopsony arises when an input is much more productive to a particular firm or use than to other firms or uses. It can also result from lack of geographical or occupational mobility.

5. A monopsonist hiring a single variable input maximizes profits by hiring the input until the marginal revenue product (MRP) of the input equals the marginal expense (ME) for the input. The price of the input is then determined by the corresponding point on the market supply curve of the input. A monopsonist hires less of the variable input and pays the input a lower price than would a perfectly competitive firm in the input market. The excess of the MRP over the price of the input at the point where MRP = ME is called monopsonistic exploitation.

6. To maximize profits a firm should hire any variable input until the marginal revenue product of the input equals the marginal expense of hiring it. If the firm is a perfect competitor in the product market, the marginal revenue product of the input is identical to the value of the marginal product of the input. If the firm is a perfect competitor in the input market, the marginal expense of the input equals the input price.

7. Monopsonistic exploitation can be eliminated by the government setting the minimum price of an input at the point where the MRP curve intersects the market supply curve of the input. Bilateral monopoly occurs when the monopsonist buyer of a product or input faces the monopolist seller of the product or input. Unions seem to have increased wages only slightly. Among the most important goals of unions are higher wages and greater employment of union labor. Discrimination in employment reduces the wages and/or the employment of the discriminated category. The marginal expense of an input is related to the price of the input and the price elasticity of the input supply.

Glossary

Marginal revenue product (MRP) The marginal (physical) product of the input (MP) multiplied by the marginal revenue of the commodity (MR).

Monopolistic exploitation The excess of an input's value of marginal product over its marginal revenue product at the level of utilization of the input.

Monopsony The single buyer of an input.

Marginal expense for the input The extra cost of hiring an additional unit of the input.

Marginal expense of labor (ME_L) The extra cost of hiring an additional unit of labor.

Marginal expense of capital (ME_K) The extra cost of hiring an additional unit of capital.

Oligopsony One of a few firms hiring a homogeneous or differentiated input.

Monopsonistic competition One of many firms hiring a differentiated input.

Monopsonistic exploitation The excess of the marginal revenue product of an input over the price of the input at the level of utilization of the input.

Bilateral monopoly   The case where the monopsonist buyer of a product or input faces the monopolist seller of the product or input.

Labor union   An organization of workers devoted to increasing the wages and welfare of its members through bargaining with employers.

Discrimination in employment   The (illegal) unwillingness on the part of employers to hire some group of equally productive workers based on sex, color, religion, or national origin under any circumstances or at the same wage rate.

Questions for Review

1. For a firm that is an imperfect competitor in the product market but a perfect competitor in the input market,
   (a) what is the best level of output?
   (b) what is the condition for profit maximization?
   (c) how much of each variable input should the firm hire to maximize profits?

2. (a) What is the value of the marginal product of an input?
   (b) What is the relationship between the marginal revenue product and the value of the marginal product of an input?
   (c) Why is the marginal revenue product curve of a firm negatively sloped?
   (d) Under what condition does the marginal revenue product of an input represent the firm's demand curve for the input?

3. (a) What happens to the marginal revenue product curve of an input if the amount employed of a complementary input rises? If the amount employed of a substitute input declines?
   (b) How is a firm's demand curve of an input derived when all inputs are variable and the firm is a monopolist in the product market but a perfect competitor in the input markets?
   (c) What is monopolistic exploitation? How is it measured?

4. (a) How is the market demand curve for an input determined when all firms hiring the input are monopolists in their respective product markets?
   (b) How is the market demand curve for an input determined when all firms hiring the input are oligopolists or monopolistic competitors in their respective product markets?
   (c) How is the equilibrium price and employment of an input determined when the firms hiring the input are imperfect competitors in the product market but perfect competitors in the input market?

5. With respect to the input market, what is
   (a) perfect competition?
   (b) monopsony?
   (c) oligopsony?
   (d) monopsonistic competition?

6. (a) What is the marginal expense of an input?
   (b) What is the relationship between the marginal expense and the price of an input?
   (c) What is the relationship between the supply curve of an input and the marginal expense of an input curve for a monopsonist?

7. (a) What is the general profit maximizing rule for a monopsonist hiring a single variable input?
   (b) How is the profit maximizing rule in part (a) modified when the firm is a perfect competitor in the product market?
   (c) How is the general profit maximizing rule of part (a) modified when the firm is a perfect competitor in the input market?

8. (a) How is the input price determined when the input is the only variable input of a monopsonist?
   (b) Why is the input price paid by a monopsonist lower than the marginal revenue product of the input?
   (c) What is monopsonistic exploitation?
   (d) How is monopsonistic exploitation different from monopolistic exploitation?

9. (a) What is the general rule for profit maximi-

zation for any firm hiring one or more variable inputs?

(b) What is the condition for the optimal or least-cost input combination for any firm?

(c) What does the ratio of the marginal expense of an input to its marginal product measure?

10. What part of the general condition for profit maximization is modified and how when the firm is a perfect competitor in the
(a) product market?
(b) input market?
(c) product and input markets?

11. (a) How can a monopsonist be made to behave as a perfect competitor in the input market?
(b) What is bilateral monopoly?
(c) Why are price and output indeterminate under bilateral monopoly?

12. (a) How can a labor union seek to increase the wages of its members?
(b) What are some of the most important goals of labor unions?
(c) What is the effect of discrimination in employment?
(d) What is the relationship among the marginal expense of an input, the input price, and the price elasticity of the input supply?

Problems

1. For a firm that is a monopolist in the product market but a perfect competitor in the input markets, express the condition prevailing if the firm
(a) utilizes too much labor or too little capital at the best output level. What is the graphical interpretation of this?
(b) utilizes the least-cost input combination but with its marginal cost exceeding its MR. What is the graphical interpretation of this?
(c) minimizes the cost of producing an output that is too small to maximize profits. What is the graphical interpretation of this?

2. Given the following data where: L is the number of workers hired per day by a firm (the only variable input), Q_x is the quantity of the commodity produced per day, and P_x is the commodity price:

L	1	2	3	4	5
Q_x	10	20	28	34	38
P_x	$5.00	4.50	4.00	3.50	3.00

(a) Find the marginal revenue product of labor and plot it.

(b) How many workers per day will the firm hire if the wage rate is $40 per day? $22? $7? What is the firm's demand curve for labor?

★3. From Table 15-1 in the text,

(a) find the MR_x, the MRP_L by multiplying MR_x by MP_L, and the VMP_L.

(b) On the same graph, plot the VMP_L and the MRP_L on the assumption that labor is infinitesimally divisible. How many workers would the firm employ if it were a perfect competitor in the product market? What is the amount of monopolistic exploitation?

4. Repeat the procedure in Problem 3 for the data in Problem 2 and on the assumption that the daily wage is $22.

5. Assume that (1) labor is infinitesimally divisible (i.e., workers can be hired for any part of the day) in the production function of Problems 2 and 4, (2) all inputs are variable, and (3) when the wage rate falls from $40 to $22 per day, the firm's value of the marginal product curve shifts to the right by two labor units. Derive the demand curve for labor of this firm. How many workers will the firm hire per day at the daily wage rate of $22?

6. (a) Derive the market demand curve for labor if there are 100 monopolistically competitive firms identical to the firm of Problem 5 in the labor market and each individual firm's demand curve for labor shifts to the left by one unit when the wage rate falls from $w = $40 to $w = $22 per day.

(b) If 200 workers are willing to work at the daily wage of $10 and 600 are willing to work at the daily wage of $40, what is the equilibrium wage and level of employment? How many workers would each firm hire at the equilibrium wage?

7. (a) From the following market supply schedule of labor faced by a monopsonist, derive the firm's marginal expense of labor schedule.

   (b) Plot on the same set of axes the firm's supply and marginal expense of labor schedules.

L	1	2	3	4	5
w	$10	11	16	40	100

8. On your graph for Problem 7b, superimpose the monopsonist's value of marginal product and marginal revenue product of labor curves from Problem 15-4. Assuming that labor is the only variable input, determine the number of workers that the firm hires, the wage rate, and the amount of monopolistic and monopsonistic exploitation if the firm is a monopolist in the product market and a monopsonist in the input market.

★9. Starting with Figure 15-4, explain what happens if the government set the minimum wage at

   (a) $35.
   (b) $50.

★10. Assume that all workers in a town belong to the union and there is a single firm hiring labor in the town. Suppose that the demand for labor function of the firm (monopsonist) is $S_L = 2w$ (where w refers to wages, measured in dollars per day) and the supply of labor function by the union (the monopolist seller of labor time) is $D_L = 120 - 2w$. Find the wage rate and number of workers that the firm would like to hire and the wage and level of employment that the union would seek if it behaved as a monopolist. What is the likely result?

★11. Draw a figure showing that an increase in union wages usually reduces employment in unionized industries, and increases employment and lowers wages in nonunionized industries.

12. Given that (1) $ME_L = w(1 + 1/\epsilon_L)$ where ϵ_L is the price (wage) elasticity of the supply curve of labor (this formula is derived in Section A14 of the Mathematical Appendix), and (2) S_L is a straight line through the origin, find the value of ME_L if

   (a) $w = \$40$.
   (b) $w = \$80$.

Supplementary Readings

For a problem-solving approach to the topics covered in this chapter, see

Dominick Salvatore, *Microeconomic Theory,* 2nd ed. (New York: McGraw-Hill, 1983), Sections 13.9–13.14.

On the theory of wages and employment, see

John R. Hicks, *The Theory of Wages* (New York: Macmillan, 1932).

Allan M. Cartter, *Theory of Wages and Employment* (Homewood, Ill.: Irwin, 1959), pp. 11–74.

Intertemporal Choice: Interest and Capital

Chapter 16

16-1   Lending-Borrowing Equilibrium

16-2   Saving-Investment Equilibrium

16-3   Investment Decisions

16-4   Determinants of the Market Rates of Interest

16-5   Applications

Examples

16-1   Personal Savings

16-2   Personal and Business Savings, and Gross and Net Private Domestic Investment

16-3   Fields of Education and Lifetime Earnings

16-4   Nominal and Real Rates of Interest: 1970–1983

Applications

Application 1:   Investment in Human Capital

Application 2:   Investment in Human Capital and Hours of Work

Application 3:   Pricing of Exhaustible Resources

Application 4:   Management of Nonexhaustible Resources

Application 5:   Socialism and the Rate of Interest

Preview Questions

Why do some people lend and some people borrow resources?

What is investment? Why do some people and firms invest resources?

Why do some people and firms save and invest, lend or borrow?

How is the market rate of interest determined? What are its determinants?

What is human capital?

What is the effect of education on hours of work?

How is the price of a nonrenewable resource, such as petroleum, determined?

How can renewable resources, such as forests, be managed?

In this chapter we examine intertemporal choices or the optimal allocation of resources *over time*. We examine the choice between consuming now or saving a portion of this year's income in order to consume more in the future. The other side of the coin is borrowing against future income in order to increase present consumption. The ability of an individual to exchange present for future income or consumption (by lending or borrowing) enables him or her to maximize the total or joint satisfaction of present and future income and consumption. For example, people individually and collectively (through the social security system) save during their working lives to provide for retirement, and by doing so, they maximize the lifetime satisfaction from their earnings. On the other hand, students often borrow against their future income (i.e., they dissave).

Another way by which present income can be exchanged for future income is to free some resources from the production of final commodities for present consumption (i.e., save) to produce more capital goods (i.e., invest in machinery, factories, and so on), which will lead to larger output and consumption in the future. The ability of individuals and firms to trade present for future income and output and vice versa (through lending and borrowing, saving and investing) is very crucial in all societies. Indeed, a great deal of the increase in the standards of living in modern societies is the result of investments in physical capital (machinery, factories, etc.) and human capital (education, skills, health, and so on).

An individual usually requires a reward for postponing present consumption (i.e., saving) and lending a portion of this year's income. The reward takes the form of a repayment that exceeds the amount lent. This premium is the interest payment. The other side of the coin is the borrowing of a given sum today and the repaying of a larger sum in the future (the

513

principal plus the interest). Similarly, individuals and firms will only invest in machinery, factories, or in acquiring or providing skills if they can expect a return on their investment in the form of higher future incomes or outputs than the amounts invested.

In this chapter we will examine the determination of the rate of interest that will balance the quantity of resources lent and borrowed and that equilibrates saving and investment. Then we examine the criteria used by individuals, business firms, and government agencies in their investment decisions. Subsequently, we discuss the reasons for differences in interest rates in the same nation, in different nations, and over time. Finally, several important applications of the theory presented in the chapter are analyzed. These range from investment in human capital to the pricing and management of nonrenewable and renewable resources.

16-1

Lending-Borrowing Equilibrium

In this section we examine how an individual maximizes the total or joint satisfaction from spending his or her present and future income by lending or borrowing. We will then show how the equilibrium market rate of interest is determined at the level at which the total quantity demanded of loans (borrowings) equals the total quantity supplied of loans (lendings).

16-1a Lending

We begin by examining how a consumer can maximize satisfaction over time by lending. For simplicity we assume that the consumer's income is measured in terms of the quantity of a commodity (say corn) that he or she has or expects to receive. Also to simplify matters we will deal with only two time periods: this year and the next. This assumption is relaxed in Section 16-3. We also begin by assuming that the consumer has an **endowment position** or receives $Y_0 = 7.5$ units of corn this year and $Y_1 = 3$ units of corn next year (point A in the left panel of Figure 16-1).[1]

The consumer, however, is not bound to consume the $Y_0 = 7.5$ units of corn this year and the $Y_1 = 3$ units of corn next year since he or she can lend part of this year's corn or borrow against next year's corn. The question is how should the consumer distribute his or her consumption between this year and next so as to maximize the total or joint satisfaction over the two periods. This is analogous to the consumer's choice between

---

[1] Uncertainty is ruled out here so that the consumer knows exactly how much of the commodity he or she gets this year and next year. This assumption is relaxed in Section 16-4. In what follows, subscripts 0 and 1 denote, respectively, this year (or the present) and next year (or the future).

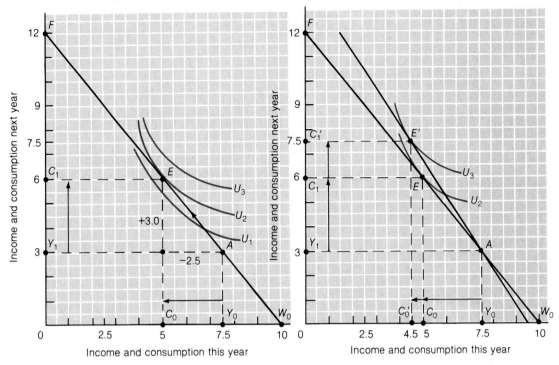

FIGURE 16-1.   Lending
Starting from endowment A (Y_0 = 7.5 and Y_1 = 3), the consumer maximizes satis-
faction at point E, where budget line FW$_0$ is tangent to indifference curve U$_2$ in the
left panel. The consumer reaches point E by lending Y$_0$ − C$_0$ = 2.5 units from this
year's endowment and receiving three additional units next year. Thus, the slope of
the budget line is 3/(−2.5) = −1.2 or −1(1 + 0.2) and the interest rate r = 0.2 or
20 percent. At r = 50 per cent, the optimal point is E′ (in the right panel), where the
steeper budget line through point A is tangent to indifference curve U$_3$. Point E′ is
reached by lending 3 units (instead of 2.5).

hamburgers (commodity X) and soft drinks (commodity Y) examined in
Section 3-4 and Figure 3-8. The only difference is that here the choice is
between the consumption of corn this year or next.

In the left panel of Figure 16-1, the consumer's tastes between consumption this year and next is given by indifference curves U_1, U_2, and U_3. The
consumer also faces budget line FW_0. The latter shows the various combinations of present and future income and consumption available to the
consumer. Starting from endowment position A (Y_0 = 7.5 and Y_1 = 3), the
consumer can lend part of this year's corn endowment so that he or she
will consume less this year and more next year. This is represented by an
upward movement from point A along budget line FW_0. On the other hand,
the consumer could increase consumption this year by borrowing against
next year's endowment or income by moving downward from point A
along FW_0.

The consumer maximizes satisfaction by reaching the highest indifference curve possible with his or her budget line. The optimal choice is given by point E, where budget line FW_0 is tangent to indifference curve U_2. At point E, the individual consumes $C_0 = 5$ units of corn this year and $C_1 = 6$ units of next year (see the left panel of Figure 16-1). The consumer reaches point E by lending $Y_0 - C_0 = 2.5$ units of corn out of this year's endowment or output and receiving three additional units next year.

The slope of the budget line gives the premium or the rate of interest that the lender receives. For example, the movement from point A to point E indicates that the consumer receives 3 units of the commodity next year by lending 2.5 units this year. Thus, the slope of the budget line is $3/(-2.5) = -1.2$ or $-1(1 + 0.2)$, so that the interest rate $r = 0.2$ or 20 per cent. That is,

$$\frac{C_1 - Y_1}{C_0 - Y_0} = -(1 + r) = -(1 + 0.2) \tag{16-1}$$

The negative sign reflects the downward-to-the-right inclination of the budget line. This simply means that for the consumer to be able to consume more next year, he or she will have to consume less this year. In this case, the consumer lends (i.e., reduces consumption by) 2.5 units this year and gets $2.5(1 + 0.2) = 3$ next year. If the consumer lends all of this year's income or endowment of $Y_0 = 7.5$ units at 20 per cent interest, he or she will receive $7.5(1 + 0.2) = 9$ additional units next year (and reaches point F on budget line FW_0). The consumer could do this, but does not, because he or she would not be maximizing satisfaction.

Returning to the slope of the budget line or interest rate, we can say more generally that the **rate of interest (r)** is the premium received by an individual next year by lending one dollar today. Another way of stating this is that the rate of interest is the price next year (P_1) of a dollar this year (P_0). That is,

$$P_1 = P_0 (1 + r) \tag{16-2}$$

The individual receives (\$1) $(1 + r)$ next year (P_1) by lending one dollar this year (P_0). If the interest rate r is 0.2 per cent or 20 per cent, the individual receives (\$1) $(1 + 0.2) = \$1.20$ next year by lending \$1 this year. Of course, the person that borrows one dollar today must repay \$1.20 next year if the rate of interest is 20 per cent. Thus, the interest rate can be viewed as the price next year of a dollar lent or borrowed this year.

If the interest rate rises (i.e., if the budget line becomes steeper), lenders will usually lend more. For example, starting with endowment position A in the *right* panel of Figure 16-1, if the interest rate rises to 50 per cent (so that the slope of the budget line becomes $-(1 + 0.5)$, the optimal choice of the consumer is at point E', where the new steeper budget line through point A is tangent to higher indifference curve U_3. The consumer can reach point E' by lending $Y_0 - C_0' = 3$ units (instead of 2.5), for which he or she receives $C_1' - Y_1 = 4.5$ units next year. That is, by lending 3 units at 50 per cent interest, the consumer receives $3(1 + 0.5) = 4.5$ next year. Thus, the increase in the rate of interest from 20 per cent to 50 per cent leads this individual (the lender) to increase lending from 2.5 to 3 units.[2]

16-1b Borrowing

We will now show that if the endowment position of the consumer in the left panel of Figure 16-1 had been to the left of point E on budget line FW_0 (rather than at point A), the consumer would have been a borrower rather than a lender. This is shown in the left panel of Figure 16-2. Specifically, suppose the endowment position of the consumer had been at point B ($Y_0 = 2.5$ and $Y_1 = 9$) on budget line FW_0. The consumer would maximize satisfaction at point E ($C_0 = 5$ and $C_1 = 6$), where budget line FW_0 is tangent to indifference curve U_2 (the highest the consumer can reach with budget line FW_0). To reach point E, the consumer would have to borrow $C_0 - Y_0 = 2.5$ units of the commodity this year and repay $Y_1 - C_1 = 3$ units next year.

Since $3/2.5 = 1.2$, the rate of interest $r = 0.2$ or 20 per cent, as found before in Section 16-1a. This means that in order to borrow 2.5 units this year, the individual must repay 3 units next year if the market rate of interest is 20 per cent. That is, $2.5 = 3/(1 + 0.2)$. The reason for this is that 2.5 units this year will grow to 3 units next year at $r = 0.2$ or 20 per cent. More generally, we can say that the price of a dollar today (P_0) is equal to one dollar next year (P_1) divided by $(1 + r)$. That is,

$$P_0 = P_1/(1 + r) \tag{16-3}$$

This is obtained by dividing both sides of Equation (16-2) by $(1 + r)$. For example, at $r = 20$ per cent, \$1 next year is equivalent to $\$1/(1 + 0.2) = \$0.83$ this year because \$0.83 lent this year at 20 per cent will grow to \$1 next year.

If the individual borrowed all of next year's income of $Y_1 = 9$, he or she could increase consumption this year by $\$9/(1 + 0.2) = 7.5$ and be at point $W_0 = 10$. Point $W_0 = 10$ gives the **wealth** of the individual. This is equal to the individual's income or endowment this year plus the present value

---

[2] The increase in the rate of interest will usually, but not always, increase the amount of lending. The reason is that (as in the case of an increase in the wage rate), an increase in the rate of interest gives rise to a substitution and an income effect. According to the substitution effect, the increase in the rate of interest leads the individual to lend more. However, by increasing the future income of the individual, the increase in the rate of interest also gives rise to an income effect, which leads the individual to lend less. At a sufficiently high rate of interest, the negative income effect exceeds the positive substitution effect and the individual's supply curve of loans bends backward. This is examined in Problem 5a, with answer at the end of the text.

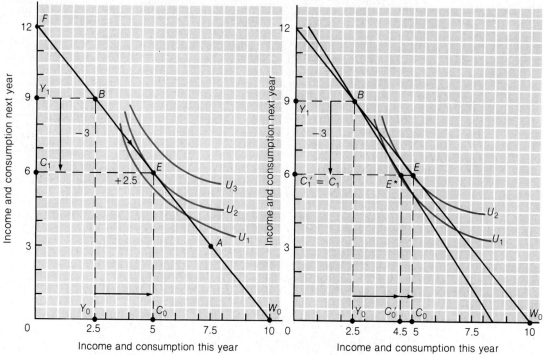

FIGURE 16-2. *Borrowing*
Starting from endowment B ($Y_0 = 2.5$ and $Y_1 = 9$), the consumer maximizes satis-faction at point E, where budget line FW_0 is tangent to indifference curve U_2 in the left panel. The consumer reaches point E by borrowing $C_0 - Y_0 = 2.5$ and repaying $Y_1 - C_1 = 3$ next year. Thus, the slope of the budget line is $3/(-2.5) = -1.2$ or $-1(1 + 0.2)$ and the interest rate $r = 0.2$ or 20 percent. At $r = 50$ per cent, the optimal point is E^* in the right panel, where the steeper budget line through point B is tangent to indifference curve U_1. Point E^* is reached by borrowing 2 units (instead of 2.5).

of next year's income or endowment. That is, the consumer's wealth is given by

$$W_0 = Y_0 + [Y_1/(1 + r)] \tag{16-4}$$

In our example, the income this year is $Y_0 = 2.5$ and the present value of next year's income is $Y_1/(1 + r) = 9/(1 + 0.2) = 7.5$, resulting in the indi-vidual's wealth of 10. Graphically, the wealth of the individual or consu-mer is given by the intersection of the budget line with the horizontal axis. Thus, wealth plays the same role in intertemporal choice as the consumer's income plays in the consumer's choice between two commodities during the same year. An increase in wealth, like an increase in income, will shift the consumer's budget line outward and allows the consumer to purchase more of every normal good or to consume more, both this year and next.

518

An increase in the rate of interest leads to a reduction in the amount the individual wants to borrow. Since present consumption becomes more expensive in terms of the future consumption that must be given up, the borrower will borrow less. This is shown in the right panel of Figure 16-2. Starting once again with endowment position B in the right panel of Figure 16-2, an increase in the rate of interest to 50 per cent will result in a new budget line with slope of $-(1 + 0.5)$. The optimal choice of the consumer is then at point E^*, where the steeper budget line through point B is tangent to lower indifference curve U_1. Indifference curve U_1 is the highest that the consumer can reach with his or her initial endowment position B and $r = 50$ per cent. To reach point E^* ($C_0' = 4.5$ and $C_1' = C_1 = 6$), the consumer will have to borrow $C_0' - Y_0 = 2$ units (instead of 2.5) this year and will have to repay $C_1' - Y_1 = (-)3$ units next year. That is, $2 = 3/(1 + 0.5)$. Thus, the increase in the rate of interest from 20 per cent to 50 per cent leads this individual to borrow less.[3]

16-1c The Market Rate of Interest with Borrowing and Lending

We now examine how the equilibrium rate of interest is determined in the market for borrowing and lending. For simplicity, we assume that we have only two individuals in the market for loans: individual B with endowment position B and individual A with endowment position A on budget line FW_0 (see the left panel of Figure 16-2). That is, instead of assuming as above that an individual has either endowment B (and is a borrower) or endowment A (and is a lender), we now assume that we have two individuals, one with endowment B (the borrower) and the other with endowment A (the lender) on FW_0. We also assume for now that both individuals have the same tastes or time preferences for present (this year) versus future (next year) consumption, as shown by indifference curves U_1, U_2, and U_3 in the left panel of Figure 16-2.

As we can see from the left panel of Figure 16-2, the optimal choice for individual B is to move from point B to point E along budget line FW_0 by borrowing 2.5 units of the commodity this year at the rate of interest of 0.20 or 20 per cent (so that he or she will have to repay 3 units next year). Thus, the quantity demanded of loans (borrowing) by individual B is 2.5 units at $r = 20$ per cent. On the other hand, the optimal choice of individual A is to move from point A to point E along budget line FW_0 by lending 2.5 units of the commodity this year at the rate of interest of 0.20 or 20 per cent (so that he or she will receive an additional 3 units next year). Thus, the quantity supplied of loans (lending) by individual A is 2.5 units at $r = 20$ per cent.

---

[3] As opposed to the supply curve of loans, which could bend backward at a sufficiently high rate of interest, the demand curve for loans is always negatively sloped (see Problem 5b, with answer at the end of the text).

FIGURE 16-3.
Borrowing-Lending
Equilibrium

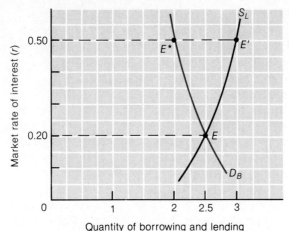

Borrowing-lending equilibrium occurs at point E, where the demand curve for borrowing (D_B) intersects the supply curve for lending (S_L). Point E shows that r = 20 per
cent and 2.5 units are borrowed and lent. At r = 50 per cent, the quantity supplied
of lending of 3 units (point E') exceeds the quantity demanded of borrowing of 2 units
(point E*) and the rate of interest falls to 20 per cent (point E). The opposite is true
at r lower than 20 per cent.

Since we have assumed that A and B are the only two individuals in the
market, the equilibrium market rate of interest is 0.20 or 20 per cent. This
is the only market rate of interest at which the desired quantity demanded
of loans (borrowing) of 2.5 units equals the desired quantity supplied of
loans (lending) of 2.5 units, and the market for loanable funds is in equilibrium. This is shown by point E in Figure 16-3, where the demand curve for
borrowing (D_B) intersects the supply curve for lending (S_L). The figure also
shows that at r = 50 per cent, individual B wants to borrow only 2 units
(point E* on D_B, from the right panel of Figure 16-2) and individual A wants
to lend 3 units (point E' on D_L, from the right panel of Figure 16-1). The
resulting excess in the quantity supplied over the quantity demanded of
loans of 1 unit (E*E') at r = 50 per cent causes the rate of interest to fall to
the equilibrium level of r = 20 per cent (point E).

In the above analysis we have assumed for simplicity that there are only
two individuals, A and B, in the market and that both have identical tastes
or time preference.[4] In the real world, however, there are many individuals
with different tastes. Yet, the process by which the equilibrium market rate
of interest is determined is basically the same. That is, the equilibrium
market rate of interest is the one at which the total or aggregate quantity
demanded of borrowing matches the aggregate quantity supplied of lending. At a market rate of interest above the equilibrium rate, the supply of
lending exceeds the demand for borrowing and the interest rate falls. On

[4] The determination of the market rate of interest when consumers have different time
preferences is examined in Problem 4 (with answer at the end of the text).

the other hand, at a market rate of interest below the equilibrium rate, the demand for borrowing exceeds the supply of lending and the market rate of interest rises toward equilibrium. Only at the equilibrium market rate of interest the quantity demanded matches the quantity supplied and there is no tendency for the interest rate to change.

Example 16-1 Personal Savings

The Facts: Table 16-1 presents the total or aggregate amount of personal savings (PS) in the United States in terms of 1972 prices for the years 1950, 1960, 1970, 1975, and 1980 through 1983. It also shows the level of personal disposable (i.e., after tax) income (PDI) and the percentage of PS to PDI during the same years. Personal savings ranged from $22 billion in 1950 to $75 billion in 1975. It was $52.5 billion in 1983 or 4.8% of personal disposable income.

Comment: Prior to the establishment of Social Security in 1935, individuals provided for their retirement by saving a portion of their earnings during their working years. With Social Security, a retirement income was provided by the government, thus reducing the need for personal savings. If the government had saved the social security taxes it levied, net savings (personal plus government) would have been more or less unchanged. Since the government chose not to "fund" the system but to use social security taxes for current expenditures and pay future social security benefits out of future taxes, the nation's level of aggregate savings declined. Michael R. Darby estimated that the Social Security program reduced the nation's savings by 5–20 percent.

Source: Michael R. Darby, *The Effects of Social Security on Income and Capital Stock* (Washington, D.C.: American Enterprise Institute, 1979).

TABLE 16-1   Personal Savings and Personal Disposable Income (in Billions of 1972 Dollars)

Year	PS	PDI	PS as % of PDI
1950	$22.2	$ 362.8	6.1
1960	28.7	489.7	5.9
1970	61.0	751.6	8.1
1975	75.0	874.9	8.6
1980	61.8	1,021.6	6.0
1981	69.3	1,054.7	6.6
1982	60.6	1,060.2	5.7
1983	52.5	1,094.3	4.8

Source: Council of Economic Advisers, *Economic Report of the President* (Washington, D.C.: U.S. Government Printing Office, 1984), pp. 249–250.

16-2

Saving-Investment Equilibrium

In Section 16-1 we analyzed borrowing-lending equilibrium. For simplicity we assumed that no part of the current endowment or output was invested to increase future productive capacity. In this section we begin with the opposite situation and examine saving-investment equilibrium without borrowing or lending. That is, we begin (in Section 16-2a) by examining the case where an isolated individual (a Robinson Crusoe) consumes less than he or she produces in this period (saves) in order to have more seeds or to produce a piece of equipment to increase production in the next period (invests). Then, in Section 16-2b, we relax the assumption that the individual is isolated and that he or she cannot borrow or lend and examine saving-investment equilibrium with borrowing and lending. Finally (in Section 16-2c), we will show how the equilibrium rate of interest is determined with saving and investment, and borrowing and lending.

16-2a Saving-Investment Equilibrium Without Borrowing and Lending

Suppose that an individual lives alone on an island and produces and consumes a single commodity. This Robinson Crusoe has no possibility to borrow or lend (or trade) the commodity and can only consume what he produces. Suppose that under present conditions he can count on producing $Y_0 = 7.5$ units of the commodity during this year and $Y_1 = 3$ units next year. This is shown by point A on his production-possibilities curve FQ in Figure 16-4.

Production-possibilities curve FQ shows how much Crusoe can produce and consume next year by saving part of this year's output and invest it to increase next year's output. **Saving** refers to the act of refraining from present consumption. **Investment** refers to the formation of new capital assets. For example, Crusoe may use part of the year to construct a rudimentary net rather than catching fish with a spear. Since he is not catching fish while he is building the net, he is refraining from present consumption (saving). The net is an investment that will allow him to catch more fish in the future. Note that in this case, the saving and the investment are done by the same person, and are one and the same thing.

Disregarding for the moment the indifference curves in Figure 16-4, we see that the FQ curve shows that if the individual consumes $C_0 = 6$ units of the commodity this year, he can produce and consume $C_1 = 6.5$ units of the commodity next year (point G on FQ). Starting from point A, this means that by saving and investing $Y_0 - C_0 = 7.5 - 6 = 1.5$ units of the commodity this year, the individual can increase output by $C_1 - Y_1 = 6.5 - 3 = 3.5$ units next year. Thus, the average yield or return on investment (in terms of next year's output) is $3.5/1.5 = 2.33 = (1 + 1.33)$ or 133 per cent.

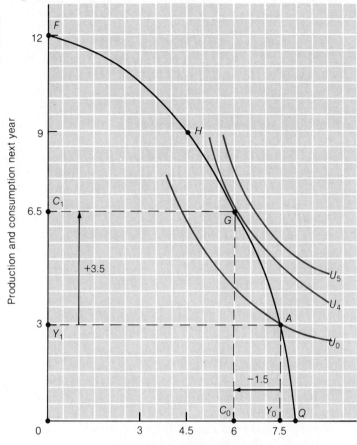

Production and consumption this year

*Production-possibilities curve FQ shows how much an isolated individual can pro-
duce and consume next year by saving and investing part of this year's output. Starting at point A on FQ, the optimal level of saving and investment is 1.5 units. This
allows the individual to reach point G on the highest indifference curve possible (U_4).
Saving and investing 1.5 units this year allows the individual to produce and consume 3.5 units more next year. Thus, the average yield on investment is 133 per cent.*

Should the individual save and invest 3 units of the commodity this year,
his output will increase by 6 units next year (the movement from point A
to point H on FQ), so that the average yield or rate of return would be 6/3
= 2 = (1 + 1) or 100 per cent. Note that the larger is the amount invested,
the lower is the rate of return (because of the operation of the law of diminishing returns).

Given the individual's production-possibilities curve FQ, the question is,
"what is the optimal amount of saving and investment for this individual?." The answer is 1.5 units. The reason is that this will permit the individual to reach point G on indifference curve U_4. Indifference curve U_4 is
the highest that Crusoe can reach with his production-possibility curve.

523

Note that indifference curves here show the trade-off or time preference between consumption this year and next. Thus, starting from point A, Crusoe should save and invest 1.5 units of this year's output so as to reach point G next year and maximize his total or joint utility or satisfaction over the two years.

16-2b Saving-Investment Equilibrium with Borrowing and Lending

Suppose that more people get stranded on Crusoe's island and they also start producing and consuming the commodity. Now, borrowing and lending become possible. The optimal chioce of Crusoe is now to save and invest, borrow or lend so as to reach the highest indifference curve possible (higher than U_4).

To show this, we must realize that from every point of the production-possibilities curve there is a **market line,** the slope of which shows the rate at which the individual (Crusoe) can borrow or lend in the market. For example, starting at point A on the FQ curve in Figure 16-5, the individual can borrow or lend along market line FAW_0 at the rate of interest of $r = 20$ per cent (as in the left panel of Figures 16-1 and 16-2). If starting from point A the individual only borrows or lends (or does neither), his wealth is $W_0 = 10$ (given by the intersection of market line FOW_0 with the horizontal axis).

However, with the possibility of saving and investment, and borrowing or lending now open, the optimal choice for Crusoe is to invest first (so as to maximize wealth), and then to borrow (so as to reach the highest indifference curve possible). Wealth is maximized by reaching the highest market line (with slope reflecting the market rate of interest) that is possible with the FQ curve. This is given by market line $HE''W_0'$, which is parallel to market line FAW_0 (so that $r = 20$ per cent) and tangent to production-possibilities curve FQ at point H. Market line $HE''W_0'$ shows that the maximum attainable wealth is $W_0' = 12$. Starting from point A on the FQ curve, the individual can attain market line $HE''W_0'$ and maximize wealth by investing $Y_0 - Q_0 = 3$ units of this year's output. This allows him to reach point H on this production-possibilities curve and produce $Q_1 = 9$ units of the commodity next year.

Having attained the highest wealth possible by investing 3 units of the commodity (point H on market line $HE''W_0'$), the individual can then borrow $C_0 - Q_0 = 2.5$ units (i.e., move to the right of point H on market line $HE''W_0'$) and reach point E'' on U_5. This is the highest indifference curve that the individual can reach with optimal investment and borrowing. Point E'' on indifference curve U_5 is superior to point A on U_0 (see Figure 16-4) without borrowing or investing, it is superior to borrowing alone (to the left of point A along budget line FEW_0), and it is superior to point G on U_4 (see Figure 16-4) with saving equal to investment and no borrowing.

To summarize, the optimal choice of the individual is to invest $Y_0 - Q_0$

FIGURE 16-5.
Saving-Investment
Equilibrium with
Borrowing and
Lending

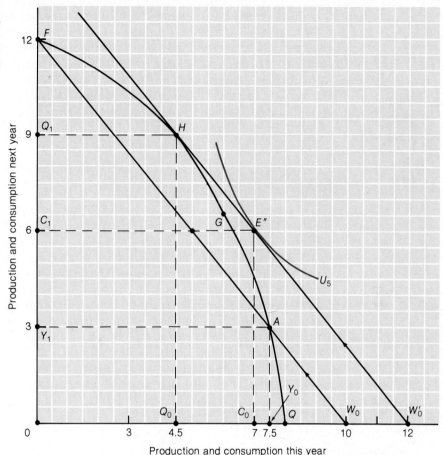

Starting from point A, *the individual maximizes wealth (at* $W_0' = 12$ *units) by investing 3 units of the commodity and reaching point* H, *where market line* $HE''W_0'$ *(with
slope reflecting the market rate of interest) is tangent to production-possibilities
curve* FQ. *The individual then borrows 2.5 units (i.e., moves to the right of point* H
on market line $HE''W_0'$*) and reaches point* E'' *on* U_5 *(the highest indifference curve
possible). The individual invests 3 units, borrows 2.5, and saves 0.5.*

$= 3$ units (i.e., to move from point A to point H on the FW_0' line) in order
to maximize wealth (at $W_0' = 12$) and to borrow $C_0 - Q_0 = 2.5$ units (the
movement from point H to point E'' on indifference curve U_5) to maximize
his total or joint satisfaction or utility over both years. Of the total amount
of $Y_0 - Q_0 = 3$ invested, the individual borrows $C_0 - Q_0 = 2.5$ and saves
$Y_0 - C_0 = 0.5$. That is, the individual is saving a portion of his current
output, but not enough to "finance" all of his investment. Therefore, other
individuals must be saving 2.5 units of the commodity more than they
invest in order to lend this amount to our individual.

If the market rate of interest rises above $r = 20$ per cent, the market line

525

becomes steeper and tangent to production-possibilities curve FQ to the right of point H, and the individual will invest less (see Figure 16-6 and Problem 6, with answer at the end of the text). If the individual borrows more than he invests, he will be dissaving (see Problem 7). If indifference curve U_5 had been tangent to market line HW_0' to the left of point H in Figure 16-5, the individual would have been investing and lending (rather than borrowing) so that his saving would equal the sum of the two (see Problem 8).

16-2c The Market Rate of Interest with Saving and Investment, Borrowing and Lending

We now examine how the equilibrium rate of interest is determined in the market with borrowing and lending, and saving and investment. For simplicity we assume that only our individual borrows and invests while all other individuals collectively only want to lend 2.5 units of the commodity at the rate of interest of $r = 20$ per cent. The equilibrium rate of interest is then 20 per cent and is shown in Figure 16-6 in two different ways: (1) by point E, where the demand curve of borrowing of our individual (D_B) intersects the supply curve of lending of all other individuals (S_L) as in Figure 16-3, or equivalently (2) by point E'', where the demand curve for investment of our individual (D_I) intersects the total supply curve of savings of this and other individuals (S_S).

FIGURE 16-6.
The Rate of Interest
with Borrowing,
Lending, Saving,
and Investment

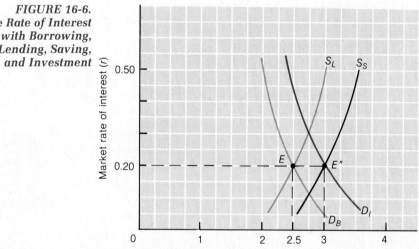

The equilibrium rate of interest is 20 per cent and is shown (1) by point E, where the demand curve for borrowing (D_B) intersects the supply curve of lending (S_L), and (2) by point E'', where the demand curve for investment (D_I) intersects the total supply curve of savings (S_S). At r > 20 per cent, desired lending exceeds desired borrowing and desired saving exceeds desired investments and r falls. The opposite is true at r < 20 per cent.

At the equilibrium market rate of interest of $r = 20$ per cent, the quantity of desired borrowing of 2.5 units (done exclusively by our individual) equals the quantity of desired lending of 2.5 units (supplied by all other individuals). In addition, at $r = 20$ per cent, the total amount of desired savings of 3 units (2.5 units by other individuals and 0.5 units by our individual) matches the desired level of investment of 3 units (undertaken exclusively by our individual). That is, at equilibrium, desired borrowing equals desired lending (point E) and desired savings equals desired investment (point E''). Note that the excess between the saving-investment equilibrium and the borrowing-lending equilibrium refers to the amount of investment that is self-financed from the investor's own savings rather than from borrowing in the market.[5]

At a rate of interest above equilibrium, there will be (1) an excess in the quantity supplied of lending over the quantity demanded of borrowing and (2) an excess in the total quantity supplied of savings over the total quantity demanded of investment (see Figure 16-6). As a result, the interest rate will fall to the equilibrium level. The opposite is true at rates of interest below equilibrium. Of course, in the real world, there are many borrowers and many lenders, and many savers and investors, but the principles by which the equilibrium rate of interest is determined is the same (when capital markets are perfectly competitive). That is, at equilibrium, aggregate desired borrowing equals aggregate desired lending, and aggregate desired investment equals aggregate desired saving.

Example 16-2   **Personal and Business Savings, and Gross and Net Private Domestic Investment**

The Facts: Table 16-2 presents the total or aggregate amount of personal savings (PS), business savings (BS), gross private domestic investment (GPDI), and net private domestic investment (NPDI) in the United States in terms of 1972 prices for the years 1950, 1960, 1970, 1975, and 1980 through 1983. NPDI equals GPDI minus capital consumption allowances or depreciation resulting from the production of the given year's output. Table 16-2 also shows the level of real net national product (NNP) and the percentage of NPDI to NNP during the same years.

Comment: Business savings are from 2 to 4 times larger than personal savings. Net private domestic investment is the net addition to society's capital stock and an important contributor to the growth of the economy and standards of living. Personal and business savings are required to provide for

---

[5] Just as some people can borrow more than they invest so that they dissave, so some individuals can consume more than the sum of what they produce, borrow, and invest. Such individuals would be *disinvesting* or failing to maintain (i.e., not replacing depreciated) capital stock. To some extent, these individuals are "living off their capital." This may also be true for society as a whole during periods of war or natural disaster.

Table 16-2   Personal and Business Savings, and Gross and Net Private Domestic Investment in the United States (in Billions of 1972 Dollars)

Year	PS	BS	GPDI	NPDI	NNP	NPDI as % of NNP
1950	$22.2	$ 57.3	$ 93.5	$50.7	$ 491.7	10.3
1960	28.7	84.9	104.7	41.1	669.9	6.2
1970	61.0	112.4	158.5	62.4	989.2	6.3
1975	75.0	149.7	154.8	34.0	1,104.9	3.1
1980	61.8	182.2	208.5	58.7	1,310.7	4.5
1981	69.3	191.8	227.6	71.6	1,345.0	5.3
1982	60.6	191.5	194.5	32.0	1,311.8	2.4
1983	52.5	210.9	218.4	49.3	1,359.8	3.6

Source: Council of Economic Advisers, *Economic Report of the President* (Washington, D.C.: U.S. Government Printing Office, 1984), pp. 239, 242, 249–250.

the replacement of the capital consumed during the course of producing current output and for the net additions to the capital stock of the country. Not included in the table are government savings and investments, and foreign investments. As indicated in Example 16-1, Michael R. Darby estimated that the establishment of Social Security in 1935 reduced the nation's savings by 5–20 per cent. He also estimated that this reduced the level of national income by 2–7 per cent.

Source: See Example 16-1.

16-3

Investment Decisions

The above discussion has very important practical applications and is the basis for very valuable decision rules used by firms and government agencies in determining which investment project to undertake. For example, a bank may have to decide whether to purchase or rent a large computer, a government agency whether or not to build a dam, and a manufacturing firm whether it should purchase a more expensive machine that lasts longer or a cheaper one that lasts a shorter period of time. The decision rule to answer these questions and for ranking various investment projects is called **capital budgeting.** Our discussion of capital budgeting will begin by considering a two-period time framework. We then extend and generalize the discussion to a multiperiod time horizon.

16-3a Present-Value Rule for Investment Decisions: The Two-Period Case

An investment project involves a cost (to purchase the machinery, build the factory, acquire a skill, and so on) and a return in the form of an increase in output or income in the future. In a two-period framework, the cost is usually incurred in the current year and the return or benefit will come the following year. However, since one unit of a commodity or a dollar next year is worth less than a unit of the commodity or a dollar today, cost and benefits occurring at different times cannot simply be added together to determine whether or not to undertake the project.

For example, for a project that involves the expenditure of $1 this year and results in $1.50 next year, we simply cannot add the −$1 of cost this year to the $1.50 return next year and say that the net value of the project is $0.50. The reason is that $1.50 next year is worth less than $1.50 today.[6] Specifically, if the rate of interest is 20 per cent, $1.50 next year is worth $1.50/(1.02) = $1.25 today. The reason is that $1.25 today will grow to $1.50 next year. That is, $1.25(1 + 0.2) = $1.50. Thus, to determine the net return of an investment we must compare the cost incurred today with the value of the benefits *today*.

The **present value (V_0)** of an investment is the value today of all the net cash flows of the investment. Costs or outflows are subtracted from revenues or inflows in each year to find the net cash flow. For a two-period time horizon, V_0 is given by

$$V_0 = R_0 + \frac{R_1}{1 + r} \tag{16-5}$$

where, R_0 is the net cash flow (usually negative during the current year when the investment is made), R_1 is the net cash flow next year, and r is the rate of interest. For example, suppose that a firm purchases a machine this year for $100, and this increases the firm's net income by $120 next year. Suppose also that the rate of interest is 10 per cent and the machine has no salvage or scrap value at the end of the next year. The present value of the machine (V_0) is

$$V_0 = -\$100 + \frac{\$120}{(1 + 0.1)} = -\$100 + \$109.09 = \$9.09$$

This means that the purchase of the machine will increase the wealth of the firm by $9.09.

Suppose the firm had to decide between the above project (with present value of $9.09) and another project which costs $150 and generates an income of $180 next year. The firm should choose the second project because its present value of −$150 + $180/(1 + 0.1) = $13.64 exceeds the present value of $9.09 for the previous project. Such a choice arises because firms do not usually have or cannot usually borrow all of the

---

[6] We assume throughout this discussion that there is no price inflation. This assumption is relaxed in Section 16-4.

529

resources required to undertake all of the projects that have a positive present value.

We will see in the next section that the rule to undertake a project if its present value is positive or to choose the project with the highest present value is a general rule and applies to all projects regardless of the number of periods or years over which the costs and returns of the project are spread. Furthermore this rule is independent of the tastes or time preference of the investor. That is, regardless of the shape and location of the indifference curves of investors, the general investment or capital budgeting rule is to maximize the wealth of the firm. This is achieved by investing in projects with the highest (positive) present value. The tastes of investors will then determine whether they will borrow or lend and how they will choose to use their (maximized) wealth. This means that the owners or stockholders of a firm can appoint an agent or a manager, and they can objectively evaluate his or her performance based exclusively on whether or not he or she has maximized the wealth of the firm in his or her investment decisions. This is the **separation theorem.** However, this holds only if capital markets are perfect and costless (i.e., if borrowers and lenders are too small individually to affect the rate of interest and can borrow or lend at the same rate).

16-3b Present-Value Rule for Investment Decisions: The Multiperiod Case

Most investment projects last longer than (i.e., give rise to cash flows over more than) two periods. Thus, the investment rule given above must be extended to consider many periods (years). This can easily be done by "stretching" Equation (16-5) to deal with many (n) years. This is given by

$$V_0 = R_0 + \frac{R_1}{1 + r} + \frac{R_2}{(1 + r)^2} + \cdots + \frac{R_n}{(1 + r)^n} \tag{16-6}$$

where V_0 is the present value of the investment, R_0 refers to the net cash flow (usually negative during the current year when the investment is made), R_1 is the net cash flow from the investment next year, R_2 is the net cash flow in two years, R_n is the net cash flow in n years, and r is the rate of interest. Net cash flows refer to the revenue of the firm resulting from the investment during any given year minus the expenses or costs of the project during the same year. Thus, Formula (16-5) is a special case of Formula (16-6) applicable when there are no cash flows after the first year.

For example, suppose that a firm purchases a machine this year for $150, and this increases the firm's net income by $100 in each of the next two years. If the rate of interest is 10 per cent and the machine has no salvage value after two years, the present value of the machine (V_0) is

$$V_0 = R_0 + \frac{R_1}{1 + r} + \frac{R_2}{(1 + r)^2} = -\$150 + \frac{\$100}{1 + 0.1} + \frac{\$100}{(1 + 0.1)^2}$$

$$= -\$150 + \$90.91 + \$82.64 = \$23.55$$

This means that the purchase of the machine will increase the wealth of the firm by \$23.55. Specifically, \$100 received next year is worth $\$100/(1 + 0.1) = \$90.91$ this year because \$90.91 this year grows to \$100 next year at $r = 10$ per cent. On the other hand, \$100 received two years from now is worth $\$100/(1 + 0.1)^2 = \$82.64$ this year because \$82.64 this year grows to \$90.91 next year at $r = 10$ per cent,[7] and the \$90.91 next year grows to \$100 the year after (i.e., two years from now) at $r = 10$ per cent. Another way of saying this is that \$82.64 today times $(1 + 0.1)^2$ or 1.21 equals \$100 two years from now.

If the project generated a net cash flow of \$100 in the third year also, this would be "worth" $\$100/(1 + 0.1)^3 = \$100/(1.331) = \$75.13$ this year because \$73.13 this year will grow to \$100 (except for rounding errors) in three years at $r = 10$ per cent. Similarly, \$100 in 10 years is worth $\$100/(1 + 0.1)^{10} = \$38.55$ this year because \$38.55 this year will grow to \$100 in 10 years at $r = 10$ per cent. Finally, \$100 in n years (where n is any number of years) is worth $\$100/(1 + 0.1)^n$ this year because this sum today will grow to \$100 in n years at $r = 10$ per cent.

We can go one step further and say that the present value (V_0) of an investment that yields a constant stream of net cash flows in each future year indefinitely, starting with the next year, is given by

$$V_0 = \frac{R}{r} \tag{16-7}$$

where R is the constant net cash flow received the next year and in every subsequent year (i.e., in perpetuity) and r is the rate of interest. That is,[8]

$$V_0 = \frac{R}{1 + r} + \frac{R}{(1 + r)^2} + \cdots$$

$$= R\left[\frac{1}{1 + r} + \frac{1}{(1 + r)^2} + \frac{1}{(1 + r)^3} + \cdots\right] = \frac{R}{r} \tag{16-7A}$$

[7] Actually (\$82.64) (1.1) equals \$90.904 rather than \$90.91 (as indicated above) because of rounding errors.

[8] For the mathematical derivation of Formula (16-7A), see Section A15 of the Mathematical Appendix.

For example, the present value of $100 next year and in every subsequent year is

$$V_0 = \frac{\$100}{0.1} = \$1,000$$

The reason for this is that $1,000 invested today at $r = 10$ per cent will give a stream of net cash flows of $100 at the end of each future year, starting with next year. Thus, an individual should be indifferent between receiving $1,000 today or $100 for every year into the future. An example of this is the British "consols," which are never repaid, but pay a constant sum forever.

If the interest rate fell to $r = 0.05$, then V_0 in the above example would be $100/0.05 = $2,000$. On the other hand, if r rose to 20 per cent, $V_0 = $100/0.2 = 500. Thus, the present value for any cash flow stream rises when r falls and falls when r rises. This is true not only for an infinite stream of cash flows, but also for a finite one. This can be illustrated by returning to the case where the firm purchased a machine this year for $150 and received net cash flows of $100 in each of the next two years (after which the machine has zero salvage value). We have seen earlier that if $r = 10$ per cent, $V_0 = 23.55. Had $r = 5$ per cent, V_0' would have been

$$V_0' = -\$150 + \frac{\$100}{(1 + 0.1)^1} + \frac{\$100}{(1 + 0.1)^2}$$
$$= -\$150 + \$95.24 + \$90.70 = \$35.94$$

Had $r = 20$ per cent,

$$V_0'' = -\$150 + \frac{\$100}{(1 + 0.2)^1} + \frac{\$100}{(1 + 0.2)^2}$$
$$= -\$150 + \$83.33 + \$69.44 = \$2.77$$

The decline in V_0 when r rises is due to the fact that when r rises, the revenues from the project are "discounted" more heavily than costs since revenues arise later in time than costs.

Finally, note that the cost of an investment need not be incurred entirely during the current year, but may be spread over many years. For example, a firm which purchases a piece of machinery incurs not only the cost of purchasing it, but also the subsequent maintenance costs. It may also have to hire a more skilled operator for the machine at a higher wage. The machine may also have a positive salvage value at the end of its useful life for the firm. All these factors can and should be included in calculating the present value of the machine. Specifically, the cash flows used by the firm to calculate the present value of the machine should be the *net* cash flows. That is, they should include the extra income generated by the machine minus the extra expense to operate the machine during each year. Similarly, the value today of the salvage value of the machine should also be included.

For example, suppose that the benefit and cost of an investment project (the purchase of a piece of machinery) are as given in Table 16-3. The table shows that the machine costs $1,000 to purchase this year and also gives rise to $200, $300, $300, and $400 maintenance and other costs in each of the subsequent four years. The revenues from the investment are $600, $800, $800, and $800, and the salvage value of the machine is $200 at the end of the fourth year. The net revenue is the revenue from the investment minus the cost in each year. The present value coefficient is $1/(1 + 0.1)^n$. For example, for the first year the present value coefficient is $1/(1.01)^1 =$ 0.909. For the second year, it is $1/(1 + 0.1)^2 = 0.826$, and so on. The present value of the net revenue in each year is obtained by multiplying the net revenue (R) by the present value coefficient for that year. By adding together all present values of the net revenues, we get the present value of the project (V_0) of $563. Since V_0 is positive, the firm should purchase the machine.

Sometimes, complications may arise in applying the present-value rule for investment decisions. First, projects may be interdependent so that the stream of net cash flows from a project depends on whether or not other projects are undertaken at the same time. In such a case, the present value of a group of projects may have to be evaluated together and compared with the present value of other groups of projects. Second, it may some- times be difficult to accurately forecast the future stream of net cash flows from a project. Third, the firm may not have the resources and may not be willing or able to borrow to undertake all of the projects that have a posi- tive present value. The firm should then choose those projects with the highest present value.

TABLE 16-3   Benefit-Cost Analysis of an Investment Project

End of Year	Investment (Year 0) and Cost	Revenue	Net Revenue	Present Value Coefficient $1/(1 + 0.1)^n$	Present Value of Net Revenue
0	$1,000	. . .	−$1,000	. . .	−$1,000
1	200	$600	400	0.909	364
2	300	800	500	0.826	413
3	300	800	500	0.751	376
4	400	800	400	0.683	273
4	. . .	200*	200	0.683	137
					$563

*Salvage value.

Example 16-3 **Fields of Education and Lifetime Earnings**

The Facts: Table 16-4 gives the present value of the higher lifetime earnings from receiving the bachelor's degree in various fields. Present values were estimated from National Science Foundation data for the year 1968. The interest rate used to find the present values was 3 per cent. Earnings were assumed to begin on the fifth year after entering college and to continue until retirement, which was assumed to occur 44 years after entering the labor force. Note that only the benefits of going to college are included; the earnings foregone or opportunity costs and other costs (tuition, books, and so on) of going to college are not included.

Comment: The higher earnings of the recipients of the bachelor's degree over the earnings of non-college graduates cannot be attributed entirely to college education. At least in part, the higher incomes of college graduates may be due to their higher level of intelligence, longer working hours, and more inherited wealth than non-college graduates. The higher lifetime earnings in some fields than in others greatly affected the number of students pursuing the bachelorate in the various fields (the costs were probably very similar). For example, nearly 42 per cent of all bachelor's degrees in 1984 were issued in occupation-oriented fields such as business and engineering, up from 23 per cent in 1965–1966, while degrees in liberal arts fell to 7 per cent of the total, from 20 per cent in 1965–1966.

Source: "Liberal-Arts Colleges Bow to the Future," *U.S. News and World Report,* May 23, 1984, p. 67.

TABLE 16-4   **Present Values of Bachelor's Degrees in Various Fields**

Field of Study	Lifetime Earnings*
Mathematics	$342,000
Economics	339,000
Computer Science	307,000
Political Science	300,000
Physics	283,000
Psychology	262,000
Biology	216,000
Sociology	214,000

*Rounded to the nearest thousand.
Source: Assaf Razin and James D. Campbell, "Internal Allocation of University Resources," *Western Economic Journal,* September 1972, pp. 313–317.

16-4

Determinants of the Market Rates of Interest

Until now we have discussed "the" interest rate. However, the rate of interest varies at different times and in different markets. Even at a given point in time and in a specific capital market, there is not a single rate of interest but many. That is, there is a different interest rate on different loans or investments depending on differences in (1) risk, (2) duration of the loan, (3) cost of administering the loan, and (4) tax treatment. We will now briefly examine each of these in turn.

The major reason for differences in rates of interest at a given point in time and place is the risk of the loan. In general, the greater is the risk, the higher is the rate of interest. Two types of risk can be distinguished: default risk and variability risk. **Default risk** refers to the possibility that the loan will not be repaid. If the chance of default is 10 per cent, the lender will usually charge a rate of interest 10 per cent higher than on a loan with no risk of default, such as a government bond. Similarly, loans unsecured by collateral (such as installment credit) usually charge higher rates of interest than loans secured by collateral (such as home mortgages). **Variability risk** refers to the possibility that the yield or return on an investment, such as a stock, may vary considerably above or below the average. Given the usual aversion to risk, investors generally demand a premium or a higher yield for investments whose returns are more uncertain.

The second reason for differences in rates of interest is the duration of the loan. Loans for longer periods of time usually require higher rates of interest than loans for shorter durations. The reason is that the lender has less flexibility or liquidity with loans of longer duration, and so he or she will require a higher rate of interest. It is for this reason that savings deposits offer lower rates of interest than six-months certificates of deposit.[9]

The third reason for differences in rates of interests is the cost of administering the loan. Smaller loans and loans requiring frequent payments (such as installment loans) usually involve greater bookkeeping and service costs per dollar of the loan and, as a result, usually involve a higher interest charge. Finally, the tax treatment of interest and investment income can lead to differences in rates of interest among otherwise comparable loans and investments. For example, state and municipal bonds are exempted from federal income tax, and since investors look at the after-tax return, state and local governments can usually borrow at lower interest rates than corporations.

Thus, at a given point in time and in a given capital market there are a large number of interest rates depending on relative risk, term structure,

---

[9] Regulation may also account for part of the difference.

administration costs, and tax treatment. Yet, all of these rates of interest are related. If individuals and firms collectively decide to save less (a leftward shift in the aggregate supply curve of savings), interest rates will rise. Interest rates will also rise if the time preference of consumers shifts in favor of the present or if the net productivity or yield of capital increases. In addition, a rise in short-term rates will lead to higher long-term rates, and vice versa. Furthermore, higher interest rates for comparable instruments in one market than in another market will lead to an outflow of funds from the latter to the former. These flows of funds will reduce (and may eventually eliminate) interest rate differences between the two markets. Specifically, the supply curve of funds will shift to the left (i.e., the supply of funds decreases) and interest rates will rise in the market with lower rates of interest. The opposite occurs in the market with the higher rates of interest and interest rates will fall there.

Finally, a distinction must be made between real and nominal or money interest rates. Until this point, we have been discussing the **real rate of interest** (**r**). This refers to the premium on a unit of a commodity or real consumption income today compared to a unit of the commodity or real consumption income in the future. However, in the everyday usage of the term, the interest rate refers to the nominal or money rate of interest. The **nominal rate of interest** (r') refers to the premium on a unit on a monetary claim today compared to a unit of monetary claim in the future. The nominal rate of interest (r') is affected by the anticipated rate of price inflation (i), while the real rate of interest is not. Thus, the nominal rate of interest equals the real rate of interest plus the anticipated rate of price inflation. That is,

$$r' = r + i \tag{16-8}$$

The reason for this is that during the period of the loan, the general price level may rise (i.e., inflation may occur) so that the loan is repaid with dollars of lower purchasing power than the dollars borrowed. Therefore, the nominal rate of interest must be sufficiently high to cover any increase in the price level (or in the price of real claims) during the loan period. It is primarily to avoid this complication (and to deal with the real rate of interest) that we chose to borrow and lend a commodity in Sections 16-1 and 16-2.

Anyone who borrows money now and repays in money in the future must expect to pay an additional monetary amount to cover any anticipated increase in the monetary price of real claims by the time of repayment. Only if anticipated inflation is zero will $r' = r$. Since some price inflation is always occurring, r' usually exceeds r. For example, if $r' = 11$ per cent and $i = 6$ per cent, then $r = 5$ per cent. We concentrated on the real rate of interest throughout most of the chapter because it is the real, and not the nominal, rate of interest that primarily affects incentives to borrow and lend, and to save and invest.

Example 16-4 **Nominal and Real Rates of Interest: 1970–1983**

The Facts: Table 16-5 shows the nominal, before-tax and after-tax, annual interest rates on 6-month U.S. Treasury bills and the change in the Consumer Price Index from 1970 through 1983. The assumed tax rate is 40 per cent. Note that from 1974 through 1980, the nominal before-tax interest rate was smaller than the change in the Consumer Price Index. Thus, the real rate was negative. The real after-tax interest rate was negative in every year except 1982 and 1983.

Comment: U.S. investors have earned very low or negative real after-tax interest rates for over a half century. This is certainly one of the causes for the relatively low rate of savings in the United States and resulted in a smaller rate of growth of the economy.

16-5

Applications

In this section we discuss some important applications of the theory presented in the chapter. These include investment in human capital, the effect of investment in human capital on hours of work, the pricing of

TABLE 16-5   Nominal and Real Interest Rates on
6-Month U.S. Treasury Bills: 1979–1983

Year	Nominal Interest Rate Before Tax	Nominal Interest Rate After 40% Tax	Change in Consumer Price Index
1970	6.56	3.94	5.9
1971	4.51	2.71	4.3
1972	4.47	2.68	3.3
1973	7.18	4.31	6.2
1974	7.93	4.76	11.0
1975	6.12	3.67	9.1
1976	5.27	3.16	5.8
1977	5.51	3.31	6.5
1978	7.57	4.54	7.7
1979	10.02	6.01	11.3
1980	11.37	6.82	13.5
1981	13.78	8.27	10.4
1982	11.08	6.65	6.1
1983	8.75	5.25	3.2

Source: Council of Economic Advisers, *Economic Report of the President* (Washington, D.C.: U.S. Government Printing Office, 1984), pp. 283, 298.

537

exhaustible resources, the management of nonexhaustible resources, and socialism and the rate of interest. These applications clearly indicate the usefulness and applicability of the theory presented in this chapter.

Application 1: Investment in Human Capital

Investment in human capital is any activity on the part of a worker or potential worker that increases his or her productivity. It refers to expenditures on education, job training, health, migration to areas of better job opportunities, and so on. Like any other investment, investments in human capital involve costs and entail returns. For example, going to college involves explicit and implicit or opportunity costs. The explicit costs are tuition, books, fees, and all other out-of-pocket expenses of attending college. The implicit costs are the earnings or opportunities foregone while attending college (the individual could have worked or could have worked more by not attending college). As we have seen in Example 8-1, the implicit or opportunity costs of attending college are generally higher than the explicit costs. The returns of attending college take the form of higher lifetime earnings compared to the lifetime earnings without a college education (see Example 16-3).

As with any other investment, we can find the present value of the stream of net cash flows from the college degree. Net cash flows are negative during the college years (because of the explicit and implicit or opportunity costs of attending college) and positive during the working life of the college graduate until retirement. The same is generally true for other investments in human capital. That is, they also lead to a stream of net cash flows and should be undertaken only if their present value (V_0) is positive or higher than the present value of other investments (such as the purchasing of a stock). Using this method, it was estimated that the return to a college education was about 10 per cent to 15 per cent per year during the 1950s and 1960s. This was substantially higher than the return on similarly risky investments (such as the purchasing of a stock). Since the early 1970s, and as a result of the sharp increases in tuition and relatively lower starting salaries, the returns to a college education declined to about 7 per cent to 8 per cent per year.[10]

These studies, however, face a number of statistical problems. For example, not all expenditures for education represent an investment (as, for example, when a physics student takes a course in Shakespeare). In addition, at least part of the higher earnings of college graduates may be due to their being more intelligent or from working harder than non-college graduates (see the next application). On the other side of the coin, there are benefits from a college education that cannot be easily measured. These are that college graduates seem to enjoy their jobs more than non-college graduates, have happier marriages, and generally suffer less mental illness.

---

[10] Richard B. Freeman, "The Decline in the Economic Rewards to College Education," *The Review of Economics and Statistics,* February 1977, pp. 18–29.

In spite of these measurement difficulties, the concept of investment in human capital is very important and commonly used. Most differences in labor incomes can be explained by differences in human capital. Juries routinely determine the amount of damages to award injury victims (or their survivors, in case of fatal accidents) on the basis of the human capital or income lost by the injured party. Developing countries complain about the "brain drain" or the emigration to rich nations of their young and skilled people (who embody a great deal of human capital), and so on.

Application 2: Investment in Human Capital and Hours of Work

People may work more hours as a result of investment in human capital. This can be shown with the aid of Figure 16-7. Figure 16-7 is similar to Figure 14-11, used to analyze the effect of a negative income tax on work effort. In Figure 16-7, the movement from left to right on the horizontal axis measures hours of leisure per day. The movement from right to left measures the hours of work. The sum of the hours of leisure and the hours of work always add up to the 24 hours of the day. The vertical axis measures the daily income of the individual.

We begin by assuming that the individual portrayed in Figure 16-7 has a daily property income of FC ($30). If the hourly wage is $2.50, the individual's budget line is FB (so that the negative of the slope of the budget line gives the wage rate). Before investing in education, the individual maximizes utility or satisfaction at point E, where indifference curve U is tangent to budget line FB. The individual works 8 hours per day and has a daily income of $50 (FC or $30 from property income plus HE or $20 from working 8 hours at the wage rate of $2.50 per hour).

Suppose that now the individual decides to invest all of his or her endowed property income in education (i.e., sacrifice all of his or her non-human capital) and that as a result he or she can earn a wage rate of $5 per hour. The budget line of the individual is now CA (see the figure), reflecting zero property income available for consumption and the wage of $5 per hour (the negative of the slope of budget line CA). Assuming that the individual's tastes remain unchanged as a result of the education, the individual will now maximize utility at point G, where indifference curve U is tangent to budget line CA. The individual now works 14 hours per day for a daily income of $70 (all of which is labor income).

Thus, education seems to induce individuals to work more hours (i.e., have fewer leisure hours) and earn higher incomes. Having made the investment in education, the individual will work more hours and earn a higher income to maximize utility. This seems to be confirmed in empirical studies. For example, Lindsay found that physicians work on average 62 hours per week, far more than the average worker.[11] The same seems to be true for other professionals as opposed to nonprofessionals.

[11] C. M. Lindsay, "Real Returns to Medical Education," *Journal of Human Resources*, Summer 1982, p. 338.

539

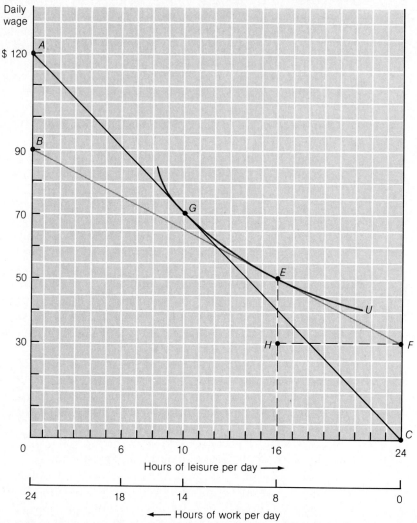

FIGURE 16-7.
Education and
Hours of Work

The individual has a daily property income of FC = $30 and faces budget line FB
(with the negative of the slope giving the wage of $2.50 per hour). The individual
maximizes utility at point E, where indifference curve U is tangent to FB. He or she
works 8 hours and has a daily income of $50 (of which HE = $20 is labor income).
Suppose the individual invests all property income in education and as a result earns
$5 per hour. The budget line is now CA. The individual maximizes utility at point G,
where U is tangent to CA and works 14 hours for a daily income of $70.

Application 3: Pricing of Exhaustible Resources
One of the great concerns of modern societies is that the world's resources
will become depleted. Resources can generally be classified as exhaustible
or nonexhaustible. **Exhaustible resources** are those, such as petroleum and
othr minerals, which are available in fixed quantities and are nonreplen-
ishable. **Nonexhaustible resources** are those such as fertile land, forests,

rivers, and fish which can last forever, if they are properly managed. We examine the pricing of exhaustible or nonrenewable resources here and will look at the pricing of nonexhaustible or renewable resources, under proper management, in Application 4.

Since the early 1970s (and to large extent as a result of the petroleum crisis), there has been great concern that exhaustible resources may soon be depleted. Doomsday models were built that predicted when various exhaustible resources would run out, thereby threatening the living standard and the very future of mankind.[12] Economists, while not entirely shrugging off the danger, have been skeptical for the most part. They have indicated that the price of exhaustible resources tend to rise over time, and this leads to conservation and to the discovery of substitutes. Thus, doomsday models should not be taken too seriously. Let us see more precisely why this is so.

We begin by pointing out that the owner of an exhaustible resource will keep it in the ground and available for future use if the present value of the resource in future use in greater than its current price. For example, suppose that the price of the resource is $100 per unit today, it is expected to be $120 next year, and the market rate of interest is 10 per cent per year. The owner will sell the resource next year since the present value of a unit of the resource sold next year is $120/(1 + 0.1) = $109.09, and this exceeds its price of $100 today.

In a perfectly competitive market, the net price of the resource (i.e., the price minus the cost of extraction) will rise at a rate equal to the market rate of interest, and this will spread available supplies over time (see Applications 10-1). If the net price of a resource is expected to rise faster than the market rate of interest, more of the resource will be held off the market for future sale. This increases the current price and reduces the future price until the present value of the future price is equal to the present price. On the other hand, if the net price of the resource is expected to rise at a slower rate than the market rate of interest, more of the resource will be sold in the present. This will reduce the present price and increase the future price until the present value of the expected future price equals the present price. This is shown in Figure 16-8.

In the left panel of the figure, time is measured along the horizontal axis, and the price of the exhaustible resource and its average total cost (assumed to be constant, and thus equal to marginal cost) are measured along the vertical axis. The right panel shows the market demand curve for the resource (input). The net price or benefit to the owners of the resource is given by the difference (AB at time zero) between the (gross)

[12] See Jay W. Forrester, *World Dynamics* (Cambridge, Mass.: Wright-Allen Press, 1971), Donella H. Meadows et al., *The Limits to Growth: A Report for the Club of Rome's Project on the Predicament of Mankind* (New York: Universe Books, 1972), and Mihajlo Mesarovic and Eduard Pestel, *Mankind at the Turning Point: The Second Report to the Club of Rome* (New York: The American Library, 1974).

FIGURE 16-8. The Price of Exhaustible Resources

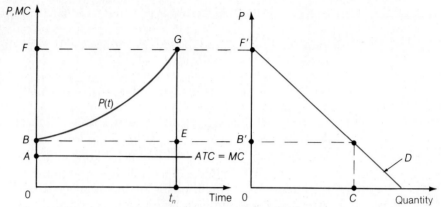

In the left panel, time is measured along the horizontal axis, and the price of the exhaustible resource and its average cost (assumed constant and equal to MC) is measured along the vertical axis. The right panel shows the demand curve for the resource. At P = OB, the net benefit is AB per unit and the quantity demanded is OC. Over time, the net benefit or net price rises at the same rate as the market rate of interest until at P = OF, the supply of the resource is exhausted (point G in the left panel) and the quantity demanded is zero (point F′ in the right panel).

price of the resource and the assumed constant cost of extracting it. The owner can obtain these net benefits now or in the future (by leaving the resource in the ground). For the owner of the resource to be indifferent between extracting the resource now or in the future, the net benefit or net price of the resource must appreciate over time at a rate equal to the market rate of interest.

The right panel of Figure 16-8 shows that at the resource (gross) price P = OB′, the quantity demanded of the resource is OC. Over time, the net price rises at the same rate as the market rate of interest (from AB to EG in the left panel) until at P = OF, the supply of the resource is exhausted (point G in the left panel) and the quantity demanded of the resource is zero (point F′ in the right panel). Thus, in perfectly competitive markets, exhaustion of the resource coincides with zero quantity demanded. If exhaustion occurs before time t_n at P = OF, owners of the resource could have sold the resource at a higher price (and net benefit) over time than indicated by line BG. On the other hand, if the resource is not exhausted by t_n at P = OF, owners would have gained by selling the resource at a lower price over time. In the real world, the net price of most resources increased at a smaller rate than the market rate of interest (and the net price of many resources actually fell) over time because of new discoveries, technological improvements in extraction, and conservation.

Application 4: Management of Nonexhaustible Resources
Nonexhaustible or renewable resources such as forests and fish grow naturally over time. Unless the rate of utilization of the resource exceeds its

rate of natural growth, the resource will never be depleted.[13] If the renewable resource is trees, the question is when should the trees be cut? The answer (as you might suspect by now) is that the trees should be allowed to grow as long as the rate of growth in the net value of the trees exceeds the market rate of interest. Cutting the trees when the rate of growth in their net value exceeds the market rate of interest would be equivalent to taking money out of a bank paying a higher rate of interest and depositing the money in another bank that pays a lower rate of interest. We can analyze this with the aid of Figure 16-9.

The top panel of Figure 16-9 shows the net value of the trees if harvested at time t. This is given by the $V(t)$ curve. The net value is the total market value of the trees minus the cost of harvesting them. We assume zero maintenance or management costs. The top panel shows that $V(t)$ grows at an increasing rate at first. At time $t = 3$ (point A), diminishing returns begin. $V(t)$ reaches the maximum value of \$14 million at $t = 9$ (point B), after which disease, age, and decay set in.

When should the trees be cut? The answer is not at $t = 9$ when $V(t)$ is maximum. That would be the case only if the market rate of interest were zero. With a positive market rate of interest, the correct answer is to cut the trees when the growth in the net value of the standing trees (ΔV) is equal to the growth of the net receipts from cutting the trees and investing the proceeds at the market rate of interest (rV). That is, the trees should be cut when

$$\Delta V = rV \tag{16-9}$$

or

$$\Delta V/V = r \tag{16-9A}$$

This says that trees should be cut when the *rate* of growth in the value of the standing trees ($\Delta V/V$) equals the market *rate* of interest (r).

In terms of Figure 16-9, the trees should be cut at $t = 6$ when the ΔV curve crosses the rV curve (point C' in the bottom panel). The ΔV curve (in the bottom panel) is the marginal value curve or slope of the $V(t)$ curve in the top panel (i.e., $\Delta V = MV$). The rV curve in the bottom panel is 0.25 or 25 per cent of the $V(t)$ curve, at $r = 25$ per cent. To the left of point C', MV exceeds rV (i.e., $\Delta V/V > r$) and it pays for the firm to leave the trees to continue to grow. To the right of point C', MV is smaller than rV (i.e., $\Delta V/V < r$) and it pays for the firm to cut the trees. The optimal choice is to

[13] The term renewable is, perhaps, more appropriate than nonexhaustible because if the rate of utilization of the resource exceeds its natural growth rate, the resource can be exhausted. For example, if you cut all trees or catch all the fish now, there will be no trees or fish in the future.

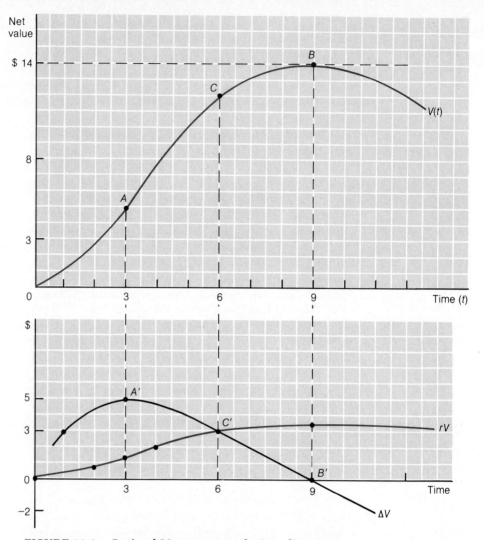

FIGURE 16-9.   *Optimal Management of a Standing Forest*
The top panel shows the net value of the trees if harvested at time t, V(t). The trees should be cut when the growth in the net value of the standing trees (ΔV) is equal to the growth in the net receipts from cutting the trees and investing the proceeds at the market rate of interest (rV). This occurs at t = 6 when the ΔV or MV curve crosses the rV curve (point C' in the bottom panel) and ΔV/V = r.

cut the trees at point $t = 6$ (point C', where MV = rV). This is the usual marginal rule applicable in all optimization decisions.

Application 5: Socialism and the Rate of Interest
Throughout history, interest has been attacked as immoral by many, including Moses, Aristotle, and more recently, Karl Marx. The latter

viewed interest as capitalistic exploitation by the idle rich. Today, communist nations, such as the Soviet Union, assert that interest plays no role in their system. This is not true. In the Soviet Union, implicit interest rates are now used (even though they are not so called) in making intertemporal decisions.

Originally, Soviet planners did not use interest rates in their investment decisions but simply added together the benefits and the costs of a project regardless of when these were received or incurred. One ruble today was considered to be equivalent to one ruble in the future. As a result, they were unable to determine the most productive use of scarce resources over time. That is, planners implicitly assumed a zero rate of interest. At the implicit zero rate of interest, many more projects were proposed than could be undertaken with their limited resources, and no clear rule was readily available for choosing the most productive among the proposed projects. This certainly proved costly in terms of missed opportunities for more rapid growth.

Subsequently, in order to choose among the most worthwhile investment projects, Soviet planners started to exclude all projects with a payback period of four years or more. The **payback period** refers to the number of years it takes for the project to pay for itself (i.e., generate enough output to cover the cost of the project). A project that cost 120 rubles this year and generated an output worth 40 rubles in each of the next four years was said to have a payback of 3 years. On the other hand, a project that cost 100 rubles this year and generated an output of 25 rubles in each of the next four years was said to have a payback period of 4 years. According to the decision rule that a project should have a payback period of less than four years, planners would adopt the first, but not the second, project.

Yet, the use of a payback period was a decision rule roughly equivalent to the use of the rate of interest (whether Soviet planners want to admit it or not). For example, the project that cost 120 rubles this year and generated output of 40 rubles in each of the four subsequent years has a productivity of 33 per cent (the total output of 160 rubles over the four years divided by the original cost of the project of 120 rubles *at a zero rate of interest*). The second project that cost 100 rubles this year and generated an output of 25 rubles in each of the four subsequent years has a zero productivity at $r = 0$ per cent and would not be undertaken. Adopting a rule of a payback period of less than four years for the above projects is equivalent to using a positive rate of interest. Using a payback period of 3 years, the first project should have been undertaken, but not the second. However, resources would certainly have been used more efficiently in the Soviet Union if the rate of interest had been used explicitly in investment decisions and if interest rates had been applied uniformly across all sectors of the economy.[14]

[14] See Judith Thornton, "Differential Capital Charges and Resource Allocation in Soviet Industry," *Journal of Political Economy*, May/June 1971, pp. 545–561.

Summary

1. Given the consumer's income or endowment for this year and the next, and the rate of interest, we can define the consumer's budget line. The rate of interest is the premium received next year for lending or borrowing one dollar this year. The optimal consumer's choice involves lending or borrowing so as to reach the highest possible indifference curve showing the consumer's time preference between present and future consumption. The wealth of an individual is given by the sum of the present income and the present value of future income. If the rate of interest rises, the borrower will borrow less and the lender will usually lend more. The equilibrium rate of interest is determined at the intersection of the market demand curve for borrowing and the market supply curve for lending.

2. For an isolated individual, the optimal saving and investment is given by the point where the production-possibilities curve is tangent to an indifference curve. With saving and investment, and borrowing and lending, the optimal choice of the individual is first to maximize wealth (by reaching the market line that is tangent to the production-possibilities curve) and then to borrow or lend along the market line until he or she reaches the highest indifference curve possible. The equilibrium rate of interest is given by the intersection of (1) the aggregate demand curve for borrowing and the aggregate supply curve of lending, or (2) the aggregate demand curve for investment and the aggregate supply curve of savings.

3. A firm should undertake an investment only if the present value of the investment is positive. The present value (V_0) of the investment is the value today from the stream of the net cash flows (positive and negative) from the investment. In choosing between any two projects, the firm will maximize attained wealth by undertaking the project with the highest present value. The separation theorem refers to the independence of the optimum production decision from the individual's preferences in perfect capital markets. The present value of a constant sum received at the end of each year, indefinitely, is given by the net revenue in one year divided by the rate of interest.

4. The rate of interest usually varies at different times and in different markets. Even at a given point in time and in a specific capital market, there is not a single rate of interest, but many. That is, there is a different interest rate on loans or investments depending on differences in (1) default and variability risks, (2) duration of the loan, (3) cost of administering the loan, and (4) tax treatment. Interest rates rise if society decides to save less or to borrow and invest more. The nominal rate of interest equals the real rate of interest plus the anticipated rate of price inflation.

5. Investment in human capital refers to expenditures on education, job training, health, or migration to areas of better job opportunities that increase the productivity of an individual. Like any other investment, investments in human capital involve costs and entail returns. Education seems to induce people to work more hours. The net price of exhaustible resources tends to rise at the same rate as the market rate of interest, and this spreads the available supply over time and stimulates the discovery of substitutes. A nonexhaustible resource should be harvested when the growth in its net value equals the market rate of interest. An implicit and approximate rate of interest is used in investment decisions under socialism.

Glossary

Endowment position   The quantity of a commodity that the consumer receives in each year.

Rate of interest (r)   The premium received in one year for lending one dollar this year.

Wealth   The individual's income this year plus the present value of future income.

Production-possibilities curve   It shows the various increases in output in the next period by investing various quantities during the present period.

Saving   The refraining from present consumption.

Investment   The formation of new capital assets.

Market line   A line from any point on the production-possibilities curve showing the various amounts of a commodity that the individual can consume in each period by borrowing or lending.

Capital budgeting   The ranking of all investment projects from the highest present value to the lowest.

Present value (V_0)   The value today from the stream of net cash flows (positive and negative) from an investment project.

Separation theorem   The independence of the optimum investment decision from the individual's preferences.

Default risk   The possibility that a loan will not be repaid.

Variability risk   The possibility that the return on an investment, such as on a stock, may vary considerably above or below the average.

Real rate of interest (r)   The premium on a unit of a commodity or real consumption income today compared to a unit of the commodity or real consumption income in the future.

Nominal rate of interest (r')   The real rate of interest plus the anticipated rate of price inflation.

Investment in human capital   Any activity, such as education and training, that increases an individual's productivity.

Exhaustible resources   Nonrenewable resources, such as petroleum and other minerals, which are available in fixed quantities and are non-replenishable.

Nonexhaustible resources   Renewable resources, such as fertile land, forests, rivers, and fish, which need never be depleted, if they are properly managed.

Payback period   The number of years it takes for the project to pay for itself.

Questions for Review

1. (a) What is intertemporal choice?
   (b) Why are intertemporal choices important?
   (c) In what way is intertemporal choice similar to consumer demand theory?

2. (a) What is meant by endowment position? Rate of interest? Wealth?
   (b) What does the budget line measure in intertemporal choice?
   (c) What happens to the budget line if the individual's wealth increases?
   (d) What do indifference curves measure in intertemporal choice?

3. (a) Why do some individuals lend part of their present income?
   (b) How does an individual determine the optimal amount to lend?
   (c) What happens to the amount that an individual lends if the rate of interest increases?

4. (a) Why do some individuals borrow against their future income?
   (b) How does an individual determine the optimal amount to borrow?
   (c) What happens to the amount that an individual borrows if the rate of interest increases?

5. (a) How is the market rate of interest determined in a purely exchange economy?
   (b) What happens if the rate of interest rises above its equilibrium level?
   (c) What happens if the rate of interest falls below the equilibrium level?

6. (a) How are saving and investment shown on production-possibilities curve?
   (b) How is the average yield or return on investment shown on the production-possibilities curve?
   (c) What happens to the average yield as the amount invested increases? Why?
   (d) What is the optimal choice of saving and investment for an isolated individual?

7. (a) What does a market line show?
   (b) What level of investment maximizes the wealth of the individual?
   (c) What level of borrowing or lending will maximize the individual's satisfaction after he or she has invested the optimal amount?

(d) Why is the individual's optimal choice with saving and investment, and borrowing or lending, superior to saving and investing alone, or to borrowing or lending only?

8. (a) What is the relationship between borrowing and lending at equilibrium?
   (b) Must savings equal investment for the economy as a whole at equilibrium?
   (c) Must savings equal investment for any one individual in the economy at equilibrium?
   (d) What happens if the rate of interest is above equilibrium? Below equilibrium?

9. What is
   (a) capital budgeting?
   (b) present value?
   (c) net revenue?
   (d) the separation theorem?

10. (a) What is the formula to find the present value of a project?

(b) When should a project be undertaken?
(c) How can we compare two projects?
(d) How can the present value of a constant stream of revenue received indefinitely at the end of each year be found?

11. (a) What is default risk? Variability risk?
    (b) What are the reasons for differences in rates of interest?
    (c) What is the real rate of interest? The nominal rate of interest?

12. (a) What is investment in human capital?
    (b) Why does education seem to induce people to work more hours?
    (c) How is the price of an exhaustible resource determined?
    (d) How should nonexhaustible resources be managed?
    (e) Are there interest rates under socialism?

Problems

1. Suppose that an individual is endowed with $Y_0 = 7.5$ units of a commodity this year and $Y_1 = 2.75$ units next year. Draw a figure showing that the individual lends 2.5 units of this year's endowment for 2.75 units next year. What is the rate of interest? On the same figure show that the individual lends 3 units for 4.2 units. What would the rate of interest be then?

2. Suppose that an individual is endowed with $Y_0 = 2.5$ units of a commodity this year and $Y_1 = 8.25$ units next year. Draw a figure showing that the individual borrows 2.5 units this year and repays 2.75 units next year. What is the rate of interest? On the same figure show that the individual borrows 2 units this year and repays 2.80 units next year. What would the rate of interest be then?

3. Assume that (1) the consumer of Problem 2 (call him or her individual B or the borrower) is a different individual than the consumer of Problem 1 (call him or her individual A or the lender), and (2) both individuals A and B have the same tastes or time preference. Draw a figure showing how the equilibrium rate of interest is determined if A and B are the only

individuals in the market. What would happen at $r = 40$ per cent? At $r = 5$ per cent?

★4. Assume that (1) individual A and B have identical endowments of a commodity of $Y_0 = 5$ this year and $Y_1 = 6$ next year, and (2) the optimal choice for individual B is to borrow 2.5 units this year and repay 3 units next year, while the optimal choice for individual A is to lend 2.5 units this year and receive 3 units next year. Draw a figure similar to Figure 16-1 and 16-2 for the above. What is the equilibrium rate of interest if A and B are the only individuals in the market? On the same figure show that at $r = 50$ per cent, individual B wants to borrow 2 units instead of 2.5 this year and repay 3 units next year, while individual A wants to lend 3 units this year and receive 4.5 units next year. Why is $r = 50$ per cent not the equilibrium rate of interest?

★5. (a) Why does a lender's supply curve of loans (lending) bend backward at sufficiently high rates of interest?
    (b) Why is a borrower's demand curve for loans (borrowing) negatively sloped throughout?

★6. Draw a figure similar to Figure 16-5 showing

that a rise in the rate of interest will reduce the individual's level of investment and borrowing.

7. Starting from Figure 16-5, draw a figure showing that if indifference curve U_5 had been tangent to market line HW_0' to the right of point A, the individual would have been dissaving.

8. Starting from Figure 16-5, draw a figure showing that if indifference curve U_5 had been tangent to market line HW_0' to the left of point H, the individual would have been saving more than he invested.

9. Draw a figure showing the value today of $100 received at the end of each of 10 years at the rate of interest of 10 per cent.

10. Find the value to which $1 this year grows in each of the next five years at (round values to 4 decimal places) (1) $r = 5$ per cent, (2) $r = 10$ per cent, (3) $r = 15$ per cent, (4) $r = 20$ per cent, and (5) $r = 25$ per cent.

★11. Reestimate the present value of the project given in Table 16-3 for $r = 5$ per cent.

12. Draw a figure showing the effect of the following on the price of an exhaustible resource.
    (a) A decrease in the market rate of interest.
    (b) An increase in the demand for the resource.

Supplementary Readings

An excellent presentation of the topics covered in this chapter is found in

George J. Stigler, *The Theory of Price,* 3rd ed. (New York: Macmillan, 1966), Chapter 17.

The classical reference for the theory of interest is

Irwin Fisher, *The Theory of Interest* (New York: Macmillan, 1930).

For investment theory, see

Robert M. Solow, *Capital Theory and the Rate of Return* (Amsterdam: North-Holland, 1964).

On human capital, see

Theodore W. Shultz, "Investment in Human Capi-

tal," *The American Economic Review,* March 1961, pp. 1–17.

Gary S. Becker, *Human Capital: A Theoretical and Empirical Analysis with Special Reference to Education.* (New York: Columbia University Press, 1975).

For the economics of exhaustible resources, see

Harold Hotelling, "The Economics of Exhaustible Resources," *The Journal of Political Economy,* April 1931, pp. 137–175.

Robert M. Solow, "The Economics of Resources or the Resources of Economics," *The American Economic Review,* May 1974, pp. 1–14.

General Equilibrium, Welfare Economics, and the Role of Government

SIX

Part Six (Chapters 17–19) presents the theory of general equilibrium and welfare economics, and examines the role of government. Chapter 17 presents general equilibrium theory. This examines the interdependence or relationship among all products and input markets and shows how the various individual markets (studied in Parts Two through Five) fit together to form an integrated economic system. Chapter 18 studies welfare economics within a general equilibrium framework. It examines questions of economic efficiency in the production of output and equity in the distribution of income. Finally, Chapter 19 examines externalities, public goods, and the role of government. It studies why externalities (such as pollution) and the existence of public goods (such as national defense) lead to economic inefficiencies. It also presents policies that can be used to overcome these inefficiencies.

General Equilibrium Analysis

Chapter 17

17-1 Partial vs. General Equilibrium Analysis

17-2 General Equilibrium of Exchange

17-3 General Equilibrium of Production

17-4 Derivation of the Production-Possibilities Frontier

17-5 General Equilibrium of Production and Exchange

17-6 Applications

Examples

17-1 The Effect of a Reduction in the Demand for Domestically Produced Automobiles in the United States

17-2 Exchange in POW Camps

17-3 International Specialization in Production, and International Trade

Applications

Application 1: Input-Output Analysis: The General Concept

Application 2: Input-Output Analysis: Numerical Example

Application 3: The Basis and the Gains from Trade Between Two Nations

Application 4: Measures of Income Inequality

Preview Questions

What is general equilibrium analysis?

What is partial equilibrium analysis?

What is the relationship between partial and general equilibrium analyses?

Under what conditions is partial equilibrium analysis appropriate?

When is an economy in general equilibrium of exchange?

When is an economy in general equilibrium of production?

How is the production-possibilities frontier derived?

When is an economy simultaneously in general equilibrium of production and exchange?

What is input-output analysis?

What is the relationship between input-output analysis and general equilibrium theory?

Until this point we have examined the behavior of individual decision-making units (individuals as consumers of commodities and suppliers of inputs, and firms as employers of inputs and producers of commodities) and the workings of individual markets for commodities and inputs under various market structures. Generally missing from our presentation was an examination of how the various individual pieces fit together to form an integrated economic system.

In this chapter we take up this topic and examine the interdependence or relationship among the various decision-making units and markets in the economy. This allows us to trace both the effect of a change in any part of the economic system on every other part of the system, and also the repercussions from the latter on the former. We begin the chapter by distinguishing between partial equilibrium analysis and general equilibrium analysis and examining the conditions under which each type of analysis is appropriate. Then, we present the conditions required for the economy to be in general equilibrium of exchange, production, and of production and exchange simultaneously. In the process, we also derive the production-possibilities frontier.

Subsequently, we examine input-output analysis as an important and practical application of general equilibrium analysis. Then, we apply the tools of analysis presented in the chapter to examine the basis for specialization in production and the gains from trade between two nations. Finally, we discuss measures of income inequality. These applications and the examples presented in the chapter clearly indicate the usefulness and relevance of the theory.

17-1

Partial vs. General Equilibrium Analysis

In Parts II–V (Chapters 3–16) we conducted **partial equilibrium analysis.** That is, we studied the behavior of individual decision-making units and individual markets, *viewed in isolation.* We have examined how an individual maximizes satisfaction subject to his or her income constraint (Part II: Chapters 3–6), how a firm minimizes its costs of production (Part III: Chapters 7–9) and maximizes profits under various market structures (Part IV: Chapters 10–13), and how the price and employment of each type of input is determined (Part V: Chapters 14–16). In doing so, we have abstracted from all the interconnections that exist between the market under study and the rest of the economy (the *"ceteris paribus"* assumption). In short, we have shown how demand and supply in each market determine the equilibrium price and quantity in that market, *independently of other markets.*

However, a change in any market has spillover effects on other markets, and the change in these other markets will, in turn, have repercussions or feedback effects on the original market. These are studied by **general equilibrium analysis.** That is, general equilibrium analysis studies the interdependence or interconnections that exist among all markets and prices in the economy, and attempts to give a complete, explicit, and simultaneous answer to the questions of what, how, and for whom to produce. In terms of Figure 1-1 (showing the circular flow of economic activity), general equilibrium analysis examines simultaneously the links among all commodity and input markets, rather than studying each market in isolation.

For example, a change in the demand and price for new, domestically produced automobiles will immediately affect the demand and price of steel, glass, and rubber (the inputs of automobiles), as well as the demand, wages, and income of autoworkers and of the workers in these other industries. The demand and price of gasoline and of public transportation (as well as the wages and income of workers in these industries) are also affected. These affected industries have spillover effects on still other industries, until the entire economic system is more or less involved and all prices and quantities are affected. This is like throwing a rock in a pond and examining the ripples emanating in every direction until the stability of the entire pond is affected. The size of the ripples declines as they move farther and farther away from the point of impact. Similarly, industries further removed or less related to the automobile industry are less affected than more closely related industries.

What is important is that the effect that a change in the automobile

554

industry has on the rest of the economy will have repercussions (through changes in relative prices and incomes) on the automobile industry itself. This is like the return of feedback effect of the ripples in the pond after reaching the shores. These repercussions or feedback effects are likely to significantly modify the original partial-equilibrium conclusions (price and output) reached by analyzing the automobile industry in isolation (see Example 17-1).

When (as in the above automobile example) the repercussions or feedback effects from the other industries are significant, partial equilibrium analysis is inappropriate. By measuring only the *impact* effect on price and output, partial equilibrium analysis provides a misleading measure of the total, final effect after all the repercussions or feedback effects from the original change have occurred. On the other hand, if the industry in which the original change occurs is small and the industry has few direct links with the rest of the economy (for example, the U.S. wristwatch industry), then partial equilibrium analysis provides a good first approximation to the results sought.

The logical question is why not use general equilibrium analysis all the time and immediately obtain the total, direct and indirect results of a change on the industry (in which the change originated) as well as on all the other industries and markets in the economy. The answer is that general equilibrium analysis, dealing with each and all industries in the economy at the same time, is by its very nature very difficult, time consuming, and expensive. Happily for the practical economist, partial equilibrium analysis often suffices. In any event, partial equilibrium analysis represents the appropriate point of departure, both for the relaxation of more and more of the "*ceteris paribus*" or "other things equal" assumptions, and for the inclusion of more and more industries in the analysis, as required.

The first and simplest general equilibrium model was introduced in 1874 by the great French economist, Léon Walras.[1] This and subsequent general equilibrium models are necessarily mathematical in nature and include one equation for each commodity and input demanded and supplied in the economy, as well as market clearing equations.[2] More recently, economists have extended and refined the general equilibrium model theoretically and proved that under perfect competition, a general equilibrium solution of the model usually exists, under which all markets are *simultaneously* in equilibrium.[3] A recent simplification and important practical application of general equilibrium analysis is provided by input-output analysis. This is presented in Applications 1 and 2.

---

[1] Léon Walras, *Elements of Pure Economics*, translated by William Jaffé (Homewood, Ill.: Irwin, 1954).

[2] See Section A16 of the Mathematical Appendix at the end of the text.

[3] Kenneth J. Arrow and Gerald Debreu, "Existence of an Equilibrium for a Competitive Economy," *Econometrica*, July 1954, pp. 265–290, and Lionel W. McKenzie, "On the Existence of General Equilibrium for a Competitive Market," *Econometrica*, January 1959, pp. 54–71.

Example 17-1 The Effect of a Reduction in the Demand for Domestically Produced Automobiles in the United States

The Facts: With the sharp increase in the price of imported petroleum from 1973 to 1980, the demand for new and large, domestically produced automobiles declined, as from D to D' in panel a of Figure 17-1, while the demand for small fuel-efficient, foreign-produced automobiles increased. This reduced the real (i.e., the inflation-adjusted) price and quantity of domestically produced automobiles, as from P to P' and from Q to Q',

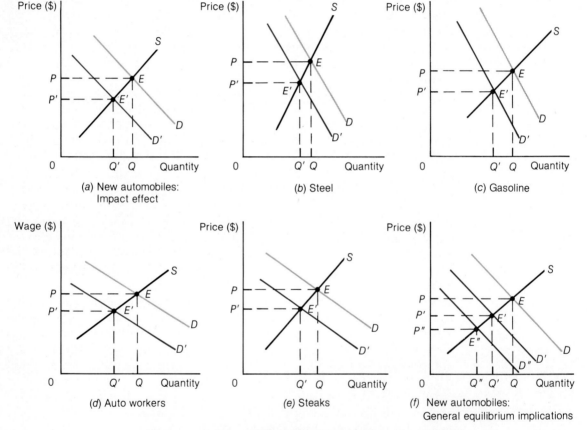

(a) New automobiles:
Impact effect

(b) Steel

(c) Gasoline

(d) Auto workers

(e) Steaks

(f) New automobiles:
General equilibrium implications

FIGURE 17-1.   General Equilibrium Implications of a Reduction in the Demand for New Domestically Produced Automobiles
The impact or partial equilibrium effect of a reduction in the demand for new domestically produced automobiles is to reduce price from P to P' and quantity from Q to Q' [panel (a)]. This reduces the demand for (and price and quantity of) steel [panel (b)] and gasoline [panel (c)], and the demand for (and wages and employment of) workers in the automobile [panel (d)] and other affected industries. This, in turn, has spillover effects on the market for steaks [panel (e)] and other commodities, and feedback effects on the domestic automobile industry itself [panel (f)].

respectively, in panel *a*. This impact effect is what partial equilibrium analysis measures. However, the reduction in the demand for the domestically produced automobiles had spillover effects that disturbed the equilibrium in the steel (panel *b*) and other industries that supply inputs to the domestic automobile industry, as well as in the petroleum industry (panel *c*). The price and quantity of steel and other inputs fell, and part of the original increase in the price of gasoline was neutralized. Other industries related to these industries were also affected.

But this is not the end of the story. The demand for workers in the automobile industry (panel *d*) and other affected industries fell, and so did real wages, employment, and incomes. The reduction in incomes reduced the demand, price, and quantity of steaks (panel *e*) and other normal goods purchased. To be sure, the demand for public transportation (buses, trains, and drivers and other attendants) and cheaper substitutes for steaks increased, but the net effect of the reduction in the demand for domestically produced cars was to reduce the demand and income of labor. This, in turn, had feedback effects on the automobile industry, further reducing the demand, price, and output of domestically produced automobiles (panel *f*).

Comment: Panel *f* of Figure 17-1 shows that the feedback effects on the domestic automobile industry were significant. Price fell from P to P'' rather than to P', and quantity fell from Q to Q'' instead of falling only to Q'. Thus, partial equilibrium analysis gives only a rough first approximation to the final solution. Note that a first round of spillover and feedback effects (as shown in the above analysis) can be measured by the cross and income elasticities (see Sections 5-2 and 5-3), but these only carry us part of the way. The complete, final effects on the domestic automobile and on all other industries can only be measured through full-fledged general equilibrium analysis. This is necessarily mathematical in nature—words and graphs simply fail us.

Source: "U.S. Giving up on Making Small Cars," *U.S. News and World Report,* December 19, 1983, p. 56.

17-2

General Equilibrium of Exchange

In this section, we examine general equilibrium of exchange for a very simple economy composed of only two individuals (A and B), two commodities (X and Y), and no production. This allows us to present the general equilibrium of exchange graphically.[4] The general equilibrium of

---

[4] However, the analysis can be generalized mathematically to more than two individuals and more than two commodities. The graphical presentation in the text follows the well-known article by Francis M. Bator, "The Simple Analytics of Welfare Maximization," *The American Economic Review,* March 1957, pp. 22–59.

exchange for this simple economy of two individuals, two commodities, and no production was already presented in Application 3 in chapter 4. That analysis is now summarized and extended, and it will be utilized in the rest of this chapter and in the next chapter.

The **Edgeworth box diagram for exchange** of Figure 17-2 is that of Figure 4-10, except that the indifference curves of individual A, convex to origin O_A, are given by A_1, A_2, and A_3 (rather than by U_1, U_2, and U_3 as in Figure 4-10) and the indifference curves of individual B, convex to origin O_B, are given by B_1, B_2, and B_3 (rather than by U_1', U_2', and U_3'). The dimension of the box is given by the total amount of the two commodities ($10X$ and $8Y$)

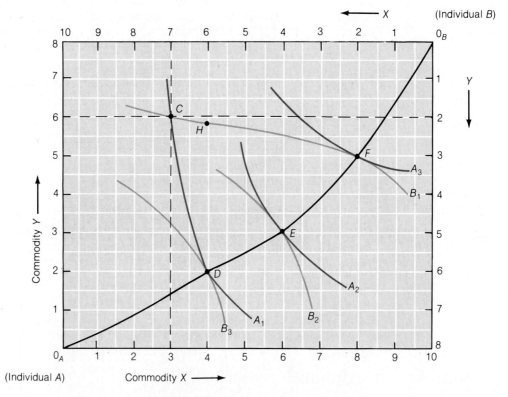

FIGURE 17-2.   Edgeworth Box Diagram for Exchange
A point such as C indicates that individual A has 3X and 6Y (viewed from origin O_A), while individual B has 7X and 2Y (viewed from origin O_B) for a total of 10X and 8Y (the dimension of the box). A's indifference curves (A_1, A_2, and A_3) are convex to O_A, while B's indifference curves (B_1, B_2, and B_3) are convex to O_B. Starting from point C where A_1 and B_1 intersect, individuals A and B can reach points on DEF, where one or both individuals gain. Curve $O_A DEFO_B$ is the contract curve for exchange. It is the locus of tangencies of the indifference curves (at which the MRS_{xy} are equal) for the two individuals and the economy is in general equilibrium of exchange.

owned by the two individuals together.[5] Any point inside the box indicates how the total amount of the two commodities is distributed between the two individuals. For example, point C indicates that individual A has $3X$ and $6Y$, while individual B has $7X$ and $2Y$, for the combined total of $10X$ and $8Y$ (the dimensions of the box).

Suppose that point C does in fact represent the original distribution of commodities X and Y between individuals A and B. Since at point C, indifference curve A_1 and B_1 intersect, their slope or marginal rate of substitution of commodity X for commodity Y (MRS_{xy}) differs. Starting at point C, individual A is willing to give up $4Y$ to get one additional unit of X (and move to point D on A_1), while individual B is willing to accept $0.2Y$ in exchange for one unit of X (and move to point H on B_1).[6] Since A is willing to give up much more Y than necessary to induce B to give up $1X$, there is a basis for exchange that will benefit either or both individuals. This is true whenever, as at point C, the MRS_{xy} for the two individuals differs.

For example, starting from point C, if individual A exchanges $4Y$ for $1X$ with individual B, A moves from point C to point D along his or her indifference curve A_1, while B moves from point C on B_1 to point D on B_3. Thus, individual B receives all of the gains from exchange while individual A gains or loses nothing (since A remains on A_1). At point D, A_1 and B_3 are tangent, so that their slopes (MRS_{xy}) are equal, and there is no further basis for exchange.[7]

Alternatively, if individual A exchanged $1Y$ for $5X$ with individual B, individual A would move from point C on A_1 to point F on A_3, while individual B would move from point C to point F along B_1. Then, A would reap all of the benefits from exchange while B would neither gain nor lose. At point F, MRS_{xy} for A equals MRS_{xy} for B and there is no further basis for exchange. Finally, if A exchanges $3Y$ for $3X$ with B and gets to point E, both individuals gain from exchange since point E is on A_2 and B_2. Thus, starting from point C, which is not on line DEF, both individuals can gain through exchange by getting to a point on line DEF between D and F. The greater A's bargaining strength, the closer the final equilibrium point of exchange will be to point F, and the greater will be the proportion of the total gains from exchange going to individual A (so that less will be left over for individual B).

Curve O_ADEFO_B is the **contract curve for exchange.** It is the locus of tan-

---

[5] As explained in Application 3 in chapter 4, the Edgeworth box was obtained by rotating individual B's indifference curves diagram by 180 degrees (so that origin O_B appears in the top right-hand corner) and superimposing it on individual A's indifference curves diagram (with origin at O_A) in such a way that the size of the box refers to the combined amount of the X and Y owned by the two individuals together.

[6] That is, $MRS_{xy} = 4$ for A and $MRS_{xy} = 0.2$ for B.

[7] At point D, the amount of Y that A is willing to give up for $1X$ is exactly equal to what B requires to give up $1X$. Any further exchange would make either individual worse off than he or she is at point D.

gency points of the indifference curves of the two individuals.[8] That is, along the contract curve for exchange, the marginal rate of substitution of commodity X for commodity Y is the same for individuals A and B, and the economy is in general equilibrium of exchange. Thus, for equilibrium,

$$MRS_{XY}^{A} = MRS_{XY}^{B} \tag{17-1}$$

Starting from any point not on the contract curve, both individuals can gain from exchange by getting to a point on the contract curve. Once on the contract curve, one of the two individuals cannot be made better off without making the other worse off. For example, a movement from point D (on A_1 and B_3) to point E (on A_2 and B_2) makes individual A better off but individual B worse off. Thus, the consumption contract curve is the locus of general equilibrium of exchange. For an economy composed of many consumers and many commodities, the general equilibrium of exchange occurs where the marginal rate of substitution between every pair of commodities is the same for all consumers consuming both commodities.

Example 17-2 Exchange in POW Camps

The Facts: Prisoner-of-war (POW) camps during World War II provide an example of pure exchange. In these camps, little or no production took place, but prisoners received rations of many products from the detaining power, the Red Cross, and from private parcels. The products ranged from canned milk, sugar, butter, chocolates, cookies, cigarettes, razor blades, and writing paper. Soon after receiving rations, prisoners voluntarily began to exchange the received products among themselves, in order to end up with a bundle of goods that better fit their different tastes. People who did not smoke much, exchanged some of their ration of cigarettes for cookies, chocolate, or other products. People who did not care much for chocolate exchanged much of it for other products, and so on.

Comment: Since exchange was voluntary, the strong presumption is that all parties to the exchange benefitted. Equilibrium would be reached and exchange would come to an end when the marginal rate of substitution between all pairs of products was more or less equal for all prisoners consuming each pair of products.

Source: R. A. Radford, "The Economic Organization of a POW Camp," *Economica*, November 1945, pp. 189–201.

---

[8] Such tangency points are assured because indifference curves are convex and the field is dense (that is, there is an infinite number of indifference curves).

17-3

General Equilibrium of Production

In the previous section, we examined general equilibrium in a pure exchange economy with no production. In this and in the next section, we examine general equilibrium of production in a simple economy in which no exchange takes place. Then, in Section 17-5, we bring the two parts together and examine general equilibrium of production and exchange simultaneously.

To examine general equilibrium of production, we deal with a very simple economy that produces only two commodities (X and Y) with only two inputs, labor (L) and capital (K). We construct an Edgeworth box diagram for production from the *isoquants* for commodities X and Y in a manner completely analogous to the Edgeworth box diagram for exchange of Figure 17-2. This is shown in Figure 17-3.

The **Edgeworth box diagram for production** shown in Figure 17-3 was obtained by rotating the isoquant diagram for commodity Y by 180 degrees (so that origin O_Y appears in the top right-hand corner) and superimposing it on the isoquant diagram for commodity X (with origin O_X) in such a way that the size of the box refers to the total amount of L and K available to the economy ($12L$ and $10K$). Any point inside the box indicates how the total amount of the two inputs is utilized in the production of the two commodities. For example, point R indicates that $3L$ and $8K$ are used in the production of X_1 of commodity X, and the remaining $9L$ and $2K$ are used to produce Y_1 of Y. Three of X's isoquants (convex to origin O_X) are X_1, X_2, and X_3. Three of Y's isoquants (convex to origin O_Y) are Y_1, Y_2, and Y_3.

If this economy were initially at point R, it would not be maximizing its output of commodities X and Y because, at point R, the marginal rate of technical substitution of labor for capital ($MRTS_{LK}$) in the production of X (the absolute slope of X_1) exceeds the $MRTS_{LK}$ in the production of Y (the absolute slope of Y_1).[9] By simply transferring $6K$ from the production of X to the production of Y and $1L$ from the production of Y to the production of X, the economy can move from point R (on X_1 and Y_1) to point J (on X_1 and Y_3), and increase its output of Y without reducing its output of X.

Alternatively, this economy can move from point R to point N (and increase its output of X from X_1 to X_3, without reducing its output of Y_1) by transferring $2K$ from the production of X to the production of Y and $6L$ from Y to X. Or, by transferring $4K$ from the production of X to the production of Y and $4L$ from Y to X, this economy can move from point R (on X_1 and Y_1) to point M (on X_2 and Y_2), and increase its output of both X and Y. At

---

[9] Review, if necessary, the definition and measurement of the marginal rate of technical substitution in Section 7-4a.

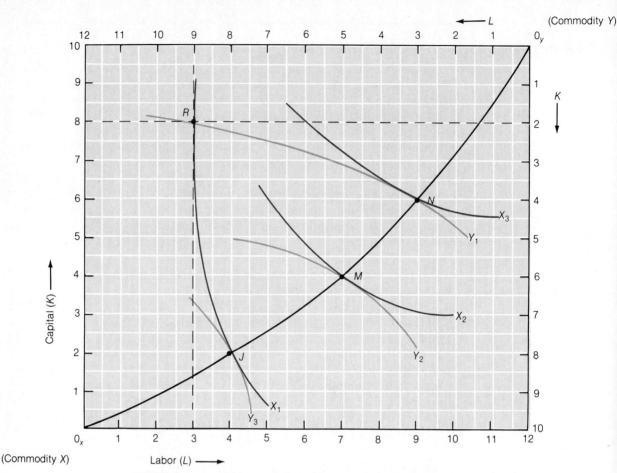

FIGURE 17-3.   Edgeworth Box Diagram for Production

A point such as R indicates that 3L and 8K (viewed from origin O_X) are used to produce X_1 of commodity X, and the remaining 9L and 2K (viewed from origin O_Y) are used to produce Y_1 of Y. The isoquants for X (X_1, X_2, and X_3) are convex to O_X, while the isoquants of Y (Y_1, Y_2, and Y_3) are convex to O_Y. Starting from point R, where X_1 and Y_1 intersect, the economy can produce more of X, more of Y, or more of both by moving to a point on JMN. Curve $O_X JMNO_Y$ is the contract curve for production. It is the locus of tangencies of the isoquants (at which the $MRTS_{LK}$ are equal) for both commodities, and the economy is in general equilibrium of production.

points J, M, N, and X isoquant is tangent to a Y isoquant so that the $MRTS_{LK}$ in the production of X equals $MRTS_{LK}$ in the production of Y.

Curve $O_X JMNO_Y$ is the **contract curve for production.** It is the locus of tangency points of the isoquants for X and Y at which the marginal rate of technical substitution of labor for capital in the production of X and Y are equal. That is, the economy is in general equilibrium of production when

$$MRTS_{LK}^X = MRTS_{LK}^Y \qquad (17\text{-}2)$$

Thus, by simply transferring some of the given and fixed amounts of available L and K between the production of X and Y, this economy can move from a point not on the contract curve for production to a point on it and increase its output of either or both commodities. Once on its production contract curve, the economy can only increase the output of either commodity by reducing the output of the other. For example, by moving from point J (on X_1 and Y_3) to point M (on X_2 and Y_2), the economy increases its output of commodity X (by transferring $3L$ and $2K$ from the production of Y to the production of X) but its output of commodity Y falls. For an economy of many commodities and many inputs, the general equilibrium of production occurs where the marginal rate of technical substitution between any pair of inputs is the same for all commodities and producers using both inputs.

17-4

Derivation of the Production-Possibilities Frontier

From the production contract curve, we can derive the corresponding production-possibilities frontier or transformation curve by simply plotting the various combinations of outputs directly. For example, if isoquant X_1 in Figure 17-3 referred to an output of 4 units of commodity X and isoquant Y_3 referred to an output of 13 units of commodity Y, we can go from point J (X_1, Y_1) in Figure 17-3 to point J' (4X, 13Y) in Figure 17-4. Similarly, if isoquant X_2 referred to an output of 10X and isoquant Y_2 to an output of 8Y, we can go from point M (X_2, Y_2) in Figure 17-3 to point M' (10X, 8Y) in Figure 17-4. Finally, if $X_3 = 12X$ and $Y_1 = 4Y$, we can plot point N (X_3, Y_1) from Figure 17-3 as point N' (12X, 4Y) in Figure 17-4. By joining points $J'M'N'$ and other points similarly obtained, we derive the production-possibilities frontier or transformation curve of X for Y, TT, shown in Figure 17-4. Thus, the production possibilities frontier is obtained by simply mapping or transferring the production contract curve from input space to output space.

The production-possibilities frontier or transformation curve shows the various combinations of commodities X and Y that the economy can produce by fully utilizing all of the fixed amounts of labor and capital with the best technology available. Since the production contract curve shows all points of general equilibrium of production, so does the production-possibilities frontier. That is, the production-possibilities frontier shows the maximum amount of either commodity that the economy can produce, given the amount of the other commodity that the economy is producing. For example, given that the economy is producing 10X, the maximum amount of commodity Y that the economy can produce is 8Y (point M' in Figure 17-4), and vice versa.

A point inside the production-possibilities frontier corresponds to a point

FIGURE 17-4.
The Production-Possibilities Frontier

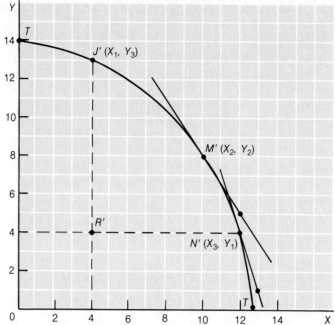

Production-possibilities frontier or transformation curve TT shows the various combinations of X and Y that the economy can produce given the fixed amounts of labor and capital and technology available. It is derived by mapping the production contract curve of Figure 17-3 from input to output space. Starting from point R', the economy could increase its output of Y (point J'), of X (point N'), or of both X and Y (point M'). The absolute slope or $MRT_{xy} = 3/2$ at point M' means that 3/2 of Y must be given up to produce one additional unit of X. MRT_{xy} increases as we move down the frontier. Thus, at point N', $MRT_{xy} = 3$.

off the production contract curve and indicates that the economy is not in general equilibrium of production, and it is not utilizing its inputs of labor and capital most efficiently. For example, point R', inside production-possibilities frontier TT in Figure 17-4, corresponds to point R in Figure 17-3, at which isoquant X_1 and Y_1 intersect. By simply reallocating some of the fixed labor and capital available between the production of X and Y, this economy can increase its output of Y only (and move from point R' to point J' in Figure 17-4), it can increase the output of X only (and move from point R' to point N'), or it can increase its output of both X and Y (the movement from point R' to point M'). On the other hand, a point outside the production-possibilities frontier cannot be achieved with the available inputs and technology.

Once on the production-possibilities frontier, the output of either commodity can be increased only by reducing the output of the other. For example, starting at point J' ($4X$ and $13Y$) on the production-possibilities frontier in Figure 17-4, the economy can move to point M' and produce $10X$ only by reducing the amount produced of Y by 5 units (i.e., to $8Y$). The

564

amount of commodity Y that the economy must give up, at a particular point on the production-possibilities frontier, so as to release just enough labor and capital to produce one additional unit of commodity X, is called the **marginal rate of transformation of X for Y (MRT$_{xy}$)**. This is given by the absolute value of the slope of the production-possibilities frontier at that point. For example, at point M' on production-possibilities frontier TT in Figure 17-4, $MRT_{xy} = \frac{3}{2}$ (the absolute value of the slope of the tangent to the production-possibilities frontier at point M').

The marginal rate of transformation of X for Y is also equal to the ratio of the marginal cost of X to the marginal cost of Y. That is, $MRT_{xy} = MC_x/MC_y$. For example, at point M', $MRT_{xy} = \frac{3}{2}$. This means that $\frac{3}{2}$ of Y must be given up to produce one additional unit of X. Thus, $MC_x = \frac{3}{2}MC_y$, and $MRT_{xy} = \frac{3}{2}$. Another way of looking at this is that if $MC_y = \$10$ and $MC_x = \$15$, this means that to produce one additional unit of X requires 1.5 or $\frac{3}{2}$ more units of labor and capital than to produce one additional unit of Y, so that $\frac{3}{2}$ of Y must be given up to produce one additional unit of X. This is exactly what the MRT_{xy} measures. Thus, at point M', $MRT_{xy} = MC_x/MC_y = \frac{3}{2}$.

As we move down the production-possibilities frontier (and produce more X and less Y), the MRT_{xy} increases, indicating that more and more Y must be given up in order to produce each additional unit of X. For example, at point N', the MRT_{xy} or absolute value of the slope of the production-possibilities frontier is 3 (up from 3/2 at point M'). The reason for this is that, as the economy reduces its output of Y (in order to produce more of X), it releases labor and capital in combinations that become less and less suited for the production of more X. Thus, the economy incurs increasing MC_x in terms of Y. It is because of this imperfect input substitutability between the production of X and Y (and rising MC_x in terms of Y) that the production-possibilities frontier is concave to the origin.[10]

17-5

General Equilibrium of Production and Exchange

We now combine the results of the previous three sections and examine how our very simple economy composed of two individuals (A and B), two commodities (X and Y), and two inputs (L and K) can reach *simultaneously* general equilibrium of production and exchange. This is shown in Figure 17-5.

The production-possibilities frontier of Figure 17-5 is that of Figure 17-4, which was derived from Figure 17-3. That is, the production iso-quants for commodity X and commodity Y and the input base of the econ-

---

[10] If labor and capital were perfectly substitutable in the production of X and Y, MC_x would be constant in terms of Y, and the production-possibilities frontier would be a straight line.

FIGURE 17-5.
General
Equilibrium of
Production and
Exchange

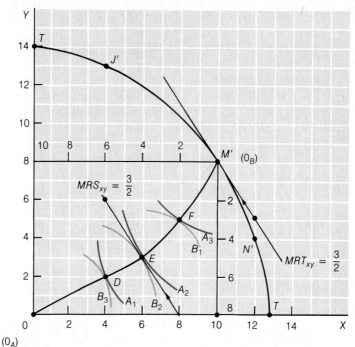

Production possibilities frontier TT is that of Figure 17-4. Every point on TT is a point of general equilibrium of production. Starting from point M' (10X, 8Y) on the pro-duction-possibilities frontier, we constructed in the above figure the Edgeworth box diagram for exchange between individuals A and B of Figure 17-2. Every point on contract curve $O_A DEFO_B$ is a point of general equilibrium of exchange. Simultan-eous general equilibrium of production and exchange is at point E, at which $MRT_{XY} = MRS^A_{XY} = MRS^B_{XY} = 3/2$.

omy (12L and 10K) were used to derive production contract curve $O_X JMNO_Y$ in Figure 17-3. By mapping the production contract curve from input to output space, we derived the production-possibilities frontier of Figure 17-4, which is reproduced in Figure 17-5. Every point on produc-tion-possibilities frontier *TT* is a point of general equilibrium of production.

    Suppose that this economy produces 10X and 8Y, given by point M' on production-possibilities frontier TT in Figure 17-5.[11] By dropping perpen-diculars from point M' to both axes, we can construct in Figure 17-5 the Edgeworth box diagram for exchange between individuals A and B of Fig-ure 17-2. Note that the top right-hand corner of the Edgeworth box diagram for exchange of Figure 17-2 coincides with point M' on production-possi-bilities frontier TT in Figure 17-5. Given the indifference curves of indi-viduals A and B and the output of 10X and 8Y, we derived contract curve $O_A DEFO_B$ for exchange in Figure 17-2. This is reproduced in Figure 17-5.

---

[11] How this particular output level is determined is examined in Section 18-3.

Every point on the contract curve for exchange in Figure 17-5 is a point of general equilibrium of exchange.

Thus, every point on production-possibilities frontier TT in Figure 17-5 is a point of general equilibrium of production, and every point on the contract curve for exchange is a point of general equilibrium of exchange. However, to be *simultaneously* in general equilibrium of production and exchange, the marginal rate of transformation of commodity X for commodity Y in production must be equal to the marginal rate of substitution of commodity X for commodity Y in consumption for individuals A and B. That is,

$$MRT_{XY} = MRS_{XY}^A = MRS_{XY}^B \tag{17-3}$$

Geometrically, this corresponds to the point on the contract curve for exchange at which the common slope of an indifference curve of individual A and individual B equals the slope of production-possibilities frontier TT at the point of production. In Figure 17-5, this occurs at point E, where

$$MRS_{XY}^A = MRS_{XY}^B = MRT_{XY} = \tfrac{3}{2} \tag{17-3A}$$

Thus, when producing $10X$ and $8Y$ (point M' on production possibilities frontier TT), this economy is simultaneously in general equilibrium of production and exchange when individual A consumes $6X$ and $3Y$ (point E on his or her indifference curve A_2) and individual B consumes the remaining $4X$ and $5Y$ (point E on his or her indifference curve B_2).

If Condition (17-3) did not hold, the economy would not be simultaneously in general equilibrium of production and exchange. For example, suppose that individuals A and B consumed at point D on the contract curve for exchange rather than at point E in Figure 17-5. At point D, the MRS_{xy} (the common absolute value of the slope of indifference curves A_1 and B_3) is 3. This means that individuals A and B are willing (indifferent) to give up $3Y$ to obtain one additional unit of X. Since in production, only $\tfrac{3}{2}Y$ needs to be given up to produce an additional 1 unit of X, society would have to produce more of X and less of Y to be simultaneously in general equilibrium of production and exchange. Put in another way, if $MRS_{xy} = 3$, this society would not have chosen to produce at point M', but would have produced at point N' ($12X$ and $4Y$), where $MRS_{xy} = MRT_{xy} = 3$.

The opposite is true at point F. That is, at point F, $MRS_{xy} = \tfrac{1}{2}$. Since $MRT_{xy} = \tfrac{3}{2}$ at point M' (the point of production), more of Y needs to be given up in production to obtain one additional unit of X than individuals A and B are willing to give up in consumption. If this were the case, this society would have chosen to produce at point J' ($4X$ and $13Y$), where $MRS_{xy} = MRT_{xy} = \tfrac{1}{2}$, rather than at point M'. Only by consuming at point E will $MRT_{xy} = MRS_{xy}$ for both individuals, and society will be simultaneously in general equilibrium of production and exchange when it produces at point M'.

We conclude the following about this simple economy when it is in general equilibrium of production and exchange: (1) it produces $10X$ and $8Y$ (point M' in Figure 17-5)[12]; (2) individual A receives $6X$ and $3Y$ and individual B receives the remaining $4X$ and $5Y$ (point E in Figure 17-5); (3) to produce $10X$, $7L$ and $4K$ are used, while to produce $8Y$, the remaining $5L$ and $6K$ are used (see point M in Figure 17-3).[13]

Example 17-3 International Specialization in Production, and International Trade

The Facts: An important example of general equilibrium of production and exchange is provided by international trade, say, between nations A and B. Suppose that nation A is endowed with an abundance of labor (L) relative to capital (K) with respect to nation B, and commodity X is labor intensive (i.e., the L/K ratio in the production of X is greater than in the production of Y). Given the same technology and tastes in the two nations, the cost (in terms of the amount of Y to be given up) of producing an additional unit of X (i.e., the MRT_{xy}) is lower in nation A than in nation B. Then, we say that nation A has a **comparative advantage** in commodity X and nation B has a comparative advantage in commodity Y. With trade, nation A specializes in the production of commodity X (i.e., it produces more of X than it demands for internal consumption) in order to exchange it for commodity Y from nation B. On the other hand, nation B specializes in the production of commodity Y (i.e., it produces more of Y than it demands for internal consumption) in order to exchange it for commodity X from nation A. With each nation specializing in the production of the commodity of its comparative advantage (nation A in commodity X and B in Y), the combined output of X and Y by the two nations is larger than without specialization. Both nations then share the increased output of X and Y through voluntary exchange (trade), and both are better off than without trade.

Comment: As each nation specializes in the production of the commodity of its comparative advantage, it will incur increasing opportunity costs. Specialization in production reaches the equilibrium level when MRT_{xy} is the same in both nations. The two nations are then simultaneously in general equilibrium of production and exchange (trade) when $MRT_{XY} = MRS_{XY}^A = MRS_{XY}^B$. (A graphical analysis of general equilibrium of production and exchange that shows the gains from specialization in production and trade is presented in Application 3.)

Source: Dominick Salvatore, *International Economics*, 2nd ed. (New York: Macmillan, 1985), Chapter 5.

---

[12] As pointed out in Footnote 11, we will see how this level of output is determined in Section 18-3.

[13] In Section 18-4, we will also determine the relative price of commodity X (i.e., P_x/P_y) and the relative price of labor time (i.e., P_L/P_K or w/r) for this simple economy, when it is simultaneously in general equilibrium of production and exchange.

17-6

Applications

In this section we examine some important applications of the theory presented in the chapter. These are input-output analysis, the basis and the gains from trade between two nations, and measures of income inequality.

Application 1: Input-Output Analysis: The General Concept

One important practical application of general equilibrium theory is input-output analysis, introduced by Wassily Leontief.[14] **Input-output analysis** is the empirical study of the interdependence among the various sectors of the economy. It shows the uses of the output of a particular sector or industry in the economy as input by the other industries or sectors, and the uses of the output of these other sectors or industries as inputs in the particular sector or industry. This is done for all the sectors or industries in the economy. For example, the output of the steel industry is used as input by the construction and transportation industries, and the steel industry, in turn, uses the output of the construction and transportation industries as inputs in its own steel production. A change in the output of the construction and transportation industries requires a change in the output of the steel industry, and a change in the output of the steel industry requires a change in the output of the construction and transportation industries. Such interdependence generally exists not only between the steel industry, on the one hand, and the construction and transportation industries, on the other, but more or less among practically all industries and sectors of the economy. Thus, input-output analysis seeks to determine what can be produced and the amount of each input or intermediate good that is required to produce a given output.

Input-output analysis makes several important simplifications to reduce general equilibrium analysis to manageable proportions. *First*, it deals with the *total* or aggregate quantity of each commodity demanded by all consumers and produced by all firms together, rather than with the quantity demanded by each consumer and produced by each firm separately. This greatly reduces the number of variables and equations in the system. *Second*, in its simplest form, input-output analysis assumes a given demand for each commodity (rather than the quantity demanded depending on prices and income).[15] *Third*, it assumes constant returns to scale and fixed input proportions in the production of each commodity. That is, 100 tons of steel require exactly 100 times the amount of each input needed to pro-

---

[14] Wassily W. Leontief, *The Structure of the American Economy* (New York: Oxford University Press, 1951).

[15] This assumption is partially relaxed in Wassily W. Leontief, *Input-Output Analysis* (New York: Oxford Universtiy Press, 1966), and in Hollis B. Chenery and Paul G. Clark, *Interindustry Economics* (New York: Wiley, 1959).

duce one ton of steel. This assumption does not allow any substitutability of inputs in production as a result of changes in relative input prices.[16] While this is grossly incorrect in the long run, it is roughly true in the short run in the production of many basic products, where input substitution is often slow and gradual.

Input-output analysis has been widely applied during the past forty years to analyze a wide range of problems. During World War II, the U.S. government was the first to develop input-output tables, which it used to analyze the national production requirements for the war effort. Over the past thirty years or so, economists have made extensive use of input-output analysis for planning economic development. They frequently started with a given output or growth target for the economy as a whole and used input-output analysis to determine the output or growth of the various sectors of the economy that were required to achieve the targeted output or growth rate for the economy as a whole. Economists in centrally planned economies routinely utilize input-output analysis for similar purposes. Another application of input-output analysis was to estimate the consequences of disarmament for the various sectors of the economy.[17] More recently, input-output analysis has been utilized to investigate the effect of the 1973–1974 oil embargo and sharp increase in petroleum prices on other industrial and consumer prices in the United States and on the level of employment in various industries.

Despite its many useful applications, input-output analysis has many shortcomings, the most serious of which being its assumption of fixed input proportions or coefficients. Over time, technology and input prices change and these are likely to greatly affect the proportions with which inputs are combined in the production of many commodities. This necessitates frequent and continuous updating of input-output tables, which are very costly and time consuming. For the U.S. economy, input-output tables are available for 1947, 1958, 1963, and 1969.[18]

Application 2: Input-Output Analysis: Numerical Example

In order to explain input-output analysis in greater technical detail, we consider a very simple economy composed of only four sectors: service, manufacturing, agriculture, and household. Table 17-1 gives the hypothetical flows of inputs and outputs, in billions of dollars per year, among the various sectors of the economy.[19]

The columns in Table 17-1 indicate the input requirements of each sec-

---

[16] This assumption was also made in linear programming (see Sections 9-3 and 9-4).

[17] Wassily W. Leontief and Marvin Offenberg, "The Economic Effects of Disarmament," *Scientific American*, April 1961, pp. 47–55.

[18] The 1969 data on 370 industries are found in *Survey of Current Business* (Washington, D.C.: U.S. Government Printing Office, November 1969), pp. 16–47.

[19] The analysis could also be carried out in physical, rather than in monetary, units of output.

TABLE 17-1   Annual Flows of Inputs and Outputs Among the Various Sectors of the Economy (in Billions of Dollars)

Sector Producing	Service	Manufacturing	Agriculture	Household	Total Sales
Service	$ 200	$ 600	$ 300	$ 900	$2,000
Manufacturing	800	900	200	1,100	3,000
Agriculture	400	300	100	200	1,000
Household	600	1,200	400	. . .	2,200
Total Production	$2,000	$3,000	$1,000	$2,200	$8,200

tor or how much each sector purchased from other sectors and from itself in order to produce its output. For example, by reading down the service column of the table, we find that the service sector purchased $200 billion of its own output, $800 billion from the manufacturing sector, $400 billion from the agricultural sector, and $600 billion of labor and capital inputs from the household sector.

On the other hand, the rows of Table 17-1 indicate the uses of the output of each sector. For example, the first row shows that of the total output of $2,000 billion of the service sector, $200 billion was supplied to itself, $600 billion was sold to the manufacturing sector, $300 billion to the agricultural sector, and the remainder of $900 billion was sold to households. The service, manufacturing, and agricultural sectors used the services supplied by the service sector as *inputs* to produce their own output, while the household sector used the services purchased from the service sector for *final* consumption.

From the data in Table 17-1, we can derive the technical coefficients (also called production coefficients or input coefficients) for the three producing sectors. These are given by the structural matrix of Table 17-2. The technical coefficients for each producing sector are obtained by dividing the entries in each column of Table 17-1 by the overall total output of the sector given at the bottom of the column in Table 17-1. For example, the first entry of the first column of Table 17-2 is obtained by 200/2,000 = 0.1 (from Table 17-1). The second entry of the first column in Table 17-2 is obtained by 800/2,000 = 0.4 (from Table 17-1), and so on. As a result, the sum of the technical coefficients in each column equals 1. Thus, the **technical coef-**

TABLE 17-2   Structural Matrix

Sector Producing	Sector Purchasing		
	Service	Manufacturing	Agriculture
Service	0.1	0.2	0.3
Manufacturing	0.4	0.3	0.2
Agriculture	0.2	0.1	0.1
Household	0.3	0.4	0.4
Total	1.0	1.0	1.0

ficients in each column of Table 17-2 give the dollar value of each input required to produce one dollar's worth of output in each industry or sector. For example, the first column of Table 17-2 shows that to produce one dollar's worth of service output, $0.10 of service inputs, $0.40 of manufacturing inputs, $0.20 of agricultural inputs, and $0.30 of labor and capital inputs from the household sector are required.

The structural matrix of Table 17-2 can be used to determine the total amount of output required from each sector of the economy in order to meet the specified final demand requirements of the household sector. For example, suppose that the household sector demands $200 billion of services, $300 billion of manufactured goods, and $100 billion of agricultural commodities. The question is, by how much should the output of each of these sectors increase in order to meet these final demand requirements of the household sector? Since each sector must also supply its output (as input) to the other sectors, it is clear that each sector must produce more of its output than the quantity demanded by the household sector. The question is, how much more?

This question can be answered by setting up and solving the following system of three simultaneous linear equations, where S = service, M = manufacturing, and A = agriculture (all measured in billions of dollars):

$$S = 0.1S + 0.2M + 0.3A + 200$$
$$M = 0.4S + 0.3M + 0.2A + 300$$
$$A = 0.2S + 0.1M + 0.1A + 100$$

The first equation postulates that to meet the final consumption target of the household sector, the service sector must supply $0.1S$ to meet its own service needs, $0.2M$ to meet the needs of the manufacturing sector, $0.3A$ to meet the needs of the agricultural sector, as well as the $200 billion to meet the household consumption target for services. Note that we are using the technical coefficients in the first row of Table 17-2, but using the target *amount* of services demanded for final consumption by the household sector. Thus, the total output of the service sector must equal the sum of the four terms in the first equation. The second and third equations can be interpreted similarly.

The solution (with all values rounded to the nearest billion) is

$$S = \$505 \text{ billion}, M = \$807 \text{ billion}, A = \$313 \text{ billion.[20]}$$

To meet the final output requirements of the household sector, the household sector, for its part, will have to supply the following total amounts of labor and capital inputs (H):

$$H = 0.3S + 0.4M + 0.4A$$
$$H = 0.3(505) + 0.4(807) + 0.4(313) = \$600 \text{ billion}$$

[20] To see how these were obtained, see the solution to Problem 12 at the end of the text.

(rounded to the nearest billion). If the total amount required of labor and capital inputs is not available in the economy, the solution is not feasible and the targets must be scaled down.

Application 3: The Basis and the Gains from Trade Between Two Nations

We can show general equilibrium of production and exchange and the gains from specialization in production and trade with the aid of Figure 17-6. The production-possibilities frontier is AA for nation A and BB for nation B. The different shape of the two production-possibilities frontiers results from nation A having a relative abundance of labor and commodity X being labor intensive. We assume that technology is constant in both nations. In the absence of trade, nation A is observed to be producing and consuming at point C, while nation B is at C'. Since the MRT_{xy} (the absolute value of the slope of the production-possibilities frontier) is lower at point C for nation A than at point C' for nation B, nation A has a comparative advantage in commodity X, while nation B has a comparative advantage in commodity Y.

With the opening of trade, nation A specializes in the production of X (moves down its production-possibilities frontier from point C) and incurs

FIGURE 17-6.
Graphical Proof of
the Law of
Comparative
Advantage

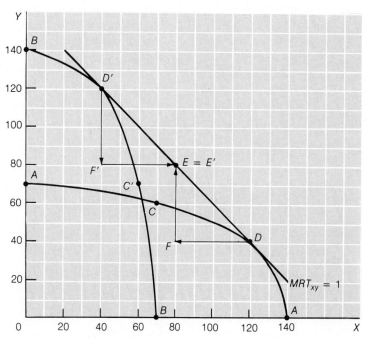

The production-possibilities frontier is AA for nation A and BB for nation B. In the absence of trade, A is at point C and B is at point C'. Since MRT_{xy} (the absolute value of the slope of the production-possibilities frontier) is lower at point C than at point C', nation A has a comparative advantage in X while nation B has a comparative advantage in Y. With trade, A produces at point D, exchanges 40X for 40Y with B, and consumes at E > C. B produces at point D', exchanges 40Y for 40X with A, and consumes at E' > C'.

573

increasing opportunity costs in the production of more X (the MRT_{xy} rises). Nation B specializes in the production of Y (moves up its production-possibilities frontier from point C') and incurs increasing opportunity costs in the production of more Y (the MRT_{yx} rises, which means that the MRT_{xy} falls). Specialization in production proceeds until nation A has reached point D and nation B has reached point D', at which MRT_{xy} is the same in both nations. Nation A might then exchange $40X$ (DF) for $40Y$ (FE) with nation B and reach point E. At point E, nation A consumes $10X$ and $20Y$ more than at point C without trade. With trade, nation B consumes at point E' ($= E$) or $20X$ and $10Y$ more than at point C' without trade. Production and trade is in (general) equilibrium, and both nations gain.

Note that with trade, both nations consume $80X$ and $80Y$. This means that nations A and B are of equal size and have the same tastes. This was implicitly assumed to simplify the graphical analysis. However, the law of comparative advantage is equally valid for more general cases.

Application 4: Measures of Income Inequality

We have seen in Section 17-2 that once individuals A and B are on the contract curve for exchange, one of the two individuals cannot be made better off without making the other worse off. Thus, different points on the contract curve refer to different distributions of income between the two individuals. The best-known summary measure of income inequality is provided by the Lorenz curve and the Gini coefficient. A **Lorenz curve** shows the cumulative percentages of total income (from 0 to 100 per cent) measured along the vertical axis, for various cumulative percentages of the population (also from 0 to 100 per cent) measured along the horizontal axis. The Gini coefficient is calculated from the Lorenz curve as indicated below.

An illustration of two Lorenz curves, obtained by plotting the data of Table 17-3, is given in Figure 17-7.

The table and the figure show that the 20 per cent of the families with the lowest income received only 0.3 per cent of the national income before

TABLE 17-3 Distribution of Annual Family Income Before and After Taxes and Transfers in the United States in 1976

Cumulative Per Cent of Families	Cumulative Per Cent of Total Income	
	Before Taxes and Transfers	After Taxes and Transfers
Lowest 20	0.3	7.2
40	7.5	18.7
60	23.8	35.3
80	49.8	58.7
100	100.0	100.0

Source: U.S. Congress, *Congressional Budget Office*, "Poverty Status of Families Under Alternative Definitions of Income," January 13, 1977, Table A-4.

FIGURE 17-7.
Lorenz Curves

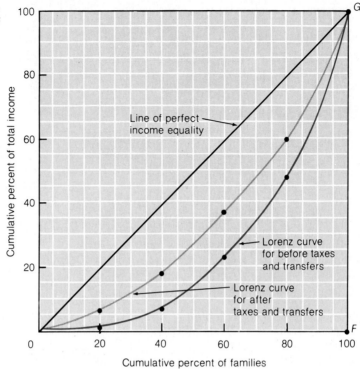

A Lorenz curve gives the cumulative percentages of total income (measured along the vertical axis), for various cumulative percentages of the population or families (measured along the horizontal axis). The after-taxes and after-transfers Lorenz curve has a smaller curvature (or outward bulge from the diagonal) than the before-taxes and before-transfers Lorenz curve, indicating a smaller income inequality after than before taxes and transfers.

all taxes and transfers to aid low-income families, but 7.2 per cent of national income after all taxes and transfers. The 40 per cent of the families with the lowest income received 7.5 per cent of total income before taxes and transfers, but 18.7 per cent afterwards, and so on, until 100 per cent of the families received the entire national income. Note that the after-taxes and after-transfers Lorenz curve has a smaller curvature than the before-taxes and before-transfers Lorenz curve, indicating a much smaller income inequality after than before taxes and transfers.

If income were equally distributed, the Lorenz curve would coincide with the straight-line diagonal. On the other hand, if one family received the entire income of the nation, the Lorenz curve would be at right angle (OFG in the figure). The **Gini coefficient** is given by the ratio of the area between the Lorenz curve and the straight-line diagonal to the total area of triangle OFG. The Gini coefficient can range from 0 with perfect equality (when the Lorenz curve coincides with the diagonal) to 1 with perfect inequality (when only one family receives all the income and the Lorenz curve is given by *OFG*). For the United States, the Gini coefficient is about 0.45 before all taxes and transfers and about 0.35 afterwards. The Gini coefficient in the United States is generally lower than for most other nations and it has remained relatively constant over time.

Summary

1. Partial equilibrium analysis studies the behavior of individual decision-making units and individual markets, viewed in isolation. On the other hand, general equilibrium analysis studies the interdependence that exists among all markets in the economy. Only when an industry is small and has few direct links with the rest of the economy is partial equilibrium analysis appropriate. The first general equilibrium model was introduced by Walras in 1874. Under perfect competition, a solution to the general equilibrium model usually exists.

2. General equilibrium of exchange for a very simple economy of two individuals, two commodities, and no production can be shown diagrammatically using an Edgeworth box diagram. The economy is in general equilibrium of exchange when it is on its contract curve. This is the locus of tangency points of the indifference curves (at which the MRS_{xy} are equal) for the two individuals. Starting from any point not on the contract curve, both individuals can gain from exchange by getting to a point on the contract curve. Once on the contract curve, one of the two individuals cannot be made better off without making the other worse off.

3. General equilibrium of production for a very simple economy that produces two commodities with two inputs, and in which no exchange takes place, can be shown diagrammatically using an Edgeworth box diagram. The economy is in general equilibrium of production when it is on its production contract curve. This is the locus of tangency points of the isoquants (at which the $MRTS_{LK}$ are equal) for the two commodities. Starting from any point not on the contract curve, the output of both commodities can be increased by moving to a point on the contract curve. Once on the contract curve, the output of either commodity can only be increased by reducing the output of the other.

4. By mapping or transferring the production contract curve from input to output space we can derive the corresponding production-possibilities frontier. This shows the various combinations of commodities X and Y that this economy can produce by fully utilizing all of its fixed amount of labor and capital with the best technology available. Points inside the production-possibilities frontier are inefficient while points outside cannot be reached. The absolute slope of the production-possibilities frontier measures the amount of Y that must be given up in order to release just enough labor and capital to produce one additional unit of X. This is called the marginal rate of transformation of X for Y (MRT_{xy}). The MRT_{xy} increases as we move down the production-possibilities frontier.

5. Every point on the production-possibilities frontier is a point of general equilibrium of production, and every point on the contract curve for exchange is a point of general equilibrium of consumption. For the economy to be simultaneously in general equilibrium of production and exchange, the marginal rate of transformation of X for Y in production must be equal to the marginal rate of substitution of X for Y in consumption for individuals A and B. That is, $MRT_{XY} = MRS_{XY}^{A} = MRS_{XY}^{B}$. Geometrically, this corresponds to the point on the contract curve for exchange at which the common slope of the indifference curve of the two individuals equals the slope of the production possibilities frontier at the point of production.

6. Input-output analysis is an important practical application of general equilibrium theory. It is the empirical study of the interdependence among the various sectors of the economy. As such, it shows the flow of outputs and inputs among all sectors and industries in the economy. Input-output analysis assumes a given demand for each commodity, constant returns to scale,

and constant technical coefficients. The latter refer to the dollar value of each input required to produce one dollar's worth of output in each sector or industry. Input-output analysis has been applied to a wide variety of uses over the past forty years. Another application of general equilibrium theory is provided by the law of comparative advantage, which shows the basis and the gains from trade among nations, based on different input endowments. Measures of income inequality are given by the Lorenz curve and the Gini coefficient.

Glossary

Partial equilibrium analysis   It studies the behavior of individual decision-making units and individual markets, *viewed in isolation.*

General equilibrium analysis   It studies the interdependence that exists among all markets in the economy.

Interdependence   The relationship among all markets in the economy, such that a change in any of them affects all the others.

Edgeworth box diagram for exchange   A diagram constructed from the indifference curves diagram of two individuals that can be used to analyze voluntary exchange.

Contract curve for exchange   The locus of tangency points of the indifference curves (at which the MRS_{xy} are equal) for the two individuals, when the economy is in general equilibrium of exchange.

Edgeworth box diagram for production   A diagram constructed from the isoquants diagram of the two commodities that can be used to analyze general equilibrium of production.

Contract curve for production   The locus of tangency points of the isoquants (at which the $MRTS_{LK}$ are equal) for the two commodities, when the economy is in general equilibrium of production.

Production-possibilities frontier   The curve showing the various amounts of commodities X and Y that the economy can produce with the fixed quantities of labor and capital and technology available. It is also called the transformation curve.

Marginal rate of transformation of X for Y (MRT_{xy})   The amount of Y that must be given up in order to release just enough labor and capital to produce one additional unit of X. It is equal to the absolute value of the slope of the production-possibilities frontier and to the ratio of the marginal cost of X to the marginal cost of Y.

Comparative advantage   The cost advantage that a nation has over another in the production of the commodity requiring a great deal of its relatively abundant and cheap input.

Input-output analysis   The empirical study of the interdependence among the various sectors and industries in the economy; it usually assumes fixed input proportions in production.

Technical coefficients   Coefficients in input-output analysis that indicate the dollar value of each input required to produce one dollar's worth of output in each industry or sector; also called production or input coefficients.

Lorenz curve   A curve showing income inequality by measuring cumulative percentages of total income along the vertical axis, for various cumulative percentages of the population (from the lowest to the highest income) measured along the horizontal axis.

Gini coefficient   A measure of income inequality calculated from the Lorenz curve and ranging from 0 (for perfect equality) to 1 (for perfect inequality).

Questions for Review

1. (a) What is partial equilibrium analysis?
   (b) What is general equilibrium analysis?

(c) What is the relationship between partial and general equilibrium analysis?

577

(d) When is partial equilibrium analysis appropriate?

2. (a) How is the Edgeworth box diagram for exchange constructed?
   (b) What determines the dimensions of the box?
   (c) What does any point inside the box indicate?

3. (a) How is the contract curve for exchange derived?
   (b) What does a movement from a point not on the contract curve for exchange to a point on it indicate?
   (c) What does a movement from one point to another on the contract curve for exchange indicate?

4. (a) How is the Edgeworth box diagram for production constructed?
   (b) What determines the dimensions of the box?
   (c) What does a point inside the box indicate?

5. (a) How is a contract curve for production derived?
   (b) What does a movement from a point not on the production contract curve to a point on it indicate?
   (c) What does a movement from one point to another on the production contract curve show?

6. (a) What does a production-possibilities frontier show?
   (b) How is a production-possibilities frontier derived?
   (c) What is an input space? An output space?
   (d) What does a point inside the production-possibilities frontier show? A point outside?

7. (a) What does the marginal rate of transformation of X for Y (MRT_{xy}) measure?

(b) How can MRT_{xy} be measured graphically?
(c) What is the relationship between MRT_{xy} and MC_x and MC_y?
(d) Why does MRT_{xy} increase as we move down a production-possibilities frontier?

8. What is the algebraic and graphical condition for general equilibrium in
   (a) production?
   (b) exchange?
   (c) production and exchange simultaneously?

9. If production takes place at point M' in Figure 17-5, why is general equilibrium
   (a) not achieved, if consumption takes place at point D?
   (b) not achieved, if consumption takes place at point F?
   (c) achieved if consumption takes place at point E?

10. In what way is Figure 17-5
    (a) a general equilibrium model?
    (b) a great simplification of a general equilibrium model?
    (c) incomplete, as a general equilibrium model?

11. (a) What is input-output analysis?
    (b) What is the relationship between input-output analysis and general equilibrium theory?
    (c) What are technical coefficients?
    (d) What are some applications of input-output analysis?

12. What is
    (a) comparative advantage?
    (b) the Lorenz curve?
    (c) the Gini coefficient?

Problems

1. Starting from a position of general equilibrium in the entire economy, if the supply curve of commodity X falls (i.e., S_x shifts up), examine what happens (a) in the markets for commodity X, its substitutes, and complements, (b) in the input markets, and (c) to the distribution of income.

★2. Suppose that the indifference curves of individuals A and B are given by A_1, A_2, A_3, and B_1, B_2, B_3, respectively, in the table below. Suppose also that the total amount of commodities X and Y available to the two individuals together are 14X and 9Y. Draw the Edgeworth box diagram for exchange and show the contract curve for exchange.

A's Indifference Curves

A_1		A_2		A_3	
X	Y	X	Y	X	Y
3	7	5	6	6	7.5
4	3	6	4	8	6
6	1	8	3	9.5	5.5

B's Indifference Curves

B_1		B_2		B_3	
X	Y	X	Y	X	Y
7	2	6	4	8	4
2	3	4	5	6	6
1	4	3	7	5.5	8

3. For the Edgeworth box diagram of Problem 2 (shown at the end of the text), (a) explain how, starting from the point at which A_1 and B_1 intersect, mutually advantageous exchange can take place between individuals A and B; (b) what is the value of the MRS_{xy} at point E, D, and F?

★4. Suppose that the isoquants for commodities X and Y are given by X_1, X_2, X_3, and Y_1, Y_2, Y_3, respectively, in the table below. Suppose also

X's Isoquants

X_1		X_2		X_3	
L	K	L	K	L	K
5	7	8	5	10	7
6	2	9	3	11	5
7	1	11	2	13	4.5

Y's Isoquants

Y_1		Y_2		Y_3	
L	K	L	K	L	K
9	2	7	4	10	4
3	4	5	6	8	7
1	6	4	8	7.5	8.5

that the total of 14L and 9K are available to produce commodities X and Y. Draw the Edgeworth box diagram for exchange and show the production contract curve.

5. For the Edgeworth box diagram of Problem 4 (shown at the end of the text), (a) explain how, starting from the point at which X_1 and Y_1 intersect, the output of both commodities can be increased by simply reallocating some of the fixed amounts of L and K available between the production of X and Y; (b) what is the value of the $MRTS_{LK}$ at points M, J, and N?

6. Suppose that in the figure in the answer to Problem 4, $X_1 = 4X$ and $Y_3 = 13Y$, $X_2 = 10X$ and $Y_2 = 9Y$, and $X_3 = 14X$ and $Y_1 = 4Y$. Derive the production-possibilities frontier corresponding to the production contract curve given in the figure in the answer to Problem 4. What does a point inside the production-possibilities frontier indicate? A point outside?

7. Find (a) the MRT_{xy} at points J', M', and N' for the production-possibilities frontier of Problem 6. (b) If $MC_y = \$100$ at point M', what is MC_x? (c) Why is the production-possibilities frontier concave to the origin? (d) When would the production-possibilities frontier be a straight line?

★8. Superimpose the Edgeworth box diagram for exchange of Problem 2 on the production-possibilities frontier of Problem 4 (both shown at the end of the text) and determine the general equilibrium of production and exchange.

9. Explain why the economy portrayed in the answer to Problem 8 would not be simultaneously in general equilibrium of production and exchange at points D and F.

10. Given that the economy of Problem 8 produces at point M' on its production-possibilities frontier, determine (a) how much of commodities X and Y it produces, (b) how this output is distributed between individuals A and B, (c) how much labor (L) and capital (K) are used to produce commodities X and Y, (d) What questions have been left unanswered in the model?

11. Suppose that the economy represented by the figure in the answer to Problem 8 (shown at

the end of the text) grows over time and/or has available a more advanced technology. Explain how this affects the figure and general equilibrium analysis.

★12. Show how the solution of the set of three simultaneous linear equations in Application 2 was obtained.

Supplementary Readings

For a problem-solving approach to the topics presented in this chapter, see

Dominick Salvatore, *Microeconomic Theory,* 2nd ed. (New York: McGraw-Hill, 1983), Chapter 14 (Sections 14.1 to 14.6).

The first general equilibrium model presented mathematically is found in

Léon Walras, *Elements of Pure Economics,* translated by William Jaffé (Homewood, Ill.: Irwin, 1954).

For a more recent and advanced treatment of general equilibrium theory, see

James Quirk and Rubin Saposnick, *Introduction to*

General Equilibrium Theory and Welfare Economics (New York: McGraw-Hill, 1968).

A very advanced presentation and extension of general equilibrium theory is found in

Gerard Debreu, *Theory of Value* (New Haven, Conn.: Yale University Press, 1959).

Kenneth J. Arrow and F. H. Hahn, *General Equilibrium Analysis* (San Francisco: Holden-Day, 1972).

The original input-output application of general equilibrium theory is found in

Wassily W. Leontief, *The Structure of the American Economy* (New York: Oxford Universtiy Press, 1951).

Welfare Economics

18-1   Welfare Economics—The General Concept

18-2   Utility-Possibilities Frontiers

18-3   The Social Welfare Function and the Point of Maximum Social Welfare

18-4   Perfect Competition and Economic Efficiency

18-5   Social Policy Criteria

18-6   Applications

Examples

18-1   "The Painful Prescription: Rationing Hospital Care"

18-2   Income Redistribution and Social Welfare

18-3   Watering Down Efficiency in the Pricing of Water

18-4   Trade Adjustment Assistance

Applications

Application 1:   The Welfare Effects of Monopoly

Application 2:   The Welfare Effects of Monopsony

Application 3:   The Welfare Effects of Price Controls

Application 4:   Marginal Cost Pricing in Planned Economies and in Government-Owned Enterprises

Application 5:   Perfect Competition and Dynamic Efficiency

Chapter 18

Preview Questions

What does welfare economics study?

What is Pareto optimality?

What is the relationship between Pareto optimality and interpersonal comparison of utility?

What does a utility-possibilities frontier measure?

What does a social welfare function portray?

What is the relationship between Pareto optimality and the point of maximum social welfare?

How does Adam Smith's "law of the invisible hand" ensure economic efficiency?

What does Arrow's impossibility theorem postulate?

What is the theory of the second best?

What are the welfare effects of monopoly?

In this chapter, we examine the welfare implications of the general equilibrium model developed in the previous chapter. That is, we utilize the economic conditions for efficiency in the production of output and in the exchange of commodities (which were developed in Chapter 17) to determine the conditions under which the well-being of society is maximized. To do so, we must squarely face the problem of interpersonal comparison of utility. Somewhat more manageable problems are encountered if we simply wish to determine the conditions under which a given change leads to an improvement in social welfare. As the case for Chapter 17, this is a crucial and challenging chapter because it brings together or makes use of most of the theory developed in Parts II–V of the text.

The chapter begins with the definition of welfare economics, economic efficiency, and Pareto optimum. Then, we see how the utility-possibilities frontier can be derived from the contract curve for exchange examined in Chapter 17. Subsequently, we discuss the social welfare function and its use in determining the point of maximum social welfare. Finally, we examine the relationship between perfect competition and economic efficiency, and the way to measure the effect of economic changes on social welfare. In the section on applications, we analyze the welfare effects of monopoly, monopsony, and price controls, and we discuss marginal cost pricing in government-owned enterprises, and the meaning and importance of dynamic efficiency. These applications and the examples presented in the chapter clearly indicate the usefulness and relevance of the theory of welfare economics.

18-1

Welfare Economics—The General Concept

In this section, we define the meaning of welfare economics and Pareto optimality, and review the marginal conditions for economic efficiency and Pareto optimum. These concepts represent the link between the theory of general equilibrium presented in Chapter 17 and the conditions required for maximizing the well-being of society examined in this chapter.

18-1a The Meaning of Welfare Economics and Pareto Optimality

Welfare economics studies the conditions under which the solution to the general equilibrium model presented in Chapter 17 can be said to be optimal. It examines the conditions for economic efficiency in the production of output and in the exchange of commodities, and equity in the distribution of income. This is to be clearly distinguished from the everyday usage of the term "welfare," which refers mostly to government programs to aid low-income families. That topic is only a very small part of what welfare economics covers.

The maximization of society's well-being requires the optimal allocation of inputs among commodities and the optimal allocation of commodities (i.e., distribution of income) among consumers. The conditions for the optimal allocation of inputs among commodities and exchange of commodities among consumers were discussed in Chapter 17 and will be summarized below. These are objective criteria devoid of ethical connotations or value judgments. On the other hand, it is impossible to objectively determine the optimal distribution of income. This necessarily requires interpersonal comparisons of utility and value judgments on the relative "deserving-ness" or merit of various members of society, and different people will inevitably have different opinions on this. For example, taxing $100 away from individual A and giving it as a subsidy to individual B will certainly make B better off and A worse off. But who is to say that the society composed of both individuals is better or worse off as a whole? This involves comparing the utility lost by individual A to the utility gained by individual B, and even if A has a high income and B has a low income to begin with, different people will have different opinions on whether this increases social welfare, reduces it, or leaves it unchanged. Therefore, no entirely objective or scientific rule can be defined.

It was primarily to distinguish between the scientific and objective, from the subjective and controversial aspects of welfare economics, that Vilfredo Pareto, the great Italian economist of the turn of the century, devised in 1909 the efficiency rule that became known as **Pareto optimality.**[1] This is the cornerstone of modern welfare economics. According to this, a distribution of inputs among commodities and of commodities among consumers is Pareto optimal or efficient if no reorganization of production and consumption is possible by which some individuals are made better off (in their own judgment) without making someone else worse off. Any change that improves the well-being of some individuals without reducing the well-being of others, clearly improves the welfare of society as a whole, and should be undertaken. This will move society from a Pareto nonoptimal position to Pareto optimum. Once at Pareto optimum, no reorganization of production and exchange is possible that makes someone better off without, at the same time, making someone else worse off. To evaluate such changes requires interpersonal comparisons of utility, which are subjective and controversial.

Example 18-1   "The Painful Prescription: Rationing Hospital Care"

The Facts: The great difficulty with interpersonal comparison of utility in making social choices is aptly exemplified by the need to ration hospital care. New therapeutic techniques (such as open-heart surgery) and new diagnostic devices (such as CAT scanners) have improved medical care, but have greatly added to costs. For example, open-heart surgery costs tens of thousands of dollars and replaces the much cheaper (but somewhat less effective) use of drugs in treating heart patients. This raises difficult choices for society in general and for physicians and hospitals in particular, as they try to contain ever rising costs of medical care. In England, only a handful of patients with chronic kidney failure over the age of 55 are referred for expensive dialysis, the others are simply allowed to die of chronic renal failure. The idea of rationing medical care is generally alien to Americans, accustomed as they are to expect the best care that can be medically provided. However, ever rising medical costs are likely to lead to rationing in the use of some new and expensive techniques and diagnostic devices.

Comment: As pointed out by Fuchs, medical care has always been rationed in the United States and elsewhere, since "no nation is wealthy enough to provide all the care that is technically feasible and desirable...." Therefore, the change is not between "no rationing and rationing, but rather in the way rationing takes place—who does the rationing and who is affected by it." The way hospital care (particularly the use of the more advanced and costly new diagnostic techniques) are to be rationed in the future is

---

[1] Vilfredo Pareto, *Manual of Political Economy*, translated by William Jaffé (New York: August M. Kelley, 1971).

likely to give rise to a prolonged national debate and a period of great turmoil. In addition, unless the courts redefine negligence in view of the need to restrain rising medical costs, physicians are likely to face more and more malpractice suits.

Source: V. R. Fuchs, "The 'Rationing' of Medical Care," *The New England Journal of Medicine,* December 13, 1984, pp. 1572–1573, and H. J. Aaron and W. B. Schwartz, *The Painful Prescription: Rationing Hospital Care* (Washington, D.C.: Brookings, 1984).

18-1b Marginal Conditions for Economic Efficiency and Pareto Optimum

The conditions for Pareto optimality are those for general equilibrium or **economic efficiency** in exchange, production, and simultaneously in production and exchange, as discussed in Chapter 17. In a very simple economy of two individuals, two commodities (X and Y), and no production, the contract curve for exchange (along which the MRS_{xy} is the same for both individuals) is the locus of Pareto optimum in exchange and consumption. As we have seen in Section 17-2, a movement from a point off the contract curve to a point on it improves the condition of either or both individuals, with the given quantities of the two commodities. Once on the contract curve, the economy is in general equilibrium or Pareto optimum in exchange in the sense that either individual can be made better off, only by making the other worse off. In an economy of many individuals and many commodities, Pareto optimum in exchange requires that the marginal rate of substitution between any pair of commodities be the same for all individuals consuming both commodities.

In a very simple economy of two commodities, two inputs (L and K), and no exchange, the production contract curve (along which the $MRTS_{LK}$ is the same for both commodities) is the locus of Pareto optimum in production. As we have seen in Section 17-3, a movement from a point off the production contract curve to a point on it makes it possible for the economy to produce more of either or both commodities, with the given inputs and technology. Once on the production contract curve, the economy is in general equilibrium or Pareto optimum in production in the sense that the economy can increase the output of either commodity, only by reducing the output of the other. In an economy of many commodities and many inputs, Pareto optimum in production requires that the marginal rate of technical substitution between any pair of inputs be the same for all commodities and producers using both inputs.

Finally, Pareto optimum in production and exchange simultaneously, in an economy of many inputs, many commodities, and many individuals requires that the marginal rate of transformation in production equal the marginal rate of substitution in consumption for every pair of commodities and for every pair of individuals consuming both commodities. In the case

585

of a very simple economy composed of only two commodities and two individuals (A and B), Pareto optimality in production and consumption requries that

$$MRT_{XY} = MRS_{XY}^{A} = MRS_{XY}^{B}$$

This was shown graphically in Figure 17-5 by the point on the contract curve for exchange at which the common slope of an indifference curve of individual A and individual B is equal to the slope of the production frontier at the point of production. Note that the above marginal conditions for economic efficiency are independent of institutional settings and are equally applicable to free enterprise as to planned economies (see Application 4).

If we assume that there is only one individual (a Robinson Crusoe) in society, we achieve considerable graphical simplification in showing the point of economic efficiency in production and consumption.[2] This is given by point M^* in Figure 18-1, at which indifference curve A_2 for individual A (the only individual in society) is tangent to his or her production-possibilities frontier $T'T'$. Any point on $T'T'$ represents a point of efficient production. Given $T'T'$, A_2 is the highest indifference curve that the individual can reach with his or her production-possibilities frontier. At point M^* (the tangency point of A_2 to $T'T'$), output is $6X$ and $3Y$, and $MRT_{xy} = MRS_{xy} = \frac{3}{6}$. Production and consumption is economically efficient and society (the individual) maximizes welfare.

18-2

Utility-Possibilities Frontiers

In this section we derive the utility-possibilities frontier from the contract curve for exchange. We will also derive the grand utility-possibilities frontier from points of Pareto optimum in both production and exchange.[3]

18-1a The Utilities-Possibilities Frontier

By assigning utility rankings to the indifference curves of individual A and individual B in Figure 17-5, we can map or transfer the contract curve for exchange of Figure 17-5 from output or commodity space to utility space, and thus derive utility possibilities frontier $U_{M'}U_{M'}$ in Figure 18-2. Specifi-

---

[2] Since in this very special case there is no problem of interpersonal comparison of utility, the point of maximum economic efficiency in production and consumption also represents the point of maximum social welfare.

[3] This section is based on Francis M. Bator, "The Simple Analytics of Welfare Maximization," *The American Economic Review*, March 1957, pp. 22–59.

FIGURE 18-1.
Efficiency in
Production and
Exchange in a
"Robinson Crusoe"
Economy

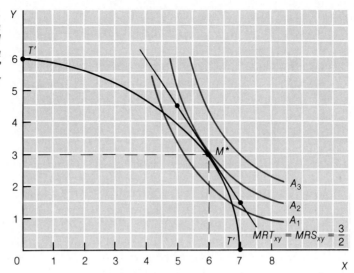

In a single-person economy, economic efficiency in production and exchange (and maximum social welfare) is achieved at point M*, at which indifference curve A_2 for individual A (the only individual in society) is tangent to his or her production possibilities frontier T'T'. Output is 6X and 3Y, and $MRT_{xy} = MRS_{xy} = 3/2$.

FIGURE 18-2.
The Utility-
Possibilities
Frontier

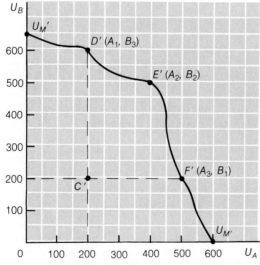

Utility-possibilities frontier $U_M U_{M'}$ shows the various combinations of utilities received by individuals A and B (i.e., U_A and U_B) when the economy composed of individuals A and B is in general equilibrium or Pareto optimum in exchange. It is obtained by mapping exchange contract curve $O_A DEFO_B$ in Figure 17-5 from output or commodity space to utility space. Specifically, if A_1 refers to $U_A = 200$ utils and B_3 to $U_B = 600$ utils, point D in Figure 17-5 can be plotted as point D' in the above figure. Point E can be plotted as point E', and point F as F'. By joining points D'E'F', we get utility-possibilities frontier $U_M U_{M'}$.

587

cally, if indifference curve A_1 in Figure 17-5 referred to 200 units of utility for individual A (i.e., $U_A = 200$ utils) and B_3 referred to $U_B = 600$ utils, we can go from point D (on A_1 and B_3) in commodity space in Figure 17-5 to point D' in utility space in Figure 18-2. Similarly, if A_2 refers to $U_A = 400$ utils and B_2 refers to $U_B = 500$ utils, we can go from point E (on A_2 and B_2) in Figure 17-5 to point E' in Figure 18-2. Finally, if A_3 refers to $U_A = 500$ utils and B_1 refers to $U_B = 200$ utils, we can go from point F (on A_3 and B_1) in Figure 17-5 to point F' in Figure 18-2.[4] By joining points $D'E'F'$ and other points similarly obtained, we derive utility-possibilities frontier $U_{M'}U_{M'}$ in Figure 18-2. Thus, the utility-possibilities frontier is obtained by mapping or transferring the contract curve for exchange from output or commodity space into utility space.

The **utility-possibilities frontier** shows the various combinations of utilities received by individuals A and B (i.e., U_A and U_B) when the simple economy of Chapter 17 is in general equilibrium or Pareto optimum in exchange. It is the locus of maximum utility for one individual for any given level of utility for the other individual. For example, given that $U_A = 400$ utils, the maximum utility of individual B is $U_B = 500$ utils (point E'). A point such as C in Figure 17-2 (at which indifference curves A_1 and B_1 intersect off exchange contract curve O_ADEFO_B) corresponds to point C' inside utility-possibilities frontier $U_{M'}U_{M'}$ in Figure 18-2. By simply redistributing the $10X$ and $8Y$ available to the economy (point M' in Figure 17-5) between individuals A and B, the economy can move from point C' to point D' in Figure 18-2 and increase U_B, to point F' and increase U_A, or to point E' and increase both U_A and U_B. A point outside the utility-possibilities frontier cannot be reached with the available amounts of commodities X and Y. Of all points of Pareto optimality in exchange along utility possibilities frontier $U_{M'}U_{M'}$ in Figure 18-2, only point E' (which corresponds to point E in Figure 17-5) is also a point of Pareto optimality in production. That is, at point E', $MRS_{XY}^A = MRS_{XY}^B = MRT_{XY} = \%$.

18-2b The Grand Utility-Possibilities Frontier

We have seen that utility-possibilities frontier $U_{M'}U_{M'}$ in Figure 18-2 (repeated below in Figure 18-3) was derived from the contract curve for exchange drawn from point O to point M' on the production-possibilities frontier in Figure 17-5. If we picked another point on the production-possibilities frontier of Figure 17-5, say, point N', we can construct another

---

[4] Note that the scale along the horizontal axis refers only to individual A, while the scale along the vertical axis refers only to B. Thus, $U_A = 400$ utils is not necessarily smaller than $U_B = 500$ utils since no interpersonal comparison of utility is implied. Furthermore, the scale along either axis is ordinal, not cardinal. That is, $U_A = 300$ utils is greater than $U_A = 200$ utils, but not necessarily 1.5 times larger. Note also that utility-possibilities frontier $U_{M'}U_{M'}$ is negatively sloped, but irregularly rather than smoothly shaped.

FIGURE 18-3.
The Grand Utility-
Possibilities
Frontier

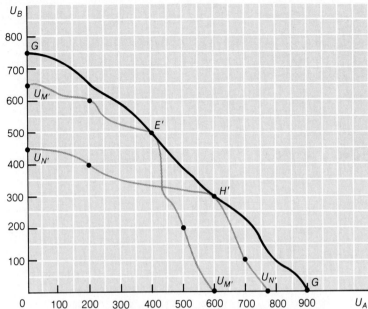

Utility-possibilities frontier $U_{M'}U_{M'}$ *is that of Figure 18-2. Utility-possibilities frontier* $U_{N'}U_{N'}$ *is derived from the contract curve for exchange in the Edgeworth box diagram constructed from point N' on the production-possibilities frontier of Figure 17-5. By joining E', H', and other Pareto optimum points of production and exchange similarly obtained in the above figure, we get grand utility-possibilities frontier GE'H'G.*

Edgeworth box diagram and get another contract curve for exchange, this one drawn from point O to point N' in Figure 17-5. From this different contract curve for exchange (not shown in Figure 17-5), we can derive another utility-possibilities frontier ($U_{N'}U_{N'}$ in Figure 18-3) and obtain another Pareto optimum point in production and exchange (point H' in Figure 18-3). By then joining points E', H', and other points similarly obtained, we can derive grand utility-possibilities frontier $GE'H'G$ in Figure 18-3.[5]

Thus, the **grand utility-possibilities frontier** is the envelope to the utility-possibilities frontiers at Pareto optimum points of production and exchange. It indicates that no reorganization of the production-exchange process is possible that makes someone better off without, at the same time, making someone else worse off. This is as far as objective analysis goes. In order to determine the Pareto optimum point in production and exchange at which social welfare is maximum, we need a social welfare function. This is examined next.

---

[5] Note that the various utility-possibilities frontiers, and the grand utility-possibilities frontier derived from them are negatively sloped but are usually irregularly shaped as in Figure 18-3.

18-3

The Social Welfare Function and the Point of Maximum Social Welfare

In this section we define a social welfare function that will allow us to determine the point of maximum social welfare.

18-3a The Social Welfare Function

We have seen in the last section that every point on the grand utility-possibilities frontier is a Pareto optimum point of production and exchange. In order to determine which of these points refers to the maximum social welfare, we need a social welfare function derived from the positions of individual A and individual B on their own preference scale. A **social welfare function** measures the aggregate utility of individuals A and B and can be represented by a family of social or community indifference curves, three of which are W_1, W_2, and W_3 in Figure 18-4. It might be assumed that the aim of society is to reach the highest social indifference curve possible.

FIGURE 18-4.
Social Indifference
Curves

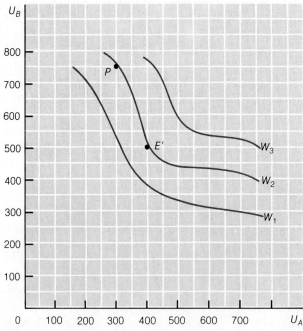

W$_1$, W$_2$, and W$_3$ are three social indifference curves. Each one shows the various combinations of U_A and U_B that give the same level of welfare to the society composed of individuals A and B. Since individual A is better off at point E' than at point P on W$_2$, while the opposite is true for individual B, the construction of social indifference curves involves interpersonal comparisons of utility. The aim of society is to reach the highest social indifference curve possible.

Social indifference curves are negatively sloped, but need not be convex to the origin at every point. Points on the same social indifference curve, such as point P and E' on W_2, refer to the same level of social welfare. However, since individual A is better off at point E' than at point P, while the opposite is true for individual B, the construction of social indifference curves involves interpersonal comparisons of utility, or a decision on the part of society regarding the relative "deservingness" or merit of the two individuals.

In a dictatorship, a social welfare function (and social indifference curves) reflects the value judgment of the dictator. In a democracy, it is extremely difficult or impossible to construct a social welfare function by voting. The reason for this is discussed in Section 18-5b. Here, we simply assume that a social welfare function and social indifference curves exist in order to be able to proceed with the analysis.

18-3b The Point of Maximum Social Welfare

The **maximum social welfare** or "constrained bliss" is given by the point at which a social indifference curve is tangent to the grand utility-possibilities frontier. This is given by point E' in Figure 18-5, at which social indifference curve W_2 (from Figure 18-4) is tangent to grand utility-possibilities frontier GG (from Figure 18-3). Social indifference curve W_2 is the highest that this society can reach with its grand utility-possibilities frontier. Society would like to reach W_3 but cannot. Thus, by assuming a social welfare function and social indifference curves we were able to determine which of the infinite number of Pareto optimum points of production and exchange on the grand utility-possibilities frontier maximizes social welfare.

At point E' (the point of maximum social welfare in Figure 18-5), U_A = 400 utils and U_B = 500 utils. For this to be the case individuals A and B must be at point E in Figure 17-5, with individual A on indifference curve A_2 and receiving 6X and 3Y, and individual B on indifference curve B_2 and receiving 4X and 5Y. Thus, this society maximizes its welfare by producing a total of 10X and 8Y (point M' on the production possibilities frontier in Figure 17-5). We have now determined that the output of 10X and 8Y (which was assumed in Section 17-5) is the output that maximizes social welfare. We were able to do this only by assuming a social welfare function that is based on interpersonal comparisons of utility (and which, as we will see in Section 18-5b, is extremely difficult or impossible to arrive at by democratic vote).

At this point, it is useful to take stock of what was done up to now and summarize the answer to the general equilibrium model presented in this chapter and in Chapter 17. The following has been established: (1) U_A = 400 utils and U_B = 500 utils (point E' in Figure 18-5); (2) the economy produces 10X and 8Y (point M' in Figure 17-5), of which individual A receives

591

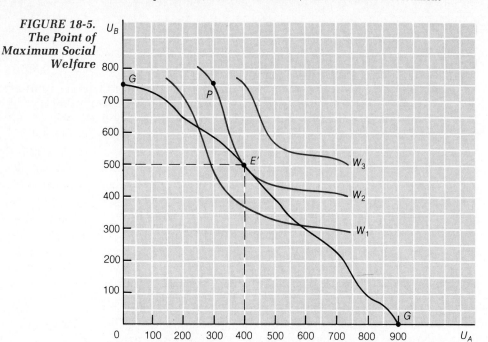

FIGURE 18-5.
The Point of
Maximum Social
Welfare

The maximum social welfare or "constrained bliss" is given by point E', at which social indifference curve W_2 (from Figure 18-4) is tangent to grand utility-possibilities frontier GG (from Figure 18-3). W_2 is the highest social indifference curve that this society can reach with its grand utility-possibilities frontier. At point E', $U_A = 400$ utils and $U_B = 500$ utils.

$6X$ and $3Y$ and individual B receives the remainder of $4X$ and $5Y$ (point E in Figure 17-5); (3) of $12L$ and $10K$ available to this economy, $7L$ and $4K$ are used to produce $10X$ and the remainder of $5L$ and $6K$ to produce $8Y$ (point M in Figure 17-3).[6] Aside from dealing with only two individuals, two commodities, and two inputs, this is a complete general equilibrium model dealing with production, exchange, distribution, and welfare. It can be used to show how a change in any part of the model affects every other part of the model.

For example, an increase in the amount of inputs available will increase the size of the Edgeworth box diagram for production and change the production contract curve inside it. This will cause the production-possibilities frontier to shift outward, indicating that more of commodities X and Y can now be produced. This, in turn, affects the size of the Edgeworth box diagrams for exchange inscribed under the production-possibilities frontier, and the contract curve for exchange inside them. Finally, this outward shift in the utility-possibilities frontier and the grand utility-possibilities frontier allows society to reach a higher social indifference curve.

[6] We will see in the next section that if we assume perfect competition in all input and commodity markets, we can also determine P_L/P_K or w/r and P_X/P_y.

Example 18-2 **Income Redistribution and Social Welfare**

The Facts: Table 17-3 and Figure 17-7 showed that the after-taxes and after-transfers inequality in the distribution of income is much smaller than the before-taxes and the before-transfers inequality. Presumably, income redistribution from high- to low-income families increases social welfare. However, this conclusion is based on interpersonal comparisons of utility, which is subjective and controversial (except, perhaps, if the before-taxes and the before-transfers income distribution is so unequal as to lead to starvation for some people and/or social turmoil).

Comment: While economists generally shy away from making interpersonal comparisons of utility, other social scientists and politicians do not. This is inevitable, as practically all government policies benefit some members of society but harm others (as, for example, progressive taxation, transfer payments, industrial subsidies, tariff reductions, and so on). Thus, without implicit or explicit interpersonal comparisons of utility, it is practically impossible to make any policy decision. We will return to this topic in Section 18-5.

Source: U.S. Congress, *Congressional Budget Office*, "Poverty Status of Families Under Alternative Definitions of Income," January 13, 1977.

18-4

Perfect Competition and Economic Efficiency

With perfect competition in all input and commodity markets, the three marginal conditions for economic efficiency or Pareto optimum in production and exchange (discussed in Chapter 17 and summarized in Section 18-1b) are automatically satisfied. This is the basic argument in favor of perfect competition. We can easily prove that perfect competition leads to economic efficiency.

We have seen in Section 3-4a that a consumer maximizes utility or satisfaction when he or she reaches the highest indifference curve possible with his or her budget line. This occurs where an indifference curve is tangent to the budget line. At the tangency point, the slope of the indifference curve (the MRS_{xy}) is equal to the slope of the budget line (P_x/P_y). Since P_x and P_y, and thus P_x/P_y, are the same for all consumers under perfect competition, the MRS_{xy} is also the same for all consumers consuming both commodities. This is the first marginal condition for economic efficiency or Pareto optimum in exchange. We can now also establish that for the simple economy examined in Chapter 17, $P_x/P_y = \frac{3}{4}$ (the absolute value of the slope of the common tangent to indifference curves A_2 and B_2 at point E in Figure 17-5).

We have also seen in Section 8-2b that efficiency in production requires that the $MRTS_{LK}$ (the absolute value of the slope of an isoquant) be equal to P_L/P_K or w/r (the ratio of the input prices given by the absolute value of the slope of the isocost line). Since P_L or w and P_K or r, and thus P_L/P_K or w/r, are the same for all producers under perfect competition, the $MRTS_{LK}$ is also the same for all producers using both inputs. This is the second marginal condition for economic efficiency or Pareto optimum in production. We can now also establish that for the simple economy examined in Chapter 17, P_L/P_K or $w/r = \frac{2}{3}$ (the absolute value of the common tangent to isoquants X_2 and Y_2 at point M in Figure 17-3).[7]

Finally, we have seen in Section 17-4 that $MRT_{xy} = MC_x/MC_y$, and in Section 10-3b that perfectly competitive firms produce where $MC_x = P_x$ and $MC_y = P_y$. Therefore, $MC_x/MC_y = P_x/P_y = MRT_{xy}$. Since we have also seen above that under perfect competition $MRS_{xy} = P_x/P_y$ for all consumers consuming both commodities, we conclude that $MRT_{xy} = MRS_{xy}$ for all consumers consuming both commodities. This is the third marginal condition for economic efficiency and Pareto optimum in production and exchange. For example, when the simple economy of Chapter 17 produces $10X$ and $8Y$ (point M' in Figure 17-5), $MRT_{XY} = MRS_{XY}^A = MRS_{XY}^B = \frac{3}{4}$. Individual A should then consume $6X$ and $3Y$ and individual B should consume the remaining $4X$ and $5Y$ (point E in Figure 17-5) for the economy to be simultaneously in Pareto optimum of production and exchange. Note, however, that perfect competition only leads to a Pareto optimum point of production and exchange on the grand utility-possibilities frontier.

To determine which of the infinite number of Pareto optimum points of production and exchange on the grand utility-possibilities frontier maximizes social welfare, we need a social welfare function. Yet, the fact that perfect competition leads to maximum economic efficiency and Pareto optimum in production and exchange is no small achievement. It proves Adam Smith's famous **law of the invisible hand** stated over two hundred years ago, which postulates that in a free market economy, each individual by pursuing his or her own selfish interests is led, as if by an *invisible hand*, to promote the well-being of society, more so than he or she intends or even understands. This is true, however, only in the absence of **market failures.** These arise from the existence of monopoly, monopsony, price controls, externalities, and public goods that lead to economic inefficiencies. The first three conditions (i.e., monopoly, monopsony, and price con-

---

[7] Note that in microeconomic theory, we are only concerned with *relative*, not absolute, input and commodity prices. This means that proportionate changes in (e.g., doubling or halving) all input prices and/or all commodity prices do not change the solution to the general equilibrium model. If we want to get unique absolute (dollar) values for P_x, P_y, P_L, (or w), and P_K (or r), we would have to add a monetary equation, such as Fisher's "equation of exchange" to our model. This is done in a course in macroeconomic theory but is not needed in microeconomics.

trols) are examined in Applications 1 to 3 in this chapter. *Externalities* and *public goods* are examined in Chapter 19.

Finally, note that perfect competition leads to maximum efficiency and Pareto optimum in production and exchange *at a particular point in time.* Over time, tastes, the supply of inputs, and technology change, and what is most efficient at one point in time may not be most efficient over time. In short, perfect competition leads to *static, but not necessarily to dynamic, efficiency.* This is discussed in Application 5.

Example 18-3 Watering Down Efficiency in the Pricing of Water

The Facts: In some cities (Los Angeles, for example), the price of water is lower for irrigation than for most other purposes. This reduces economic efficiency because the marginal rate of technical substitution between water and other inputs will differ in irrigation than in other uses. For example, suppose that the price of 1,000 cubic feet of water is equal to the daily wage of an unskilled worker when used for irrigation, but it is twice the daily wage of the unskilled worker when used to wash cars. Then, a farmer will use water until the marginal rate of technical substitution between water and labor is equal to 1, but a car-washing firm until $MRTS = 2$. Water and labor inputs are then utilized as at a point (such as R in Figure 17-3) at which the isoquants intersect off the production contract curve, and production is inefficient. In this case, the farmer will use too much water and too little labor, while the car-washing firm will underutilize water and overutilize labor.

Comment: If the price of water were the same for both the farmer and the car-washing firm in the above example, economic efficiency in production would increase. Each producer would then use water and labor until the MRTS between water and labor would be equal to the relative price of these two inputs. The result is that the output of either or both commodities or services would increase, with the given quantity of water and unskilled labor available. This is equivalent to moving from point R to a point from J to N on the production contract curve of Figure 17-3.

Source: J. Hirschleifer, J. Milliman, and J. De Haven, *Water Supply* (Chicago: University of Chicago Press, 1960).

18-5

Social Policy Criteria

In this section we examine (1) some very important criteria for measuring changes in social welfare, (2) Arrow's impossibility theorem, and (3) the theory of the second best.

18-5a Measuring Changes in Social Welfare

There are four different criteria to determine whether or not a particular policy raises social welfare. The *first* is the **Pareto criterion,** discussed in Section 18-1, and accepted by nearly all economists. According to this, a policy increases social welfare if it benefits some members of society (in their own judgment) without harming anyone. In terms of Figure 18-6, a movement from point C^*, inside grand utility-possibilities frontier GG, to points E', H', or any point between E' and H' (such as point V) on GG, benefits one or both individuals and harms none, and thus, it passes the Pareto criterion. However, a movement from point C^* to point Z on GG makes individual B much better off but individual A a little worse off and, so, it does not pass the Pareto criterion. Since most policies will benefit some and harm others,[8] the Pareto criterion does not go very far and it is biased in favor of the *status quo*.

It is to overcome this limitation of the Pareto criterion that Kaldor and Hicks introduced the *second* welfare criterion, which is based on the **compensation principle.**[9] According to the **Kaldor-Hicks criterion,** a change is an improvement if those who gain from the change can fully compensate the losers and still retain some gain. In terms of the movement from point C^* to point Z in Figure 18-6, individual B (the gainer) could fully compensate individual A for his or her loss, so that society could move from point C^* to point E' (instead of from point C^* to Z) on GG, and we can determine that social welfare is higher. Yet, this conclusion is not as clear-cut as it may seem.

First of all, it is possible (though unusual) for the Kaldor-Hicks criterion to indicate that a given policy increases social welfare but also to indicate that, after the change, a movement back to the original position also increases social welfare. This limitation can be overcome with the *third* or **Scitovsky criterion.**[10] This is a double Kaldor-Hicks test. That is, according to Scitovsky, a change is an improvement if it satisfies the Kaldor-Hicks criterion, and after the change, a movement back to the original position *does not* satisfy the Kaldor-Hicks criterion.

Another shortcoming of the Kaldor-Hicks criterion is more serious. It arises because the compensation principle measures the welfare changes of the gainers and losers in monetary units. For example, if a policy increases the income of individual B by $100 but lowers the income of individual A by $60, social welfare has increased according to the Kaldor-Hicks

---

[8] For example, a tax on high-income people to finance aid to low-income families, benefits the latter but harms the former. Even the breakup of a monopoly harms someone (the monopolist who loses the source of profits).

[9] Nicholas Kaldor, "Welfare Propositions in Economics and Interpersonal Comparisons of Utility," *Economic Journal*, December 1939, pp. 549–552; and John R. Hicks, "The Foundations of Welfare Economics," *Economic Journal*, December 1939, pp. 696–712.

[10] Tibor Scitovsky, "A Note on Welfare Propositions in Economics," *Review of Economics and Statistics*, November 1941, pp. 77–78.

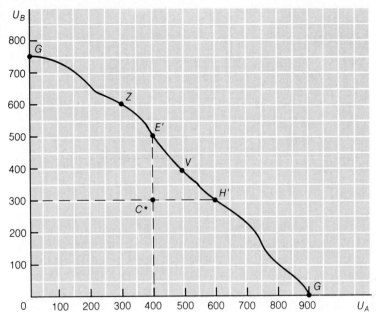

FIGURE 18-6.
Measuring Changes
in Social Welfare

A movement from point C* to a point from E' to H' on grand utility-possibilities frontier GG benefits one or both individuals and harms no one. Thus, it increases social welfare according to the Pareto criterion. A movement from point C* to point Z increases social welfare according to the Kaldor-Hicks criterion, since individual B could fully compensate individual A for his or her loss and still retain some gain. However, since this type of reasoning is based on interpersonal comparisons of utility, social welfare need not be higher.

criterion (because individual B could transfer $60 of his or her $100 income gain to individual A and retain $40).[11] Since compensation is not actually required, the Kaldor-Hicks criterion is based on the assumption that the gain in utility of individual B (when his or her income rises by $100) is greater than the loss of utility to individual A (when his or her income falls by $60). Yet, this line of reasoning is based on interpersonal comparisons of utility and social welfare need not be higher.

The only way to overcome this limitation of the Kaldor-Hicks criterion is to squarely face the problem of interpersonal comparison of utility. This leads us to the *fourth* welfare criterion, which is based on the construction of a **Bergson social welfare function** (of the type discussed in Section 18-3a) from the explicit value judgments of society.[12] A particular policy can then be said to increase social welfare if it puts society on a higher

[11] If compensation actually took place (something that is not required by the Kaldor-Hicks criterion), the Pareto criterion would suffice (since individual B is better off and individual A is not harmed), and the Kaldor-Hicks criterion would be superfluous.

[12] Abram Bergson, "A Reformulation of Certain Aspects of Welfare Economics," *Quarterly Journal of Economics*, February 1938, pp. 310–334.

social indifference curve. However, as it will be seen in the next section, a social welfare function is extremely difficult or impossible to construct by democratic vote.

Example 18-4   **Trade Adjustment Assistance**

The Facts: The reduction in import tariffs provides benefits to society as a whole (as the price of imports fall) but harms workers and firms of import-competing goods. In order to share adjustment costs and reduce objections to tariff reductions, the Trade Expansion Act of 1962 provided retraining and moving assistance to displaced workers and tax relief, low-cost loans, and technical assistance to injured firms.

Comment: The above is an example of actual compensation from the harm imposed on some segments of society by tariff reductions. Since significant gains were estimated to remain even after fully compensating the harmed workers and firms, the reduction in tariff barriers was deemed socially desirable. However, this line of reasoning is based on implicit interpersonal comparison of utility.

Source: Dominick Salvatore, *International Economics* (New York: Macmillan, 1983), pp. 217–218.

18-5b Arrow's Impossibility Theorem

Nobel laureate Kenneth Arrow proved that a social welfare function cannot be derived by democratic vote (i.e., reflecting the preferences of all the individuals in society). This is known as **Arrow's impossibility theorem.**[13]

Arrow lists the following four conditions that he believes must hold for a social welfare function to reflect individual preferences:

1. Social welfare choices must be transitive. That is, if X is preferred to Y and Y is preferred to Z, then X must be preferred to Z.
2. Social welfare choices must not be responsive in the opposite direction to changes in individual preferences. That is, if choice X moves up in the ranking of one or more individuals and does not move down in the ranking of any other individual, then choice X cannot move down in the social welfare ranking.
3. Social welfare choices cannot be dictated by any one individual inside or outside the society.
4. Social choices must be independent of irrelevant alternatives. For example, if society prefers X to Y and Y to Z, then society must prefer X to Y even in the absence of alternative Z.

Arrow showed that a social welfare function cannot be arrived at by

[13] Kenneth J. Arrow, *Social Choice and Individual Values* (New York: Wiley, 1951).

TABLE 18-1   Rankings of Alternatives X, Y, and Z by Ann, Bob, and Charles

	Alternative		
Individuals	X	Y	Z
Ann	1st	2nd	3rd
Bob	3rd	1st	2nd
Charles	2nd	3rd	1st

democratic voting without violating at least one of the above four conditions. This can easily be proved for the first of the above conditions. For example, suppose that Ann, Bob, and Charles (the three individuals in a society) rank alternatives X, Y, and Z as in Table 18-1.

Consider first the choice between alternative X and Y. The majority (Ann and Charles) prefers X to Y. Now consider the choice between alternatives Y and Z. The majority (Ann and Bob) prefers Y to Z. It might then be concluded that since the majority prefers X to Y and Y to Z, the society composed of Ann, Bob, and Charles would prefer X to Z. However, from Table 18-1, we see that the majority (Bob and Charles) prefers Z to X. Therefore, the preference of the majority is inconsistent with the preferences of the individuals making up the majority. In short, this society cannot derive a social welfare function by democratic voting even if individual preferences are consistent. This is sometimes referred to as the "voting paradox."

While disturbing, it must be noted that the above conclusion is based on considering only the rank and not the intensity with which various alternatives are preferred. Thus, if half of society *mildly* preferred more space exploration while the other half *strongly* preferred more aid to low-income families instead, the difference in the intensities of these preferences would have to be disregarded in the decision process according to Arrow.

18-5c   The Theory of the Second Best

The **theory of the second best** postulates that if all of the conditions required to achieve Pareto optimum cannot be satisfied, trying to achieve as many of the conditions as possible does not necessarily increase social welfare (i.e., it is not necessarily the second best position).[14] For example, if some markets in the economy are monopolistic, Pareto optimum cannot be achieved. However, breaking up as many monopolies as possible, when all of them cannot be broken down (e.g. natural monopolies), does not necessarily increase social welfare or represent the second best welfare position for the society. This can be shown with Figure 18-7 (which is similar to Figure 18-1).

[14] R. G. Lipsey and Kelvin Lancaster, "The General Theory of the Second Best," *Review of Economic Studies*, 1956–1957, pp. 11–32.

FIGURE 18-7.
The Theory of the
Second Best

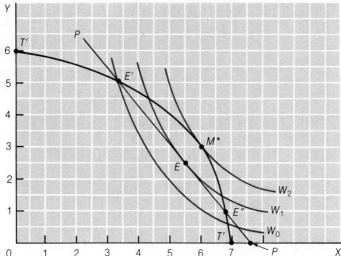

Society achieves Pareto optimum and maximum social welfare at point M*, as in Figure 18-1. If, because of some institutional constraint, combinations to the right of line PP are unattainable, the second best welfare position is achieved at point E on W_1, rather than at point E′ or E″ on production-possibilities frontier T′T′ (where one more of the Pareto optimum conditions are fulfilled than at point E).

Society achieves Pareto optimum and maximum social welfare at point M* in Figure 18-7, at which social indifference curve W_2 is tangent to production-possibilities frontier T′T′.[15] Suppose that because of some institutional constraint, such as monopoly, combinations to the right of line PP are unattainable. A point such as E on W_1 and inside T′T′ is then superior to point E′ or E″ on T′T′ (and satisfying one more of the Pareto optimum conditions). In short, piecemeal welfare economics can be very misleading.

18-6

Applications

In this section we analyze the welfare effects of monopoly, monopsony, and price controls with the tools of analysis developed in this chapter; we evaluate the usefulness of marginal cost pricing in government-owned enterprises, and examine the long-run efficiency implications of perfect competition.

Application 1: The Welfare Effects of Monopoly
We have seen in Part IV of the text that a profit maximizing firm always produces where marginal revenue (MR) equals marginal cost (MC). If com-

---

[15] Note that in Figure 18-7 (and 18-1), social indifference curves are drawn in commodity space, rather than in utility space, as in Figures 18-4 and 18-5.

600

modity Y is produced in a perfectly competitive market, $P_y = MR_y = MC_y$. On the other hand, if commodity X is produced by a monopolist (or other imperfect competitor), $P_x > MR_x = MC_x$. Then,

$$MRT_{xy} = \frac{MC_y}{MC_x} = \frac{MR_x}{MR_y} < \frac{P_x}{P_y} = MRS_{xy}$$

That is, $MRT_{xy} < MRS_{xy}$, so that the third condition for Pareto optimum and economic efficiency (discussed in Section 18-1b) is violated. This is shown in Figure 18-8, which is similar to Figure 17-4. In Figure 18-8, consumption takes place at point D (on indifference curves A_1 and B_3) at which $MRS_{xy} = 3$. With production taking place at point M', $MRT_{xy} = \frac{3}{2}$ or 1.5 (the absolute value of the slope of production-possibilities frontier TT). Consumers are willing to give up $3X$ for $1Y$, but only $1.5X$ need be given up in production to get $1Y$. Thus, too little of X (and too much of Y) is being produced. This confirms the conclusion of Part IV that monopoly restricts output. To achieve Pareto optimum and maximum economic efficiency, monopoly in the production of X would have to be eliminated, so that more

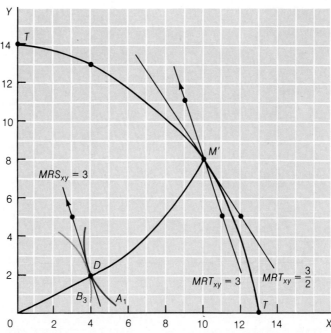

FIGURE 18-8.
The Welfare Effects
of Monopoly

If consumption takes place at point D (on indifference curves A_1 and B_3), at which $MRS_{xy} = 3$, but production takes place at point M' (on production-possibilities frontier TT), at which $MRT_{xy} = 3/2$, one of the conditions for Pareto optimum and economic efficiency is violated. In this case, too little of commodity X and too much of commodity Y is being produced.

of X and less of Y can be produced, until $MRT_{xy} = MRS_{xy}$ for both consumers. This will increase social welfare.

Application 2: The Welfare Effects of Monopsony

We have seen in Part V of the text that a profit maximizing firm always produces where the marginal revenue product (MRP) of each input equals the marginal expense (ME) for the input. If P is the price of the input, and the input market is perfectly competitive, $MRP = ME = P$. Otherwise, $MRP = ME > P$. Now suppose that all markets in the economy are perfectly competitive, except that the firm producing commodity X is a monopsonist in its labor market (i.e., it is the sole employer of labor in its labor market). Therefore, $MRP = ME > P$ in the production of commodity X, while $MRP = ME = P$ in the production of commodity Y. Then,

$$MRTS_{LK}^X = \frac{ME_L}{ME_K} > \frac{P_L}{P_K} = MRTS_{LK}^Y$$

That is, $MRTS_{LK}^X > MRTS_{LK}^Y$, so that the first of the conditions for Pareto optimum and economic efficiency (discussed in Section 18-1b) is violated. This was shown in Figure 17-3, reproduced below as Figure 18-9 for ease of reference.

At point R off production contract curve $O_X JMNO_Y$, (the absolute value of) the slope of isoquant X_1 (i.e., $MRTS_{LK}^X$) exceeds the slope of isoquant Y_1 (i.e., $MRTS_{LK}^Y$). This corresponds to point R' inside production-possibilities frontier TT in Figure 17-4. In this case, too little labor and too much capital

FIGURE 18-9.
The Welfare Effects
of Monopsony

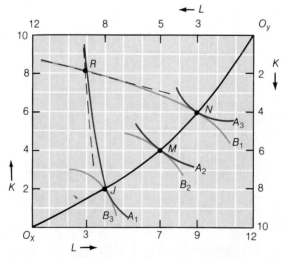

Monopsy in the labor market in the production of commodity X may lead the economy to produce at point R, at which $MRTS_{LK}^X > MRTS_{LK}^Y$, so that one of the conditions for Pareto optimum and economic efficiency is violated. In this case, too little labor and too much capital are used in the production of commodity X.

are used in the production of commodity X, while too much labor and too little capital are used in the production of commodity Y.

To achieve Pareto optimum and economic efficiency in production, the monopsony in the market for labor used in the production of commodity X would have to be eliminated. Then, the economy would be at a point from J to N on production contract curve $O_X JMNO_Y$ in Figure 18-9, at which $MRTS^X_{LK} = MRTS^Y_{LK}$. By so doing, the production of either or both commodities would increase with the given supply of inputs and technology, and social welfare would increase.

Application 3: The Welfare Effects of Price Controls

Effective price controls prevent the attainment of Pareto optimum and maximum economic efficiency. This can be shown by returning to Application 1 in chapter 2 on rent control. As pointed out in Chapter 2, rent control is a price ceiling or a maximum rent below the equilibrium rent. This results in a shortage of apartments, as shown in Figure 18-10 (the same as Figure 2-8).

Figure 18-10 shows that without rent control, the equilibrium rent would be $500 and the equilibrium number of apartments rented would be 2.4 million (point E). At the controlled rent of $300 per month, 3 million apartments could be rented. Since only 1.8 million apartments are available at that rent, there would be a shortage of 1.2 million apartments (AB in the figure).

With only 1.8 million apartments available for rent under rent control,

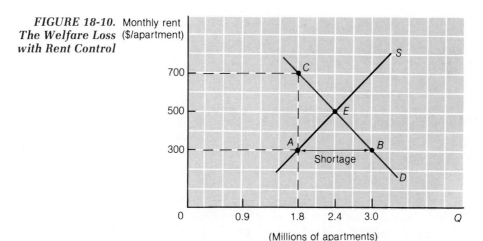

FIGURE 18-10.
The Welfare Loss
with Rent Control

With a rent ceiling of $300 per month, only 1.8 million apartments would be supplied and there would be a shortage of 1.2 million apartments (AB in the figure). The welfare loss with rent control is given by the area of triangle CEA. This measures the difference between what consumers would be willing to pay in order to be able to rent the equilibrium number of apartments (of 2.4 million, rather than 1.8 million available under rent control) and the cost per month of supplying the 0.6 million additional apartments.

603

apartment seekers would be willing to pay $700 per month (point C on the demand curve) rather than go without an apartment, while the cost of supplying an additional apartment is only $300 per month (point A on the supply curve).[16] Only at equilibrium point E is the marginal value of the last apartment to consumers (the height of the demand curve at $Q = 2.4$ million) equal to the marginal cost of supplying the last apartment (the height of the supply curve at $Q = 2.4$ million). Therefore, by reducing the number of apartments available from 2.4 million to 1.8 million, rent control leads to a welfare loss equal to the area of triangle CEA.

The welfare loss to society arises because rent control prevents inputs from flowing into the housing industry where they are more productive than in alternative uses. In other words, too little housing and too much of other commodities are supplied. Consumers would be willing to give up more of other commodities than is required in production in order to get more housing. This means that $MRS > MRT$ so that the third of the Pareto optimum conditions is violated. If rent control were the only distortion in the economy, the elimination of rent control would certainly increase social welfare.

Application 4: Marginal Cost Pricing in Planned Economies and in Government-Owned Enterprises

In Section 18-4 we proved that the three marginal conditions for economic efficiency and Pareto optimum in production and exchange are automatically satisfied under perfect competition. Competitive prices could also be utilized to increase economic efficiency in planned economies, in development projects, and in pricing by government-owned enterprises.

In centrally planned economies (such as the U.S.S.R. and communist China), the government owns all means of production and the price system is not allowed to operate. However, Lerner[17] noted that by utilizing sophisticated computers, the government could solve the general equilibrium model of the economy for the prices that would prevail under perfect competition. Then, the government could set those prices, and allow consumers and managers decentralized decisions to maximize satisfaction and profits, respectively, subject to the established prices. In such a case, the economy could theoretically achieve maximum economic efficiency, as under perfect competition. Economic efficiency could also be maximized if development projects utilized equilibrium prices rather than actual prices when the latter do not reflect the true relative scarcities of inputs and commodities in the nation (the usual case in developing countries).

Economic efficiency would also increase if government-owned enterprises behaved as perfect competitors and charged a price equal to the marginal cost of producing the commodity. However, a problem arises when

---

[16] This assumes insignificant income redistribution effects from rent control.

[17] Abba Lerner, *The Economics of Control* (New York: Macmillan, 1944).

the long-run average cost curve falls over the range of outputs of the government-owned enterprise. Then, the long-run marginal cost curve will be below the long-run average cost curve.[18] In such a case, if the government-owned enterprise set the price equal to the long-run marginal cost, it would not cover its total costs, and the enterprise would incur a loss or deficit. Raising taxes to cover the deficit may also lead to violations of the conditions for economic efficiency.

Application 5: Perfect Competition and Dynamic Efficiency

We have seen in Section 18-4 that perfect competition leads to Pareto optimum and maximum economic efficiency at a particular point in time. However, over time, tastes, the supply of inputs, and technology change, and what is most efficient at one point in time may not be most efficient over time. The question of what is the institutional setting most conducive to technological change and innovations over time is a crucial one because technological change and innovations are the forces responsible for most of the long-term growth in standards of living in modern societies.

According to Schumpeter and others, perfect competition is not conducive to promoting long-run growth through technological change and innovations.[19] Since long-run profits tend toward zero in perfectly competitive markets, firms will not have the necessary resources to undertake sufficient research and development to maximize growth. Furthermore, with free entry under perfect competition, a firm introducing a cost-reducing innovation or a new product would quickly lose its source of profits through imitation. Thus, Schumpeter argued that large firms with some degree of monopoly power were essential to provide the financial resources required for research and development (R&D) and to protect the resulting source of profits. Although monopoly leads to some inefficiency at one point in time (static inefficiency), over time, it is likely to lead to much more technological change and innovation (dynamic efficiency) than perfect competition.

In addition, according to Schumpeter, large firms with some monopoly power are not sheltered from competition. On the contrary, they face powerful competition from new products and new production techniques introduced by other large firms. For example, aluminum is replacing steel in many uses, and plastic is replacing aluminum. This competition is much more dangerous and affects the very existence of the firm. This is the process of **creative destruction** as new products and technologies constantly lead to new investments and the obsolescence of some existing capital stock. In this process of creative destruction, the role of the entrepreneur is crucial. In terms of our general equilibrium model, an economy composed of large firms with some monopoly power may never be on its grand

---

[18] This is the same as in the case of natural monopolies (see Sections 8-5 and 11-1a).

[19] Joseph Schumpeter, *Capitalism, Socialism and Democracy* (New York: Harper & Row, 1942).

utility-possibilities frontier, but this frontier may be pushed out so much more rapidly than under perfect competition that social welfare would be much larger.

Other economists disagree. They point out that it is not at all clear that monopoly power leads to more R&D and faster long-run growth than perfectly competitive markets. Furthermore, a more decentralized market economy is more adaptable and flexible to changes and is much more consistent with individual freedom of choice than an economy characterized by great economic concentration. The challenge is to devise policies that correct the most serious economic distortions in the economy and encourage a high level of R&D, while retaining a large degree of decentralization, equity, and individual freedoms.

Summary

1. Welfare economics studies the conditions under which the solution to the general equilibrium model can be said to be optimal. It examines the conditions for economic efficiency in the production of output and in the exchange of commodities, and for equity in the distribution of income. A distribution of inputs among commodities and of commodities among consumers is Pareto optimal or efficient if no reorganization of production and consumption is possible by which some individuals are made better off without making someone else worse off. The marginal conditions for Pareto optimum are the same as those for economic efficiency and general equilibrium.

2. A utility-possibilities frontier is derived by mapping or transferring a contract curve for exchange from output or commodity space to utility space. It shows the various combinations of utilities received by two individuals at which the economy is in general equilibrium or Pareto optimum in exchange. We can construct an Edgeworth box and contract curve for exchange from each point on the production-possibilities frontier. From each contract curve for exchange we can then construct the corresponding utility possibilities frontier and determine on it the point of Pareto optimum in production and exchange. By joining points of Pareto optimality in production and exchange on each utility-possibilities frontier, we can derive the grand utility-possibilities frontier.

3. In order to determine which of the various Pareto optimum points of production and exchange along the grand utility-possibilities frontier represents the maximum social welfare, we need a social welfare function. This measures the aggregate utility of the two individuals in society and can be represented by social indifference curves. Because a movement along a social indifference curve makes one individual better off but the other worse off, the construction of social indifference curves involves interpersonal comparisons of utility. The maximun social welfare or constrained bliss is given by the point at which a social indifference curve is tangent to the grand utility-possibilities frontier.

4. Under perfect competition in all input and commodity markets, the three marginal conditions for economic efficiency and Pareto optimum in production and consumption are automatically satisfied. This is the basic argument in favor of perfect competition and can be regarded as a proof of Adam Smith's law of the invisible hand. In proving that perfect competition leads to maximum economic efficiency we also determine the equilibrium relative input and commodity prices. Perfect competition leads to maximum economic efficiency only in the absence of market failure (monopoly, monopsony, price controls, and so on).

5. A change that benefits some but harms others can be evaluated with the Kaldor-Hicks-Scitovsky criterion. However, this is based on the compensation principle, which measures the welfare

changes of the gainers and the losers in monetary units. The only way to overcome this shortcoming is with a social welfare function. Arrow proved that a social welfare function cannot be derived by democratic vote. This is known as Arrow's impossibility theorem. The theory of the second best postulates that if all the conditions required to achieve Pareto optimum cannot be satisfied, trying to achieve as many of the conditions as possible does not necessarily lead to the second best welfare position for the society.

6. If the market for commodity X is monopolized but that for commodity Y is not, too little of X and too much of Y is produced for Pareto optimum to be achieved. Imperfect competition in an input market will also prevent the achievement of Pareto optimum. Effective price controls similarly prevent the attainment of Pareto optimum and maximum economic efficiency. Competitive prices could also be utilized to increase economic efficiency in planned economies, in development projects, and in pricing by government-owned enterprises. Perfect competition leads to static but not necessarily dynamic efficiency. Nevertheless, perfect competition may be preferred because of the greater flexibility in the economy and because it is more consistent with individual freedoms of choice.

Glossary

Welfare economics It examines the conditions for economic efficiency in the production of output and in the exchange of commodities, and for equity in the distribution of income.

Pareto optimality The situation where no reorganization of production and consumption is possible by which some individuals are made better off without making someone else worse off.

Economic efficiency The situation in which the marginal rate of transformation in production equals the marginal rate of substitution in consumption for every pair of commodities and for every pair of individuals consuming both commodities.

Utility-possibilities frontier It shows the various combinations of utilities received by two individuals at which the economy (composed of the two individuals) is in general equilibrium or Pareto optimum in exchange.

Grand utility-possibilities frontier The envelope to utility-possibilities frontiers at Pareto optimum points of production and exchange.

Social welfare function It measures the aggregate utility of the two individuals in society and can be represented by a family of social or community indifference curves. It is based on interpersonal comparisons of utility.

Maximum social welfare The point at which a social indifference curve is tangent to the grand utility-possibilities frontier; also called constrained bliss.

Law of the invisible hand The law stated by Adam Smith over two hundred years ago that postulates that in a free market economy, each individual by pursuing his or her own selfish interests, is led, as if by an invisible hand, to promote the welfare of society more so than he or she intends or even understands.

Market failures The existence of monopoly, monopsony, price controls, externalities, and public goods that prevent the attainment of economic efficiency or Pareto optimum.

Pareto criterion It postulates that a change increases social welfare if it benefits some members of society (in their own judgement) without harming anyone.

Compensation principle The amount that those who gain from a change could pay to the losers to fully compensate for their losses.

Kaldor-Hicks criterion It postulates that a change is an improvement if those who gain from the change can fully compensate the losers and still retain some of the gain.

Scitovsky criterion It postulates that a change is an improvement if it satisfies the Kaldor-Hicks criterion and, if, after the change, a movement back to the original position does not satisfy the Kaldor-Hicks criterion.

Bergson social welfare function A social welfare function based on the explicit value judgments of society.

Arrow's impossibility theorem The theorem that

postulates that a social welfare function cannot be derived by democratic vote to reflect the preferences of all the individuals in society.

Theory of the second best The theory that postulates that if all the conditions required to achieve Pareto optimum cannot be satisfied, trying to achieve as many of the conditions as possible does not necessarily lead to the second best position for society.

Creative destruction The process stressed by Schumpeter whereby growth depends primarily on investments to introduce new technology and new products and that also leads to the obsolescence of some existing capital stock.

Questions for Review

1. What is meant by
   (a) welfare economics?
   (b) economic efficiency?
   (c) Pareto optimality?

2. For an economy of many inputs, many commodities, and many individuals, what is the condition for Pareto optimality in
   (a) consumption?
   (b) production?
   (c) production and consumption?

3. Answer the following questions about a utility-possibilities frontier.
   (a) How is it derived?
   (b) What does it show?
   (c) What does a point inside it show?
   (d) What does a point outside it show?

4. Answer the following questions about a grand utility-possibilities frontier.
   (a) How is it derived?
   (b) What does it show?
   (c) What is its relationship to maximum social welfare?

5. (a) What does a social welfare function measure?
   (b) Why is it needed?
   (c) How can it be represented graphically?
   (d) What is its shortcoming?

6. (a) How is the point of maximum social welfare determined?
   (b) What is another name for it?
   (c) What question left unanswered in Chapter 17 can now be answered?

7. How does perfect competition lead to the satisfaction of the conditions for economic effi-

ciency or Pareto optimum in
   (a) exchange?
   (b) production?
   (c) production and exchange simultaneously?

8. What is the meaning and importance of each of the following.
   (a) The law of the invisible hand?
   (b) Market failure?
   (c) Static and dynamic efficiency?

9. What is the
   (a) Pareto criterion?
   (b) compensation principle?
   (c) Kaldor-Hicks criterion?
   (d) Scitovsky criterion?

10. (a) What are the four conditions that Arrow believes must hold for a social welfare function to reflect individual preferences?
    (b) What is Arrow's impossibility theorem?
    (c) What is meant by the "voting paradox"?
    (d) What does the theory of the second best postulate?

11. How can the analysis of this chapter be used to determine that economic efficiency is not maximum with
    (a) monopoly?
    (b) monopsony?
    (c) price control?

12. How can the principles discussed in this chapter be useful to increase economic efficiency in
    (a) planned economies?
    (b) development projects?
    (c) government-owned enterprises?
    (d) the long run?

Problems

1. Explain the relationship between
   (a) Pareto optimality and interpersonal comparison of utility.
   (b) Pareto optimality and maximum social welfare.

2. Suppose that in the figure in the answer to Problem 8 in Chapter 17 (see Figure 17-4 at the end of the text), A_1 refers to 100 utils, A_2 = 300 utils, A_3 = 450 utils and B_1 = 200 utils, B_2 = 400 utils, B_3 = 450 utils.
   (a) Derive the utility-possibilities frontier corresponding to contract curve $O_A DEFO_B$ for exchange in Figure 17-4 at the end of the text.
   (b) At what point is the economy at Pareto optimum in production and exchange?

★3. From Figure 17-4 at the end of the text,
   (a) derive the grand utility-possibilities frontier.
   (b) what do points on the grand utility-possibilities frontier show?

4. Suppose that three social indifference curves for the economy of Problem 3 are given in the following table.

W_1		W_2		W_3	
U_A	U_B	U_A	U_B	U_A	U_B
100	450	100	650	200	750
200	300	300	400	400	500
600	200	600	300	700	400

   (a) Plot these social indifference curves and indicate what they show.
   (b) What is involved in constructing a social welfare function and social indifference curves?

★5. Determine from the grand utility-possibilities frontier of Problem 3 and the social indifference curves of Problem 4 the point of maximum social welfare.

6. Determine how much of commodities X and Y the economy of Problem 5 should produce in order to maximize social welfare.

7. Assuming perfect competition in all markets, determine for the simple economy examined in problems 5 and 6 and in problems 4 and 8 in Chapter 17, the general equilibrium value of
   (a) P_x/P_y.
   (b) P_L/P_K or w/r.

★8. Suppose that in the simple perfectly competitive economy examined in problems 5–7 and in problems 4 and 8 in Chapter 17, P_x = $10 and the marginal (physical) product of labor in the production of commodity X (i.e., MP_L^X) is 6.
   (a) What is P_y?
   (b) What is P_L?
   (c) What is M_K^X?
   (d) What is P_K?
   (e) What would be P_y, P_L, and P_K if P_x = $20?

9. If the institutional constraint preventing the attainment of Pareto optimum and the maximum social welfare in Figure 18-7 is the existence of a monopoly, is the monopoly in the market for commodity X or in the market for commodity Y if production occurred at point E'? At point E''? Why?

10. Starting with Figure 17-4, showing production taking place at point M' and consumption at point F, show why Pareto optimum is not achieved if the government gives a subsidy to the producers of commodity X such that $P_x/P_y = \frac{1}{2}$.

★11. With reference to Figure 18-9, explain why if $P_L/P_K = \frac{2}{3}$ with perfect competition in all markets $MRTS_{LK}^X > \frac{2}{3}$ even though both the labor and capital markets are perfectly competitive in the production of commodity Y, if the firm producing commodity X is a monopsonist in its labor market.

12. Explain in terms of the frontiers examined in Chapter 17 where the economy would be located if each of the Pareto optimum conditions discussed in Section 18-1b were violated.

Supplementary Readings

For a problem-solving approach to the topics presented in this chapter, see

Dominick Salvatore, *Microeconomic Theory,* 2nd ed. (New York: McGraw-Hill, 1983), Chapter 14 (Sections 14-7 to 14-13).

The presentation of welfare economics of the chapter is based on

Francis M. Bator, "The Simple Analytics of Welfare Maximization," *The American Economic Review,* March 1957, pp. 22–59.

The Pareto conditions for economic efficiency were introduced in

Vilfredo Pareto, *Manual of Political Economy,* translated by William Jaffe' (New York: August M. Kelley, 1971).

For an advanced treatment of welfare economics, see

J. Quirk and R. Saposnik, *Introduction to General Equilibrium Theory and Welfare Economics* (New York: McGraw-Hill 1968).

J. de V. Graff, *Theoretical Welfare Economics* (London: Cambridge Universtiy Press, 1957).

A very advanced presentation of welfare economics and of the impossibility theorem is found in

Kenneth J. Arrow, *Social Choice and Individual Values* (New York: Wiley, 1951).

Externalities, Public Goods, and the Role of Government

Chapter 19

19-1 Externalities

19-2 Externalities and Property Rights

19-3 Public Goods

19-4 Benefit-Cost Analysis

19-5 Applications

Examples

19-1 The Case for Government Support of Basic Research

19-2 The Fable of the Apples and the Bees

19-3 The Economics of a Lighthouse

19-4 Benefit-Cost Analysis and the SST

Applications

Application 1: Environmental Pollution

Application 2: Optimal Pollution Control

Application 3: Direct Regulations and Effluent Fees for Optimal Pollution Control

Application 4: The Case Against Government Intervention

Preview Questions

What is an externality?

Why do externalities prevent the attainment of Pareto optimum?

What is the relationship between externalities and property rights?

What does the Coase theorem postulate?

What are public goods?

What is meant by nonrival consumption and nonexclusion?

Why are public goods usually underproduced and underconsumed?

What is benefit-cost analysis?

What is the usefulness of benefit-cost analysis?

When is government intervention justified?

We have seen in Section 18-4 that perfect competition leads to maximum economic efficiency and Pareto optimum. However, this conclusion holds only in the absence of market failures. These arise from the existence of monopoly, monopsony, price controls, externalities, and public goods. (The reason that monopoly, monopsony, and price controls prevent the attainment of economic efficiency and Pareto optimum was discussed in Applications 1 through 3 in Chapter 18).

In this chapter, we examine why the existence of externalities and public goods also leads to economic inefficiencies and to an allocation of inputs and commodities that is not Pareto optimum. We will then examine how the government (through regulation, taxes, and subsidies) could attempt to overcome or at least reduce the negative impact of these distortions on economic efficiency. Because these distortions and government attempts to overcome them are fairly common in most societies, including our own, the importance of the topics presented in this chapter can hardly be overstated.

19-1

Externalities

In this section we define externalities and examine why their existence prevents the attainment of maximum economic efficiency or Pareto optimum, even under perfect competition.

19-1a Externalities Defined

In the course of producing and consuming some commodities, harmful or beneficial side-effects arise that are borne by firms and people not directly involved in the production or consumption of the commodities. These are called **externalities** because they are felt by economic units (firms and individuals) not directly involved with (i.e., that are external to or outside) the economic units that generate these side effects.[1] Externalities are called **external costs** when they are harmful and **external benefits** when they are beneficial. An example of an external cost is the air pollution that may accompany the production of a commodity. An example of an external benefit is the reduced chance of the spreading of a communicable disease when an individual is innoculated against it.

Externalities are classified into five different types. These are external diseconomies of production, external diseconomies of consumption, external economies of production, external economies of consumption, and technical externalities. Each of these will be examined in turn. **External diseconomies of production** are uncompensated costs imposed on others by the expansion of output by some firms. For example, the increased discharge of waste materials by some firms along a waterway may result in antipollution legislation that increases the cost of disposing waste materials for all firms in the area. **External diseconomies of consumption** are uncompensated costs imposed on others by the consumption expenditures of some individuals. For example, the riding of a snowmobile by an individual imposes a cost (in the form of noise and smoke) on other individuals who are skiing, hiking, or ice fishing in the area.

On the other hand, **external economies of production** are uncompensated benefits conferred on others by the expansion of output by some firms. An example of these arises when some firms train more workers to increase output, and some of these workers go to work for other firms (which, therefore, save on training costs). **External economies of consumption** are uncompensated benefits conferred on others by the increased consumption of a commodity by some individual. For example, increased expenditures to maintain his or her lawn by a homeowner increases the value of the neighbor's house. Finally, **technical externalities** arise when declining long-run average costs as output expands leads to monopoly, so that price exceeds marginal cost. Not even regulation to achieve competitive marginal cost pricing is then viable (see Application 3 in Chapter 11).

19-1b Externalities and Market Failure

We have seen in Section 18-4 that perfect competition leads to maximum economic efficiency and Pareto optimum. However, this is true only when

---

[1] The presentation of this section and of Section 19-3 follows Francis M. Bator's "The Anatomy of Market Failure," *Quarterly Journal of Economics*, August 1958, pp. 351–379.

FIGURE 19-1.
Competitive
Overproduction
with External Costs

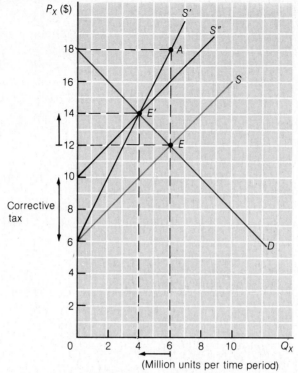

With perfect competition, $P_x = \$12$ and $Q_x = 6$ million units (given by point E at which D and S intersect). S reflects only marginal private costs, while S′ equals marginal private (internal) costs plus marginal external costs. Efficiency and Pareto optimality require that $P_x = \$14$ and $Q_x = 4$ million units (given by point E′, at which D and S′ intersect). This can be achieved with a $4 per-unit corrective tax on producers that shifts S to S″.

private costs equal social costs and when private benefits equal social benefits (i.e., in the absence of externalities). This was implicitly assumed to be the case until now. When externalities are present, the "invisible hand" is led astray and Pareto optimum is not achieved, even under perfect competition. This is shown in Figure 19-1.

We assume that commodity X in Figure 19-1 is produced by a competitive industry. The industry supply curve (S) is the horizontal summation (above minimum average variable costs) of the individual firm's marginal (private) cost curves (i.e., $S = \Sigma MPC$). Given market demand curve D for the commodity, the equilibrium price is $12 and the equilibrium quantity is 6 million units per time period (given by the intersection of D and S at point E in the figure). Suppose that the production of commodity X involves rising external costs (in the form of air pollution, water pollution. traffic congestion, and so on) that the firms producing commodity X do not take into account. The industry supply curve that includes both the private and external costs might then be given by S' (see the figure). Curve S' shows that the marginal *social* cost *(MSC)* of producing 6 million units of commodity *X* exceeds the marginal private cost *(MPC)* of $12 by an amount equal to the marginal external cost *(MEC)* of $6 *(AE* in the figure).

Thus, efficiency or Pareto optimality requires that $P_x = \$14$ and $Q_x = 4$ million (given by the intersection of *D* and *S'* at point *E'* in the figure). Only then would the commodity price reflect the full social cost of producing it. Starting with S (showing the *MPC*), this could be achieved with a $4 per-unit corrective tax on producers of commodity *X*, which shifts S up to *S"* and defines equilibrium point *E'* at the intersection of *D* and *S".*[2] As we will see in the next section, efficiency and Pareto optimality might also be achieved by the proper specification of property rights. Without any such corrective action, the perfectly competitive industry would charge too low a price and produce too much of commodity *X* (compare points *E* with *E'* in the figure).

Efficiency and Pareto optimality are not achieved whenever private and social costs or benefits differ. With external diseconomies of consumption, consumers do not pay the full marginal social cost of the commodity and consume too much of it. Corrective action would then require a tax on consumers rather than on producers. On the other hand, with external economies of production and consumption, the commodity price exceeds the marginal social cost of the commodity so that production and consumption falls short of the optimum level. Efficiency and Pareto optimum in production and in consumption would then require a subsidy (rather than a tax) on producers and on consumers, respectively (see Problems 3 and 5, with answers at the end of the text). Finally, technical externalities (economies of large scale production) over a sufficiently large range of outputs lead to the breakdown of competition (natural monopoly). In that case, marginal cost pricing is neither possible nor viable, and Pareto optimum cannot be achieved.

Example 19-1 The Case for Government Support of Basic Research

The Facts: Basic research refers to efforts to discover fundamental relationships in nature, such as natural laws. Often, these cannot be patented and do not have immediate commercial applications. It is also practically impossible for the firm that makes a discovery of this nature to be able to take advantage of the full range of commercial applications that might result from its discovery. Thus, the social benefits from basic research greatly exceed private benefits. As a result, there is likely to be underinvestment in basic research by the private sector. Since technological

---

[2] However, the marginal external costs created by firms in different areas of the market are likely to be different so that different corrective per-unit taxes may be required to achieve Pareto optimality. Furthermore, *MEC* may be constant rather than rising. The corrective tax may also have some unintended side effects that lead to inefficiency (such as the utilization of a less efficient technology).

change and innovations are the most important contributors to growth in modern societies, there is a strong case for government support of basic research.

Comment: The same arguments that apply to firms in a nation apply to nations in the world. That is, the government of a nation may support less than the optimal level of basic research because additions to fundamental knowledge made by a nation can easily be utilized by other nations. For example, until recently, Japan stressed the finding of commercial applications for basic discoveries made by other nations, mostly the United States, rather than basic research itself.

Source: National Academy of Science, *Basic Research and National Goals* (Washington, D.C.: U.S. Government Printing Office, 1965).

19-2

Externalities and Property Rights

We have seen in the previous section that externalities, by driving a wedge between private and social costs or benefits, prevent the attainment of economic efficiency and Pareto optimality. But why do externalities arise in some cases and not in others? To see this, suppose that you own a car. You have a clear property right in the car and anyone ruining it is liable for damages. The courts will uphold your right to compensation. In this case there are no externalities. Private and social costs are one and the same thing. Compare this to the case of a firm polluting the air. Neither the firm nor the people living next to the firm own the air. That is, the air is **common property.** Since no resident owns the air, he or she cannot sue the firm for damages resulting from the air pollution generated by the firm. The firm imposes an external (i.e., an uncompensated) cost on the individual. These two simple examples clearly demonstrate that externalities arise when property rights are not adequately specified. In the first case, you have a clear property right to the car and there are no externalities. In the second case, no one owns the air and externalities arise. This leads to the famous Coase theorem.[3]

The **Coase theorem** postulates that when property rights are clearly defined and transaction costs are zero, perfect competition results in the internalization of externalities, regardless of how property rights are assigned among the parties (individuals or firms). For example, suppose that a brewery is located downstream from a paper mill that dumps waste into the stream. Suppose also that in order to filter and purify the water to

[3] Ronald R. Coase, "The Problems of Social Costs," *Journal of Law and Economics,* October 1960, pp. 1–44.

make beer, the brewery incurs a cost of $1,000 per month, while the paper mill would incur a cost of $400 to dispose its waste products by other means and not pollute the stream. If the brewery has the property right to clean water, the paper mill will incur the added cost of $400 per month to dispose of its waste without polluting the stream (lest the brewery sue it for damages of $1,000 per month). On the other hand, if the paper mill has the property right to the stream and can freely use it to dump its wastes in it, the brewery will pay to the paper mill $400 per month not to pollute the stream (and thus avoid the larger cost of $1,000 to purify the water later).

The cost of avoiding the pollution is *internalized* by the paper mill in the first instance and by the brewery in the second. That is, the $400 cost per month of avoiding the pollution becomes a regular business expense of one party or the other and *no externalities results*. The socially optimal result of **internalizing external costs** and avoiding the pollution at $400 per month, rather than cleaning up afterwards at a cost of $1,000 per month, is achieved regardless of who has the property right to the use of the stream.[4] Thus, externalities are avoided (and economic efficiency and Pareto optimum achieved) under perfect competition, if property rights are clearly defined and transferable, and if transaction costs are zero.[5]

Transaction costs are the legal, administrative, and informational expenses of drawing up, signing, and enforcing contracts. These expenses are small when the contracting parties are few (as in the above example). When the contracting parties are numerous (as in the case of a firm polluting the air for possibly millions of people in the area), it would be practically impossible or very expensive for the firm to sign a separate contract with each individual affected by the pollution it creates. Contracting costs are then very large and externalities (and inefficiencies) arise. This is especially true in the case of environmental pollution (see Application 1).[6]

Example 19-2   **The Fable of the Apples and the Bees**

The Facts: For decades economists have used the tale of the apples and the bees as a classic example of externalities. That is, the owner of beehives receives an external benefit, in the form of free nectar, which his or her bees extract from the neighbor's apple blossoms to produce honey. At the

---

[4] Note that the cost of pollution abatement is minimized rather than entirely eliminated. The only way to completely avoid the cost of pollution is for the paper mill to stop production. But this would result in the greater social cost of the lost production. The above conclusion is also based on the assumption of a zero income effect on the demand curve for the use of the stream regardless of who has the property right of it.

[5] Even if neither the brewery nor the paper mill had a property right to the use of the stream, the conclusion would generally be the same as long as transaction costs are zero. That is, it pays for the brewery to pay the paper mill $400 per month not to pollute. This is equivalent to the paper mill having the right to the use of the stream.

[6] However, the recent development of class action lawsuits has greatly reduced transaction costs in this area.

same time, the apple grower receives an external benefit in the form of free pollinating services for his or her apple blossoms from the neighbor's bees, which increase crops. Both the apple grower and the owner of the beehives receive external (i.e., unpaid) benefits from the other.

At least so it was taught, until Steven Cheung took the time to investigate the case in the state of Washington. He found that apple growers and bee-keepers were quite aware of the external benefits that each conferred on the others and routinely attempted to internalize (i.e., extract a payment for) the benefits they provided. This was done by contracts for the place-ment of beehives on farms. These contracts specified the number of bee-hives, the average number of bees in each, the dispersion of hives through-out the farm, the time period, and even bee protection against insecticides. When honey production was very large, beekeepers paid farmers (i.e., signed apiary leases) for the right to place hives on the farm. On the other hand, when honey production was very little, farmers paid beekeepers to have hives placed on their farm for pollinating purposes (i.e., signed pol-linating contracts). Indeed in many localities one can find the entry "pol-linating services" in the yellow pages. The amount of actual payment in one direction or the other also depends on the size of the net external ben-efits received by one of the two parties. By so doing, externalities were, for the most part, internalized.

Comment: By inventing the tale of the apples and the bees in order to pro-vide an example of externalities, it seems that economists have themselves created an external cost by theorizing without adequate empirical inves-tigation. As pointed out in Section 1-4, theoretical speculation (in the form of hypotheses) and empirical verification should go hand in hand.

Source: Steven N. S. Cheung, "The Fable of the Bees: An Economic Inves-tigation," *Journal of Law and Economics,* April 1973, pp. 11–33.

19-3

Public Goods

We have seen in Section 18-4 that perfect competition leads to maximum economic efficiency and Pareto optimum in the absence of market failures. One type of market failure results from the existence of public goods. In this section we examine the nature of public goods and their provision.

19-3a The Nature of Public Goods

If consumption of a commodity by one individual does not reduce the amount available for others, the commodity is a public good. That is, once the good is provided for someone, others can also consume it at no extra cost. Examples of **public goods** are national defense, law enforcement, fire and police protection, and flood control (provided by the government), but also radio and TV broadcasting (which are provided by the private sector in many nations, including the United States).

The distinguishing characteristic of public goods is **nonrival consumption.** For example, when one individual watches a TV program, he or she does not interfere with the reception of others. This is to be contrasted to private goods, which are rival in consumption, in that if an individual consumes a particular quantity of a good, such as apples, these *same* apples are no longer available for others to consume.

Nonrival consumption must be distinguished from nonexclusion. **Nonexclusion** means that it is impossible or prohibitively expensive to confine the benefits of the consumption of a good (once produced) to selected people (such as only to those paying for it). While nonrival consumption and nonexclusion often go hand in hand, a public good is defined in terms of nonrival consumption only. For example, since national defense and TV broadcasting are nonrival in consumption (i.e., the same amount can be consumed by more than one individual at the same time) they are both public goods. However, national defense also exhibits nonexclusion (i.e., when it is provided for some individuals, others cannot be excluded from also enjoying it free), while TV broadcasting can be exclusive (e.g., only paying customers can view cable TV). We will see in the next section that public goods (i.e., goods that are nonrival in consumption) will not be provided in the optimal amount by the private sector under perfect competition, thus requiring government intervention. However, first we must determine what is the optimal amount of a public good.

Since a given amount of a public good can be consumed by more than one individual at the same time, the aggregate or total amount of a public good is obtained by the vertical (rather than by the horizontal) summation of the demand curves of the various individuals who consume the public good. This is shown in Figure 19-2. In the figure, D_A is the demand curve of Ann and D_B is the demand curve of Bob for public good X. If Ann and Bob are the only two individuals in the market, the aggregate demand curve for good X, D_T, is obtained by the *vertical* summation of D_A and D_B. The reason for this is that each unit of public good X can be consumed by both individuals at the same time.[7]

Given market supply curve S_X for public good X, the optimal amount of X is 8 units per time period (given by the intersection of D_T and S_X at point E in the figure). At point E, the sum of the individuals' marginal benefits or marginal social benefit equal the marginal social cost (i.e., $AB + AC = AE$). The problem is that, in general, less than the optimal amount of public good X will be supplied under perfect competition, and this prevents the attainment of maximum efficiency and Pareto optimum.

---

[7] This is to be contrasted with the *market* demand curve for a private or rival good, which, as we have seen in Section 5-1, is obtained from the *horizontal* summation of the individuals' demand curves (see Problem 10, with answer at the end of the text).

FIGURE 19-2.
The Optimal
Amount of a Public
Good

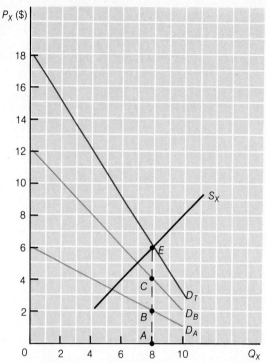

Aggregate demand curve D_T for public good X is obtained by the vertical summation of individual demand curve D_A and D_B. The reason for this is that each unit of public good X can be consumed by both individuals at the same time. Given market supply curve S_X, the optimal amount of X is 8 units per time period (given by the intersection of D_T and S_X at point E). At point E, the sum of the individuals' marginal benefits equals the marginal social costs (i.e., AB+ AC = AE).

Example 19-3   **The Economics of a Lighthouse**

The Facts: A lighthouse is a good example of a public good. Once a lighthouse is built, it can send additional signals to ships during storms at practically zero extra cost. That is, lighthouse signals are nonrival in consumption. However, lighthouse signals are not exclusive, as it was originally believed. That is, each user *can* be charged for the service. Indeed, historical research showed that lighthouses were privately owned in England from 1700 to 1834, and that they must have been doing a good business since their number increased over the period. Lighthouse owners charged ships at dock (according to their tonnage) for their land-demarcation light signals during storms. Usually only one ship at the time was in sight of the lighthouse and ships were identified by their flag. If a ship had not paid for the service, the light signals were not shown.

Comment: The lighthouse provides an example of a public good that is exclusive (so that users can be charged for the service). A similar public good is education. Entrepreneurs often show great ingenuity in making public goods exclusive. An example is the provision of in-place paying binoculars at Niagara Falls and other scenic sights. Another example is the placing of super large TV screens in some bars. These and other similar services would not be provided if they were not or if they could not be made exclusive (i.e., if consumers could not be charged for them).

Source: Ronald R. Coase, "The Lighthouse in Economics," *Journal of Law and Economics,* October 1974, pp. 357–376.

19-3b The Provision of Public Goods

We have seen above that the optimal amount of a public good is that at which the sum of the marginal benefits of all the individuals consuming the good equals its marginal cost. Graphically, this is given by the point at which the aggregate demand curve for the good (obtained from the vertical summation of the individuals' demand curves) intersects the market supply curve of the good. However, less than this optimal amount of the public good is likely to be supplied by the private sector.

There are two related reasons for this. First, when the public good is non-exclusive (i.e., when those individuals not paying for it cannot be excluded from also consuming it), there is a tendency for each consumer to be a free rider. A **free-rider problem** arises because each consumer believes that the public good will be provided anyway, whether he or she contributes to its payment or not. That is, since there are many people sharing the cost of providing the public good, each individual feels that withdrawing his or her financial support will practically go unnoticed by others and will have little or no effect on the provision of the good. The problem is that since many individuals behave this way (i.e., behave as free riders), less than the optimal amount of the public good will be provided.[8] In general, as the group size increases, the free-rider problem becomes more acute. This problem can and is generally overcome by the government taxing the general public to pay for the public good. A good example of this is national defense.[9]

The second (related) problem cannot be resolved as satisfactorily by government intervention. This arises because each individual has no incentive to accurately reveal his or her preferences or demand for the public good. Therefore, it is practically impossible for the government to know exactly what is the optimal amount of the public good that it should provide or induce the private sector to provide. Then there is the problem of

---

[8] Note that even a private (rival) good leads to market failure if it is characterized by nonexclusion (i.e., if each individual consuming it cannot be adequately charged for it).

[9] Sometimes a free-rider problem can partially be resolved by the private sector. Examples are educational television stations, tenants' associations, and charitable associations such as the Salvation Army.

government inefficiency in providing public goods and in otherwise intervening in the market (see Application 4).

19-4

Benefit-Cost Analysis

Governments play many roles in modern societies. These range from the provision of public goods, to the redistribution of income, the regulation of monopoly, and pollution control. In carrying out these functions, government agencies must constantly decide which projects to implement and which to reject. A useful procedure for determining which are the most worthwhile projects is **benefit-cost analysis.** This compares the present value of the benefits to the present value of the costs of a project. Government should carry out a project only if the present value of the social benefits from the project exceeds the present value of its social costs (i.e., if the benefit-cost ratio for the project exceeds 1). Often, the government does not have the resources (i.e., cannot raise taxes or borrow sufficiently) to undertake all the projects with a benefit-cost ratio exceeding 1. In such cases, government should rank all possible projects from the highest to the lowest (but exceeding 1) benefit-cost ratio and, starting at the top of the list, it should undertake all projects until its resources are fully utilized.

While the above sounds pretty much straightforward, a number of serious difficulties arise in the actual application of benefit-cost analysis because it is often very difficult to correctly estimate the social benefits and the social costs of a project and determine the appropriate rate of interest to use to calculate the present value of benefits and costs. First, since the benefits and the costs of most public projects (such as a dam, a highway, a training program, and so on) take place over many years, it is difficult to estimate them correctly so far into the future.

Second, benefits and costs are frequently estimated on the basis of current or projected prices, even though these prices may not reflect the true scarcity value or opportunity cost of the outputs resulting from or the inputs used in the project. For example, commodity prices under imperfectly competitive commodity markets exceed their marginal cost. Similarly, if a project results in the employment of otherwise unemployed labor, the real cost of hiring labor is zero, in spite of the positive wage paid to these workers. In other words, it is the real or opportunity value of the benefits and costs of the project that should be used in benefit-cost analysis. But it may be difficult to estimate these. Real costs may also rise as the project increases the demand for inputs.

Third, some of the benefits and costs of a project may not be quantifiable. For example, while it may be possible to estimate the rise in workers' income resulting from a training program, it is next to impossible to assign a value to their enhanced self-esteem and to their becoming more responsible citizens. Similarly, it is practically impossible to assign a value to the loss of scenery resulting from the construction of a dam. Yet all of these social benefits and costs should be included in benefit-cost analysis for it to lead to correct public investment decisions.

Fourth, and perhaps the most serious difficulty with benefit-cost analysis, arises in the choice of the proper interest rate to be used to find the present value of the benefits and costs of the project. That is, since the benefits and costs of most projects occur over a number of years, they must be discounted to the present. For this a rate of interest must be used, as indicated in Section 16-3b[10] The question is *which* is the proper interest rate to use? As indicated in Section 16-4, there are a large number of rates of interest in the market (ranging from nearly zero to 40 per cent) depending on the risk, duration, cost of administering, and the tax treatment of the loan. Since the use of resources by the government competes with their private use, the interest (discount) rate to be used to find present values should reflect the opportunity cost of funds for a project of similar riskiness, duration, and administrative costs in the private sector. However, since different people may come up with a different rate of interest to use, benefit-cost analysis is usually prepared for a range of interest rates (from a low, to a medium, and a high one) rather than for a single interest rate. The lower the interest rate (or range of interest rates) used, the higher the benefit-cost ratio usually is and the greater the likelihood of the project being undertaken. The reasons for this is that the benefits of a project usually arise later or over a longer period of time than its costs.

In spite of the great difficulties inherent in benefit-cost analysis, it is nevertheless a very valuable procedure for organizing our thoughts on the social benefits and the social costs of each project. If nothing else, it forces government officials to make explicit all the assumptions underlying the analysis. Scrutiny of the assumptions has sometimes led to decision reversals. For example, in 1971, the Federal Power Commission (now the Federal Energy Regulatory Commission) approved the construction of a hydroelectric dam on the Snake river, which flows from Oregon to Idaho and forms Hell's Canyon (the deepest in North America). The decision was based on a benefit-cost analysis that ignored some environmental costs. Because of that, the Supreme Court, on appeal from the Secretary of the Interior, revoked the order to build the dam pending a new benefit-cost analysis that properly included *all* benefits and costs. Finally, Congress passed a law prohibiting the construction of the dam.[11]

---

[10] In Section 16-3b we showed how to find the present value of a project. For benefit-cost analysis we need to find the present value of the benefits and costs of the project *separately*. The procedure, however, is the same. Note that a positive present value for a project is equivalent to a greater-than-one benefit-cost ratio.

[11] John V. Krutilla and Anthony C. Fisher, *The Economics of Natural Environments: Studies in the Valuation of Commodity and Amenity Resources* (Baltimore: The Johns Hopkins University Press, 1975), pp. 101–103.

Although benefit-cost analysis is still more of an art than of a science and is somewhat subjective, its usefulness has been proven in a wide variety of projects ranging from water projects, to transportation, health, education, and recreational projects. In fact, in 1965, the federal government formally began to introduce benefit-cost analysis for its budgetary procedures under the Planning-Programming-Budgeting System (PPS). The practice has now spread to state and local governments as well.

Example 19-4   Benefit-Cost Analysis and the SST

The Facts: Based on benefit-cost analysis, the development of a supersonic transport plane (SST) was abandoned in the United States in 1971. The benefits were simply not sufficient to justify the costs. However, the British and French governments jointly continued to pursue the project and built the Concorde at a huge cost. Today, there are only a handful of such planes operated exclusively by the British and French national airlines. With operating costs more than four times higher than the Boeing 747, the Concorde must be classified as a clear market failure and would not fly without heavy government subsidies. Specifically, a one-way seat from New York to London or Paris on the Concorde would have to be priced at over $4,000 (as compared with less than $1,000 on the Boeing 747) for the Concorde to break even. This means that the person would be paying about $1,000 for each of the three hours saved in flying on the Concorde. Modern man is hurried but not that hurried! As it is, the British and the French governments subsidize about half of the operating costs of the Concorde. Still, business is not brisk for the Concorde.

Comment: It seems that in their benefit-cost analysis, the British and the French greatly overestimated the benefits arising from building and operating the Concorde and grossly underestimated its costs. This only points to how imprecise benefit-cost analysis can sometimes be. The question is why do the British and the French governments continue to heavily subsidize flying the Concorde now, thereby "throwing good money after bad." The answer may be national pride in being the only two nations flying a supersonic passenger plane. If that is true, it only points to how expensive national pride can be.

Source: "The Concorde's Destination," *The New York Times*, September 28, 1979, p. 26 and "Crise du Concorde," *New York*, October 29, 1984, p. 28.

19-5

Applications

In this section we utilize the tools of analysis developed in the chapter to analyze environmental pollution, optimal pollution control, direct regulation and effluent fees for pollutants, and the case against government intervention in the economy. These applications and the several examples presented in the chapter highlight the great importance and relevance of the theory of externality and public goods.

Application 1: Environmental Pollution

We have seen in Section 19-2 that externalities (and inefficiencies) may be eliminated by the clear definition of property rights if the parties involved are not very numerous. Otherwise, transaction costs are too high and externalities persist. This is precisely the case with **environmental pollution,** which refers to air pollution, water pollution, thermal pollution, pollution resulting from garbage disposal, and so on. Environmental pollution has become one of the major political and economic issues in recent decades. Environmental pollution results from and is an example of negative externalities.

Air pollution results mostly from automobile exhaust, and smoke from factories and electrical generating plants through the combustion of fossil fuels, which release particles into the air. While it is difficult to measure precisely the harmful effects of sulfur dioxide, carbon monoxide, and other air pollutants, they are known to create damage to health (in the form of breathing illnesses and aggravating other diseases, such as circulatory problems) and to property (in the form of higher cleaning bills, and so on). *Water pollution* results from the dumping into streams, lakes, and sea shores of raw (untreated) sewage, chemical waste products from factories and mines, and runoff of pesticides and fertilizers from farms. This reduces the supply of clean water for household uses (drinking, bathing, and so on) and recreational uses (swimming, boating, fishing, and so on). There is then *thermal pollution* resulting from the cooling off of electrical power plants and other machinery. This increases water temperature and kills fish. The disposal of garbage such as beer cans, newspapers, cigarette butts, and so on, also spoil the natural scenery, as do billboards and posters. To this visual pollution must be added noise pollution and many others.

Environmental pollution results whenever the environment is used (abused) as a convenient and cheap dumping ground for all types of waste products. It is convenient and cheap from the private point of view to use the environment in this manner because no one owns property rights to it. As a result, air and water users pay less than the full social cost of using these natural resources, and by so doing they impose serious external costs on society. In short, society produces and consumes too much of products that generate environmental pollution. Since property rights are ambiguous and the parties involved are numerous (often running into the millions), it is impossible or impractical (too costly) to identify and negotiate with individual agents. The external costs of environmental pollution cannot be internalized by the assignment of clear property rights and so government intervention is required. This can take the form of regulation or taxation (see Application 3). However, appropriate corrective action on the part of the government requires knowledge of the exact cost of pollution. This is examined in Application 2.

Application 2: Optimal Pollution Control

If one asked a stout environmentalist how much environmental pollution society should tolerate, his or her answer would probably be zero. This would be the wrong answer. The optimal level of pollution is the level at which the marginal social cost of pollution equals the marginal social benefit (in the form of avoiding alternative and more expensive methods of waste disposal). Zero pollution is an ideal situation, but as long as pollution is the inevitable by-product of the production and consumption of commodities that we want, it is downright silly to advocate zero pollution. Economists advocate optimal pollution control instead. That is, we should be prepared to accept (as inevitable) that amount of pollution which, at the margin, just balances the social costs and benefits of pollution. This is shown in Figure 19-3.

In Figure 19-3, the horizontal axis measures the quantity of pollution per year and the vertical axis measures costs and gains in dollars. The MC curve, for example, could measure the value of the marginal loss of fish suffered by fishermen for various amounts of water pollution generated by a firm. The marginal loss (cost) increases with rising amounts of pollution. The MB curve would then measure the marginal benefit or saving that the firm that pollutes the water receives by being able to freely dump its waste into the water rather than disposing of it by the next best alternative method (at a positive cost). The MB is negatively sloped, indicating declin-

FIGURE 19-3.
Optimal Pollution
Control

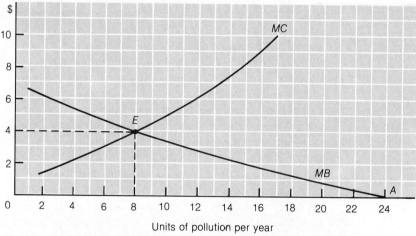

The MC *curve shows the rising marginal cost or loss to society from increasing amounts of pollution. The* MB *curve shows the declining marginal benefit to the polluter (and to society) by being able to freely dump increasing amounts of waste into the water rather than disposing of it by other costly alternatives. Since the firm does not pay for discharging its waste into the water, it will do so until* MB = *0 (point A). From society's point of view, the optimal level of pollution for the firm is 8 units per year (point E, at which* MC = MB).

ing benefits for the firm for each additional unit of pollution that it discharges into the water.

When the firm does not incur any cost for discharging waste into the water, it will do so until the marginal benefit is zero (point A in the figure). That is, as long as the firm saves some cost by discharging its waste into the water, it will do so until the MB is zero. However, pollution does impose a cost on society as a whole. The optimal amount of pollution from society's point of view is 8 units, given by the intersection of the MC and the MB curves at point E. Only when pollution is 8 units per year is the marginal benefit to the individual and to society equal to the marginal social cost of pollution. To the left of point E, MB > MC and it pays for society to increase the level of pollution (see the figure). The opposite is true to the right of point E. As strange as it might have sounded earlier, we now know that the optimal level of pollution is not zero, but it is positive.

Application 3: Direct Regulation and Effluent Fees for Optimal Pollution Control

We have seen in Application 2 that the optimal level of pollution from society's point of view is not zero, but given by the level at which the marginal cost of pollution is equal to the private (and social) marginal benefit of disposing waste by the cheapest method possible. While this prescription is theoretically precise, it is often very difficult to actually estimate the marginal social costs and benefits of pollution. As also seen in Application 1, without government intervention, environmental pollution is certainly likely to be excessive (compare point A to point E in Figure 19-3).

There are generally two ways to achieve the optimal amount of pollution control: direct regulation and effluent fees. By direct regulation, government could legislate that the industry must limit pollution to the optimal level (8 units per year in Figure 19-3) or install a particular polluton-abatement device. Alternatively, government could set the **effluent fee** that brings the private cost of pollution equal to its social cost. An effluent fee is a tax that a firm must pay to the government for discharging waste or otherwise polluting. For example, an effluent fee of $4 per unit of waste or pollution per year in Figure 19-3 results in the optimal level of pollution of 8 units per year. That is, an effluent fee of $4 per unit will make the marginal private (and social) cost of pollution equal to its marginal private (and social) benefit.

While direct regulation is sometimes necessary (as in the case of radio-active and other very dangerous waste materials), economists generally prefer effluent fees to achieve optimal pollution control. There are two reasons for this. First, effluent fees generally require less information on the part of the government than direct regulation. Secondly, and more importantly, effluent fees minimize the cost of optimal pollution control, while direct regulation does not. The reason for this is that with effluent fees, each polluter will pollute until the marginal benefit of pollution equals the effluent fee. Thus, the optimal amount of pollution is allocated to those firms that benefit most from polluting. As a result, the social cost of pollution is minimized. Actual pollution control has stressed effluent fees in Europe (particularly in Germany, where they were useful to maintain water quality in the Rhur Valley) but the regulatory approach is used in the United States (by the Environmental Protection Agency).[12]

Application 4: The Case Against Government Intervention

We have seen in this and in the previous chapter that governments generally intervene in the market to provide public goods, redistribute income, and correct distortions (such as monopoly, externalities, and so on) in the private sector. However, government intervention is justified only if government demonstrates efficiency and "equity." That is, market failures do not, in and of themselves, justify government intervention since government can be even less efficient than the private sector, and can do more harm than good. There are generally two reasons for this.

First, bureaucrats can be very inefficient and only interested in maximizing their own selfish gains (such as tenure in office and agency growth) rather than the welfare of society. Great social waste can arise from laziness, inefficiency, incompetence, and corruption on the part of bureaucrats. For example, there is often no presumption that bureaucrats have or can gather more relevant information for the proper conduct of benefit-cost analysis than businessmen in their private investment decisions. Therefore, if a public good is exclusive (i.e., users can be properly charged for it), it should perhaps be provided by the private sector, whenever possible.[13]

Second, government may not be always responsive to the wishes of the majority that elected it. Specifically, in democratic societies, individuals reveal their preferences by voting for those candidates that most closely represent the set of public expenditures and taxes that individuals prefer. Yet government may not be always responsive to those wishes. This may results because pressure groups are often successful in lobbying government to pass measures which further their narrow interests at the expense of the more-or-less silent majority. For example, steel producers in the United States successfully lobbied Congress to impose import restrictions on steel. This raised steel prices and, through these, most other prices in the U.S. Special interest groups, being made up of relatively few people or firms (so that the free-rider problem is not serious) and having much to gain

---

[12] The U.S. government also provides tax credits to firms that introduce antipollution equipment. However, these are generally not very effective because it may still be cheaper to pollute. In addition, subsidizing the introduction of antipollution equipment is usually not the most economical way of optimal pollution control. For example, a Congressional report indicated that allowing utilities to devise their own method to control sulfur dioxide could save over $1 billion, or about ⅕ of the cost of mandated controls ("Acid Rain Controls Examined," *The New York Times*, June 21, 1984, p. 18).

[13] See William A. Niskanen, *Bureaucracy and Representative Government* (Chicago: Aldine, 1971), and Thomas E. Borcherding, *Budgets and Bureaucrats: The Sources of Government Growth* (Durham, N.C.: Duke University Press, 1975).

or lose from a specific government measure, are often willing and able to spend vast sums of money to influence legislation. Frequently, they carry much more weight in influencing government decisions than their small number justifies. On the other hand, the vast majority, being often only slightly and indirectly affected, remains mostly indifferent and unable to organize to oppose minority interests. The result is that small special interest groups often gain at the expense of the majority.[14]

Thus, because of government inefficiency and waste and because of special groups' pressures, government functions should perhaps be limited to only provide public goods of a nonexclusive character and correct the most glaring cases of market failures. For the most part, the "invisible hand" should be allowed to operate unhampered, lest private sector inefficiencies be replaced with perhaps even greater public sector ones and do more harm than good.

Summary

1. Externalities are harmful or beneficial side effects borne by those not directly involved in the production or consumption of a commodity. Externalities are classified into external economies or diseconomies of production or consumption, and technical externalities. With external diseconomies of production or consumption, the commodity price falls short of the full social cost of the commodity and too much of the commodity is produced or consumed. With external economies of production or consumption, the commodity price exceeds the full social cost of the commodity and too much of the commodity is produced and consumed. Technical externalities may prevent marginal cost pricing.

2. Externalities arise when property rights are not clearly defined and transaction costs are very high. The Coase theorem postulates that when property rights are clearly defined and transaction costs are zero, perfect competition results in the absence of externalities, regardless of how property rights are assigned among the parties involved.

3. Public goods are commodities that are nonrival in consumption. That is, consumption of a public good by some individual does not reduce the amount available for others (at zero marginal cost). Some public goods, such as national defense, exhibit nonexclusion. That is, once the good is produced, it is impossible to confine its use to only those paying for it. Other public goods, such as TV broadcasting, can exhibit exclusion. Because of the free-rider problem, public goods are usually underproduced and underconsumed.

4. Benefit-cost analysis is based on the government calculating the ratio of the present value of all the benefits to the present value of all the costs for each proposed public project. The projects are then ranked from the highest to the lowest in terms of benefit-cost ratios. Government should undertake those projects with the highest benefit-cost ratio (as long as that ratio exceeds 1) and until government resources are fully employed. There are many difficulties in estimating all benefits and costs of a project and in determining the interest rate to use to find the present value of the benefits and costs.

5. Enviromental (air, water, thermal, scenic, and noise) pollution arises because of unclearly

---

[14] See Anthony Downs, *An Economic Theory of Democracy* (New York: Harper & Row, 1957), and Mancur Olson, *The Logic of Collective Action* (Cambridge, Mass.: Harvard University Press, 1965). Also see "Lobbyists' Spending in the First Quarter was $11.75 Million," *The New York Times*, September 4, 1984, p. 19.

defined property rights and too high transaction costs. The optimal level of pollution from society's point of view is not zero, but given by the level at which the marginal cost of pollution to society is equal to the private (and social) marginal benefit of disposing waste by the cheapest method available. Optimal pollution control can be achieved by direct regulation or effluent fees. While direct regulation is sometimes necessary (as in the case of dangerous waste materials), economists generally prefer effluent fees. Government intervention is justified only if it is efficient and "equitable."

Glossary

Externalities   Harmful or beneficial side effects borne by those not directly involved in the production or consumption of a commodity.

External benefits   Beneficial side effects received by those not directly involved in the production or consumption of a commodity.

External costs   Harmful side effects borne by those not directly involved in the production or consumption of a commodity.

External diseconomies of production   Uncompensated costs borne by those not directly involved in the production of a commodity.

External diseconomies of consumption   Uncompensated costs borne by those not directly involved in the consumption of a commodity.

External economies of production   Uncompensated benefits received by those not directly involved in the production of a commodity.

External economies of consumption   Uncompensated benefits received by those not directly involved in the consumption of a commodity.

Technical externalities   Economies of scale.

Common property   Property, such as air, owned by no one.

Coase's theorem   It postulates that when property rights are clearly defined and transaction costs are zero, perfect competition results in the absence of externalities, regardless of how property rights are assigned among the parties involved.

Internalizing external costs   The process whereby an external cost becomes part of the regular business expense of the firm.

Public goods   Commodities for which consumption by some individuals does not reduce the amount available for others. That is, once the good is provided for someone, others can consume it at no additional cost.

Nonrival consumption   The distinguishing characteristic of a public good whereby its consumption by some individuals does not reduce the amount available to others.

Nonexclusion   The situation in which it is impossible or prohibitively expensive to confine the benefit or the consumption of a good (once produced) to selected people (such as only to those paying for it).

Free-rider problem   The problem that arises when a individual does not contribute to the payment of a public good in the belief that it will be provided anyway.

Benefit-cost analysis   A procedure for determining the most worthwhile public projects for the government to undertake. It prescribes that government should undertake those projects with the highest benefit-cost ratio, as long as that ratio exceeds 1, and until government resources are fully employed.

Environmental pollution   The lowering of air, water, scenic, and noise qualities of the world around us that results from the dumping of waste products. It arises because of unclearly defined property rights and too high transaction costs.

Effluent fee   A tax that a firm must pay for discharging waste or polluting.

Questions for Review

1. What are
   (a) externalities?
   (b) external costs?
   (c) external benefits?
   (d) free-rider problem?
2. What is
   (a) external diseconomy of production?
   (b) external diseconomy of consumption?
   (c) external economy of production?
   (d) external economy of consumption?
3. Why does each of the following prevent the attainment of Pareto optimality?
   (a) external diseconomy of production.
   (b) external diseconomy of consumption.
   (c) external economy of production.
   (d) external economy of consumption.
4. What are technical externalities?
   (b) Why do technical externalities prevent the attainment of Pareto optimality?
   (c) How can technical externalities be overcome?
5. (a) What is a property right?
   (b) What is meant by common property?
   (c) How do externalities arise?
6. (a) What is meant by internalizing external costs?
   (b) When are external costs internalized?
   (c) Why does Pareto optimality result when external costs are internalized?
7. (a) What does Coase's theorem postulate?
   (b) What are transaction costs?
   (c) When are transaction costs high?
   (d) Why does Coase's theorem fail when transaction costs are high?
8. What is meant by

   (a) public good?
   (b) nonrival consumption?
   (c) nonexclusion?
9. Answer the following questions with respect to a public good.
   (a) How is its aggregate demand curve determined?
   (b) What is its optimal amount?
   (c) Why is too little of its usually supplied without government intervention?
   (d) How could the government ensure that the optimal amount of it is provided?
   (e) How can the government determine the optimal amount of it?
10. Answer the following questions with respect to benefit-cost analysis.
    (a) What is it?
    (b) How is it carried out?
    (c) What is its usefulness?
    (d) What are the difficulties in carrying it out?
11. (a) What is environmental pollution?
    (b) Why is this an important political and economic problem?
    (c) How does it arise?
    (d) Why does it arise?
12. (a) Why is the optimal level of pollution not equal to zero from society's point of view?
    (b) How is the optimal level of pollution determined from society's point of view?
    (c) What is an effluent fee? How can it be used to achieve optimal pollution control?
    (d) What are the relative benefits of direct regulation and effluent fees to achieve optimal pollution control?

Problems

1. Explain why
   (a) in a system of private education (i.e., a system in which individuals pay for their own education), there is likely to be underinvestment in education.

   (b) the discussion of external economies and diseconomies is in terms of marginal rather than total social costs and benefits.
2. Start with D and S as in Figure 19-1.
   (a) Draw D′ with the same vertical intercept

suming various quantities of the commodity.

(b) Does D' indicate the existence of external economies of production or consumption?

(c) What is the marginal external benefit or cost and the marginal social benefit or cost at the competitive equilibrium point?

(d) What is the socially optimal price and consumption of the commodity?

★3. (a) Draw a figure showing the corrective tax or subsidy that would induce society to as D but with twice the absolute value of its slope. Suppose that D' portrays the marginal social benefit of the public con-consume the socially optimum amount of the commodity.

(b) What is the total value of the economic gain resulting from the imposition of the corrective tax or subsidy?

4. Start with D and S as in Figure 19-1.

(a) Draw S' with the same vertical intercept as S but with half of its slope. Suppose that S' portrays the marginal *social* costs of supplying various quantities of the commodity.

(b) Does S' indicate the existence of external economies or diseconomies of production or consumption?

(c) What is the marginal external cost or benefit and the marginal social cost at the competitive equilibrium point?

(d) What is the socially optimum price and output of the commodity?

★5. (a) Draw a figure showing the corrective tax or subsidy that would induce the industry to produce the socially optimal amount of the commodity.

(b) What is the total value of the economic inefficiency eliminated by the corrective tax or subsidy?

6. Start with D and S as in Figure 19-1.

(a) Draw D' with the same vertical intercept as D but with half the absolute value of its slope. Suppose that D' portrays the marginal social benefit of the public consuming various quantities of the commodity.

(b) Does D' indicate the existence of external economies or diseconomies of production or consumption?

(c) What is the marginal external benefit or

cost and the marginal social benefit or cost at the equilibrium point?

(d) What is the socially optimum price and consumption of the commodity?

7. (a) Draw a figure showing the corrective tax or subsidy that would induce the society to consume the socially optimal amount of the commodity.

(b) What is the total value of the economic gain resulting from the imposition of the corrective tax or subsidy?

8. Explain what would be the outcome if the cost of avoiding polluting the stream (with its waste products) by the paper mill of Section 19-2 was $1,200 rather than $400 per month and property rights to the stream were assigned to the

(a) brewery.

(b) paper mill.

(c) When would the socially optimal solution be reached?

★9. Explain why in each of the following cases, externalities arise and how they would be avoided or corrected when

(a) one individual owns an oil field next to another oil field owned by another individual.

(b) a firm develops a recreational site (golf, skiing, boating, and so on).

★10. (a) Draw a figure showing the market demand curve for good X for Figure 19-2 if good X were a private rather than a public good.

(b) State the condition for the Pareto optimal output of commodity X when X is a private good and when it is a public good.

(c) What is the relationship between public goods and externalities?

11. Three possible solutions were proposed at the time of the severe water shortage experienced by New York City in 1949–1950. These were (1) building a dam that would cost $1,000 per million of gallons of water supplied, (2) sealing leaks in water mains that would cost about $1.60 per million gallons of water gained, (3) or installing water meters that would cost $160 per million gallons of water saved. The city chose the first project. Was New York's choice correct? If not, why might New York have chosen it?

12. With reference to Figure 19-3, calculate the total social gains by
    (a) increasing the level of pollution from 4 to 8 units per year.
    (b) reducing pollution from 12 to 8 units per year.

Supplementary Readings

For a very brief problem-solving approach to the topics presented in this chapter, see

Dominick Salvatore, *Microeconomic Theory,* 2nd ed. (New York: McGraw-Hill, 1983), pp. 303, 316–317.

The presentation of externalities in the chapter follows

Francis M. Bator, "The Anatomy of Market Failure," *Quarterly Journal of Economics,* August 1958, pp. 351–379.

Coase's theorem was introduced by

Ronald R. Coase, "The Problems of Social Costs," *Journal of Law and Economics,* October 1960, pp. 1–44.

The major references for public goods and benefit-cost analysis are

James Buchanan, *The Demand and Supply of Public Goods* (Chicago: Rand McNally, 1968).

Richard and Peggy Musgrave, *Public Finance in Theory and Practice* (New York: McGraw-Hill, 1980).

Paul A. Samuelson, "The Pure Theory of Public Expenditures," **Review of Economics and Statistics,** *November 1954, pp. 387–389.*

For pollution and pollution control, see

Allen Kneese and Charles Schultze, *Pollution, Prices, and Public Policy* (Washington, D.C.: Brookings Institution, 1975).

Robert and Nancy Dorfman, *Economics of the Environment* (New York: Norton, 1977).

Mathematical Appendix

A-1   Indifference Curves

A-2   Utility Maximization

A-3   Elasticities

A-4   Relationship Among Income Elasticities

A-5   Consumer Surplus

A-6   Relationship Among Marginal Revenue, Price, and Elasticity

A-7   Isoquants

A-8   Cost Minimization

A-9   Profit Maximization

A-10 Price Determination

A-11 The Cobweb Model

A-12 Price Discrimination

A-13 Employment of Inputs

A-14 Input Price, Marginal Expense, and the Price Elasticity of Input Supply

A-15 Derivation of the Formula to Find the Present Value of an Investment

A-16 A Model of General Equilibrium

Appendix
A

A-1

Indifference Curves

Suppose that a consumer's purchases are limited to commodities X and Y, then

$$U = U(X,Y) \qquad (1A)$$

is a general utility function. Equation (1A) postulates that the utility or satisfaction that the consumer receives is a function of, or depends on, the quantity of commodity X and commodity Y that he or she consumes. The more of X and Y the individual consumes, the greater is the level of utility or satisfaction that he or she receives.

Using a subscript on U to specify a given level of utility or satisfaction, we can write

$$U_1 = U_1(X,Y) \qquad (2A)$$

This is the general equation for an indifference curve. Equation (2A) postulates that the individual can get U_1 of utility by various combinations of X and Y. Of course, the more of X the individual consumes, the less of Y he or she will have to consume in order to remain on the same indifference curve. Higher subscripts refer to higher indifference curves. Thus, $U_2 > U_1$.

Taking the total differential Equation of (1A), we get

$$dU = \frac{\partial U}{\partial X}\, dx + \frac{\partial U}{\partial Y}\, dy \qquad (3A)$$

Since a movement along an indifference curve leaves utility unchanged, we set $dU = 0$ and get

$$\frac{\partial U}{\partial X}\, dx + \frac{\partial U}{\partial Y}\, dy = 0 \qquad (4A)$$

so that

$$\frac{\partial U}{\partial Y}\, dy = -\frac{\partial U}{\partial X}\, dx \qquad (5A)$$

and

$$-\frac{dy}{dx} = \frac{\partial U/\partial X}{\partial U/\partial Y} = \frac{MU_x}{MU_y} = MRS_{xy} \qquad (6A)$$

Equation (6A) indicates that the negative value of the slope of an indifference curve ($-dy/dx$) is equal to the ratio of the marginal utility of X to the marginal utility of Y (MU_x/MU_y), Which, in turn, equals the marginal rate of substitution of X for Y ($MRSxy$).

A-2

Utility Maximization

We now wish to maximize utility [i.e., Equation (1A)] subject to the budget constraint. The budget constraint of the consumer is

$$P_xX + P_yY = I \qquad (7A)$$

where P_x and P_y are the price of commodity X and commodity Y, respectively, X and Y refer to the quantity of commodity X and commodity Y, and I is the consumer's income, which is given and fixed at a particular point in time.

To maximize Equation (1A) subject to Equation (7A), we form

$$V = U(X,Y) + \Lambda(I - P_xX - P_yY) \qquad (8A)$$

where Λ is the Lagrangian multiplier.

Taking the first partial derivative of V with respect to X and Y and setting them equal to zero gives

$$\frac{\partial V}{\partial X} = \frac{\partial U}{\partial X} - \Lambda P_x = 0 \,, \frac{\partial V}{\partial Y}$$
$$= \frac{\partial U}{\partial Y} - \Lambda P_y = 0 \quad (9A)$$

It follows that

$$\frac{\partial U}{\partial X} = \Lambda P_x \,, \frac{\partial U}{\partial Y} = \Lambda P_y \quad (10A)$$

Dividing, we get

$$\frac{\partial U/\partial X}{\partial U/\partial Y} = \frac{P_x}{P_y} \quad (11A)$$

Equation (11A) indicates that the consumer maximizes utility at the point where the marginal rate of substitution of X for Y, $\frac{\partial U/\partial X}{\partial U/\partial Y}$, equals the ratio of the price of X to the price of Y. Graphically, this occurs at the point where the budget line is tangent to the highest indifference curve possible (and their slopes are equal). Equation (11A) is only the first order condition for maximization (and minimization). The second order condition for maximization is that the indifference curves be convex to the origin.

A-3

Elasticities

In Section 2-2c we defined the *price elasticity of demand*, η, as the percentage change in the quantity demanded of a commodity divided by the percentage change in its price. That is, for $Q = f(P)$,

$$\eta = - \frac{\Delta Q/Q}{\Delta P/P} = - \frac{\Delta Q}{\Delta P} \frac{P}{Q} \quad (12A)$$

We also pointed out that since quantity and price move in opposite directions, we multiply by -1 in order to make the value of η positive. Equation (12A) can be used to measure *arc elasticity*. In that case, P and Q refer to the average price and the average quantity, respectively.

As the change in price approaches zero in the limit, we can measure *point elasticity* by

$$\eta = - \frac{dQ}{dP} \frac{P}{Q} \quad (13A)$$

If the demand curve is linear and given by

$$Q = a - bP \quad (14A)$$

the slope of the demand curve is constant and is given by

$$\frac{dQ}{dP} = \frac{\Delta Q}{\Delta P} = - b \quad (15A)$$

and

$$\eta = - b \frac{P}{Q} \quad (16A)$$

For example, if $b = -2$ and $P/Q = 1$, then $\eta = 2$. Since P/Q is different at every point on the negatively sloped, straight-line demand curve, η varies at every point.

For a curvilinear demand curve of the form

$$Q = aP^{-b} \quad (17A)$$

$$\frac{dQ}{dP} = -abP^{-b-1} \quad (18A)$$

and

$$\eta = -abP^{-b-1}\frac{P}{Q} = -\frac{abP^{-b}}{Q} = -b \qquad (19A)$$

since $aP-b = Q$. Thus, Equation (16A) is a demand curve with a constant price elasticity equal to the exponent of P (i.e., $\eta = -b$). Thus, if $b = 2$, $\eta = -2$ at every point on the demand curve. As pointed out in Section 5.2, demand is elastic if $|\eta| > 1$ and inelastic if $|\eta| < 1$.

The *income elasticity of demand*, η_I, is defined as the ratio of the relative change in the quantity purchased (Q) to the relative change in income (I), other things remaining constant. That is, for $Q = f(I)$,

$$\eta_I = \frac{dQ}{dI}\frac{I}{Q} \qquad (20A)$$

For the following linear income-demand function

$$Q = a + cI \qquad (21A)$$

where $c > 0$, the derivative of Q with respect to I is

$$\frac{dQ}{dI} = c \qquad (22A)$$

Therefore,

$$\eta_I = c\frac{I}{Q} \qquad (23A)$$

For the following nonlinear income-demand function

$$Q = aI^c \qquad (24A)$$

the derivative of Q with respect to I is

$$\frac{dQ}{dI} = acI^{c-1} \qquad (25A)$$

Therefore,

$$\eta_I = acI^{c-1}\frac{I}{Q} = \frac{acI^c}{Q} = c \qquad (26A)$$

As pointed out in Section 5.3, a commodity is normal if $\eta_I > 0$ and inferior if $\eta_I < 0$. A normal good is a luxury if $\eta_I > 1$ and a necessity if η_I is between 0 and 1.

The *cross elasticity of demand* of commodity X for commodity Y, η_{xy}, is defined as the ratio of the relative change in the quantity purchased of commodity X (Q_x) to the relative change in the price of commodity Y (P_y). That is,

$$\eta_{xy} = \frac{dQ_x/Q_x}{dP_y/P_y} = \frac{dQ_x}{dP_y}\frac{P_y}{Q_x} \qquad (27A)$$

Consider the following linear demand function for commodity X:

$$Q_x = a + bP_x + cP_y \qquad (28A)$$

The above function indicates that Q_x depends on P_x and P_y. The derivative of the function with respect to P_y is

$$\frac{dQ_x}{dP_y} = b\frac{dP_x}{dP_y} + c \qquad (29A)$$

If the P_x remains unchanged when P_y changes, then

$$\frac{dP_x}{dP_y} = 0 \text{ while } \frac{dQ_x}{dP_y} = c \qquad (30A)$$

Therefore,

$$\eta_{xy} = c\frac{P_y}{Q_x} \qquad (31A)$$

As pointed out in Section 5-4, commodities X and Y are substitutes if $\eta_{xy} > 0$ and complements if $\eta_{xy} < 0$.

Price elasticity of supply, ϵ, is defined as the ratio of the relative change in the quantity supplied of a commodity (Q_s) to the relative change in its price (P). That is, for $Q_s = f(P)$,

$$\epsilon = \frac{dQ_s/Q_s}{dP/P} = \frac{dQ_s}{dP}\frac{P}{Q_s} \tag{32A}$$

Since the quantity supplied and price move in the same direction (i.e., supply curves are usually positively sloped), ϵ is positive.

For the following linear supply function

$$Q_s = a + bP \tag{33A}$$

the derivative of Q_s with respect to P is

$$\frac{dQ_s}{dP} = b \tag{34A}$$

Therefore,

$$\epsilon = b\,\frac{P}{Q_s} \tag{35A}$$

Substituting Equation (33A) for Q_s into Equation (35A), we get

$$\epsilon = \frac{bP}{a + bP} \tag{36A}$$

Thus, if $a = 0$ (so that the supply curve starts at the origin), $\epsilon = 1$ throughout the supply curve, regardless of the value of its slope (b). If $a > 0$ (so that the supply curve cuts the quantity axis), $\epsilon < 1$ throughout the supply curve. If $a < 0$ (so that the supply curve cuts the price axis), $\epsilon > 1$ throughout. When $a = 0$, ϵ varies with price.

A-4

Relationship Among Income Elasticities

If a consumer's income increases, say by 10 per cent, and the consumption of some commodities increases by less than 10 per cent, the consumption of other commodities must increase by more than 10 per cent for the entire increase in the consumer's income to be fully spent. This leads to the proposition that the income elasticity of demand must be unity, on the average, for all commodities. Assuming, for simplicity, that the entire consumer's income is spent on commodities X and Y, we can restate the above proposition mathetmatically as

$$K_x\eta_{Ix} + K_y\eta_{Iy} \equiv 1 \tag{37A}$$

where K_x is the proportion of the consumer's income (I) spent on commodity X (i.e., $K_x = P_xX/I$), ηIx is the income elasticity of demand

for commodity X, K_y is the proportion of income spent on Y (i.e., $K_y = P_yY/I$), and η_{Iy} is the income elasticity of demand for Y.

Starting with the consumer's budget constraint (7A)

$$I = P_xX + P_yY \tag{7A}$$

we can prove proposition (37A) by differentiating Equation (7A) with respect to income, while holding prices constant. This gives

$$\frac{dI}{dI} \equiv 1 \equiv P_x\frac{dX}{dI} + P_y\frac{dY}{dI} \tag{38A}$$

If we multiply the first term on the right-hand side by $(X/X)\,(I/I)$, which equals one, and the second term by $(Y/Y)(I/I)$, which equals one, the value of the expression will not change, and we get

$$1 \equiv P_x \frac{dX}{dI} \frac{X}{X} \frac{I}{I} + P_y \frac{dY}{dI} \frac{Y}{Y} \frac{I}{I} \quad (38A')$$

Rearranging Equation (38A'), we get

$$\frac{P_x X}{I} \frac{dX}{dI} \frac{I}{X} + \frac{P_y Y}{I} \frac{dY}{dI} \frac{I}{Y} \equiv 1 \quad (39A)$$

Since $P_x X/I = K_x$, $(dX/dI)(I/X) = \eta_{Ix}$, $P_y Y/I =$

K_y, and $(dY/dI)(I/Y) = \eta_{Iy}$, we have

$$K_x \eta_{Ix} + K_y \eta_{Iy} \equiv 1 \quad (37A)$$

That is, with the K's providing the weights, the weighted average of all income elasticities equals unity. Thus, the income elasticity of demand of a commodity on which the consumer spends a great proportion of his or her income cannot be too different from unity (see Problem 12 in chapter 5).

A-5

Consumer Surplus

In Application 2 in chapter 4, we defined consumer surplus as the difference between what a consumer is willing to pay for a given quantity of a good and what he or she actually pays for it. Graphically, consumer surplus is given by the difference in the area under the demand curve and the area representing the total expenditures of the consumer for the given quantity of the good that he or she purchases.

Starting with $P = g(Q)$, where g is the inverse of $Q = f(P)$, for a given price (P_1) and

its associated quantity (Q_1),

consumer surplus

$$= \int_{P_1}^{Q_1} g(Q)dQ - P_1 Q_1 \quad (40A)$$

where the integral sign ($\int$) represents the process of calculating the area under inverse demand function $P = g(Q)$ between zero quantity of the commodity and quantity Q_1, and $P_1 Q_1$ is the total expenditure of the consumer for Q_1 of the commodity.

A-6

Relationship Among Marginal Revenue, Price, and Elasticity

Let P and Q equal the price and the quantity of a commodity, respectively. Then the total revenue of the seller of the commodity (TR) is given by

$$TR = PQ \quad (41A)$$

and the marginal revenue is

$$MR = \frac{d(TR)}{dQ} = P + Q \frac{dP}{dQ} \quad (42A)$$

Manipulating Expression (42A) mathematically, we get

$$MR = P\left(1 + \frac{Q}{P} \frac{dP}{dQ}\right) = P\left(1 - \frac{1}{\eta}\right) \quad (43A)$$

where, η equals -1 times the coefficient of price elasticity of demand. For example, if $P = \$12$.

$12 and $\eta = 3$, MR = \$8. If $\eta = \infty$, $P = MR = \$12$.

A-7

Isoquants

Suppose that there are two inputs, labor and capital. Then

$$Q = Q(L,K) \qquad (44A)$$

is a general production function. Equation (41A) postulates that output (Q) is a function of or depends on the quantity of labor (L) and capital (K) used in production. The more L and K are used, the greater is Q.

Using a subscript on Q to specify a given level of output, we can write

$$Q_1 = Q_1(L,K) \qquad (45A)$$

This is the general equation for an isoquant. Equation (45A) posulates that output Q_1 can be produced with various combinations of L and K. The more L is used, the less K will be required to remain on the same isoquant. Higher subscripts refer to higher isoquants. Thus, $Q_2 > Q_1$.

Taking the total differential of Equation (44A), we get

$$dQ = \frac{\partial Q}{\partial L} d_L + \frac{\partial Q}{\partial K} d_K \qquad (46A)$$

Since a movement along an isoquant leaves output unchanged, we set $dQ = 0$ and get

$$\frac{\partial Q}{\partial L} d_L + \frac{\partial Q}{\partial K} d_K = 0 \qquad (47A)$$

so that

$$\frac{\partial Q}{\partial K} d_K = -\frac{\partial Q}{\partial L} d_L \qquad (48A)$$

and

$$-\frac{d_K}{d_L} = \frac{\partial Q/\partial L}{\partial Q/\partial K} = \frac{MP_L}{MP_K} = MRTS_{LK} \qquad (49A)$$

Equation (49A) indicates that the negative value of the slope of an isoquant $(-d_K/d_L)$ is equal to the ratio of the marginal product of L to the marginal product of K (MP_L/MP_K), which, in turn, equals the marginal rate of technical substitution of L for K $(MRTS_{LK})$.

A-8

Cost Minimization

A firm may wish to minimize the cost of producing a given level of output. The total cost of the firm (C) is given by

$$C = wL + rK \qquad (50A)$$

where w is the wage rate of labor and r is the

rental price (per unit) of capital. A given level of output $(\overline{Q})$ can be produced with various combinations of L and K:

$$\overline{Q} = \overline{Q}(L,K) \qquad (51A)$$

To minimize Equation (50A) subject to

Equation (51A), we form

$$Z = wL + rK + \lambda^* [\overline{Q} - \overline{Q}(L,K)] \qquad (52A)$$

where λ^* is the Lagrangian multiplier.

Taking the first partial derivative of Z with respect to L and K and setting them equal to zero gives

$$\frac{\partial Z}{\partial L} = w - \lambda^* \frac{\partial Q}{\partial L} \text{ and}$$

$$\frac{\partial Z}{\partial K} = K - \lambda^* \frac{\partial Q}{\partial K} \qquad (53A)$$

It follows that

$$w = \lambda^* \frac{\partial Q}{\partial L} \text{ and } r = \lambda^* \frac{\partial Q}{\partial K} \qquad (54A)$$

Dividing, we get

$$\frac{w}{r} = \frac{\partial Q/\partial L}{\partial Q/\partial K} = MRTS_{xy} \qquad (55A)$$

Equation (55A) indicates that a firm minimizes the cost of producing a given level of output by hiring labor and capital up to the point where the ratio of the input prices (w/r) equals the ratio of the marginal products of labor and capital, $\frac{\partial Q/\partial L}{\partial Q/\partial K}$, which equals the marginal rate of technical substitution of labor for capital $(MRTS_{LK})$. Graphically, this occurs at the point where a given isoquant is tangent to an isocost line (and their slopes are equal). Equation (55A) is only the first order condition for minimization (and maximization). The second order condition for minimization is that the isoquant be convex to the origin.

A-9

Profit Maximization

A firm usually wants to produce the output that maximizes its total profits. Total profits (π) are equal to total revenue (R) minus total cost (C). That is,

$$\pi = R - C \qquad (56A)$$

where H, R, and C are all functions of Q.

Taking the first derivative of H with respect to Q and setting it equal to zero gives

$$\frac{d\pi}{dQ} = \frac{dR}{dQ} - \frac{dC}{dQ} = 0 \qquad (57A)$$

so that

$$\frac{dR}{dQ} = \frac{dC}{dQ} \qquad (58A)$$

Equation (55A) indicates that in order to maximize profits, a firm must produce where marginal revenue (MR) equals marginal cost (MC).

Equation (58A) is only the first order condition for maximization (and minimization). The second order condition for profit maximization requires that the second derivative or π with respect to Q be negative. That is,

$$\frac{d^2\pi}{dQ^2} = \frac{d^2R}{dQ^2} - \frac{d^2C}{dQ^2} < 0 \qquad (59A)$$

so that

$$\frac{d^2R}{dQ^2} < \frac{d^2C}{dQ^2} \qquad (60A)$$

According to Equation (60A), the algebraic

value of the slope of the MC function must be greater than the algebraic value of the MR function. Under perfect competition, MR is constant (i.e., the MR curve of the firm is horizontal) so that Equation (60A) requires that the MC curve be rising at the point where $MR = MC$ for the firm to maximize its total profits.

A-10

Price Determination

At equilibrium, the quantity demanded of a commodity (Q_d) is equal to the quantity supplied of the commodity (Q_s). That is,

$$Q_d = Q_s \tag{61A}$$

The demand function can be written as

$$Q_d = a - bP \; (a,b > 0) \tag{62A}$$

where a is the positive quantity intercept, and $-b$ refers to the negative slope of the demand curve (so that the P rises, Q_d falls). The supply function can take the form of

$$Q_s = -c + dP \; (c,d > 0) \tag{63A}$$

where $-c$ refers to the negative quantity intercept (so that the supply curve crosses the price axis at a positive price), and d refers to the positive slope of the supply curve (so that when P rises, Q_s also rises).
Setting $Q_d = Q_s$ for equilibrium, we get

$$a - bP = -c + dP \tag{64A}$$

Solving for P, we have

$$\overline{P} = \frac{a + c}{b + d} \tag{65A}$$

where the bar on P refers to the equilibrium price. Since parameters a, b, c, and d are all positive, $\overline{P}$ is also positive.
To find the equilibrium quantity ($\overline{Q}$) that corresponds to $\overline{P}$, we substitute Equation (65A) into Equation (61A) or (62A). Substituting Equation (65A) into Equation (61A), we get

$$\overline{Q} = a - \frac{b(a + c)}{(b + d)}$$
$$= \frac{a(b + d) - b(a + c)}{b + d} = \frac{ad - bc}{b + d} \tag{66A}$$

Since the denominator of Equation (66A), $(b + d)$, is positive, for $\overline{Q}$ to be positive (and for the model to be economically meaningful) the numerator, $(ad - bc)$, must also be positive. That is, $ad > bc$.

A-11

The Cobweb Model

The cobweb model is an example of dynamic analysis where the quantity supplied of a commodity adjusts with a lag to a change in demand. For example, for some agricultural commodities, this year's prices determine next year's quantity supplied, and the quantity supplied this year (Q_{st}) depends on last year's prices (P_{t-1}). That is,

$$Q_{st} = -c + dP_{t-1} \; (c,d > 0) \tag{67A}$$

Assuming the usual demand curve where the quantity demanded this year (Q_{dt}) depends on this year's price (P_t), we have

$$Q_{dt} = a - bP_t \ (a,b > 0) \qquad (68A)$$

For equilibrium in the present period,

$$Q_{dt} = Q_{st} \qquad (69A)$$

Substituting Equations (68A) and (67A) into Equation (69A), we have

$$a - bP_t = -c + dP_{t-1} \qquad (70A)$$

Solving for P_t, we get

$$P_t = \left(-\frac{d}{b}\right)P_{t-1} + \frac{a + c}{b} \qquad (71A)$$

Therefore,

$$P_1 = \left(-\frac{d}{b}\right)P_0 + \frac{a + c}{b} \qquad (72A)$$

and

$$P_2 = \left(-\frac{d}{b}\right)P_1 + \frac{a + c}{b} \qquad (73A)$$

Substituting Equation (72A) into Equation (73A), we get

$$P_2 = \left(-\frac{d}{b}\right)^2 P_0$$

$$+ \left(-\frac{d}{b}\right)\left(\frac{a + c}{b}\right) + \left(\frac{a + c}{b}\right) \qquad (74A)$$

It can be shown that the general solution for any time period, t, is

$$P_t = \left(-\frac{d}{b}\right)^t P_0 + \left(\frac{a + c}{b + d}\right)$$

$$\times \left[1 - \left(-\frac{d}{b}\right)^t\right] \qquad (75A)$$

We now have three possible outcomes (cases): (1) uniform oscillation, (2) damped oscillation, and (3) explosive oscillation.

Case 1: Uniform Oscillation

If the slope of the supply curve equals the absolute value of the slope of the demand curve (i.e., $d = |b|$), then $-d/b = -1$ and

$$P_t = (-1)^t P_0 + \left(\frac{a + c}{b + d}\right)[1 - (-1)^t] \qquad (76A)$$

If $t = 0$ or any even number, then

$$P_t = P_0 + \left(\frac{a + c}{b + d}\right)(1 - 1) = P_0 \qquad (77A)$$

On the other hand, if t is an odd number,

$$P_t = -P_0 + \left(\frac{a + c}{b + d}\right)(1 + 1)$$

$$= 2\left(\frac{a + c}{b + d}\right) - P_0 \qquad (78A)$$

Therefore, if $d = b$, price will constantly oscillate between P_0 (in even years) and the value of Equation (78A) (in odd years).

Case 2: Damped Oscillation

If $d < b$, then $d/b < 1$ and P_t approaches $(a + c)/(b + d)$ as t increases. That is, the amplitude of the price oscillations will decrease over time and price will converge toward the price given by the intersection of the supply and demand curves (see Figure 2-12).

Case 3: Explosive Oscillation

Finally, if $d > b$, then $d/b > 1$ and $(-d/b)^t$ approches infinity as t increases. That is, the time path of the price oscillations will be divergent and the oscillation explosive. Over time, price and quantity will then move farther and farther away from equilibrium.

A-12

Price Discrimination

Suppose that a monopolist sells a commodity in two separate markets. The monopolist must then decide how much to sell in each market in order to maximize its total profits. The total profits of the monopolist (π) is equal to the sum of the total revenue that it receives from selling the commodity in the two markets (i.e., $R_1 + R_2$) minus the total cost of producing the total output (C). That is,

$$\pi = R_1 + R_2 - C \tag{79A}$$

Taking the first partial derivative of π with respect to Q_1 (the quantity sold in the first market) and Q_2 (the amount sold in the second market), and setting them equal to zero, we get

$$\frac{\partial \pi}{\partial Q_1} = \frac{\partial R_1}{\partial Q_1} - \frac{\partial C}{\partial Q_1} = 0,$$

$$\frac{\partial \pi}{\partial Q_2} = \frac{\partial R_2}{\partial Q_2} - \frac{\partial C}{\partial Q_2} = 0 \tag{80A}$$

or

$$MR_1 = MR_2 = MC \tag{81A}$$

That is, in order to maximize its total profits, the monopolist must distribute its sales between the two markets in such a way that the marginal revenue is the same in both markets and equal to the common marginal cost. If $MR_1 > MR_2$, the monopolist could increase its total profits by redistributing sales from market 2 to market 1, until $MR_1 = MR_2$.

Since we know from Equation (43A) that

$$MR = P(1 - 1/\eta) \tag{82A}$$

profit maximization requires that

$$P_1(1 - 1/\eta_1) = P_2(1 - 1/\eta_2) \tag{83A}$$

where P_1 and P_2 are the prices in market 1 and market 2, respectively, and η_1 and η_2 are the coefficients or price elasticity of demand in market 1 and market 2. If $\eta_1 < \eta_2$, Equation (83A) will hold only if $P_1 > P_2$. That is, in order to maximize total profits the monopolist must sell the commodity at a higher price in the market with the lower price elasticity of demand (see also Figure 11-11). For example, if $\eta_1 = 2$, $\eta_2 = 3$, and $P_2 = \$6$, then $P_1 = \$8$.

A-13

Employment of Inputs

A firm employs the quantity of inputs that allows it to produce the profit maximizing level of output. As indicated by Equation (56A), total profits (π) are equal to total revenue (R) minus total cost (C). Total revenue is given by

$$R = PQ \tag{84A}$$

where P is the price of the commodity that the

firm produces and Q is the output, such that $Q = Q(L,K)$. The total cost of the firm was defined by Equation (50A). Thus, the firm employs labor and capital so as to maximize:

$$\pi = PQ(L,K) - (wL + rK) \tag{85A}$$

When P, w, and r are constant, the firm is a perfect competitor in the product and input markets.

Taking the first partial derivative of π with respect to L and K and setting them equal to zero gives

$$\frac{\partial \pi}{\partial L} = P \frac{\partial Q}{\partial L} - w = 0,$$

$$\frac{\partial \rho}{\partial K} = P \frac{\partial Q}{\partial K} - r = 0 \qquad (86A)$$

It follows that

$$P \frac{\partial Q}{\partial L} = w \; , \; P \frac{\partial Q}{\partial K} = r \qquad (87A)$$

or

$$VMP_L = w \; , \; VMP_K = r \qquad (88A)$$

Equation (60A) indicates that a firm maximizes profits by hiring labor and capital up to the point where the value of the marginal product of labor $[VMP_L = P \, (\partial Q/\partial L)]$ equals the wage rate (w) and the value of the marginal product of capital $[VMP_K = P \, (\partial Q/\partial K)]$ equals the rental price of capital (r). Geometrically, this occurs where the VMP_L curve intersects the (horizontal) supply curve of labor and the VMP_K curve intersects the (horizontal) supply curve of rental capital. Equation (60A) is only the first order condition for maximization. The second order condition is that the VMP_L and VMP_K curves be negatively sloped (i.e., that the firm be in stage II of production or produce in the area of diminishing returns).

A-14

Input, Price, Marginal Expense, and the Price Elasticity of Input Supply

The total cost (C) of a firm hiring only labor is given by

$$C = wL \qquad (89A)$$

where w is the wage rate and L is the number of workers hired.

If the firm is a monopsonist (i.e., the only employer of labor in the market) it will have to pay higher wages the more labor it wants to hire. That is, the wage rate is a function of or depends on the amount of labor the firm hires (and the amount of labor the firm hires depends on the wage rate).

The firm's marginal expense for labor (ME_L) is then given by

$$ME_L = \frac{dC}{dL} = w + L \frac{dw}{dL} \qquad (90A)$$

Rearranging Equation (90A), we get

$$ME_L = w \left(1 + \frac{L}{w} \frac{dW}{dL} \right) \qquad (91A)$$

Therefore,

$$ME_L = w \left(1 + \frac{1}{\epsilon_L} \right) \qquad (92A)$$

where ϵ_L is the price (wage) elasticity of the supply curve of labor. Graphically, this means that the ME_L curve lies above the (positively sloped) S_L curve (see also Figure 15-3). The same would be true for capital or any other input for which the firm is the only employer in the market.

If the firm were a perfect competitor in the labor market, $\epsilon_L \to \infty$ and $ME_L = w$ (i.e., the ME_L curve would coincide with the horizontal S_L curve faced by the firm at the given level of w).

A-15

Derivation of the Formula to Find the Present Value of an Investment

We have seen in Section 16-3b that the present value (V_0) of an investment that yields a constant stream of net cash flows in each future year indefinitely, starting with the next year, is given by Equation (16-7), repeated below as Equation (93A):

$$V_0 = \frac{R}{r} \tag{93A}$$

where R is the constant net cash flow received the next year and in every subsequent year (i.e., in perpetuity), and r is the rate of interest.

To derive Equation (93A), we start with

$$V_0 = \frac{R}{(1 + r)} + \frac{R}{(1 + r)^2}$$
$$+ \cdots \frac{R}{(1 + r)^n} \tag{94A}$$

which is similar to Equation (16-6) in Section 16-3b.

If we let $1/(1 + r) = k$, then

$$V_0 = R(k + k^2 + \cdots k^n) \tag{95A}$$

Multiplying both sides of Equation (95A) by k, we get

$$kV_0 = R(k^2 + k^3 + \cdots k^{n+1}) \tag{96A}$$

Subtracting Equation (96A) from Equation (95A) we have

$$V_0 - kV_0 = R(k - k^{n+1}) \tag{97A}$$

From Equation (97A), we get

$$V_0 = \frac{R(k - k^{n+1})}{1 - k} \tag{98A}$$

Since $k = 1/(1 + r)$ is smaller than 1, for n very large, k^{n-1} is very small and can be ignored. Thus, we are left with

$$V_0 = R\left(\frac{k}{1 - k}\right) \tag{99A}$$

Substituting $1/(1 + r)$ for k into Equation (99A), we get

$$
\begin{aligned}
V_0 &= R\left(\frac{\dfrac{1}{1 + r}}{1 - \dfrac{1}{1 + r}}\right) \\
&= R\left(\frac{\dfrac{1}{1 + r}}{\dfrac{1 + r - 1}{1 + r}}\right) \\
&= R\left(\frac{1}{1 + r}\right)\left(\frac{1 + r}{r}\right) \\
&= \frac{R}{r}
\end{aligned} \tag{100A}
$$

A Model of General Equilibrium

In this section we outline the Walras-Cassel general equilibrium model.*

Let $x_1, x_2, \ldots, x_n$ refer to the quantity of the n commodities in the economy, with prices $p_1, p_2, \ldots, p_n$. Let $r_1, r_2, \ldots, r_m$ refer to the quantity of the m resources or inputs in the economy, with prices $v_1, v_2, \ldots, v_m$.

The market demand equations for the n commodities can be written as

$$x_1 = f_1(p_1, p_2, \ldots, p_n; v_1, v_2, \ldots, v_m)$$
$$x_2 = f_2(p_1, p_2, \ldots, p_n; v_1, v_2, \ldots, v_m) \quad (101A)$$
$$\cdots\cdots\cdots\cdots\cdots\cdots\cdots\cdots\cdots$$
$$x_n = f_n(p_1, p_2, \ldots, p_n; v_1, v_2, \ldots, v_m)$$

The market demand for each commodity is the sum of the demand for the commodity by each consumer and is a function of, or depends on, the prices of all commodities and of all inputs. Input prices affect individuals' incomes and, thus, influence the demand for commodities.

Since in long-run perfectly competitive equilibrium, commodity prices equal their production costs, we have

$$a_{11}v_1 + a_{21}v_2 + \cdots + a_{m1}v_m = p_1$$
$$a_{12}v_1 + a_{22}v_2 + \cdots + a_{m2}v_m = p_2 \quad (102A)$$
$$\cdots\cdots\cdots\cdots\cdots\cdots\cdots\cdots\cdots$$
$$a_{1n}v_1 + a_{2n}v_2 + \cdots + a_{mn}v_m = p_n$$

where a_{11} refers to the quantity of input 1 required to produce one unit of commodity 1. Since v_1 is the price of input 1, a_1v_1 is then the dollar amount spent on input 1 to produce one unit of commodity 1. On the other hand, a_{21} refers to the quantity of input 2 required to produce one unit of commodity 1, so that $a_{21}v_2$

is the dollar amount spent on input 2 to produce one unit of commodity 1. Finally, a_{m1} is the amount of input m required to produce one unit of commodity 1 and $a_{m1}v_m$ is the expenditure on input m to produce one unit of commodity 1. Therefore, the left-hand side of Equation (102A) refers to the total cost of producing one unit of commodity 1. This is equal to the unit price of commodity 1 (p_1). The second equation gives the expenditure on each input to produce one unit of commodity 2, and this is equal to p_2. The same is true for each of the n commodities. The a_{ij}'s are called input or production coefficients, and they are assumed to be fixed in our simple model.

Setting the total demand for each resource or input (required to produce all commodities) equal to the total supply of the input, we have

$$a_{11}x_1 + a_{12}x_2 + \cdots + a_{1n}x_n = r_1$$
$$a_{21}x_1 + a_{22}x_2 + \cdots + a_{2n}x_n = r_2 \quad (103A)$$
$$\cdots\cdots\cdots\cdots\cdots\cdots\cdots\cdots\cdots$$
$$a_{m1}x_1 + a_{m2}x_2 \cdots + a_{mn}x_n = r_m$$

where $a_{11}x_1$ is the quantity of resource or input 1 required to produce x_1 units of commodity 1, $a_{12}x_2$ is the quantity of input 1 required to produce x_2 of commodity 2, and $a_{1in}x_n$ is the quantity of input 1 required to produce x_n of commodity n. Thus, the first equation sets the total quantity demanded of input 1 (required to produce x_1, x_2, to x_n) to equal the total supply of resource or input 1 (r_1). Similarly, the second equation sets the total quantity demanded of input 2 used in all commodities to equal the quantity supplied of input 2, and so on for each of the m resources or inputs.

---

* The presentation is adapted from Robert Dorfman, Paul A. Samuelson, and Robert M. Solow, *Linear Programming and Economic Analysis* (New York: McGraw-Hill, 1958), pp. 351–355.

The last step to close the model is to specify the set of equations that relate the supply of each resource or input to prices. This is given by

$$r_1 = g_1(p_1, p_2, \ldots, p_n; v_1, v_2, \ldots, v_m)$$
$$r_2 = g_2(p_1, p_2, \ldots, p_n; v_1, v_2, \ldots, v_m) \quad (104A)$$
$$\cdots\cdots\cdots\cdots\cdots\cdots\cdots\cdots\cdots\cdots$$
$$r_m = g_m(p_1, p_2, \ldots, p_n; v_1, v_2, \ldots, v_m)$$

That is, the supply of each resource or input is a function of or depends on the price of all inputs (the v_i's) and the price of all commodities (the p_j's). For example, the supply of steel depends on the price of steel, the price of aluminum, the wages of autoworkers, and other input prices. The price of steel also depends on the price of automobiles, washing machines, steaks, and other commodity prices. There-fore, a change in any part of the system affects every other part of the system.

Summing up in Equation (101A) to Equation (102A), we have $2n + 2m$ equations and an equal number of unknowns (the x_j's, the p_j's, the v_i's, and the r_i's). However, according to Walras' law Equations (101A) and (104A) have only $n + m - 1$ independent equations, since if all but one of these $n + m$ equations are satisfied, the last one must also be satisfied. However, we can arbitrarily set any commodity price, say, $p_1 = 1$ and express all other prices in terms of p_1 (the *numéraire*). This reduces the number of unknowns in the system by 1 so as to equal the number of independent equations. The system may then have a unique solution (i.e., set of prices and quantities that simultaneously satisfies all the equations of the model).

Appendix B

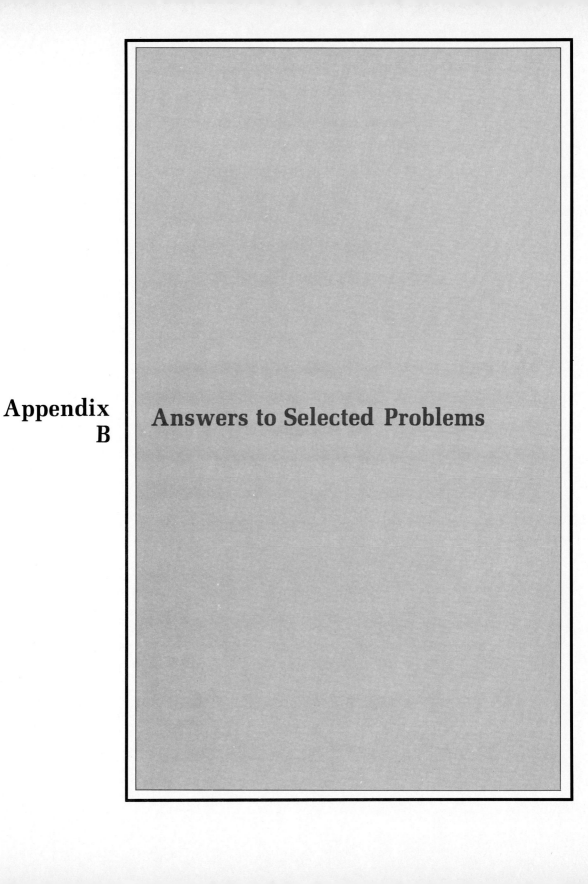

Answers to Selected Problems

Chapter 2

2. (a)

P($)	8	7	6	5	4	3	2	1	0
QD'	0	10	20	30	40	50	60	70	80

(b) See Figure 1.

(c) D' represents an increase in demand because consumers demand more of the commodity at each and every price.

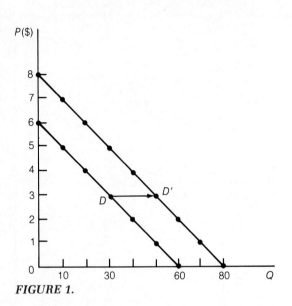

FIGURE 1.

5. (a)

Market Supply Schedule, Market Demand Schedule and Equilibrium

Price	Quantity Supplied	Quantity Demanded	Surplus (+) Shortage (−)	Pressure on Price
$6	60	0	60	Down
5	50	10	40	Down
4	40	20	20	Down
3	30	30	0	Equil.
2	20	40	−20	Up
1	10	50	−40	Up
0	0	60	−60	Up

(b) See Figure 2.

9. (a) The demand for hamburgers increases, and this results in a higher equilibrium price and quantity.

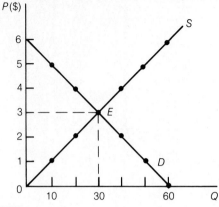

FIGURE 2.

(b) The supply of hamburgers declines, and this results in an increase in the equilibrium price and a reduction in the equilibrium quantity.

(c) The supply of hamburgers increases and this lowers the equilibrium price and increases the quantity purchased.

(d) The demand for hamburgers increases and this has the same effect as in part (a).

(e) A per unit subsidy is the opposite of a per unit tax; the per unit subsidy increases the supply of hamburgers and this has the same effect as in part (c).

11. (a) See Figure 3.

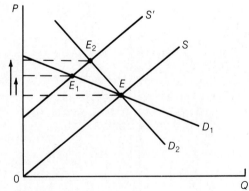

FIGURE 3.

(b) See Figure 4.

B2

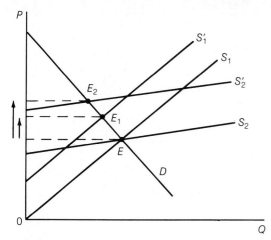

FIGURE 4.

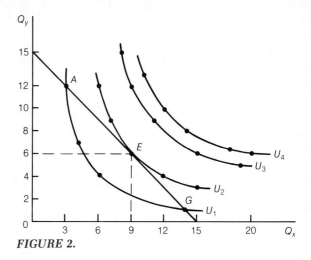

FIGURE 2.

Chapter 3

3. (a) See Figure 1.

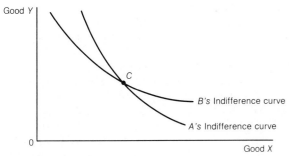

FIGURE 1.

(b) Point C is the original equal endowment of good X and good Y of individual A and individual B. Since A prefers X to Y, A's indifference curve is steeper than B's indifference curve. That is, A is willing to give up more of Y for an additional unit of unit of X and MRS_{xy} for A at point C is greater than for B.

7. (a) See Figure 2.
   (b) The individual maximizes utility at point E, where U_2 is tangent to the budget line by purchasing 9X and 6Y. To maximize utility, the individual should spend all income in such a way that MRS_{xy} (the absolute slope of

the indifference curve) equals P_x/P_y (the absolute slope of the budget line).
   (c) Points A and G are on U_1 even though the individual spends all income.
   (d) The individual does not have sufficient income to reach U_3 and U_4.

9. (a) The individual should spend $4 to purchase 4X and the remaining $3 to purchase 3Y.
   (b) $MU_x/P_x = MU_y/P_y = 6/\$1$ and ($1) (4X) + ($1) (3Y) = $7.
   (c) The individual would receive 41 utils from consuming 4X (the sum of the MU_x up to 4X) plus 27 utils from purchasing 3Y (the sum of the MU_y up to 3Y) for a total utility of 68 utils. If the individual spent all $7 on 7X he or she would get 49 utils (the sum of all MU_x). If the individual would spend all income on 7Y, he or she would get 38 utils (the sum of all MU_y).

12. Fringe benefits are more likely to grow faster in relation to cash compensation in periods of rapid inflation because they provide the opportunity to avoid being pushed into higher income-tax brackets by inflation (the so-called bracket creep), or at least to slow down the process. That is, by increasing fringe benefits instead of income compensation, bracket creep can be avoided.
   This benefit has been essentially eliminated by the federal government indexing of taxes for inflation that started in 1985. However, the

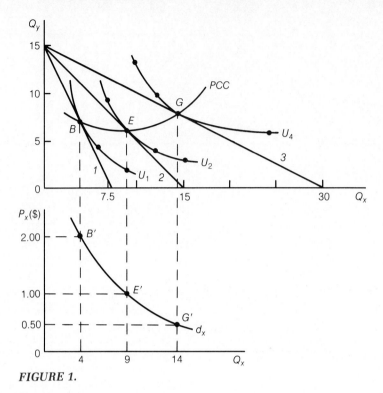

FIGURE 1.

more basic benefit of fringe benefits resulting from their tax-deductible status remains. The Regan tax proposal, if passed would tax most fringe benefits.

Chapter 4

3. (a) See Figure 1.
   (b) At P_x = $0.50, the consumer maximizes utility at point G where U_4 is tangent to budget line 3 by purchasing 14X. This gives point G' in the bottom panel. With P_x = $1, optimum is at point E where U_2 is tangent to budget line 2 and the consumer purchases 9X. This gives point E' in the bottom panel. Finally, with P_x = $2, the consumer is at optimum at point B where U_1 is tangent to budget line 1 by purchasing 4X. This gives point B' in the bottom panel. Joining points G'E'B' in the bottom panel we derive dx.
6. See Figure 2.
   The sequence in Figure 2 is from A to B to C.
8. In very poor Asian countries people can pur-

chase very little else besides rice. If the price of rice falls, the substitution effect tends to lead people to substitute rice for other goods. However, if rice is an inferior good in these nations, the increase in real income resulting from the decline in the price of rice leads people to purchase less rice. Since people spend most of their income on rice, a decline in the price of rice will lead to a relatively large increase in purchasing power, which will allow people to purchase so much more of other goods that they need to purchase less rice.
That is, it is conceivable that the substitution effect (which leads people to purchase more rice when its price falls) could be overwhelmed by the opposite income effect. The net effect would then be that people purchase less rice when its price falls, so that the demand curve for rice would be positively sloped in these countries. However, there is no proof that this is indeed the case.

10. See Figure 3.
    The poor family is originally maximizing utility

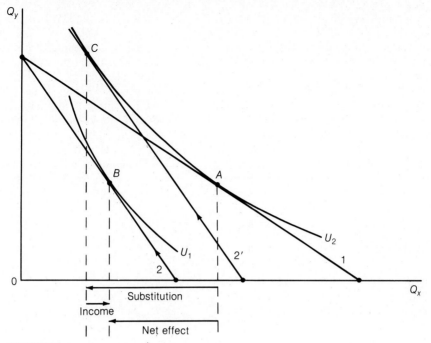

FIGURE 2.

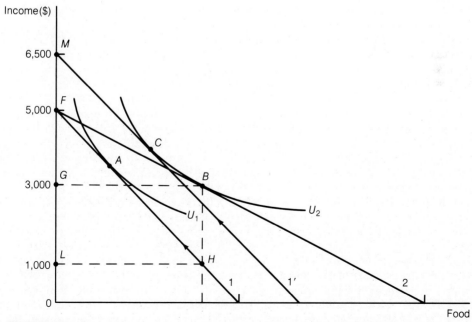

FIGURE 3.

at point A where U_1 is tangent to budget line 1. With the government paying half of the family's food bill, we have budget line 2. With budget line 2, the poor family maximizes utility at point B on U_2. To get the point B, the family spends $2,000 of its income (FG). Without the subsidy the family would have to pay $4,000 (FL).

Thus, the cost of the subsidy to the government is $2,000. The family, however, could reach U_2 at point C with a cash subsidy of only $1,500 (FM). The government may still prefer to subsidize the family's food consumption (even if more expensive) if one of its aims is to improve nutrition.

Chapter 5

3. (a) When two demand curves are parallel, their slopes $(- \Delta P/\Delta Q)$ and their inverse $(- \Delta Q/\Delta P)$ are the same at every price. However, P/Q (the other component of the price elasticity formula) is smaller (since Q is larger) for the demand curve further to the right at every price. Therefore, the price elasticity of the demand curve further to the right is smaller.

   (b) When two demand curves intersect, P/Q is the same for both demand curves at the point of intersection. However, $- \Delta Q/\Delta P$ is larger for the flatter demand curve. Therefore, the flatter demand curve is more elastic at the point where the demand curves intersect.

7. (a) In a two-commodity world, both commodities cannot be luxuries since that would imply that a consumer could increase the quantity purchased of both commodities by a percentage larger than the percentage increase in his or her income. This is impossible if the consumer already spent all income on the two commodities before the increase in income (and does not borrow money).

   (b) A 10% increase in income results in a 25% increase in the quantity of cars purchased if the income elasticity is 2.5. That is, since 2.5 $= \%\Delta Q/10\%$, $\%\Delta Q = (2.5)(10\%) = 25\%$.

9. (a) Since $\eta = 0.13$ in the short run and 1.89 in the long run, the demand for electricity is inelastic in the short run and elastic in the long run. With a 10% increase in price, the quantity demanded of electricity will decline by 1.3% in the short run and 18.9% in the long run.

   (b) Since the income elasticity of demand exceeds unity, electricity is a luxury. With a 10% increase in incomes, consumers would purchase 19.4% more electricity.

   (c) Since the cross elasticity of demand between electricity and natural gas is positive, natural gas is a substitute for electricity. However, a 10% increase in the price of natural gas increases electricity consumption by only 2%.

12. (a) Since $Kx = 0.75$, Ky must be 0.25. Then,

$$(0.75)(0.90) + (0.25)(\eta_{IY}) = 1$$
$$0.25\eta_{IY} = 0.325$$
$$\eta_{IY} = 1.3$$

   (b) Commodity Y is a luxury and commodity X is a necessity. For Y to be an inferior good, η_{IY} must be negative. For this to occur, (0.75) (η_{IY}) must be larger than 1, which means that η_{IX} must exceed 1.33. Since most goods are normal, the income elasticity of demand of a commodity on which the consumer spends a great proportion of his or her income cannot be too much higher than 1.

Chapter 6

1. (a) See Figure 1.
   Since the Slutsky substitution effect of the reduction in Px puts the consumer on a higher indifference curve, the Slutsky substitution effect is larger than the corresponding Hicksian substitution effect, and so d^*x is more elastic than $d'x$.

   (b) The Slutsky method of measuring the substitution effect is more useful in empirical work because it can be obtained from actual price-quantity observations and does not require knowledge of the exact shape of indifference curves (as the Hicksian substitution effect does). However, the difference between the Slutsky and the Hicksian substitution effect is very small for small price changes.

3. (a) Starting with $\eta = \%\Delta Q/\%\Delta P$ and substitut-

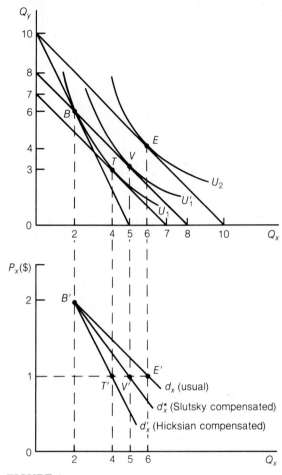

FIGURE 1.

ing the values from the given, we have 0.56 = %Δ Q/0.50. Therefore, %Δ Q = 28% reduction. Then, (0.28) (930) = 260 gallons (the total reduction in the family yearly gasoline consumption.)

(b) The 50% increase in gasoline price is equal to $0.60 (from $1.20 times 0.50). Then $0.60 times 930 gallons gives $558 for the tax collected per family per year. This represents 2.66% of the median family income of $21,000 in 1980. Substituting the appropriate values into the formula for n_j, we have 1.36 = %Δ Q/2.66. Therfore, %Δ Q = 3.62 or about 34 gallons (930 times 0.0362). This is the income effect. The substitution effect is

then a 226 gallons reduction per family per year.

8. (a) Since the individual requires better than even odds to accept the bet, he or she is an insurer.

(b) In choices involving risk, the individual maximizes expected utility. Since the individual is just willing to accept the bet with 60% odds of winning, this means that

Expected gain in utility =
Expected loss of utility
(0.6) (utils gained) =
(0.4) (150 utils)
Utils gained =
(0.4) (150)/0.6 = 100 utils

Thus, MU declines, confirming the conclusion of part (a) that the individual is an insurer.

(c) This is not really a cardinal measure of utility because the results obtained are arbitrary with respect to both origin and scale. That is, if the utils lost had been 300, the utils gained would have been 200. But 200 utils can only be interpreted as being more utility than 100, and not twice as much. Thus, we have an ordinal rather than a cardinal measure of utility.

9. (a) See Figure 2.
With a 50% reduction in the price of pork,

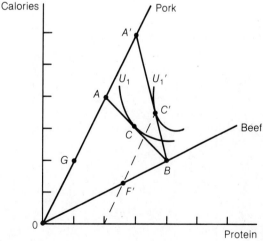

FIGURE 2.

budget line *AB* will shift outward to *A'B*. The consumer maximizes satisfaction at point *C'* on U'_1 by obtaining *OF'* characteristics from spending $6.67 on beef and $F'C'$ (= *OG*) characteristics from spending the remaining $3.37 on pork.

(b) See Figure 3.

With a 50% increase in the consumer's income, budget line *AB* shifts outward to *A'B'* and the consumer maximizes satisfaction at point *C''* on U_3.

Chapter 7

3. (a) See Figure 1.
   (b) The law of diminishing returns begins to operate past point *G* on the total product

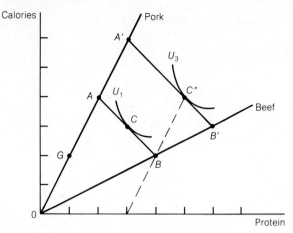

FIGURE 3.

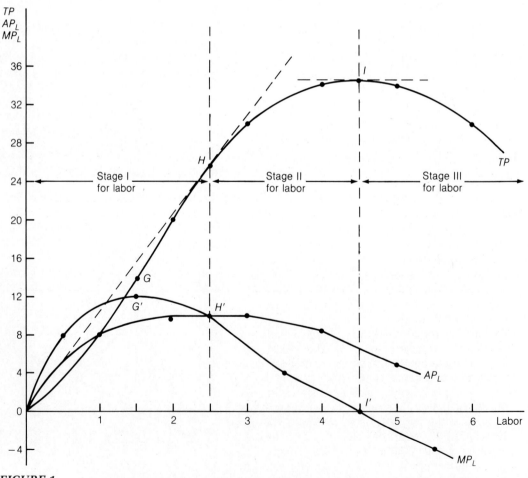

FIGURE 1.

curve. This corresponds to point G' on the marginal product of labor curve. As more and more units of the variable input (here labor) is used on one acre of land, eventually, "too much" labor is used and the marginal product of labor begins to fall.

8. See Figure 2.

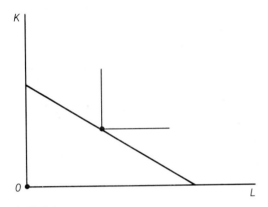

FIGURE 2.

The right angle or L-shaped isoquant shows no possibility of substituting one input for the other in production. The straight line isoquant shows that inputs are perfectly substitutable for each other in production ($MRTS_{LK}$ is constant). That is, the given level of output could be produced with only labor or only capital.

10. (a) The production function $Q = 10 \sqrt{LK}$ exhibits constant returns to scale throughout. For example, when $L = 1$ and $K = 1$, $Q = 10 \sqrt{1} = 10$. When $L = 2$ and $K = 2$, $Q = 10 \sqrt{4} = 20$. When $L = 3$ and $K = 3$, $Q = 10 \sqrt{9} = 30$. With $L = 4$ and $K = 4$, $Q = 10 \sqrt{16} = 40$, and so on.

(b) The production function exhibits diminishing returns to capital and labor throughout. For example, holding capital constant at $K = 1$ and increasing labor from $L = 1$ to $L = 2$, increases Q from 10 to $Q = 10 \sqrt{2} = 14.14$. Therefore, the marginal product of labor (MP_L) is 4.14. Increasing labor to $L = 3$, results in $Q = 10 \sqrt{3} = 17.32$. Thus, the MP_L declines to 3.18. The law of diminishing returns operates throughout, but the MP_L remains always positive. The same is

true if labor is held constant and capital changed.

11. (a) False.
The quantity of fertile land can be increased through reclamation and reduced through the depletion of fertility and through soil erosion.

(b) False.
As long as returns are diminishing but positive, the student still benefits from additional hours of study.

(c) True.
If economies of scale were present, larger and more efficient firms would drive smaller and less efficient firms out of business.

Chapter 8

1. (a) The explicit costs are $10,000 + 30,000 + 15,000 = 55,000$.

(b) The implicit cost is the forgone earning of $15,000 in the previous occupation.

(c) The total costs are equal to the $55,000 of explicit costs plus the $15,000 of implicit cost, or $70,000. Since the total earnings or revenues are only $65,000, from the economist's point of view, the woman actually lost $5,000 for the year by being in business for herself.

6. (a) Since to expand output in the short run to meet peak electricity needs, electrical utilities bring into operation older and less efficient equipment, their short-run marginal costs rise sharply.

(b) New generating equipment would have to run around the clock or nearly so for its AFC to be sufficiently low to make its ATC lower than for older equipment. To meet only peak demand, older *and fully depreciated* equipment is cheaper.

9. (a) The *LTC* curve would be a positively-sloped straight line through the origin when constant returns to scale operate at all levels of output.

(b) The *LAC* and the *LMC* curves would coincide and be horizontal at the value of the constant slope of the *LTC* curve.

(c) Horizontal *LAC* and *LMC* curves are consistent with U-shaped *SATC* curves. That is,

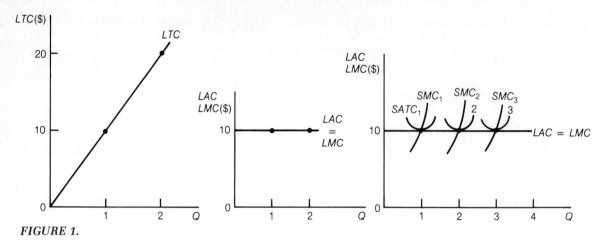

FIGURE 1.

the *LAC* curve would be tangent to and be formed by the lowest points of the *SATC* curves.

(d) See Figure 1.

12. (a) With the isoquant for 10Q L-shaped with origin at point A in Figure 8-15, the firm cannot substitute labor for capital in production when the wage rate falls, and its *TC* = (7)($5) + (7)($10) = $105.

(b) See Figure 2.

(c) *TC* = $105 now as compared with *TC* = $100 in application 4. Thus, *TC* is higher when substitution of *K* for *L* in production is not possible.

Chapter 9

2. (a) $AP_L = Q/L = AL^\alpha K^{1-\alpha}/L =$

$$AL^{\alpha-1} K^{1-\alpha} = A\left(\frac{K}{L}\right)^{1-\alpha}$$

Since A and α are given parameters, the AP_L = $f(K/L)$ only. This means that the AP_L is the same at every point on the expansion path.

(b) $MP_L = \alpha A^{\alpha-1} K^{1-\alpha} = \alpha A \left(\frac{K}{L}\right)^{1-\alpha}$

Since A and α are given parameters, the MP_L = $f(K/L)$ only. This means that the MP_L is

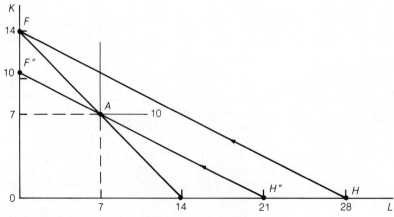

FIGURE 2.

B10

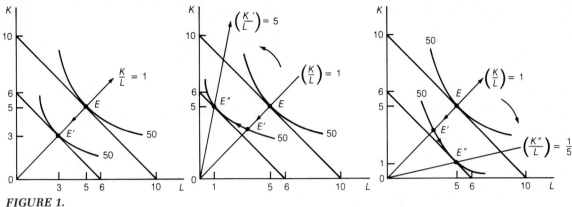

FIGURE 1.

the same at every point on the expansion path.

6. See Figure 1.

Since neutral technological progress increases the MP_K and MP_L in the same proportion, there is no substitution between L and K in production at unchanged w/r, so that the K/L ratio remains unchanged at $K/L = 1$ (point E' in the left panel).

Since K-using technological progress raises MP_K proportionately more than the MP_L, the firm substitutes K for L in production at constant w/r, so that K/L rises to $K/L = 5$ (point E'' in the middle panel). Since L-using technological progress raises the MP_K proportionately less than the MP_L, K/L falls to $K/L = 1/5$ (point E'' in the right panel).

8. The objective function to maximize is $\pi = \$10X + \$10Y$. Therefore, $Y = \pi/\$10 - X$.
   A constraint: $1X + 2Y \leq 12$.
   Therefore, $Y = 6 - \frac{1}{2}X$
   B constraint: $1X + .5Y \leq 6$.

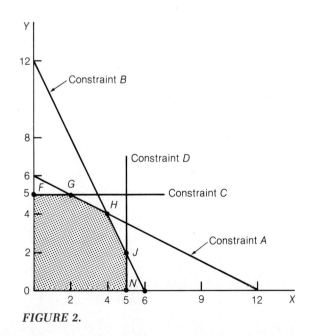

FIGURE 2.

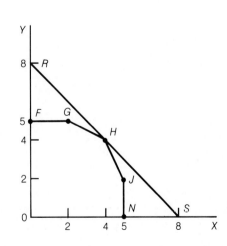

B11

Therefore, $Y = 12 - 2X$.
C constraint: $0X + 1Y \leq 5$.
Therefore, $Y = 5$.
D constraint: $1X + 0Y \leq 5$.
Therefore, $X = 5$.
Nonnegative constraints: $X, Y \geq 0$
Treating the inequalities as equations and plotting them, we get area of feasible solutions OFGHJN (the shaded area in the left panel of Figure 2). The right panel shows that the area of feasible solutions touches highest isoprofit line RS at point H (4X and 4Y). The highest total profits of the firm is thus $80. Note that here only constraints A and B are binding.

12. (a) *Reducing* nutrient B from 14 to 13 units shifts its constraint line down so that the new feasible region is the area above $DE'F'G$ in Figure 3 and TC are minimized at point F' (8X, 5Y) at ($2) (8) + ($3) (5) = $31, or $1 less than before. Therefore, the shadow price of nutrient B is $1.

   (b) Nutrient C is a slack input, and so its shadow price is zero.

Chapter 10

1. (a) $QD = QS$
   $$4,750 - 50P = 1,750 + 50P$$
   $$3,000 = 100P$$
   $$P = \$30 \text{ (equilibrium price)}$$

   (b)

Market Demand and Supply Schedules

P ($)	QD	QS
50	2,250	4,250
40	2,750	3,750
30	3,250	3,250
20	3,750	2,750
10	4,250	2,250

   (c) See Figure 1.
   (d) $P = \$30$.

4. (a) See Figure 2.
   In Figure 2, the slope of the TR curve refers to the constant price of $10 at which the perfectly competitive firm can sell its output. The TC curve indicates total fixed costs

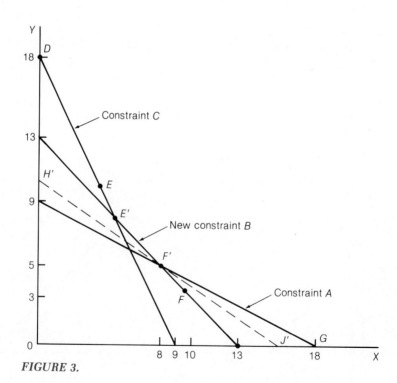

FIGURE 3.

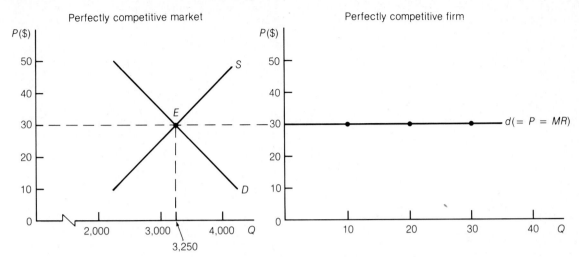

FIGURE 1.

of $200 and a constant average variable cost of $5 (the slope of the *TC* curve). This is often the case for many firms for small changes in outputs. The firm breaks even at *Q* = 40 per time period (point *B* in the figure). The firm incurs a loss at smaller outputs and earns a profit at higher output levels. A figure such as Figure 2 is called a *break-even chart*.

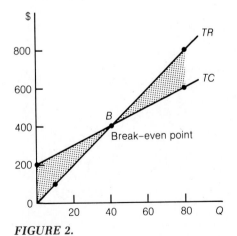

FIGURE 2.

(b) An increase in the price of the commodity can be shown by increasing the slope of the

TR curve; an increase in the total fixed costs of the firm can be shown by an increase in the vertical intercept of the *TC* curve, and an increase in average variable costs by an increase in the slope of the *TC* curve. The chart will then show the change in the break-even point of the firm and the profits or losses at other output levels. Thus, the break-even chart is a flexible tool to analyze quickly the effect of changing conditions on the firm.

(c) An important shortcoming of break-even charts is that they imply that firms will continue to earn larger and larger profits per time period with greater output levels. From our discussion in chapter 8, we know that, eventually, the *TC* curve will begin to rise faster than *TR*, and total profits will fall. Thus, break-even charts must be used with caution. Nevertheless, under the appropriate set of circumstances, they can be a useful tool and they are being used extensively today by business executives, government agencies, and nonprofit organizations.

8. See Figure 3.
12. See Figure 4.

The original long-run equilibrium point is *E* (where *D* crosses *S* and *LS*). If *D* shifts up to *D'*, the equilibrium point is *E'* in the market period (where *D'* and *S* cross). *E''* in the short run

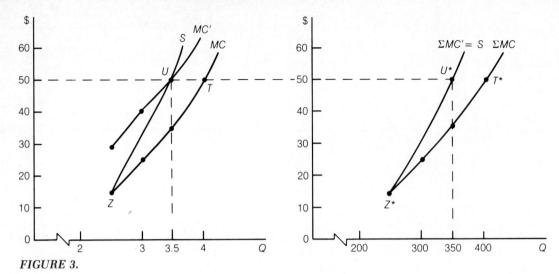

FIGURE 3.

(where D' and S' cross), and E^* in the long run (where D' crosses S'' and LS). Thus, the adjustment to an increase in demand falls entirely on price in the market period, mostly on price in the short run, and mostly on output in the long run. With a constant cost industry, long-run adjustment would fall entirely on output.

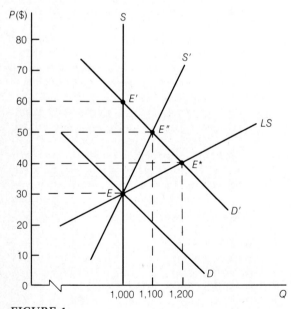

FIGURE 4.

Chapter 11

4. (a) See Figure 1. The best level of output is about $Q = 2$, where the MC curve intersects the MR' curve from below.

(b) Since at $Q = 2$, $P = \$20$ while $ATC = \$30$, the firm incurs a loss of $10 per unit and $20 in total. However, since $AVC = \$15$, the monopolist covers $10 out of its $30 of total fixed costs. Were the monopolist to go out of business, it would incur a total loss equal to its $TFC = \$30$. The shut-down point of the monopolist is at $Q = 2.5$, where $P = AVC = \$14$.

7. (a) See Figure 2.
(b) See Figure 3.

10. With third degree price discrimination $MR_1 = MR_2$.
Also with formula (5 − 6), $MR_1 = P_1 (1 − 1/\eta_1)$
and $MR_2 = P_2 (1 − 1/\eta_2)$
Setting MR_1 equal to MR_2, we get:
$P_1 (1 − 1/\eta_1) = P_2 (1 − 1/\eta_2)$
so that

$$\frac{P_1}{P_2} = \frac{1 − 1/\eta_2}{1 − 1/\eta_1}$$

and

$$P_1 = \left(\frac{1 − 1/\eta_2}{1 − 1/\eta_1} \right) 4.5$$

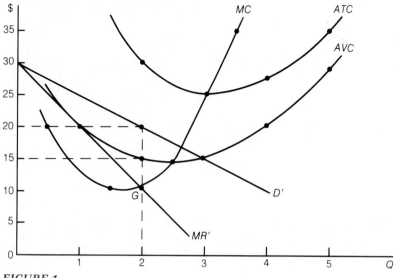

FIGURE 1.

Since we were given that $P_2 = \$4.50$, we need only to calculate η_1 and η_2 in order to prove that P_1 should be $7. By extending D_1 to the horizontal axis and labeling H the intersection point at $Q = 11$ and also labeling J the point on the horizontal axis directly below point A, we get that $\eta_1 = JH/OJ = 7/4$. Doing the same for D_2, we get that $\eta_2 = 3$. Substituting the η_1, η_2 and P_2 val-

ues into the formula for P_1 derived above, we get:

$$P_1 = \left(\frac{1 - 1/3}{1 - \frac{1}{4/7}}\right) 4.5 = \left(\frac{2/3}{1 - 7/4}\right) 4.5$$

$$= \left(\frac{2/3}{3/7}\right) 4.5 = \left(\frac{2}{3}\right)\left(\frac{7}{3}\right) 4.5 = 7$$

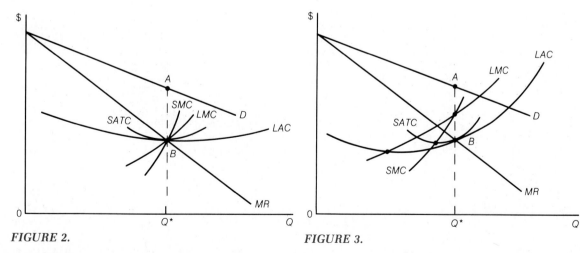

FIGURE 2.   **FIGURE 3.**

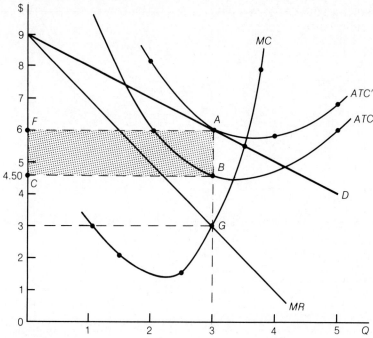

FIGURE 4.

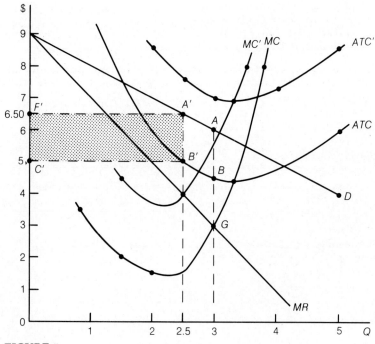

FIGURE 5.

12. (a) See the following table and Figure 4 where the prime indicates the effect of the lump-sum tax of $4.50.

Q	STC	MC	ATC	STC'	ATC'
0	$ 6	—	—	$10.50	—
1	10	$ 4	$10	14.50	$14.50
2	12	2	6	16.50	8.25
*3	13.50	1.50	4.50	18	6
4	19	4.50	4.75	23.50	5.88
5	30	11	6	34.50	6.90
6	48	18	8	52.50	8.75

The STC' values are obtained by adding $4.50 to the STC values. ATC' = STC'/Q. Since the lump-sum tax is like a fixed cost, it does not affect MC. Thus, the best level of output of the monopolist remains at 3 units, at which P = $6, ATC' = $6 and the monopolist breaks even.

(b) See the following table and Figure 5, where the prime indicates the effect of a $2.50 per-unit tax.

Q	STC	MC	ATC	STC'	MC'	ATC'
1	$10	$ 4	$10	$12.50	—	$12.50
2	12	2	6	17	$ 4.50	8.50
3	13.50	1.50	4.50	21	4	7
4	19	4.50	4.75	29	8	7.25
5	30	11	6	42.50	13.50	8.50

The STC' values are obtained by adding $2.50 per unit of output to STC. ATC' = STC'/Q. MC' = Δ STC'/Δ Q. Since a per-unit tax is like a variable cost both the ATC and the MC curves shift up to ATC' and MC'. The new equilibrium point is 2.5 units given at point G' where the MC' curve intersects the MR curve from below. At Q = 2.5, P = $6.50, ATC' = $7.50, and the monopolist incurs a loss of $0.50 per unit and $1.25 in total (as opposed to a profit $4.50 before the per-unit tax). Thus, the monopolist can shift part of the burden of the per-unit tax to consumers.

Chapter 12

3. See Figure 1.
The best level of output of the firm in the short-

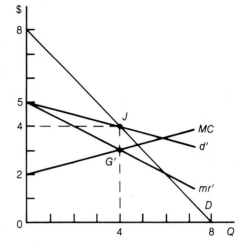

FIGURE 1.

run is given by point G' where the firm's MC curve intersects the mr' curve from below. The firm should thus charge P = $4 and sell Q = 4 (point J on demand curve d'). At point J, demand curve d and D intersect and so there is no incentive for the firm to change its price and output.

5. Because the demand curve facing a monopolist-ically competitive firm is negatively sloped (so that its marginal revenue curve lies below the demand curve) we cannot derive the short-run supply curve of the firm, just as in the case of monopoly. That is, as shown in Figure 11-5 for a monopolist, a given quantity can be supplied at different prices, and so there is no unique relationship between price and quantity (i.e., there is no supply curve for the monopolist). Exactly the same is true for a monopolistically competitive firm. The only difference is that the demand curve that the monopolistically com-petitive firm faces is usually more elastic than the demand curve facing a monopolist.

7. See Figure 2.
Figure 2 is identical to the right panel of Figure 12-3, except that curve de has been added. Curve de is parallel to curve d** and intersects demand curve D* at point Z. Starting from P = $3, the monopolistically competitive firm believes that de is its relevant demand curve in the long run. Thus, the firm believes that if it increased the commodity price to $4, it will not

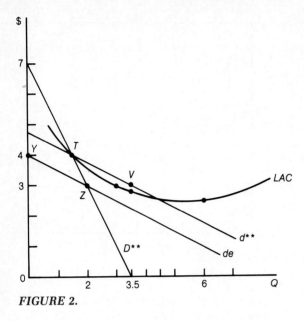

FIGURE 2.

return to point T on D^* and break even, but it will move instead along de to point Y and $Q = 0$ and the firm incurs a loss equal to its total fixed costs of $12.

11. The more price elastic is the demand curve faced by a monopolistically competitive firm, when in long-run equilibrium, the closer to the lowest point on its LAC curve will the firm be when in long-run equilibrium. Since excess capacity is measured by the distance between the two points, the more elastic the demand curve is, the smaller is the amount of excessive capacity under monopolistic competition (see Figure 12-5).

Chapter 13

4. (a) See Figure 1.

If the demand curve that the oligopolist faces shifts up by $0.50 but the kink remains at $P = $8, we get demand curve d^*

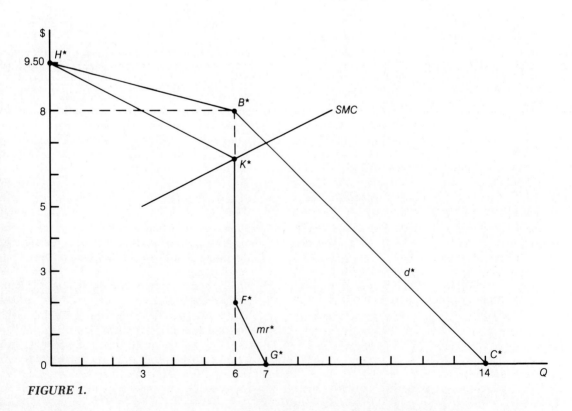

FIGURE 1.

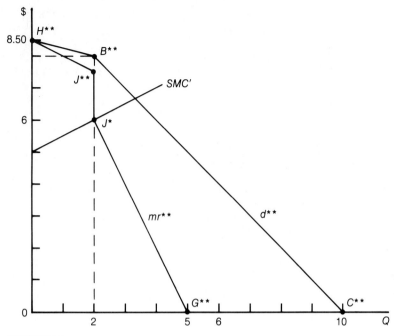

FIGURE 2.

or $H^*B^*C^*$. The marginal revenue curve is then mr^* or $H^*K^*F^*G^*$. Since the SMC curve intersects the mr^* curve at point K^*, $Q = 6$ and price remains at $P = \$8$.

(b) See Figure 2.

If the demand curve that the oligopolist faces shifts down by \$0.50 but the kink remains at $P = \$8$, we get demand curve d^{**} or $H^{**}B^{**}C^{**}$. The marginal revenue curve is then mr^{**} or $H^{**}J^{**}J^*G^{**}$. Since the SMC' curve intersects the mr^{**} curve at point J^*, $Q = 2$ and price remains at $P = \$8$.

6. If we interchange the payoff of 0 and −1 in the second column of Table 13-2, the zero-sum game is no longer strictly determined and there is no saddle point (see the following table).

The reason is that the payoff of the maximin strategy of firm A (−1, with A1), is not equal to the payoff of the minimax strategy of firm B (0, with B2). Specifically, if firm A knows in advance that firm B will choose strategy B2, firm A can do better by choosing strategy A2, with which it loses no market share (compare A2B2 with A1B2).

But if firm B knows in advance that firm A will

Matrix of Firm A's Gain (+) and Loss (−) of Market Share (in Percentages)

		Firm B			
		B1	B2	B3	Row Minimum
Firm A	A1	1	−1	2	−1
	A2	−2	0	0	−2
Column Maximum		1	0	2	1 = −1

choose A2, firm B can do better by choosing strategy B1, with which A loses and B gains 2% of the market (compare A2B1 with A2B2). If firm A knew in advance that firm B will choose B1, firm A would choose A1, with which A gains 1% of the market. In short, there would be no stable solution or equilibrium unless firms A and firm B adopt a mixed strategy. For that we would need additional information.

7. The high-advertising strategy by firm A is better than (i.e., dominant over) the low-advertising strategy because no matter how firm B responds, firm A earns a higher net profit. That is, when firm A incurs a high expenditure for

advertising, it will earn profits of $4 million (after paying for the advertising) if firm B responds with a low advertising expenditures and a profit of $1 million if firm B responds with high advertising expenditures.

On the other hand, if firm A had a low advertising budget it would have profits of $2 million if firm B also had a low advertising budget, and would have zero profits if firm B had a large advertising budget. Then the best that firm B can do is to also have a large advertising budget and earn $2 million in profits (instead of earning no profits with a low advertising budget). Thus, both firms adopt a maximin strategy.

Note that both firms could increase profits by agreeing to spend less on advertising. That is, when both firms are considered together (rather than separately), each is spending too much on advertising (i.e., the marginal revenue from advertising expenditures is negative).

10. (a) See Figure 3.

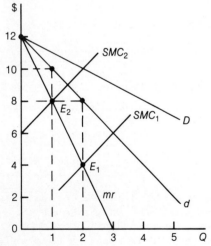

FIGURE 3.

Duopolist 1 (the low-cost duopolist) produces 2 units of the commodity and charges $P = \$8$ (given by point E1, at which $SMC1 = mr$, as in Figure 13-6). Duopolist 2 produces 1 unit of the commodity and would like to charge $P = \$10$ (given by point E2, at which $SMC2 = mr$). However, since the

commodity is homogeneous, duopolist 2 (the high-cost duopolist) is forced to also sell at $P = \$8$ set by low-cost duopolist 1.

(b) With $P = \$8$ and $SATC1 = \$5$ at $Q = 2$, duopolist 1 earns a profit of $3 per unit and $6 in total. With $P = \$8$ and $SATC2 = \$8$ at $Q = 1$, duopolist 2 breaks even. At $P = \$10$ duopolist 2 would have earned a profit of $2. Thus, only duopolist 1 maximizes profits.

If the high-cost duopolist would go out of business at the profit-maximizing price set by the low-cost duopolist, the latter would probably set a price sufficiently high to allow the high-cost duopolist to remain in the market and avoid possible prosecution under antitrust laws for monopolizing the market. In that case the low-cost firm would not be maximizing profits.

Chapter 14

5. (a) See Figure 1.

The left panel of Figure 1 shows that the individual maximizes satisfaction at point H (with 16 hours of leisure per day, 8 hours of work, and a daily income of $8) on U_1 with $w = \$1$; at point E (with 14 hours of leisure, 10 hours of work, and an income of $20) on U_2 with $w = \$2$; at point N (with 15 hours of leisure, 9 hours of work, and an income of $27) on U_3 with $w = \$3$; and at point R (with 17 hours of leisure, 7 hours of work, and an income of $28) on U_4 with $w = \$4$. Plotting the hours of work per day at various wage rates, we get the individual's supply curve of labor (s_L) in the right panel. Note that s_L bends backward at the wage rate of $2 per hour.

(b) An increase in the wage rate, just like an increase in the price of a commodity, leads to a substitution effect and an income effect. The substitution effect leads individuals to substitute work for leisure when the wage rate (the price of leisure) increases. On the other hand, an increase in wages increases the individual's income, and when income rises, the individual demands more of every normal good, including leisure. Thus, the income effect, by itself, leads the individual

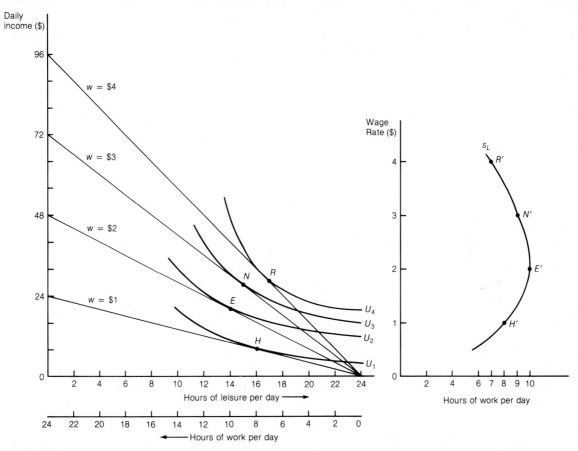

FIGURE 1.

to demand more leisure and work fewer hours.

Up to $w = \$2$ (point E' on s_L in the right panel of Figure 1, the substitution effect exceeds the opposite income effect and the individual supplies more hours of work (i.e., s_L is positively sloped). At $w = \$2$, the substitution and the opposite income effect are in balance and the individual supplies the same number of hours per work (s_L is vertical). Above $w = \$2$, the substitution effect is smaller than the opposite income effect and the individual works fewer hours (i.e., s_L is negatively sloped or bends backward).

9. See Figure 2.

The movement from point E to point R is the

combined substitution and income effects of the wage increase from $\$2$ to $\$4$ (as in Figure 1). The substitution effect can be isolated by drawing the budget line with slope $w = \$4$ which is tangent to U_2 at point M. The movement along U_2 from point M to point E measures the substitution effect. By itself, it shows that the increase in w leads the individual to reduce leisure time and increase work by 4 hours per day.

The shift from point M and U_2 to point R and U_4 is the income effect of the wage increase. By itself, the income effect leads the individual to increase leisure and reduce work by 7 hours. The net result is that the individual increases leisure (works less) by 3 hours per day *(ER)*.

11. See Figure 3.

In occupation or region A in the left panel, D_L

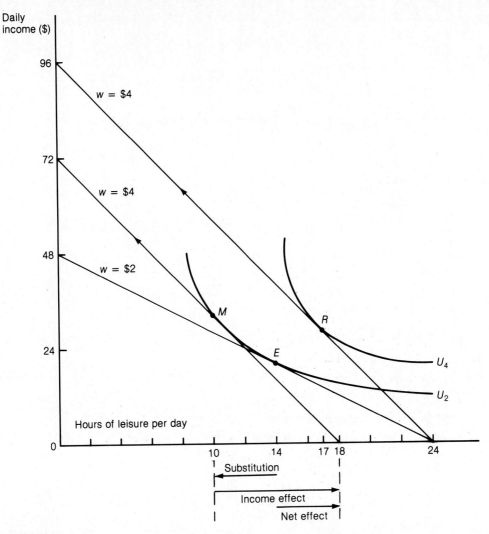

FIGURE 2.

and S_L intersect at point E so that the wage rate is w_1 and the level of employment is L_2. In occupation or region B in the right panel, D_L and S_L intersect at point E so that the wage rate is w_3 and the level of employment is L_1. Since the wage rate is higher in occupation or region B, workers will leave A and seek employment in B. This reduces the supply of labor A and increases in B. This process continues until S_L has shifted up to S'_L in A and *down* to S'_L in B until, at point E' in both figures, the same wage rate (w_2) prevails in both occupations or regions.

12. (a) See Figure 4.

By supplying 8 hours of work per day with the NIT, the family would reach higher indifference curve U'_2 (point J). However, the family would maximize utility by not working at all and reaching still higher indifference curve U''_2 (point F).

(b) See Figure 5.

If the family's indifference curve U_2 had been as indicated in Figure 5 rather than as in Figure 4, the family would have maximized utility at point M without the NIT and have an (earned) income of $80 per day and would supply 16 hours of work. With

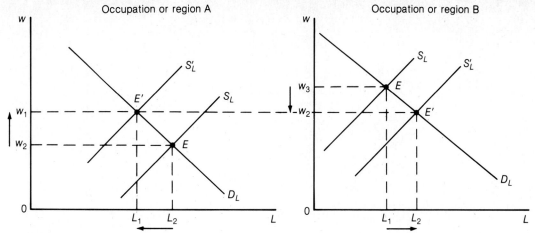

Occupation or region A

Occupation or region B

FIGURE 3.

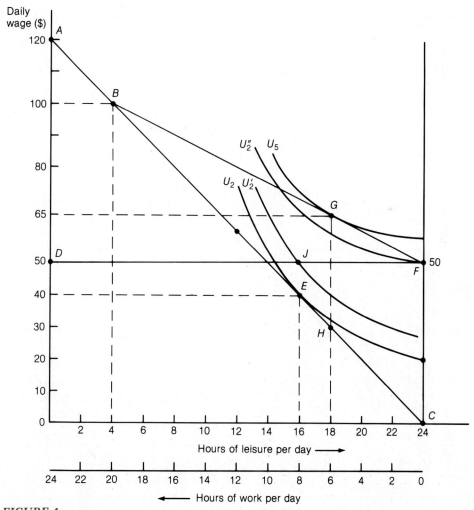

FIGURE 4.

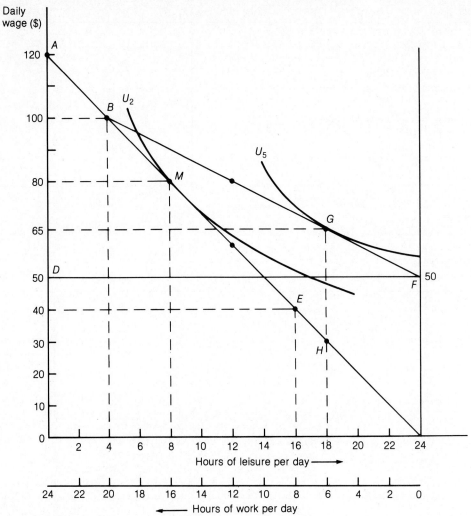

FIGURE 5.

the NIT, the same family would be at point G on U_5 and have a total income of $65 per day ($30 earned plus the $35 subsidy) and supply only six hours of work. This, however, need not be the case. It is more likely to occur, the closer the family's earned income without the NIT is to the break-even income with the NIT.

Chapter 15

3. (a) See the following table.

L	Qx	MP_L	Px	TRx	MRx	MRP_L	VMP_L	w
1	12	12	$13	$156	—	—	—	$40
2	22	10	12	264	$10.80	$108	$120	40
3	30	8	11	330	8.25	66	88	40
4	37	7	10	370	5.71	40	70	40
5	43	6	9	387	2.83	17	54	40
6	48	5	8	376	−1.80	−9	40	40

MRx is obtained by the change in TRx per unit change in the quantity of the commodity sold. That is, $MRx = \Delta TRx/\Delta Qx = \Delta$

TRx/MP_L. For example, when the firm increases the number of workers it hires from one to two, Qx rises from 12 to 22 units (i.e., $MP_L = 10$) and TRx rises from $156 to $264 or by $108. Thus, $MRx = \$108/10 = \$10.80$. When the firm increases the number of workers it hires from 2 to 3, TRx increases by $66 and Qx increases by (i.e., MP_L equal to) 8 units. Thus, $MRx = \$66/8 = \$8.25$, and so on.

$MRP_L = (MP_L)(MRx)$. For example, when the firm increases the number of workers hired from 1 to 2 workers, $MP_L = 10$ and $MRx = \$10.80$. Thus, $MRP_L = (10)(\$10.80) = \$108$. This is equal to $\Delta TRx/\Delta L$ or $\$108/1 = \$108$ (as found in the text).

$VMP_L = (MP_L)(Px)$. For example when the firm increases the number of workers it hires from 1 to 2, $MP_L = 10$ and $Px = \$12$, so that the $VMP_L = (10)(\$12) = \$120$.

(b) See Figure 1.

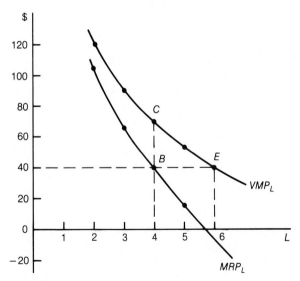

FIGURE 1.

If the firm were a perfect competitor in the product market as well as in the labor market, the firm would hire 6 workers (point E) because only by hiring 6 workers $VMP_L = w = \$40$.

Since the firm is a monopolist in the product market but a perfect competitor in the labor market, it hires only 4 workers (point B) because only by hiring 4 workers the $MRP_L = w = \$40$. The difference between the VMP_L and the MRP_L at $L = 4$ ($BC = \$30$ per worker and $120 in total) is the amount of monopolistic exploitation.

9. (a) See Figure 2.

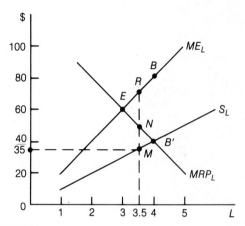

FIGURE 2.

The monopsonist's supply curve becomes HMB' and the ME_L curve becomes $HMNRB$. The monopsonist maximizes profits by hiring 3 workers on a full time basis and one worker on a half-time basis (given by point N, where the MRP_L curve intersects the vertical segment of the new ME_L curve). Monopsonistic exploitation is NM or $15 per worker.

(b) See Figure 3.

The monopsonist's supply curve becomes TNF and the ME_L curve becomes $TNFG$. The monopsonist maximizes profits by hiring 3 workers on a full time basis and one worker on a half-time basis (given by point N, where the MRP_L curve intersects the horizontal segment of the new ME_L curve). Now, $MRP_L = w = \$50$ at $L = 3.5$ and the monopsonistic exploitation of labor is zero.

10. See Figure 4.

The union (the monopolist seller of labor time) would like to have 40 workers employed (given by point E, where $MR = MC$) at the daily wage

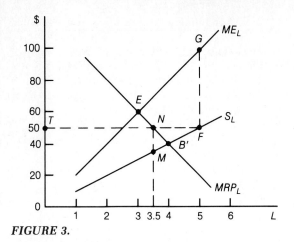

FIGURE 3.

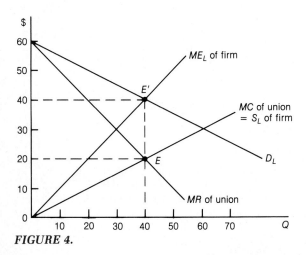

FIGURE 4.

of \$40 (point E' on D_L). The firm (the monopsonist employer of labor) would maximize profits by employing 40 workers (given by point E', where its D_L or MRP_L curve intersects its ME_L curve) at w = \$20 (point E on its S_L).

Thus, there is agreement between the union and the firm on the number of workers to be employed but not on the wage. The greater is the relative bargaining strength of the union, the closer the wage rate will be to \$40. The greater is the relative bargaining strength of the firm, the closer the wage rate will be to \$20. Note that it is not entirely certain that the union will behave entirely as a monopolist (see application 4).

11. See Figure 5.

In the figure, the demand for union labor (D_U) plus the demand for nonunion labor (D_N) gives the total demand for labor (D_T). The intersection of D_T and S_T (the market supply of labor) at point E determines the equilibrium daily wage of \$60 for union and nonunion labor (in the absence of any effect of unions on the wages). At w = \$60, 4 million union workers (point E') and 8 million nonunion workers (point E'') are employed.

If unions are now successful in raising union wages from \$60 to \$65, the employment of union labor falls from 4 to 3 million (point A on D_U). The one million workers who cannot find union employment will now have to find employment in the nonunion sector. This increases employment in the nonunion sector

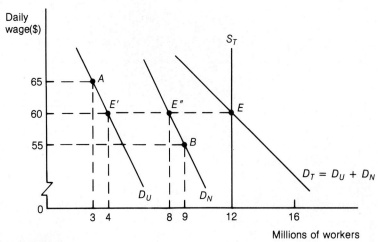

FIGURE 5.

from 8 to 9 million workers. But 9 million workers can only be employed in the nonunion sector at $w = \$55$ (point B on D_N).

Thus, when unions increase wages in the
unionized sector, employment in the unionized
sector falls. More workers must find employment in the nonunionized sector and nonunion
wages fall. Thus, what union workers gain
come mostly at the expense of nonunion
workers.

Chapter 16

4. See Figure 1.
   Starting at point B ($Y_0 = 5$ and $Y_1 = 6$) in the
   figure, individual B moves to point E (7.5, 3) on
   indifference curve U_2 by borrowing 2.5 units of
   the commodity at $r = 20$ percent. On the other

hand, starting from point A ($Y_0 = 5$ and $Y_1 = 6$)
in the figure, individual A moves to point E'
(2.5, 9) on indifference curve U'_1 by lending 2.5
units of the commodity at $r = 20$ percent. Since
at $r = 20$ percent, desired borrowing equals
desired lending, this is the equilibrium rate of
interest.

On the other hand, at $r = 50$ percent, individual
B moves from point B to point E* on U_1 by borrowing only 2 units of the commodity this year
and repaying 3 units next year, while individual A moves from point A to point E" on U'_2 by
lending 3 units this year for 4.5 units next year
(so that $r = 50$ percent). Since at $r = 50$ percent
desired lending exceeds desired borrowing, $r =$
50 percent is higher than the equilibrium rate
of interest and r will fall toward 20 percent.

5. (a) The supply curve of loans (lending) is usu-

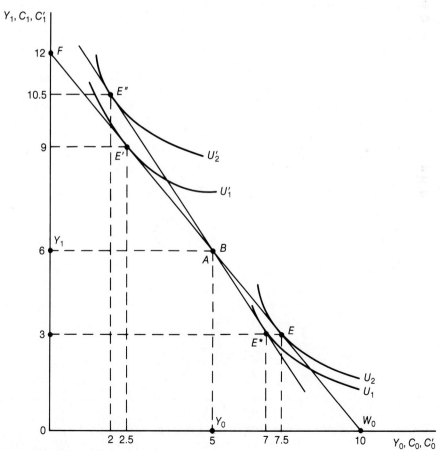

FIGURE 1.

ally positively sloped, indicating that lenders will lend more at higher rates of interest. However, when the interest rate rises,
the lender will face a substitution effect and
an income or wealth effect (just as a worker
does when the wage rate rises). The substitution effect induces the lender to substitute future for present consumption and
lend more since the reward for lending has
increased.

On the other hand, when the interest rate
rises, the lender's wealth rises and he or she
will want to consume more both in the present (and lend less) and in the future. Thus,
the substitution effect tends to lead the
lender to lend more while the wealth effect
leads the lender to lend less.

Up to a point, the substitution effect overwhelms the wealth effect and the lender
will lend more at higher rates of interest.

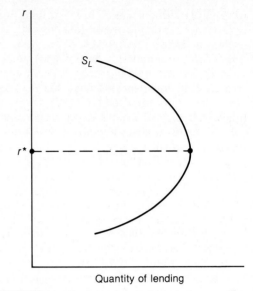

FIGURE 2.

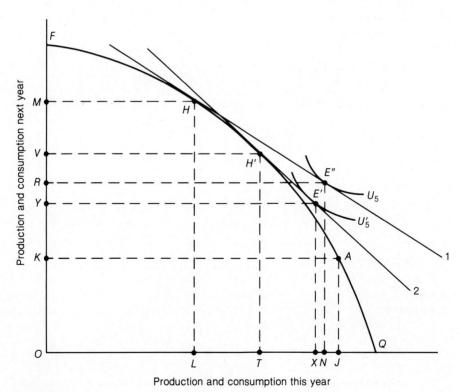

FIGURE 3.

B28

However, after a point, higher rates of inter-est will cause the wealth effect to exceed the opposite substitution effect so that the lender will lend less. Thus, at a sufficiently high rate of interest, the lender's supply curve will bend backward (as at r^* in Figure 2).

(b) For borrowers both the substitution and the wealth effect operate to reduce the amount of desired borrowing when the rate of inter-est rises, so that the demand curve for bor-rowing is negatively sloped throughout. The substitution effect reduces the amount of borrowing as the rate of interest rises, because future consumption becomes more expensive in terms of the present consump-tion to be given up. The wealth effect also tends to reduce the amount of borrowing because an increase in the rate of interest reduces the borrower's wealth.

6. See Figure 3.

In the figure, FQ is the hypothetical production-possibilities curve of the individual. The indi-vidual has endowment A (OJ this year and OK next). With the interest rate shown by the slope of market line 1, the individual maximizes wealth by investing JL this year so as to reach point H on curve FQ. He or she then borrows NL in order to reach point E'' on the highest indifference curve possible (U_5). Thus, the indi-vidual saves JN.

If the interest rate rises so that the market line is steeper as indicated by market line 2, the individual maximizes wealth by investing JT this year (which is less than before) so as to reach point H' on curve FQ. He or she then bor-rows XT (which is less than before) in order to reach point E' on the highest indifference curve possible (U'_5). Thus, the individual now saves JX (which is larger than before).

11. See the following table.

Note that the present value of the project is higher with $r = 5$ percent than with $r = 10$ percent.

Benefit-Cost Analysis of an Investment Project

End of Year n	Investment (Year 0) and Cost	Revenue	Net Revenue	Present Value Coefficient $1/(1 + 0.05)^n$	Present Value of Net Revenue
0	$1,000		−$1,000	—	−$1,000
1	200	$600	400	0.952	381
2	300	800	500	0.907	454
3	300	800	500	0.864	432
4	400	800	400	0.823	329
4	—	200*	200	0.823	165
					$761

*Salvage value

Chapter 17

2. See Figure 1.

The Edgeworth box diagram of Figure 1 was obtained by rotating individual B's indifference curve diagram by 180 degrees (so that O_B appears in the top right-hand corner) and super-imposing it on individual A's indifference curve diagram (with origin O_A), in such a way that the size of the box is $14X$ and $9Y$ (the com-bined amount of X and Y owned by individuals A and B). The contract curve for exchange is $O_A DEFO_B$ and is given by the tangency points

of the indifference curves (at which MRS_{xy} are equal) for the two individuals.

4. See Figure 2.

The Edgeworth box diagram of Figure 2 was obtained by rotating the isoquant diagram for commodity Y by 180 degrees (so that O_Y appears in the top right-hand corner) and superimpos-ing it on the isoquant diagram for commodity X (with origin O_X) is such a way that the size of the box is $14L$ and $9K$ (the total amount of L and K available). The production contract curve is $O_X JMNO_Y$ and is given by the tangency points of

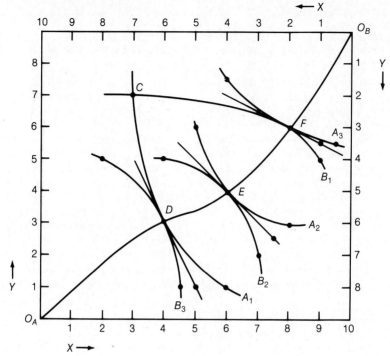

FIGURE 1.

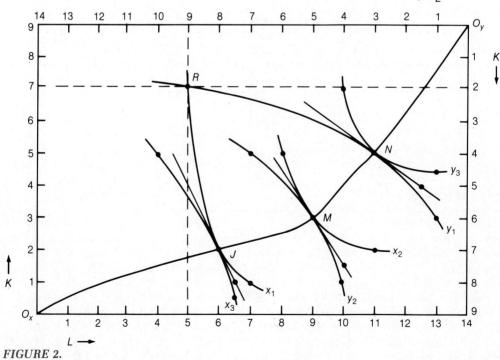

FIGURE 2.

B30

the isoquants (at which $MRTS_{LK}$ are equal) for commodities X and Y.

8. See Figure 3.

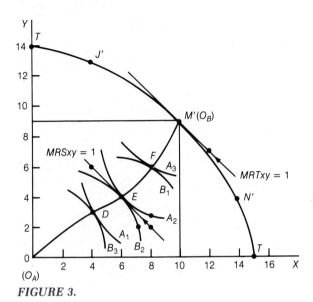

FIGURE 3.

The simple economy portrayed in Figure 3 would be simultaneously in general equilibrium of production and exchange at point E, where

$$MRTxy = MRS^Axy = MRS^Bxy = 1$$

12. We can solve the following set of three simultaneous linear equations by substitution, as follows:

(1) $S = .1S + .2M + .3A + 200$
(2) $M = .4S + .3M + .2A + 300$
(3) $A = .2S + .1M + .1A + 100$

(1A) $-.9S + .2M + .3A = -200$
(2A) $.4S - .7M + .2A = -300$
(3A) $.2S + .1M - .9A = -100$

Solving equation (3A) for S, we get

$S = -.5M + 4.5A - 500$

Substituting into equations (1A) and (2A), we get

$-.9(-.5M + 4.5A - 500) + .2M + .3A = -200$
$.45M - 4.05A + 450 + .2M + .3A = -200$

and

$.4(-.5M + 4.5A - 500) - .7M + .2A = -300$
$-.2M + 1.8A - 200 - .7M + .2A = -300.$

B31

(1B) $.65M - 3.75A = -650$

and

(2B) $-.9M + .2A = -100$

Multiplying (2B) by 1.875, we get

(2C) $-1.6875M + 3.75A = -187.5$

Adding (1B) and (2C), we get

$$\begin{array}{r} .65M - 3.75A = -650 \\ -1.6875M + 3.75A = -187.5 \\ \hline -1.0375M = -837.5 \end{array}$$

Therefore, $M = \$807$ (rounded to the nearest billion dollar)
Substituting $M = \$807$ into equation (2B), we get $-.9(807) + 2A = -100$
Therefore, $A = \$313$ billions (rounded to the nearest billion).
Substituting the calculated values of $M = \$807$ and $A = \$313$ into equation (3A), we get

$.2S + .1(807) - .9(313) = -100$

Therefore, $S = \$505$ billions (rounded to the nearest billion).
A much quicker method of solving this system of three simultaneous equations is by matrix inversion.

Chapter 18

3. (a) See Figure 1.
Utility-possibilities frontier U_M, U_M, is that of problem 2. Utility-possibilities frontier U_N, U_N, is derived from the contract curve for exchange in the Edgeworth box diagram drawn from point N' on the production pos-

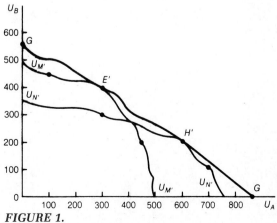

FIGURE 1.

sibilities frontier in Figure 17.4 at the end of the text (not shown in that figure). By joining E', H', and other Pareto optimum points of production and exchange, we get grand utility-possibilities frontier GE'H'G in Figure 1.

(b) The grand utility-possibilities frontier is the locus of Pareto optimum points of production and exchange. From any point inside the grand utility-possibilities frontier, U_A, U_B, or both U_A and U_B can be increased with the given production-possibilities frontier. Once on the grand utility-possibilities frontier, no reorganization of the production-exchange process is possible that makes someone better off without, at the same time, making someone else worse off.

Points above the grand utility-possibilities frontier cannot be reached. The aim of society is to choose from among the infinite number of Pareto optimum points along the grand utility-possibilities frontier the one point that refers to the maximum social welfare.

5. See Figure 2.

The point of maximum social welfare or constrained bliss is given by point E' in the figure, at which social indifference curve W_2 is tangent to grand utility-possibilities frontier GG. That is, of all the infinite number of Pareto optimum points of production and exchange on the grand

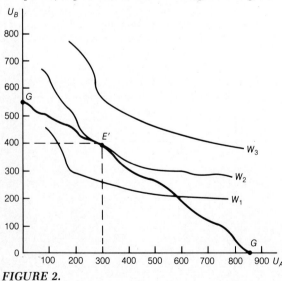

FIGURE 2.

utility-possibilities frontier, point E' is the one at which social welfare is maximized. At point E', U_A = 300 utils and U_B = 400 utils.

8. (a) Since Px/Py = 1 (see your answer to problem 18.7a) and Px = $10, Py = $10 also.

(b) In perfectly competitive input and output markets, each profit-maximizing firm employs each input up to the point where the value of the marginal product of the input equals the input price. Thus,

$$P_L = VMP_L^x = (Px)(MP_L^x) = (\$10)(6) = \$60.$$

(c) In equilibrium, $P_L = VMP_L^x = VMP_L^y = \$60$. Since $VMP_L^y = (Py)(MP_L^y)$, and $P_Y = \$10$. MP_L^y = 6 also.

(d) Since P_L/P_K = 3/2 (from problem 18.7b) and P_L = $60, P_K = $2/3P_L$ = (2/3)($60) = $40.

(e) If Px = $20, then Py = $20, P_L = $120 and P_K = $80. That is, Px is the *numeraire* and all other prices are proportionate to Px. Thus, there are no unique absolute equilibrium values for Px, Py, P_L, and P_K. Note that we could have used an input price as the *numeraire*.

11. We have seen in application 2, that when the firm producing commodity X is a monopolist in its labor market, too little labor and too much capital are used in the production of commodity X, as compared with the case where all markets are perfectly competitive. This leaves more of the given amount of labor and less of the given amount of capital to produce commodity Y.

Thus, $MRTS_{LK}^y$ and P_L/P_K would have to be smaller than 2/3 (the value of the MRT_{LK} in the production of X and Y when all markets in the economy are perfectly competitive) for both labor and capital in the economy to be fully employed. Thus, $MRTS_{LK}^x > MRTS_{LK}^y$ and one of the conditions required for Pareto optimum and economic efficiency is violated.

Chapter 19

3. (a) See Figure 1.

A corrective tax of $4 per unit imposed on the consumers of commodity X will make D'' the new industry demand curve. With D'', Px = $10 and Qx = 4 million units per time period (given by the intersection of D''

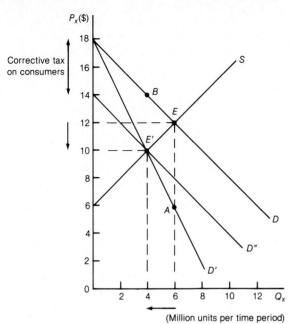

FIGURE 1.

the figure). This is the excess of the marginal social value (shown by demand curve D) over the MSC (shown by supply curve S′) between $Qx = 6$ and $Qx = 8$ million units.

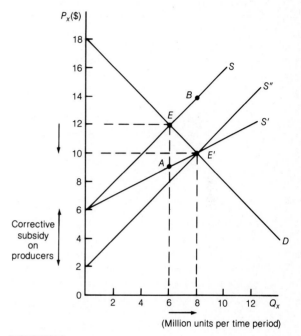

FIGURE 2.

and S at point E′). This is the socially optimum price and output. Consumers would now pay $Px = \$10$ plus the $4 tax per unit ($E'B$) or a net $Px = \$14$ (as compared with $Px = \$12$ under the previous competitive equilibrium at point E).

(b) The total value of the economic gain resulting from the imposition of the corrective tax is equal to $6 million (given by area $EE'A$ in the figure). This is the excess of the MSC (shown by supply curve S) over MSB (shown by demand curve D') between $Qx = 4$ and $Qx = 6$ million units.

5. (a) See Figure 2.

A corrective subsidy of $4 per unit given to producers of commodity X will make S'' the new industry supply curve. With S'', $Px = \$10$ and $Qx = 8$ million units per time period (given by the intersection of D and S'' at point E′). This is the socially optimal price and output. Producers would now receive $Px = \$10$ plus the $4 subsidy per unit ($BE'$) for a total of $14 per unit.

(b) The total value of the economic inefficiency eliminated by the corrective subsidy is equal to $3 million (given by area $EE'A$ in

9. (a) Each individual will drill more wells and pumps oil faster than he or she would if no other oil field was located adjacent to his or hers, in order to prevent some of the oil under his or her field to flow to the neighbor's field. The external diseconomies arise because oil is pumped faster than socially desirable. The external diseconomies can be avoided by merging the two adjacent oil fields under joint ownership, by government regulation, or by taxation.

(b) The development of a recreational site confers external benefits to shops, gasoline stations, and motels in the area. In order to internalize the external benefits, the recreational site developer may also set up and operate establishments that provide these other services near the recreational site.

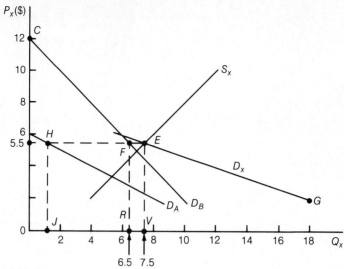

FIGURE 3.

10. (a) See Figure 3.

Market demand curve D (CFEG) is obtained by the *horizontal* summation of demand curves D_A and D_B. Dx and Sx intersect at point E and define equilibrium price of Px = $5.5 and the equilibrium quantity of Qx = 7.5, if the market for commodity X is perfectly competitive. Individual A consumes 1X and individual B consumes 6.5X.

(b) When X is a private good, the condition for Pareto optimal output is $MRTxy = MRS^Axy = MRS^Bxy$. That is, at the optimal output level, the marginal benefit that each consumer receives from an additional unit of commodity X equals its marginal cost. That

is, $HJ = FR = EV$ in Figure 3.

On the other hand, when X is a public good, the condition for the Pareto optimal output is $MRTxy = MRS^Axy + MRS^Bxy$. That is, since each consumer can consume the *same* quantity of commodity X when X is a public good, it is the *sum* of the marginal benefits that each consumer receives from the additional unit of commodity X that must equal its marginal cost (i.e., $AB + AC = AE$ in Figure 19-2).

(c) Public goods that exhibit nonexclusion convey external economies of consumption on free riders (i.e., on the consumers not paying for the public goods).

Glossary Index

Activity, 293
Alternative or opportunity cost doctrine, 258
Arc elasticity of demand, 52
Arc elasticity of supply, 52
Arrow's impossibility theorem, 607–608
Average fixed cost (AFC), 258
Average product (AP), 225
Average revenue, 155
Average total cost (ATC), 258
Average variable cost (AVC), 258

Bad, 90
Bandwagon effect, 155
Barometric firm, 441–2
Benefit-cost analysis, 630
Benefit reduction rate, 480
Bergson social welfare function, 607
Bilateral monopoly, 509
Break-even income, 479–480
Break-even point, 330
Budget constraint, 90
Budget line, 90

Capital budgeting, 547
Capital-using technological progress, 293
Cardinal utility, 89
Cartel, 441
Centralized cartel, 441
Chamberlin model, 441
Characteristics approach to consumer theory, 189
Circular flow of economic activity, 22
Coase's theorem, 630
Cobb-Douglas production function, 293

Cobweb model, 53
Common property, 630
Collusion, 441
Comparative advantage, 577
Compensated demand curve, 189
Compensation principle, 607
Complementary inputs, 479
Complements, 155
Concentration ratio, 441
Conscious parallelism, 441
Consistent, 188
Constant cost industry, 330
Constant returns to scale, 225
Constrained utility maximization, 90
Consumer equilibrium, 90
Consumer optimization, 90
Consumer surplus, 124
Contract curve for exchange, 577
Contract curve for production, 577
Corner solution, 90
Cost-plus pricing, 442
Cournot model, 441
Creative destruction, 608
Cross elasticity of demand (n_{xy}), 155

Decreasing cost industry, 331
Decreasing returns to scale, 225
Default risk, 547
Derived demand, 479
Differentiated oligopoly, 441
Differentiated product, 398
Discrimination in employment, 509
Disemployment effect, 479
Dominant strategy, 441
Dual problem, 293
Duopoly, 441

Economic efficiency, 22, 607
Economic goods, 21
Economic growth, 22
Economic rent, 479
Economic resources, 21
Economics, 21
Edgeworth box diagram, 124
Edgeworth box diagram for exchange, 577
Edgeworth box diagram for production, 577
Edgeworth model, 441
Efficiency frontier, 189
Effluent fees, 630
Elasticity of substitution of L for K (e_{LK}), 293
Engel curve, 123
Engel's law, 155
Endowment position, 546
Entrepreneurship, 224
Environmental pollution, 630
Equalizing wage differentials, 479
Equilibrium, 53
Equilibrium price, 52
Excess capacity, 398
Excise tax, 53
Exhaustible resources, 547
Expansion path, 258
Expected income, 189
Expenditure index (E), 188
Explicit costs, 258
External benefits, 630
External costs, 630
External diseconomies of consumption, 630
External diseconomies of production, 630
External diseconomy, 331
External economies of consumption, 630
External economies of production, 630

External economy, 331
Externalities, 630

Feasible region, 189
Feasible solutions, 293
Firm, 224
First degree price discrimination, 370
Fixed inputs, 224
Food stamp program, 124
For whom to produce, 22
Free-enterprise system, 22
Free goods, 22
Free resources, 22
Free-rider problem, 630
Fringe benefits, 90
Fundamental economic fact, 22

Game theory, 441
General equilibrium analysis, 577
Giffen paradox, 124
Gini coefficient, 577
Good, 90
Grand utility possibilities frontier, 607

Hedonic price, 189
Hicksian substitution effect, 188
Homogeneous of degree 1, 293
Hotelling paradox, 442
How to produce, 22
Human wants, 21

Ideal output, 398
Ideal plant, 398
Identification problem, 189
Implicit costs, 258
Incidence of a tax, 53
Income-consumption curve, 123
Income effect, 124
Income elasticity of demand (n_I), 155
Income or expenditure index (E), 188
Increasing cost industry, 331
Increasing returns to scale, 225

Indifference curve, 90
Indifference map, 90
Individual demand, 124
Inequality constraints, 293
Inferior good, 124
Input-output analysis, 577
Inputs, 224
Interdependence, 577
Intermediate good, 479
Internalizing external costs, 630
Investment, 547
Investment in human capital, 547
Isocost line, 258
Isoquant, 225

Kaldor-Hicks criterion, 607
Kinked-demand curve model, 441

Labor union, 509
Labor-using technological progress, 293
Laspeyres price index (L), 188
Law of demand, 52
Law of diminishing marginal utility, 89
Law of diminishing returns, 225
Law of the invisible hand, 607
Least-cost input combination, 258
Limit pricing, 442
Linear programming, 293
Linearly homogeneous, 293
Long run, 224
Long-run average cost (LAC), 258
Long-run marginal cost (LMC), 258
Long-run total cost (LTC), 258
Lorenz curve, 577
Luxury, 155

Macroeconomic theory, 22
Managerial theories of the firm, 442
Marginal cost (MC), 258

Marginal expense of capital (ME_K), 508
Marginal expense of labor (ME_L), 508
Marginal expense of the input, 508
Marginal product (MP), 225
Marginal productivity theory, 479
Marginal rate of substitution (MRS), 90
Marginal rate of technical substitution (MRTS), 225
Marginal rate of transformation of X for Y (MRT_{xy}), 577
Marginal revenue, 155
Marginal revenue product (MRP), 508
Marginal utility, 89
Market, 52
Market demand curve, 155
Market demand schedule, 52
Market failures, 607
Market line, 547
Market period, 330
Market-sharing cartel, 441
Market supply curve, 52
Market supply schedule, 52
Markup, 442
Maximin strategy, 441
Maximum social welfare, 607
Methodology of economics, 22
Microeconomic theory, 22
Minimal income maintenance, 479
Minimax strategy, 441
Mixed economy, 22
Mixed strategy, 441
Model, 22
Monopolistic competition, 398
Monopolistic exploitation, 508
Monopsonistic competition, 508
Monopsonistic exploitation, 508–509
Monopsony, 508
Multiple regression, 189

Natural monopoly, 370
Necessity, 155

Negative income tax, 155, 479
Neuter, 90
Neutral technological progress, 293
Nominal rate of interest (r'), 547
Noncompeting groups, 479
Nonexhaustible resources, 547
Nonexclusion, 630
Nonnegative constraints, 293
Nonprice competition, 442
Nonrival consumption, 630
Nonzero sum game, 441
Normal good, 124
Normative economics, 22

Objective function, 293
Oligopoly, 441
Oligopsony, 508
Opportunity cost doctrine, 258
Optimal solutions, 293
Ordinal utility, 89
Output elasticity of capital (β), 293
Output elasticity of labor (α), 293
Overtime pay, 479

Paasche price index (P), 188–189
Pareto criterion, 607
Pareto optimum, 607
Partial equilibrium analysis, 577
Payback period, 547
Payoff, 441
Payoff matrix, 441
Perfectly competitive market, 52, 330
Planning horizon, 258
Point elasticity of demand, 52
Point elasticity of supply, 52
Positive economics, 22
Present value (V_0), 547
Price ceiling, 53
Price-consumption curve, 124
Price discrimination, 370
Price elasticity of demand (n), 52
Price elasticity of supply (e), 52
Price floor, 53

Price leadership, 441
Price system, 22
Price theory, 22
Primal problem, 293
Prisoner's dilemma, 441
Private costs, 258
Process, 293
Product differentiation, 398
Product group, 398
Product variation, 398
Production, 224
Production function, 224
Production-possibilities curve or frontier, 22, 546–547, 577
Proportional demand curve, 398
Public goods, 630
Pure monopoly, 370
Pure Oligopoly, 441
Pure strategy, 441

Quasirent, 479

Rate of interest, 546
Rational consumer, 90
Rationing, 90
Rationing over time, 22
Real rate of interest, 547
Relative price, 124
Resources, 21
Ridge lines, 225

Saddle point, 441
Satisficing behavior, 442
Saving, 547
Scitovsky criterion, 607
Second degree price discrimination, 370
Selling expenses, 398
Separation theorem, 547
Shadow price, 293
Sherman Antitrust Act, 441
Short run, 224
Shortage, 52
Shut-down point, 330
Simplex method, 293
Slack variable, 293
Slutsky substitution effect, 188
Snob effect, 155

Social costs, 258
Social welfare function, 607
Stage I of production, 225
Stage II of production, 225
Stage III of production, 225
Strictly determined game, 441
Substitutes, 155
Substitution effect, 124
Surplus, 52

Technical coefficients, 577
Technical constraints, 293
Technical externalities, 630
Technological progress, 293
Technology, 22
Theory of revealed preference, 188
Theory of the second best, 608
Third degree price discrimination, 370
Time budget line, 124
Total costs (TC), 258
Total fixed costs (TFC), 258
Total product (TP), 224
Total revenue, (TR), 155
Total utility, 89
Total variable costs (TVC), 258
Transaction costs, 398
Transformation curve, 22
Transitive, 188

Unemployment gap, 479
Util, 89
Utility, 89
Utility possibilities frontier, 607

Variability risk, 547
Variable inputs, 224
Veblen effect, 155

Water–diamond paradox, 124
Wealth, 546
Welfare economics, 607
What to produce, 22

Zero-sum game, 441
Zone of ignorance, 188

Name Index

Aaron, H. J, 585
Adams, W., 132, 243, 319, 338
Addison, W., 38
Adelman, D., 351
Allen, R. D. G., 64, 191
Anderson, John B., 111
Arrow, Kenneth J., 491, 555, 580, 598, 610

Bacon, N., 405
Bain, J., 429
Baumol, William J., 191, 296, 433
Bator, Francis M., 577, 586, 610, 613, 633
Becker, Gary S., 126, 507, 549
Bell, F. W., 43, 251
Benham, L., 391–2
Bergson, Abram, 597
Berndt, E. R., 222
Bertrand, J., 407
Bierman, H., 418
Borcherding, Thomas E., 628
Boulding, K., 373
Brown, Murray, 296
Buchanan, James, 633

Campbell, James D., 534
Capron, W., 491
Carlin, A., 243
Cartter, Allan M., 482, 511
Cassady, R., 304
Cassels, John M., 227
Chamberlin, Edward H., 377, 392, 400
Charnes, A., 286
Chenery, Hollis B., 569
Cheung, Steven N. S., 618
Christensen, L., 250, 251
Clark, John M., 227
Clark, Paul G., 569
Coase, Ronald R., 616, 621, 633

Cobb, C. W., 296
Cohen, H., 251
Cooper, W. 286
Cournot, A., 405
Cyert, R., 435, 437

Dahl, C. A., 151
Dantzig, G. B., 274
Darby, Michael R., 521, 528
de Graff, J. V., 610
De Haven, J., 595
Debreu, Gerald, 555, 580
Denison, E., 273
Dirlam, J., 444
Dorfman, Nancy, 633
Dorfman, Robert, 296, 633, A13
Douglas, Paul H., 227, 296
Downs, Anthony, 629
Dunlop, J., 504
Dupuit, A. J., 118

Eads, G., 251
Edgeworth, F., 64, 121, 407
Ehrenberg, R., 505, 507
Ehrlich, I., 78
Engel, Ernst, 98
Ericsson, N., 312

Feldstein, M., 463–4
Fellner, William J., 444
Ferber, R., 478
Ferguson, C. E., 227
Fisher, Anthony C., 623
Fisher, F., 430
Fisher, Irving, 549
Forrester, Jay W., 541
Freeman, Richard B., 538
Frey, B. S., 18
Friedman, Milton, 24, 191
Fuchs, V. R., 585

Gaskins, Darius W., 444
Giffen, Robert, 113
Grabowski, H. G., 82
Green, H., 250, 251
Griliches, Z., 251, 430

Hahn, F. H., 580
Halvorsen, R., 143, 180
Harberger, A., 353, 354
Harrison, D., 176
Heady, H. O., 205, 216
Hicks, John R., 64, 93, 143, 158, 162, 296 373, 482, 511, 596
Hirsh, W., 478
Hirschleifer, J., 595
Hotelling, H., 439, 549
Houthakker, H., 33, 137, 141, 158, 163

Jaffé, William, 555, 584
Jansson, J. O., 223
Jevons, William Stanley, 63
Johnston, Jack, 296
Jureen, L., 141, 143

Kagel, J. H., 78, 105
Kaldor, Nicholas, 596
Kantorovich, V. L., 274
Kaplan, A. D. H., 444
Karmarker, N., 275, 285
Kaysen, C., 430
Kearl, J., 18
Khan, Alfred E., 373
Klarman, H., 251
Kneese, Allen, 633
Koenker, R., 251
Krutilla, John V., 623
Kuenne, Robert E., 400

Lancaster, Kelvin, 174, 191, 599
Landes, W., 105

Lanzillotti, R., 338, 444
Leibenstein, Harvey, 158
Leontief, Wassily W., 569, 570, 580
Lerner, Abba, 604
Lewis, H., 504
Lindsay, C. M., 539
Lipsey, R. G., 599
Luttrell, B., 314

MacCrimmon, K. R., 72
Machlup, Fritz, 227
Manne, A., 286
Mansfield, Edwin, 373
March, J., 435, 437
Marshall, Alfred, 31, 56, 93, 118, 333, 373
Masson, R. T., 433
McKenzie, Lionel W., 555
Meade, James E., 400
Meadows, Donella H., 541
Mellon, B., 286
Menger, Karl, 63
Mesarovic, Mihajlo, 541
Milliman, J., 595
Morgan, P., 312
Morgenstern, O., 413
Moroney, J., 219, 269
Murphy, N., 251
Musgrave, Peggy, 633
Musgrave, Richard, 633

Nerlove, M., 38, 251
Niskanen, William A., 628

Offenberg, Marvin, 570
Oi, W., 470
Olson, Mancur, 629

Pareto, Vilfredo, 64, 580, 610
Park, R., 243
Pashigian, B., 494
Pestel, Eduard, 541

Quirk, James, 580, 610

Radford, R. A., 560
Raduchel, W., 251
Razin, Assaf, 534
Rees, A.. 153
Reynolds, L., 318–319
Robbins, Lionel, 24
Robbins, P., 478
Robinson, Joan, 373, 400, 488, 496
Rogerson, W., 354
Rubinfeld, D., 176

Salvatore, D., 24, 56, 93, 126, 158, 177, 191, 227, 261, 295, 333, 373, 400, 444, 482, 511, 580, 598, 610, 633
Samuelson, Paul A., 164, 296, 633, A13
Saposnick, Rubin, 580, 610
Savage, L. J., 191
Scherer, F. M., 354, 444
Schmalensee, Richard L., 400
Schultz, H., 33
Schultze, Charles, 633
Schumpeter, Joseph, 605
Schwartz, W. B., 585
Scitovsky, Tibor, 596
Scully, G., 496
Shaanan, J., 433
Shepard L., 494

Shneerson, D., 223
Shubik, Martin, 444
Shultz, Theodore W., 549
Siegfried, J., 354
Simon, H., 435
Slutsky, Eugene, 161
Smith, R., 505, 507
Solow, R., 296, 549, A13
Sternlieb, G., 46
Stigler, George J., 24, 93, 126, 261, 333, 373, 400, 412, 482, 549
Stone, R., 143
Suits, D., 132, 243
Sweezy, P., 411

Taylor, L. D., 33, 137, 141, 158, 163
Thornton, Judith, 545
Tiemann, T., 354
Toda, M., 72
Tollison, R., 418
Traywick, T., 319

Veblen, Thorstein, 131
Vernon, J. M., 82
Viner, Jacob, 261
von Neumann, J., 413

Walras, Leon, 63, 555, 580
Walters, A. A., 296
Watts, H. W., 153
Waud, R., 458
Welch, F., 475
West, R., 478
Wold, H., 141, 143
Wood, D. O., 222

Subject Index

Activity level, 275, 278, 293

Advertising
  as creating false needs, 396–397
  in monopolistically competitive markets, 386–388
  informative, 388–389, 396, 431
  price of eyeglasses and, 391

Agricultural programs, 46–48, 150

Allocation over time, 4, 9, 16, 303–304, 323–324, 513

Alternative or opportunity cost doctrine, 197, 230, 237, 258, 317, 538, 622–623

Aluminum Company of America (Alcoa), 336, 338, 426

American Telephone and Telegraph (AT&T), 3, 275, 427, 501

Antitrust laws, 337–338, 419, 427

Apple and the bees, fable of, 617–618

Arc elasticity of demand, 32, 52

Arc elasticity of supply, 37, 52

Arrow's impossibility theorem, 595, 598–599, 607

Assets, 184–185, 522

Assumptions in theory, 15–16, 64, 392

Attributes (characteristics) of goods, 174–176, 189

Average fixed cost, 238–242, 258

Average product, 199–205, 219–220, 225, 265–266

Average total cost, 238–243, 246–249, 255–256, 258, 286–287, 306–309, 315–317, 344–347, 349–350

Average variable cost, 238–243, 252, 258, 308–310

Backward-bending supply curve of labor, 459–463, 470–471

Bad, 65, 67, 71, 90, 101

Barometric firm, 424, 441

Barriers to entry, 338, 428

Basic research
  and growth, 605–606
  case for government support of, 615–616
  defined, 615

Basis and the gains from trade, 118–121, 573–574

Benefit-cost analysis
  defined, 622–624, 630
  examples of, 17–18, 82, 533
  of the SST, 624

Benefit reduction rate, see Taxes

Bergson social welfare function, 597–598, 607

Bertrand model, 407

Best level of output, 306–308, 315, 342–347, 349, 355–356, 364–365, 380–382, 411, 430, 449

Bilateral monopoly, 501–502, 504, 509

Black markets, 46, 84–85

Blocked entry, 336, 349, 394–395, 428

Borrowing, 513, 515, 517–527, 529–530

Break-even income, 477, 479–480

Break-even point, 305–306, 308, 318, 330

Breakfast cereals, 376, 384–385

Budget constraint, 72–73, 90

Budget line
  defined, 72–73, 90, 121, 124, 459–460
  rotation of, 75, 102, 105–106, 162, 182
  shifts in, 74–76, 96, 518
  slope of, 73–77, 81, 459–460, 516

Business firms, see Firms

Capital, 5, 10, 12

Capital budgeting, 528–533, 547, A12

Capital-labor ratio, 214, 217, 244, 254, 256, 265, 270–273, 275–277, 289–290, 568

Capital-using technological progress, 272–273, 289–290, 293

Cardinal utility, 16, 63–64, 80, 89, 162

Cartels
  antitrust laws and, 338, 419, 427
  centralized, 419, 441
  collusion and, 338, 419–427, 441
  defined, 338, 419, 441
  in petroleum, 338, 421–422
  instability of, 420–421
  market-sharing, 422–423, 441
  price leadership in, 424–427, 441

Cellophane, 153–154, 337

Centralized Cartel, 419, 441

Centrally planned economy, 570, 604–605

Chamberlin model, 409–410, 441

Characteristics approach to consumer theory, 174–176, 189

Charitable behavior, 85–87

Circular flow of economic activity, 10–11, 13–14, 22, 447, 554

Coase's theorem, 616–617, 630

Cobb-Douglas production function
estimation, 268–269
formula, 264, 293
illustration, 205, 215–216, 264–267

Cobweb model, 49–51, 53, A8–A9

Collective bargaining
bilateral monopoly and, 504
considerations in, 502–504

Collusion
cartels and, 338, 409–410, 419–427, 441
in electrical equipment, 423–424

Commodities, see Goods

Common property, 616, 630

Comparative advantage, 568, 573, 577

Compensated demand curve, 180–184, 189

Compensation principle, 596, 607

Competition
nonprice, 385–388, 429, 442
price, 379–383
see also Perfect competition: Monopolistic competition

Complementary commodities, 141–143, 155, 179

Complementary inputs, 222, 452–453, 479, 488–489

Concentration ratio, 404–405, 441

Conscious parallelism, 427, 441

Consistency assumption, 164, 188

Constant cost industry, 319–320, 330–331

Constant returns to scale, 216–219, 225, 246, 251, 265, 267, 275, 277, 351, 569

Constrained utility maximization, 69, 76–84, 90, 96, 105, 108, 175, 234, 516, 539, A1–A2

Constraints, 72–74, 76, 121–123, 274, 277, 279–285, 290–291, 293

Consumer
demand, 102–104
equilibrium, 76, 90, 175
tastes and preferences, 15, 27, 29, 59–60, 62, 64–66, 76, 83–84, 90, 99–101, 104, 163–165, 391, 395–396, 431, 515, 520, 539, 568, 574

Consumer price index (CPI), 169–170

Consumer surplus, 116–118, 124, 352, 357–358, A5

Contract curve
in exchange, 119–121, 558–560, 566–567, 577, 585–589, 592

in production, 562–564, 566, 577, 592, 602–603

Corner solution, 78–81, 86, 90

Cost curves, long run
average, 246–251, 258, 288–289, 315–318, 336, 349–350, 365–366, 541
marginal, 247–249, 258, 287–289, 315–317, 349–350, 365–366, 541
relation to production functions, 244–245
total, 244–245, 258, 287–289

Cost curves, short run
average fixed, 238–242, 258
average total, 238–243, 246–249, 255–256, 258, 286–287, 306–309, 315–317, 344–347, 349–350
average variable, 238–243, 252, 258, 308–310
derivation of, 241–243
marginal, 239–243, 249, 252, 255–256, 258, 286–287, 306–311, 315–317, 344–350, 353–356
relation to long run, 247–249
relation to production functions, 252–253
total, 236–239, 258, 286–288, 304–307, 341–347
total fixed, 236–239, 258, 308–309
total variable, 236–239, 252–253, 258

Cost-plus pricing, 436–437, 442

Costs of production
alternative or opportunity, 197, 230, 237, 258, 317, 538, 622–623
explicit, 230–231, 237, 258, 317, 538
implicit, 230–231, 237, 258, 317, 538
private, 231, 258, 614
social, 231, 258, 614

Cotton, textile industry, 318–319

Cournot model, 405–407, 441

Creative destruction, 605–606, 608

Cross elasticity of demand
defined, 142, 155
formula, 142
for selected commodities, 143

Decreasing cost industry, 321–322, 331

Decreasing returns to scale, 216–219, 225, 246, 250

Default risk, 535, 547

Demand
consumer, 102–104
determinants of, 27
excess, 12, 40, 42, 45, 52
for inputs, 448, 450–454, 456–457, 479
law of, 28, 52, 104, 113, 129, 179, 182

market, 27
  schedule, 27–28, 39, 52, 486–488
  theory, 15–16
Demand curve
  compensated, 180–184, 189
  constant elasticity, 135–136
  facing monopolist, 336, 339–340
  facing monopolistic competitor, 378–379, 398
  facing perfectly competitive firm, 301, 340
  elasticity of, *see* Elasticity of demand
  for Giffen good, 112–113
  for inferior good, 111–112
  for input, 450–456, 486–489
  kinked, 411–413, 441
  linear, 29, 132, 145
  market, 28, 52, 104, 128–132, 149, 155, 464,
    489–490, 541–542
  measurement of, 28
  movement along, 30–31, 42, 44, 104
  nonlinear, 103, 134, 147
  of individual consumer, 102–104, 124, 129, 357
  shifts of, 29–30, 41–43, 104, 129, 490
  see also Market demand curve
Depreciation, 527
Derived demand, 448, 450, 456–457, 479
Diamond–water paradox, 118, 124
Differentiated oligopoly, 403, 441
Differentiated products, 376–377, 392–394, 398,
  403, 429, 431, 437–439
Diminishing marginal utility, 60–62, 89
Diminishing returns, law of, 202–205, 218, 220,
  225, 237–238, 246, 250, 252–253, 265–266,
  287–288, 304, 341–342, 487, 523, 543
Discrimination in employment, 505–507, 509
Diseconomies of scale, 223, 246, 323
Disemployment effect, 474–475, 479, 503
Distribution, 8, 14, 22, 447
Dominant firm model, 424–426
Dominant strategy, 415
Dual problem, 290, 293
Duopoly, *see* Oligopoly
du Pont, 154, 337–338, 422
Dynamic efficiency, 595, 605–606

Economic efficiency, 18, 22, 583, 585–587, 593–
  595, 601–605, 607, 612–613
Economic goods, 5, 21, 121–123
Economic growth, 9, 16, 22
Economic profit, 197, 316–317, 389

Economic rent, 466–469, 479
Economic resources, 4–5, 21
Economics, 3–4, 7, 21
Economies of scale, 216, 223, 246, 323, 336–337,
  404
Edgeworth box diagram
  for exchange, 118–121, 124, 558–560, 566, 577,
    589, 592
  for production, 561–563, 577, 592
Edgeworth model, 407–409, 441
Efficiency frontier, 174–175, 189
Effluent fees, 627–628, 630
Elasticity of demand
  cross, 141–143, 153, 155, A3
  income, 138–141, 155, A3
  price, 31–34, 52, 105–107, 132–138, A2–A3
Elasticity of supply, *see* Price elasticity of supply
Elasticity of substitution, 270–272, 293
Electricity
  demand, 179–180
  forecasting demand for, 180, 185–187
  price discrimination in, 360–362
  rates, 187, 337, 361
Emission controls, 625, 627–628
Empirical demand curves, 176–179
Engel curves, 96–101, 138–140
  defined, 98
  income consumption curve and, 96–98
  income elasticity of demand and, 138–140
  shapes of, 98–101
Engel law, 98–99, 139
Engineers' shortage, 490–491
Endowment position, 514
Entrepreneurship, 5, 11, 197–198, 605
Envelope curve, 247
Environmental pollution, 625–628
  defined, 625
  direct regulation of, 627–628
  effluent fees and, 627–628
  optimal control of, 626–627
Equalizing wage differentials, 472–473
Equilibrium
  defined, 41
  demand-supply model, 39–44, 45–51
  in monopoly, 341–345, 349–350
  in monopolistic competition, 377, 381–382, 389
  in oligopoly, 407, 409–411
  in perfect competition, 313–314
  of consumer, 76–77, 80–81, 636
Equilibrium price, 39–44, 48–49

Equilibrium price *(cont.)*
  defined, 39–41
  demand curve shifts and, 41–43
  excise tax and, 48–49
  supply curve shifts and, 41, 43–44, 48–49
Excess capacity, 389–390, 395–396
Excess demand, 12, 40–41, 45–46
Excess supply, 12, 39–41, 47–48
Exchange, 118–121
Exchange in POW camps, 560
Excise taxes, 48–49, 326–327, 362–363
Exhaustible resources
  defined, 540
  pricing of, 541–542
Expansion path, 244–245
Expected income, 171–173
Expenditure index, 166–169
Explicit costs, 230
Exploitation
  monopolistic, 488
  monopsonistic, 496
External benefits, 613, 617–618
External costs, 613–614, 625
External diseconomies
  of consumption, 613, 615
  of production, 323, 613–615
External diseconomy, 323, 613
External economies
  of consumption, 613, 615
  of production, 323, 613–615
External economy, 323, 613
Externalities, 612–618

Factors of production, *see* Inputs
Feasible region, 122, 174, 276–277
Feasible solutions, 277, 279–284, 290–291
Firms
  entrepreneurship and, 197–198
  existence of, 10, 196
  goals of, 196–197, 433–436
  management of, 196–197
  monopolistic, 336–337, 339–340, 342–345, 349–350
  monopolistic competitive, 376–378, 380–384
  oligopolistic, 403–404, 405–411
  perfectly competitive, 301–302, 304–310, 313–318
First degree price discrimination, 356–358
Fish auctions, 303–304

Fixed costs, 236–238
Fixed inputs, 198
Food stamp program, 114–116
For whom to produce, 7–8, 13
Free-enterprise system, 7–10, 13–14, 18
Free goods, 5
Free resources, 5
Free-rider problem, 621
Fringe benefits, 87–88

Gambling, 172–173
Game theory
  defined, 413
  dominant strategy in, 415
  maximin strategy in, 414
  minimax strategy in, 415
  mixed strategy in, 415–416
  non-zero sum game in, 416–417
  payoff, 413
  payoff matrix, 414
  prisoner's dilemma and, 417–418
  pure strategy in, 415
  saddle point in, 415
  strictly-determined, 415
  zero-sum game, 413
Gasoline
  consumption, 150–152, 163
  price control of, 14
  price elasticity of demand, 31, 150–152
  rationing of, 14
  speed limit and consumption of, 221–222, 252, 254
  tax-rebate proposal, 110–111, 163
General equilibrium
  defined, 554, A13–A14
  existence of, 555
General equilibrium analysis
  input-output analysis and, 569–573
  of exchange, 557–560
  of production, 561–563
  of production and exchange, 565–568
  partial equilibrium analysis vs., 554–555
  welfare economics and, 583–589, 591–592
Giffen paradox, 113–114
Gini coefficient, 575–576
Goods
  Giffen, 112–114
  inferior, 99–101, 111–114, 138–139, 181–182, A3

normal, 99–101, 138–139, 181–182, A3
public, 618–619, 621–622
Government
  benefit-cost analysis and, 622–624
  externalities and, 615–616, 621–622
  intervention, case against, 14, 628–629
  public goods and, 14, 20, 618–619, 621–622
  regulation of monopoly price, 363–365
  regulation of natural monopoly, 250, 365–366
  warnings, 83–84
Grand utility-possibilities frontier, 588–589, 591–
    592, 596–597, 605–606

Hedonic price, 175–176
Heterogeneous commodity, 376–377
Hicksian substitution effect, 108–114, 162–163,
    182
Homogeneous commodity, 300
Hotelling paradox, 437–439
How to produce, 7–8, 13
Human capital, 538–539
Human wants, 4, 6–7, 21, 60

IBM (International Business Machines), 388, 427
Ideal output, 389
Ideal plant, 389
Identification problem, 177
Imperfect competition, 13, 302, 336–338, 376–377,
    403–404
  see also Monopolistic competition; Monopoly;
    Oligopoly
Implicit costs, 230
Incidence of tax, 48–49
Income
  constraint, 72–74, 121–123
  consumption curve, 96–97
  distribution, 289–290, 447, 574–576, 593
  effect, 29–30, 108–114, 161–162, 180–184, 461–
    462, 470–471
  elasticity of demand, 138–141, 153, A3–A5
  leisure choice, 459–461, 470–471
  money and real, 108–110, 162
Income or expenditure index, 166–169
Increasing cost industry, 320–321
Increasing returns to scale, 216–219, 250
Index numbers
  changes in consumer welfare and, 165–170
  expenditure, 166–169

Laspeyres, 166–169
Paasche, 167–169
Indifference curve
  characteristics, 66–67
  convexity of, 67–69, 71
  defined, 64–66, 635
  experimental determination of, 71–72
  marginal rate of substitution and, 68–69,
    A1
  negative slope of, 66–67, 69–70, 635
  nonintersection of, 67
  revealed preference and, 163–165, 182–184
Indifference map, 65–66, 118–120
Individual demand curve
  derivation of, 102–104
  location and shape of, 104, 113–114
  money income and, 180–182
  price consumption curve and, 102–104
  price elasticity of, 105–108, A2–A3, A5–A6
Industry
  constant cost, 319–320
  decreasing cost, 321–322, 331
  defined, 142
  increasing cost, 320–321
  long-run adjustment, 317–318, 329, 349–350,
    428
  short-run adjustment, 314, 329
Inequality constraints, 279–284
Inferior good, 99–101, 111–114, 138–139, 181–
    182, A3
Innovation, 616
Input–output analysis
  applicability, 570
  defined, 569
  example of, 570–573
  technical coefficients in, 571–572
Inputs
  average product of, 199–203, 239, 252
  defined, 4, 8, 197
  fixed, 198
  imperfect competition and, 486–490, 491–496,
    498, 501
  least-cost combination of, 234–235
  marginal expense of, 492–493, A11
  marginal product of, 199–204, 240, 252
  optimal combination of, 485, 499
  perfect competition and, 449–450, 464–465
  price and employment of, 464–465, 489–490,
    495–496, 498, 501, A10–A11
  price elasticity of demand of, 456–458, A11

Inputs (*cont.*)
  substitution among, 211–212, 214–216, 222, 254–256
  technology and, 272–273
  variable, 198
Insurance, 171–173
Interdependence, 403
Interest rates
  defined, 516
  determinants of, 535–536
  intertemporal choice and, 514–533, 622–623
  real vs. nominal, 536–537
  socialism and, 544–545
Intermediate good, 459
Internalizing external costs, 616–617
International specialization, 568
International trade, 568, 573–574
Intertemporal choice
  investment decisions, 528–533
  lending–borrowing equilibrium, 514–521
  saving–investment equilibrium, 522–527
Investment, 522, 646
Investment decisions, 184–185, 528–534, A12
Investment in human capital
  and hours of work, 539–540
  defined, 538
  education and lifetime earnings, 534
Isocost line
  defined, 232, A6
  rotation of, 233
  shifts in, 233
  slope of, 232–233, 235, A6
Isoquant
  characteristics, 209–210
  defined, 206
  derived from production functions, 206–207
  for Cobb-Douglas production function, 265–267
  marginal rate of technical substitution and, 211–212
  nonintersection of, 210
  slope of, 211–212, 235
  substitution among inputs and, 211–212, 214–216, 236, 254–255

Kaldor-Hicks criterion, 596
Kinked-demand curve model, 411–413

Labor, 5, 197
Labor union
  collective bargaining and, 502

objectives of, 504–505
  wage effect of, 502–504
Labor-using technological progress, 272–273
Land, 5, 197
Laspeyres price index, 166, 169–170
Law of demand, 28, 104
Law of diminishing marginal utility, 61
Law of diminishing returns, 202–205, 240–241
Law of the invisible hand, 594
Lawyers, glut of, 465–466
Least-cost input combination, 234–235, 252
Leisure, 459–462
Lending, *see* Intertemporal choice, 514–517
Lighthouse, the economics of, 620–621
Limit pricing, 428–429, 432–433
Linear programming
  applications of, 274
  cost minimization in, 282–285
  dual problem in, 290–291
  feasible solution in, 276–277
  in the petroleum industry, 285–286
  inequality constraints in, 279
  nonnegative constraints in, 279
  objective function in, 279
  optimal solution of, 276–277
  primal problem in, 290
  profit maximization in, 279–282
  shadow price in, 290–291
  simplex method of solution of, 285
  slack variable in, 290
  technical constraints in, 279
Long run
  allocation process in, 9, 323–324, 329
  cost function in, 244–251, 287–289
  defined, 198
  price and quantity determination in, 235–236
  supply curve in, 317–318
Long-run average cost, 246–247, 250–251
Long-run equilibrium
  in monopolistic competition, 382–385
  in oligopoly, 428–429
  in perfect competition, 315–319
  in pure monopoly, 349–351
Long-run marginal cost, 247
Long-run total cost, 244
Lorenz curve, 574–575
Loss minimization, 308–310
Lump-sum tax, 372–373
Luxury, 138

Macroeconomic theory, 10
Major league baseball, monopsonistic exploitation
   in, 496–497
Managerial theories of the firm, 435–436
Marginal benefit, 614–615
Marginal cost
  law of diminishing returns and, 240–241
  long run, 247–249
  pricing, 604–605
  relation to average cost, 241
  short run, 239–243
Marginal expense
  of capital, 493
  of input, 492–493, A11
  of labor, 492–493, A11
Marginal product, 199–205
Marginal productivity theory, 464–465
Marginal rate
  of substitution, 68–69
  of technical substitution, 211–212
  of transformation, 565
Marginal revenue curve
  defined, 144–145
  formula for, 144
  graphical estimation of, 145–148
  price elasticity of demand and, 148–149, A5–A6
  kinked demand curve and, 411–413
  market demand curve and, 306–308
  of perfectly competitive firm, 306–308
  of monopolist, 339–341, 342–345
  of monopolistic competitor, 379–381
  third degree price discrimination and, 358–362
Marginal revenue product, 486–487
Marginal social benefit, 614–615
Marginal social cost, 614–615
Marginal utility, 60–63, 80–82
Market
  for stocks, 27, 301–302, 325–327
  government intervention in, 13–14
  perfect vs. imperfect, 27
Market demand curve
  consumers' income and, 27, 29–30, 41–42
  consumers' tastes and, 27, 29–30, 41–42
  defined, 27–29
  derivation of, 28–29
  estimation of, 176–180
  for an input, 454–456, 489–491
  for a commodity, 27–30, 104, 129–132
  for electricity, 179, 185–187
  see also Demand curve

Market demand schedule, 27–29
Market failures, 594
Market organization, 299–300
Market period, 302–304
Market-sharing cartel, 422–424
Market supply curve
  defined, 34–36
  derivation of, 34–35
  elasticity of, 37–39
  for an input, 462–464
  for a commodity, 34–36
  short run, 43–44, 310–314
  market period, 302–304
  long run, 316–318
  technological change and, 36
  see also Supply curve
Market supply schedule, 34–36
Markup, 436
Maximin strategy, 414
Maximum social welfare, 591–593
Medicare and Medicaid, 327–329, 464
Methodology of economics, 15–16
Microeconomic theory, 3–4
Military draft, cost of, 468–470
Minimal income maintenance, 475
Minimum wage
  levels, 473
  laws, 473
  effects of, 473–475
Minimax strategy, 415
Mixed economy, 14
Mixed strategy, 415–416
Model, 15–16
Money income
  as constraint, 72–76
  individual demand curve and, 104
  of consumers, 96–99
Monopolistic competition
  advertising, 386, 391–392, 396–397
  compared with other models, 389–391
  criticism of theory of, 392–393
  defined, 376–378
  demand curves, 378–379
  excess capacity, 390, 395–396
  long-run equilibrium, 382–385
  nonprice competition, 385–389
  price and output, 379–385
  product differentiation, 376
  product group, 377
  selling expenses in, 386–389

Monopolistic competition (cont.)
    short-run equilibrium, 379–382
Monopolistic exploitation, 488
Monopoly
    bilateral, 501–502
    defined, 336–338
    natural, 337
    price and output, 341–350
    profits, 342–347, 349–351
    regulation of, 363–366
    sources of, 336–337
    welfare effect of, 600–602
    see also Pure monopoly
Monopsonistic exploitation, 496
Monopsony
    defined, 491–494
    exploitation in, 496
    pricing and employment, 494–499
    regulation, 500–501
    sources of, 492
    welfare effect of, 602–603
Multipart pricing, 358
Multiplant firm, 354–356
Multiple regression, 177–179

Natural monopoly, 337
Natural resources, 5, 197
Necessity, 138
Negative income tax, 153, 475–478
Neuter, 69–70
Neutral technological progress, 272–273
New York Stock Exchange, 301–302
Nominal rate of interest, 536–537
Noncompeting groups, 473
Nonexhaustible resources
    defined, 540–542
    management of, 542–544
Nonexclusion, 619
Nonnegative constraints, 279
Nonprice competition, 385–389, 429
Nonrival consumption, 619
Nonzero sum game, 416–417
Normal good, 96, 99–101
Normative economics, 17–19

Objective function, 279, 292–293
Oligopoly
    barriers to entry in, 428–429, 440
    Bertrand model, 407

centralized cartel model, 419–422, 440–441
Chamberlin model, 409–410, 440–441
collusion in, 410, 419–424, 427, 440–441
compared with other models, 392, 430–431, 485
Cournot model, 405–407, 409, 440–441
defined, 301, 403, 439–441
Edgeworth model, 407–409, 440
efficiency, 430–431, 440
game theory, 413–419, 440–441
kinked demand curve model, 411–413, 440–441
market-sharing cartel model, 422–424, 440–441
nonprice competition, 429, 437–439, 440, 442
price leadership by dominant firm, 424–426, 440
price leadership by low-cost firm, 424, 440
price and output, 407, 408–409, 410–411, 424–425
sources of, 404
Oligopsony, 493, 508
OPEC (Organization of Petroleum Exporting Countries), 421–422
Opportunity cost, 230, 258, 350
Optimal combination of inputs, 232–236, 448–450, 485
Optimal rate of output, 246–247, 306, 307, 315, 330, 342–347, 349–350, 369, 380–382, 387, 397
Optimal scale of plant, 246–247, 315, 349–350, 369, 382, 397
Optimal solution, 277, 279, 292–293
Ordinal utility, 63–64, 89
Output
    in monopolistic competition, 380–382, 382–384, 386, 395, 397–398
    in monopoly, 342, 344–345, 349, 352, 369, 501
    in oligopoly, 407, 408–411, 420, 428
    in perfect competition, 304–308, 315, 330, 453, 455
Output elasticity
    of capital, 264, 269, 293
    of labor, 264, 269, 293
Overtime pay, 470–471

Paasche price index, 167, 187–189
Pareto criterion, 596, 607
Pareto optimum, 584, 585–586, 588–589, 591, 593–595, 599–603, 606–607, 614–615, 617, 619
Partial equilibrium analysis, 553, 554–555, 576–577
Partnership, 196

Patents, 336, 354
Payback period, 545, 547
Payoff, 413, 441
Payoff matrix, 414, 441
Per-unit costs
    defined, 238–239
    derived, 239–241
    geometry of, 241–242
Per-unit tax, 362–363
Perfect competition
    adjustment in the very short run, 302–303
    compared with other models, 300–301, 339–
        340, 341, 348–350, 351–352, 362–363, 376,
        384–391, 392, 397
    constant cost industries in, 319–320, 330
    decreasing cost industries in, 321–323, 330
    defined, 27, 52, 300, 329–330
    efficiency and, 300–301, 317, 593–595, 605–
        606, 613–615, 619
    firm demand curve in, 450–454, 478
    firm marginal cost in, 306–308, 310
    increasing cost industries in, 320–321, 330
    long run adjustment, 315–318
    market demand curve in, 455–456
    price and employment of inputs, 449–451, 455–
        456, 478
    price and output, 39–41, 310–311, 313–314,
        449, 478
    short run adjustment, 304–310, 313–314
    supply curve in, 310–311, 315–316
Physicians' services, supply of, 463–464
Planning horizon, 247, 258
Point elasticity of demand, 32, 52
Point elasticity of supply, 37
Pollution, see Environmental pollution
Positive economics, 16–17, 21–22
Potatoes, estimation of demand for, 131–132
Preferences of consumers
    changes in, 164
    defined, 164
    graphed as indifference curves, 164–165
    transitivity of, 164
Present-value rule
    intertemporal choice and, 528–533, 546–547
    in multiperiod case, 530–533, A12
    in two-period case, 528–530
Price
    absolute, 594
    controls, 44, 55, 603–604, 606–607
    ceiling, 45–46, 53

floor, 46–48, 53
    relative, 109, 124, 568, 594
    rigidity, 411, 412, 440
    war, 411
Price-consumption curve
    defined 102, 123–124
    derivation of individual's demand curve and,
        102–104
    price elasticity of demand and, 105–108, 123
Price determination
    in a centrally planned economy, 14, 18–19, 604
    in long run, 315–318, 352, 382–384
    in market period, 302–303
    in a mixed economy, 14
    in monopolistic competition, 380–384, 386, 389
    in monopoly, 339, 342, 346–349, 351–352, 363–
        365, 369, 501
    in oligopoly, 407, 408–411, 429, 432–433, 436–
        437, 440, 442, 489
    in perfect competition, 39–42, 43–44, 310–314,
        316
    in short run, 313–314, 330, 348–349, 380–381
    of commodities, 12, 323–324, 489, 615
    of inputs, 12–13, 447, 464–466, 479, 490, 492,
        508, 540–542
Price discrimination
    first degree, 356–357, 369, 370
    second degree, 358, 369–370
    third degree, 358–361, 367, 370, 393, 398, A10
Price dispersion, 393–394, 398
Price elasticity of demand
    arc, 32, 51–52
    defined, 32, 51–52, A2
    determinants of, 135–137
    formula for, 32, 636
    graphical measurement of, 132–135, 154
    point, 32, 52, A2
    price discrimination and, 360, 393
    for selected commodities, 33–34, 150–153
    substitutes and, 33
    total expenditures and, 134–135, 154
Price elasticity of supply
    arc, 37
    defined, 37, 52, A3–A4
    formula for, 37, A4
    for selected commodities, 38–39
    point, 37
Price leadership
    by dominant firm, 424–426
    by low-cost firm, 424

Price support, agricultural, 46–48
Price system, 7–9, 12, 21–22
Price taker, 301, 424
Price theory, 13, 22
Primal problem, 290, 292–293
Prisoner's dilemma, 417–418, 440–441
Private costs, 231
Private marginal benefit, 619, 627
Private marginal cost, 614–615, 627
Product curves
  average, 199–203
  marginal, 199–204
  total, 199–203, 207–209, 252
Product differentiation, 376, 393, 395, 397–398,
  429, 437
Product group, 377, 392, 398
Product variation, 385, 398
Production
  defined, 196, 223–224
  three stages of, 204–225, 265, 292
Production costs
  fixed, 236, 257–258
  long run, 244–252, 254, 258, 287–289
  per unit, 238–241, 242, 246–247, 286
  private, 231, 257–258
  short run, 236–243, 247–249, 252, 254, 257–
    258, 286
  social, 231, 257, 258
  total, 236–238, 244–245, 252, 254, 257, 258, 286
  variable, 236, 252, 257
Production function
  Cobb-Douglas, 264–269, 270–271, 286–289,
    292–293
  defined, 199, 224
  estimation of, 268
  fixed proportions, 214
Production-possibilities frontier, 6–7, 22, 522–523,
  546–547, 563–567, 573–577
Production techniques, 8, 22
Production theory, 195
Productivity growth, 273–274
Profit
  economic, 197, 223, 316–319, 386, 389, 430
  normal, 316–317, 365, 426
Profit maximization
  as objective of firm, 196
  in linear programming, 279–282, 292
  marginal revenue–marginal cost approach, 308–
    310, 342–346, 411, 641–642
  in monopolistic competition, 379–384

  in monopoly, 341–345, 349–350, 369, 501
  in monopsony, 494–496, 497–498, 508
  in oligopoly, 406–407, 410–411, 433–437, 485
  in perfect competition, 308–310, 330, 448–450,
    478
  total revenue–total cost approach, 304–306, 346–
    347, 382–384, 408–410, A10–A11
Property rights, 616–617, 629
Proportional demand curve, 378, 398
Proprietorships, 196
Public goods
  Coase theorem and, 616–617, 629–630
  defined, 618–619, 629–630
  free-rider problem in, 621, 628–630
  nonexclusion of, 619, 629–630
  nonrival consumption of, 619, 629–630
  provision of, 621–622
Public utilities, 337, 365
Pure monopoly
  bilateral, 501–502, 508–509
  compared with other models, 339–341, 348–
    352, 362–363, 376
  defined, 336, 369, 370
  demand curve in, 339
  efficiency and, 350, 601, 605–606
  long-run equilibrium, 349–350, 369
  marginal revenue in, 339, 341, 344–345, 348–
    349, 359–360
  multiplant, 354–356, 369
  natural, 337, 365–366, 370
  price discrimination in, 356–367, 369–370
  price and output in, 347, 348–349, 369
  profits in, 342, 344–345, 349–351
  short-run equilibrium and, 341–349
  sources of, 336–337
  regulation of, 363–366, 370
  welfare effect of, 351–354, 600–602
Pure oligopoly, 403
Pure strategy, 415

Quantity demanded, 8
Quantity supplied, 7
Quasirent, 468–479

Rate of interest, see Interest rates
Rational consumer, 76, 90
Rationing
  defined, 9, 22, 84–85, 89–90

hospital care, 584–585
in the very short run, 303–304, 323–324
Raw materials, 336
Real income, 109–110, 113, 162, 166–170, 182, 183–184
Real rate of interest, 536, 537, 546, 547
Regression analysis, 177–179, 188
Regulation (of monopoly), 363–366
Relative price, 594
Rent, 466–469, 479
Rent control, 325–326, 330
Research and development (R&D), 430, 605–606
Resources
 allocation, 4, 21
 defined, 4–5, 21
 exhaustible, 540, 541–542
 nonexhaustible, 540, 542–544
 see also Inputs
Return on investment, 365, 528–529
Returns to scale
 constant, 216–218, 225, 250, 257, 292
 decreasing, 216–218, 225, 250, 257, 292
 increasing, 216–218, 223, 225, 250, 257, 292
 law of diminishing, 203–205, 218–220, 238, 246, 265, 341–342, 451–452, 487
Revealed preference, theory of:
 assumptions of, 164, 187
 derivation of individual's indifference curve and, 164–165, 187
Revenue
 average, 145, 155
 marginal, 144–149, 154, 155, 306, 315, 330, 339, 342, 485, 493, 498, 502, 505, 507, A5, A8, A10
 total, 144–148, 150, 152, 154, 155, 306, 330, 487, A7, A10
Ridge lines, 212, 224
Risk
 analysis of, 170–173, 184–185
 defined, 170–173
 expected income and, 171–173
Rivalry, 301, 329, 403, 409

Saddle point, 415
Sales, maximization model, 433–435
Satisficing behavior, 435
Saturation point, 60
Saving
 amount of, 522, 525

and investment, 522–527, 536, 546
 and the rate of interest, 526–527
 business, 527–528
 personal, 521, 527–528, 547
Scale of plant, 247, 382, 397, 428
Scale, returns to, 216, 223, 224, 250, 257, 264, 267, 292
Scarcity, 5–8, 18, 21, 604
Scitovsky criterion, 596
Second best, theory of, 599
Second degree price discrimination, 358, 369, 370
Selling expenses, 386, 397, 398
Separation theorem, 530, 546, 547
Services (as goods), 5
Shadow price, 290, 293
Sherman Antitrust Act, 427, 441
Short run
 allocation process in, 323–324
 cost function in, 236–243, 304–306
 defined, 198, 223
 fixed inputs in, 198
 price and quantity determination in, 313, 330
 supply curve in, 310, 330, 348
 variable inputs in, 198
Short-run equilibrium
 in monopolistic competition, 379–382
 in monopoly, 341–345, 354, 369, 397
 in oligopoly, 411, 420, 425, 440
 in perfect competition, 304–314, 329
Shortage, 12, 40, 44, 52, 365, 603
Shut-down point, 308–310, 345
Simplex method, 285, 292, 293
Slack variable, 290, 293
Slutsky substitution effect, 161–164, 165, 180–184, 187, 188
Snob effect, 131, 154–155
Social benefit, 614, 616, 622, 629
Social costs, 231, 257, 258, 351, 354, 614, 622, 629
Social security, and savings, 547
Social welfare function, 590, 596–598, 606, 607
Socialism, 544–545
Specialization in production, 568–573
Speculation, 535
Stage of production
 first, 204, 225
 relevant, 204, 225
 second, 204, 225, 265
 third, 204, 225
Static efficiency, 595
Strictly determined game, 415, 440

Subsidy, 114–116, 123, 364, 475
Substitutes
  defined, 29, 155
  characteristics approach,175
  cross elasticity and, 141–143, 154, 179, A3
Substitution (in production)
  among inputs, 214, 222, 252, 254, 457, 461, 570
  elasticity of, 270, 292, 293
  marginal rate of, 68, 89, 120, 585
  shape of isoquants and, 214, 254
Substitution effect
  according to Hicks, 162–164, 182, 187, 188
  according to Slutsky, 161–164, 165, 180–184, 187, 188
  defined, 108–114, 123, 124, 517
Supply and demand model, 41–44
Supply curve
  defined, 34–36, 51, A11
  excise tax and, 48, 326
  for an input, 451, 462, 478, 491–492, 494, 500, 508
  for capital, 493
  for a commodity, 34, 51, 52
  for labor, 459–461, 478, 493, 495–496, 500–502, 505–507, A11
  for physicians' services, 328, 463
  for shale oil, 312
  of constant cost industries, 319, 330
  of decreasing cost industries, 321, 330
  of increasing cost industries, 320, 330
  see also Market supply curve
Surplus, 12, 39, 43, 47, 51, 52
Sweezy model, see Kinked-demand curve model

Tastes, 27, 29, 41, 51, 68, 84, 519–520, 530, 605
Taxes
  benefit reduction rate, 622–625
  excise, 48, 53, 362, 370
  incidence of, 48, 53
  lump sum, 182
  negative income tax, 153, 155, 475–478, 479, 539
  on gasoline, 110, 163, 362
  per unit, 48, 53, 362, 370, 627
  to control pollution, 625–627
  to finance public goods, 621
Taxicab regulation, 350
Technical coefficients, 571–572, 577
Technical constraints, 279, 280, 283

Technical externalities, 613, 629
Technologically fixed factor proportions, 275, 278, 292
Technological progress
  defined, 272, 292, 293
  capital-using, 272, 292, 293
  labor-using, 272, 292, 293
  neutral, 272, 292, 293
Technology, 7, 22, 198, 199, 219, 264, 292, 605
Theory, 15, 21
Theory of revealed preference, see Revealed preference
Theory of the second best, see Second best
Third degree price discrimination, 358–361, 367, 369, 370
Time as an economic good, 121, 252
Time budget line, 121, 124
Time preference, 519, 520, 524, 530, 536
Total costs, 232, 236, 257, 258, 286
Total fixed costs, 236, 257, 258, 286
Total product, 199, 201, 207, 224
Total revenue, 144–148, 150, 152, 154, 155, 306, 330, 342
Total utility, 60, 89, 170–173
Total variable costs, 236–243, 252–253, 257–258
Trade adjustment assistance, 598
Transformation curve, see Production-possibilities frontier
Transaction costs, 387, 397, 398, 617
Transitivity assumption, 64, 89, 164, 187, 188

Unemployment, 469
Unemployment gap, 474, 479
Unions, see Labor union
Unitary elasticity, see Price and income elasticities
Util, 60–89
Utility:
  cardinal, 63–64, 89
  defined, 16, 60, 89, 635
  expected, 173
  marginal, 60, 61, 80, 81, 89, 171
  maximization of, 76–78, 80, 85, 87, 89, 97, 102, 105, 180, 187, 234, 524–525, 539, A1–A2
  ordinal, 63–64, 89
  total, 60, 89, 171–173
Utility theory, 60–64
Utility possibilities frontier, 586–588, 606

Value of marginal product, 450, 478, 486, 488, 508, A11
Variability risk, 535, 546, 547
Variable costs
  average, 238–243, 257–258
  total, 236–243, 252–253, 257
Variable Inputs, 198, 205–209, 223, 329, 486–489, 494–497, 507–508
Veblen effect, 131, 154–155
Very short run
  defined, 302, 330
  pricing under, 302
  rationing among consumers, 303
  rationing over time, 323, 330

Wage
  differences, 8–9, 472, 504
  income-leisure choice and, 459–461, 477
  labor unions and, 502–505, 508
  minimum wage laws, 14, 16, 473, 502
  rate, 485, 487–489, 495–496
  substitution and income effect of change in wage, 470
Wants, see Preferences of consumers

Water–diamond paradox, 118, 124
Wealth, 517, 518, 524–525, 530, 546
Welfare economics
  defined, 583, 606–607
  Arrow's impossibility theorem in, 598, 607
  externalities in, 613, 616
  general equilibrium analysis and, 577
  grand utility possibilities frontier and, 588, 606, 607
  interpersonal comparison of utility and, 582, 597
  maximum social welfare and, 591–593, 606, 607
  Pareto optimum and, 583, 596–601, 606, 607
  perfect competition and, 593–595, 606, 607
  public goods and, 619
  theory of second best and, 599, 607, 608
  social welfare function in, 590, 596–598, 606, 607
  utility possibility frontier and, 587, 606, 607
What to produce, 7, 12, 16, 21, 22

Zero-sum game, 413, 441
Zone of ignorance, 164, 187, 188